INTERNATIONAL STUDIES

of the
Committee on International Relations
University of Notre Dame

INTERNATIONAL STUDIES

of the
Committee on International Relations
University of Notre Dame

CHRISTIAN DEMOCRACY
IN WESTERN EUROPE
1820–1953

by

MICHAEL P. FOGARTY

UNIVERSITY OF NOTRE DAME PRESS

NOTRE DAME, INDIANA

Library of Congress
Catalog Card Number 57–7387

First published 1957
by University of Notre Dame Press
Notre Dame
Indiana
© Michael P. Fogarty
Printed in Great Britain
by William Clowes and Sons, Limited
London and Beccles

CONTENTS

vi

CONTENTS

PART IV

LIST OF TABLES

PREFACE

THIS book is a preliminary survey of one aspect of the social influence of the Christian Churches. It is not about their social message, in the sense of the principles of social action proclaimed by each Church as such and by its clergy on its behalf. Nor is it about the religious aims of Church organisations, like those of Catholic Action, which, though concerned with practical economic and social activities, are formally or in fact auxiliaries of the clergy. Its subject is Christian Democracy, the area in which lay men and women, inspired by their Christian faith, take independent responsibility for the running of political parties, trade unions, farmers' unions, and the like. Christian Action organisations, the direct auxiliaries of the clergy, are considered in so far as they too have activities parallel or allied to those of Christian Democracy.

The business reason (so to speak) for studying Christian Democracy is in my case that, as an economist responsible for the last four years for a Department of Industrial Relations, I wanted to find out more about some of the Christian Democratic economic and social organisations, especially the trade unions and employers' associations. These organisations have been particularly interested in workers' control in industry, and especially in the part to be played in it by the rank and file as apart from full-time union officials. They have tried to work out a balance between the centralisation and decentralisation of economic control, and this has led them among other things to pay special attention to the role of the organised industry. It seemed that these and other aspects of the Christian Democrats' industrial policy should contain lessons of general importance, and therefore I set out to write a specialised study covering that field.

For several reasons this original limited project expanded into a plan for a general survey. One, I must admit, was personal interest. I have been active for a good many years in various Catholic and inter-denominational groups, which have brought me a wide range of international contacts. I am a member of the International Union of Social Studies (Union of Malines), and have lectured at the *Semaine Sociale de France* and opened a discussion group at the *Deutscher Katholikentag*. I have found myself in various more or less official capacities at meetings of all kinds and degrees of publicity, from the Annual Congresses of the N.E.I.—the Christian Democratic

xiii

parties' International—by way of the International of Catholic employers and workers, to a series of Protestant-Catholic conversations on the common ground between the Churches in economic and social affairs. As a member of the Labour Party I found myself present at the Socialist International's Bentveld Conference in 1953 on *Religion and Socialism*, and so in direct contact with the 'religious socialist' movement. The extent and unity of Christian Democracy gradually came home to me; a unity extending even beyond the limits of what are conventionally known on the Continent as the Christian Democratic movements. If I was to spend time and raise money for a study in this field at all, it seemed tempting to use the opportunity to bring all this experience into focus.

I dare say I could have resisted this temptation and stuck to my professional last if it had not been for certain other very practical reasons for making a general survey first. The Christian Democratic movements hang together in the sense not only of mutual aid but of mutual inspiration. If one examines their programmes and finds out what they are trying to do, it turns out that the very essence of it is catholicity. They are trying to create a broad synthesis incorporating and bringing into perspective elements which tend, Christian Democrats would say, to be one-sidedly emphasised in the traditions of conservatism or liberalism or socialism; together with certain other federalist or 'pluralist' ideas which are the characteristic contribution of the Christian social movement itself. It is this catholic, synthetic view which makes the Christian Democratic parties —for instance—tend to appear at or about the centre of the political stage. And the synthesis which Christian Democrats aim at creating is not arrived at only by abstract thought, or by any one movement on its own. A main factor in it is the interplay, with reference to concrete problems, of organisations and interest groups each of which influences the rest. To understand one movement it is necessary to cast at least a glance at all. This would not be difficult if Christian Democracy had been studied as thoroughly as, for instance, Socialism. But it quickly became apparent, so far as my own original project was concerned, that I was unlikely to find in any language the background material needed to put the trade unions and employers' organisations in their right perspective unless I dug so far into other subjects and examined so much first-hand material as to provide myself with the material for a general survey.

However, there are limits to human endurance and to the time which can be spared from other work, and the upshot inevitably is that this study is limited to Christian Democracy in one group of countries in Western Europe, and to that one form of it which is characteristic there. I have not examined here what Christian Democracy may mean, or rather has meant, in the different conditions of Britain and America. What is written here is also preliminary rather than conclusive. Before a conclusive study can be written a great deal more research will be needed, and I hope one result of this book will be to stimulate it; primarily in the English-speaking countries, but not only there. There are already a number of first-class histories of particular aspects of Christian Democracy. In France, for example, there are the superb theses of Duroselle and Henri Rollet on the growth of the Catholic social movement down to 1900. In Holland there are massive biographies of several of the leading figures of both the Protestant and the Catholic movements; De Savornin Lohman, for instance, or on the Catholic side Schaepman and Ariens. The religious socialist movement has been studied by Van Gestel (against) and Wilzen and Van Biemen (for). There are a number of good party or union histories; for instance Zirnheld's *Cinquante Années de Syndicalisme Chrétien,* brought up to date in Levard's slighter *Chances et Périls du Syndicalisme Chrétien.* But the literature even in the original languages of the various movements shows great gaps, and English-language literature is in this field a desert. Some important contributions towards cultivating this desert are beginning to come now from the United States. From Britain and Ireland there is as yet little or nothing. Dutch Protestants, for example, have built up over the last century one of the most successful and in many ways the most instructive political, economic, and social movements to be found anywhere in the Christian world. But this achievement has been neglected to an astonishing extent by their co-religionists in the Churches of the Calvinist tradition in the British Isles. Academic readers of this book will find subjects for Ph.D. theses sparking off right and left. And I hope that Ph.D. candidates will not be the only ones to take the hint.

One thing which this study is not is a tract for the times. It is a voyage of exploration in the history and current aims and achievements of one of the major social movements of modern times; indeed, so far as Continental Western Europe is concerned, of the most influential single movement of recent years. This is a study worth making in the interests of history, of the social sciences, and of the development of Christian doctrine, and it is for these academic purposes that it has in fact been made. But in studying a movement of this kind it is impossible not to reflect on how its experience might be relevant in one's own country. What stands out from this point of view is the convergence of British and Continental conditions in recent generations. Britain sixty or seventy years ago was a broadly Christian country in which even the labour movement was still deeply marked with the stamp of the Free Churches. The dividing line ran not between

Christians and non-Christians but between those who took one or another view on politics or economics or social policy. The main issues of political and social controversy had been those characteristic of Liberalism—free trade, for instance—and were coming to be those of Socialism and the 'managerial' society. On the Continent on the other hand large sections of society had already been lost to Christianity. Atheism was militant, and the dividing line in political and social life often ran between Christians and non-Christians. And when the Christian Democratic movements in due course emerged, the issues in which they were interested were not those characteristic of either Liberalism or Socialism, though they were prepared to learn from both. What interested them above all was problems of human relations; of the family, the small working group, the social group of every shape and size, with no exaggerated concentration after the Liberal manner on the individual or after the Socialist manner on the State. They were often also rather traditional in their outlook, at a time when Britain, with all its conservatism, was still the leading example of the new dynamic, mobile industrial society.

But today the lines have converged. It is no longer true that Britain is a Christian country in a sense in which other countries of Western Europe are not. The proportion of believing, understanding, and practising Christians—the sort of Christians who are statistically distinguishable as such—is very much smaller today in Britain as a whole than in the belt along the Rhine, from Flanders to the North of Italy, in which Christian Democracy has its greatest strength. It is doubtful whether it is even as high as in France. There is not yet much militant atheism or 'humanism'. But then neither is there anything like so much of this on the Continent as there used to be. In Britain and on the Continent alike, the problem for the Christian believer today is more likely to be to attract attention in an indifferent environment than to beat off the assaults of militant anti-clericals. It is no longer true that the chief dividing line in Continental politics and social life runs between Christians and non-Christians. It runs between democrats and authoritarians, whether of the right or the left; and Christian Democrats and 'humanist' Liberals and Social-Democrats are grouped together on the democratic side. And it is rapidly ceasing to be true that Christian Democrats talk about one set of social problems while British politicians or trade unionists talk about another. The problems of the family and local community or of human relations in industry are coming to the front in Britain, while the Christian Democrats on their side have learnt to appreciate such things as State economic planning or the Rights of Man. They are still conservative, in the sense that they understand the meaning of stability and continuity, and, in general, of the time factor in human affairs. But they have long ceased to be traditionalist: their eyes are turned to the future, not the past.

It seems very likely, therefore, that the problems faced by the movements studied in this book, and the formulas found for solving them, will have some relevance in British conditions. It is perhaps worth underlining that 'formulas' is used here in the plural. It is a common error to think that Christian Democracy is identified with one political and social formula; that which leads in politics, for example, to the party with a 'Christian' label, and particularly to the party which tries to group all Christians. If this book teaches one idea of current practical significance, it is that this conception of a single formula has no relation to the facts. There are many formulas, and much of the internal debate in the Christian Democratic world is concerned precisely with choosing between them. Just because of this, Britain in turn may have a good deal to teach the Christian Democratic movements. It is often rather embarrassing, at some Christian Democratic international meeting, to experience the deference paid to the obscure representative of what is often a frankly microscopic British group. For British ideas on the way to handle political and social problems attract a great deal of interest and respect in Christian Democratic circles, and have provoked a good deal of controversy. There has been an active debate in several countries, for example, over the British Labour Party, its ability to embrace Christians and non-Christians alike, its special relation to the trade unions, and the case for and against developing similar parties under Christian leadership in countries such as France or Holland.

May I also emphasise that this is *not* particularly a study of the Christian Democratic political parties? People in the Anglo-Saxon countries have a way of being blinded by the parties and forgetting the social movements and the movements of Christian Action: that weightier part of the iceberg which lies for the most part below the vision of the British or American press. Nor is this primarily a study of current political or trade union tactics. There are such studies—books like Einaudi and Goguel's *Christian Democracy in Italy and France*, for example—and there ought to be many more. But this book, as its title implies, is written in a longer perspective, and the reference to recent and current affairs cannot be as detailed as some might wish.

Leaders and officials of many of the organisations mentioned in this book have supplied material and given me the opportunity of talking over with them questions about the history and current position of their organisations. I take this opportunity of expressing my appreciation of their help. There are also three more special acknowledgements. First, to

Fr. L. O'Hea, S.J., formerly Principal of the Catholic Workers' College at Oxford, to whom this book is dedicated. I owe to Fr. O'Hea my first introduction to this field and stimulus to take an active interest in it. Secondly, to Mr. A. E. de Schryver, Belgian Minister of State and Chairman of the N.E.I., who gave support and material encouragement at a time when it seemed doubtful whether I would have either the opportunity or the means to make this study. It is due to him that the study proceeded at all. And last, but not least, to the Rockefeller Foundation, which in 1952–3 and 1953–4 gave me the travel grants without which a large part of the interviewing and collection of material—much of which is not available in Britain—would have been impossible.

M. P. F.

Cardiff,
June 1955

PART I

PART I

CHAPTER I

INTRODUCTION

THE IDEA OF CHRISTIAN DEMOCRACY

CHRISTIAN DEMOCRACY is an idea, a movement, and the product of a process of history reaching far back through the centuries. This book is concerned with all three aspects. Writing in 1901 in his Encyclical *Graves de Communi*, Leo XIII defined Christian Democracy in terms of ideas and aims. It was:

> concerned primarily, though not exclusively, with the problems of the working class.
> aimed at so improving the conditions of life as to allow people to 'feel themselves to be men, not mere animals; Christian men and not pagans'.
> a means, in these ways, of enabling people 'to strive with more facility and earnestness to attain that one thing needful, that final good for which we came into the world'.

This definition is both wider and narrower than would be appropriate today. It is narrower, since, especially in the more socially advanced countries, the problems at the top of the agenda today are no longer exclusively or even specially those of the working class. Problems such as those of unemployment, sweated wages, or slum housing, which used to weigh specially heavily on the working class, are in many countries either solved or on their way to solution. In their place attention is beginning to be given to problems of human relations, in the family or the firm or the local community, which may affect people of any class. In so far as economic problems do remain important, they are today often the problems of farmers, or the middle class, as well as of workers, or else problems of quite general significance such as that of inflation. Christian Democracy today does not regard itself as class-bound even to that limited extent implied in Leo XIII's definition.

Yet at the same time the old definition is too wide, in that it sweeps into one net a whole range of activities which today are more carefully distinguished, not least in the Catholic Church itself. The Catholic Church recognises in principle, and the Protestant Churches usually recognise in practice, three levels of action inspired by Christian ideals. There is that specific to the clergy, in preaching the Gospel and maintaining the tradition

3

and services of the Church. There is that of Catholic Action, or, as one might say in order to bring in the corresponding Protestant bodies, of Christian Action. Catholic Action:

> In its strict sense, and properly speaking, consists of the organised totality of those associations in which the laity carry on some form of apostolate as auxiliaries of the ecclesiastical Hierarchy; and not merely with the approval of the Hierarchy, but under its special mandate, in direct dependence on it, and under rules called for and sanctioned by it. (Civardi, *Manuale di Azione Cattolica*, 12th Italian ed., 1952, p. 22.)

Christian Action in this, strict, sense aims primarily at religious and moral development, though with special emphasis on training for political, economic, or social activity. Its 'prime task' (Civardi, p. 55) is 'the formation of consciences'. It is not to be confused with the third level of action, at which the laity take over entirely and act on their own initiative and responsibility, though within the normal framework of the beliefs, rules, and practice of their church. The 'laity' in this case includes members of the clergy who may, for instance, enter politics on the same footing as laymen, leaving behind for that purpose the special authority of their clerical office. However Christian and apostolic these activities not directly controlled by the Hierarchy may be in their aims, it is only 'in a loose sense' (Civardi, p. 22) that they can be said to belong to Catholic or Christian Action. So for instance the French Christian trade unions, though of overwhelmingly Catholic inspiration, appear in the Yearbook of French Catholic Action not in the main text but in an appendix 'For Information', and the French Christian Democratic political party, the M.R.P., does not appear there at all. The primary aim of bodies working in this third area is to solve political, economic, or social problems, though naturally keeping in mind the relevance of these to religious and moral development.

It is here, in this third area, that Christian Democracy is to be found, though it is not the only inhabitant of it. The militant Catholic employers whose activities fill so many pages of the history of the French Christian social movement in the nineteenth century were certainly Christian laymen acting on their own initiative and responsibility, but were hardly an example of Christian Democracy. 'Christian Patriarchalism' might have been a better title, not least since many of them were in fact influenced by the patriarchalist school of Le Play. Contemplating the class-conscious aristocrats who led a number of other Christian movements at that time, one is tempted to comment like Karl Marx:

> In this way arose feudal socialism: half lamentation, half lampoon; half echo of the past, half menace of the future; at times, by its bitter, witty, and incisive criticism, striking the bourgeoisie to the very heart's core, but always ludicrous in effect, through total incapacity to comprehend the march of modern history. The aristocracy, in order to rally the people to them, waved the proletarian

alms-bag in front for a banner. But the people, so often as it joined them, saw on their hind-quarters the old feudal coats of arms, and deserted with loud and irreverent laughter. . . . (*Communist Manifesto*, III. 1. a.)

This 'Christian Feudalism'—the phrase is not too strong—can also not be identified with Christian Democracy. And there is no need to confine examples to the past. In politics, or among employers and managers, there are still many sincere Christians who uphold patriarchal or feudal principles.

Then what is Christian Democracy? It might be crudely defined as the movement of those laymen, engaged on their own responsibility in the solution of political, economic, and social problems in the light of Christian principles, who conclude from these principles and from practical experience that in the modern world democracy is normally best: that government, in the State, the firm, the local community, or the family, should be not merely of and for the people but also by them. More precisely: Christian Democracy is the movement of those who, having regard to the Christian revelation, accept the personalist and pluralist principles to be outlined in later chapters, and conclude from these that conditions in the modern world call for the widespread use of such techniques as political democracy, joint responsibility in industry, or the withering away of the patriarchal family.

These distinctions between and within the various levels of activity inspired by Christianity are often blurred. A Christian Democratic politician in France or Austria or Italy may protest indignantly that he has nothing in common with the Christian monarchists or anti-semites or clericals of seventy years ago. Yet to the historian it is perfectly clear that monarchist, anti-semitic, or clerical politics is one of the stocks out of which Christian Democracy in these countries has grown. It is impossible (as will be obvious in Part III) to write the history of one without the other, and there are still many issues, such as that of Church schools, on which the Democratic and the Right-wing Christian join together against the world. The lines between the three levels of activity—of the clergy, of Christian Action, and of the laity on their own—are also often uncertain. The priest in his pulpit belongs clearly to the first level, the politician in parliament to the third. Economic and social movements belong in general to the third; but those of them which, though directed to economic or social ends, have a particularly high educational content, lie on the margin between the third and the second, and may even be absorbed into the level of Christian Action altogether. Women's and youth movements and the social services are particularly often treated in this way. Thus the Young Christian Workers would ordinarily be classified as an organisation of Catholic Action, indeed one of the most important of them. Yet this is also certainly an organisation in which laymen have a very high degree of responsibility, and which aims at and achieves important political, economic, and social ends. For certain purposes it is convenient to think of it rather as a branch of Christian Democracy. And there are a number of what in a business would probably be called 'service' activities, such as the research carried on by religious sociologists, or as—Civardi's example—a Christian publishing house, which may be formally classified as clerical or Christian or lay action, but may in fact assist action at all three levels at once. Such activities are not formally a part of Christian Democracy, but no study of Christian Democracy can afford to neglect them.

Yet, though sometimes blurred, these various distinctions must be upheld. Christian Democracy *is* in fact something very different from Christian Patriarchalism or Feudalism. And the division between Christian Action and clerical action on the one hand and the 'third sphere' of lay action on the other corresponds to nothing less than the traditional distinction between the two supreme powers of Church and State.

> God, therefore, has appointed the charge of the human race between two powers, the ecclesiastical and the civil, the one being set over divine and the other over human things. Each in its kind is supreme. . . . One of the two has for its proximate and chief object the well-being of this mortal life; the other the everlasting joys of heaven. Whatever, therefore, in things human is of a sacred character, whatever belongs either of its own nature or by reason of the end to which it is referred, to the salvation of souls, or to the worship of God, is subject to the power and judgment of the Church. Whatever is to be ranged under the civil and political order is rightly subject to the civil authority. Jesus Christ has Himself ordered that what is Caesar's is to be rendered to Caesar, and what is God's to God. (Leo XIII, Encyclical *Immortale Dei*, 1885, CTS ed. in *The Pope and the People*, pp. 51 and 52.)

There has been repeated conflict through the centuries over the precise meaning of this distinction and the best way of upholding it. But this conflict has arisen precisely because the distinction is recognised as vital, and to be upheld at all costs. Christian Democracy, we might say again, is the movement of those who aim to solve—with the aid of Christian principles and 'democratic' techniques—that range of temporal problems which the Church has repeatedly and solemnly declared to lie within the 'supreme' competence of lay society, and outside direct ecclesiastical control. We are concerned here essentially with those Christian movements, or movements of Christians, which fall under the definition of Christian Democracy given here and above. We touch only incidentally—however often or at length—those other movements, of Christian Action or otherwise, which overlap into the Christian Democratic movements' field or contribute to their growth.

CHRISTIAN DEMOCRACY AS A MOVEMENT

The idea of Christian Democracy as just defined is quite general; it applies anywhere, at any time. But the forms in which it has been embodied are many and various, and it is impossible to study them all at once. We are concerned here with one major geographical area and, chiefly, one pattern of Christian Democracy; that area and pattern in which Christian Democracy has been most obviously manifested in the last few years.

Across Western Europe, from Flanders to Venice, there lies a belt of high religious observance, where people are more likely than elsewhere not only to profess a religion but to practise it; a sort of heartland of European Christianity. The mainly Protestant lands to the north and east are, if not precisely a religious desert, at any rate an area of what in the National Farm Survey would be called Grade C culture. The statistics of religious practice are everywhere imperfect, and need to be carefully interpreted in the light of the theology and customs of the various churches. Allowing for this, it can be shown for example in Germany that religious observance among Protestants falls off rather consistently from the west and south towards Berlin and the north coast. During the Nazi period it was in the north and east that the paganised 'German Christian' movement made most progress. But the tendency to a low level of observance goes back to before the war and the Nazi period; it is not simply an effect of the strains of recent years. One explanation might be that religion thrives on competition, since the areas of low observance tend also to be those where the proportion of Protestants in the total population is highest. Silesia, an eastern territory, but one where the balance between Catholics and Protestants was till the Second World War more equal than elsewhere, showed till then a rather high level of observance among Protestants. But if there is such a rule it should apply also to Catholics, whereas in fact the statistics show that Catholic observance is high in the mainly Catholic west and south, but falls away, like observance among Protestants, towards the mainly Protestant east and north.

There is a similar, mainly Catholic, desert on the other side of the heartland, covering most of France, Spain, and Italy. A glance at the map of France, taken on its own, would suggest that religious observance there is a matter of the fringe areas; Brittany and Vendée, parts of the south-west and south, and various departments round the eastern and northern frontiers. But when the map of France is set in its place among the other countries of the Continent, a fairer interpretation seems to be that the eastern and northern zone of France, like the Veneto and certain of the sub-Alpine lands of Italy, is part of the outer edge of the central belt of high observance. West and south of this there are great sanctuaries, such as Lourdes or Rome; islands of intellectual and missionary activity, as at Paris or Madrid; even zones of high observance, as in western France or north-western Spain. But the main impression, by contrast with the central belt, is of a standard of observance always uneven and often low. Rome and Wittenberg, curiously enough, thus turn out both to lie in 'religious

7

deserts'. Wittenberg, in Saxony, lies well away in the eastern Protestant desert. The proportion of practising Catholics in Rome is comparable to that in central France, and scandalously low by the standards of, say, Holland or western Germany.

High observance, at any rate, is most commonly to be found in the belt which includes Holland, Belgium, French Flanders, Alsace-Lorraine, Westfalia, the Rhineland, most of south Germany and Austria, Switzerland (though here statistics are lacking), and parts of north Italy. There are large Protestant as well as Catholic populations in this area, and the tendency to high observance applies to both. As the case of Germany shows, competition between religions is probably not by itself enough to explain this. But it may be that competition of a more general kind is at the bottom of it; for this is a land not only of political but also of linguistic and cultural frontiers. However, let the reason be what it may, the relatively high degree of religious observance in this region is a fact. And it is in the eight countries which either lie within or touch on this belt— Holland, Belgium, Luxemburg, Switzerland, Austria, Germany, Italy, France—that Christian Democratic movements have in recent years taken their most clear-cut and self-conscious form, and have had the solidest support. Parties officially known as Christian Democratic, and grouping both Protestants and Catholics, held in 1955 nearly two-fifths of the seats in lower houses of parliament in these countries. Christian Democratic trade unions held a majority over the Socialist unions in Holland and Belgium, fell short of the Communists but substantially exceeded the Socialists in Italy and France, and constituted an appreciable and organised minority in Switzerland, Austria, and Germany. Christian Democratic organisations had a substantial footing among farmers and the smaller employers, and at least a foothold among larger firms. Massive youth and family movements (not to be confused with the ordinary Church youth and women's movements) gave Christian Democracy and Christian Action a strong position among these groups as well. And the Christian Democratic movements had the help of a strong Press, of the Protestant and Catholic universities and schools, and of a variety of research and other service agencies.

Actually, Christian Democracy in recent years has achieved its greatest strength and found its main sources of initiative and inspiration not merely in these eight countries but in those parts of them which lie inside the central belt. This is least true, though there is still much truth in it, in France. The Nord and Alsace-Lorraine, the parts of France within the central belt, have played a great part in the history of French Christian Democracy in all its aspects. But they cannot be said to have dominated it. In Germany on the other hand both the Protestant and the Catholic movements have been led primarily from the west, with the south playing second string and the rest nowhere. It is characteristic that when Adolf Stöcker was struggling to found the Protestant political movement—what has since become the Protestant component of the C.D.U.—he was forced out of Berlin and driven back on a group of constituencies in west Germany, notably round Bielefeld and Siegen. The weight of the German Protestant social movement has also been predominantly in the west. The first generation of the German Catholic social movement was dominated by the Westfalian Bishop Ketteler, whose see was at Mainz. The second was inspired by the 'München-Gladbach school', whose centre lies a few miles from the Dutch frontier. Its greatest internal controversy, early in the twentieth century, was the 'trade union conflict' between the leaders in München-Gladbach and Cologne on the one hand and Berlin on the other: and it is characteristic that the west Germans won. In Italy the outstanding Christian Democratic leader, Don Sturzo, built his original bailiwick in Sicily. But when his Popular Party went to work after the First World War the heaviest support for political Christian Democracy came, as it still does, from Lombardy, the territory around Venice, and the Alpine districts. And the original Christian Democratic social move-ment—rural credit societies, trade unions, and the rest—was overwhelm-ingly a creation of the north. The München-Gladbach of Italy was Bergamo, north-east of Milan on the edge of the Alps. The effective founder of the Austrian Christian Social movement, Karl Lueger, was Mayor of Vienna, but the movement's solidest support has always come from the Alpine lands to the west. And of all the national Christian Democratic movements the solidest, most stable, and most compre-hensive are those of Holland and Belgian Flanders, and perhaps secondly of the Catholics in Switzerland: countries wholly within the central belt.

Though the central belt of Europe has been the most conspicuous base of Christian Democracy for some years, this was not always so. A history of Christian Democracy in the nineteenth century would have to give much more prominence to Great Britain and the United States. The only Continental European Christian Democratic movement which general historians treat as of major importance at that time was the German Centre Party, and that only from the eighteen-seventies onwards. The contribution of the Free Churches to the British Liberal or Labour move-ments, or of Anglicanism to Tory democracy, bulked far larger then than the brilliant but ineffectual efforts of a Lamennais in France or of the early continental Christian Socialists in Germany or Holland or Switzer-land. The work of men like Kuyper in Holland or Helleputte in Belgium was no doubt effective enough, but was confined to these smaller countries. There were massive and organised Catholic forces in the political and social life of Italy and France, but their aims and methods defined them at most as precursors of Christian Democracy, and certainly not as

Christian Democratic themselves. It is only in the last forty or fifty years that Continental Christian Democracy as a whole has emerged as a movement of first-class importance.

It has tended in doing so to monopolise the name of Christian Democracy, accidentally and rather misleadingly, for its own characteristic form of organisation. The Anglo-Saxon Christian Democracy of the nineteenth century grew up through participation by individual Christians, each acting for himself, in any and all of those political or economic or social movements which happened to offer themselves. The unions they joined had no religious division. The parties they voted for were Republican or Democratic, Liberal or Conservative: their connection with this or that denomination, where it existed at all, was incidental, local, and in no way constitutional. Continental Christian Democracy has on the contrary been identified, at least up to the present, with the idea of the specifically Christian party or social organisation. So far as the theory of Christian Democracy is concerned, either form of organisation would seem to be acceptable. Which one is appropriate depends on the circumstances of each time and place, and it is not for the supporters of either to claim a monopoly of the Christian Democratic name. To quote Leo XIII again, Christian Democracy rests on principles which:

> Are and remain . . . completely outside party rivalries and political changes. (Encyclical *Graves de Communi*, 1901, CTS ed. in *The Pope and the People*, p. 172.)

The 'Continental' and 'Anglo-Saxon' approaches both have wide support among Christians today, and remain characteristic of action by Christian Democrats in their respective areas. Ideally it would be best to study them in parallel. But they are so different, have so many varieties and sub-varieties, and are found in such a remarkably wide range of geographical and social conditions, that no one investigator could hope to do this well. It is for this reason that this study is confined to the Continental movement and to the countries in or touching on the central belt. That will not necessarily prevent its conclusions from being relevant in other cases. The ideas of Christian Democracy are, or can be, universal. The form of organisation traditional among Christians in the Anglo-Saxon countries exists also on the Continent, and several of the Continental movements have been debating seriously in recent years whether they should not go over to it altogether. These debates have thrown a great deal of light, revealing for British or American as well as Continental practice, on the conditions to which each form of organisation is appropriate. And in general, as has been suggested in the Preface, the position of Christians in the life of the Continental and the Anglo-Saxon countries has today become similar enough to make a study of either side relevant to the other.

INTRODUCTION

CHRISTIAN DEMOCRACY AS THE PRODUCT OF HISTORY

Christian Democracy, finally, is the product not only of recent history but of tendencies which reach far back into past centuries, indeed to the beginning of Christianity itself. It can be understood, as will be shown in Part IV, as the answer in the political, economic, and social field to questions posed by Ernst Troeltsch half a century ago about the division of Christianity since the Reformation and the schism between East and West and the way to overcome it. Be that as it may, it is certain that a movement as wide and deep as Christian Democracy can be understood only as part of the general ebb and flow of Christianity, which proceeded for centuries before recognisably Christian Democratic movements began. Part IV will try to put it in this longer perspective.

PART II

CHAPTER II

THE SOURCES OF CHRISTIAN DEMOCRATIC PROGRAMMES

CAN one speak of 'a' doctrine or programme of Christian Democracy? At first sight the answer might well be 'no'. The Christian Democratic movements, even if one confines oneself to those of Continental Europe studied here, have grown up separately, in many different countries and social environments, and in response to widely different needs. Their initiators include rich and poor, clergy and laity, Protestants and Catholics. Their interests often differ or conflict. Family movements have one set of interests, and a programme to correspond; small business movements have another. The Christian workers' movements stand for a degree of workers' control in industry which the Christian employers' movements indignantly reject. There are denominational differences and national differences. One does not have to attend many gatherings of Christian Democrats to realise that the Dutch approach is of one kind, the French approach very much of another. Where there are both Protestant and Catholic documents on the same subject, they will often appeal to different authorities, use a different line of argument, even be written in a different style.[1] And sometimes there is a plain and straightforward lack of co-ordination. The Christian Democratic political parties complain in their own international congresses at the lack of co-ordination even on matters of international policy, such as the integration of Europe.

But this diversity fades quickly when a longer view is taken. When one has followed through the history of Christian Democracy, soaked oneself in its literature, and caught the atmosphere of its meetings, one is left with the feeling not of divergence but of fundamental, impressive, and growing unity between people and movements who do indeed share one world of ideas. Through the programmes of all the movements run common characteristics, which stand out particularly in the case of the political parties. For these embrace all classes, regard themselves as responsible for the common good, and tend therefore to represent the

[1] See for instance the pair of pamphlets published by the French Christian trade unions (CFTC) on *Syndicaliste chrétien—Pourquoi?*

15

highest common denominator of Christian Democratic opinion. Their programmes are characteristically:

(1) Comprehensive and balanced, a catholic (with a small 'c') synthesis of views from all quarters of the political universe on the whole range of problems with which government is concerned.
(2) Based consciously and, usually, explicitly on the Christian revelation and the tradition and teaching of the Churches.
(3) Empirical, built up in the light of history and current experience rather than of any systematic, *a priori*, theory.

THE CATHOLIC SYNTHESIS

The Christian Democratic movements have been criticised both by their own supporters and from outside for their desire to equip themselves with a comprehensive doctrine.

> One of the characteristics of secular movements or organisations whose inspiration is religious is their pretension to possess, define, or recall a 'doctrine'. A strange and dangerous pretension, revealing a basic confusion. The Catholic Church, as guardian of faith and morals, has a doctrine. But it is far otherwise with purely secular organisations. (Bernard Georges in *Problèmes du Catholicisme Français*, 1953, p. 145.)

Or as Stefano Jacini, who was a leading member of the Italian Popular Party, says of the programme which the party adopted in 1919:

> If there is one comment to be made today, in the light of experience, on this list of demands, it is that which appeared repeatedly from the start in the Liberal press; it was too complete, one might almost say too stuffed. There is no doubt that in practice this completeness damaged the party in its early days. Experience has in fact shown that to draft a detailed political programme, to proclaim it to the people and remain tenaciously attached to it through the precipitous changes of events, and to take as an aim the realisation of this programme point by point through legal channels, over many years of administrative and political action, in a sort of slow-moving frontal attack— all this pays less well than to create forthwith a nucleus of strength, and to set out with this to win power, adapting the programme from hour to hour, without fear of inconsistency, to the changing moods of the electorate and the needs of the battle for power. (*Storia del Partito Popolare Italiano*, 1951, ed., p. 24.)

And yet, says Jacini:

> I for one still believe that the intrinsic goodness of a programme does something to establish and maintain the standards of public life. (Ibid., p. 24.)

Or, to quote Senator Houben of the Belgian Christian Social Party:

> If politics are important and it is right for Christians to play their part in them, their action, to be effective, needs to be guided by a political doctrine. As soon, in fact, as one has in mind political action spread over a period, and proposes to attain aims defined in advance, a political doctrine is necessary to guarantee continuity and co-ordination, seeing the number of people who must act simultaneously or in succession in the different sectors and positions of political life. This is certainly true in our countries on the Continent of

Europe and in our age; for we are faced with grave problems and a rapid evolution, and are at one and the same time deeply logical (to the point of regarding a precedent as an argument) and very little bound by tradition. A doctrine is indispensable, notably, to Christians, who intend to base their policy on the common good, and have in their ranks people of all environments and classes. (Houben, 'Les Chrétiens devant la Politique', in *Revue Politique*, III (5), p. 13 (1953).)

From the side of the trade unions:

No one, no society or collectivity of any kind, can do without a doctrine or a guide to life. . . . And this is above all true of trade union action. Trade unionism is in fact not merely—as has too often been said of it—a question of stomachs. To draw and hold a mass membership it needs not only a material bait but also an ideal which encourages them, in the hope of an uncertain result, to make sacrifices which are not repaid in immediate satisfaction or through any personal profit. Even the most apparently neutral trade union movements fall under this rule. They may claim to be solely concerned with the economic interests of their members. But inevitably there arise occasions when their members understand the satisfaction of these interests, or the means to be employed to achieve it, quite differently according to each one's opinions and personal beliefs. . . . (Zirnheld, *Cinquante Années de Syndicalisme Chrétien*, 1937, p. 178.)

It is at any rate a fact that the Christian Democratic movements do in general try to equip themselves with a comprehensive doctrine, covering both aims and methods. And it is also true that the programmes in which these doctrines are expressed are marked off from those of other movements by their synthetic or catholic quality. The parties, especially, draw material from all the corners of the political universe, and criticise and rework it into a pattern in which each element finds its place in the perspective of the rest. They are as much preoccupied as liberals with the status, role, and security of the individual: with such things as human rights and the value of individual initiative. But a Christian Democrat will criticise the liberal approach as too individualist, and as 'humanist' in the sense of secularist. His own view, he would say, is 'personalist' in the sense of bringing into account all the dimensions of personality; social as well as individual, supernatural (and therefore Church) as well as purely human. Christian Democrats share with socialists an appreciation of the importance and rights of the collectivity, and especially of the State. But they hasten to add that they are not 'collectivist' either, in the sense of over-stressing the role of any particular social grouping, and notably that of the State. They are on the contrary 'solidarist' in the sense of thinking always of collectivities as being at the service of the individual, not as superior to him. And they are 'pluralist' or 'federalist' in that they appreciate the value of social groupings of every size from the individual up to the community of all the peoples of the world, and try to mark out the functions and organisation appropriate to each and its rights and duties over against the rest. The State takes its place as merely one, and not necessarily or always the most important, in a hierarchy of social groups.[1] Christian Democrats are also conservative, in that they share with conservatives an appreciation of the time factor, of the difficulties of successful change, and of the importance of smooth, continuous development. But they are convinced also of man's right and duty to advance towards mastering his environment by the power of his reason and will. They will stoutly deny that they are 'traditionalist', in the sense of being particularly attached to the shape of things as it now is or once was.

This tendency to catholicity exists not only in the Christian Democratic parties but also in the trade unions, employers', farmers', and women's and youth organisations. Christian trade unions like to think of themselves as pursuing with equal vigour the defence of class interests and an ideal of inter-class collaboration. Socialist or Communist unions are for them one-sidedly class-conscious, interested in industrial collaboration only as a tactic of the class war. And in the same way the Christian employers', business middle class, and farmers' organisations criticise their neutral opposite numbers for being 'liberal' in the Manchester school sense; as tending, that is, to be one-sidedly interested in the pursuit of profit.

THE RELEVANCE OF REVELATION

Coming from the more secularised atmosphere of a country like Britain, one cannot help being struck by the way in which even the language of the Christian Democratic movements and their leaders betrays their Christian inspiration. Visit an official of one of the Dutch Protestant parties, and within five minutes one may be debating the political consequences of Karl Barth, or of the 'Separation' and 'Complaint' which split the Hervormde Kerk in the nineteenth century. Have lunch with his Catholic opposite number, and one finds the conversation channelled, often quite unconsciously, by *Quadragesimo Anno* and solidarist philosophy. The life and language of a political party like the French M.R.P., or the Italian *Democrazia Cristiana*, and of many of the social movements, is deeply coloured by the training so many of their leaders received in the Catholic youth movements. This impression is confirmed by an inspection of parties' and movements' rules and constitutions which regularly include references to revelation and the Christian tradition of the natural law. 'Our road', declared the representatives of the German Christian Dem-

---

[1] There is sometimes confusion among the theorists of Christian Democracy between the juridical conception of the 'State' as a 'perfect society', that is as a society which contains within itself all those functions which need to be performed collectively; and the State as commonly understood, that is the organ with final responsibility for most of the functions of government in a given territory. The latter is merely one social grouping among others. The former is a theoretical concept, a concrete approximation to which can be found in the modern world only at the level of the United Nations, or at least of the governments of the U.S.A. and U.S.S.R.

ocratic Union at the annual conference of the Christian Democratic political international (the N.E.I.) at Bruges in 1954,

> cannot be one of mere political pragmatism, concentrating on immediate practical decisions. Neither however can we accept a programme based purely on theory. Decisions must first and foremost make sense in the current political situation. But there must also be a place for reference to intellectually and spiritually based principles.

The form of the reference to Revelation and the natural law varies from case to case. The Protestant parties and social movements are particularly downright in insisting that their foundation is in Scripture.

> In exercising authority in the State the guide and standard must be Revelation, as set down in Scripture. (Principles of the Christian Historical Union (Holland), Art. 1.)

The Evangelical Party in Switzerland is the party of those citizens who 'base their view of public affairs on the Gospel'. But the Catholic People's Party in Holland also claims to base its programme on:

> the principles of the moral law and divine Revelation, and on respect for the pronouncements of the teaching authority of the Church. (General Political Programme of the K.V.P., Art. 1.)

In Germany the inter-confessional Christian Democratic Union cannot adopt formulas so characteristic of particular denominations, but makes clear that it is based on principles worked out in, though not directly taken over from, each of the two main churches. The Christian Social Party (P.S.C.) in Belgium:

> is Christian because it defends the human values which are the foundation of our Western civilisation; and historically, it is Christianity which put them there. (P.S.C., *Les Chantiers sont Ouverts*, 1945, p. 10.)

The M.R.P. avoids any reference to Christianity in its statutes. But its trade-union opposite number, the French Confederation of Christian Workers (C.F.T.C.)

> attaches itself to and inspires its action by the principles of Christian social ethics. (Statutes, I. 1.)

But what exactly do these references to revelation and the natural law mean? There are few if any matters of politics or economics or social life of which Christian Democrats would say that Christianity allows them to see the truth clearly, whereas non-Christians cannot see it at all. It is precisely to the possibility of agreement among all men of good will that parties like the P.S.C. and M.R.P. appeal when they speak of 'the values of Western civilisation', or in the case of the M.R.P. simply of the principles of 'political, economic, and social democracy'. But to say that men of good will *can* agree is one thing; to say that all of them *will* agree is another. What Christian Democrats maintain is that their Christianity

19

gives them an extra assurance, a certainty of touch, and a capacity for recognising and recovering from their mistakes which enables them to grasp and solve the problems of life more completely and competently than if they relied on human reason alone. At point after point, Revelation steps in to confirm conclusions which could be reached by reason, but which reasonable men in one age or country or another have in fact denied. By under-pinning and supplementing natural knowledge it makes possible a certain breadth and sureness of judgment, which, it is claimed, marks off Christian Democratic views from the more one-sided, partial, and often misleading views of others. If Christian Democracy achieves catholicity it is—so the claim goes—thanks first and foremost to this grasp of certain central truths demonstrable by national reasoning but confirmed by revelation. And these truths are in fact none other than the 'characteristic values of Western civilisation', though always with the essential theological footnote to confirm them.

(1) *Everyone has a right to the fullest and freest development of which he is capable*; to become all that he has it in him to become.

This is a judgment of the natural law, but the Christian revelation steps in to confirm and explain it. Man is made in the image of God, who reveals himself as a Creator and as he who IS; he who, by definition, is already in the fullest sense all that he has it in him to be. It is the right and duty of everyone, man or woman, to perfect the image of God in himself by becoming all he has it in him to become, and by taking the fullest share of which he is capable in God's work of creation.

(2) *People can become all that they have it in them to become only through co-operation with others. Social co-operation is therefore a duty*.

Since all, as individuals, have the same basic rights, duties, and destiny, all are equally entitled to benefit from this co-operation. Social life should be based on solidarity, not exploitation: human beings are ends, not means. There is no reason why solidarity and co-operation should be limited by class, race, religion, or anything except the need to give priority to those forms of them which are most urgent and effective. Nor, where there is a clash of interests or question of priority, can there be any question of weighting one man's claim more heavily than another's, so that needs of his which in all the circumstances are less important and urgent take precedence over the more urgent needs of others. Since all have the same basic rights, the calculation must be made strictly in terms of the urgency of each claim to each individual concerned.

Christian revelation confirms this judgment by showing that all men are indeed basically equal, and in what sense this is so. It insists that no conflicts between individuals, groups, or classes are ultimately irreconcilable. In the last resort all clashes of interest and claims for priority can be resolved, since every person without exception can in fact attain his highest destiny. And Christianity also shows, with its doctrine of the Mystical Body of Christ, what the necessary co-operation among men should ideally mean. It is that, not of master and servant, but of the mutually dependent and indispensable members of one body.

Christianity sums up these two basic judgments in the Great Commandments, to love God and to love one's neighbour as oneself.

(3) Science and practical action proceed on the assumption that the world is *rational*, in the sense of an order which *reason and will can master*, and which in the interests of full personal development and social solidarity they *should be used to master*. Even those forces which are studied by the natural sciences are hard to understand and harness, and still more those studied by the social sciences. Mastery can in any case not be achieved in a day. A great deal has been found out about the process of learning both for individuals and for social groups; the operations, the stages of development, and the time needed to enable an individual or group to break through an existing frame of reference and achieve a new view of a problem. Nevertheless, the assumption remains that in the last resort reason and will are decisive.

Revelation steps in with a whole series of clarifications. What reason and will lead up to is a genuine choice or series of choices. Actions are never completely determined, whether for worse or for better. It is possible to sin against the light even when the light is unimaginably clear; that is one main point of the story of the Fall of Satan. On the other hand the margin of choice is always great enough, for any individual, to allow him to attain the essential purpose of human life. It is always possible to choose between Heaven and Hell. The created world is indeed rational and capable of being mastered by man, and it is in fact man's duty to master it, to 'fill the earth and make it his'. And, with its account of sin and the forces of evil, revelation underscores and explains the difficulties, delays, and diversions which lie in the way of actually carrying out this duty.

(4) Sociology and anthropology can show on purely natural grounds the value of *religious ritual* and of a detached, dedicated class of priests. These help to symbolise and define the highest values of a society, to encourage a detached, impartial judgment of how they are or are not being realised in practice, and to win people's attention both for these values themselves and for the judgment on their application. They help to develop what a psychologist such as Allport, arguing purely on natural grounds, labels the 'mature religious sentiment' and defines in effect as the highest level of maturity and integration in individuals and groups. Examples of how the value of ritual, detachment and dedication is recognised even in purely secular affairs are the ritual of royalty or the special independence accorded to the Universities.

Revelation steps in to define the purpose, nature, and authority of what is in a pre-eminent way *the* Church, and so, by implication, the place religion and the Church should take in social life.

THE CONTRIBUTION OF HISTORY AND EXPERIENCE

These broad orientations can give rise to rules for day to day conduct only in the light of factual, historical study and experience showing how they apply in a particular time and place.

There is no equivalent in the Christian Democratic tradition of Marx's *Manifesto*. . . . Just as the first French socialists preferred to talk of justice, democracy, and equality rather than of surplus value and dialectics, so Christian Democratic thought was stimulated first by certain social or political aspirations. Reaction to facts was decisive rather than deliberate systematisation, and experience of life rather than abstract concepts. . . . What matters above all is to retain enough moral dynamism not to be caught at a loss by any new set of conditions; which implies a certain relativism, if not of principles

THE SOURCES OF CHRISTIAN DEMOCRATIC PROGRAMMES

then at any rate in the choice of means and methods. It also explains why Christian Democracy expresses itself better in its questions than in its positive statements. But one must not be misled by this refusal of a degree of systematisation such as would fail to take account of the contingency and approximation implied by action. It leads neither to softness and scepticism nor to cynical realism. Between systematisation and opportunism there is room for a doctrine hard enough to face up to any of the closed systems which oppose it, yet supple enough to benefit from the dialogue which the Christian Democrat, on the basis of his own conception of pluralism, sets out to maintain with those who hold other views. (Biton, *La Démocratie Chrétienne dans la Politique Française*, 1954, pp. 71–2.)

Zirnheld's account of why the C.F.T.C. thinks it necessary to have a doctrine was quoted above. But it does not imply that the C.F.T.C. or its predecessors had a fully worked-out doctrine from the start. The Clerical Workers' Union, which took the lead in the early days, defined its objective at first simply as 'security in our jobs, comfort in our families, and a higher social status'. At its 1909 Congress the question of a programme was raised. The General Secretary replied:

We are holding an organising congress, to consolidate what we have done so far. Later, when there is a whole network of unions, we can go on to define an economic and social doctrine, work out the problems raised by collaboration with the employers or by State intervention, and so on. . . . (Zirnheld, op. cit., p. 186.)

This cautious view was unanimously approved. A doctrine was necessary, but first there must be experience on which to build it. *En forgeant on devient forgeron*,[1] though not by forging to the exclusion of everything else. The Christian ideal is not activism but contemplation, that is 'leisure' in the sense of the σχολη from which are derived 'school' and 'scholarship'. The Christian Democratic and Christian Action movements agree that to understand events it is necessary to be immersed in them. But they also try to ensure through retreats, recollections, and study courses, and through the role of personal religion and the clergy in keeping the first principles of revelation and the natural law continually in view, the element of 'leisure' and contemplation which saves their policy from mere empiricism.

The 'hard yet supple' doctrine of which Biton speaks crystallises out of experience at two levels. The Churches, and the philosophers and theologians who speak in their name, have built up a large body of principles on political, economic, and social affairs. There are the Papal Encyclicals, and the corresponding official statements of the Protestant Churches. There are commentaries on and expansions of these documents, like the vast commentaries on *Quadragesimo Anno* by Fr. Hentzen and on Papal social teaching generally by Fr. Villain. There are the philosophers who have developed the Christian tradition of the natural law with special

[1] The smith's trade is learnt in the smithy.

reference to modern social problems, such as—picking books at random from the shelves—Pesch or Leclercq or Messner or Maritain. These statements and writings are stimulated by particular social conditions and problems, and summarise, in the light of the general orientations supplied by revelation and the natural law, experience in dealing with them. They are concerned chiefly with drawing the more general conclusions which can be reached in this way; the conclusions on which there is substantial agreement in the Church, and those of permanent value, most likely to stand the test of time. And what they say has to do largely with the ideal state of affairs which might be realised if the culture to which they apply were fully permeated with Christian principles.

The Christian Democratic movements draw heavily for their training and propaganda and for the general framework of their thought on this general philosophical and theological, though also existential, doctrine built up by and in the Churches. But there is also a level at which they themselves elaborate doctrine in the light of experience, independently and in their own right; the level of 'middle principles' or strategy. A political party or trade union can of course survive only with the help of a great deal of tactical and organising skill; what line to take in this committee, whether or not it is opportune to press that wage claim, how best to organise a movement for such and such a group. But it is not enough to have tactical and organising skill plus sound general philosophical principles. In between comes the level of strategy, of those working rules which may govern political or social action in a country for years or even generations together, but are not permanent or general enough to be incorporated into the general political and social doctrine of the Churches. They constitute the practical working 'hypothesis' as apart from the ideal 'thesis' of the theologians and philosophers. A labour movement may—as the British labour movement did—pursue for one or two generations typically 'liberal' objectives, such as political emancipation, or self-help through co-operatives and trade unions. Then for another couple of generations it may pursue socialist ideals and the Welfare State. It may turn in a third phase to federalist or pluralist objectives, and put the accent on workers' control in the firm and industry. It has not necessarily changed its principles, nor does it necessarily value one set of objectives more highly than another. It is merely that in each period one out of the various limited sets of objectives which might contribute to the overall purpose of the movement seems not merely desirable but realisable, and so to deserve priority at that stage. The question is one of strategy. When eighteenth- or nineteenth-century diplomatists applied the principle of the balance of power, that too was a question of strategy and the 'hypothesis'. What they had in mind was obviously not one of the unchanging constants of the natural law. Yet it was certainly a rule with stable and continuing validity in that particular environment, something much more than a matter of mere day to day tactics.

This sphere of strategy or 'middle principles' is important not only in its own right, so to speak, but because it belongs properly and exclusively to Christian Democracy. There is a difference here between the Catholic and Protestant views, due to differing conceptions of the nature and authority of the Church. But this difference is more apparent in theory than in practice. To summarise, define, and teach the broader principles of political and social conduct, those most immediately following from revelation and the natural law, is seen even by Protestants as the business in the first instance of the trained theologian or philosopher, and in the second of Christian Action movements, more or less formally under the official Church's control. But to decide how these principles can best be carried into effect in a given political, economic, or social environment is seen even by Catholics as primarily and essentially the responsibility of the lay Christian Democratic movements. And this covers the long-term, strategic judgments as well as day to day tactics. It is precisely in these long-term, strategic judgments, so the N.E.I. insisted when it considered this question at its annual conference at Fribourg in 1952, that the political or social or economic doctrine specific to a Christian Democratic movement consists; or, it is perhaps better to say, would consist if it were more fully worked out. As the main report at Fribourg said:

> Over and above these individual deficiencies, we note [in the programmes of the various Christian Democratic parties] the lack of a basic concept, that of . . . a political doctrine in the full sense; this we have attempted to define. At the risk of exaggeration, let us state this point schematically. It is possible to distinguish two parts in each of our programmes. One lays down philosophical concepts, and is the work of moral philosophers. The other says what it is intended to do immediately; it is the work of employers, trade unionists, farmers, and representatives of the business middle class. But we fear that the juxtaposition of these two sections does not add up to the definition of a political doctrine. Part I is not political: it is philosophy. Part II is not a matter of doctrine: it is a programme of action. (Houben, 'Force et faiblesse des chrétiens sur le plan de la doctrine', published in *Revue Politique*, Dec. 1952, p. 22.)

This self-criticism must not be pressed too far. Strategy has not been entirely neglected. The history of all the Christian Democratic movements shows, as will appear, that particular strategic conceptions of aims and method have dominated them for long periods together. Strategic aims can be, and in the next few chapters will be, read out of the programmes of the Christian Democratic movements today. But there is certainly reason to think, and not only in the case of the political parties, that the deliberate and conscious analysis of strategy has tended to lag behind the acquisition of tactical and organising skills and the build-up of a body of general principles. In the early days there were deficiencies in all three spheres.

Trade unions could not find competent organisers, new parties needed time to find their feet in parliament, and the textbooks and manifestoes which now lay down general principles for Christians in political and social life had still to be written. Looking back over fifty years of participation in the Christian social movement by the French Catholic institute *Action Populaire*, a member of its staff notes three stages in the process by which in French experience these gaps have been or are being filled. Down to the First World War the problem was to convince people of the need to organise on specifically Christian lines; to draw out the general principles which call for a special Christian contribution to public life. In a second period, down to the 'thirties, the problem was not, usually, whether to organise, but how to organise; the question of tactics and of movements' structure and management. But since the Second World War an organisation which asks for *Action Populaire*'s advice is more likely to be concerned with the best way of attacking some problem or range of problems; no longer with general principles or with tactics, but with the strategy of action. This new accent on strategy shows itself in international exchanges as well as within individual countries. It has led the N.E.I. to devote two of its recent annual congresses, at Fribourg in 1952 and Bruges in 1954, to comparing and, in a modest way, co-ordinating the aims of the Christian Democratic political parties. In the economic field it will be shown below[1] how the debate since the Second World War on the major unresolved issue of industrial relations, workers' control, began with a vigorous international exchange on the level of principles, but has now moved on to a discussion of the strategy of advance in a direction which in principle is broadly defined.

Since the programmes of Christian Democracy have been and are being shaped by experience, there is and can be no moment at which they attain their final form. While growth goes on it is not surprising that the differen experience in different countries and movements leads at times to divergences or even contradictions and to marked and sometimes rapid swings of opinion. Rapid swings have occurred in recent years notably in movements which are new or have suffered a break in continuity, and so have not had time to stabilise their opinions. So for example in Germany the C.D.U. emerged in 1945 after a twelve-year break in democratic political life, and in a form to which no previous parallel existed. The main previous Christian Democratic party had been overwhelmingly Catholic, and dead-centre or even at times centre-left in its views. Now the Catholics were joined by a large block of Protestants, many of them from right-wing movements, liberal or conservative. The Germany into which the new party was born had suffered unprecedented devastation, and was subject for an uncertain period to an in many ways unpredictable Allied control.

[1] Pp. 65ff.

It is not surprising that the C.D.U.'s policy took some time to settle down. Its first programme, the Köln Principles, placed it in the centre, if not actually on the left, of the Christian Democratic parties in Western Europe as a whole. Later programmes contained a much heavier dose of liberalism, and by the time of the Düsseldorf Principles of 1949 the pendulum had swung well over to the right; though, as will appear below, not quite so far in reality as in appearance. So also in Italy the *Democrazia Cristiana* came to the surface in 1943 after seventeen years of repression, and several years were needed for the movement's views to settle down; if indeed they can be said to have settled at all. The swing of the pendulum in Italy has on the whole been in the opposite direction from Germany. The Christian Democrats' initial policy was strongly liberal, but the left wing of the party has emerged more strongly as time went on.

CHAPTER III
PERSONALIST, NOT INDIVIDUALIST

T HE Christian Democrats' ideal of the good society is, as has been said, 'personalist'.

Man is not a tool of production, nor may he be reduced to a mere servant of society. He is a free and reasonable being, endowed by God with an eternal destiny, and equipped to that end with a supreme value as a person, with inalienable rights, and with high responsibilities. (C.F.T.C., Workers' Action Programme, 1945, p. 5.)

Or, as the Christian Social Party in Belgium puts it:

The liberal and capitalist order of the past was based on the individual. In theory, the individual was guaranteed complete freedom. But no one troubled about the way this freedom was used, or its results. When freedom is unlimited, the advantage goes to the strongest. Great masses of men live like beasts in slums, with no share in those spiritual goods in which civilisation consists. . . . Freedom of work is proclaimed, for the manual and white-collar worker alike. What does that mean? A wage which they can take or leave; passive submission to unemployment; no voice in the management of the economy on which their welfare depends. . . . Private enterprise is held in honour; but in practice this leads to the effacement of personality. A great part of the economy is controlled by limited companies . . . depersonalised business. Who carries the final responsibility for production and human relations? An indefinite majority of unknown shareholders. As concentration proceeds and companies become more important, even their staff lose their individuality and make up a numbered, ticketed, interchangeable mass. . . . In many sectors there build up, over these limited companies, trusts, holding companies, finance companies, some of which have a useful task of co-ordination, but which often are merely the expression of financial dictatorship. Where in all this is Man? In politics the sovereign elector still has his vote. But this freedom is a mockery, since more and more human personality comes to be buried under the dictatorship of the bureaucracy. . . .

Marxism has reacted strongly against these excesses of liberal capitalism, but has fallen into the opposite extreme. It gives all power to the State. The human person merely changes masters. Whereas before it risked oppression by too powerful private interests, now it has the certainty of being enslaved by the State. . . . Marxists believe in the materialist explanation of history. The succession of events is explained for them chiefly by economic conflicts. They do not attach enough importance to the spiritual forces which direct human effort, and human personality thus comes to be threatened in its highest attributions. Logically, Marxism leads to a civilisation dominated by technology, in which spiritual and personal freedom are stifled. A State monopoly of the means of production, along with bureaucracy and the

27

reduction of one social class after another to a proletariat, and accompanied by a network of formal and informal controls, must mean for society a stifling economic and political dictatorship. . . .

In the face of these contradictions and deficiencies there rises up the coherent and human doctrine of the Christian Social Party, based entirely on the central conception of the human person. Where there is a problem to be solved the party has only one standard for the choice of a solution. Will the formula proposed lead to the full development of the greatest possible number of personalities? (P.S.C., *Les Chantiers sont Ouverts*, 1945, pp. 11–13.)

The P.S.C. works out these general orientations into a series of specific programme points, alternative policies being judged in each case by the extent to which each contributes, or fails to contribute, to developing human personality. The problem of the family is not simply one of more births, or of social stability. It is that of an area where several personalities meet and must find a chance of satisfactory development. The problem of the Health Service is to find a form of management which respects the human dignity and differing ideals of doctor and patient alike. The problem of education is to educate the whole man, one and indivisible, in all his aspects. The problem of industry is not simply production; it is to ensure the primacy of man over money and technique. The human aspects of production must have priority over technical needs, and these in their turn over purely financial conditions such as the maintenance of profits. Industrial leadership itself needs to be 'personalised',[1] notably by giving the active managers of a business a stronger position over against their shareholders.

The P.S.C.'s views happen to be rather explicit. But pages can easily be filled with quotations illustrating thinking on similar lines in the other Christian Democratic movements. The M.R.P.'s statutory object is a political, economic, and social democracy which will:

Guarantee respect for personal rights and civic freedoms, and ensure the primacy of labour over capital and of merit over birth or wealth. (Statutes, Art. 2.)

The starting point is man, not as a member of a mass, but as an individual with reason, responsibility, and potentially infinite value. For the C.D.U. 'Man is the centre'. Labour is valued as 'a moral achievement, not a mere commodity'. For the Conservative People's Party in Switzerland the basis is 'the Christian conception of human personality and society'.

Respect for human dignity demands that work be valued as a personal and social achievement and as the basis of the physical and spiritual development of the individual and the family. (Programme, S. 5.)

The Dutch and Swiss Protestant parties derive their programmes not so much from a philosophical doctrine of personality as directly from

---

[1] The English version of one movement's history says that in the Christian Democratic view it should be 'parsonalised'.

Scripture and history. But they do not forget to underline the meaning and importance of personal freedom and responsibility. Thus the Evangelical People's Party in Switzerland calls for a social order which:

> Allows man to fulfil his divine destiny and freely develop his personality to that end. . . . The solution of the social question . . . lies in the spiritual renewal of the individual. Injustice and the absence of love and truth have their origin in the individual person, not in his environment. (Programme, S. 5.)

Personalism, as distinct from individualism, is held by Christian Democrats to imply a certain 'solidarist' conception of the individual's responsibility to and for the society around him, and, following from this, a 'federalist' or 'pluralist' ideal of the structure of society and the processes which go on within it. It has three main implications for practical policy.

(1) All social action should be oriented to enabling personalities to form themselves along certain ideal lines; to acquire certain basic characteristics and social and technical skills.
(2) These ideal personalities should be grouped in a pluralist social structure, in which scope is left for the free though socially responsible development of groups of all shapes and sizes, from the family up to international society. Different 'spiritual families' should have freedom and opportunity to work out their own salvation: 'vertical' pluralism, referring to the ideological divisions which cut through society from top to bottom, as apart from 'horizontal' pluralism between the different levels of society.
(3) The social structure should be tied together by and operated through sanctions (political, economic, or social) and mechanisms (competition, direction, consultation) combined so as to maintain its personalist and pluralist character.

CHRISTIAN DEMOCRACY'S IDEAL PERSONALITY TYPE

The training of individual personality is above all the field of the Christian Action movements, including the youth and women's movements and the workers' leagues or similar social class organisations, and it is from these that the Christian Democratic ideal of personality for the modern world can best be learnt. They themselves did not learn it all at once: like the Christian Democratic movements, they were not born with their ideals fully formed. The ideal of the Catholic Workers' Movement in Germany, for example, took a full generation to come to maturity. When the movement began, around 1880, it was concerned simply with plugging the most obvious gaps in the culture of the apathetic and ignorant proletariat with whom it then had to deal. Its objects were drawn widely enough, but the actual activities of local groups were, says their historian Hans Zeck, 'primitive enough to make you think'. What the members, and even many chaplains and local lay leaders, wanted was sing-songs and beer-hall politics. They had little class consciousness or pride in their standards of work and family life. Still less had they any idea of effective political and economic action. Nor did they want to learn. Lectures were a penance. The movement accordingly at first kept out of the political and trade union field, and did only a limited amount of religious education, largely apologetic, to refute the arguments of the rising Socialist movement. It concentrated for the time being on activities in which members could see a quick personal return, such as legal aid, friendly benefits, and consumer education. As the social insurance system developed in the eighteen-eighties, the local associations advised and guided their members in matters arising from it.

But little by little the field expanded. New methods of religious education among workers developed, and this side of the work became more positive. In the last half of the eighteen-nineties Christian trade unions began to be formed on a large scale, and members of the workers' associations woke up to the value of education in such things as economics and public speaking. As the years drew on towards the First World War the rising standard of workers' life and education led to a new interest in politics and demand for civic education, which the associations promptly began to provide. They also began to discover that, with the emergence of a new body of working-class leaders trained in their courses and schools, a gap was opening between the intellectually-trained spear-point and the general mass of workers who could or would not follow in their footsteps. Too much attention, the Movement concluded—or rather too exclusive attention—was being paid to intellectual training, and not enough to the qualities of temperament in which leaders and led stood on the same footing. Such qualities as inwardness, depth of feeling, honesty, loyalty, and above all 'a feeling for the family' in any case deserved cultivation for their own sake. Programmes began, therefore, to be slanted in this direction. Courses in literature, music, home management, and the history of the homeland were introduced. And finally, in the new general 'Würzburg Programme' of 1921, all this was brought into focus around the idea of the Catholic working man as cultured, self-confident, shaping his own life in the light of religion. The ideal Catholic worker appeared as 'a human being in overalls, not a dervish of the class war'; one with a cultivated family life, a sense of vocation in his work, and with this a responsible citizen and an active member of the Church.

Let us put all this more precisely. The ideal man (or woman), as the world of Christian Action or Christian Democracy sees him, has certain general personality traits. His personality is mature; well adjusted and integrated in itself, and adapted to the outside world. He is 'cultivated' in the sense that:

A cultivated man is one who, knowing what he, a man, is, and what is his vocation—knowing, therefore, the whole meaning of his existence—organises his whole life in the light of the ultimate goal of his being, and develops and

30

expands all his faculties in order to achieve the fullest possible life. . . . Culture is the expansion of all a man's faculties under the guidance of the spirit. It consists not so much in a certain quantity of knowledge as in the quality of knowledge. It consists in whatever makes it possible for a man to find his place, as a man, in the universe. . . . (Mouvement Ouvrier Chrétien (Belgium), XVth Congress, 1949, report by R. Hulpiau on *Current Problems*, pp. 10–11.)

In the words of a Young Christian Workers' pamphlet, he will have been 'converted' to his view of life, not merely 'conquered' for it; he will have thought, and felt, his whole position through. Though suitably suspicious of intellectualism, he will have used his intellect to the full. He will be steady and conscientious, capable of taking a long view, alive to his responsibilities as an individual and a member of various social groups. He will know how to take a positive line and stick to it: but he must also be able to say 'No'. As the Dutch Protestant trade unions' journal says,[1] he must be able to work with and for others who do not share his views, and yet to steer his own course without being led away by them or dragged down to their level. The histories of the Christian workers' movements recount with pride episodes where they looked ahead and refused to be stampeded into badly prepared strikes, or unity movements based purely on sentiment, or attempts at revolution. Stability, persistence, and self-control are valued highly. Fernand Tonnet, one of the 'Big Three' of the Y.C.W.'s early days, was an eager reader of Samuel Smiles, and the names of Smiles' heroes—George Stephenson, for instance—appeared often in the reading lists he made out for study groups. When H. Amelink, historian and formerly Treasurer of the Dutch Protestant trade unions, speaks his mind on the 'fiddling with the coinage' ('knoeien met de munt') of the nineteen-thirties, one seems to hear the very accents of Viscount Snowden. And Sir Stafford Cripps would have fitted well into the austere, gleaming, traditional Dutch interior of those unions' head office.

But the ideal man of the Christian Democrats is not only steady and conscientious. He is also open and sensitive to the movements of his time, quick to adapt to new situations, and on his guard against what another Belgian report calls the 'individual sectarianism' of the 'activist who shuts himself up with his own ideas in complacent self-satisfaction'. He is cheerful and resilient. And he is a leader, and above all an apostle.

There is a very strong element of truth in Communism. An element which we have not sufficiently recognised—the fact that Marx gave the working class a mission to fulfil; a redemptive mission, a messianic mission. (Cardijn, *The Hour of the Working Class*, 1948, Australian ed., p. 17.)

One cannot circulate among the Christian Democratic movements—the social movements, perhaps, more than the political—without being impressed with this sense of apostolate; and not only among younger

[1] *Evangelie en Maatschappij*, Jan. 1954.

31

people, or leaders of youth or educational movements. The middle-aged leader of an employers' federation may say half-jokingly over a dinner table, 'Of course we are great apostles here, in this country and out of it'. It is only later, on getting to know him and his organisation better, that one realises that what he says is seriously meant and literally true.

TECHNICAL SKILLS

On these basic qualities of personality various skills are ideally to be built up. Technical skills, first of all, including such things as personal hygiene and physical capacity. The Young Christian Workers began in the slums of Brussels, and their journal quoted in the early days the following piece of advice from an unspecified poet:

> No riot or general strike will give you the same moral force for victory as fresh water, a tooth-brush, a bath, a shower, or pumice stone and soap. (*Jeunesse Syndicaliste*, September 1923.)

A couple of years later the 'Leaders' Bulletin' of the same movement included a 38-item questionnaire on personal hygiene, running from cleanliness ('which of us has never had a bath?'), via clothing, meals, fresh air, and a group of questions which might be classified as 'poison', to temper ('who goes off the deep end about nothing at all?') and one question marked 'Special': 'Whose bowels move every day?' A quarter of a century later essentially the same questions turn up in the international questionnaire for the Y.C.W.'s Jubilee Congress: more sophisticated in form, but with the same basic aim. The women's and girls' movements preach the same gospel with an appropriately different accent. In all movements, drink and the 'brutalising passion for sport' come in for their share of condemnation. The ideal Young Christian, Worker or otherwise, is a sportsman, but chiefly in the sense that he plays himself. Games, hiking, cycling, or for that matter dancing or a hobby like gardening or carpentry, all come in for strong recommendation, and the Christian youth movements have introduced vast numbers of their members to active participation in them. The need has naturally been greatest in the towns, but has been felt in the country as well. The youth movement of the Belgian Farmers' Union, for instance, has encouraged the growth of riding clubs all over Flanders. In general, the Christian movements stress strongly the need to acquire 'leisure' skills, physical as well as social, not merely for their own sake but also as compensation for the deficiencies of industrial life.

Master of himself, the ideal Christian Democrat is also master of his craft. Living in a torrent of change, the age of 'Humanity conquering the earth',[1] he:

[1] Chapter heading from Lebret, *Montée Humaine*, 1953.

Witnesses every day the colossal advance of technique, transforming every aspect of our personal life and the life of the world. And we accept this as normal. . . . This progressive mastery over matter . . . proclaims the grandeur of human labour, which day by day, from the leaders of science to the boy on the factory floor, is transforming the face of the earth, embellishing it and putting it at the service of humanity. . . . The whole world appears to us as a vast project under construction. And the Creator himself points out to us the meaning and grandeur of this labour. 'Fill the earth, and make it yours'. He calls us to complete the work of creation with Him. . . . So we assist at the birth of a new world, built of many elements. . . . At dizzy speed, this revolution . . . is creating a new humanity. And these aspirations, efforts, and transformations are, more and more, crystallised and sanctioned by international institutions. . . . The working class is no stranger to this drive towards the unity of the world. So far from ignoring it, or living on its fringe, it commits itself totally to it; for it sees its own evolution and revolution proceeding in the heart of and simultaneously with the universal transformation. Indeed, more; the working class is today the most important factor, the most numerous and dynamic, in the revolution of our time. (Young Christian Workers, *Une Étape de l'Internationale Jociste*, 1951, pp. 101–4.)

The technical revolution, and the accompanying social revolution, are seen as perfectly compatible with the growth and development of human personality. Robert Schuman, of the M.R.P., writes of a new steel strip mill in his native Lorraine:

Here the roles are happily reversed [as compared with old-style sheet mills]. Man resumes his place as the being who observes and reflects. Teachers and other intellectuals have taken up this work in place of their old profession, and have no feeling of constriction of their personality or of loss of social status. (In *Tour d'Horizon*, 1954, No. 13; published by the International Federation of Catholic Workers' Movements.)

The task of Christian managers, technicians, and workers is to ensure that the reconciliation of technical and personal development does in fact take place, without loss to either. But for this it is first necessary to understand modern techniques, though without losing a grip on the sound traditions of the past.

The [ideal] craftsman is fully open to technical developments. He is resourceful enough to adapt quickly to them, yet retains his basically conservative nature. . . . His basic strength lies in a healthy tension between tradition and progress, as well as in responsibility towards his fellow-workers, fellow-craftsmen, and fellow-men; and in acceptance of his craftsman's status out of the pride, self-respect, and joy of his craft. (Kolping Associations, *Werkende Hand, wirkender Geist*, 1951, pp. 32 and 34.)

The young member of a Christian farmers' organisation finds himself expected to attend an agricultural college and take part in the management of experimental plots. A visitor to the Farmers' Union in Belgium is likely to find his attention drawn with pride to statistics showing how, due largely to the Union's efforts, productivity in Belgian farming, per beast or per acre of land, was 50% greater by 1935–9 than it had been in 1890. The housewife is expected to be a technician in her own field, and marriage preparation and home management courses are made available to help her. A movement such as the M.L.P. (French workers' family movement) works to spread a knowledge of home mechanisation and to provide the means, notably through co-operatives, of putting machines at housewives' disposal. And for the higher, scientifically trained managers and technicians is reserved the highest responsibility of all for reconciling technique and respect for human personality. For:

> To achieve a synthesis between technique and the whole man, it is obviously necessary to have mastered both sides. One must know Man, in all his essential elements and needs, and one must know and possess technique . . . for this synthesis cannot be imposed from outside; it can be realised only from within technique itself. Only, for instance, someone who knows both Man and Architecture can achieve the synthesis between man and his house; that is, can build a house worthy of man, one really at his service. And normally it is in fact only laymen who are technically competent. . . . (Mgr. P. Pavan, Chairman of the Italian Social Weeks, address to the delegates of the Catholic International Organisations, 15th March, 1954.)

'It is precisely on the Christian line', so the Dutch Protestant trade unions sum it all up, 'to be, in the right sense of the word, completely practical'.

A man should, the Christian movements feel, have another skill beyond even that of the craftsman. His aesthetic abilities must be developed. He must have learnt to recognise and appreciate beauty.

> It is proper to man to be open to beauty, elegance, and art, in their highest forms; and this is closely linked to a feeling for truth and true freedom. In the contemplation of beauty man raises himself above his own selfish level and opens his mind to Reality, which reveals itself in all its inexhaustible wealth and brilliance. He thus nourishes in himself the respect for what Is, and in particular for that unsurpassed marvel, man himself. The sense of beauty is rooted, in short, in respect for truth, and leads to the unfolding of love. The Christian social movement must develop in the working class this feeling for beauty, elegance, and art in all their forms. (Belgian Christian Trade Unions (C.S.C.)—*Le Syndicalisme Chrétien*, 1951, p. 28.)

SOCIAL SKILLS

A fully cultivated man needs social as well as technical skills, and the Christian Action and Christian Democratic organisations set out to provide him with them. The 'cultivated man' does not acquire his culture in a vacuum.

> Man is not a hermit, withdrawn into the solitude of an Aventine hill, and living in the contemplation of the truth. It is through full and entire involvement in the structures of society, through participation in social life in a variety of environments, that he achieves the perfection of his nature. It is for that reason essential that the environments in which he is called upon to live should be healthy and educative. . . . (Hulpiau, report to the XV Congress of the Mouvement Ouvrier Chrétien (Belgium), 1949, p. 13.)

He must be able to establish and make the most of numerous social contacts, in a wide range of environments.

The highest level of social training is achieved through the union of classes, and this can only be attained by combining in a single association, outside the family, young people of different social classes. . . . The wealth of the Italian Catholic Youth Movement is in its parish associations, in which rich and poor, students and workers, learned and ignorant, are to be found side by side.[1] (L. Gedda, *Addio Gioventù*, 1947, p. 22.)

But above all he must be prepared to take a full part in the life of the various associations and communities which he meets in the course of his life. He belongs of course first of all to his family and his age-group. Secondly, he must identify himself with his neighbourhood, region, and country.

The community, for the people, means first of all the street, the neighbourhood, where people know one another, exchange services, discuss all the events of social life from parish and world politics to the worries of daily life, and where they work, suffer, and rejoice together; where they make up an active brotherhood. In this small-scale community everyone has the chance to exercise the social virtues and to increase his generosity and understanding. The community also means for the people the town or district, with its civil and religious celebrations and its own special character. It includes the parish and its circle of activities. It means the choral society, the brass band, the drama and athletic clubs; everything, in short, which creates the local atmosphere and customs to which all of us like to come home. The community means, too, the region one lives in, with its own particular temper and myths, religious or profane, with the special features of its villages and industries, with its favourite walks, perhaps also with that special degree of community created by a common language and set of attitudes; making it a nation, in Wallonia or Flanders, with its own history and distinct character. And finally there is the fatherland itself, and all the love and pride that springs from it. All these things that link men to other men, to their land, their customs, and their traditions, are irreplaceable and essential to the people's culture. (Hulpiau, loc. cit., pp. 24–5.)

It is not suggested that every neighbourhood does in fact measure up to this ideal. Sociologists attached to the Christian Democratic movements have in fact made a number of valuable studies underlining the deficiencies of existing neighbourhood and regional cultures. The social skill which members of these movements are called on to acquire consists in entering into an—as is usually to be expected—imperfect neighbourhood, in order to reform it from within.

A man is also expected to participate actively in the social life of his firm, his industry, and his social class; meaning not only leisure and entertainment but also management, or formal or informal discussion, or political activity. The German word characterising a Christian industrial order, *'berufsständisch-leistungsgemeinschaftlich'*, sums up the idea of the common obligations of those engaged in any line of production and the social organisation which flows from it. They are a 'community based on function', therefore also 'a distinct social group based on vocation'. And

[1] On Gedda's view, see p. 275.

each individual should equip himself to play his part in such a group. Yet at the same time he must play his part as a member of a social class whose interests may cut across vocational group lines. 'Our ancestors in the Middle Ages', the Y.C.W. journal once quoted from an article by Fr. Vermeersch,

> Were outspoken Christians. But this did not stop them, one day when a riot broke out, from throwing fifteen of the city councillors of Louvain through the town hall windows. (*Jeunesse Syndicaliste*, February 1922.)

The ideal which is held out by the Christian movements today is not simply that of a man who rises out of his class to the highest point his abilities will command. It is that of one who recognises that though individuals may rise, classes remain, and that the social ascent of a class must be achieved by collective action, embracing the class as a whole. A man who recognises and accepts this will indeed develop his abilities to the fullest possible extent. But he will do so to remain in and with his class, helping in its collective ascent; as a trade union official, for instance. Or, if he does in fact move into another profession and class, he will keep his contact with the class from which he came and work in its interests in whatever way his new position makes possible.[1] And for that great majority of people who do not change classes, at least after their early years, an essential element in personality is awareness of what their class is, of its interests and way of life, and readiness to accept and participate in this life to the fullest possible extent.

To belong to and accept the obligations of a social class, a firm, a family, and the rest obviously involves a risk of conflicting loyalties; of a clash between what Chester Barnard calls 'moral systems'. These conflicts can be reduced by skilful social organisation, and particularly by applying the principle of pluralism (of which more in the next chapter), which makes it easier for individuals to build up a set of compatible associations. Conflict is also reduced inasmuch as no one can be active in more than a few of the associations to which he does or could belong. The Christian Democratic movements, like any others, prefer militants to mere subscribers. But they are less inclined than many to minimise the value of the 'mere' subscription of someone who is preoccupied in other ways.

> It is so easy to speak slightingly of 'passive' or 'paper' members. Plain membership is already an act of witness to Catholic principles, showing readiness to make some sacrifice for them. (*De Katholiek in het Openbare Leven van deze Tijd*, Dutch Bishops' Lenten Pastoral, 1954, p. 21.)

There is a whole *mystique*, says the Leaders' Bulletin of the Belgian Y.C.W. in 1951, about the payment of a subscription. It links the member to the

---

[1] For some interesting comments on this, see an address by Canon Leclercq, of Louvain, to the Semaine Sociale Wallonne, Liége 1950.

movement, guarantees the movement's independence, and thereby also creates an obligation of the movement towards the member and makes its help available to him.

But there is no way—and least of all if a 'mere' subscription is to be treated as so weighty a matter—of getting rid entirely of a clash such as that between vertical association in the firm and industry and horizontal association in a social class. To work through the conflicts of loyalty which then arise calls for a mature personality in the sense already described: a strong central direction, with infinite flexibility in adjusting to detailed circumstances. It also calls for a special set of skills. Fr. S. de Lestapis, in a textbook[1] intended for the French Catholic family movements, illustrates this combination of basic qualities and skills in terms of the relations to each other and to the world in general of a husband and wife. Their behaviour should be inspired by clear-cut norms, firmly upheld in practice; they should know their own mind and stick to it. Each goal or line of action should be checked against the ultimate, over-riding standard of revelation and the natural law; to which in any case it is directly referred thanks to the fact that marriage, unlike most other social relationships, is a sacrament. But with all this their attitude should be 'open'; they should be interested in and capable of appreciating others' points of view, ready to accept others' interests as their own. It should be creative, preferring positive solutions, which lead to the expansion and fulfilment rather than the restriction of the personality of all concerned. It should include also an accurate understanding of social process, particularly as applied to situations of change and conflict; of when to consult, or to give an order, or to act on one's own initiative. This implies among other things appreciation of the need for time to think. A certain detachment is desirable: time for contemplation. And other writers add that people who hope to produce a flexible response to varying social demands must limit their own needs, that is their demands on society. For those whose needs are great have little room for manoeuvre in their social relations, since only a few positions in the social system can satisfy them.

Successful participation in groups calls not only for well-prepared personalities in the rank and file but also for an élite willing and equipped to take up leadership roles. One of the standard complaints of the Christian Democratic movements against social conditions since the Industrial Revolution is that they have led to an unfair distribution of opportunities for potential leaders to develop their qualities.

> Modern businesses have piled up upon the shoulders of top management heavy duties and vast responsibilities. But they have cut to within the narrowest possible limits the tasks and responsibilities of the general mass of the workers.

[1] *Amour et Institution Familiale*, 1948.

For some they have created immense opportunities to grow in personal stature and accumulate wealth. But for far too many others they have cut these same opportunities below any reasonable limit. A democratic economy, centred on the human person, is bound to set out to correct these gross inequalities. (Statement by the International Union of Social Studies, 1953, on *Workers' Control*, drafted by Mgr. Brys, Chaplain-General to the Christian Workers' Movement of Belgium.)

It is the proud boast of the Christian Action and Christian Democratic movements in general, and in particular of the farmers' and workers' movements, that they have in fact trained up a new élite matching the Christian ideal. They like to think of themselves as a school of education through action; 'in the working class, for the working class, by the working class', as the Y.C.W. phrase goes. The training of leaders serves the purposes of the movements as institutions. But it is also regarded as worth while for its own sake, or rather for the sake of those who thus have opportunities which otherwise would not come their way. To quote the Y.C.W. again, this time from its general programme:

Experience shows that the surest way to save [the movement's militants] is to give them the job of saving someone else.

RELIGIOUS SKILLS

The foundation of culture is knowledge of the religious truth which conveys the meaning of human life and the truth about its destiny, and about the role of human society and the reason of all things. (Hulpiau, op. cit., p. 22.)

The faith which is the foundation of membership of the Christian Church cannot properly be described either as 'knowledge' or as a 'skill'. But before it can become the foundation of a culture there need to be built upon it a number of what can perfectly properly be called skills. Prayer, except at the most elementary level, is neither easy nor straight-forward. Scripture can be the study of a lifetime. The liturgy of the Church symbolises and involves truths essential to the faith. To know the constitution of the Church, and the rights and responsibilities of each branch or unit within it, is essential for anyone who proposes to work effectively in the field of Christian Democracy; let alone in that of Christian Action, more closely identified with the ecclesiastical machine. It is not surprising, in the light of all this, that in the last two generations the rise of Christian Action and Christian Democracy has gone hand in hand, in both the Catholic and Protestant Churches, with such things as a revival of Bible studies, a liturgical movement, and a new and growing appreciation of the role of the Church. Personal religion, thought through and capable of leading to apostolic action, has tended to replace religious practice based merely on tradition. And this is at least as much a by-product of Christian Action and Christian Democracy as a revival in, so to speak, its own right.

LIMITS AND VARIATIONS

It goes without saying that Christian Democrats' ideal of personality is interpreted rather differently from country to country and from class to class. Indeed, this is essential to that ideal itself, calling as it does for participation, 'in all things except sin', in class, national, and other group cultures. There is naturally also a difference in its application to men and women.

> Let us sketch here the Christian ideal of life for a modern woman. What sort of woman do we have in mind in this ideal?
> One who develops all her personal qualities, and still remains a woman; who wins equality with man in one field after another, but still keeps her femininity.
> One who prefers work which touches life directly, rather than any purely material, technical, or administrative task; and who regards the vocation of wife and mother as the highest of all.
> One who is ready to strike out into the life of today, who is trained for a profession, knows how to play a part in social and public life, and can reconcile her vocation in the family with her duties as a member of a class, a community, and a State.
> One who can drive her path through life, come what may, and who prefers to devote the best of her efforts to the service of the family, of charity, of justice, of peace, of humanity and of religion. (Hulpiau, op. cit., p. 57.)

There are also differences of accent between denominations. There is a family resemblance between the ideals of different Catholic groups, and another between Protestant groups whose theological background is similar. Article XV of the Anti-Revolutionaries' *Statement of Principles*, for instance, on decency, temperance, and public blasphemy, could have been written in the chapels of Wales: something very unlike what one finds in documents from the Catholic side. And, of course, the Christian ideal of personality is not universally achieved among even the leaders of the Christian Democratic movements, let alone the rank and file.

> Too few Christians have bothered to expand their vision of the world to its full dimensions. It is easier to wall oneself in and reject *en bloc* what one chooses to regard as 'hostile' systems of thought. (Lebret, *Montée Humaine*, 1953, p. 170.)

Often, especially in the youth movements, where leaders quickly grow older and pass on, there is backsliding and the work has to be begun again.

But these qualifications should not be overstressed. What impresses one on actually meeting leaders of the Christian Action and Christian Democratic movements is not their divergences but their underlying unity of purpose. From decade to decade these movements have come to define more precisely and agree more fully on the type of personality they wish to create. And, starting with the poverty in human material as well as ideas which the story of the German Catholic Workers' Movement illustrates, they have succeeded in making this ideal today the guiding light of their activities as organisations, and the inspiration of an increasing proportion of their membership. Moreover, their ideal of personality corresponds with the findings of psychologists such as Kurt Lewin and David Riesman on the type of personality best suited to the modern world. The ideal is not, these writers suggest, a tradition-based personality, rather fixed and inflexible in even its more superficial aspects, and conversely over-flexible, because supported by nothing more than a long departed tradition, in its innermost convictions. In modern, changing, conditions, where the crutches of tradition cannot be relied on, an ideal personality will have a hard inner core of conviction, mature and fully 'interiorised'; one which will not yield to outside pressures, but will instead provide a compass through the changing conditions of life. To that extent the ideal personality will be, in Riesman's phrase, 'inner-directed'. But it will also be 'other-directed', that is highly flexible in all its ordinary, more superficial relationships, sensitive and adaptable to changing circumstances and others' needs. Taking both characteristics together, it will be 'autonomous': combining, that is, participation with detachment and independence. And on these basic qualities will of course be built up the full kit of technical and social skills needed to make adaptation to changing conditions effective.

But this is precisely the personality type just outlined as the Christian Democratic ideal. Consider again the picture of the 'open', adaptable family, steered by hard, precise, norms, participating in yet detached from and 'contemplating' the world around it. Or take the case of the worker or technician accepting fully a world of change, and the need to participate in many 'moral systems', and equipped with the maturity and skills needed to steer him through the resulting conflicts. These are just the types which Lewin or Riesman would seem to have in mind. Only, of course, a Christian Democrat would add that the hard inner core of conviction needed to steer a steady course in modern times is far more likely to be achieved by those who have the Christian revelation for their guide than by those who have to rely on natural reasoning alone, however scientific it may be.

CHAPTER IV

PLURALIST, NOT COLLECTIVIST—

1. 'HORIZONTAL' AND 'VERTICAL' PLURALISM

THE Catholic and the Reformed (notably Dutch Reformed) Churches express in slightly different terms an essentially similar idea about social structure. Catholics speak of the 'principle of subsidiarity'.

> It is an injustice, a grave evil, and a disturbance of right order for a larger and higher organisation to arrogate to itself functions which can be performed efficiently by smaller and lower bodies. . . . Of its very nature the true aim of all social activity should be to help individual members of the social body, but never to destroy them. (Pius XI, Encyclical *Quadragesimo Anno*, 1931, CTS ed., p. 37.)

For the Reformed churches the corresponding principle is that of 'sovereignty in one's own circle', or 'the special task and vocation of each social group'. There is obviously a difference of accent. The Protestant conception underlines the separate and exclusive responsibility of the individual and the small group, though only within defined limits and subject to a vocation of service to others. The Catholic phrasing stresses rather the inclusion of these small units of society in greater wholes, within which however they have a sphere of autonomy on which they have a right to insist. But in practice the two conceptions come to much the same thing. There is work to be done at every level of social organisation from the individual to the international community, and the responsibility for what can be done at lower levels must not be allowed to gravitate to the top. Every social unit or group has a sphere of work which it can do efficiently in the interests not only of its members but of society as a whole, and this sphere must be defined and reserved for it. A higher authority may of course insist that some subordinate group live up to its responsibilities. It may call on the subordinate group to justify its independence by proving that there is indeed some sphere in which it can work efficiently on its own. It may check excesses or suggest new lines of development. It may 'direct, watch, stimulate, and restrain', as the passage of *Quadragesimo Anno* just quoted goes on to say. But only in the last, extreme resort may it take over its subordinates' responsibilities and discharge them itself. A phrase sometimes used to cover this whole conception, from both the Protestant and the Catholic side, is 'autonomisation'; the

41

'autonomisation', that is, of individuals and social groups. It can also be described as *'horizontal pluralism'*; a policy which insists on the independence, rights, and responsibilities of each individual or group which can show that it has a legitimate sphere of its own: independence firstly as against others on the same level of social organisation, and secondly as against those at other and particularly higher levels.

Horizontal pluralism is defended primarily as a way of helping the growth of human personality. It offers the greatest number of openings for leaders to develop and show their ability, and for effective participation by the rank and file. It avoids the dangers of both 'massification' and 'atomisation'.

> The danger of massification is not merely that the individual is swallowed up in the mass and becomes an undifferentiated element of it. It is also that he is simultaneously isolated within the mass. He hesitates to open himself to others. He tries to ensure that only superficial contacts develop between himself and others, his neighbours; contacts based on common interests, or public events, things which affect his group, his class, his neighbourhood, his workmates as a whole. But he loses the true, warm, contact with other human beings. He and his neighbour slip by one another, not knowing the reality and basis of each other's life, or the reality of each other's need. (From *Evangelie en Maatschappij* (Dutch Protestant trade unions), November 1953, pp. 154–5.)

A well thought out and decentralised division of powers is also seen as making possible a higher degree of executive efficiency than could be achieved under either pure individualism or central direction. We shall show in the following chapters how Christian Democracy works out its ideas on 'horizontal' pluralism in practice.

The Christian Democratic movements also support the idea of *'vertical' or ideological pluralism*. 'Vertical' refers to the way in which ideologies cut vertically through all the layers and groups of society, so as 'to set a man at variance with his father, and the daughter with her mother . . .: a man's enemies will be the people of his own house' (Matt. x, 35–6); as by contrast with the 'horizontal' division between, for example, the State and the local community or the Board of Directors and the primary working group. Different 'spiritual families', in a common French phrase, —Catholics, Protestants, Marxists, 'humanists', or whoever they may be— should on the principle of 'vertical' pluralism be permitted and enabled to follow their own way of life, even when they are in a minority in a nation or group as a whole.

'Vertical' pluralism is defended, like horizontal, on grounds of social efficiency. It reduces conflicts, since it allows everyone, without discrimination or loss to himself, to build up a set of associations which fits his own ideals. Since, in an imperfect world, some conflicts of ideals and loyalties are inevitable, the essential thing is that they should be fought out in a way which lets the truth eventually emerge and form the basis for a

(1) 'HORIZONTAL' AND 'VERTICAL' PLURALISM

settlement. But this is likely to happen only if the parties in conflict hold firm, clear, views which provide a solid basis for argument, and yet are open and sensitive to the views of others; respectful of their good faith and ready to admit their good points. Everyone must sail 'under his own flag' or 'with banners unfurled', the title of the standard history of one of the Protestant movements. Society must make it easy for him to do this by ensuring that he loses nothing by it, whether in cash and convenience or in social status and respect. And organisations have a right and duty to 'sail under their own flag' in the same way as individuals; for association with others is needed even to reach a full understanding of one's own ideals, let alone to express them effectively in action. 'Tolerance' is hardly the word for this attitude, for tolerance suggests a state like that of the Laodiceans, neither hot nor cold. 'Co-existence' might be a better word, if it had not been captured recently for the idea of a permanent cold war. Perhaps the nearest formula is that of Sarah Battle on whist: 'a clean hearth, a clear fire, and the rigour of the game'. There is in 'vertical pluralism' a warmth of common humanity and common responsibility before God. But 'the rigour of the game' is also part of its essence.

A classic passage on tolerance in a sense equivalent to 'vertical pluralism' occurs in a statement by Pius XII to a congress of Italian lawyers in 1954:

> Thus the two principles are classified . . . concerning the attitude which the jurist, the statesman, and the sovereign Catholic State is to adopt . . . in regard to a formula of religious and moral toleration as described above.
> First: that which does not correspond to truth or to the norm of morality objectively has no right to exist, to be spread, or to be activated.
> Secondly: failure to impede this with civil laws and coercive measures can nevertheless be justified in the interests of a higher and more general good. Before all else the Catholic statesmen must judge if this condition is verified in the concrete. This is the question of fact. . . . (Pius XII, address to the National Convention of Italian Catholic Jurists, 6th December, 1953.)

It is irrational, the case runs, to argue that it is right to teach what is not true or to promote policies which are wrong. But if different opinions arise and are held in good faith, it may be perfectly rational to say that the way to bring back to the truth those whose views are wrong is to give them what they themselves will accept as a fair chance to argue their case. And this means adopting a policy of 'vertical pluralism', with full freedom and scope for each 'spiritual family'. Whether that policy is or is not right depends on the facts of each situation. But if it turns out that 'vertical pluralism' is in fact normally right in the situations met in the modern world, it becomes reasonable to accept and state this as a general principle. And that is precisely what the Christian Democratic movements do.

Few subjects have inspired more passionate debates, in and out of the Christian Democratic movements, than the idea of 'vertical pluralism'.

43

The churches which inspire Christian Democracy have often shown this kind of pluralism little respect, and even among Christian Democrats themselves the old Adam is not quite dead. Holland, for instance, has a discriminatory ban on certain Catholic religious processions; this is kept in force by the votes not only of Liberal and Socialist anti-clericals but of Protestant Christian Democrats. The attitude to be taken towards agnostic or atheistic humanism, notably in the schools, is often a test case. There is a tendency, even in those countries where the philosophy of the State schools is normally 'humanist', for the Christian Democrats, in the words of the Christian Social Party in Belgium, to:

> See in the State and private [Church] schools, not competitors, success for one of whom is measured by the defeat of the other, but friendly rivals whose ambition should be to co-operate to the greatest possible extent, each in its own field, for the success of the national system of education. (*Les Chantiers sont Ouverts*, p. 24.)

But one also meets, though much more rarely than in the past, statements such as appear in a Pastoral Letter of the Dutch Catholic Bishops, which ranks as one of the fundamental documents of Catholic Christian Democracy in Holland today. The letter is discussing the efforts of the 'Humanist League' to establish the same right to State grants for its services to atheists and the churchless as the Churches enjoy for services to believing Christians. It concludes:

> We feel bound to raise our voice against any attempt to place on an equal footing, in law or in fact, the religious provision of the Church and the provision of the Humanist League. It must at all costs be avoided that the State should appear to encourage what is in fact a religion without God. (*De Katholiek in het Openbare Leven van deze Tijd*, 1954, pp. 40–1.)

The difficulty arises not merely from reluctance in some cases to adopt the principle of vertical pluralism, but also from the fact that this principle itself neither applies everywhere nor always gives clear guidance. Like that of horizontal pluralism, it does not apply unconditionally. A group which claims to benefit from it must, in Christian Democratic theory, have good reason to think that independence is needed to safeguard and develop its special point of view, and the independent action at which it aims must not prevent the co-operation which is called for if people are to live together in society at all. A group which proposes to disturb public order or decency or to avoid its members' normal civic obligations—to violate, that is, the natural law which is common ground for Catholic, Protestant, humanist, and all other men of goodwill—puts its claim for freedom to develop its own ideals out of court. So does a group which sets out to destroy the principle of vertical pluralism itself. Christian Democracy does not admit that there is freedom to destroy freedom. And when is organisation on ideological lines in fact necessary? This has been a major question for the Christian Democratic movements themselves. They agree that some organisation on ideological lines is needed in the modern world, and insist that where this is so, Christian movements have a right to claim and a duty to concede treatment on an equal footing with organisations of any other kind. But which are the cases in which specifically Christian organisations do more good than harm? Opinions have differed, the debate is still proceeding, and much of the last part of this book will be concerned with it.

Or take the question of the legal relations between Church and State. What exactly is to be the legal connection between one and the other, given that, as Christian Democrats agree, the two have distinct and sovereign spheres which, however, interlock? Should the Church be under the common law applicable to all associations and citizens, or should it, or any particular church, have a special legal status? 'Vertical' pluralism might seem to imply that the State's legislation should leave the Church entirely to itself, except in so far as the Church's business or other secular dealings might bring it under the common law. But a moment's thought will show half-a-dozen reasons, quite consistent with the principle of pluralism, why special and more detailed regulation of the relation between Church and State may be justified. The Church or churches are bodies of exceptional public importance. They have important public functions, as in education or the social services. They administer a great deal of property under rather special conditions. There are cases where this property has been taken over by the State; compensation has then to be provided for by way of capital or income. There are often opportunities for friendly co-operation between Church and State, even in primarily ecclesiastical matters, where no violation of pluralism arises. Membership of the Church, for example, implies a duty to 'contribute to the support of one's pastors', and the Church accordingly makes levies on its members. In some countries the State lends the services of its officials to collect this levy from those who declare themselves to be Church members. The State's act is friendly to the Church. But so long as no attempt is made to enforce Church requirements on those who are not Church members, it is not clear that it in any way violates the principle of vertical pluralism, any more than horizontal pluralism is violated when the State collects a local income tax or a local authority collects State licence duties. More generally, a great many citizens, in some countries a large majority, attach a deep importance to their religion in public as in private affairs. It might well be a greater violation of pluralism for the State to ignore this than to admit it and to act accordingly. In view of all these considerations, so the main report of the Fribourg Congress of Christian Democratic parties (N.E.I.) pointed out, the Christian Democrats themselves do not yet agree what the legal status of the Church or churches should be.

45

This difficulty in seeing clearly how the principle of 'vertical' pluralism applies is sometimes aggravated by becoming entangled with similar difficulties over 'horizontal' pluralism. When for instance at the end of the Second World War an independent and Neutral Staffs' Federation (C.G.C.) sprang up in the French trade union movement, the Christian trade unions were in no hurry to have it admitted to equal treatment with themselves and with the at that time united Communist-Socialist General Confederation of Labour (C.G.T.). There was an issue here of 'vertical' pluralism, that is of the right of the adherents of a certain ideology to form organisations of their own. If that had been the only issue, the Christian unions' position would have been, on their own principles, hard to defend. But there was also a question of 'horizontal' pluralism, namely the claim of workers in certain firms and occupations to be allowed to break away from the existing organisations and establish a new 'sovereign sphere' or area of 'subsidiary responsibility' of their own. Here the position was much less clear, for it takes a great deal, and for good reason, to convince any trade union movement that a breakaway union fulfils the conditions justifying a claim to an independent 'sphere'.

The Christian Democrats' application of the principle of 'vertical' pluralism is thus neither simple nor always assured. But the main difficulties are practical ones, and reservations to the principle itself are essentially marginal. The principle of pluralism, 'vertical' even more than 'horizontal', is rooted very deeply indeed in Christian Democrats' minds. For, apart from any merely intellectual acceptance, its value has been burnt into their consciousness by generations of bitter experience of what happens when 'spiritual families' ' freedom is denied. It is barely a century since Catholics were emancipated in Holland. The State abandoned administrative control of the Protestant Church in Germany and the Catholic Church in France only within the last half-century. In Germany and Italy attempts were made to resume it in the Fascist period. Nearly all even of the Christian Action, let alone the Christian Democratic, movements in Germany and Italy were suppressed or reduced to impotence. In due course Fascist occupation extended to all Western Europe except Sweden and Switzerland. And when it ended, the persecution of Christians in Eastern Europe and China remained to keep the lessons of the resistance years alive in Western minds. Even in officially Catholic Spain Christian Democracy has been driven underground.

It would indeed be hard to name even one Christian Democratic movement which has not in the last three or four generations known what it was to be a minority, and often a seemingly permanent minority, to which even elementary justice was denied. The political movements have had to fight for generations for freedom for the Churches to manage their own affairs, or to obtain equality for Christians within the fiscal and educational system: especially to prevent tax funds being reserved for non-Christian schools. In some even of those countries which have strong Christian Democratic movements, notably France and parts of Germany, little or nothing has yet been done to put Christian and non-Christian education on an equal footing. The Christian workers' movements, especially in their early days, had to meet opposition which did not stop at violence. It was not for nothing that Adolf Hitler learnt his first lessons in totalitarian discipline and political terror among the Austrian Social-Democrats.[1] The legend of the early struggles of the Y.C.W. in some French industrial areas, particularly at the time of the great strikes of 1936, is enshrined in Van der Meersch's *Fishers of Men*. The employers' and middle-class organisations have had to face, not indeed violence, but a cold war of suspicion, misrepresentation, and attempts to ignore their existence. To all this has been added opposition inside the Christian body itself. Christian Democracy has grown out of several generations of struggle and debate among Christians themselves, and its enemies have not always observed the courtesies of debate. The 'red curates' of the Ruhr, the 'abbés démocrates' in France, or the 'devils in bedroom slippers' who destroyed the peace of ages in the Dutch Reformed Church by founding a Protestant workers' movement, were hounded by their own people as well as by their anti-Christian opponents.

These experiences of life as a minority might have led Christian Democrats to safeguard their freedom, not by organising on their own, but by entering united (that is, non-plural) unions or associations or parties, on condition however that their neutrality should be genuine. And so in some places, and for some purposes, they do. But their experience with 'neutral' organisations has often been bad, and has convinced even those least inclined to confessionalism that for some purposes only a pure and unadulterated Christian organisation will do. Almost the whole Continental Christian Democratic movement, indeed, owes its existence to the discovery that in Western Europe in recent generations Christians have been unlikely to get their due unless—subject always to the doubts about particular spheres recorded above—they organised apart. No body, Protestant or Catholic, in the main stream of Continental Christian Democracy, supports the agreed syllabus approach to religious teaching.

[1] For a balanced comment on this see Weinberger, *Tatsachen, Begegnungen und Gespräche*, 1948. Weinberger is a Christian trade unionist who emerged from a concentration camp in 1945 to take a leading part, in collaboration with the Socialdemocrats, in founding the present united Austrian trade union movement. See also the earlier Congress reports of the International Federation of Christian Trade Unions.

CHAPTER V

PLURALIST, NOT COLLECTIVIST—

2. 'HORIZONTAL' PLURALISM—INDIVIDUAL, FAMILY, AND AGE GROUP

INDIVIDUAL RIGHTS

THE spreading of power at which Christian Democrats aim begins with the individual. He has a right to an inviolable sphere of action and to the means of acting within it. The International Union of Social Studies makes its own a Declaration of Rights drafted by the National Catholic Welfare Conference of the U.S.A. in 1947:

The dignity of man, created in the image of God, obligates him to live in accordance with law imposed by God. Consequently he is endowed as an individual and as a member of society with rights which are inalienable. Among these rights are:

(1) The right to life and bodily integrity from the moment of conception, regardless of physical or mental condition, except in just punishment for crime.

(2) The right to serve and worship God in private and public.

(3) The right to religious formation through education and association.

(4) The right to personal liberty under just law.

(5) The right to the equal protection of just law regardless of sex, nationality, colour or creed.

(6) The right to freedom of expression, of information, and of communication in accordance with truth and justice.

(7) The right to choose and freely to maintain a state of life, married or single, lay or religious.

(8) The right to education suitable for the maintenance and development of man's dignity as a human person.

(9) The right to petition the government for redress of grievances.

(10) The right to a nationality.

(11) The right of access to the means of livelihood, by migration when necessary.

(12) The right of association and peaceable assembly.

(13) The right to work and choose one's occupation.

(14) The right to personal ownership, use, and disposal of property subject to the rights of others and to limitation in the interest of the general welfare.

(15) The right to a living wage.

(16) The right to collective bargaining.

(17) The right to associate by industries and professions to obtain economic justice and the general welfare.

(2) 'HORIZONTAL' PLURALISM—INDIVIDUAL, FAMILY, AGE GROUP

(18) The right to assistance from society, if necessary from the State, in distress of person or family.

(Declaration of Rights drafted by a committee of the National Catholic Welfare Conference, 1947, Part I. The Declaration is adopted as an Appendix to the third edition of the International Union of Social Studies' *Code of Social Principles*; initial French edition 1948, English edition by the Catholic Social Guild, 1952.)

The Christian Democratic parties took a leading share in drafting the charters of human rights written into the constitutions of several Western European countries after the Second World War, and also the Charter and Convention on Human Rights established by the Council of Europe. The International Federation of Christian Trade Unions, as the only specifically Christian organisation with the necessary status, played a conspicuous part in the drafting of the United Nations' Charter of Human Rights.

THE FAMILY

But it is for their views on the rights of social groups that the Christian Democratic movements have chiefly been remarkable, and in the first place for their defence of the family. They claim with justice to be the special upholders of the family's needs and rights. So for instance the C.F.T.C., outlining what it regards as 'the distinctive contribution of the C.F.T.C.', makes the first sub-heading read:

[The C.F.T.C.] feels itself specially responsible for defending the FAMILY. Under this it includes, along with all those material questions which affect the standard of living in a home, also moral questions concerned with restoring the stability of family life and protecting it against direct and indirect attacks. (*Programme d'Action Ouvrière*, 1945, p. 58.)

The 'material questions' referred to include such things as taxation, family allowances, housing and town planning, home help, health services, and education. The State as well as the unions and other voluntary organisations is expected to help in solving them. Several of the countries studied here have acquired Ministries or Departments of Family Affairs, and it is chiefly the Christian Democrats who have been responsible. But there is a marked difference even over these material questions between the Christian Democratic programmes and those of, say, the Swedish family movement. The Christian Democrats think in terms not so much of providing families with services, particularly State services, as of ensuring them, through a modification of the wage system, the income with which to provide services for themselves, on their own or through co-operation with others. All of them support strongly the idea of a family living wage. Some interpret this in a traditional sense as a flat-rate wage, paid to married and single alike, on a level high enough to keep not only a man but his wife and children. Family allowances may be admitted as a supplement to inadequate wages, or even strongly recommended for families with an unusually large number of children. But:

> Family allowances are only a first stage, previous to the achievement of an actual family living wage. The Catholic Workers' Movement stands for equal pay for equal work, and warns against the deception and self-deception involved in expecting equal standard of living for equal work. (Programme of the K.A.B. (Germany), 1950, p. 19.)

More and more of the Christian Democrats, however, support both equal pay for equal work and also 'equal standard of living for equal work'. The two are reconciled by means of a generous system of family allowances, financed from premiums paid out of the basically equal wage of workers doing equal work. The usual system is to pay these premiums to an industry-wide or regional compensation fund, from which employers receive whatever is needed to meet their particular family allowance bill.[1] The French have led the way along this road, beginning with the initiative of a number of Catholic employers at the time of the First World War. A semi-skilled French worker with four or five children finds today, thanks chiefly to the efforts of the Christian movements, that the family allowance more than doubles his wage. The International Union of Social Studies, under French and Belgian influence, wrote 'equal standard of living for equal work' into its *Code of Social Principles* in 1948. And even the Catholic Workers' Movement of Germany began to show signs of second thoughts not long after the vigorous blast against 'equal standard of living' quoted above.[2]

This stress on income for rather than services to the family reflects a fundamental characteristic of the Christian Democrats' view of the family and its role. Their aim is not merely to ensure the family justice but to increase its responsibility and independence. The family is by all means 'the cornerstone of the structure of society' (P.S.C.). But that does not make it a mere tool or ward of society; the instrument of a State population policy, for instance. Like every other human group—indeed more than any other—it has to be judged as a centre where personalities are

---

[1] Strictly, it should be said that the premiums are paid not out of wages but out of the wages fund, since it is necessary to take account of sums not formally recorded as wages, but set aside for workers' benefit. In France in 1948, for example, it is estimated that for every thousand francs paid out by employers to or on behalf of workers:

730 francs were paid			direct in wages
117	,,	,,	,, in premiums to family allowance funds
73	,,	,,	,, in social insurance premiums
51	,,	,,	,, for workmen's compensation and industrial health
29	,,	,,	,, for paid holidays

1,000

Source: *Bulletin d'Étude et de Documentation Sociale.*
[2] See an article by Dr. J. David on 'Familienzulagen', in *Priester und Arbeiter*, Chaplains' magazine of the K.A.B., 1952/IV.

shaped and formed. And personalities cannot be shaped and formed to any good purpose without independence and responsibility. The ideal is the 'open', 'creative', family described by Fr. de Lestapis, aware of its responsibility for the good of society as well as its own members, and ready and able to discharge it by the collective action of family movements as well as the efforts of individual families acting on their own. To quote the P.S.C. again, the family should 'participate, on the same footing as organised labour, in the exercise of power'. Hence the tendency to prefer equalisation of incomes to the provision of services in kind, and to link family allowances to the wage-earner's efforts rather than turn them into State grants. And hence also the efforts of Christians all over Western Europe to build up family movements, big and small scale, of the trade union or the discussion group type.

A glance down the list of organisations represented in the International Union of Family Organisations shows immediately how the land lies. From Scandinavia, or Britain, or North America there come organisations *for* the family. But from countries like France, or Belgium, and today also from Germany, there come organisations *of* families, defending their rights and advancing their interests with the same formidable efficiency as is shown in their own field by the trade unions. The small-scale, discussion-group type of family association, for its part, is seen increasingly, by people connected with the Christian Action and Christian Democratic movements, not merely as a means of raising the spiritual and material level of family life itself, but as a key point where the lines of other Christian organisations meet and unity between them is maintained: where family ties and friendships cut across organisation lines. So for Workers' Catholic Action in France the inter-family group is the place where the parish worker, the youth organiser, and the officials of half a dozen different unions or associations sit down, with their wives, to talk things over at the basic human level. So far from being a ward of society, the family appears here as the root and centre of the whole Christian social apostolate.

The ideal of the open, creative, socially responsible family, concerned with developing the personalities of all its members, and also working actively and positively for the good of society, is still rather new in Western Europe. What in Britain would probably be called a Victorian ideal of the family, well-cushioned, in-turned, patriarchal, is still widespread in middle-class Christian circles. But family action constitutes today one not only of the most important but of the most rapidly developing fields of work in the whole Christian social movement, and new views are forming fast not only on the family's external relations but on relations within it. For one thing, ideas are changing on the general code of sex behaviour of which the marriage code forms a part. The traditional Christian respect

51

for purity and virginity still stands. The primary purpose of sexual intercourse is still seen as being to have children. Chastity is upheld inside and
outside marriage. And marriage continues to be seen as a vocation, and
as constituting a more permanent social group than any other contract.
It is indeed seen as conferring the only absolutely permanent social status
apart from those arising from baptism and Holy Orders. But even Catholic
or Catholic-inspired movements are usually prepared today to tolerate
divorce as a concession to the hardness of their fellow-countrymen's
hearts, though under no circumstances for believing Catholics themselves.[1]
And marriage is becoming much more a matter of personal choice—at
least in the middle and upper class—than it once was. The questions of
dowries and social status which fill the novels of the nineteenth century
have been dropping into the background. There is still however a good
deal of pressure to keep this choice within the limits of each Church. The
traditional attitude of the Churches on this has been reinforced by the
recent work of Christian sociologists, who show that in modern conditions
mixed marriages tend to lead not to a switch of faiths—one Church's loss
but another's gain—but to indifference to any religion at all. In Dutch
Catholic experience 45–50% of the children of mixed marriages are brought
up as agnostics.

Within marriage, the idea of 'responsible parenthood' is gaining ground.
A statement on this was issued early in 1954 by the International Union
of Social Studies. Later in the year Fr. de Lestapis, one of its authors,
representing the Vatican at the World Population Conference at Rome,
made a further statement which attracted a good deal of attention. The
guiding rule in this as in all other matters affecting human relations, the
two statements insist, must be the growth and development of human
personality. Parents must decide how many children to aim at after
allowing:

> Not merely for the personal welfare of husband and wife—their health and
> their physical and psychological strength—but also for the welfare of the
> children and the best possible upbringing for them; for the welfare of the
> family as a group, with its principles of unity, order, and love; and finally for
> the general welfare, now and in the future, of the whole human community
> in each place and region and in the world as a whole. (International Union
> of Social Studies, Statement on *World Population and Food Resources*, 1954.
> This passage is quoted from par. 5 of an earlier *Family Code* published by
> the Union. English translation of the statement published by the Sword of the
> Spirit, 1954.)

It is parents' responsibility that is underlined, for it is to them, not to the
State or any other group, that the judgment as to what in all the circumstances is appropriate belongs. The State has the right to guide and inform,

---

[1] See for instance the very cautious line of the P.S.C. (*Les Chantiers sont Ouverts*,
p. 41), accepting the fact of divorce but hedging it around with as many limitations and
precautions as possible.

but not in any way to compel. It may not, for instance, use family allowances as an instrument of population policy. They are a matter of social justice, not a means of forcing on parents decisions which they should be free to take. Parents' responsibility must be exercised positively and creatively, and society must help them in this. If there are economic or social obstacles to the command 'increase and multiply', the first reaction must be to break through them. Family allowance systems must be set up, under-developed countries must be developed. But there are cases, for families and whole societies, where a slowing up in the rate of growth of the population is desirable. In these cases, the Union's statement says, it is necessary to judge, by the usual standard of helping or hindering the growth of personality, between the different forms of birth regulation available. And the statement proceeds to list these in orders of desirability, according to the contribution each makes or fails to make to developing qualities of self-control and foresight, and to whether it does or does not directly contradict the primary purpose of intercourse. To use mechanical or chemical contraceptives involves a direct contradiction of this basic purpose and is to be condemned on that ground alone, even apart from being consistent with a very low degree of foresight and self-control. On both counts the safe period method, simple abstention, or the dedicated chastity of priests and nuns appear as—in that order—increasingly acceptable.

Ideas have also changed a good deal on the internal structure of the family, and particularly on the relation of husband and wife. There is an analogy here with the thinking of the Christian social and political movements in other fields. It is traditional for these movements to emphasise the need for strong leadership in formally organised groups of all kinds. They underline the role of the prime minister, the managing director, or the union chairman or secretary in initiating legislation, in directing executive action, and in co-ordinating the two. But for leadership to be strong it does not need to be authoritarian, and as the years have gone by, and the movements have become not only Christian but Democratic, they have become less and less inclined to confuse the two. The prime minister may lead the legislature, but he does not pass acts. He is chairman of the cabinet, but it is the cabinet as a whole, not the prime minister alone, which constitutes the government of the country. And though the prime minister is head of the executive, other ministers have independent responsibility for their own spheres.

There has been an analogous change in conceptions of the structure of the family. St. Paul's well-known passage in Ephesians v, 22–3 reads:

> Wives must obey their husbands as they would obey the Lord. The man is the head to which the woman's body is united, just as Christ is the head of the Church.

53

This could be and traditionally was usually interpreted as conferring, in principle at least, authoritarian power on the 'head of the house'. This interpretation is hard to reconcile with the personalist aims of the Christian movements today, and has been progressively abandoned. The family as a system of formal rights and duties has moved into the background, and the role of informal relations, of love and mutual understanding, has been emphasised instead. The husband retains formal 'prime ministerial' status, an extra overall responsibility for leadership and decision. There must be some point within the family at which a final decision can be reached in business matters, or the children's education, or other matters affecting people other than the parents themselves. For these decisions must be made, and if the family cannot make them for itself, it must call in some outside authority: which conflicts with the Christian social movement's cardinal principle that every social group, and the family more than any other, needs to be autonomous within the widest possible sphere.[1] But the husband's right to a casting vote arises only in a limited field and in the last resort. The policy of a family is seen as in the normal way the work of husband and wife together, and they have independent and equal, though not identical, responsibilities for action; with the children sharing in responsibility for both policy and action to the extent that their age permits and that they remain attached to the family group. Here for instance is Frau Praetorius opening the debate on 'Family and Education' at the Hamburg Congress of the C.D.U. in 1953:

God made humanity to be man and woman. . . . We must once again recognise that this community, this mutual dependence, is the basis of our existence. It is this meeting with the 'thou' of our fellow-man which first makes us truly human. It is to humanity, man and woman together, that God has given the direction to increase and multiply and make the earth subject to them. Therefore the family, with its responsibility for bringing up children, and the whole responsibility for life and work on earth, is a task for both sexes, without difference or division of labour . . . Woman is man's helpmate. Man has the primacy (loud applause). But listen a minute to see what that means! His is the prime duty to serve (laughter and cries of 'Oh'!) and to lead. But his weak point is his need for completion and help (laughter). . . . Man and wife stand together on an equal footing, and the two are of equal value. . . . They are subject to one another in the fear of God. . . . The relation of mutual dependence described in Ephesians v is unfortunately often forgotten. Paul says particularly to the wife that she must be subject to her husband in the Lord. She brings joyfully to her husband the surrender of her whole being, because her husband brings her in return his love, as Christ loved his Church, even to his death on the Cross. This love involves every sacrifice of which a human being is capable. And if a husband takes his dignity as head of the family in an autocratic sense and compels his wife to submit to him, the community between them is dissolved. . . . A husband does what his position really

[1] See the analysis of this in *Priester und Arbeiter*, 1951 IV (K.A.B., Germany), and later articles on the same theme.

demands if he follows the command of love and forgets that he wears the crown of headship. . . . And the children are the responsibility of both. (Report of the Fourth Federal Congress of the C.D.U., 1953, pp. 169-70.)

The stress on strong leadership remains. Family life, in itself and in relation to the rest of the world, requires a high degree of dynamism; everyone must know his or her part and play it to the full. But the parts are now more fairly and carefully distributed than under the authoritarian conceptions of the past. And ideas continue to evolve. At the N.E.I. congress at Fribourg in 1952, Mlle de Meeus, then Assistant General Secretary of the P.S.C., pointed out the wide divergence of views still found not only on the headship of the family but on such consequent matters as the more or less joint ownership of family property. The Belgian Christian trade unions raised the same point earlier:

There are still important gaps in the legal rights of the married woman. The father's authority, as our law defines it, follows from the Roman law's conception of the 'Pater familias', and has therefore an absolute character. This absolute authority no longer operates in the patriarchal society in which it originated, but has not been, or has scarcely been, modified, on its insertion into a Code drafted with a view to the rights of the individual, to take account of the father's responsibility towards those dependent on him. The family community is not sufficiently protected against possible abuse on the part of the husband and father. . . . We wish for a reform of the law which will in future prevent the husband from alienating or selling the furniture and equipment of the family home without his wife's consent. . . . And why does the Code regard a wife as a minor, to be protected like lunatics and children under age? Should not collaboration between husband and wife, which is the basis of Christian marriage, be taken as the normal rule for their relations? Why also does the Code deny the mother any legal authority over her children while the father is alive? . . . Fourthly, bearing in mind that a woman has a personal destiny, each woman should be free to choose the work in which she can best realise the full development of her personality. As a social being, she has the duty to render, in and through this freely chosen task, the greatest possible service to human welfare. . . . (Hulpiau, report to the XV Congress of the Belgian Christian Workers' Movement, 1949, pp. 60-1.)

The discussion of policy on the family has at many points, and not only in Belgium, still to get beyond the level of general principles. It continues to be about 'man', 'woman', and 'the family', and has still to take account of the variety of family circumstances and the enormous and overlapping range of personality types found among men and women as individuals.

Several of the Christian Democratic parties owe their existence to the schools question, and it remains one of their most important and distinctive concerns. But here too ideas have changed. A clearer understanding of 'vertical' pluralism has emerged, and, as in other fields, the parties have come to be concerned less with ecclesiastical issues and more with general social policy. The battle in the early days was to retain for the Church, Protestant or Catholic, a place in the school. That battle is still being fought. But the accent now is more on another principle, that parents have the first right to decide how their children are to be educated. The State can properly insist that children be given the chance to learn what a citizen needs to know. The Church has a right to insist that they be given access to the truths of Christianity. But how and through what agency these requirements are to be met, and what further requirements are to be laid down, is in the Christian movements' view for parents to decide. The State has a duty to support those schools which parents choose, at least so far as is needed to enable them to reach the standards the State requires, and provided that they do in fact reach them. But it has no right to decide what schools there are to be, or to reserve public finance for schools of its own choice.

The family movement is as has been said unevenly spread, and its ideas do not receive equal support everywhere. Comparing countries, there has been a particularly striking recent change in Germany: a typical case of the uncertainty and re-focusing of ideas after a period during which their evolution was blocked. For some years after the collapse of 1945, Germany was for all practical purposes left out of the main stream of the Christian family movements. The most important provisions for the family were in kind, not cash, particularly after programmes for rehousing and the repair of war damage got under way. There were no State family allowances. When it was finally proposed to introduce them, a writer in *Sozialer Fortschitt* had to point out that the proposed level was far below that prevailing in such countries as France, Belgium, or even Denmark. A Christian Democratic government altered taxation actually to the disadvantage of the family, as compared with the war years. Leading Christian social theorists in Germany, such as Fr. Oswald von Nell-Breuning, agreed with the Catholic Workers' Movement in rejecting the principle of 'equal standard of life for equal work'.[1] The German Catholic movements were also distinctly hesitant in their approach to women's rights and to a revision of the position of the 'head of the house'. And there was no real family movement. But in the early 'fifties the current changed. By 1954 a massive family movement had come into existence, family allowances were on the way, and a Ministry for Family Affairs was set up. And Frau Praetorius, in spite of 'laughter and cries of Oh!', was expressing a new view of what family life should mean. Germany was re-entering the main stream.

YOUTH MOVEMENTS

The idea of developing personality through autonomy and responsibility is applied in the Christian movements to youth, as a group, as well as to the family. The activities of the Young Christian Workers, for example,

[1] See his preface to the *Sozialer Katechismus*, the German edition (1949) of the International Union of Social Studies' *Code of Social Ethics*.

are built up on four main principles. Young workers are a distinct group, with their own way of living and thinking, and need therefore an organisation to meet their special needs.

> The Y.C.W. demands . . . acceptance of the absolute necessity, especially for young wage-earners, of an organisation genuinely independent, fully special-ised, and adapted to their mentality, needs, and conditions of life. (*Statut du Jeune Travailleur*, 1944, s. 15.)

This does not exclude collaborating with parallel movements for other classes; far from it. As a matter of principle, all Catholic youth organisations in Belgium affiliate to the A.C.J.B. (Catholic Association of Belgian Youth), all in France to the corresponding French federation (A.C.J.F.) and so on. But it is organisation by class or social environment which is basic.

Secondly, a youth organisation which hopes to be effective and educative must be 'integral', concerned with the whole of life. It must bring into account all the activities of a given group of young people—their religion, their work, their sport, their family life—over a period of their lives which itself constitutes a complete whole; in the case of the Y.C.W., the period of transition from school to work and of settlement in work, up to marriage or the age of 25.

Thirdly, it must be young people's *own* organisation, resting essentially on comradeship, 'standing on its base, not on its head', 'of them, by them, for them'. In it they:

> Organise freely for their general education and development, for mutual aid and assistance of all kinds, and to represent and defend young people's interests in the face of authority of all kind, public and private. . . . The youth movements, each in its own field, should be accepted as the representatives of young people in every public or private organisation in which young people have a contribution to make or interest on which to insist. (Loc. cit.)

Whether or not through the youth organisations, young people in industry should send representatives to all the industrial boards or committees on which decisions concerning them are taken. Services which depend particularly on young people's own confidence and co-operation, such as vocational guidance, should preferably be provided through their own organisations, though this of course does not exclude the possibility of outside grants. The Belgian Y.C.W., for instance, has a highly efficient office for vocational guidance, and has fought hard for its right to receive as full government support as vocational guidance services provided in any other way.

Fourthly, an effective youth organisation must be effectively organised. It must have a clear-cut organisation chart, adequate finance, and efficient executive procedures. This is necessary not only for the organisation's own purposes but also because contact with executive efficiency is itself part

57

of the process of young people's education. We no longer find it startling, comments a former Y.C.W. member in *Notes de Pastorale Jociste* (October–November 1949), that even a young trade union official can draft a report or conduct an investigation, understand a legal text, speak in public, or conduct a meeting. And the credit for this basic training belongs largely to the youth movements.

There is an old tradition in youth movements of patronage and control from above, and this has helped to block the spread of the Y.C.W.'s principles. In some countries, notably Italy (on which more below), there is felt to be a risk that specialisation by social class may be carried too far. But the Y.C.W. principles are today the basis of the work of the main Christian youth federations in both Belgium and France. They have been spreading into Holland and Germany, and have begun to affect Italy. Germany has in many ways a similar home-grown tradition of its own, though not so much in Kolping, whose attraction has lain in material, social, and religious advantages rather than in young workers' chance to run their own life, as in the youth sections attached to the Catholic Workers' Movement.

CHAPTER VI

PLURALIST, NOT COLLECTIVIST—

3. 'HORIZONTAL' PLURALISM—INDUSTRY, FIRM, SOCIAL CLASS

THE INDUSTRY OR PROFESSION

THE Christian Democratic movements appreciate, like Liberals, the value of competition, and, like Socialists, that of State planning and control. But in the field of work, as everywhere, they are chiefly interested in human personality, and so in building up the co-operative, self-governing, industrial communities which seem to them most likely to favour its development. Their ideas about industrial organisation centre chiefly round two problems, those of industry-wide organisation and of workers' participation in the firm.

Concern for industry-wide organisation has been one of the traditional hall-marks of Christian Democratic doctrine. 'The principal part' of the Encyclical *Quadragesimo Anno*, so Pius XII wrote in 1952, is that which 'contains . . . the idea of the corporative professional organisation of the economy as a whole'. What this 'corporative professional organisation' means can be shown most easily from an example, and an outstanding one is available in the Dutch scheme of 'Statutory Industry Councils'. The Councils' parentage is claimed with equal enthusiasm by Protestants and by Catholics, and they represent the translation into fact of an aspiration found in some degree—however mild—in every Christian Democratic programme. The scheme is usually known as P.B.O., from the initials of its Dutch title (*Publiekrechtelijke Bedrijfsorganisatie*).

P.B.O. has appeared in Christian Democratic programmes in Holland for at least two generations. Its progress since before the First World War has been bound up notably with the propaganda of Professor J. Veraart, who had devoted to it a lifetime of study and public work. Already by 1918 a large section of Dutch public opinion was convinced that something of the kind was needed. The people living together in a certain geographical space have common interests and need common services; therefore they can properly be called a community and ask for the law to make special provision for their needs. It was now coming to be seen that the body of owners, managers, and workers engaged in operating a given

59

set of processes, or in turning out a given product, also have enough duties and interests in common to justify speaking of them as a 'community' and equipping this community with legal power to manage its common affairs. But it was not yet clear just what needed to be done, and attempts, notably by some Catholic organisations, to force the pace after the First World War had little practical result. It was not until after the Second World War that ideas had matured enough for permanent and comprehensive legislation to be passed in the shape of the Industrial Organisation Act of 1950.

This Act was passed with the approval of all parties, including the Socialists and (with much less enthusiasm) the Liberals. But the debates leading up to it brought out an essential difference between the Christian Democratic and the Social-democratic approach. For the Socialists, the basic purpose of the Act was to cheapen and increase the supply of goods and services. The consumer must come first. Since, in the Socialist view, the consumer could only be effectively represented by the State, the State must keep a firm grip on the machinery to be set up. The first, Socialist, draft accordingly provided that each industry council should be headed by a Government commissioner with considerable powers, responsible directly to a Ministry. The Christian parties and social organisations rejected this view on two grounds. They, and above all the Protestant movements, were less impressed than the Socialists with the efficiency of the Civil Service in protecting consumer interests and promoting economic dynamism, and a good deal more impressed with the possibilities of competition; or at any rate of competition if effectively policed. But also, and at least equally important, they felt that the Socialists were forgetting that the main objective of social policy is to develop human personality. To advance consumers' welfare is certainly a useful contribution to this. But it is also important to build up a sense of social responsibility and offer the widest possible circle of people the chance to exercise it: and whereas self-governing industry councils would have been a contribution to this, State-controlled machinery was not. For Catholics in particular the Socialist proposals awakened unpleasant memories of the State-controlled Fascist 'corporations' in Italy, which were nominally self-governing but in fact controlled by the government and the Fascist party. *Quadragesimo Anno* condemned them for that reason, and recommended genuine industrial self-government. In Holland both Catholics and Protestants joined in pressing for this, and their view prevailed.

Under the Act as finally passed Industry Councils can be set up for firms operating similar processes (cotton spinners, for instance), and Commodity Councils for those who contribute to the supply of a particular product; from cotton spinners, for example, through to piece-goods retailers. Commodity Councils have a Government-appointed chairman.

(3) 'HORIZONTAL' PLURALISM—INDUSTRY, FIRM, SOCIAL CLASS

Otherwise, council members are appointed by the appropriate employers' organisations and trade unions. Non-manual workers are guaranteed a place or places on the trade union side. The number of members from each side on a Council may or may not be equal, but their voting strength is equalised by crediting each member on the weaker side with an extra fraction of a vote. Ministries may send representatives to Council meetings, but these representatives have no vote. Councils may be given power to regulate a vast range of matters, including:

Registering the businesses with which each is concerned and collecting from them a levy and any necessary information, subject to safeguards against the publication by a council of business secrets.

Production and distribution, including such aspects as mechanisation, rationalisation, standardisation, management methods, and competition (this covers price-fixing, or the prevention of price-fixing).

Wages, working conditions, and welfare schemes, including such ancillary activities as arrangements for recruitment and training, schemes for preventing or minimising unemployment, and 'funds and other institutions for the benefit of those in the industry'.

Social, economic, and technical research.

A Council may not make any order which is 'an impediment to fair competition'. Nor may it regulate such matters as business reserves and investment, nor the establishment, expansion, and closing of businesses. Its decisions can be suspended or annulled by the Government 'in so far as they are contrary to the law or the public interest'.

It is not intended that all the powers under the Act should be available in every industry or commodity group, nor that all Councils should have the same constitution. Each industry or commodity group is to have a scheme tailor-made to its own requirements. At the time of writing these are being worked out under the supervision of a national Social and Economic Council also set up by the Act. This, the Introductory Note to the Act is careful to insist, is in no way a separate 'economic Parliament'. It is, like the industry and commodity councils, an advisory body to which may be delegated powers to execute certain aspects of Government policy. One-third each of its members are appointed by employers' associations and by trade unions, and the remaining third by the Government.

P.B.O. builds on the foundations of a wide range of industry-wide activities which have grown up in Holland over the years. The Dutch system of unemployment pay, for example, seen through British and American eyes, looks more like an industry-wide guaranteed wage scheme than a scheme of State social insurance. It is indeed a major contribution, passed into law primarily through the Christian parties and social movements, to the idea of the industry as a community with a collective responsibility for all those who work for it. Under the Unemployment

61

Insurance Act of 1949 each industry is expected to set up a joint management-union council, which pays 'waiting money' to workers unemployed in that industry during the first six months they are out of work. The 'waiting money' is equivalent to 80% of the normal wage in the case of family breadwinners, and to 70% in that of other workers living on their own. After six months a State scheme takes over; but this too is administered by a body one-third of whose members are nominated by the employers and one-third by the unions, with a further third of State nominees.

But in spite of such past experience as this, a scheme as comprehensive as P.B.O. obviously raises a number of new questions. Can and will a fair balance be kept between competition and control? And what is to happen to trade unions and employers' associations? They certainly retain their freedom. The tradition of Christian Democracy, in Holland as elsewhere, is of 'the free trade union in the organised profession'. The quarrel between Christian Democrats and Fascists arose not merely because under Fascism the statutorily organised profession was State-controlled, but also because the State kept its thumb on what should have been the free associations underlying it. Trade associations receive positive encouragement under P.B.O., since Art. 126 of the Act allows their members in certain circumstances to deduct part or all of their subscriptions from the levies payable under the Act. But though unions and associations remain, complete with the right to strike or lock-out, they will not necessarily in the long run have a great deal to do. Professor Veraart himself has suggested that they might dwindle into little more than educational organisations, a training ground for industry council members. Their bargaining functions would be replaced by the debates and decisions of the joint Councils. It goes without saying that this view is not shared by the Christian employers' associations and trade unions. It will be interesting to see what experience makes of this and a number of other issues about P.B.O. which in these early days remain open.

Every Christian Democratic organisation concerned with industry expresses at least some interest in organisation on P.B.O. lines, but in practice none has achieved as much as the Dutch. In Belgium the Christian Democrats have brought into existence Joint Councils for wage fixing and similar functions, and also a number of Industrial Economic Councils which advise the Government on the affairs of their industries. But this latter move is still somewhat experimental. The Christian trade unions would like to give the Economic Councils compulsory powers, but there is no sign as yet of the Christian Social Party supporting them. The Federation of the Middle Classes in Belgium has some interesting ideas of its own, differing rather markedly from the Dutch model. It would like to see Industry Councils built up directly from firms which would elect both employer and worker delegates. The trade unions and employers' associations, as important elements in the organised industry, would be entitled to representation in their own right. But they would not themselves, as in Holland, be the main basis of industry-wide organisation. The F.M.C. also suggests reserving seats specially for small and medium firms. And, like the unions, it would like to give councils some executive power.

In France the M.R.P. stresses the value of the 'natural structures' of society, including the idea of the profession as a community. The C.F.T.C. in 1945 outlined a full-scale scheme of Industry Councils, on lines similar to P.B.O., though following the Socialist first draft rather than the model finally adopted in the Act. The C.F.T.C. saw no objection to including State and independent members in Industry Councils, and stressed the idea of a national plan which the councils would be expected to help in carrying out. But nothing much has come of these moves by either the unions or the party. The Swiss Conservative People's Party and Christian unions and employers would also have liked to establish P.B.O., but have been unable to get the necessary support from other parties or from the Socialist unions and Liberal employers' organisations. In Germany, Italy, and Austria the Christian Democratic political movements have made little more than a formal bow—if as much—to the idea of industry-wide organisation. Some of the social organisations have gone further. The Austrian Christian workers, for instance, put a demand for Industry Councils into their Vienna Programme, drafted just after the war, and the Catholic Workers' Movement in Germany did the same in its Gelsenkirchen programme in 1950.

There are several reasons for this lack of progress outside Holland and perhaps Belgium. The French Christian Democrats, like the Swiss, would have gone further if other parties or trade unions had been willing to join in. Their German, Italian, and Austrian colleagues were preoccupied for several years with recovery from the Second World War, a problem to which industry-level organisation had much less to contribute than action at the level of the firm and the State. Its benefits, as the Dutch have correctly seen, lie in stabilising production, prices, and employment, and in promoting long-range programmes of education, research, and the exchange of information. For Germany, Italy, and Austria these possibilities did not have high priority in the first post-war years. The most urgent needs were short-term and concerned with increasing production rather than stabilising it. These countries were also, after years of Fascist government during which the idea of 'corporatism' or 'industrial communities' was misused in the interests of State power, allergic to anything which even remotely suggested a return to the conditions of that time.

Another factor is that there are few if any countries where the Christian Democrats' theory of industrial self-government has been as fully thought

63

out as in Holland. The pioneers of modern 'corporatist' thinking in many parts of Europe—Vogelsang in Austria, La Tour du Pin in France, Toniolo in Italy—were medievalist and romantic in outlook. They drew their lessons from the remote and often idealised past rather than from current reality. Many of them confused economic and social with political objectives. Disliking democracy as today understood, they wished to make professional organisations, not territorial constituencies, the basis of representation in Parliaments. In Austria in particular this view was strongly represented in Christian social circles right down to the Nazi occupation in 1938. It inspired the constitution introduced there in 1934, under which representatives in the Austrian Parliament were to be appointed by six employer-worker corporations. The most obvious effect of this system, as critics were quick to point out, was to reduce worker representation from over 50% to about 15% of the total. Ideas of this kind are thoroughly discredited today, in Austria as elsewhere.[1] But they lasted long enough to spread confusion and discredit over the Industry Council movement as a whole.

In Germany and Italy the discussion of industry-wide organisation was cut short by Fascism. The effect was particularly striking in Germany, where both discussion and experience of industry-wide organisation had gone far. In March 1933, as Hitler was coming to power, the German Christian trade unions outlined in their 'Essen Principles' a far-reaching scheme of organisation on P.B.O. lines. But in the circumstances of that time this scheme was still-born: the discussion was cut off in just those years when, in Holland, it was becoming most practical and fruitful. In Italy the break was earlier and the interruption longer. Alcide de Gasperi, the leader of Italian Christian Democracy from the collapse of Fascism till his death in 1954, was himself an expert in this field. One of the best short introductions to it is the study of 'The Evolution of Corporatism' which he published while on the run from the Fascist police in the inter-war years. But in the Italian Christian social movement as a whole the thread was broken, and when in 1950 a group of Christian Democratic intellectuals tried to come back to the subject, in a book on 'Towards a Democratic Corporatism', their thinking seemed wildly out of touch with reality. In a country engaged in one of the most striking and successful applications of liberal economics attempted anywhere since the war, they made no serious attempt to work out the relative spheres of competition and of the control to be exercised by Industry Councils. The largest trade union federation in Italy, which presumably would be a main pillar of industry-wide organisation, is Communist-controlled, and the Christian and Socialist unions object to any rigid legal framework which would

[1] Below, pp. 95–96.

64

prevent the flexible adjustment of power relations as their strength grows. But the neo-corporatists cared for none of these things, and their initiative, not surprisingly, had no practical effect. If Europe has a spell of peaceful and continuous development the Dutch example is likely to find more and more imitators among Christian Democrats. But in a case like that of Italy this move is likely to be spread over a long time.

THE FIRM

(a) The workers' movements' claim

The idea that people working together in the service of consumers constitute a community, responsible to and for all its members and also to and for the wider community of which it forms part, extends of course to the firm as well as to the industry or 'commodity group'. A number of the Socialist, and still more of course the Communist, movements in Western Europe have at one time or another pressed the doctrine of the class war so far as to doubt whether fruitful collaboration with management in the plant or firm is possible. The Christian workers' movements have never gone so far, though they have not denied that collaboration may be and often is difficult. They agree that management and workers have common interests and joint responsibility. This should eventually, they insist, be reflected in joint control of the firm. For only full industrial democracy, with not merely a consultative but a decisive voice for all, can provide full opportunity for the 'promotion of the working class', the widest chance for workers to take responsibility and develop their power to lead. But by joint control the Christian workers' movements mean literally 'joint' control and honest collaboration, not a step towards total victory in the class war. For they do not dispute the right of investors to earn such profits as the Christian theory of the just price permits, nor the responsibility of managers towards consumers and shareholders as well as towards workers.

It has not always been clear exactly on what grounds the Christian workers' movements claim a share in control of the firm, or how their claim can best be given practical effect. At the annual German Katholiken-tag (Catholic Assembly) in 1949, at Bochum, the Chaplain-General of the Catholic Workers' Movement, Dr. H. J. Schmitt, read the following declaration on behalf of a joint working party of Catholic industrialists, distributors, and trade unionists:

Man stands at the centre of every economic and management problem. We recognise the right of all who work in a business to share in control over its decisions in social, personal, and economic matters. The right to joint control belongs to the natural law, under the order willed by God. For this requires that all should share in responsibility. It is to be approved in the same way as the right to property. (From the official Press hand-out at the Katholikentag.)

It quickly became apparent that Dr. Schmitt had put his foot not merely in it but clean through it. After a vigorous debate extending over the next five years, the official view of the Catholic Church was stabilised something as follows:

(1) There is in general no absolute or 'natural' right to joint control of industrial decisions of any kind.

(2) But joint control is in modern conditions often very desirable, for the usual reason of promoting the growth of human personality and opening up new opportunities of leadership and responsibility. The statement quoted earlier from the International Union of Social Studies is a good example of this line of thought.[1]

(3) Each contributor to a firm's activities brings with him needs and interests which others must respect. Any decision which involves solely the interests of a given individual or group is a matter solely for that individual or group. A decision exclusively affecting the value of a firm's capital assets, for instance, is a matter exclusively for those who provide these assets. But decisions which affect the rights and interests of two or more groups are a legitimate matter for joint control.

(4) No formula or set of formulas can yet be said to have proved definitely the best. For the moment, therefore, what is needed is the greatest possible amount of experiment under varying conditions.

These are quite general rulings. They amount essentially to giving the green light for experiment and argument on the most suitable forms of joint control. A number of Protestant churches and organisations have made statements to the same effect.

Experiment has been duly forthcoming, and on a big scale. J. Zamanski, the Chairman of the French Catholic employers' organisation, was able in 1948 to fill a book[2] with some dozens of schemes in firms of all shapes and sizes, ranging from elementary joint consultation to fully shared control, and helping to clarify ideas not only on consultation and workers' control but also on such matters as profit-sharing, workers' shares, or the 'autonomisation' of departments and working groups. The Christian-Democratic parties have been largely responsible for the Works Council laws now in force all over Europe; in France from 1945–6, in Austria from 1947, in Belgium from 1948, in Holland from 1950, in Germany (the most far-reaching of all) from 1951 and 1952. They have not been solely responsible, and the content of these laws has not always been what they would have wished: most notably in the case of the German co-determination law of 1951. But the difference has been over what the law should contain, or whether this or that purpose is best attained by law; there has been no question of the need to move in the direction of joint control. From all this experiment has emerged, not indeed detailed agree-

1 This statement by the International Union of Social Studies, on *Workers' Control*, is a useful summary of the whole Catholic position. English translation in *The Christian Democrat*, March 1954.
2 *L'Avenir de l'Entreprise—un Patronat qui S'Engage.*

ment as to what should be done, but at any rate a broad agreement among Christian Democrats on what is to be the line of approach.

(b) *Autonomy of the firm*

In the first place, the works community must have a high degree of autonomy. It is difficult enough in any case to find workers, or managers mature enough to operate a fully developed system of joint control, and 'they never will be mature unless put to the test'.[1] Maturity depends on full, independent, responsibility, and this calls for a self-denying ordinance on the part both of the class organisations (trade unions and employers' associations) and of the higher organs of the profession and the State. Sharp disputes have more than once arisen over this between the Christian and the social-democratic movements. In Germany the Socialist majority of the trade unions called for joint control of the firm mainly because, after their experience of the support given by employers to the National Socialists, they were afraid of the misuse of firms' resources and influence for political ends. They disliked any close identification of the worker with his firm, and, when the law provided for workers' seats on Boards of Directors, wished to fill these largely with trade union nominees from outside the firm. The Christian-Democratic Union and Christian workers' movements allowed that these arguments had some truth in them. They did not object to *some* outside representation, and, in case of disputes within a firm, they were ready to agree that an outside arbitrator—a genuinely independent one—should be brought in. But the primary purpose of joint control was for them to improve relations within the firm and offer an additional opening for workers' participation and responsibility.

> The right, recognised [by law], for a firm's workers to collaborate through their representatives in its management should be exerted by these workers themselves, and contribute first and foremost to restoring a direct relation of confidence between all engaged in the firm. Persons who have the confidence of a firm's staff, but are not themselves engaged in the firm, should be allowed to assist their constituents' efforts, but nothing more: they should not be called in as arbitrators, nor should they be allowed to intervene in their own right. The trade unions are competent to establish collective agreements, but not to join in applying these in individual firms. (Reply of the C.D.U. to preliminary questionnaire of the Bruges Conference of the N.E.I., 1954.)

The Socialist view was on the whole accepted in the case of the coal and steel industries, in which three of the normal five workers' seats on Boards of Directors are allotted directly by trade union head offices, with only the nominal consent of the workers concerned. The more general Works Constitution Law of 1952 inclines more to the Christian view.

In Holland also the Socialists wished works councils to be the lowest rung of a national planning mechanism, whereas Protestants and Catholics

[1] Taviani, *Problemi del Lavoro*, 1947 Congress of the Christian Democratic party in Italy, p. 51.

insisted on their independence. In Belgium the law on works committees requires them to report and advise on matters submitted to them by the appropriate Industry Councils, and the Christian trade unions agree that in the absence of provisions of this kind—if, that is, firms were left entirely to govern themselves—there would be a danger of what they call 'corporatism in the enterprise'. The Belgian law also lays down that candidates for works councils are to be put forward by the unions. But the union intervention in works council affairs envisaged in Belgium does not go beyond that outlined as an ideal by the French Christian union (C.F.T.C.):

> The trade unions work on the level of the profession and the national economy. It is not for them to take directly in hand the organs which deal with the life of each firm, and its reform. These organs must have a real autonomy. But action in the firm must, lest it turn selfishly in on itself and go wrong in a variety of ways, be linked to the industry-wide organisation of which the unions are the driving force. A link must therefore be carefully planned between the unions and the various organs through which the solidarity of the firm is expressed. It is for the unions to:
> (a) Study, on the spot, the constitution of these organs.
> (b) Raise in Industry Councils, at the appropriate level, difficulties arising on the operation and authority of works councils.
> (c) Present lists of candidates at shop stewards' and works council elections.
> (d) Educate and document shop stewards and works council members.
> (e) Stand guard over their independence and security.
>   (*Programme d'Action Ouvrière*, 1945, p. 56.)

This, it will be noticed, suggests a rather greater degree of union intervention than would be approved in principle by the Christian-Democratic union, though no greater than is actually permitted in Germany under the legislation which the C.D.U. has passed. It also calls for a great deal more union intervention than French or Belgian employers, Christian or otherwise, have in general been willing to accept. Belgian employers have complained that the presentation of lists of candidates by unions leads to:

> Trade union interests taking priority over those of the firm, violation of professional secrecy, failure to provide representation for non-trade unionists, and use for collective bargaining purposes of data obtained about the firm. (David (ed.), *La Participation des Travailleurs à la Gestion des Entreprises Privées*, Paris 1954, p. 103.)

There have also been disputes over the standardisation of procedure, with the unions pressing for at least a minimum common list of standing orders for works councils, and the employers insisting that standing orders should be not only 'very simple' but also established separately for each firm in the light of its special characteristics.[1] The unions have been inclined to dismiss these complaints by employers as arising out of incomprehension and bad faith.

---

[1] Statement by the Belgian engineering employers, June 1950.

We cannot say—the praiseworthy exceptions are very rare indeed—that we are any more satisfied with the general employers' attitude in this matter than in that of industry-wide organisation. From the very first meetings of the works councils the employers, backed by their organisations, have tried to limit their range of action or at least to impede their functioning. (XVII Congress of the C.S.C. (Belgian Christian trade unions), 1951. Report on *L'Activité de la C.S.C.*, p. 127.)

However, some of the Christian unions have felt that additional precautions are in fact needed. It is quite probable that in Belgium or France, where a large works will often have two, three, or more unions competing for the allegiance of each group of employees, provision for the nomination of candidates by the unions will not lead to 'union domination' in the sense of excessive control by union officials or by branch committees outside the works. Competition will save members' wishes from being neglected. But the danger is reduced, not eliminated, and in any case even in these countries one-union plants exist. The Dutch Protestant unions therefore propose that union nomination for works elections should be retained, but that each union should choose its candidates by a primary election held with all due formality among its members in each works.

Under 'education and documentation' it is of course possible for many other organisations besides trade unions, including the Churches and the Christian Action organisations, to take a hand without interfering with firms' proper autonomy. The Evangelical Church in Germany, for instance, is making a great effort in this direction, notably through its Social Academy at Friedewald.

(c) The authority of management

Within the firm, the Christian Democratic movements agree in the first place that the authority and personal responsibility of top management must be preserved, or even strengthened. It is not surprising to find this emphasised by the employers' organisations; but the trade unions and other workers' organisations do not dispute it. There seem to be three factors here. One is a feeling, not always very clearly expressed, that the manager of an ordinary competitive firm, in a well-organised profession, is more an executive than a policy-maker. What he is to produce, and on what conditions, has been largely settled for him by the market and by industry-wide or national decisions. As regards what is left, his role is chiefly that of a leader in an executive chain, a role which calls principally for leader-subordinate relations. Dutch Christian Democrats have particularly insisted that the (largely policy-making) organisation at the national and industry-wide level must be straightened out before the place of top management. or anyone else, in the constitution of the firm can be accurately defined.

Secondly, however, it is of course agreed that there is some policy-making to be done in the firm. Indeed, it is very important policy-making.

It is the Idea (conception) which gives birth to the enterprise, and therefore also to the works community. And the Idea carries with it the right of decision. (National Federation of the Middle Classes (Belgium): *Les Travailleurs Indépendants dans l'Economie Nationale*, 1953, p. 33.)

Here too, top management's rights and responsibilities have to be safeguarded. The conception is very like that found in the British Constitution. The conventions of the Cabinet and Parliament are designed to ensure that there shall be strong, united, executive power, and that the Cabinet which exerts this power shall also be responsible for the main initiatives in legislation; for in this way legislation is consistent and practical, and leads to effective action. So also the Christian Democrats see the main initiative in policy-making within the firm, as well as the main responsibility for execution, as falling on top management. Managers must certainly follow a policy in the interests and with the consent of their constituents, inside as well as outside the firm. But they must themselves take the lead in making it.

Top management, it is also insisted, can carry its responsibilities effectively only if it constitutes a small and definite enough group, with a sufficiently clear-cut legal status, to make its responsibility truly personal. What is called for is what Holden, Fish, and Smith,[1] in a study of big American firms, name a 'general management group' of one or more recognisable individuals in whom is concentrated, by law and custom, the ultimate responsibility for both execution and legislative leadership; precisely the conception of the British Cabinet. Belgian Christian Democrats have particularly stressed the need to revise company law so as to put the legal as well as the effective leadership of companies in the hands of a group of this kind.

(*d*) *Control over policy and senior appointments: the position of the workers' movements*

These conceptions do not make the industrial manager an autocrat. Executive leadership is a matter largely of leader-subordinate relations. But effective legislative leadership implies readiness to consult on an equal footing with the various interests concerned, and accept the decisions at which they as a group arrive. Top managers—so Christian Democrats on the whole see it—should be bound by decisions reached at the level of the firm as well as of the industry or the nation. Only who is to take part in these decisions? That raises a number of unresolved questions. Several of the workers' movements support, as has been said, the idea of equal shares in control, half to those who supply the capital of a business

---

[1] *Top Management Organisation and Control*, McGraw Hill, 1941.

and half to those who do its work. This means, concretely, that workers' representatives should have half the seats on Boards of Directors. The French and (more cautiously and in a slightly different form) the Belgian Christian trade unions demand as much. In Germany, where the workers have in fact equal representation on the boards of coal, iron, and steel firms[1] the Christian workers' movement dislikes the particular constitution adopted but agrees with the French and Belgians that the principle of this 'exemplary law, unique in the world'[2] is good. The German trade unions have also secured one-third of the seats on the boards of other companies (excluding family firms employing fewer than 500), and the Catholic Workers' Movement has proclaimed that this is merely a step towards equal representation. The Christian trade unionists in the German Parliament, though members of the Christian Democratic Union, abstained from voting on this law on the ground that it did not go far enough. In Austria also works councils have won the right to nominate two members to the boards of companies with above a certain minimum of capital. The Italian Christian (or Christian-inspired) unions have been more doubtful about moves in this direction; but this is chiefly because workers' representation is likely in that country to mean usually representation of and by Communists. The only clear exception to the rule that the Christian workers' movements demand joint control of the firm seems to be the Swiss Protestant Workers' and Clerks' Union (S.V.E.A.) which calls for joint control only over wages and similar matters, plus the right to be informed on and to discuss matters of technique, welfare and safety, and the general progress of the business.

Several of the Christian Workers' movements underline that overall joint control implies joint responsibility between capital and labour for the appointment of top managers.

> A firm is a matter of co-operation between capital and labour. . . . And why exactly should only the supplier of capital have an influence on the appoint- ment and dismissal of the leaders of this joint effort, and not the supplier of labour? (From M. Ruppert, *De Nederlandse Vakbeweging*. Ruppert is Pres- ident of the C.N.V.—the Protestant trade unions.)

Here too the German workers have actually achieved their objective in the coal and steel industries. The joint worker-shareholder Boards in these industries appoint two of the normal three members of each firm's general management group (*Vorstand*). The third, the Labour Director, is in effect directly appointed by the trade unions.

---

[1] The actual formula is five management and five workers' representatives with an 'eleventh man' acceptable to both sides. The point objected to by the Catholic Workers' Movement is, as has been said, what is regarded as undue influence from outside the works in the appointment of workers' representatives.

[2] Even, *Das Betriebsverfassungsgesetz*, K.A.B. pamphlet, 1952, p. 9.

(e) Control over policy and senior appointments: the position of the Christian employers' organisations

The Christian employers' organisations have been reluctant to see workers sharing control equally with shareholders, though some at least of them have come out in favour of giving workers a minority of the seats on Boards. The French Catholic employers, for instance, took this view in a 'Joint Plan' which they drafted with the Christian trade unions in 1944. But, though views are changing, a more typical opinion among both Catholic and Protestant employers would still be that of the Dutch Protestant Employers' Association:

> The worker should have a voice in drawing up the labour agreement. As regards stipulations essential to the agreement, we reject one-sided decisions by the employer. As regards its incidental details, the workers should be consulted, but the right of the employer to take decisions, as the responsible leader, should be maintained. The technical and commercial management of the business should remain in the hands of the employer, though workers should be given ample opportunity to make suggestions. (*What We Believe and What We Do,* English-language pamphlet of the Protestants-Christelijke Werkgevers in Nederland, c. 1938, 3.3.)

The 'constitutional firm' and the works council with executive powers are ruled out. An intermediate position is taken by certain groups—the Austrian People's Party also takes this view—which are prepared to accept joint control if, but only if, it is based on joint ownership, that is on workers' shareholdings. They feel that ownership of a financial as well as a personal stake in a firm is needed to produce the right sense of responsibility. The workers' movements do not entirely reject this idea. They are strongly in favour of building up workers' investments in industry, notably with the help of profit-sharing. But they do not feel that these investments should of necessity be in workers' own firms, nor that the sharing of control in these firms should depend on the investment of a man's money in addition to that of his labour and life. The Belgian Christian trade unions go so far as to describe the issue of workers' shares, as a basis for participation, as 'a useless fiction'.

(f) Control over policy and senior appointments: the position of the Christian Democratic parties

The Christian Democratic parties have not been willing, at least as yet, to go the whole way with the workers' movements on joint control. The one which has gone furthest is the Christian Democratic Union in Germany. In its Ahlen Programme of 1947 the C.D.U. laid down that:

> In plants which are too large for the relationship between worker and employer to remain on a personal basis, the workers should be guaranteed a share in control over the basic issues of economic planning and social policy. . . . The plant's employees should have an appropriate representation in its trusteeship

management, as for instance in the Board of Directors. For this purpose . . .
the Board should be placed in a stronger position over against the senior
executives. In large plants which have a management committee [instead of a
single chief executive], long-service employees . . . should be given the
opportunity to take part in the direction of the business through appointment
as members of the management committee. Such appointments should be
made on the proposal of the plant's employees, who should nominate at least
three candidates for consideration by the Board of Directors. (C.D.U.,
Neuordnung der Industriellen Wirtschaft (Ahlen Programme), 1947, s.3.)

Other recommendations dealt with the right of the works council to be
informed and to co-operate with management, and with profit-sharing.
The Düsseldorf Programme of 1949 confirmed in general terms that in the
party's view workers have a right to 'joint consultation, co-operation, and
joint control', though 'without destroying management's responsibility'.
A year later the party's *Political ABC* once again confirmed that it regards
joint control as properly extending not merely to personnel questions but
to matters of general business policy. In 1951 it was a primarily C.D.U.
government which passed the law on joint control in coal and steel.

The C.D.U. was, however, frankly unwilling to go as far as it did in
1951, and did so only under severe trade union pressure. This pressure
was helped by the fact that the occupation authorities had already set
up a system of joint control in steel on which it was difficult to go back.
Like the Catholic Workers' Movement, the C.D.U. disliked the degree of
trade union head office control finally written into the law. Its own policy,
as the quotation above shows, was for representation of and nomination
by 'the plant's employees', that is the rank and file. And a large proportion
of the party's employer and middle-class members interpreted its
programme declarations about joint control of business decisions and the
need to preserve management responsibility in—from the point of view of
the workers' claims—a very restrictive sense. Views typical of many of
them were expressed in the report of a working party issued in 1949 by
Cardinal Frings of Cologne.[1] The working party agreed without difficulty
that workers had a right to share in the control of personnel matters and
welfare services, though even here only within limits. Appointments and
dismissals, for instance, should in the last resort be a matter for decision
by management. But in decisions affecting the general policy of the
business workers' representatives were to be entitled only to information,
and to a right of protest and delay in a few cases involving mass dismissals.

The Works Constitution Law of 1952, which revived and strengthened
the general German law on works councils of 1920, much more accurately
represented the C.D.U.'s own views. The previous law had allowed
workers to nominate one or two members to Boards of Directors. The law
of 1952, as already recorded, granted workers in limited companies, other

[1] *Verantwortung und Mitverantwortung in der Wirtschaft*, Cologne, 1949.

than family firms employing fewer than 500, the right to one-third of the seats on Boards, whatever their number. It also strengthened the position of works councils, partly by facilitating their work and partly by adding to their rights of control over management. Councils have joint control with management, and the right to appeal to compulsory and binding outside arbitration, in so-called 'social' matters, which include such things as works rules, the fixing of job and piece rates and introduction of incentive schemes—except in so far as collectively agreed at higher levels—and welfare, holiday schedules, and vocational training. They have a legal right to intervene in safety and health matters, and can veto appointments and transfers which are in breach of a law or collective agreement, constitute discrimination on personal, racial, religious, or other similar grounds, or are likely to lead to 'disturbance of the peace of the firm through anti-social or illegal behaviour'. Through an Economic Committee, established jointly with management, a works council is entitled to quarterly and annual reports on the production and financial position of the firm, and to such details to complete this information as it may require. It is entitled to express its views on all dismissals, and to receive special advance information of all large-scale dismissals. This power is limited, since there is a separate law, also passed by the C.D.U. to guarantee workers against arbitrary dismissal and to provide for a special procedure and notice in the case of dismissals on a large scale. The 1952 law allows the works council to appeal to an outside conciliator, in the absence of agreement within the firm, in the event of major changes which affect employment prospects:

> Contraction or closing of the entire works, or of substantial parts of it.
> Transfer of the entire works, or of substantial parts of it.
> Fusion with other works.
> Basic changes in the purpose or structure of the works, unless manifestly consequent on changes in the market.
> Introduction of basically new working methods, unless manifestly required to keep up with or promote technical progress. (Betriebsverfassungsgesetz, s. 72.)

Where an agreement is reached in this way, or a formula is put forward by the conciliator though not accepted by the parties, the Industrial Court will award damages to workers dismissed in breach of the agreement or formula.

The law does not recognise any formal connection between the works councils and the trade unions. There is no provision such as is found in France or Belgium for councillors to be union members or nominees. In fact, however, it seems that about 80% of councillors are union members, and council elections are one of the main occasions for the different fractions in the unions—Socialist, Christian, Liberal, Communist—to try their strength. It can be said that union influence is strong, but in accordance with the views of the Catholic Workers' Movement as well as the C.D.U., only to the extent that it is transmitted through and secures the support of the rank and file in the firm itself.

Looking back at the element of joint control introduced into German industry by the laws of 1951 and 1952, the C.D.U. comment two years later that:

> We are watching the practical effect of legal regulation in this matter. Its primary purpose must be to avoid one-sided and capricious measures, not to form a basis for positions of collective power.... [These measures are] approved to the extent that they do in fact promote confident co-operation and mutual responsibility. (Answer to the questionnaire for the Bruges Conference of the Christian-Democratic parties' international (N.E.I.), Bruges, 1954.)

'Positions of collective power' refers of course to the usual fear of excessive control by union officials outside the firm.

The Austrian People's Party has gone almost as far as the C.D.U., indeed in some ways further: though there is reason to think that much of what it has done has been more due to pressure from the Social-Democrats, who are equal partners with the People's Party in the coalition which has governed Austria since the war, than to the goodwill of the People's Party itself. The People's Party supported in 1946 a Co-Partnership Act, the effect of which could eventually be to transfer to employee ownership the capital, and following this also the control, of nationalised firms whose employees decide to set up a co-partnership association. Until 1955 this Act remained in cold storage thanks at least in part to difficulties created by foreign occupation. It remains to be seen what effect it will have now that the occupation is ended. In 1947 the Party also let through Parliament (the exact phrase in *Programm Österreich* is that the law 'could never have been passed against the will of the People's Party') a Works Council Law under which the works council in a company with more than a low minimum of capital is entitled to nominate two members to the Board. Works councils in Austrian firms employing over 500 have, as under the German law of 1952, the right to appeal to an outside authority if it is proposed to close a plant, or if the management ignores works council proposals on specified aspects of production and economic development. And, also as in the German law, the works council has veto rights over appointments, dismissals, transfers, disciplinary measures, holiday arrangements, and other so-called 'personal' matters.

Christian Democratic parties elsewhere have usually felt that it was enough to encourage collective agreements, which may of course cover such matters as profit-sharing, shop stewards' rights, and grievance procedures, and to promote and uphold works councils as established by agreement or law. The M.R.P. would have liked to go further, and in 1946 promoted a bill under which companies which so wished could reconstitute themselves with Boards consisting of one-third or more of workers' representatives, and for the rest, of shareholders' representatives and independents. It wished constitutions on these lines to be made compulsory in the case of firms sequestrated on account of collaboration with the Nazis. But neither the special proposal for these firms nor the more general measure actually passed into law, and the general bill in any case called only for voluntary reorganisation: there was to be no such compulsion as in Germany or Austria. It is more usual for works council laws supported by Christian Democrats outside Germany and Austria to give the councils four much more restricted sorts of power:

(1) The right to elect a council, and to meet management on specified occasions.
(2) The right to supervise, and often to administer, their firm's welfare work.
(3) Varying responsibilities for 'personal' matters such as dismissals, appointments, or works rules; that is, the matters most directly affecting the personnel.
(4) The right to be informed about the technical and economic progress of the business, and to discuss it. This in some countries includes the right to send in an accountant to establish and (in Belgium) to report and advise on the facts about the firm's economic position.

Under all these heads, ideas as to what the law is to require or Ministries are to encourage remain very fluid. Under (1), for example, what is to be the basis of representation? Where do supervisors and technicians, or clerical workers, fit in? Under (2), does or should this right, where it exists, include the right to demand that a certain sum be made available for this work, or is it a case merely of administering what the employer makes available? Under (3), it is not always clear just what are the respective spheres of the works council, of shop stewards and the normal grievance machinery, and of outside union officials. And, under (4), different importance is attached in different countries to the various types of policy open for discussion: to technical matters of production, for instance, or to the overall economies of the firm.

(g) Co-responsibility in general: obstacles from outside the Christian movements

The hesitations of the Christian Democratic parties and employers' organisations must be seen in the light not only of their doubts about the final validity of the workers' movements' claims—and such doubts are certainly widespread—but also of the unsettled state of the question, and of the general political and social atmosphere in which it is being discussed. Managers are naturally more sensitive than the rank and file to the question, for example, of securing proper representation on works committees for supervisors and technicians. They do not want to freeze the machinery, or give it too much power, till this and other open questions are settled. They are also, and just as naturally, sensitive to the danger of

76

putting the levers of decision into the hands of workers' representatives who have not been fully proved and trained. And both managers and politicians are sensitive to the point insisted on by the Italian Christian trade unions, that any general measure must apply to Communist and Socialist unions and 'liberal' employers as well as to Christians. If the Italian government were tomorrow to pass a law establishing joint control of industrial firms, the result would usually be to divide power between 'liberal' managers, who have what the Christian employers' organisations regard as an exaggerated view of shareholders' and managers' rights, and Communist trade unionists interested only in the class war. The results, judging by actual experience of co-determination in Italy just after the war, would be unlikely to satisfy liberals, Communists, or indeed anyone else. In Italy and France in particular, the way forward would seem at present to be through experiment in individual firms where conditions are suitable rather than through new general legislation.

The present position of the debate among Christian Democrats on the works community, as on so many other matters, can be summed up in the title of the Belgian Christian Social Party's programme, *Les Chantiers sont Ouverts*; roughly speaking, 'Men at Work'. The pace of discussion has died down since the immediate post-war years. But the idea of a works community based on co-responsibility remains very much alive, and debate and experiment are proceeding steadily. It does not seem likely that any *general* move from present positions will occur for ten or fifteen years. But the ideas and material are building up out of which an important body of new models should be forthcoming then.

SOCIAL CLASS

The class structure cuts across the collaborative systems of the firm and industry, as well as of other communities and social groups. The Christian Democratic and Christian Action movements duly recognise the existence of classes, with distinct ways of life and separate interests which they are legitimately entitled to develop and defend. The growth of personality requires not merely that each individual find a role and status appropriate to him, but also that he enjoy a certain measure of security. One of the main foundations of security, as the Christian movements see it, is to belong to a class of people like oneself, among whom one meets understanding and feels at home, and to know that this class is organised and indispensable enough to be a power in the land. And this all the more so since the vast majority of people are today fixed for life in one or other class, once their school and college years are over.

Class organisation is seen as having value first of all in industrial relations. Christian Democratic movements may sometimes fear trade union interference with self-government in the firm. But none would claim that it was possible to build mutual confidence and ready collaboration in the firm or the industry against, or even without, the trade unions and employers' organisations. For mutual confidence is impossible without mutual respect, and this must be based not only on character and common ideals but on organisation and strength. One of the last serious challenges to this principle from a professedly Christian Democratic source dates from 1924. As a result of disputes in the textile industries in the north of France, the employers' federation chiefly involved—a 'neutral' body, but in fact led largely by Catholic employers active as such—appealed to Rome to condemn the Christian trade unions. The reply was long delayed, but was finally known in Lille in 1928, and officially published in 1929.[1] It reaffirmed the value of class collaboration, but at the same time made clear that in the view of the Roman Congregation concerned:

(1) Trade unions, entirely independent of the employers, are necessary.
(2) The defence by these unions of 'legitimate economic and temporal interests' is entirely justifiable. In the particular case under review, the Christian unions on strike had committed at most 'some tactical errors', and used some unfortunate expressions.
(3) This defence may quite properly be carried on in collaboration, from case to case as conditions demand, with other, non-Christian, working-class organisations.
(4) A special value of separate class organisations lies in their potentialities for education—hence the special importance of keeping them on a Christian basis.

Class organisation is also seen to have its value in politics, though there has been a great deal of argument over the form which the political influence of classes should take. There was a long battle around the turn of the nineteenth into the twentieth century to persuade the then Christian parties to give due weight to working-class interests. During and after that debate several parties grew into a federal way of thinking and regarded themselves as composed of, or at least based on, a series of organised interest groups. The Austrian People's Party is to this day a federation resting on three fractions, of the workers, the farmers, and the employers and middle class, together with a women's and individual members' section. The workers' group figures at one and the same time as the Christian fraction of the 'neutral' trade unions and the workers' fraction of the Christian Democratic party. The Swiss Conservative People's Party has the same triple foundation. The Catholic Party in Belgium, the predecessor of the P.S.C., was down to the second World War a federation of regions and social classes. This type of party organisation is today unfashionable, for reasons very well put in a study of the Dutch Catholic workers' movement:

In principle, the movement opposes class parties and politics because the aim of the Government should be to advance the common good, not that of some

[1] *Trade Unions and Employers' Associations—the Catholic View*, English translation by the Catholic Social Guild, Oxford, 1929.

(3) 'HORIZONTAL' PLURALISM—INDUSTRY, FIRM, SOCIAL CLASS

particular group or class. . . . And furthermore, in practice, political action involves risks, compromises, and personal competition which can seriously disturb the action of social movements, to the point of completely compromising them by absorbing the best part of their efforts and provoking splits. (du Bois de Vroylande, *L'Organisation du Milieu Ouvrier en Hollande*, 1926, p. 116.)

But the parties and social movements continue to appreciate the value to both sides of, not indeed formal or organic links—these now rarely exist—but regular contact and representations. It is on the whole those Christian Democratic parties which are most solidly underpinned with class organisations, notably in Holland, Belgium, and Switzerland, which have the most stable policy and have done—taking account of all the circumstances—the most effective work.

The Christian Action movements, for their part, have tended more and more to specialise their work by social class. This is partly for the sake of good communication; they will not be listened to if they do not speak in the terms current in each environment. But it is also because they value positively the culture of a class as a contribution to the welfare both of its members and of society as a whole. In France this idea often takes on a distinct class war tinge, the idea of 'the working class movement as the driving force of the ascent of humanity and of the new society which will bring it about', thanks to 'a clean break with the capitalist regime . . . a broad re-grouping of anti-capitalist, popular, progressive, revolutionary forces'.[1] But it is in the Dutch and German Catholic movements, above all the workers' movements, that the idea of class culture ('Standes-Kultur') is most fully worked out.

> The father's vocation as a worker is also the foundation of the special culture of the worker's family and home. The Catholic Workers' Movement expresses its appreciation of this and demands positive support for it. The worker in his self-consciousness rejects any imitation of others' customs and style of life. The worker's family has no need to copy the style of any other. In the consciousness of their own values, out of their own experience, from life in their own calling, and to fulfil their own tasks in public life, Catholic workers set out to build the culture of their own class. (Programm der K.A.B., German Catholic Workers' Movement, 1950, pp. 33–4.)

Some sections of the Christian social movement feel that this tendency to specialise by classes goes, or may go, too far. The Dutch Protestant trade unions, for instance, insist that:

> They have never felt themselves to be a class—'Stand'—movement, which considers 'the worker' apart from other classes. They are organisations of free men who demand their rightful place in society, that is their place as co-partners of all others who work and produce. (R. Hagoort in *Evangelie en Maatschappij*, December 1954.)

The nearest Protestant equivalent to the Catholic 'Stand' organisations in Holland, the workers' leagues such as 'Patrimonium', have always had,

[1] The quotations are from *Travaux* 1951, M.P.F./M.L.P., pp. 44 and 47.

79

and wished in principle to have, some middle-class members. In the Protestant Social movement generally, not only in Holland, doubts have been growing about the value of mass, class-based organisations for at any rate educational and cultural work—there is no doubt of their value for trade union action—in the diversified, fractionated, and mobile conditions of modern society.[1] Among Catholics in Italy, Luigi Gedda finds the specialisation of youth organisations by social class a second-rate substitute for the ideal of all classes in one organisation; a substitute whose use may sometimes be inevitable, but which aggravates the difference between classes and often does more harm than good. In France the A.C.J.F., the federation of the main Catholic youth movements, notes that in its own ranks two or three generations of effort were needed to reach a sound co-operation between classes, and that at one period specialisation by classes threatened to lead to complete disunity:

> Till the rise of the specialised movements, the middle and upper class ran the A.C.J.F. It saw its task as being to educate the mass of the people by 'condescending' to them without giving up its own superior position. Specialisation produced an A.C.J.F. run by the leaders of the different classes on a footing of equality. But within each specialised movement the limited point of view of that class tended to prevail exclusively. The Young Christian Workers answered its problems in the light of the wishes and interests of the working class, the Young Farmers concerned themselves mainly with the farming world, the Young Independents were interested essentially in problems of the middle and upper class. It is only since the Liberation that the A.C.J.F. has reached a third stage in which . . . what counts is no longer the consideration of class interests but that of functions to be performed. . . . The 'Social Christians' who tried to improve the life of the proletariat without taking away from the upper and middle class their monopoly of the top jobs were succeeded by . . . those . . . who wished to base society on collaboration between the leaders of the workers', farmers', and employers' unions. The society which we are now trying to build must on the contrary be the work of men of every class, but all of them respectful of the common good. (*Devenir Membre Actif de la Société des Hommes*, report of the Federal Committee of the A.C.J.F., December 1950.)

It has been a fairly general observation in recent years that, though co-ordination between the specialised Christian movements is often (not always) good at the top, it may be almost non-existent at the bottom. It would scarcely be claimed anywhere that the right balance between class organisation and collaboration has yet been found.

But these are, so to speak, marginal notes on the general approval given to independent class-wise organisation. It is agreed that class defence must not be allowed to obscure the need for class collaboration. But it is also remembered that, if the purpose of organising the members of a social class is first of all to give them a sense of security, the first essential is that the organisation should be run by as well as for the members of that class.

[1] See below, p. 227.

(3) 'HORIZONTAL' PLURALISM—INDUSTRY, FIRM, SOCIAL CLASS

There was a time when the idea of the 'mixed guild' prevailed, and when no Christian workers' organisation was complete without its middle or upper class patrons. That day is over, and the International Federation of Christian Trade Unions has for many years been the most tenacious defender in the whole trade union world of the principle that class organisations must be fully independent and democratically run. It has the distinction of being the only major trade union body never to admit the right of State or party-controlled 'trade unions' to rank as genuine organisations of the working class. Others, including the T.U.C., have for instance been prepared to admit the Soviet 'trade unions' to the I.L.O.: but never the I.F.C.T.U. And the I.F.C.T.U. has stood by this principle even in the face of appeals from former affiliates of its own. A number of former Christian trade unionists in Austria joined the State-sponsored 'unions' set up by Chancellor Dollfuss after the civil war of 1934. The General Secretary of the I.F.C.T.U. gave their leaders to understand that they would be welcome in his office as old personal friends or as representatives of their government, but could no longer be recognised as trade unionists or representatives of the working class.

Though insisting that it is basically for the members to determine policy, the leaders of Christian Democracy and Christian Action show the same appreciation of strong, stable leadership on both the policy-making and the executive side in the case of class organisations as in that of the firm. The history of the Belgian Christian trade unions is in this respect typical.

To 1904. Slow emergence of local, independent, unions.

1904–14. Gathering of these into industrial federations, and from 1912 into a national confederation.

1918–39. Increasing centralisation within the federation, and nationally. The local unions become branches of the industrial federations, now better called industrial unions. These are now the main negotiating, financial, benefit, and general service agencies. The power of the Confederation also increases. In 1922 it establishes a strike reinsurance fund. In 1928 all strike funds are centralised.

1945 ff. New drive for central control of trade policy, finance, propaganda, and staff appointments. 'The new statutes have helped to build the Christian trade unions into a solid block'. (From a special article in *I.S.C.*, published by the International Federation of Christian Trade Unions, May 1949.)

The French Christian unions have always insisted that policy-making should be decentralised, and their finances have been distinctly casual. Jules Zirnheld, for many years their President, wrote in 1937 that the prime cause of the easy collapse of the German and Italian unions in the face of Fascism was:

The excessively concentrated, rather undemocratic, form of these organisations, and the non-existence of the branch. Activity and authority were transmitted not from the base to the top but from the top down, and through agents of the central executive, not through delegates freely chosen by the

F—C.D. 81

members concerned. The German, Italian, and Austrian trade unions were mass movements, perfectly organised no doubt; but, instead of the personal, independent, support of the branch members, they depended wholly on appointed officials, capable of making known the wishes of the executive, but acting solely on its responsibility, and often failing to win a hearing among the mass of the membership. It was enough to lay hands on the men and money at the centre to bring all activity to a stop and destroy the movement at one blow. (*Cinquante Années de Syndicalisme Chrétien*, 1937, p. 119.)

The problem may not have been as simple as Zirnheld thought. There *was* resistance by Christian trade unionists in Germany, Austria, and Italy once the occasion offered. And the highly centralised Belgian or Dutch unions proved as hard nuts for the Nazi occupants to crack as the C.F.T.C. itself. But Zirnheld's sentiment is significant of a difference of atmosphere between the French and the rest which still remains.

What may however be still more significant is that this difference has diminished with time. As Zirnheld himself records, the history of the C.F.T.C. from its foundation in 1919 until the middle of the 'thirties was made up of the effort to achieve:

Cohesion, formation, discipline . . . unity of doctrine and principles, cohesion in the mass of the membership, friendly discipline in action. . . . (Ibid., p. 88.)

And since the Second World War there has been:

A centralisation of finance which would have made the hair of regional and branch officials in the heroic years stand on end, but which was absolutely necessary if the Confederation was to operate with full efficiency. (G. Levard, *Chances et Périls du Syndicalisme Chrétien*, 1955, p. 51.)

Catholic Action movements such as the Catholic Workers' Movement in Germany have, of course, an additional degree of centralisation and stability through being directly linked to the Church and ultimately under the control of the Hierarchy.

CHAPTER VII

PLURALIST, NOT COLLECTIVIST—

4. 'HORIZONTAL' PLURALISM—FROM THE NEIGHBOURHOOD TO THE INTERNATIONAL COMMUNITY. CONCLUSION

THE NEIGHBOURHOOD

THE exact, scientific study of urban and rural sociology has emerged in the Christian social movement chiefly since the 'thirties and has developed particularly far in France. Several studies have been made on French ports, from the docks of Marseilles to the little fishing harbour of Paimpol. There is a series of studies of urban neighbourhoods and regions, some slanted mainly towards helping the work of the clergy, others, like those of Michel Quoist or Chambard de Lauwe, of a type more familiar to town planners and sociologists in the English-speaking countries. Quoist, in his *The Town and Man*, makes an excellent and detailed analysis of the social life of a Rouen neighbourhood. He studies its geography, population, housing, commercial or cultural or administrative equipment, its work and leisure, its religious life, its links with other areas; above all, the way its people group themselves among neighbours, or by streets, or by interests, and its meeting places and centres of influence. Canon Boulard, in his *Missionary Problems of the French Countryside*, incidentally paints an excellent picture of social change in rural France over the last two or three generations. Studies like these are now beginning to influence the whole way of thinking of the French Christian Action movements. The research centre *Economie et Humanisme* supplies outlines for local schemes of research on particular areas—a parish or group of parishes, for instance —or particular problems, such as juvenile delinquency. Fr. P. Virton, in a series of *Studies in the Sociology of the Parish*, brings together typical case studies commissioned in various parts of France in connection with Church mission work. They cover such things as the change in the grouping of the people and the spheres of influence of institutions in a developing town; problems of bomb damage and slum clearance; the impact on social life of shift working and the journey to work; the disadvantages of the dominance of a region by a single industry; or the social problems of rapid industrialisation and high prosperity.

83

This new approach to the neighbourhood and community is not confined to France. In Holland the Hervormde Kerk's social research centre, 'Church and World', has produced a number of studies like Fr. Virton's. It has a special series on industrial areas—on the life and problems of iron and steel workers, for instance—and has reported on a number of individual towns and villages at the request of their church authorities. The corresponding Catholic 'Institute for Social-Ecclesiastical Research' has also made a number of neighbourhood and community studies, as well as large-scale studies on such questions as the level of religious belief and practice in the country as a whole. And there is a rising tide of similar studies from Belgium, Germany, and Italy. The Young Christian Workers, beginning in Belgium, can indeed claim to have led the way for the whole Christian social movement, for they have been practising their 'enquiry method' since the end of the First World War. Their work starts from a detailed enquiry into social organisation and ways of life in the community in which each Y.C.W. section is embedded.

It is nothing new for the Churches and the movements associated with them to recognise the neighbourhood, community, and region as important social units. The parish church is traditionally the church of the neighbourhood, and diocesan boundaries usually coincide, at least in principle, with those of political or social regions. What is new, and accounts for the growing interest in precise, scientific investigation, is appreciation of the complications of the local community under modern conditions. These complications are apparent in the first place at the level of the neighbourhood. The rural neighbourhood may still have a fairly straightforward structure. In a Flemish village, for example, the boundaries of the religious parish, the civil commune, and the main organisations for work and leisure will normally coincide, and these three main elements in local life are likely to be closely integrated. The parish is the basic unit for the Farmers' Guilds, the Young Farmers' Clubs, and the women's and girls' organisations of the Belgian Farmers' Union. The parish priest is ex-officio chaplain of the farmers' guild, and the whole machinery of the Farmers' Union is closely linked to the Church. And so, though less formally, is the political machinery, since local politics are likely to be dominated by the P.S.C. But even in the countryside what Canon Boulard calls the 'totalitarian parish' is disappearing:

> The parish where the priest, master of his vessel under God, used to hold in his powerful hands the whole spiritual domain, and a good part of his flock's temporal affairs as well. (*Problèmes Missionaires de la France Rurale*, 1945, II, 141.)

A wider range and greater specialisation of interests is coming in. National services and national organisations are reaching into the parish. As in the towns, a new, more personal and independent way of life is developing, and the civil community is becoming, if not necessarily divorced from the religious, at any rate more and more clearly distinct from it. And in the towns, of course, these tendencies have gone much further. Town life has a pattern. But it is not a regular nor, as yet, an easily predictable one. Neighbours' groups, street groups, 'service' neighbourhoods, and special interests and associations cut across one another in a bewildering tangle.

The response of militant Christians to these new complications has been threefold. There is first the movement for organised, scientific study of them. Secondly, there has been a movement to revive and re-think the life of the parish, the *Gemeinde* of the Evangelical and the *Gemeente* of the Hervormde as well as the parish normally so-called of the Catholics. This includes an effort to re-define the relation between the parish and the other more specialised and secular Christian organisations. And, thirdly, the Christian Action organisations which most easily reach the level of the group of streets or neighbours—the youth, family, and to some extent the women's organisations—have made a steadily increasing effort to stimulate, guide, and integrate neighbourhood social life. The Y.C.W.'s jubilee Report, for example, pictures model sections as concerned at least as much with doorstep and street and shopping or cinema life as with life in the office or works. They are expected to study and understand the social structure and groupings of their neighbourhood, the main centres of influence, the problems of family life, housing, leisure, religion, and the journey to work. They are to help young people to see and solve these problems as they affect not only themselves personally but the whole of the social group or groups, beginning with the group of neighbours, to which they belong. The Y.C.W. section itself is expected to adapt its organisation to the structure of its neighbourhood. It has its general meetings, and perhaps its own central club. These provide a means of integration at the level of the wider neighbourhood: the ward or town district, possibly with several thousand inhabitants, that is the 'service' neighbourhood as the town-planner understands it. But 'the essential thing is to establish a team [group or sub-section] in each homogeneous and distinctive environment'; in street groups or other 'quarters' in particular. The small-scale family movements, which basically are informal groups of neighbours, also aim to do this, following on from the work of the youth movements from which their recruits largely come. The Young Farmers and the adult farmers' movements have a similar conception of their task in the country parish.

In line with the actual evolution of the neighbourhood, the ideal which these movements pursue is today coming to be that of the 'open and integrated' neighbourhood. They do not deny the attraction of the village or small town community of the old 'closed and integrated' type. It had its social system based on ideas accepted by all, bound together by a real solidarity; a system in which each was assigned a well-understood role and status, and enjoyed a high degree of security. It was in-turned, unprogressive, 'a little mummified and hard in the arteries',[1] yet from the point of view of human relations often very satisfying. But such communities have no future.

> Our investigations have brought up a number of magnificent Christian communities of the old type; I mean real Christian communities, under the reign of love as well as honesty, not merely shop fronts dressed up with impressive figures of Easter communions. But, a disturbing discovery, every one of these communities, so far as can be seen, is condemned to death. Either they are well 'preserved', but dying on their feet, like Pierrefiche-du-Larzac, in Aveyron, which has fallen from 220 inhabitants in 1880 to 90 today. . . . Or else, where these parishes are alive, they are changing. . . . (Boulard, op. cit., II, 140.)

They have become either 'closed and disintegrating', where the old values prevail but the life has gone out of them, or 'open and disintegrated', full of new interests and ideas, more open to the outside world, but not as yet having found the point of integration round which new common ideals, new frames of reference and mutual understanding, and a new security and solidarity could grow. To promote the new 'open' neighbourhood, and at the same time find this point of integration for it, is what the Christian movements take as their task.

THE LOCAL COMMUNITY AND REGION

The movements specially concerned with neighbourhood life rank as branches of Christian Action. The Christian Democratic movements strictly so-called, and the political movements in particular, come effectively into the picture only where local government begins. In rural areas the basic unit of local government, the commune, often corresponds to a neighbourhood. But it does not always do so even there, and rarely if ever does so in a town; though, following recent studies of the neighbourhood, it is beginning to be suggested that it is time that it did. Quoist's study of Rouen, for instance, suggests that the boundaries of wards and parishes (or groups of parishes) should coincide with 'natural' neighbourhoods, and that there should be some kind of neighbourhood council or community centre and association: perhaps a grouping of representatives of voluntary associations and the statutory social services rather than a local authority properly so-called. But these suggestions are looking to the future. The basic unit of town government is still everywhere the town, or in the biggest cities a major section of a conurbation.

The Christian Democratic parties have been strong supporters of local and regional government, though always as subordinate to the greater whole represented by the nation. They have been, one might say, States' Rights parties, but not in the sense of admiring parochialism or secession.

[1] Boulard, op. cit., II, 139.

Their ideal is the 'open' community in the sense among other things of one which stands on its own feet, defends its own interests, but also is conscious of its links with and responsibility towards the wider community around it. The Swiss Conservatives may declare without qualification that:

> True to its federalist tradition, the Party stands for the maintenance of the federal basis of the Confederation and the independence of the Cantons. (*Programme*, Introduction.)

But usually statements are much more carefully shaded. The Dutch Anti-Revolutionaries' 'Action Programme' asks that local authorities' freedom be restored, that more responsibility be given to regional authorities (provinces), that the power of local councils be increased over against local officials, and that local finance and local control of the police be strengthened. But a glance at the party's statement of principles puts this in perspective:

> The Party demands greater recognition—by way of decentralisation—of regional and local autonomy, *so far as this does not clash with the requirements of a unified State.* . . . (Art. X) (our italics.)

The P.S.C. in Belgium has had to face a particularly difficult problem. There is in Belgium, as in Holland, an intense and deep-rooted tradition of local autonomy. But over and above this there is a clash between two nations, Flanders and Wallonia, of different language and culture. A similar clash has been resolved over the centuries in Switzerland by strict insistence on federal principles. The Flemish section of the P.S.C.'s predecessor, the Catholic Party, was ready to agree to a federal scheme for Belgium as well. Its own constitution was made federal in 1936, and the P.S.C.'s has remained so. The Christian Workers' Movement's constitution is also federal, and the Belgian Farmers' Union distinguished itself in the nineteen-thirties by its particularly close association with the federalist, if not actually separatist, Flemish National League. But by 1945 the P.S.C. concluded that it must 'oppose federalism, at least in the sense of endowing regional authorities, legally speaking, with sovereign power' (Programme, p. 76). The Swiss system spreads sovereign power over a large number of cantons, which on particular issues may group themselves in different ways, not necessarily along language lines. In Belgium, on the other hand, federalism would involve a conflict between only two great divisions of the country, with the bilingual Brussels province as perhaps a buffer or perhaps the stakes. This permanent conflict would tend to produce permanent hostility. But though the P.S.C. thus insists on the unity of Belgium as a whole, it is prepared to go a long way towards meeting regional claims. It is ready to adapt legislation to the special conditions of Flanders and Wallonia, to make recruitment to the Civil Service proportional to the population speaking each language, and to insist that both languages be taught in the schools. It stands for far-reaching decentralisation and increased powers for the provinces, which roughly correspond to British counties. And it supports 'deconcentration', in the sense of encouraging local and regional officials of the central government to make their decisions on the spot.

> We stress that deconcentration and decentralisation can be organised in such a way that local agencies enjoy a really wide autonomy in managing the business within their competence. The intervention of the central government is to be limited to protecting the general interest. It cannot be upheld on the ground of a different view of what local interests require. (*Les Chantiers sont Ouverts*, 1945, p. 77.)

The other Christian Democratic parties take a similar view. The old German Centre Party supported the unification of Germany, though not the methods by which it was achieved. It consistently opposed, down to its dissolution in 1933, the extreme federalist or separatist views held in certain other parties and in some German States. But it also opposed with equal force all tendencies towards centralisation under the government of the Reich. The C.D.U. has carried on this tradition.

> The Union is opposed to a constitution which would place at the head of the State an excessive concentration of power, which could be misused for new experiments in dictatorship. It is for that reason against the unified state, whose over-concentration of power and tendency to standardise leads to the suppression of the special ways of life of regions and Länder, and to the drying up of the country's spirit. We wish for viable Länder, but also for a viable Federation, which should not be merely the servant of the Länder. . . . (*Geschichte und Wesen der C.D.U.*, 1949, p. 4.)

There should be a strong central government. But the Länder should also have extensive and well-entrenched rights. The second chamber of the central legislature should be designed, like the American Senate, to express and defend the rights of the Länder. And there should be a wide and strong development of local government.

In Italy the Christian Democrats have had to face in a slightly different form the same difficulties as in Belgium. The father of their movement, Don Sturzo, made his political name as Vice-Mayor (being a priest he could not at that time legally be Mayor) of his native town of Caltagirone in Sicily. He has remained a strong supporter of local and regional autonomy, and the Christian Democratic Party stands by this tradition. But Italy is divided, not indeed on language lines (apart from the small area of the south Tyrol), but between Communists and democrats; and the Communists have a substantial majority in several key provinces. It is understandable that the Christian Democrats hesitated for years over actually redeeming their promises on regionalism, though they not merely made them on the platform but caused them to be written into the Italian constitution. The Austrian People's Party has also had to deal with a divided country, thanks to the long-standing antagonism between the swollen, mainly Socialist, capital city and the largely Christian (though not always Democratic) provinces. There have been moments when this antagonism could have split the Republic in pieces. The party's solution has been very like that of the P.S.C.:

> The Party demands a unified State under unified leadership, but with respect for the historic growth and customs of the Länder, guarantees for their appropriate autonomy, and far-reaching rights of self-administration for not only the Länder but also the communes and professional bodies. (Kasamas, *Programm Österreich*, 1949, p. 118.)

In France, finally, the M.R.P. likes to think of local government as the place where it demonstrates its capacity for concrete work, as apart from 'la politique politicienne' which so often seems to electors to have the upper hand in the Chamber at Paris.[1]

THE STATE

The Christian Democrats' attitude to the State is in large part the mirror image of their attitude not only to local and regional government but also to self-government by the family, youth group, firm, industry, or social class. What appeared as a limitation of the autonomy of these smaller groups is now put positively, as the rights and duties of the State. What previously appeared positively, as the rights and duties of smaller groups, now comes up in a negative form as a limit to State power.

The State as Christian Democrats see it has a very wide competence. They agree that its competence extends not only to such classic functions as defence or justice, but also to what they would regard as the legitimate implications of the idea of the Welfare State; policy for production and employment, for social insurance and assistance, for housing and town planning, for education, scientific research, and the arts. No Christian Democratic party, for example, denies that it is the State's responsibility to set the controls of the economic system and guide its operations. The C.D.U. goes as far as any in the direction of a free economy, a point on which more will be said below. But even the C.D.U. recognises that it is for the State to decide how the economic system is to work. It stands for 'planful influencing of the economy' and 'the fulfilment of our social

---

[1] The sentiment and the phrase are taken from a report by André Colin (General Secretary of the M.R.P.), *Le Mouvement du Renouveau*, presented to the M.R.P. Congress in 1954. It is significant, though—for the M.R.P. began as a party of young men in a hurry—that some of its idealists have found the slow, seemingly petty, work of local government little to their taste. *Forces Nouvelles*, the party paper, tells how one newly elected local councillor was faced at his first committee meeting with the burning topic of firemen's uniforms. Was it for this, he rushed back in agitation to ask the party office, that he had taken up the responsibilities of public life? Was it not rather to defend the great ideals of Christian Democracy? The Secretary had some difficulty in explaining that the great ideals of Christian Democracy may sometimes be better expressed in concern with the details of what people wear, or eat, or are paid, than in orations in the Chamber.

responsibilities'. The M.R.P., at the other extreme, calls for a planned economy such as any socialist movement would be proud to claim as its own. None of the techniques normally used today to operate advanced Welfare States are shut out from consideration. Nationalisation is regarded by Christian Democrats as normally an evil, contradicting as it does the ideas of the self-governing industry and of the autonomous, co-operative community in the firm. But the accent is on 'normally', for it may be a necessary evil. The M.R.P. collaborated with a very good grace in the large French programme of nationalisation after 1944. The Italian Christian Democrats, although in some ways outstanding supporters of the liberal economy, have maintained a very large nationalised and quasi-nationalised sector inherited from Fascism, and have added to it some fine new specimens of the public corporation. Particularly impressive is the work of the corporations for developing backward areas, such as 'Ente Maremma' (for farm colonisation in central Italy) and the 'Cassa del Mezzogiorno' or Southern Development Fund.

But here comes in the negative side of the argument. Everything that has been said about the functions of the family, the youth group, the industry and firm, or local and regional autonomy, or for that matter (indeed, above all) about 'vertical' pluralism and the rights of spiritual families, implies one limit after another on the powers and functions of the State. And that is exactly how the Christian Democrats think of it. There has been an obvious danger in the twentieth century that the pendulum would swing over from the individualism of the nineteenth century to an equally exaggerated and even more dangerous collectivism, expressed chiefly through the State. The Christian Democrats have this danger continually in mind. They are not exactly anti-State. But one has always the feeling that the State figures in their thinking as a last resort, not merely because it is a very large and un-personal entity, but also because there have been so many tendencies pushing towards an expansion of State functions that it is advisable to be doubly careful where any addition or surrender to these tendencies is concerned. And they defend this view also on the ground of the State's own interest. A State is an organisation of human beings; Ministers, civil servants, M.P.s. If it is to be strong—and Christian Democrats believe in a State which is strong within its proper limits—it must restrict its responsibilities to what it can effectively carry out. To quote again from *Quadragesimo Anno*:

The State should leave to smaller groups the settlement of business of minor importance. It will thus carry out with greater freedom, power, and success the tasks which belong to it because it alone can effectively accomplish them. (CTS edition, p. 37. The translation has been slightly amended.)

The ideal State is for the Christian Democrats one which admits and exercises its responsibility to 'direct, watch, stimulate, and restrain' over the whole of that area of human welfare which is not the specific and exclusive business of the Church, but which operates in most spheres with a watching brief, intervening actively only in the last resort. It is a Welfare State in the sense that it is ready to step in, call for a public account, and enforce the necessary action in any field where the welfare of the people seems to be neglected. But its responsibility consists in defining and enforcing the responsibility of others—individuals or social groups—rather than in providing services itself. In a phrase used by Guido Gonella at the first Congress of the Italian Christian Democratic Party in 1946, it is an 'educational State': a State which shapes its citizens' characters to do what is right, rather than do it for them itself.

As regards the operation of the State, the Christian Democrats have first, as always, a high idea of the authority and responsibility of the powers that be. The Dutch Protestant parties, for instance, leave one in little doubt of their determination to enforce State authority with a strong hand. The source of sovereign authority is to be found 'neither in the will of the people, nor in the law, but in God alone' (Anti-Revolutionary Party). Governments rule by the grace of God and the authority of the divine and natural law, which positive legislation may express but not contradict or change. Their first duty is 'to preserve law and order and enforce the law of the land'. The restoration of violated justice may if necessary take place through the death penalty, 'the right to enforce which belongs, as a matter of principle, to the Government'. And there must be no surrender to unconstitutional threats. A characteristic illustration of the Dutch Christian Democrats' attitude on this occurred in 1918. Inspired by the revolution in Germany, the Socialist Party and Trade Unions threatened openly to seize power. A number of Liberal leaders, notably in Rotterdam, were impressed with their prospective new masters. Not so the Christian Democrats. A Catholic Prime Minister, Ruys van Beerenbrouck, was in power—for the first time, as it happened, in modern Dutch history—backed by a Protestant-Catholic coalition. There was no loss of nerve in the Government or its Parliamentary supporters. Protestant leaders joined with Catholic in 'the refusal of any concession to revolutionary deeds or threats'.[1] And, what is more significant, the Protestant and Catholic parliamentarians received the solid and unquestioned backing of the Christian social organisations. The C.N.V. and Catholic Workers' Movement, though they themselves had a long budget of unsatisfied demands, notably on the eight-hour day—they shortly afterwards forced this through by constitutional means—met the government and offered active cooperation in smashing any unconstitutional move. Fr. Poels, the chief organiser of the Catholic workers' leagues:

[1] Comment in the jubilee brochure of the Christian Historical Union (1948) on the attitude of its leader and founder, Baron de Savornin Lohman, in the crisis of 1918.

Travelled back to Limburg with a sealed letter for Fr. Corten, an Army chaplain. That night, after reading it, Fr. Corten roused every mayor and parish priest in Limburg. . . . Next day troops from Limburg marched into the big cities, singing their national song, and occupied town halls and government buildings. . . . And a few days later Troelstra the Socialist leader was in bed with a nervous breakdown. (Versluis, *Beknopte Geschiedenis van de Katholieke Arbeidersbeweging in Nederland*, 1949, p. 53.)

Attitudes of this kind were and are not confined to Holland. There is an equally characteristic story from Italy, dated a year or two later in 1922, of a Christian Democratic leader's reaction to aggression by Fascists:

In 1922, before the March on Rome, a Fascist column headed by Farinacci swooped down on Trento for a demonstration. At that time the city's Prefect had been replaced by a Governor, Credaro, who as a precaution had had the government offices surrounded by troops from the garrison. The troops were soon in their turn surrounded by Fascist units, which threatened to attack the building. De Gasperi, at that time a deputy, seeing this disgraceful spectacle—disgraceful both for the authority of the State and for the prestige of the Army—made his way through the Fascist ranks and the cordon of troops to the Governor's office. Credaro did not know which way to turn. Next door were two generals, who had ordered the officers to remove all ammunition. The troops' rifles were empty, and the offices at Farinacci's mercy. De Gasperi seized the telephone, rang through to Soleri, the Minister of War, and explained the situation to him, insisting that the government should resist. The voice from the other end of the line, at Rome, reassured him that the local military commander had been instructed to take all necessary measures to restore order. 'And to fire, if necessary?' De Gasperi pressed his demand till a weak voice answered 'Yes'. . . . (Tupini, *I Democratici Cristiani*, 1954, pp. 37–8.)

Twenty-odd years later, when De Gasperi became Prime Minister, Communist rioters in their turn found him a man impossible to intimidate.

A strong government needs a reliable base, and the Christian Democratic parties, seeing their central position on the political stage, have regarded it as their special responsibility to provide this. In Holland the Catholic People's Party is the natural link between the Protestant parties, to which it stands closest in its basic beliefs, and the Labour Party, with which it frequently agrees on social policy. In the face of the emergencies of recent years—war, reconstruction, floods, the defence and integration of Europe—it has taken the lead in the policy of the 'broad base', in other words of a national government. The Austrian People's Party has bridged its old enmity with the Socialists and formed a national government to face the problems of reconstruction and of foreign, particularly Russian, occupation. The M.R.P. and *Democrazia Cristiana* gave the Communist Parties of their respective countries the chance to prove their democratic good faith in national governments formed at the Liberation. When this experiment failed, they became the leaders of concentrations of democratic forces, from Liberals across to Social-Democrats, against Communists on the left and fascists and quasi-fascists on the right. The Italian Christian

Democrats held an absolute majority in parliament from 1948 to 1953. They nevertheless insisted on continuing to share the government with Liberals and Socialists in order to keep in being the concentration of democratic forces, without which they reckoned—correctly, as the 1953 elections proved—that stable government could not be maintained in the long run.

The Dutch and Swiss constitutions contain provisions, formal or conventional, to ensure that the government of the country is carried on whatever may happen in parliament. Swiss Ministers, that is members of the Federal Council, are appointed in effect for life. In Holland Ministers are formally responsible to the Crown, not parliament, and may be appointed without the guarantee of a parliamentary majority, though evidently there should normally be the expectation of one. This power is regularly used when party relationships make a stable parliamentary Cabinet difficult to achieve. Both the Dutch and the Swiss provisions have the explicit approval of the Christian Democrats. In Italy the *Democrazia Cristiana* has inherited from its predecessor, the Popular Party of 1919–26, an interest in devices for guaranteeing the winners of an election a working majority. In 1953 it voted a law whereby a party or allied group of parties winning over 50% of the votes at a general election is allocated seats as if it had won 65%. It has also insisted on a clear distinction in parliamentary procedure between votes of confidence, which may involve the fall of a government, and ordinary votes.

The M.R.P. has been plagued since its birth with the instability of French governments, but has been more sceptical than the Italians about the effectiveness of constitutional tricks. Some proposals, the party has felt, would simply substitute one instability for another. Measures to facilitate the dissolution of Parliament, for instance, would certainly increase the control of governments over the Chamber, but might lead instead to too frequent elections: one kind of instability from which France has been free. A directly elected Chief Executive, such as the President of the U.S.A., might in French conditions become too strong for Parliament to control. Nevertheless, the M.R.P. has supported some reforms of procedure, as for instance attempts to streamline Parliament's work, or to increase the Prime Minister's authority by a more clear-cut and formal procedure for investing him with office or voting him out of it. Its most striking proposal has been to stabilise economic policy by taking it out of politics.

If the State is to discharge its function of orienting the economy, it must be able to speak for the common good. But today the State is invaded by representatives of economic interests. It is dominated by them, and in no position to arbitrate. And, in so far as it is a political organ, it is subject to obligations and instabilities normal in politics, but absolutely inconsistent with the continuity required for the application of an economic plan. It is

93

essential, therefore, to have the economic functions of the State exercised by bodies independent and stable enough to be able, once they have been given a mission, to carry it out over the necessary period. We give these bodies the name of 'economic magistrature'. The 'economic magistrates' should have their place both in the organs for supervising cartels and in those for applying the Plan, for which credits should be made available for a definite length of time under skeleton Acts. (Reply to the questionnaire for the Bruges Congress of the N.E.I. 1954.)

The P.S.C., along notably with the C.D.U., stresses the importance of a properly qualified and paid Civil Service: not forgetting, it adds, an army which should be strong but silent. It also, like the M.R.P. and *Democrazia Cristiana,* insists on the need for parliamentary discipline and for stream-lining parliamentary procedure.

The State should, then, be strong. But it should also be lawful, with a strong and independent judiciary: in German a *Rechtsstaat.* And it must also be democratic, responsive to the will of the people. Government is no doubt by the grace of God, not of the people. But, to quote the Dutch Protestants again:

> Those who are charged with carrying on the work of government may properly be held to account before other persons independent of them, as for instance before Parliament. (Christian Historical Union, *Statement of Principles,* 1951 ed., Art. 2, s. 3.)

and:

> The party demands the maintenance of that justified influence which the people, by virtue of the moral bond between electors and elected, and in accordance with the march of our history, exerts on the State through Parliament. (Anti-Revolutionary Party, *Statement of Principles,* Art. 8.)

With a certain difference of accent, this conception of the people as sovereign under God is also that of the M.R.P. Representative government in France has traditionally been founded on the idea of the 'sovereignty of the nation', in the sense of the sovereignty of Parliament. In the debates on the new French constitution after the Second World War the M.R.P. defended instead the idea of the 'sovereignty of the people'. The people does not divest itself of its sovereignty at the moment of an election, nor does it merely sanction the use of power by its representatives. It retains a permanent participation in and control over it, to be exercised through any of a number of channels. Laws which modify the constitution may have to be submitted to a referendum. The government of the day may dissolve parliament and appeal to the people. Political parties may be formed to act as the transmission belt between people and parliament. They focus public opinion, supervise the work of individual representatives, but also transmit information and ideas from parliament downwards and help to educate the people in the realities of politics. The constitution should in the M.R.P.'s view lay down rules for the internal democracy of parties and ensure publicity for their finances.

A good test for the sincerity of Christian Democrats' view that respect for human personality implies democracy, once a people has enough education and maturity for self-government, has been their relations with Spain. The government of General Franco is outspokenly Catholic. It won power against forces of which—apart from the small and localised group of Basque Nationalists—even the more moderate section was anti-religious, while the more dynamic and leading elements, the Anarchists and Communists, rendered themselves guilty of one of the bloodiest persecutions of Christianity in modern times. But in the eyes even of those Christian Democrats who are Catholics this has earned for General Franco's regime at most tolerance as, perhaps, the least evil form of government available in a politically backward land. And the ground for their attitude is the lack under his rule of the civic as well as the personal freedoms for which Christian Democracy stands. The international Union of Christian Democrats affiliates the exiled Basque Nationalists on the same footing as the exiled Christian Democrats of Communist Central Europe. The Christian Democratic social organisations vary in their attitude according to whether their opposite numbers in Spain do or do not enjoy, by the standards of the rest of Western Europe, reasonable freedom of operation. The Catholic employers' international (UNIAPAC) is able to keep up useful contacts with Catholic employers in Spain, and various academic organisations in their own fields can do the same. But the Christian trade unions can maintain effective contact only underground. The International Federation of Christian Trade Unions, like the political international, affiliates representatives of the Basque Nationalists in exile.

It is not surprising, seeing the emphasis which the Christian Democrats lay on 'horizontal' pluralism, that they and their predecessors have been strongly drawn to the idea of giving social groups direct and official representation in Parliament. As the main form of political representation this idea of 'corporative' democracy has today few supporters among individual Christian Democrats, and none among their parties and social movements as such. Parliament, says the C.D.U., 'should be elected on the basis of universal, equal, secret, and direct suffrage'. (*Köln Principles*, 1945, s. 18.) For, say the Italians:

> Representation, to be truly organic, must be . . . in the first place a representation of citizens, of their individual will, channelled through groups and parties, and deriving its authority solely from the free expression of the individual's will. (Gonella, *Il Programme della Democrazia Cristiana per la nuova Costituzione*, 1946, p. 54.)

A personalist conception of politics, says the P.S.C. in Belgium, implies that politics should treat the people first and foremost as citizens, not as group members. The only qualification (if it be a qualification) is that the existence of children should be recognised by giving fathers an extra vote. But though the individual's vote is to be the primary basis of representation, a number of Christian Democratic parties are interested in making the electoral body more 'organic', 'not merely a collection of atoms' (Gonella, loc. cit.), by bringing into a Second Chamber representatives of local, regional, and other social and economic interests. The Italians took this view because not only of their general principles but of the poor showing of an Italian Senate nominated by Government favour, before and during the Fascist years. The M.R.P. would have wished to ensure representation in the French Second Chamber for local authorities and professional and family movements. The P.S.C.'s 1945 programme proposed, not indeed Second-chamber representation, but the grant of more official status to the advisory councils through which contact is maintained between interest groups and the government. Germany and Switzerland have Second Chambers representing Länder and Cantons, and this is with the C.D.U.'s and the Swiss Conservatives' full support.

The idea that political representation should be primarily of citizens, though also secondarily of interests, carries over into the Christian Democrats' conception of party life. Parties, as was said earlier,[1] should in their view be in touch with economic and social interest groups, but should not give them formal representation in the party constitution. The Christian Democratic parties are built up mainly on a local and regional basis, and regional interests like those of Flanders or of the Swiss cantons do in fact receive formal representation. There are also usually more or less formal advisory committees and study groups, like the M.R.P.'s specialised 'teams', for keeping in touch with other interests and problems. The Christian social movements see to it that their voices are heard. But, except in the Austrian People's Party, formal connections such as that between the British Labour Party and the trade unions are disapproved. The foundation of party as of Parliamentary life is seen as being the individual citizen. And though party discipline is enforced, the citizen is seen as retaining his individuality even when he holds a party card. Even in such matters as Parliamentary voting, the Christian Democrats are proud to think that their representatives use their own judgment:

> I read recently that in the present Bundestag there have been up to now 93 roll-call votes. There is one party, the Social-Democratic, which can claim that in every one of these 93 votes all its members voted solidly for the Party Executive's line. That sort of news item makes one wonder about the future of our democracy (loud applause). I believe that the good sense and intelligence of our German people will save us from ever living in a totalitarian democracy of that kind. (H. von Brentano, Chairman of the C.D.U. Parliamentary fraction, at the Hamburg Congress of the C.D.U., 1953: Report, pp. 37–8.)

[1] Pp. 78–9.

THE INTERNATIONAL COMMUNITY

Christian Democrats' thinking on the relation between States and the international community parallels their ideas on the relation between the State and local authorities. Local authorities' right to independence holds only so far as it is consistent with the needs of the wider community to which they belong. The same is true of States. When applied by metropolitan countries to colonial territories, this principle can easily look like mere imperialism. For the M.R.P.:

> Institutions may vary. But the problem posed for France by the great ferment among the under-developed nations and by the imperative need—for France's sake and theirs—to maintain a union between the peoples of the French sphere and France itself, can be solved only by association. The forms of this association may vary and evolve, but the association itself must be indissoluble. (G. Le Brun-Keris, report to the 10th National Congress of the M.R.P., May 1954.)

The Christian trade unions (C.F.T.C.) support this view, though with practical modifications.[1]

The P.S.C. admits that ultimately a fully evolved Belgian Congo may choose to become independent. But meantime the Congo remains 'an integral part of the national patrimony'.

> The P.S.C. insists on the need to develop in all native schools a spirit of civic loyalty and patriotism towards Belgium. (*Les Chantiers sont Ouverts*, p. 101.)

Strong preference and extra financial help should therefore continue to be given to schools, notably mission schools, run by Belgians. Economic links with Belgium should be developed, competition with the metropolis avoided, and a growing white Belgian population settled in the Congo. And Congo residents, being Belgian citizens, should take part in the normal Belgian elections. The Dutch, for their part, did indeed quit Indonesia not long after the British left Burma and India. But—without implying that the departure of the British was wholly voluntary—it can be said that the Dutch left with a great deal more reluctance and under heavier and more immediate pressure.

The tendency in France, Belgium, and Holland has thus been to follow Abraham Lincoln in upholding the Union, rather than Woodrow Wilson in proclaiming the right of self-determination. There is certainly a great deal of plain self-interest in this. If ever there was a colony that paid, in terms of cash and prestige alike, it is the Belgian Congo. And G. Le Brun-Keris, in the report quoted above, comments:

> What would happen to our country, a high-cost producer, if we lost our outlets in the overseas territories, which in one way or another represent 70%

[1] See *Recherches*, June 1955.

of our foreign trade? What bankruptcies, what misery, what unemployment! Anyone with a sense of national responsibility must seek to solve the colonial problem in some other way. (P. 7.)

But the argument that to preserve the Union is useful to colonies as well as the metropolis is not mere hypocrisy. The Christian Democrats are quite ready to take the arguments in favour of permanent union between colonies and metropolis, and use them to justify the permanent union of their own countries in a supra-national Europe. Sauce for the goose is sauce for the gander, and they do not mind saying so. Naturally, they are not arguing that France or Holland or Belgium, or for that matter Germany, are socially and politically under-developed in the same sense as the Belgian Congo. Nor are they under-estimating the value of their own countries' independence. They are far too conscious of the struggles by which it has been won and preserved. But most of them readily admit that the countries of Western Europe, so long as they remain isolated from one another, are economically under-developed, militarily defenceless, and subject to severe political tensions, especially that between France and Germany. The most effective form of union seems to them to be federal, with limited but strong legislative and executive powers conferred on a supra-national authority. And they see nothing particularly sacred about the—by now in any case largely nominal—sovereignty of States which need make union on these lines between the States of Western Europe less practicable or desirable than union between, say, France and French North Africa. A European Federation would it is true be an entity even less 'personal' and more remote from the man in the street than a State, and the Christian Democrats naturally insist on the maximum autonomy for their own countries within it; just as within the State they insist on a maximum of autonomy for provinces and local authorities. But this local autonomy should still, they feel, be limited, in the European Federation as in the national State, by the legislative and executive powers of the larger unit of government.

Support for a federal Europe is common to nearly all the Christian Democratic movements, and notably to all the political parties except in Switzerland and Austria. The Swiss Conservatives, along with the vast majority of their fellow-countrymen, are prepared to join with the rest of Europe in economic and social collaboration, but not to do anything which might compromise their country's neutrality. A similar position was imposed on Austria, through Russian insistence, by the peace treaty signed in 1955. But with these exceptions, the Christian Democrats have been the most united and consistent as well as the strongest supporters of moves for a united Europe since the Second World War. And when in 1954 the plan for a semi-federal European Defence Community collapsed, after being for some years the king-pin of schemes for a general European federation, the Christian Democratic parties went out of their way at the Bruges Congress of the N.E.I. in the autumn of that year to reaffirm their belief in the federal principle.

CONCLUSION

It is not always easy for people brought up in the political and social thought of modern Britain to grasp the consistency with which the Christian Democrats apply their principle of subsidiarity or 'sovereignty in one's own sphere'. To an old-fashioned individualist the Christian Democrats might seem to be aiming with only too devilish consistency to bury the individual citizen or firm beneath layer upon layer of administration and controls, local, industrial, national, and international. A modern social-democrat or social-Conservative will not complain on that score. Indeed socialists are likely to complain, and regularly do, that Christian Democrats do not lay enough stress on the authority of the higher organs of society, and particularly on State control of the economy. But though a Socialist may not think that the Christian Democrats are attributing too many functions to the larger units of society he may easily get the impression that they are inconsistent in the way they divide functions between one unit and another. For whereas at the international level they call for more centralisation and the creation of new executive authorities, within the State they demand that existing authorities be broken up and power decentralised.

But this is simply a matter of perspective. Socialists in general, and people brought up in the recent British political tradition in particular, tend to put the State at the centre of their thinking. Looking outwards from the State, it is of course true that the Christian Democrats seem to be pulling in two directions at once. But then the Christian Democrats are not looking outwards from the State. They are looking at the social structure as a whole and trying to bring the State, among other groups, into its proper perspective. This and the two previous chapters could be summed up in a series of formulas, all illustrating the same basic idea:

The young workers' own organisation—but inside the general federation of Catholic youth.
The free trade union in the organised profession.
The self-governing, democratised firm—but inside P.B.O.
Local and regional freedom within the unified State.
Free association within the indissoluble French Union.
National independence in a federal Europe.

All these are variants on one formula, which is the essence of the Christian Democrats' doctrine of subsidiarity or sovereignty in one's own sphere as applied to federalism or 'horizontal pluralism':

The highest possible status and security and the widest possible role for each social unit or group—but let there be effective, executive, power to enforce respect for the good of the wider whole.

99

For Christian Democrats the two terms of this formula, the freedom of the subordinate and the authority of the superior, carry equal weight. Which one to emphasise depends on the circumstances of each case. Feeling as they do that in recent generations power has become over-concentrated in the hands of the State, the Christian Democratic movements tend just now, when talking about internal politics, to emphasise the freedom of individuals and subordinate communities against the State. But when they come to inter-State relations, where the danger is still of anarchy rather than of over-government, they tend to stress instead the good of the wider community to which the State is subordinate.

CHAPTER VIII

CONSERVATIVE BUT NOT TRADITIONALIST

T HE Christian Democratic movements, as was said earlier, though conservative are not traditionalist. This is not for lack of tempting traditions to cling to. In Belgium, for example, the roots of the Catholic movement go back to a sort of Golden Age of rural and small-town felicity at the end of the eighteenth century; the sleepy but pleasant years before the French Revolution and Napoleon shattered the Europe of the old regime.

> The country population was prosperous and sincerely attached to the clergy and nobility, who exerted the privileges of their class with patriarchal kindness. The towns, with their cobbled streets and thrifty lighting, conveniently framed a life retired, undisturbed, quiet, whose charm—but also whose immeasurable boredom—Voltaire learnt to appreciate. In a sentence, these eighteenth-century Belgians, lacking any great intellectual culture, and too apathetic to wish to acquire one, were vegetating. (Van Kalken, *La Belgique Contemporaine*, 1950, pp. 17–18.)

The ecclesiastical principalities of Cologne, Mainz, and Trier, whose territory in more recent times has been one of the most fertile for Christian Democracy, were at that time another such sleepy land, easy-going, corrupt, intellectually and economically unprogressive, and yet in their way very pleasant places to live in:

> The people were taught to consume what was accorded them and to keep moving in their habitual grooves. . . . Distress and extreme need were rarely in evidence, but there was great poverty. The ecclesiastical territories were a paradise for contemplative spiritual inaction and highly aristocratic idleness, the true habitat for protection, sinecures, patronage, and large and small scale mendicancy. (Häusser, *Deutsche Geschichte*, I. 101, quoted in Moody (ed.), *Church and Society*, 1953, p. 354.)

Christian Democracy has had from the start the support of large numbers of farmers and craftsmen, people with an established and traditional way of life, in many ways attractive and worth preserving, and often framed in those 'Christian communities of the old type' of which Canon Boulard speaks. One can also not fail to note, in reading the history of the Christian social movement in Italy, France, or indeed any country of Western Europe except Switzerland, how plentifully it is dotted in its early years with the names of the hereditary aristocracy. Summarising the

101

attempt in 1885 to establish a Catholic Party in France, Henri Rollet[1] notes how a Count put forward the original idea in a letter to a Viscount, and drew in reply comments from one untitled commoner and a Duke, two Marquesses, and the leading figure of the Royalist party in parliament; and because these men were unfavourable the project was dropped. The small group of Catholic thinkers who prepared the way for the Encyclical *Rerum Novarum* was also meeting at about that time at Fribourg. Excluding priests and the Swiss, who by the custom of their country could have no title of nobility, the committee of the Fribourg Union had ten members, and among these were two Barons, five Counts, and a Duke. These aristocrats, particularly in France, tended to speak naively of themselves as the 'ruling classes', and to expect the deference due to their hereditary status. And before many of the more active-minded of them floated an idealised image of the Middle Ages, when Christianity inspired not only the guilds but the rights and duties of the feudal system.

National and monarchist traditions have also played their part. In France the Catholic cause was for generations also the cause of monarchy in one or other form. One of the strongholds of French Christian Democracy to this day is in Brittany and Vendée, where at the time of the Revolution nobility and people united to make the royalist defence strongest:

> We have the letter of a provincial commissioner . . . complaining that the squires of his province prefer to remain among their people in the country instead of doing their duty at the Court. But note this: the province of which this was said was Anjou, later known as the Vendée. These squires who are said to have refused to do their duty to the King were the only ones to take up arms for the monarchy in France and die fighting for it. And they owed this honourable distinction solely to having succeeded in retaining the allegiance of the country people, for preferring to live among whom they were reproached. (De Tocqueville, *L'Ancien Régime*, ed. Headlam, p. 129.)

The old Prussian monarchy had no stouter admirers than among its Protestant subjects, including those who founded the independent Protestant political movement. Reinhard Mumm, who led that movement after Stöcker, published an article on 'The Hohenzollerns—the People's Monarchy'—as late as November 11th, 1918. The mainly Catholic Centre Party also supported the German monarchy to the end, and so did the Christian trade unions:

> Our movement sees in the monarchy something more than the most convenient constitutional form. It is part of our ideology, and in ideological matters there can be no question of a transaction. (Speech by A. Stegerwald at the 4th German Workers' Congress, 1917.)

Nationalism and conflicts over nationalism have played a notable part in the history even of the Christian workers' movements. A. Vanistendael,

[1] Rollet, *L'Action Sociale des Catholiques en France*, 1947, pp. 182 ff. See also his *De Mun et le Parti Catholique*, 1949.

the present General Secretary of the International Federation of Christian Trade Unions, recalls how in Belgium in the inter-war years his section of the Young Christian Workers refused to fly the national flag or use the national colours. In Germany before 1933 the (mainly Catholic) manual workers in the Christian unions, though not precisely anti-national, were deeply suspicious of 'Hurra-Patriotismus', and identified traditional nationalism with social reaction. But on the other hand the leading Christian clerical workers' union originated as a nationalist and anti-semitic reaction, on the part of a group of Protestant clerks, against the internationalist propaganda of the social-democrats. It remained pre-dominantly nationalist as well as Protestant till its dissolution in 1933. And even the Catholics and manual workers were nationalist enough to allow the Christian unions, during the revival of German national feeling in the inter-war years, to go as far as they could short of actually 'dressing up our young men in steel helmets'[1] or falling into the arms of the National Socialists. Union congresses were regularly held in border cities such as Saarbrücken, Aachen, Danzig, and Königsberg. In 1924 the Christian unions took a prominent part in the resistance to the French occupation of the Ruhr. When it was over the youth section of the miners' union demonstrated, at the monument in the Teutoberger Wald which celebrates Hermann's defeat of Varus' legions in the reign of Augustus, against the 'slavery' imposed on Germany by the Allied powers. The 'dictate' of Versailles was regularly referred to as such.

The most dramatic clash of nationalisms in the workers' movements occurred in 1919 at the meeting where the International Federation of Christian Trade Unions was founded. The German delegation was led by Adam Stegerwald, the only trade union leader ever to reach the Prussian House of Lords: almost a caricature of a Prussian, massive, bullet-headed, crop-haired, thick-lipped, deeply convinced of the justice of Germany's cause in the war. His opposite number in the French delegation, Jules Zirnheld, was as characteristically French as Stegerwald was German, with an extra edge from the fact that he was born in Alsace. He was shot down over Germany while serving with the French Air Force, and, as an Alsatian, was deemed to be a German citizen and promptly court-martialled and condemned to death; the sentence was commuted to imprisonment for life. Under leaders such as these, in the year immediately after the war, national feeling on both sides ran high. P. J. S. Serrarens, who later became General Secretary of the I.F.C.T.U., presided, and steered the Inter-national's foundation through successfully. But he recalled this, a quarter of a century later, as the hardest meeting he handled in his life.

The very fact of being Christian of course turns the Christian movements' eyes to some extent towards the past. Their inspiration is a revelation, and

[1] Wiedefeld, *Der Deutsche Gewerkschaftsbund*, 1933, p. 117.

a tradition based on it, dating from two thousand years ago. And many of them grew up not so much to develop this tradition, or find new ways of applying it in modern conditions, but rather to defend it, and the Church as already established, against attacks by the liberals or socialists or nationalists with whom the initiative in modern society seemed to lie. Swiss Catholics rose in 1848 in defence of the ancient rights of the Church and the cantons. Catholics in Italy, and from many other countries, rallied in defence of the Temporal Power of the Popes as it had subsisted through the centuries. Dutch Protestants labelled themselves 'Anti-'Revolution-aries, if not as supporters of the *ancien régime* then at any rate as opponents of the Revolution which overthrew it. The Catholic movement in France till the end of the nineteenth century was the movement not only of the King but of the Counter-Revolution. The biggest immediate issue at the start of the Protestant political movement in Holland and the Catholic movement in Holland and Belgium was defensive, to prevent the expulsion of Christian teaching from the schools. The Centre Party in Germany consolidated to face Bismarck's attack on the freedom already enjoyed by the Church and guaranteed to it by the Prussian constitution.

All these influences have played their part. But it is one which belongs mostly to the past. Over the years the Christian movements have left behind this defensive, ecclesiastical, and backward-looking view of the role of Christianity in politics and social life. The process will be traced below. 'We are progressives', the Italian Christian Democrats now say,

> Because we know how to renew our views, and because renewal is the condition of progress. We are not traditionalists even in religion; for in religion there is presented to us mortals a model of perfection so lofty as to draw man on to an unending spiritual progress. Can anyone imagine, then, that we would be traditionalists in the world of mere contingent values, in politics and econ-omics? (Gonella. *Il Programma della Democrazia Cristiana per la Nuova Costituzione*. 1946, p. 6.)

'The perfection of man depends on civilisation', says Canon Leclercq in a lecture to an N.E.I. summer school.

> That is, on the collective conditions of life brought about by human reason. These conditions transform themselves from generation to generation, and can be improved without limit. They do not improve steadily, for there are returns to barbarism. . . . But, in spite of regression, failures, delays, practically all that is useful to us to develop our personality comes from civilisation; education, personal formation, all the tools and techniques at our service. . . . None of us could find for himself the thousandth part of what he receives from his environment. And what we receive from the environment is what men have discovered and transmitted through thousands of years past. . . . Man's duty is, in short, first of all to work out his own perfection, after such fashion as he can in the cultural conditions in which he finds himself, and then—which is also part of the process of perfecting himself—to work for the progress of humanity, so that men in the future may be able to achieve a perfection higher than his own. The Christian's duty to serve God requires

him to do all that is in his power to enable humanity to serve God better and better, and all forms of progress co-operate to this end. (N.E.I., *La Place du Travail dans la Société*, Paris 1955, pp. 22–3.)

The value of man depends on his moral value, which is expressed in action directed by love; that is in the social function of work, directed to the progress of humanity as just described. It is on work or social function in this sense, and understood widely—including, that is, all kinds of service to human progress—that the place of each in society should depend.[1]

Nationalism has died down, and the Christian Democratic movements have become the chief supporters of a United Europe. Germany has offered since the Second World War the unexpected sight of Social Democrats preaching nationalism while Christian Democrats demand the subordination of the German State to a supra-national government. Monarchy also has ceased to have the appeal that it did.

> Overnight, like spray before the wind, the glittering Empire and the—as we thought—so solidly founded dynasties of Kings, Grand Dukes, Dukes, and Princes have been swept away and their governments with them. (Stegerwald, speech at the foundation conference of the *Deutsche Gewerkschaftsbund*, 1918.)

And with them also, so far as the Christian Democrats are concerned, has gone the belief that kingdoms and dynasties are necessary. Dutch and Belgian Christians continue to find their particular monarchies attractive. In France on the other hand Christian Democracy and monarchist or quasi-monarchist politics are now mutually exclusive. There are still French Catholics who support monarchy, or its nearest convenient equivalent in presidential government. But they are to be found in right-wing parties, not specifically Christian in character, not in the M.R.P. In Italy the breach between King and Catholics which arose over the Temporal Power was largely healed by the end of the First World War. Nevertheless, at the end of the Second World War the members of the Christian Democratic party voted three to one for a Republic.[2] There are still aristocrats to be found in and around the Christian movements, and some of them are in high places; a man like Prince zu Löwenstein, for example, who became chairman of the committee of the German *Katholikentage* (Catholic Assemblies) it might almost be said by hereditary right. But in general the power today is in the hands of the trade unions and the middle class. And the bucolic bliss of pre-Revolutionary Belgium no longer has much appeal even to the farmers and business middle class of Belgium itself. The ideal of the *Boerenbond* today is as has been said the skilled

[1] Loc. cit., p. 24.
[2] The card vote at the first Congress of the *Democrazia Cristiana* showed 740,000 for the Republic, 254,000 for the monarchy. A previous referendum among the party membership gave 60% for the Republic, 17% for the monarchy, 23% 'don't know'. Figures as given in Tupini, *I Democratici Cristiani*, 1954, pp. 132 and 134.

and progressive leader of rural life, technically expert, socially active, and open and receptive to new ideas: mindful no doubt of traditions, but in all essential respects a man of the modern world of change, utterly unlike the peasant of the past.

How far has the pendulum swung? Certainly not all the way, though far enough for the accent now to be on change and development rather than on stabilising the inheritance of the past. The N.E.I. in 1954, in preparation for its annual congress at Bruges, threw some light on this by questions to its national member groups—in effect, to the various Christian Democratic parties—on economic and social policy.

Did member groups think it right that son should follow father in the same profession and class, particularly when the father was an employer? Most of them did not mind this happening in some degree and in certain social groups. They favoured sons succeeding fathers in businesses with a strong family character, and did not particularly object to their doing so in the management of larger firms, or among the rank and file of occupations such as mining. But the main stress, it was generally agreed, should be on social mobility rather than inherited status. Strong support was expressed for various means of bringing inter-class mobility about, particularly vocational guidance and general and technical education.

Was it better to favour inherited fortunes or new savings? And—a more ambiguous question in this context, but still a revealing one—to what extent should high incomes, which usually will be at least in part inherited, be redistributed by taxation? Once again, the replies showed no objection to a moderate degree of inheritance. Members positively favoured the accumulation of small fortunes and their transmission to the next generation. They were also prepared to modify death duties and other conditions of inheritance to make it possible for family businesses to be carried on as such. But the general feeling was that policy should concern itself with current savings more than with the protection of inherited wealth. Even the family firm, as the C.D.U. reply said, must be expected to re-earn its position at least in part in each generation. The Dutch Catholic group noted that after a point inheritance must be subordinated to 'fair shares in the national wealth'.

The replies on redistribution also put considerations of inherited status and wealth very much in second place. They were concerned much more with the way tax policies might affect the dynamics of the economy in future than with any modifications they might make in the inheritance of the past. So for instance the Germans saw no reason to interfere with the distribution of wealth which emerges from a free market, provided that the competition from which it results is 'free from any privilege for property or class', and that it yields a 'broadly sufficient standard of life for all classes of the population, rising with the progress of technology'.

It was better, they suggested, to equalise wealth by building up small fortunes rather than by breaking down large, and in any case equality was likely to increase automatically with the growth of a nation's wealth; for the gap between higher and lower earnings typically narrows as the national income goes up. A policy on these lines might no doubt permit the accumulation and inheritance of large fortunes and so of high social status, but this was incidental. The essential thing was to promote policies which encouraged the growth of production and its adaptation to needs, irrespective of their secondary effect on equality or inheritance. Replies from other countries, notably France and Holland, tended to put more stress on equality, though without overlooking the case for increasing production. But for them too what mattered was the present and future of the economy, much more than the preservation of what was handed down from the past.

The questionnaire also asked what stress should be laid on the preservation of existing communities, social groupings, and ways of life, particularly where this might stand in the way of economic advance. The Christian Democratic parties are well aware, as the replies and the debate on them at the Bruges Congress itself brought out, of how the abrupt widening of markets and introduction of new techniques may disrupt communities or industries and cause well-founded resentment. The 'Green Pool' which they have tried to promote for European farm products could mean the breakup or complete transformation of many rural communities, and free trade over all Western Europe in industrial products could knock the economic foundations from under whole towns and districts. The integration of Europe, most of the parties therefore insist, should be phased, and time and opportunity should be given for readaptation in each country and sector. As the M.R.P.'s reply said of farming:

> We have the right to expect plans to be made over a rather long period, and to provide for investments which will enable these units [family farms], which are capable of becoming economically viable, actually to achieve this desirable result.

The debate at Bruges showed that the Christian Democrats do not yet agree on what the measures needed to help transition and readaptation are. There is a range of opinion from the Germans and, in general, the industrialists at one end to the French and the farmers' and trade union representatives at the other. The former are inclined to minimise the need for special measures and to leave the free market to work itself out, whereas the latter think in terms of a deliberate location of industry policy and of transitional controls of the market. But this is a question of means. As regards ends, the general impression of both the debate and the replies was once again that the future must take precedence of the past. If the future welfare of the people requires higher production or the economic and political integration of Europe, then the social structures involved must adapt themselves to the new needs, though let them by all means be given time and opportunity to do so. It may be that some of the groups which answered the Bruges questionnaire assumed too easily that adjustment would always be possible, and did not face up to the choice to be made if it were not. But in principle at least they felt the priority should go not to preservation but to change.

What is left in the Christian Democratic movements is no longer traditionalism but a certain 'conservatism', in the sense that they are very much aware of the time factor in social development. Big achievements take more than one generation, and within each generation they need to proceed step by step. It is necessary to maintain continuity with the past and the future. The Anti-Revolutionary Party in Holland:

> Represents the basic character of our national culture, stamped on it, under the leadership of the House of Orange, through the influence of the Reformation in the sixteenth century. And it wishes to develop this further in a form corresponding to the needs of our time and to the changed conditions of the people. (*Principles*, Art. 1.)

The other main Protestant Party, the Christian-Historical Union, relies:

> Not only on the express statements of Scripture, but also on the judgment of the Christian Church and on God's guidance as shown in each people's history. (*Principles*, Art. 1.)

The Catholic People's Party, not to be outdone, proposes to preserve and develop 'the national virtues and customs as shaped through the centuries' (*Basic Programme*, Art. 22).

Continuity and security are important, the Christian Democrats insist, for the development not only of nations, the States, and the international community, but also of smaller social units; firms, families, social classes, neighbourhoods, individuals. Therefore, first of all, they are deeply attached to the Rule of Law, which ensures to all security to plan ahead without fear of arbitrary or retroactive interference. As is natural, attachment to the rule of law is particularly strongly emphasised in countries which have suffered from dictatorship and arbitrary government within the last generation. The C.D.U. concludes its 1953 *Hamburg Programme* with the slogan:

DEUTSCHLAND—SOZIALER RECHTSSTAAT—IM GEEINTEN EUROPA

—'Germany—a socially conscious State—under the Rule of Law—in a United Europe'. The same prominence for the idea of a 'Rechtsstaat' is found in the basic programmes of the Austrian People's Party and the *Democrazia Cristiana*.

Another phrase which sums up much Christian Democratic thinking in this field is 'deproletarisation'. 'Proletarian', in the language of Christian Democracy, is sometimes used in its original Roman sense; a propertyless man, dependent on the work of his hands and that of his wife and children. But it also has the deeper sense[1] of a man so bound to his work and the necessities of life that he never has leisure in the sense of the Greek σχολη. In the Christian conception the highest form of human activity is not work but contemplation, and the ultimate goal of life, the Beatific Vision, is contemplation in its highest form; the permanent contemplation of supreme perfection, of that which in the highest sense represents St. Augustine's 'peace', or 'rest in good order'. The proletarian is the man, whatever his wealth or status, who cannot or will not lift his head to contemplate the nature and reason of things and the wider interests of life. Answering for the Bruges Congress a question about the leading principles of its doctrine, the P.S.C. puts first 'Deproletarisation of the working class'. This is not out of a passion for small savings or for the multiplication of shopkeepers. It is because the party, like the Christian Democratic movements as a whole, believes that the conditions in which industrial workers live and work are peculiarly likely to make of them 'proletarians' in the deeper sense.

But small savings and the increase of small businesses are not irrelevant, for at a certain point the two senses of 'proletarian' meet. The contemplative man needs for himself and for the social groups to which he belongs a certain security, continuity, and resulting ease of mind. And the Christian Democratic movements set out to provide these along four main lines. First, people should have property. Our slogan, writes the *Democrazia Cristiana* in its programme for the Constituent Assembly, is not 'proletarians all!' but 'property for all!' House ownership is universally favoured. So is ownership of a small business, where that is economically practicable; a farm, a garage, a shop. The Christian Democratic movements share with the Liberals a special interest not only in farming but in the business middle class of shopkeepers, craftsmen, and the independent professions. The life of the small shopkeeper, for instance, especially when he first enters the trade, is often anything but secure; the Christian Democrats try to make it more secure through vocational training, insistence on minimum qualifications, and co-operation for credit and purchasing. They see the business middle class as a barrier against, to quote the Swiss Conservatives, 'tendencies towards proletarisation and absorption by the State'. They are also increasingly trying to promote the ownership of small packets of industrial shares, whether directly, through investment trusts, or by special arrangements for workers to invest in their own firms.

Secondly, people should have insurance rights or equivalent savings. Private insurance and individual savings are preferred, as being most effective in building up a sense of independence and therefore security. But it is agreed that social insurance is needed as a supplement. Thirdly,

[1] Cf. Pieper, *Leisure the Basis of Culture*, Faber, 1952.

the Rule of Law and a charter of human rights, written or conventional, positive as well as negative, should hold out to people and groups the certainty of being able to plan ahead, work, and develop all their potentialities. They should have security, so to speak, of opportunity. And fourthly, as already said, there should be security against the disruption of families, working groups, and other communities and societies of all kinds without reasonable time and opportunity to adjust to new needs.

What the Christian Democrats have not yet done is to work out their interest in time and continuity into a theory of political, economic, and social growth. This deficiency is particularly striking when Christian Democratic thinking is set alongside Marxist. The history of social movements shows that they proceed along a path like that of the 'learning curve' familiar to psychologists; for the learning curve turns out to describe the behaviour of very large social groups as well as of small groups and individuals. A problem begins to be felt within an established order of society. A debate develops between those seeking to solve it and those who regard it as unimportant or as a symptom of deviations to be repressed. Neither, at first, succeeds in posing the problem clearly or in perspective; they cannot break through their old frame of reference. The debate quickens, experiments are tried, and at last a preliminary 'break-through' is achieved, usually under the leadership of new men backed by a new social class or group not previously prominent. The problem is clearly posed, a new frame of reference is achieved, and new models are worked out for its solution. All this, in a big social movement, tends to take about a generation; say twenty years for the preliminaries and ten for the 'break-through'. There follows a period of 'relaxation and incubation' when the debate continues at a new level, building up and perfecting the new models and extending the discussion from the pioneers to wider and wider circles. Eventually there occurs a final, decisive break-though, in which a perfected version of the 'new models' is accepted as standard practice and as a normal part of the movement's culture. This stage too takes about a generation; twenty years for the preliminary period of 'relaxation', ten years or so for the break-through. That particular problem being solved, interest in it drops. A flat period intervenes, and then attention begins to be concentrated on whatever problem or set of problems has the next priority. Karl Marx's dialectical theory of history was a crude and distorted version of this progress along the social learning curve, one of the many flashes of genius in which he anticipated, though in a one-sided way, the later findings of social science.

This general theory of the process of growth can be applied in a vast number of fields. A great deal of information is available on such matters as the growth of population, the absorption of migrants, the formation and break-up of communities, the rise of trade unions and political parties, the growth of firms and industries, or the course of savings, investment, and industrial adaptation in both advanced and backward countries. The history of Christian Democracy itself, as will be shown, conforms to the standard pattern; two generations at a time, with a relatively slow build-up in each generation followed by a crisis or break-through. Particularised in this way, the analysis of growth processes can be both a guide to action and a strong encouragement in it. To decide what constitutes a reasonable rate and direction of growth for an economy, and to see that this is achieved, has become today one of the major questions of political and social life. And the party which sees that its particular phase of growth calls for discussion and experiment rather than for a rapid advance and break-through—or for a preliminary rather than a definitive break-through—may be spared a great deal of disappointment.

The Christian Democratic movements do not of course ignore this way of thinking. Like others, they often make comparisons which imply assumptions about the shape and time process of a society's growth. Their economists compare the growth of productivity in their own countries with that in the United States. Their colonial administrators learn from experience how to phase a development plan for an African colony. Their trade union leaders may check the progress of a union against its own or others' past progress. But with minor and often rather academic exceptions in the economic field, where Christian Democratic experts may sometimes refer to the theories of growth of Schumpeter or Colin Clark, one rarely if ever finds these casual comparisons worked out systematically into general principles of growth and development, or checked against such principles. Christian Democratic trade unions and employers' associations, for example, do not usually have any very clear idea of the proportion of a country's income which should be invested in given circumstances, or how fast the national income and wealth should be made to increase. At 1% per annum, or 2%, or 5%? Most of them would find it difficult to say, unless on a purely common sense basis which amounts to little more than keeping up with the Joneses: with Uncle Sam, or perhaps with Comrade Ivan. The traditional association of theories of social development with the Marxist movements is of course no recommendation in Christian Democrats' eyes. And this prejudice is up to now reinforced by scepticism as to whether the course of future development can be predicted or directed to any advantage at all. Very typical is the comment of the Luxembourg group of the Union of Christian Democrats on a question, before the Bruges conference, about the stages of European integration.

They will depend on the amount of good will available, and the sequence they follow will no doubt be as chance provides.

111

CHAPTER IX
SOCIAL CONTROL

1. OBJECTIVES AND SANCTIONS

THE foregoing chapters imply a theory not only of the structure of society but also—though a much less distinct one—of the processes by which it is to operate. A society may make economic welfare its chief objective and the chief sanction and incentive for its members' behaviour; in that case it will give the place of honour to business men, union leaders, and economic planners. If it is chiefly interested in government and formal power, its ideal will be the lawgiver, the civil servant, and the judge. Or it may attach the highest value to informal authority based on community, kinship, and individual consent. In practice no society pursues one of these objectives or uses one of these sanctions alone. The question is always how much of each? Whatever combination is preferred, the chosen objectives may be attained and sanctions applied through mechanisms of several kinds. A society may be competitive, one where economic and political and social success is awarded on the strength of ability to surpass others, or at least to reach certain qualifying standards; a society of economic competition, competitive party politics, and social mobility. It may be authoritarian, a 'directed' society, with economic planning, strong government and management, and rigid social customs. Or it may be based neither on direction nor on competition but on consultation and mutual aid. In practice it will probably use all three sorts of mechanism. The question, once again, is how much of each?

Marx and Lenin outlined the conception of three stages of development in a modern industrial society. First would come capitalism, an age dominated by economic sanctions and competitive mechanisms; an age not only of free enterprise but of political democracy and growing social mobility. Then would come socialism, a time of growing power for the State, of formal managerial authority, of direction and planning. And finally would dawn what Marxist-Leninists call the Age of Communism, and others might perhaps name the Age of Human Relations. That, as Marx and Lenin saw it, would be the time when the basic problems of production and distribution had been so far solved that the rigid external discipline imposed on citizens in the ages of capitalism and socialism could

112

be relaxed. Production and government would come to be the work of freely associated, informal groups, assisted but not controlled by technical advisers.

This conception has been verified in the history of Western Europe and the advanced countries of North America and Australasia. There was an Age of Competition and Economics, a Liberal Age, covering most of the nineteenth century. It was followed by an age of Direction or Managerial Revolution, dominated by the rise of Socialism in politics and scientific management in business and administration. And there are signs today of the rise of an Age of Human Relations, concerned with consultation and co-operation more than with competition or direction, and with the 'man-sized' units of social life—the small working group, the firm, the family, the neighbourhood—rather than the world economy or the State. A 'human relations' school has arisen in industrial relations. Family movements are springing up in Western Europe and, increasingly, in North America. The accent is beginning to shift among community planners from the physical shell of a local community's life to the creation of neighbourly relations within it.

Though the Marxist scheme thus fits very well the general social history of the Western countries in the nineteenth and twentieth centuries, it does not fit so accurately the development of individual social movements. Liberals have always been specially identified with competitive mechanisms —competition in trade and politics, freedom and mobility in social life— and with the economics of the market. Socialists have been identified more with questions of formal power and with its use, especially by the State, to plan and direct. And Christian Democrats, for their part, have been specially concerned with the problems of human relations, not surprisingly seeing that the centre of their thinking is personality and its development. The moral factor, they repeatedly say, comes first. The ideal is the 'educational State', not the drill-sergeant State nor the State based on a competitive scramble for economic or political power. In their early days the Christian Democrats were often charged with concentrating too much on educational methods and the 'moral factor', and not pressing hard enough for reforms of the kinds which interested liberals or socialists. The charge was often justified, and has sometimes remained so even in more recent times. So for instance Francois Goguel suggests that the M.R.P.'s industrial policy was biased too heavily towards human relations during the first years after 1944. The party was preoccupied with works councils and related matters, and paid too little attention to problems of State planning or of the competitive market.

However, in the M.R.P., as everywhere but in a few outlying corners of the Christian Democratic movement, the pendulum has swung back. Over the years the Christian Democrats have learnt Liberalism from the

Liberals and Socialism from the Socialists. They are interested today in all three types of objective, and their ideal is a balanced use of all the sanctions and incentives available, not a special preference for any one. They agree, of course, that there has been a historical progress from the Age of Liberalism to the Age of Human Relations. Indeed, they have every reason to emphasise this. For if the present age is indeed one of Human Relations, that means that it is one in which the Christian Democrats, with their generations of special interest in human relations, are better qualified than any others to take the lead. Only they would add the footnote that Stage 2 of this progress does not involve scrapping the achievements of Stage 1, nor Stage 3 those of Stage 2. Economic incentives and competitive mechanisms do not cease to be useful when the value of organised, 'scientific', management and of State planning and direction come to be better understood. They cease to be recommended for purposes for which they were in any case never useful; but that only makes them all the more useful in their right place. And so also managerial and State directives do not cease to be useful when the importance of informal, 'human', relations comes to be seen. They are only put back in their right perspective. The search for the right sanctions and mechanisms is a case, not of the progressive supersession of one by another, but of the accumulation of experience which allows the merits and limitations of each to be understood so that it may be applied to the best advantage.

THE ECONOMIC INFRA-STRUCTURE

(a) The theory of consumption

Colin Clark has shown how an under-developed economy typically concentrates heavily on the necessities of life, most of its workers being employed in farming, fishing, forestry, and hunting. As the economy develops the accent shifts to 'secondary' industries, and a range of manufactures grows up. Incomes rise and consumers' choice widens, and in due course they make use of this new freedom to demand increasing quantities not only of primary and manufactured goods, but also and above all of 'tertiary' goods and services; more comfortable and convenient shopping, more travel and transport, more and better education. In advanced economies such as Britain and the United States half, or thereabouts, of the working population may be in 'tertiary' trades and industries. Clark and Continental writers who have followed him, such as Fourastié, are quoted with interest in Christian Democratic discussions. But what they are describing is the actual course of events in a far from ideal world. The theorists of Christian Democracy have in mind a rather different conception of what ideally might happen or be made to happen.

The traditional theory of the Just Price, from which they explicitly or

114

implicitly start, focuses on the idea of 'needs'. A just price should reflect the value of a producer's output—its long-term value, not that decided by immediate conditions of scarcity, monopoly, or ignorance—in satisfying others' 'needs'. It should also reflect the producer's own personal and family 'needs', as determined by the culture of the society in which he lives, and the other 'needs' of society as a whole. These various needs, though compelling and indeed vital as far as they go, are strictly limited, and there is a 'social mortgage' on income and wealth. The private ownership of income and wealth is only a convenience, though a necessary one. The earth is for the use of all, and the private owner must use his property in the interests of society as well as himself. Whatever surplus he has after satisfying his 'needs', strictly interpreted, must be made available by gift, investment, or taxation to meet the needs of others worse off.

But what do 'needs' mean? The test, as always, is the contribution made by particular goods and services to the development of personality. The French Catholic research centre *Économie et Humanisme* suggests a three-fold division. There are 'basic' goods, which include not only economic goods such as food and shelter but also a satisfactory role, status, and degree of security in the systems of human relations to which each person belongs. The 'basic' category shades into two others, 'comfort' or 'luxury' goods and what might best be translated 'spiritual'[1] goods. The latter are those goods which, as with art or music or religion, so to speak take people out of themselves. 'Basic' goods, *Économie et Humanisme* argue, must have priority. Man must eat and be organised in society before he can think or even indeed before he can worship. But basic goods are only a point of departure, though an essential one. The economy will render its best service to humanity only if, after ensuring the basic minimum, it lays all possible emphasis on 'spiritual' goods. 'Luxury' goods are no doubt often sought after in practice. But they represent only material comfort, and surplus comfort at that: something beyond the minimum needed for living the good life. They have no spiritual value, and ideally should be done without.

Économie et Humanisme's division evidently coincides to some extent with Clark's. 'Spiritual' goods and services are often also 'tertiary'. But much of the actual increase in tertiary, secondary, or even primary consumption which Clark's statistics record as incomes rise represents what *Économie et Humanisme* would class as 'luxury'; they would deny that the increase of expenditure of this sort represents any real progress at all. Their own division between basic, spiritual, and luxury goods is practically impossible to express in statistical form. A girl buys some expensive material and, being an artist in her way, makes herself the kind

---

[1] The French word is 'dépassement'.

of dress which would look well in *Vogue*. There is a 'basic' element in this; clothing is a necessity. There is certainly also an element of artistic 'dépassement'. And there is probably a fair dose of invidious comparison and conspicuous waste, very satisfying to the lady in question, but definitely to be classed as 'luxury'. Also the dividing line varies from one person to another. One man's strong drink (luxury) is another's Château X., an exercise in connoisseurship which might well rank as 'dépassement'. But 'basic', 'spiritual', and 'luxury' elements can certainly be distinguished in the pattern of an individual's or family's consumption and in terms of that individual's or family's particular needs. It is therefore best to think of the consumption problem, as defined by *Économie et Humanisme*, as arising in two stages. The first is to induce individuals and families to revise each item of their consumption patterns so as to include the biggest possible 'spiritual' and smallest possible 'luxury' element, while giving the necessary priority to 'basic' elements. The second is to supply the goods and services corresponding to the consumption patterns as thus revised.

The 'ideal' patterns revealed in this way will certainly be immensely varied, to match the varying personality patterns and combinations of patterns in families and other social groups. They also seem likely to change, as incomes rise, more or less in the direction indicated by Clark. 'Basic' needs, on any definition, involve the supply of large quantities of primary products first of all, and then of secondary, manufactured, products. 'Spiritual' needs may be partly satisfied by varying the pattern of consumption of food or clothing or housing, but will also call, as soon as there is enough margin of income available, for the development of tertiary services such as travel, reading, education, or entertainment and sport. But it seems probable that there will be a big enough difference between the 'ideal' patterns and the actual patterns studied by Clark to make the latter a rather unreliable guide to the former. Patterns formed in the free market as actually developed in the modern world are distorted, Christian theorists argue, by:

> The unscrupulous but well-calculated speculation of men who, without seeking to answer real needs, appeal to the lowest human passions, which are aroused in order to turn their satisfaction into gain. (Pius XI, *Quadragesimo Anno*, 1931, C.T.S. ed., p. 60.)

Not only are they different in form; they also do not have as marked a ceiling as 'ideal' patterns. Christian theory admits the importance of incentives, and therefore of differences between classes in the level of consumer as well as functional expenditure. It also admits that the ceiling will be higher in a rich economy than in a poor one, since certain activities well worth while in themselves, such as travel or higher education, can be afforded in a poor economy on only a limited scale. But in any class or economy 'ideal' patterns will contain nothing which cannot be justified by

116

a reference to basic or 'spiritual' needs, strictly interpreted. And it seems likely that this will yield a bigger free margin for investment and donations than could be expected under actual conditions in the absence of State intervention.

Even State intervention will not necessarily lead to a level or pattern of expenditure satisfactory from a Christian point of view. A stock Christian Democratic criticism of the Socialist movements is that they do not see that it is dangerous for the mass of the people, as well as for the rich, to pursue wealth without limit. Luxury is bad even when shared by all:

> For according to Christian doctrine man, endowed with a social nature, is placed here on earth in order that, spending his life in society, and under an authority ordained by God, he may cultivate and evolve to the full all his faculties to the praise and glory of his Creator; and that, by fulfilling faithfully the functions of his trade or other calling, he may attain both to temporal and eternal happiness. Socialism, on the contrary, entirely ignorant of and unconcerned with this sublime end both of individuals and of society, affirms that human society was instituted merely for the sake of material well-being. . . . Indeed, the possession of the greatest possible amount of goods which serve for the conveniences of this life is esteemed so highly that man's higher goods, not even excepting liberty, must, they claim, be subordinated and even sacrificed to the exigencies of the most efficient production. . . . (*Quadragesimo Anno*, CTS/CSG ed., pars. 118–19.)

The criticism is all the sharper because, if Communist and socialist regimes do in fact make a paradise of material comfort their aim, this 'materialist' temptation may prove very hard to resist.

> Soviet propaganda does not deny the sacrifices called for by the collective economy. We know what fundamental deprivations it demands. But we know too that if stagnation continued here, whereas the East offered us the spectacle of an annual rise in incomes of more than 7%, and if, ten years from now, our workers' standard of living remained where it is, whereas that of Russian workers rose above it, the defence of freedom in Europe might well weaken. And what is one to expect of the masses in Asia and North Africa, from Indians condemned to an average expectation of life of twenty-five years, from the thousand million people recorded by the 'geographers of hunger'? How long will the 'immortal principles', translated into Hindi or Arabic, prevail against the vision of Turkestan and China marching on towards a paradise, materialist if you like, but comfortable and endowed with prestige? (Byé, Report to the 1954 Congress of the M.R.P., *Pour une Expansion Économique Libératrice*, p. 5.)

(b) The theory of work

Man as the subject of economics is a worker as well as a consumer, and work, like consumption, has evolved through history. In primitive economies the accent is on manual labour. Later it comes to be on the design and use of machines and other manufactured means of production. Then gradually, as technique advances, it shifts again to human relations and leisure. Hours are shortened, the effort required for work is reduced, and attention begins to be given to the relation between personality and work, to the social system and the structure of management and control in the working group and the plant, and to the relation between this and the social system of the community as a whole. The advanced countries of the West are in this third stage today.

Like the change in consumption patterns summarised in Clark's statistics this is an actual but not necessarily an ideal sequence. The theorists of Christian Democracy make much the same distinction here as in the case of consumption. The 'basic' work of the manual labourer or the engineer involves the commitment of human lives and efforts for purposes necessary to society, and asserts the mastery of man over matter. It is therefore honourable and dignified. But work may and often does contain an element of excess, corresponding to 'luxury' in consumption. The executive or trader as well as the rank and file worker may become 'alienated' in his work and submerged in it, a 'proletarian' as defined above. The problem is to 'deproletarise' work and to encourage the spiritual, human, element through which it contributes to the expansion of personality; or rather through which it contributes to it something over and above its basic service in satisfying consumer needs and asserting man's mastery over nature. Work can and should be the point of departure for 'leisure' in Pieper's sense; the chance and desire, whether in or out of what are formally working hours, to reflect on the nature and causes of things and achieve an all-round culture.

Up to a point, the tendency in advanced economies to shorten hours, lighten work, and emphasise human relations represents the sort of progress which the Christian tradition of work wish to promote. But what the shortening of hours leads to is not necessarily the contemplative leisure of the scholar or the creative use of free time by the good family man, sportsman, neighbour, and Christian. Within work situations, the modern interest in human relations has its bad as well as its good side. It can be a technique of exploitation, of 'false personalisation', a way of using people and their sentiments and relationships as tools for purposes alien to them. And there is no simple distinction between the 'inhuman', 'materialist' work of the engineer or the factory operative and the 'human', 'spiritual' activities of the manager, including even the personnel manager, and the trade union official. The work of the engineer, the craftsman, or even of the semi- or unskilled operative, technical and materialist as it may look, can in the right conditions be the point of departure for a culture and development of personality of a most impressive kind. The personnel manager on his side can easily become 'alienated' in the keeping of card-indexes, the administering of tests, and the upkeep of the canteen. The 'technocratic temptation' is as powerful among workers of all ranks as is the materialist temptation among consumers. It does often happen that:

Dead matter leaves the factory ennobled and transformed, whereas men are corrupted and degraded. (*Quadragesimo Anno*, C.T.S. ed., p. 62.)

And the corruption and degradation may be of the manager as well as of the workers in the rank and file. What is it, asks Emile Leonard, which draws men into the Communist Party in certain strongly Protestant farming districts in the south of France?

In actual fact, and above all, it is a Communism for technicians, a technocratic Communism, the reaction of intelligent and active men, realists, to the waste due to defects of technical even more than of social organisation. Concern for the oppressed counts for little in a country where poverty is deep-seated, but the poor, except in cases of definite misfortune, neither attract pity nor perhaps deserve it. . . . The essential factor is contempt for respectable farmers who farm badly, along with the desire for ring-fenced farms, co-operatives, and specialised farming. The idea of a collective rise of the working class also has little interest. So far as human interests are concerned, the aim is to put the most intelligent and active people in their proper place as managers; and those existing owners who come into that category are welcome to keep their place. . . . It seems to me that this desire for an aristocracy of technique . . . links up, among Protestants, with many of Calvin's ideas on government by the best citizens . . . and the eminent dignity of labour. (E. Leonard, *Le Protestant Français*, 1953, p. 253.)

It is perfectly legitimate, as not only Calvinists but Catholics would say, to wish to expand man's power over the earth. This is a true growth of human personality. But this in itself legitimate desire leads here to inexcusable, though understandable, blindness to other less pleasant consequences of some of the means by which it may be achieved.

(c) Consumption and work: the Christian Democratic Movements' practice

The policy of the Christian Democratic movements agrees in general with the principles just outlined.

The task of the economy is far from being fulfilled by merely providing for physical welfare. The economy serves also to lay the foundation for the unfolding of man's culture. Human life can achieve fulfilment only through participation in culture, and for that reason provision of the means for cultural development must also be regarded as a basic need. . . . (Werner, *Wirtschaft als Aufgabe*, 1952, p. 16. Published by the S.V.E.A.—Swiss Protestant trade unions.)

'Provision of the means for cultural development' must however follow after provision for other, more material, basic needs.

As soon as the last black spots of poverty are cleared out from our social and economic structure, we must give more place to well-utilised leisure as a product of our modern social economy. (C.D.U.—reply to questionnaire for the N.E.I. Annual Congress at Bruges, 1954.)

And at present this stage is still some way off. Recovery from the Second and even the First World Wars has taken time:

119

We are a group based on common beliefs, and for us cultural and ideal aims stand in the foreground. But so long as the severe losses of two world wars weigh down on our people, it is inevitable that economic questions should thrust themselves strongly to the front. (Austrian People's Party, reply, ibid.)

In any case, 'black spots of poverty' still stand out even in more normal conditions in all the countries covered in this study, to say nothing of the far worse situation in parts of Asia and Africa for which they are responsible. For the time being, therefore, the Christian Democrats remain rather highly production-minded, and inclined to think of economic welfare more from the angle of the consumer than from that of the share going to profit or wage earners: though they are also, because of the remaining poverty, very much concerned with ensuring a minimum 'basic' standard for all.

The accent placed respectively on production and on fair shares, with special reference to the minimum standard, varies from one country or movement to another. But even the movements which particularly stress fair shares agree on the the importance of enlarging shares through higher production. The M.R.P. stresses that workers should share in the benefits of higher production, but also and above all that the stagnation of the French economy must be ended. The Christian trade unions, though interested first and foremost in labour's share in what is produced, have shown themselves readier than unions of other tendencies to co-operate in drives to raise production. Both the parties and the social movements stress the importance of investment and savings, particularly small savings, and have some ingenious ideas for increasing them. In connection with this they believe in sound, uninflated money, though with shades varying from the C.D.U.'s 'unqualified support' for monetary stability—very understandable in the light of Germany's two great inflations—to the P.S.C.'s statement that:

Monetary policy must always remain subordinate to the needs of economic and social policy. (Reply to the Bruges questionnaire.)

And they have no hesitation in using economic incentives to bring production up. The political parties are, as was said earlier, cautious about pushing redistributive taxation so far as to damage incentives. The Austrian People's Party and the Catholic People's Party in Holland both supported drastic levelling of incomes in the poverty years just after the war, but pointed out that this often meant wiping out differentials in favour of skilled workers or risky investments, and insisted as soon as conditions improved that the differentials be restored.

On the other hand, even the most free-enterprising movements, such as the C.D.U., insist that priority must be given to a basic minimum standard of living for all. The levelling of incomes approved by the Christian Democrats in Austria and Holland while production was low and demands for war damage repair and new investment high was very drastic indeed. The C.D.U. records with pride how it raised the German social security budget by 60–65% in its first two years of office.[1] It is accepted that incomes must be stabilised through social security and full employment, and that organisations and corporations need a solid economic foundation as well as individuals. So the Dutch parties express their concern for the finance of local authorities, and the Young Christian Workers build up a *mystique* around their subscription.

The biggest contribution to the longer-term question of 'ideal' patterns of consumption is being made by the youth, family, social class, and women's organisations, and one of the chief gaps in this study is that it has not been possible to find time for a full investigation of the way their ideal is developing. It is obvious, for instance, that a certain puritanism is on its way out from the youth movements; as for example the alarm and despondency over dances which is noticeable in the early annals of the Young Christian Workers or, in France, the Young Christian Farmers. The co-operative movement has become incidentally a movement for consumers' education. It:

> Can have an educational function, particularly in educating buyers, consumers, the members of their family. In every educational activity there is liable to be transmitted a certain conception of life, inspired by an ideal more or less materialist or individualist, more or less family-minded or individualist. And we all know how in the concrete reality of the working of the co-operative movement one often finds, gravitating around the co-operative stores, a complex of other services such as restaurants, licensed premises, cinemas, games and sports clubs, social clubs, and so on—which indirectly, through their atmosphere, have an educational effect. (J. Deschuyffeleer, address to the Congress of the Catholic Workers' International [F.I.M.O.C.] May, 1955. Published by the Belgian Christian Workers' Movement, Etudes et Expériences, May 1955.)

Or again, a well-to-do French Catholic business man may be found testifying[2] to the way in which he personally tries to fix the level of his consumption. He insists, first, on accepting as income only what has been honestly earned and is clear of taxes and other obligations. He pays his taxes in full. As an investor, he takes an active interest in wages and conditions in the firms where he places his money, even if this means sacrificing dividends. As a landlord, he accepts as his own only that part of rent which remains after paying for proper maintenance and modernisation. As a tenant benefiting from rent control, he sees it as his duty to pay to the landlord, or to some housing trust, the amount by which his legal rent falls short of a fair rent. Having thus fixed his true disposable income, he makes himself an annual consumption budget, for without a definite and detailed budget the control of expenditure is unlikely to

---

[1] Report of the Fourth Party Congress, Hamburg 1953, p. 119.
[2] *Revue de l'Action Populaire*, February 1955, p. 205 ff.

be effective. He calculates a basic minimum of expenditure by reference to the official minimum family budget. He regards himself as free to spend part of his 'privilege' income above this level, but levies on it the equivalent of a progressive income tax, whose proceeds he uses for gifts and interest-free loans. The whole approach is inspired directly by the theory of the Just Price. It would be well worth while to make a special study of the direction in which this and other changes in the 'ideal' pattern of consumers' behaviour are leading.

The trade unions and political parties are also beginning to have more to say about such matters as workers' leisure or—the M.R.P.'s comparison, above, of France and the U.S.S.R. is an example—on the ideal rate of saving and investment. The parties have in the ordinary course of political business to make up their minds about consumption ceilings and the extent to which the State should enforce them through redistributive taxation. But on the whole the unions' and parties' views on the principles of consumption remain rather scattered and imprecise. Discussion of redistribution tends to stop at a few broad, rather common-sense principles, such as that a distribution of incomes is justified to the extent that it serves social welfare,[1] or that redistribution should stop when it threatened, especially by reducing incentives, to reduce welfare more than it adds to it. Much discussion is still at the level suggested by an interview with an official of one of the Christian farmers' organisations. And what, asked the interviewer, would you regard as a Just Price for such and such farm products? 'Well', said the official reflectively, 'It would be a bit more than we are getting now.' There is more interest for the moment in the minimum to which those who fall short should be raised than in the maximum beyond which what was 'basic' becomes 'luxury' and what is to be admitted as 'spiritual' must be rather carefully defined. It will be interesting to see one day what the Christian Democrats make of a situation in which the general run of incomes in Western Europe has risen to, say, something above the present American level, and the housing, town planning, and other structural difficulties which often make the ideal utilisation of income impossible have been overcome.

The theory of work outlined above is applied by the Christian trade unions and workers' leagues more explicitly than is usual in the less 'spiritual' atmosphere of labour movements in Britain or America.

> Christian trade unionism has always struggled to improve the workers' conditions of life. . . . Our workers have a right to a decent, human, standard of life . . . they have the duty and right to demand the establishment of an economic order which ensures them social security by guaranteeing their employment, and covers them against the ordinary risks of their life by a complete system of social insurance. But this material security, these improvements in workers' welfare and comfort, are not enough to ensure them the

[1] Or, more precisely, 'to the extent that the lack of it interferes with social welfare'.

freedom which the Christian trade unions wish to see them enjoy. Christian trade unionism can never forget that it cannot limit its action to reducing the material inequality between the workers and the owners of money in a capitalist regime. It must at all times see in the worker the man and recognise that the material conditions of life are not everything, that other problems are more important; those of human values, of the dignity of man, of the worker's pride, of the culture of the spirit. While stubbornly pursuing the improvement of conditions of work, the Christian unions must remain alive to the need to inculcate in workers an understanding of the value of their own personality and a desire to escape from their feeling of inferiority. They must do so by awakening in them the permanent urge to achieve a more fully human life, a new style of life, through the development of their spiritual, moral, and intellectual qualities and the safeguarding of their freedom. Here is the essential point of Christian trade union action. . . . (Henri Pauwels, Chairman of the International Federation of Christian Trade Unions, closing speech at the Amsterdam Congress of the International, 1946.)

The father's job, to quote the Catholic Workers' Movement of Germany again, should be the point of departure for a complete and highly developed culture of the working-class family. This line leads out into the field of consumption, and has been developed strongly by those movements which operate there. In the field of actual work relations, the desire of the Christian workers' movements to make work more than the pursuit of wealth and security has come out particularly in their concern for workers' control. A number of them, and of the employers' associations, have taken up actively problems of selection, training, and vocational guidance, and have been helped by the research in industrial psychology and sociology carried on in several of the Catholic and Protestant universities. Several studies, such as Michèle Aumont's *Femmes en Usine*, on women's jobs in the Paris engineering industry, have appeared on the problem of adapting the work to the worker rather than the worker to the work. Firms are feeling their way round the problem of the small working group, and the idea of 'autonomising' the working group has met with a good deal of attention. But for the time being more 'basic' economic problems tend, as on the side of consumption, to need and get most attention.

THE MORAL FACTOR. INFORMAL AUTHORITY

The Christian movements' view of economic activities is obviously ambivalent. They are necessary and therefore respected, but can have dangerous effects on personality, and must therefore be carefully scrutinised and kept within bounds. But when it comes to the 'moral factor'—friendship, community, and informal social control based on them—the atmosphere though not the principle changes completely. It is said repeatedly that the social problem is 'first of all moral and religious', that it 'begins with the inner man', and that the effectiveness of a movement, a social class, or a nation depends on how far it possesses a common culture and beliefs. Relations of friendship, community, and kinship are seen as making a particularly direct contribution to the end of all social action, the formation of personalities. For it is in this area that there occurs the direct, unconstrained, face to face meeting of 'thou' and 'I' whose value for the development of personality has been so heavily underlined by writers such as Martin Buber or Gabriel Marcel. These relations have a special value not only in themselves but as an incentive and sanction for action of other kinds. If personalities are to be shaped, as the Christian movements insist, so as to be fully aware of and responsive to social as well as individual needs, the ideal incentive or sanction must be one so deeply anchored in personality that the requirements of each situation call forth spontaneously the right response. The rather mechanical, external, sanctions of money and formal power do not pass high on this test. But informal or moral authority does. For this is that kind of authority which, not being backed by the coercive force of wealth or power, depends more than any other on individuals' own goodwill and co-operation, and on the direct influence of personal relations; with friends, fellow-workers, relatives, or fellow-members of the Church.

The same distinctions have of course to be made here as in the case of economic control. There is such a thing as 'social poverty', a state of deficiency in human relations and in the ability to respond to them. People can be left too much to themselves and can become, in Riesman's phrase, too exclusively 'inner-directed'. This is a common deficiency in modern large-scale, rapidly changing societies, in Riesman's 'Lonely Crowd'. To prevent it—to guarantee people security and a satisfactory role and status in the groups to which it is useful for them to belong—is as much a 'basic' need as the need for food and shelter. On the other hand, it is possible to become too 'other-directed', too much under the spell of others' opinions. In many systems of informal authority there is an unnecessary and undesirable element, satisfying no doubt to some people (at least in the short run), but fitting exactly *Économie et Humanisme*'s definition of a 'luxury' element. Neighbours may stifle originality by their gossip. Nation-wide prejudices may make life intolerable for those whose race or religion or politics, or even simply their way of dressing or their accent, differ from those of the majority. Solidarity among workers or employers may block a price reduction or the introduction of a new machine without, objectively considered and in the long run, bringing any compensating benefit either to the employers or workers concerned or to anyone else. 'Other-direction' in this sense has evidently to be combated.

But there remains the great difference that, though there *is* a 'spiritual' element in economic progress even beyond the point needed to ensure a basic minimum to all, it tends to taper off and can easily be offset by the 'materialist' or 'technocratic' temptation: whereas direct human relations, though they have their risks and are in themselves merely (like economic

124

or political relations) means to the end of personal development, hold out almost unlimited possibilities of contributing to that end. The Christian movements show their appreciation of this by their keen interest in families, neighbourhoods, youth groups, working groups, and all the other small social units in which face to face meetings take place and informal relations develop. Great efforts are beginning to be made to find a way into these groups:

A Christian centre in this shop
Another in that office
A Christian nucleus among those hikers
Another in that group of actors
The leaven is working in that big family lodging house
And in that great block of workers' flats
Leaven in that technical college
Leaven in that evening class, five hundred boys and young men
Leaven among the men on their allotments
Leaven among the film actors
Leaven in that neighbourhood group, among the fathers of families in that other group of streets, in that trade union branch or social work committee
Leaven in the caretakers' union of the VIIth Arrondissement, among the artists of Montmartre, among the girl shop assistants in the department stores. . . .

(From Godin and Daniel, *France, Pays de Mission?* English ed. by Maisie Ward, *France Pagan?* 1949, pp. 182–3.)

All the Christian movements, whether Christian Action or Christian Democratic, make it a prime task to train leaders for group work of this kind, and particularly to equip them for the persuasive, consultative leadership which it chiefly requires. C.F.T.C. study circles, Y.C.W. sections, the Evangelical Social Academy in Germany and the Equipes Populaires in Belgium, the family group movement in Belgium or France, or the magnificently named Credo-Pugno Clubs in Holland ('I Believe—I Fight'), aim to produce men and women who can act as a 'leaven in the lump', able to lead and influence their environment by force of character and example, not merely by the economic or formal political authority they may hold. Even for the rank and file, religious authorities insist, to quote the Dutch Catholic Bishops, on 'the primacy of the spiritual, personal, and social elements', which implies also priority for the movements which specialise in personal formation; for the workers' leagues, for example, as against the trade unions. This priority is stoutly defended but not always easy to ensure, an illustration of how the 'materialist temptation' can infect the Christian movements themselves. So for example Dutch Catholics, in spite of the lead given by their Bishops, have tended regularly to pay more attention to their trade unions and employers' organisations, and to their political party, than to the social class organisations which specialise in education. It is true that a member of the trade union section of the Dutch Catholic Workers' Movement must also join its cultural and general section: they are one and the same movement entered by one and the same subscription. But in practice Catholic workers bother much less with the educational than with the trade union side. This tendency is still more marked among Dutch Protestants. The workers' leagues which perform for Protestant workers some of the functions of the Catholic 'social class' organisations were long ago overshadowed by the C.N.V. trade unions. So also in Belgium there are half a million Christian trade unionists and only 70,000 members of the adult education movement, which concerns itself with a more personal apostolate. In Germany before 1933 the combined strength of the Protestant and Catholic workers' movements, corresponding to the Dutch 'social class' organisations, was never as much as half that of the Christian trade unions. And it has been shown above what a long struggle was needed with the German Catholic Workers' Movement itself to persuade the members to accept programmes of true, deep, personal formation, covering emotion, attitudes, and sentiments as well as intellectual development and organising techniques.

GOVERNMENTAL (INCLUDING MANAGERIAL) POWER

There are theological differences between Catholics, Lutherans, and Calvinists over the nature and status of formal non-economic, especially State, power. But taking the matter at the level of political and social practice, it seems that 'governmental' power is generally regarded in the Christian movements in a way intermediate between economic power and informal power. Like economic power, it should be limited in its scope. It is seen as justified—the doctrine of pluralism—only in so far as it makes possible the provision of services which cannot be provided by individuals or smaller groups. But within this limit it is treated with great respect. For whereas economic activities have dignity, government has majesty.

It has it in the first place, as the Christian movements see it, because those who are formally responsible for the government of any social group are endowed with total, overall responsibility for all those aspects of their people's welfare which are bound up with membership in that particular group. If a member's connection with the group is and need be only occasional, this responsibility may not amount to very much. But in the case of those groups which do, may, or should occupy a large part of their members' lives and influence them deeply, the Christian movements take the idea of the overall responsibility of government very seriously indeed. Their State is a Welfare State, with ultimate responsibility for every aspect of its people's welfare except those which are the exclusive responsibility of the Church or the international community. The Young Christian Workers and the other youth movements which have followed their model insist that, if they are to influence their members really deeply, they must take account of their life as a whole, and not merely of that part of it which is concerned with sport or work or religion or politics. The industrial manager, for the Christian movements, is not primarily concerned with profits or productivity or with the interests of any one group within his firm. His business is to focus and synthesise all the interests concerned with the firm—capital, labour, the consumer, the general public—and to take responsibility within it for decisions of all types. He is to make economic decisions, to organise and operate the firm's formal management structure, and to keep an eye on informal relations and morale. No doubt in a big firm these responsibilities will be divided among various managers. But the firm's system of management must as a whole embrace and focus every relevant aspect of the life, needs, and duties of the people whose interests it concerns. Man is one and indivisible, and it is the business of the governments of social units of every kind to see he is treated accordingly.

This emphasis on the overall responsibility of governments implies, as was noted above in dealing with the Christian Democratic idea of the State, a certain limit to their activities. The doctrine of 'horizontal' pluralism arises from two sides: from below, as a means of protecting the 'sovereign sphere' of small social groups, but also from above, to prevent the overloading of superior authorities. It is, of course, part of the duties of any government, of a social group of the State, to manage and execute as well as to supervise, initiate, and review. To make its supervision effective it must indeed be prepared to take executive action in any area of the life and activities of the group for which it is responsible. But management takes time and energy, and so does overall supervision, and there may not be enough for both. Where a clash of that sort arises, management—so the Christian movements see it—must give way. It is more important that a State should be a Welfare State[1] than that it should be a Managing State, and more important that general management should generally manage than that it should run the sales department or the works. What is essential to governments at any level, the first source of their sovereignty in their particular group's sphere, is their responsibility for thinking and acting overall.

Sovereignty is also seen as 'majestic' in the sense that its source derives directly from the law of God and nature, irrespective of constitutional forms. Its exercise corresponds to a need which is present whether the people governed are aware of it or not. No doubt it is often convenient to mediate power through the people, or through the shareholders' meeting and works council. Governments are responsible to and for all the interests which focus in their sphere, and democratic procedures help to ensure that all are in fact consulted and taken into account. The Christian Democratic movements insist, though with different degrees of emphasis

[1] In the sense defined in Chapter VII, pp. 90–91.

according to the sphere they are talking about, that to use democratic procedures is in modern conditions a duty, whether in the State, the party, the firm, or the family. But the right and duty to govern, however they may be conferred, arise not from the will of the people but from the natural law, reflected in the 'law of the situation' in each time and place. They come ultimately from the law of God, and immediately from the fact that there is a job of government to be done. It is the business of a government to do this job, and no party, group, interest, or combination of them, has a right to dictate how to do it. For no one among the various interests which converge on a social group, and no chance combination of them, is in a position, without the aid of government, to lay down a policy suitable for the group as a whole. The claims of the various interests must be pooled, worked over, re-negotiated, and synthesised, in the light of practical executive experience, into a policy which is both workable and as nearly as possible satisfactory to all concerned. And this process of collaboration and synthesis demands active and positive leadership, which it is the business of Cabinets, and higher managements, and other governments to provide, and to provide which they must use their independent judgment.

> If labour and capital wish to save themselves from impoverishment through class war, they must co-operate to promote the firm's prosperity. Harmonious co-operation is possible only if the head of the firm is exclusively responsible to neither of its two constituent elements. With his authority safeguarded over against the supplier of capital as well as of labour, though held responsible to them both for the management of the business, he should serve as the link between them. . . . (P.S.C., *Les Chantiers sont Ouverts*, p. 56.)

Management, that is, and management alone, can reconcile the interlocking interests and influences which play on a firm, because it alone stands at their centre with a general view and responsibility over them all. It has, therefore, an independent and inalienable duty to do so.

The argument from the divine and natural law of course cuts both ways. If the authority of governments comes from reflecting the law of God and nature, then it holds only to the extent that it does in fact do so. Christian Democrats, and particularly Catholics, have at their disposal a well-developed theory of the right to resist tyrannical authority. Seeing the danger and destruction which follow from revolutions, they recognise that only extreme oppression can justify actually rising in arms. A set of conditions must be satisfied similar to those long recognised by Christian theologians as justifying an external war:

(1) There must be an extraordinary abuse of political authority. Such misuse betrays itself especially in the trampling on all freedom and the supplanting of justice by might and of the common good by Party interests. What is decisive is not the personal unworthiness of the ruler but the abuse of political authority.

(2) Active resistance is considered only as the final weapon in an emergency after all peaceful constitutional methods have failed.

(3) There must be a moral certainty (i.e. a reasonably founded certainty) that active resistance can be carried through to success. An obligatory respect for the highest principle of the common good demands that nothing be undertaken which will increase rather than diminish the evils. . . . Therein lies the force of the truth . . . that the decision to resist and the conduct of the resistance are not matters for the individual but for the Estates of the Realm or similar bodies whose duty it is to represent the people and therefore to see that they get their rights. The individual comes in only as the executor of the general will. . . .
(4) Only so much force should be exerted as is required to gain the desired end. . . .

(Max Pribilla, *The Right to Resist*, 1952, pp. 21–2.)

Pribilla is an Austrian and he has in mind the Nazi period, and particularly 1944, when the General Secretary and the Chaplain General of the Catholic Workers' Movements in Germany, Bernhard Letterhaus and Mgr. Müller, were among those executed for their part in the plot of that year to overthrow Hitler. Among others deeply implicated in that plot were many, both Catholic and Protestant, who are still today leading figures in German and Austrian Christian Democracy: Jakob Kaiser in Germany, for instance, or Lois Weinberger in Austria.

The same conditions which may on occasion justify armed rebellion against the State will justify an industrial strike, except, of course, that much less provocation is needed to justify a measure so much less drastic. Christian Democrats may and do sometimes argue as if the relation between employer and employed were essentially one of contract, so that a strike would be approved or disapproved in terms of the relevant contractual conditions, or the absence of any. But this is simply to say that constitutional procedures based on mutual consent are useful, and must, where they exist, be observed, before either managerial authority or the right to strike against it can arise. The essential basis of the right to strike, as of the right of managers to manage, is still seen as lying, irrespective of contract, in the fact that managers and workers constitute a community, at the service of the community at large. Within the small community of the firm the manager derives his authority as usual from the fact that the community exists, has a function, and therefore needs government; though contracts, collective agreements, and periodic sanctioning by shareholders or a works council can and should be used to reinforce this authority and give it form. The workers for their part, once they have decided to join a firm, are bound by what Dutch Protestants speak of as the 'moral bond' between leaders and led. They are bound to accept management's authority within whatever constitution the firm for the time being possesses. But they are also entitled on the usual conditions to revolt against it. A constitution may establish forms and channels for the exercise of this right, but can never take it away.

CHAPTER X
SOCIAL CONTROL

2. MECHANISMS
COMPETITION

WHETHER power be economic, governmental, or informal or moral, how is it to be exercised? How far is society to be competitive, authoritarian, or based on consultation and co-operation? It is important not to be misled by turns of language. The literature of Christian Democracy abounds in statements to the effect that 'the proper ordering of economic affairs cannot be left to free competition alone' (*Quadragesimo Anno*), and that 'the primacy of man over economics and finance must be re-established' (P.S.C., Belgium). This disclaimer of competition, particularly in economics, has been typical for two generations of socially progressive movements all over the world, Christian and non-Christian alike. It represents their reaction from the exaggerated emphasis of the nineteenth century on business and the free market. From nineteenth-century laisser-faire arose in due course vast concentrations of private economic power, of which *Quadragesimo Anno* writes in a passage which Marx or Lenin would not have disdained:

In the first place, then, it is patent that in our days not only is wealth accumulated, but immense power and despotic domination is concentrated in the hands of a few, and that those few are frequently not the owners, but only the trustees and directors of invested funds, who administer them at their good pleasure. This power becomes particularly irresistible when exercised by those who, because they hold and control money, are able to govern credit and determine its allotment, for that reason supplying, so to speak, the life-blood to the entire economic body, and grasping, as it were, in their hands the very soul of production, so that no one dare breathe against their will. This accumulation of power, the characteristic note of the modern economic order, is a natural result of limitless free competition, which permits the survival of those only who are strongest, which often means those who fight most relentlessly, who pay least heed to the dictates of conscience. This concentration of power has led to a threefold struggle for domination. First, there is the struggle for dictatorship in the economic sphere itself; then the fierce battle to acquire control of the State, so that its resources and authority may be abused in the economic struggles; finally the clash between States themselves. This latter arises from two causes; because the nations apply their power and political influence, regardless of circumstances, to promote the economic advantage of their citizens; and because, vice versa, economic forces and economic domination are used to decide political controversies between peoples. (CTS ed., pp. 46–7.)

But this was written in 1931, in the depths of the greatest depression of modern times, and at a moment when the two generations of agitation which led up to the Welfare State and the Keynesian revolution were about to reach their peak. Today the case for far-reaching control—particularly State control—of the economy is everywhere accepted, and not least among Christian Democrats. And with this change has come a double shift in the climate of opinion. On the one hand, it has become obvious that the reaction from competition to control and from economics to politics is in danger of leading from one extreme to another; as indeed over a large part of the world it has already done. *Quadragesimo Anno*'s condemnation of nineteenth-century conditions and their consequences still stands, so far as those problems remain relevant. But the 'immense power and despotic domination' which people have in mind today is more likely to be Orwell's version of *1984* than its milder ancestor of the eighteeneighties. Even twenty or thirty years ago, though Christian Democrats agreed with Socialists in their criticism of uncontrolled economic power, they did not at all share their enthusiasm for political power and planning. With the record of Fascism and Communism before them, they are even less inclined to do so now. In recent years Liberalism has regained much of the vitality and reputability which it seemed to be losing in the 'thirties. Christian Democrats are not neo-liberals, and would indeed indignantly repudiate any such suggestion. But neo-liberal leaders such as Wilhelm Röpke are quoted with respect in their publications,[1] and when in 1949–50 the C.D.U. found its investment and employment policy under attack it called in Röpke in person to defend it.[2] Such characteristically liberal ideas as that most business should be private and competitive, that politics should be competitive, and that it is even more important to limit and control State power than economic power, are very firmly rooted among Christian Democrats today, even in the workers' movements. Socialist theses have been accepted only so far as is necessary to correct the exaggerations of liberalism, not on the ground that the liberal theses should be rejected outright.

Indeed, Christian Democrats' whole way of thinking, with their ideas of pluralism and the greatest possible autonomy for social groups and 'spiritual' families, calls for a wide use of competitive mechanisms, and not

---

[1] See for instance Kasamas, *Programm Österreich* (Austrian People's Party), 1949, p. 153, or some of the very Röpke-like doctrines proclaimed in Switzerland by the S.V.E.A. trade unions.

[2] The attack came from economists and civil servants of what is misleadingly known in some parts of the Continent as the 'Keynesian' school. Röpke's reply was based on what Keynes actually said. See the account of this episode in Piettre, *L'Économie Allemande Contemporaine*, 1952, pp. 257 ff.

only in economics. Interests, as has been seen, are to be fully and freely expressed, and there is to be full freedom of association to promote them. The family, the firm, the social class, the local authority, are to settle their own policy and decide their own destinies. In countries of mixed religion there are to be three or four different school systems operating side by side. The rule is to be the 'free trade union in the organised profession', so that there may be several unions catering for similar classes of worker, especially where there are ideological differences. Politics are to be democratic, with freedom to form independent parties. There is to be a high degree of social mobility: no privileged positions, but a chance for everyone to find and work out his or her own ideal course in life. People are not only to be autonomous and 'inner-directed' but to have the chance to behave accordingly. Social mobility is to be helped by, among other things, pluralism in the service of vocational guidance, with a separate service for each 'spiritual family', and perhaps even each social class or group.

This freedom and variety is to be kept within a framework of social control. But it must be control in a form consistent with freedom. And the form of control most consistent with freedom is competition, whose essence is to leave each social unit free to steer its own course, subject only to achieving defined standards, or to keeping pace with others. Though Christian Democrats condemn the excesses which follow from too heavy reliance on competition, their practice usually conforms to the motto which the C.D.U. set for itself in its *Düsseldorf Principles* in 1949: 'He who will be free must be competitive'. The free man learns to make his own career in competition with others. He accepts and learns to play the competitive party game in politics. He approves of parents' choice being decided by friendly competition between Christian and 'neutral' schools. And, to quote the C.D.U. again,

> He must refrain from trying to replace competition with control in the market. For he who controls a market, and is not himself controlled by competition, cannot be left free. (*Düsseldorf Leitsätze*, 1949, p. 20.)

It is not surprising that enthusiasm for competition is particularly explicit in the countries, like Germany, Austria, and Italy, which have felt most heavily the hand of dictatorship. At the Fourth Congress (1952) of the Italian Christian Democrats Alcide de Gasperi intervened characteristically as follows:

> It had been said at the Congress that Christian Democracy needed to acquire a powerful legend of its own. Legends are all very well, observed in effect De Gasperi, but Christian Democracy does not in any case lack the social vision and the historic tradition from which to draw inspiration. He reminded participants of the development of Christian-social thought, the first tendencies towards corporatism, the effort to take over from canon law the elimination of the credit system . . . and of the social ideals expressed in

132

Papal documents. 'But', he added, 'the conclusion to which experience has led us today is this. The dictatorships of the past, the dictatorship threatened for tomorrow, the unavoidable pressure of the State bureaucracy and of systematic State intervention, have brought to the fore—whatever any theory, reflection, or discussion may conclude—the need to insist on freedom, personal and political'. . . . (Tupini, *I Democratici Cristiani*, 1954, p. 298.)

CONSULTATION

Where free initiative proves inadequate, Christian Democrats turn first of all to consultation. Consultation and discussion can be formal or informal. They can serve to spread understanding of an economic situation, or of the policy of a government or management, or to create that more general, informal agreement on which informal authority rests. Christian Democrats are very well aware, from the setbacks to their own attempts at creating works councils or at collaborating politically with Communists or nationalists, of the difficulty or even futility of discussion where there does not exist at least a minimum of goodwill and common ground. But wherever this minimum exists they have a profound belief in the value of a meeting of minds.

In the political field, the unity and effectiveness of the Christian Democratic parties themselves is seen as based on a continuous exchange of views between the different classes and elements of which they are made up. Most of the parties object, as has been said, to allowing different groups and tendencies to organise fractions of their own. But they encourage the informal expression of opinions, and have usually formal machinery—joint or advisory committees—for keeping in touch with the other Christian Democratic or Christian Action movements. Giorgio Tupini's study of the Italian Christian Democrats[1] is a good illustration of the trouble often taken to keep the exchange of views going without permitting organised factions to form. And, going outside the Christian Democratic parties themselves to the coalitions to which they belong, the 'policy of the broad base' referred to in Chapter VII is seen as resting not on any formal bond but on informal understandings reached through regular contact and discussion.

In industry the Christian movements of both employers and workers have given strong and consistent support to consultation in the firm and the industry and between organisations of different ideologies. They believe, as has been said, in class collaboration, though on a basis of mutual respect resting on strength; and their traditional motto in relation to Socialist, Liberal, or even Communist organisations has been 'independence, but collaboration from case to case in matters of common interest'. How this policy may work out in favourable circumstances, in a country where the Christian organisations dominate the workers', farmers', and

[1] *I Democratici Cristiani*, 1954.

business middle class movements, and play an important part even among the larger employers, is shown by the development of consultative mechanisms in Dutch industry since the beginning of the Second World War. There have been established:

(1) A Council of Trade Union Congresses, grouping the Catholic, Protestant, and Socialist unions. This acts as a common organ for the unions in their relations with the government, and also deals with a variety of questions affecting their internal as well as their external relations. It arranged, for example, that unions in the three Congresses should have a common rate of subscription and common benefit rates, so as to eliminate transfers of members on grounds other than ideological preference or the effectiveness of each union's trade policy. The Socialist unions withdrew from the Council in 1954 as a protest against the references to them in the pastoral letter of the Catholic Bishops for Lent of that year.

(2) Joint Trade Committees and Joint Committees of Trades Councils, providing trade by trade and local co-ordination on the lines followed nationally by the Council of Trade Union Congresses.

(3) A Foundation of Labour in which the unions and the corresponding employers' organisations meet to discuss matters of common interest, such as the preparations for P.B.O., in which the Foundation played a very large part.

(4) A variety of voluntary works councils; legal compulsion to establish works councils dates only from 1950.

(5) P.B.O., which though involving compulsory powers is intended to work largely through consultation. It would never have come into existence at all if two generations of discussion, culminating in the work of the Foundation of Labour, had not shown the necessary common ground to exist.

In addition, there is regular collaboration between the Catholic employers' and workers' organisations and between them and their Protestant opposite numbers.

Even in the countries where the Christian trade unions are in a minority and find it hard to get the sort of collaboration they want, a general study in 1954 of the works council movement in Europe[1] shows that they still cling tenaciously to at least the principle of consultation. They may be cautious, like Italian Christian trade unionists afraid of opening up too many channels of influence to Communists, or like their French opposite numbers who:

Seem to fear that works councils, if they take up without careful preparation tasks above their present aptitudes and strength may later experience bitter disillusion and excessive discouragement. (David, op. cit., p. 36.)

But they remain convinced that consultation is worth while both for educating those who take part in it and for promoting production.

In these industrial and political cases consultation is used as a mechanism of government and production. But it is probably most effective when it helps to create, through the informal exchange of ideas in the family or

[1] David (ed.), *La Participation des Travailleurs à la Gestion des Entreprises Privées*, 1954. Published by the University of Strasbourg.

local community or working group, the climate of opinion by which relations of friendship and kinship, and community are governed, and which constitutes the background to economic or formal governmental relations; that is when it shapes and reinforces 'informal' authority. The Christian movements attach, as has been shown, great importance to the organisations like the Credo-Pugno Clubs or the family group movements, which specialise in training Christians to hold their own in these informal exchanges on the ordinary occasions of daily life.

DIRECTION

Direction is not the same thing as the exercise of governmental and managerial authority. A government which consults another government, a local authority which runs entertainments in competition with private business men, or a Ministry which decides to leave a certain field open to free enterprise, is certainly performing a function of government. But none of these is exercising direction. Direction means regulation by law, rules and orders, whether the ultimate sanction behind it is governmental or economic power or social custom. It is Authority fixing policies and procedures. In its most developed form it takes shape in 'bureaucracy' as Max Weber defined it.

> The assignment of roles occurs on the basis of technical qualifications which are ascertained through formalised, impersonal procedures (e.g. examinations). Within the structure of hierarchically arrayed authority, the activities of trained and salaried experts are governed by general, abstract, clearly defined rules. . . . The chief merit of bureaucracy is its technical efficiency, with a premium placed on precision, speed, expert control, continuity, discretion, and optimal returns on input. The structure is one which approaches the complete elimination of personalised relationships. (Summary in Merton, *Social Theory and Social Structure*, 1949, p. 152.)

Bureaucracy, and direction in general, are things of which the Christian Democrats are very wary. They are not indeed shy about giving orders, or about invoking 'general, abstract, clearly defined rules', whether defined by the law, by social custom, or by economic pressure. They know very well that 'personalised relationships' alone, varying from case to case, cannot provide enough security or a precise enough definition of roles and statuses to permit a satisfying development of personality in a complicated and changing society like our own. 'False personalisation' causes confusion, uncertainty, and a waste of time and effort which could be better used. The Christian youth movements set out to teach discipline and the ability to give and take orders and fit into an administrative hierarchy. The trade unions have progressively centralised and bureaucratised their own structure. The political parties want a State which is not only 'educational' but also able if need be to govern with an efficient Civil Service and a strong hand. But to rely for the management of social affairs primarily on the 'elimination of all personalised relationships' and on 'general, abstract, and clearly defined rules', would for Christian Democrats be to throw out the baby with the bathwater, since the growth of personality and, as a main incident to it, of 'personalised' relations, is the ultimate aim and test of their policy. And discipline enforced by order from above may, if pushed to excess, end in the state of affairs described in a leading article in *Engineering* early in this century:

> Modern methods . . . demand more and better foremen than the old system, because their essential principle is that the machine-man shall not exercise any discretion at all. The foreman has now to think for every man beneath him. (Quoted in Urwick and Brech, *The Making of Scientific Management*, 1949, II, 122.)

A world of 'machine-men . . . not exercising any discretion at all' directly contradicts the personalist and pluralist ideal of the Christian Democrats, and seems to them unlikely even to achieve technical efficiency. Their ideal implies minimising, though respecting, the role of direction, and making maximum use—where social control is needed at all—of competition and consultation, which offer more opportunity for self-control and self-development by individuals and groups.

The role which remains for direction is that of an essential tool, but one whose use is structural and supplementary. It is needed to provide and maintain a framework, at each level and in each sphere of social organisation—economic, governmental, informal or 'social'—within which the initiative of individuals and smaller groups can have the widest play consistent with their own welfare and that of the bigger communities to which they belong. It may serve both to set up social structures or institutions and to fix the lines on which they are to operate. But it may be used for either purpose only to the extent that what is needed cannot be done through competition or consultation. Basically, this is very like the nineteenth-century liberal idea of the State holding the ring. But only basically, for much has been added to that idea since. Right at the beginning of Christian Democracy, the German Centre Party heartily condemned the idea of the 'night watchman State'. And Christian Democrats today have incorporated into their idea of direction as a framework for freedom the lessons of the age of socialism and management, as well as their own conceptions of federalism or 'horizontal pluralism'.

(a) Direction in government and management

In the sphere of governmental and managerial authority, direction is seen first of all as a means of guaranteeing that each unit of society which needs a separate government or management gets it. Each must be equipped with the necessary institutions for legislation, execution, and judicial interpretation, and with a bill of rights defining its sphere of autonomy, though also its responsibilities towards other groups. This will of course normally be done in part through the 'free' mechanisms of competition and consultation. The initiative of individuals and groups throws up social units endowed with certain institutions and having a certain relation to the rest of society. It promotes experiment, clarifies issues, and avoids imposed changes and so creates consent, which is a necessary first step to legislation. But under conditions of pure laisser-faire there is no actual guarantee that the profession, or the working group, or the family, or Europe, will come to be equipped with just those institutions and powers, to be exercised within just those boundaries, which a careful application of the theory of pluralism would suggest. The custom and practice of the constitution of the various social groups needs to be completed and codified by the law. Here, the Christian Democrats agree, direction must step in.

By Anglo-Saxon and particularly British standards it may indeed step in rather far. One could easily get the impression of a certain legalism here; a tendency to formalise relations which in the Anglo-Saxon world would often be left to informal agreement. So for instance the British Commonwealth is a system of international government, and in many ways an effective one, tied together mainly by informal relations. But this is not the model which has appealed to the Christian-Democratic parties in their plans for the future of Europe, nor for the long-term link between European and colonial territories. So also, in industry, the English-speaking countries have for the most part left works councils, co-partnership, and the overall organisation of industries or professions to grow up by private agreement, firm by firm or trade by trade, with at most advice and persuasion from the State, whereas the Christian Democrats have sponsored P.B.O. and the whole range of works council, works constitution, and co-partnership laws enumerated above.

There is certainly a tendency to legalism here. It arises out of the national tradition of the countries concerned, and is not peculiar to the Christian Democrats. But it should not be overstressed, for another part of the difference between Christian Democratic and Anglo-Saxon practice lies simply in a different assessment of the importance of the problems of government arising in certain spheres. Seen from the Christian Democrats' pluralist and federalist angle, the Anglo-Saxons seem to be concentrating unduly on the government of one or two of the 'sovereign circles' of society, and particularly of the State. The difference between the Anglo-Saxon and the Christian Democratic view is not merely about how works councils or a government of Europe are to be set up. It is about the importance to be attached to setting them up at all.

Government—political or otherwise—needs not only institutions but working rules. The clash of parties and interests, whether in a State or in a smaller group, is partly self-regulating, but only in part: here too the Christian Democrats see scope for law and order. For government to be good it must for one thing be stable. The free expression and clash of interests contributes to this: there may well be more long-term continuity in a democracy than under a dictatorship. But the clash of interests does not always guarantee stability, and the legislator must step in. So the Christian Social Party in Belgium, as recorded earlier, demands stronger legal rights for the general management of a firm over against the competing interest groups which it serves, and the *Democrazia Cristiana* legislates to increase the chance of a government having a stable majority. The C.D.U. busies itself with securing the status of Civil Servants: the bureaucracy on which the steady and effective execution of Government policy depends. The Rule of Law is called in to prevent more generally the arbitrary and unpredictable use of power.

From another point of view, government needs to be based on a wide and long-term view of the factors in each situation. Competition and consultation between individuals and groups help to ensure this, but do not always ensure it entirely. The Christian Democratic movements, as the discussion above of their federalist ideas showed, are more uniformly willing than most others to admit the right of the larger and higher units of society to impose wide and long views on smaller and lower units, though with the reservation that this must not lead to exclusive concentration of the role of any one higher authority and notably of the State. They also insist that such directions can be justified, as the P.S.C. puts it in connection with local government, only where some interest of the larger community is at stake, and not merely where the higher authority takes a different view from the lower of what should be done on matters within the lower authority's own sphere of interest.

From yet another point of view, competition for power needs rules to ensure that all interested individuals and groups have a fair chance to influence the outcome. It has been shown that it is characteristic of Christian Democracy to insist on legal safeguards for the representation in the State machinery of the 'natural units' of society—the family, the profession, the local community—as well as of individuals. And a number of Christian Democratic political parties have identified themselves with legislation against organisations likely to aim at a monopoly of power. So for instance in Holland the Catholic People's Party begins by calling for:

> Legal guarantees for publicity for the operations of political parties, for their proper financing, and for their internal democracy. (*Immediate Programme*, 1946, p. 10.)

And then it goes further:

> We have also taken the initiative in proposing a change in the Constitution, making possible a so-called 'civil state of siege' in case of revolutionary

agitation. . . . We have demanded that it should be possible to declare revolutionaries' seats vacant in the Chambers and provincial and local councils. . . . Our efforts to suppress the poisonous and lying propaganda of the Communists, above all in the daily press, have so far had no success. . . . There are protests from all sides when it is proposed to take any action against this. . . . But for my part I can scarcely see how anyone accurately aware of the facts could fail to be convinced that of all the possible dangers—and dangers certainly exist—the greatest is to leave this poison-tap open. (Romme, *Katholieke Politiek*, 1953, p. 12.)

An Italian Christian Democrat, commenting on the new Constitution which his party took a leading share in drafting, observes that:

The Constitution which emerged is of the 'rigid' type, due chiefly to a prejudice and a fear; a prejudice against the executive, due to the recent experience of [Fascist] totalitarianism, and a fear that tomorrow a left-wing majority might use the powers made available by the Constitution to establish its own intolerant and despotic power. (Tupini, *I Democratici Cristiani*, 1954, p. 174.)

And note also how the C.D.U. and the Christian workers' movements try to ward off Socialist pressure for monopolistic control, by trade union head offices, over workers' representation on works councils and boards of directors.

(b) Direction in economic affairs

The Christian Democratic movements were at one time distinctly hesitant about economic direction or planning, and there are to this day wide differences, or at least apparent differences, between them. The workers' movements do not always see eye to eye on this with the political parties, still less with the employers' movements.

In the parties which have taken the name of Social-Christian, the representatives of the working class do not always have the influence which belongs to them . . . the forces of wealth . . . try to reserve themselves the maximum of influence. (Johannes Even, Secretary of the K.A.B., address to the Congress of the Catholic Workers' International, May 1955.)

There are also wide differences between the parties themselves. At the Bruges Congress of the N.E.I. in 1954 they tried to agree on a common economic policy for Europe. It proved possible to agree that the economy of Europe should be competitive and that the circulation of goods, services, and capital should be freed. This would require positive action by governments, and no doubt also by international organs such as the European Coal-Steel Community, which had by then already been remarkably successful in breaking down restraints of trade. But when it came to deciding what further positive powers of direction should be used by governments or attributed to new European authorities, agreement failed. Some vague phrases appeared in the final manifesto about the need for governments to have an active economic and social policy, and to harmonise their national tax and social insurance policies. But on such matters as the reconversion of firms, the re-employment of displaced workers, and the variety of other human and economic problems which might call for State or international control or for measures of organised self-help by industries or local communities, the manifesto was silent.

But these differences between the various countries and movements, though important, are smaller than appears on the surface, and in any case are diminishing. So for instance there has been a complete transformation in the economic policy of the party which twenty years ago represented the extreme liberal wing of Christian Democracy, the Dutch Anti-Revolutionaries. The Anti-Revolutionaries were led at that time by Dr. Colijn, who appeared to the outside world—his own colleagues saw another side of him—almost a laboratory specimen of the tendencies in unlimited free enterprise condemned by *Quadragesimo Anno*. A professional soldier, then an oil magnate, he dominated the Dutch Government through the slump years of the 'thirties. His policy was one of economy—except, his opponents were quick to point out, in the armed forces—and of wage and salary cuts, high indirect taxes, 'sound money', and leaving unemployment to look after itself. In the version of his party's *Statement of Principles* published in 1934 the key economic phrase was 'limitation of State initiative, leading to a powerful development of private enterprise' (Art. 12). Gladstone would not have said otherwise. Not only Socialists but many Catholics found Colijn's policy hard to swallow, and this was one reason for the widespread desire among Dutch Catholics to work with the Labour Party rather than with the Protestants after the war. But set alongside that past record the actual post-war policies and programmes of the Anti-Revolutionaries, and a very different picture appears. The lesson of the 'thirties has been well learnt, and the party's programme now abounds in such items as full employment, social insurance, State aid in the creation of new industries, P.B.O., and where necessary consumer rationing or rationing of raw materials.

Today, one of the widest of the apparent divergences among Christian Democrats about the methods and limits of economic planning is between the, on the surface, very liberal Christian Democratic Union in Germany, and the distinctly Socialist M.R.P. in France. But appearances are deceptive. There are several factors to allow for before concluding that the two parties are really divided by a gulf. The first is the difference in the problems which they face. The C.D.U. was faced when it took power with a country wrecked from end to end and with widespread social disorganisation, and dealt with this situation along the lines of Lenin's New Economic Policy of 1921. It gave free enterprise the green light, though keeping in its own hands power to guide the overall course of the economy and to guarantee a certain minimum standard of living to all. Liberal-minded leaders, and notably the Minister of Economics, Dr. Erhard, were pushed to the front. It was tacitly assumed that the German people had enough reserves of dynamism and self-discipline to make good use of a free economy, and this proved to be the case. 'This liberalism', says André Piettre in his monumental study of the German economy, 'is, one must understand, merely the reflection of the dynamism of the German people'.[1] The C.D.U.'s 'socialised market economy', the party's own phrase, did in fact prove, like Lenin's, very effective in bringing order out of chaos and securing a rapid increase in production. The M.R.P. on the other hand has had to deal with an economy which is a going concern, with a substantial degree of security for individuals and groups, but where dynamism and discipline are lacking. A policy like that of the C.D.U. could have led in France, temporarily at least, to disorganisation and a drop in the national income. The M.R.P. has therefore become specially interested in measures of planning, whether national or international, which might break the crust of stagnation in the French economy without losing those advantages which France already has.

When it comes to theorising, it is not surprising that the M.R.P. seems sometimes to fall over backwards in its abuse of neo-liberalism, or that the C.D.U. should appear almost comically afraid of planning. When for instance the N.E.I. asked, in preparation for their Bruges Congress of 1954, about the use made of national income accounts in shaping government economic policy, the C.D.U. replied:

> No special attention has as yet been given to these methods of systematically observing economic, social, and fiscal data. Statistics are used in public discussion, but have no overall framework to draw them together. It may be that a role is played in this backwardness not only by lack of knowledge of the possibilities of estimates of this kind, but also by fear of their possible misuse to instal a directed economy.

But when one penetrates behind these verbalisations, and bears in mind the difference in the problems to be solved, it turns out that the policies of the two movements have a great deal in common. The liberalism of the C.D.U. has proved compatible with 'planful influencing of the economy'[2] by methods which include price controls, 'managed' farm prices, the orientation of investment towards key industries, town planning, location of industry policy, and a housing programme whose public component alone has equalled that of Great Britain and which, overall, has achieved nearly double the British rate of construction; as well as with a massive welfare budget, including notably large-scale aid to refugees and war victims, and a remarkable redistribution of wealth in the name of war damage compensation. The M.R.P. for its part repudiates policies of general socialisation or 'total' planning, and finds it perfectly possible

---

[1] *L'Économie Allemande Contemporaine*, 1952, p. 337.
[2] C.D.U. *Düsseldorf Principles*, 1949.

and indeed normal (though with creaks and groans on its left wing) to form coalitions with the liberal and conservative parties to its right. And the particular form of direction of the economy on which it has put the accent in recent years, the idea of 'economic magistrates' managing sectors of the economy without political interference, has much in common with the 'producers' economy' which Piettre describes as the peculiarly German, and C.D.U., version of the Managerial Revolution. In general, the C.D.U. repudiates private as well as State direction of the economy. But there is a tradition which makes the Boards of German heavy industry a law unto themselves, and this, Piettre suggests, still lives on in spite of the 'socialised market economy', and of the law which has made the trade unions equal partners with the shareholders in nominating Board members.

> What one in fact finds . . . is that between neo-liberal theories and the present [German] reality there lies the whole distance which separates a consumers' economy from a producers' economy. Liberals intend that production should be directed, basically, by the votes of those to whom it is destined. The suffrage of the price system means precisely this. But, more and more, production is directed by the producers themselves. Self-financing is, fundamentally, one aspect of the Managerial Revolution. In a country where the Managers are, traditionally, the representatives of large-scale industry, it is logical that their investment policy should have received the support of the State. (Loc. cit., p. 266.)

There is in fact today wide agreement among the Christian Democratic movements on the ground which direction in economic affairs should cover, very much as in the case of governmental and managerial authority. The Austrian People's Party says of economic life that one should not attempt to plan its process in detail, but should control its structure. This means in the first place ensuring that adequately manned and equipped units—farms, firms, unions—are present where required. Competition makes it possible for progressive firms or individuals to get ahead, and even rewards them for doing so, but does not necessarily compel them to do it. There is such a thing as the 'competition of dullards', in which all are efficient as efficiency is understood, but none have the dynamism to lead the way to better standards or to open up new lines or areas. So one finds all the Christian Democratic parties, and many of the social movements, supporting State action to ensure that new economic opportunities are opened up. The French and Belgians have their colonial development plans. The Dutch and Italians sponsor plans to open up new land and develop new industries within their own territories. The M.R.P.'s schemes to break through the 'competition of dullards' in the French economy with the help of schemes of land reform, State-sponsored marketing, and selective tax and credit policies also come under this head, and so do the C.D.U.'s schemes for building up industries to absorb refugees.

Structural control of the economy, as of systems of government and

142

management, means making working rules as well as setting up operating units. Wide and long views are needed in the economy as well as in government, and may sometimes have to be imposed. The M.R.P. goes so far as to say that:

> The State must employ inducements to direct private enterprise . . . for it alone is competent to take account of very long term objectives, corresponding to the life of human collectivities. (Reply to questionnaire for the N.E.I. Congress at Bruges, 1954.)

'It alone' is more than most other Christian Democratic movements could swallow, for to look ahead to future generations, or around to the wider repercussions of a given policy, is in their view as much the duty of families or industries as of the State. But they approve the general sentiment that, since the smaller units in the economy often cannot or will not take as long and wide a view as, for instance, a P.B.O. council or the State, these higher units will often have to impose their view. They agree also that the economy cannot be expected to stabilise itself without some degree of 'management'. There have been vigorous polemics on what this 'management' implies. Some stress control of the general level of demand, on Keynesian lines. Others call for more specific measures to break bottlenecks or smooth transitions; for reconversion funds, to help firms and workers to adjust to new conditions, or for housing policies, to promote mobility of labour, or for the planned distribution of industry. The debate is however somewhat unreal, since it usually turns out that the contenders agree largely on what is to be done in given circumstances, but differ on what the circumstances are. Questions of stability, and especially of full employment, are, naturally, stressed particularly by the workers' movements. But it is interesting to note that the Catholic Employers' International (U.N.I.A.P.A.C.) devoted a special conference in 1954 and its full Congress in 1955 to the question of full employment, with special reference to the employer's contribution to it.

It is agreed, again, among the Christian Democratic movements that some degree of direction is needed to ensure a fair distribution of economic power. Even the most liberal of them, like the C.D.U., agree that the State must intervene to guarantee a minimum standard of life to all, and are interested in levelling up inequalities by helping the accumulation of small property or by raising the standard of lower paid workers' education, skill, and therefore ability to earn. Attitudes on redistributive taxation vary a good deal, as has been shown, but even a movement like the C.D.U. which dislikes it in theory accepts a great deal of it in practice. It is recognised that economic competition, like governmental, can destroy itself by leading to monopoly, and all the Christian Democratic parties accordingly support legislation or administrative measures to control monopolies, or, if possible, eliminate them; though some, notably the M.R.P., doubt whether such

143

policies are in fact really practical.[1] They have also given strong support to the efforts of the European Coal-Steel Community to break down tariffs, quotas, price-fixing arrangements, and discriminating transport rates.

(c) Direction in informal social relations

The Christian movements insist that among the fields where a certain measure of direction is needed, if only to establish the framework within which competition and discussion are to be free, is that of personal morality, habit and custom, and in general of informal social relations. At this point the Christian Democratic movements often conflict with others even when these normally—as in the case of the socialists—agree with them on the need for strong executive powers.

In so far as the powers called for are positive, no great conflict arises. Powers to promote such things as adult education or youth movements meet little opposition anywhere in principle; though there are of course plenty of conflicts over who precisely is to receive such aid. But Christian Democrats also insist on the need for negative controls, enforced not only by public opinion but by the law. The Dutch, as usual, are particularly ready to call a spade a spade:

> It is the Government's duty, our party insists, to maintain public morality on the highway and in public places; to limit opportunities for the consumption of spirits; to forbid the publication of immoral pictures, books, and other printed works; to punish any who lead minors into immoral behaviour; and to have no policy on prostitution . . . other than that of putting an end to it. . . . Measures to prevent the further growth of neo-Malthusianism are also . . . to be recommended. And the Government must likewise give its attention to the sin of drunkenness and to the public misuse of God's name. (Anti-Revolutionary Party, *Statement of Principles*, Art. 15.)

And here is a characteristic comment from the leader of the Catholic People's Party:

[1] Some of the recent statements of the M.R.P. on economic policy may give a false impression of the view of competition held in the party as a whole, since they have come notably from one pen, that of Professor Maurice Bye of Paris. He drafted the M.R.P. reply to the Bruges questionnaire, and also presented the main economic report to the party's 1954 Congress. He argues from a rather theoretical view of economic competition, on lines prevalent in the 'thirties but now becoming obsolete. All economists are agreed that competition is 'perfect' or 'effective' if it produces a certain list of results. A school grew up twenty or thirty years ago which maintained that these results would be forthcoming only if (among other things) competition was between units so small that none of them had a substantial influence in the market. Later factual research has shown that the specified results will be forthcoming under a much wider range of conditions which may be consistent with the existence—the normal state of affairs in a modern industrial market—of only rather few competitors, each with a substantial influence in the market. Professor Bye follows the former view, and argues that since in modern industrial markets the conditions called for by the older theory do not exist, effective competition neither exists nor can usefully be restored. His reports are also however coloured by the general gloomy conviction of the M.R.P. of the power and tenacity of French combines and trade associations.

144

I see as one aspect of our policy for a healthy family the bill presented early in 1949 by the late Minister Van Marseveen, to eradicate the more serious abuses of the bookselling trade. I am thinking particularly of its proposals for protecting young people against reading matter dangerous to their moral health. This proposal unchained a storm of opposition on account of what some people called its 'deadly blow to spiritual freedom', and the bill has not yet passed through many of its stages. But I remember for instance how an enquiry at Maastricht revealed horrifying facts about what is actually happening in this field. However it may be done, definite action must be taken in this matter. (C. P. Romme, *Katholieke Politiek*, 1953, p. 17.)

For both Protestants and Catholics, the Churches step in to lay down with authority what associations and communications are likely to be compatible with the growth of their personality as Christians. The Catholic Church's ruling on mixed marriages is well known. Dutch Protestant workers find that the Hervormde Kerk rules out for them membership of the Communist Party and trade unions, and discourages membership of the socialist unions. The Dutch Catholic Bishops go further and rule that:

It is forbidden for a Catholic to be a member of socialist organisations, such as the N.V.V. [Socialist trade unions] and its associated groups, or to go regularly to socialist meetings, read the socialist press regularly, or listen regularly to the socialist radio. (*De Katholiek in het Openbare Leven van deze Tijd*, 1954, p. 43.)

The Christian Democratic organisations, though not under clerical control, are expected to keep within the framework of the Churches' social teaching. Their Catholic members, in particular, will find themselves reminded of their duty with authority if they do not. And in the Christian Action organisations, specially concerned with informal social influence, the clergy are present—this again applies particularly to the Catholic organisations—and exercise direct authority. Though the lay members of these organisations have a substantial degree of day to day autonomy, they are, as has been shown, ultimately under the clergy's control:

Catholic Action is collaboration in the apostolate of the Hierarchy. But the collaborator depends on his principal . . . Catholic action is not only an auxiliary apostolate but also an official one. Its activists are not merely the collaborators of the Hierarchy but its mandatories, and its leaders are expressly delegated by the Hierarchy. (Civardi, *Manuale di Azione Cattolica*, 1952 ed., p. 182.)

Views differ among Christian Democrats about the exact degree of authority which should be exercised in these matters of personal morality and social custom. The French, for instance, would not go nearly as far as the Dutch. But a clear general distinction remains between the attitude of Christian Democrats, who insist on the exercise of authority even in matters of informal social influence, and that of liberals and social-democrats who prefer to see this field left as nearly as possible free.

PART III

PART III

CHAPTER XI

THE RISE OF CHRISTIAN DEMOCRACY, 1820–80

CHURCH AND STATE (I)

CHRISTIAN DEMOCRACY has grown by the process typical, in modern Western experience, of major social movements of all kinds and outlined above in Chapter VIII: a process whose direction is not predictable, but whose stages and rhythm very often are. A problem dawns gradually, is talked about, experimented with, and in the course of a generation is brought to the stage where workable, though as yet often very imperfect, models for a solution exist. There may be about twenty years of discovery, discussion, and feeling the way, followed by ten of break-through, when the new models are being built. A further generation is then taken up with elaborating these models and spreading the conviction of their value, till finally a definitive break-through is achieved and the new models pass into current practice. The interest of the old problem —or problems—is then exhausted, and new problems dawn. The whole cycle proceeds to repeat itself. In the case of Christian Democracy the first two-generation period was from the eighteen-twenties to the eighteen-eighties and the second from the eighteen-eighties to the nineteen-forties. The third includes the present time.

Evidently, in movements as vast and containing as many elements as this, all the elements will not move in the same direction at the same time. So for example economists, analysing the trade cycle, show that not all the components of the cycle move in the same direction or have the same turning points; some even have a counter-cyclical movement. Yet there is a very real and obvious sense, looking at the total effect of those various movements, in which prosperity was going up in 1927–9 or 1933–7, and in which 1929 and 1937 were boom years, and 1932–3 the trough of a slump. So also it is with a movement like that of Christian Democracy. Its components have changed in various ways. But there remains a very real sense in which the movement *as a whole*, in each country or in Europe in general, has had a definite rhythm and direction of advance.

It also had a definite beginning. Evidently, one can trace back this or that element of it very far into history. Chapter XXIV will try to bring out

149

some of this longer perspective. But if the ancestry of the actual movements existing today is traced back, it turns out that the eighteen-twenties were a time of pause and new beginnings from which these modern developments have directly sprung.

1820–80. OVERALL REVIEW

If the young lady of Riga (who went for a ride on a tiger[1]) had been a wise virgin instead of a foolish one, she would have noticed the danger of being permanently identified with her mount, and have jumped off and got herself a gun. That is in effect what a growing body of both Catholics and Protestants did in the two generations from 1820 to 1880 in relation to the various 'humanist', or better perhaps 'laicist' political and social movements—at that time chiefly liberal—of the modern world. After thinking about it a good deal, they quite liked the way the tiger was going, and began to climb on. But then they discovered that he actually was a tiger and hastily climbed off again and took up a position of defence.

The liberal movements of the early nineteenth century carried two messages which in principle were perfectly acceptable to Christians. First, the modern world was a very different place from that of previous centuries, and needed new forms of social organisation. The number of major inventions, technical and social, appearing in the world from decade to decade has been doubling each century from the Middle Ages on. By the nineteenth century this rising river of change had become a torrent, affecting every corner of social life. To allow for and control these new opportunities, in a society far more open and swiftly changing than in the more traditional past, the liberals proposed certain techniques; political democracy, economic competition, guarantees of the rights of man and nations. A little later socialists in their turn came forward proposing techniques of State control and class (trade union) organisation. Secondly, seeing that in the modern world beliefs are divided, the liberal movements argued that to impose by force any one set of beliefs—even the correct set—would do more harm than good. The right attitude was one of tolerance and mutual respect between different 'spiritual families'.

Both these positions are acceptable to Christians, but were not immediately or everywhere accepted by them. Many looked back to an older, less mobile, and, as they believed, happier age when the liberal techniques were neither needed nor in use; a time when kings governed the State and guilds the economic world, and each knew his place in a traditional social scale. In the face and in spite of this attitude there grew up among Christians at first a small and then a large and powerful body of opinion which accepted the liberal and in due course the socialist techniques. By

[1] They came back from the ride with the lady inside, and a smile on the face of the tiger.

about 1880 substantial Christian-liberal, if not yet Christian-socialist, bodies of opinion existed in all the churches, and their victory over traditionalism was assured. So far as the Catholic Church is concerned, the seal was set on this evolution by the Encyclicals of Leo XIII. Leo XIII was no admirer of liberalism or socialism when raised from the status of a social technique to that of a philosophy. His Encyclicals abound in denunciations of those who treat the people as the source of power and authority, as apart from those who simply regard democracy as a means, convenient in modern times, of conferring the power and authority which rest ultimately on the divine and natural law; or who do not merely found trade unions where that is useful, but erect a whole philosophy on what is assumed to be the absolute and inevitable character of the class war. But in three of his Encyclicals in particular Leo made it clear that, so long as the liberal and socialist techniques were regarded as techniques and nothing more, they could in appropriate circumstances be perfectly acceptable to Catholics. *Libertas Praestantissimum* (1888) approved in the conditions of the modern world such liberal principles as democracy and tolerance. *Rerum Novarum* (1891) accepted the essential socialist principles of class organisation and State intervention in the economy. And *Au Milieu des Sollicitudes* (1892) warned Catholic leaders in France, the most conspicuous remaining body of Catholic traditionalists in the political field, that it was time to turn their backs on the past and accept the liberal Republic.

The efforts and struggles by which this acceptance of the new social techniques was achieved are the first strand in Christian Democracy's early history. The second strand concerns the way in which even those Christians most favourable to the liberal and socialist movements found that these animals had after all essentially tigerish characteristics. It was not wise to gallop carelessly off on them or put one's head confidently in their mouth.

For one thing, though the then prevalent liberal view was no doubt founded on real needs of society, it was certainly not founded on consideration of *all* the relevant needs. It tended to omit all those which could not be satisfied by action on individualist, competitive lines. It was not, therefore, a truly synthetic approach to political and social problems. But this line of criticism, though it was heard often enough, was somewhat ineffective. It came largely, in these generations, from those who condemned the achievements of liberalism altogether, and looked back to the happier world (as they saw it) of monarchy and tradition; not from those who accepted and valued the opportunities of a more open and swiftly changing society, found the techniques of liberalism useful, but insisted that they were not in themselves enough. It was not until after 1880 that, in the hands of men who accepted modern society and criticised it from

151

within, this line of argument became a major element in Christian social policy.

What did call forth mass Christian movements—above all political movements—before 1880, and led Christians to insist on an independent voice in the modern world, was the fact that the liberal and related movements were humanist in the sense of laicist, and moreover were militantly so. They denied that the Christian revelation had any over-riding authority in matters of, particularly, politics and economics; or even, often, that it had any authority at all. And they did not stand by their own principle of tolerance and mutual respect. In country after country they insisted that the State was entitled at its convenience to interfere with, suspend, or destroy the Church's internal management, its religious foundations, and its schools: that is its machinery for preserving the message of Revelation intact, for expressing it in the highest form of Christian life, for defining and proclaiming its relevance to current problems, and for transmitting it to the next generation.

Such attacks were of course nothing new in the history of the Church. The history of the feudal age and of the absolute monarchies of modern times is full of them: and indeed the persecuting Emperors of Rome were doing precisely the same thing, asserting the right of States and peoples to over-ride the directions of Scripture and the Church. The Christian emperors at Rome and Constantinople, and many Christian kings after them, followed a subtler policy of controlling the Church—Catholic, Protestant, or Orthodox—under the pretence of allegiance to it. These, as it might be said, more traditional types of attack went on in the nine-teenth century, often (as notably in Germany) in alliance with the new liberal assault. And so it was to affirm the rights of the Church against both old and new opponents that Christians of every shade, traditionalist and modern, in this period could and did stand together and fight. In practice they found more and more that the liberal freedoms, rather than any traditional order, offered the most favourable ground on which to take their stand. In that respect Liberalism rendered Christianity a major service, as well as, along with Socialism, by teaching Christians a great many things about the management of modern communities which they should have been able to read out of their own principles for themselves. But Christianity returned the compliment. For it was the Christian resistance to attempts to assert the supremacy of the State or of majorities, and to over-ride the rights of different 'spiritual families', which in turn forced liberals and socialists to face up to the true meaning of their own principle of tolerance in a plural society.

There was as yet no clear or well-defined Christian Democratic political or social doctrine. But the lesson that Christians must be prepared to say 'yes' to the techniques and 'no' to the totalitarian claims of the movements which have made the modern world is the foundation stone, on which all subsequent developments of Christian Democracy have been built. The learning of this lesson was spread over the whole period from 1820 to 1880, within which, however, there were two distinct stages. From 1820 to 1850 the problem was being posed. From 1850 to 1880 the double line of evolution, towards the 'yes' and the 'no', was being clarified and confirmed.

1820–50. THE DAWN OF THE PROBLEM

Catholics, from 1820 to 1850, faced very different conditions in different countries. The most difficult problem—indeed, in the conditions of the time it was insoluble—was posed in *Italy*, where the Pope was at one and the same time monarch of central Italy and also head of the world-wide Church. From the eighteen-twenties onwards forces making for economic freedom and political democracy were building up steadily in Italy, and in the Papal States as well as elsewhere, and these ideas were being linked up with that of Italy as a nation. In 1846 a liberal Pope, Pius IX, was elected, and proceeded to open the prisons, grant a constitution, and undertake economic and social reforms. A movement, expressed notably in Gioberti's *Primato morale e civile degl'Italiani*, had already developed to bring the Pope to the head of a new united, federal, and democratic Italy. For a time it seemed as if the Pope had Italy at his feet. But here arose the clash. Personally, the Pope was an Italian patriot, who could (and, privately, did) cheer any progress in ridding the North of Italy of its Austrian occupiers. But as head of the universal Church he refused to lead any war unless a purely and manifestly defensive one; least of all a war against another largely Catholic people. Personally, again, he was in many ways a liberal; but as head of the Church he felt bound to refuse any constitution which would legally subordinate his acts to those of any earthly authority. The break came in 1848, when the people of Rome itself, disappointed in their hopes, rose against the Pope and drove him into exile.

Eighty years later, it seemed to the advantage of all concerned to reconcile the Pope's 'Yes' to Italian nationalism and liberalism, and his 'No' to the subordination of the Church to any State, by the creation of the State of Vatican City. But that was not how the question presented itself around 1850. The choice then was between the Temporal Power in its traditional sense and none at all. In the circumstances, modern Catholics look back to Pius IX's stand in favour of Papal independence not as a violation of the liberal principles of Christian Democracy but as the best contribution to them possible in the circumstances, particularly when it is taken with another major event about the same time. In 1854 the Pope proclaimed, in his own right and unauthorised by any Council, the dogma of the Immaculate Conception. The dogma itself was of purely religious significance. But the method of its proclamation was a ringing affirmation—the decisive affirmation, as time was to show—of the doctrine that the Pope is infallible when speaking *ex cathedra* in matters of faith and morals. The 'vertical' pluralism of modern Christian Democracy requires Catholics (among others) to make their own way in the political, economic, and social field, as merely one 'spiritual family' among many. But it is only those who feel confident and secure in themselves who can, so to speak, enter wholeheartedly into a game of that sort and abide by its rules. A major source of this self-confidence and security for Catholic Christian Democrats has been the consciousness of guidance and backing from a Church which maintains its authority and independence beyond challenge; and Pius IX's double stand, on the Temporal Power and Infallibility, is the classic reaffirmation of this authority and independence in the conditions of the modern world. It can thus be said in a very real sense that Pius IX's refusal to accept democracy as applied to himself opened the way for other Catholics to enter confidently into the democratic world.

That is not to say that they were at first willing to do so. The behaviour of *French* Catholics is an outstanding example. France presented in the eighteen-twenties a picture of luxuriant Catholic life. To take only one index, but a fundamental one, the curve of vocations to the priesthood rose in these years to a peak never since then even remotely approached. But the 'restoration' of the Bourbon monarchy was no idle word. The atmosphere in both Church and State was largely that of the pre-liberal age. Political freedom was limited, the press was censored, and reaction against the Revolution and all it had stood for was in full swing. In these respects the Church was more royalist than the king. The 'alliance of throne and altar' was in high honour in Catholic circles, democracy was discredited, and there was little sign of attempts—the essential negative side of the Church's adjustment to the modern world—to keep the State and its claims at arm's length. The Church tolerated a State monopoly of education, took the State's subsidies, and was not always reluctant to help out piety with the police. It was Rome, rather than the State, which was held at arm's length, for the French Bishops continued to teach the Gallican doctrines which prevailed before the Revolution. The gist of these was to limit the Pope's authority to pronounce on temporal affairs or to alter the national or world-wide customs of the Church, and to deny that he was infallible in his own right, that is without the consent of a General Council.

Below the surface, however, and indeed even to some extent above it, liberal political principles lived on. The characteristic social problems of the modern world, especially those of the working class, were also beginning to make themselves felt. These influences grew in strength, and in 1830 a new revolution overthrew the clerical monarchy and replaced it with a liberal, free-thinking regime. The revolution itself was accompanied by a good deal of violence against the Church, including the sacking at Paris of the Archbishop's residence, the Jesuit novitiate, and the head-quarters of the *Missions de France*. From a Christian point of view, all was manifestly not well. There accordingly appeared in the late 'twenties and 'thirties three thin but growing streams of action by Catholics pre-occupied with modern problems and the relevant social techniques. Some of the new leaders, such as Lamennais and Montalembert, were specially interested in problems of democracy, of freedom of education, or of freedom of the Church from the State. Others, often politically more conservative, were interested in relieving social distress; it was at this time that Ozanam founded the Society of St. Vincent de Paul, that Villeneuve-Bargemont was investigating workers' living conditions, and that the first 'patronages' for workers were begun. There was also a small but important Catholic working-class movement, often socialist in outlook; its chief leader was Buchez.

Significantly the leaders of many of these movements of the eighteen-thirties—and it was here that they joined hands with a growing mass of Catholics who did not share their political or social views—were not merely liberal, or socially inclined, but also 'ultramontane': men of a very different stamp from the Gallican Bishops of the Restoration. They accepted squarely the principle that for Catholics in a threatening world the unity and authority of the Church is the one rock upon which freedom can safely be built. They looked to the head of the Church as represent-ing principles above and beyond the State's authority, and on obedience to him as the best guarantee of Christian freedom against the State.

The most promising of these early Catholic liberal and ultramontane movements was that associated with the paper *L'Avenir*, founded in 1830, and edited by the Count de Montalembert, Fr. Lacordaire, Professor Charles De Coux, and above all Fr. Lamennais, who inspired the group as a whole. Historians have vied with one another in superlatives in describing the intellectual brilliance with which Lamennais analysed the problems of the Church in the society of his time, and the breadth and persistence of his influence. As regards the brilliance of his analysis they are certainly justified. The programme of *L'Avenir* anticipates in point after point that of Christian Democracy today, and particularly of that strand of Christian Democracy developed in Italy from the end of the nineteenth century onwards by Fr. Luigi Sturzo. Lamennais defended freedom of religion, education, the press, and association, along with universal suffrage—this went considerably beyond the usual demand of liberals in his time—and decentralisation, particularly for the benefit of

155

regional and local authorities.[1] He called for the separation of Church and State, not indeed as desirable in itself, but as the relationship safest for both in modern conditions. Along with his colleagues he set on foot a 'General Agency for the Defence of Religious Freedom', run by laymen, which pointed the way towards the later organisation of both Christian Democracy and Christian Action. *L'Avenir* showed a keen interest in Christian liberalism outside France, and influenced and was influenced by it: in that sense, Lamennais and his colleagues might be thought of as the ancestors of the Paris headquarters of the Christian Democratic political international (N.E.I.) today.

But as regards the breadth and persistence of Lamennais's influence superlatives are less easy to justify. He holds in the history of French Christian Democracy a place like that of Robert Owen in the British labour movement. Owen, like Lamennais, anticipated much that later generations have taken for granted. Lamennais's disciples were found all over the Church in France for a generation after him, just as Owenites were found throughout the British labour movement. But it is difficult to pinpoint anything definite and concrete which Owen achieved for the British labour movement, because he failed to judge the methods of action appropriate either to that movement itself or to the environment in which it worked. His grandiose plans for co-operative societies and communities, labour exchanges, and mass trade unionism collapsed through a combination of bad internal management and failure to pick objectives which could be achieved in the conditions of the time. And that essentially is Lamennais's story as well. He ran into doctrinal difficulties, and in some cases defended theses, in themselves acceptable, in forms which the Catholic Church then and later has been unable to approve. But the decisive factor in his case seems to have been not unorthodoxy but incompetence in Church politics. He failed to build himself a solid base among the leaders of Catholic life in France, and *L'Avenir* came to an end as a result both of lack of money and of an unnecessary, ill-timed, and unsuccessful attempt to force the reigning Pope to issue a declaration in its favour. A declaration was in fact issued in the shape of the Encyclical *Mirari Vos* (1832): but it was a condemnation of Lamennais's positions, or at the very least a solemn warning against the dangers inherent in them. The effect on Lamennais was very like that on Robert Owen of the collapse of the Grand National Consolidated Trade Union, to which he had pinned his hopes. Owen ended cut off and discredited by the movement to which he had given so much of his life, but pursuing apocalyptic visions of his own. And so also Lamennais ended cut off from the Church, and pursuing the apocalyptic vision of a new society which

[1] There is a full account of his views in Vidler, *Prophecy and Papacy*, 1954, especially Chapter V.

he defined for himself, in his *Paroles d'un Croyant*, just after *L'Avenir* was driven under.

L'Avenir and the movements associated with it finished in 1832. But other movements went on, and by the 'forties the 'new' Catholics—not necessarily liberal, but certainly ultramontane—were becoming a noticeable force in French political and social life. They also acquired at this time the services of one of the greatest journalists of the century, Louis Veuillot. A Charity Organisation Society was founded and a Catholic Party was attempted. And the first recorded social pastoral in France (by the Bishop of Cambrai) dates from these years. When in 1848 a liberal and socialist revolution broke out, it was widely welcomed by Catholics. An important new Catholic liberal paper appeared, Fr. Lacordaire's 'Ere Nouvelle'. For a short time the Christian Socialist, Buchez, was President of the Republic. And one major achievement in particular, by the joint Catholic and liberal forces, seemed to symbolise their reconciliation; the Loi Falloux of 1850, which for the first time guaranteed freedom for all, including the Church, to open secondary schools. The grip of the State on university education remained, but was at least at certain points relaxed.

But the liberal strands in French Catholicism were not yet strong enough to take a severe strain. The revolution of 1848 ended in civil war, repression, and presently the dictatorship of Napoleon III. And in this reaction Christian socialism was practically wiped out, and Catholic liberalism was left as a few scattered though at times (as with Montalembert) glorious remnants on the outer edge of political life. Ultramontanism lived on, and so did a concern for charity and the relief of distress. But over a wide area it became apparent that French Catholics were as yet more preoccupied with saying 'no' to the exaggerated claims of the promoters of modern social techniques than with discovering how these techniques might best be adapted for Christianity's own purposes.

Belgian experience went in precisely the opposite direction to that of France. After a short hesitation Belgian Catholics took hold of modern social and particularly liberal techniques with both hands, and only at the end of this generation was the case for ultramontanism and the need at times to say 'no' to their liberal allies becoming a major concern for them. At the end of the Napoleonic Wars Belgium was left under Dutch rule. Belgian Catholics disliked being ruled by a largely Protestant government, which in the middle 'twenties did in fact take a number of measures against the Catholic schools and seminaries, interfered in the nomination of Bishops, and would happily have seen a more 'national' character in the Catholic Church. Though no great admirers of liberals and their works, they came after a few years to appreciate that the sort of State the liberals had in mind offered Catholics much more hope of securing their own ends than the 'traditional' system then existing in Holland, under which the State assumed the right to control the churches and the Protestant King largely controlled the State. Belgian liberals on their side had nothing against the King's attempts to control the Church, but came to see that an alliance with the Church was an ideal means of forcing through if not precisely a liberal constitution—in Holland as in most parts of Europe, including Britain, Liberals at that time were in no hurry to give equal voting rights to the working class—at any rate a constitution which would produce the right results for liberals. Quite apart from the special interests of Catholics and Liberals, few Belgians of any sort liked being ruled by Dutchmen of whatever constitution or creed. At the end of the eighteen-twenties, after some vigorous preliminary mud-flinging, Catholics and liberals linked up into a national liberation movement, on the basis of mutual tolerance and respect. The Catholics, led by their Bishops, placed themselves squarely on the ground of liberal democracy, and approved and indeed demanded the freeing of the Church from any entanglement with the State. The Liberals on their side recognised the right of the Church to manage its own affairs, open its own schools, and even (a little illogically, in view of the general nature of the settlement) to have its clergy paid from public funds. These principles were duly incorporated into the Belgian constitution after the Dutch were driven out in 1830.

The more Belgian Catholics saw of the results of this alliance with the liberals (commonly known as Unionism) and of the double policy of independence for the Church and democracy for the State, the more they liked it. And they did not hesitate to say so, even if, as happened more than once in Rome's illiberal days, they caused alarm and despondency at the highest level of the Church itself. Their Bishops were not indeed above discouraging the circulation of Papal documents, such as the encyclical *Mirari Vos* of 1832, which manifestly contradicted their own experience of the line to take in the matter of modern liberties. But even in Belgium honeymoons end. Though Catholics continued to accept the liberal techniques of government as embodied in the settlement of 1830, frictions over the purposes for which those techniques were to be used increased. By the middle of the eighteen-forties Unionism was wearing thin. The stage was prepared for a conflict in the next generation over, as elsewhere in Europe, the limits of the authority of the liberal State over Christians and their Church.

In *Holland* developments, at least on the Catholic side, lagged rather behind those in Belgium. In Holland also a marriage took place between Catholicism and liberalism. But around 1850 it was only recently consummated, and the honeymoon was still on. Dutch Catholics proper, as apart from Belgians forcibly incorporated in Holland, were at that time a minority not merely in the general population (they are that still) but also among practising Christians. Till the French Revolution and invasion they had been a disfavoured and even a persecuted minority. The assault on Belgian Catholicism in the new twin kingdom also of course touched their Dutch co-religionists. But it was not until the middle of the eighteen-twenties that these began, under the leadership notably of Le Sage Ten Broek, to pluck up enough courage to defend actively their rights in church and school. The revolt of the largely Catholic Belgians brought the Catholics of Holland under suspicion of being anti-national elements and also deprived them of a strong ally, and for some years Catholic activity in Holland died down. But through the 'forties it recovered again. Liberals, seeking political reform, found Catholics seeking emancipation their natural allies. As in Belgium, Catholics placed themselves on the ground of freedom and democracy. In 1848 the combined Catholic and liberal forces obtained a substantial advance towards political democracy. The control of the State over the Churches (Protestant as well as Catholic) was relaxed, and freedom to open schools was guaranteed. Five years later the revival of Catholicism in Holland was crowned by the re-establishment of the Dutch Hierarchy.

Dutch Protestants' evolution was not held up by the difficulties of being a suspect and disfavoured minority. By the time a liberal constitution was finally established in Holland, what might be called the 'growing edge' of Dutch Protestantism was beginning to show the characteristic two-pronged shape: a 'yes' to modern techniques and a 'no' to the exaggerated claims of liberal majorities. The great name here is that of Groen van Prinsterer, the father of the modern Dutch Protestant political and social movement. The political world to which Groen came had few clear-cut lines. In the eighteen-forties Conservatives and Liberals were beginning to sort themselves out in the Dutch Parliament, but the distinction was as yet very blurred. In the Protestant world outside Parliament, however, and outside the then very restricted electorate, new forces were at work. An Awakening occurred, largely under Swiss and French influence, in the 'twenties and 'thirties, and under its influence there took place a Separation in the national church. Groen himself did not follow the Separation, which threw up no great individual leaders. But he was deeply influenced by the movement of which it formed part. By the end of the 'forties he was working out the concepts which today form the basis of the oldest of the Dutch Protestant parties, the Anti-Revolutionaries. Groen did not intend to be anti-all revolutions. The freedoms sought by liberals were often admirable, and in certain circumstances a revolution might be the way to achieve them. But what Groen could not and would not accept was the affirmation, which seemed to him to be embodied in the history of the French Revolution, of the supremacy of the will of man and the State over the word and authority of God. He devoted his life to arousing his fellow-Protestants to insist upon the Word of God, as interpreted in their Church, as the independent and final authority in their public as well as their private life. The affirmation of the supreme authority of the Word of God had in his thinking, and has to this day in that of the Dutch Christian Democratic movements of which he is the ancestor, the same significance as the affirmation of Papal Infallibility and the Temporal Power has in that of Catholics. Here was the essential 'no', the limit of the claims of the State and for liberal or socialist philosophy: but also the essential guide and safeguard, thanks to which Christians could place themselves confidently on the ground of modern democratic freedom. The first Anti-Revolutionary members appeared in the Dutch Parliament by the 'fifties, largely in connection with the schools question; though they were not yet an organised party.

Germany presents the most clear-cut example in Europe of an attack on the freedom of the Christian churches based at one and the same time on 'traditional' grounds and on the principles of the rising liberal movement. Protestants and Catholics found themselves in the eighteen-twenties and 'thirties faced with a sharp challenge from the State, especially in Prussia. The Evangelical churches in Prussia were equipped by royal command with a compulsory Union under an administration strictly controlled by the State. To this was added in the 'twenties a brand new, compulsory liturgy—its vestments were personally designed by the monarch—introduced in ways not always ecclesiastical. A Silesian village of Old Lutherans was occupied by troops one Christmas to make sure that the Babe of Bethlehem should be greeted with the correct drill from the Potsdam Garrison Church: quite literally from there, as that was where the new liturgy was first tried out. But Prussia in those days was no Clochemerle, where such incidents as these could be expected to end in a laugh and a bottle of wine. There was genuine persecution of those who stood out against the new rules, and the whole business had an unpleasant look to many even of those churchmen whose views on the liturgy allowed them for the moment to keep on the right side of the law. Some pastors began to speak of 'Caesaro-Papism'. And meantime Catholics in their turn had met with similar troubles, especially in the formerly independent Catholic Rhineland, incorporated with Prussia since the war. The most dramatic incident occurred in 1837. The newly installed Archbishop of Cologne refused to accept the ruling of the State on a matter of internal Church discipline, the question of which engaged couples were and were not entitled to have their marriages celebrated according to the rites of the Church. He also ordered theological students not to attend the lectures of certain unorthodox teachers in the State faculty of theology at Bonn. He was promptly charged with seditious abuse of his office and imprisoned in a fortress. Shortly afterwards another Archbishop from East Germany was dealt with in the same way.

Incidents such as these did not spring merely from the desire of un-constitutional kings to consolidate their power, nor were they found only in Prussia. Bavarian liberals around 1820, for instance, and liberals in Baden a little later, showed themselves equally unwilling to respect the freedom of the Church. And on both flanks, the traditional and the liberal, these attitudes sprang from views by then common among graduates of German secondary schools and universities. Trained in the doctrines of Kant and Hegel, they had learnt that human reason is absolutely autonomous, and that the State is the highest and most com-plete reflection of God upon earth. And to this was added, in the case of those of them in the civil service, pride in their own administrative craft. As learned men and skilled administrators, senior German civil servants tended to be doubtful and indeed contemptuous of the value of any democratic representation. They were at one and the same time anti-liberal and anti-church, except so far as bishops and pastors might be a convenient tool in the Government's hands.

The reaction of the Protestant majority to these challenges was two-fold. On the one hand, the Evangelical churches and their members had no rooted objection either to a traditional, nationalist, unconstitutional monarchy, where that suited the times, or to the new liberal social tech-niques. Many of the King of Prussia's firmest supporters came from among true Protestants. Political and economic liberalism tended to attract the unorthodox, or actual unbelievers. But more and more orthodox Protestants, particularly in West Germany, found it to their taste as well. Within the churches themselves a 'theology of mediation' concerned itself with relating the Christian tradition to the ideas of the day; sometimes, it must be admitted, by throwing most of it overboard on the way.

But Germany too, like Holland, had its Protestant Awakening. This had little effect on the educated middle class and the civil service, but did reach the people and a small but powerful circle of royalty and aristocrats. Out of the ferment which it caused there arose at least two movements by which German Protestantism affirmed, though as yet only weakly, its independence of kings and parties. One, in the short run overwhelmingly the most important, was what might be called the search for the Church. The Prussian Union was imposed on the churches from outside. But the desire for a true union which would cut across the division of sects and territories and serve as the firm foundation and expression of the faith ran very deep. It came to be expressed above all through the external and internal mission movement, which grew and spread from the Napoleonic wars on. In 1848 revolution broke out, and the king of Prussia was driven for a time from his capital. The shock provided the occasion for a major step forward in the internal mission movement. The Protestant churches felt threatened from several sides; by supposedly atheistic democrats, by Catholics, who were showing a new strength, by liberals anxious to take away from the established churches their legal privileges, and by Protestant sects, looking forward to what might fairly be called a religious free-for-all once the liberals' aim was attained. Thanks to these fears, as well as to deeper motives, there came together in 1848 the first of an annual series of Evangelical Church Assemblies. Among the delegates was J. H. Wichern, a minister, and long a pioneer in Protestant social work. Amid the manoeuvring of church politicians Wichern found his particular interest in danger of being crowded out of the Assembly. Indeed, there was a chance that he would never reach the rostrum at all.

> When he did, on the afternoon of September 22 [1848], his impatience with the petty manoeuvring of the church parties, and his anxiety lest the cause of Protestant unity be lost, moved him to deliver an incomparable sermon on the neglected tasks and the future responsibilities of German Protestantism. It was the great moment of Wichern's life. It was also a great moment in Protestant history; the force of Wichern's remarks compared in dramatic intensity with that of the young Luther before the Diet of Worms. (Shanahan, *German Protestants Face the Social Question*, Notre Dame 1954, p. 208.)

Thanks to Wichern's intervention, the so-called Inland Mission was launched. Its idea was and is to express the spirit of the united Christian community through aid to the sick, the disabled, and all others in need, and thereby to reach new classes and open up new opportunities for the preaching of the Gospel. It built up in due course one of the most remarkable complexes of charitable institutions in the world. In itself the Inland Mission was an affair of Christian charity, not of Christian Democracy. But by its mere existence it served to underline not only the unity but the independent rights and responsibility of the Church, which are one of Christian Democracy's foundation stones. Nearly a century later, under the Hitler regime in the nineteen-thirties, institutions inspired by the Inland Mission were responsible for one of the most powerful Protestant acts of witness against the claims of the totalitarian state. Standing firm on the sanctity of human life, these institutions refused admission to gangs sent by the National-Socialist government to murder mental defectives; and in the end they were able to make their protest good.

To the Evangelical Church Assemblies, concerned largely with social problems, was added from 1852 a series of Eisenach Conferences, dealing with a whole variety of matters common to the various State churches.

Some German Protestant leaders—Ludwig von Gerlach, F. J. Stahl, Moritz von Bethmann-Hollweg—were feeling their way by the eighteen-fifties towards an independent, conservative rather than reactionary, affirmation of the Church's role in politics as well as in the field of charity and of preaching the Gospel; perhaps on lines like those of the Anti-

Revolutionaries in Holland, with whom some of them presently came in contact. A characteristically Anti-Revolutionary motto before its time ('We want, not a counter-revolution, but the contrary of the Revolution') was part of the title of a Berlin conservative weekly as early as 1831. By the eighteen-fifties some conservative leaders saw the danger to the Church of State dominance from the traditionalist side, that of the national and militarist monarchy, as well as from that of the Liberals. Some were beginning to feel that the Liberal freedoms, or at least some concession to them, might provide a good ground on which to defend Christian views and interests. There might be a Protestant party, still based squarely, like more traditional conservatism, on Scripture and the ancient Protestant confessions, and aiming to establish a Christian state, but operating on modern lines and within the framework of a more or less democratic constitution. An inter-confessional party might also serve; Gerlach himself later joined the predominantly Catholic Centre Party. But views like these were rare and often incoherent. Men such as Stahl, whose own ideas were clear, often lacked insight into the political and social needs of modern life. By and large, Protestant conservatives found it hard to free themselves from patterns of thought left over from an earlier age. They continued to believe that the King's authority should be final in Church as well as State, that citizenship should be unequal and voting rights weighted heavily in favour of property, and that Liberal freedoms, such as those of the Press, should be strictly rationed. They were often readier than Liberals, Protestant or otherwise, to take action on social problems. But they were likely to insist that these problems be dealt with paternally, by the upper classes, as was done on their own estates by the best of the great East German landlords, those most deeply touched by the Awakening. The defence of these estates and of the aristocracy supported by them became in fact, over the protests of Gerlach and his associates, the chief interest of the Prussian conservative movement and the main source of its money and political influence. The so-called 'Squires' Parliament' of 1848, a convention of the great eastern landowners at Stettin, has also been called the first national convention of the Prussian Conservative Party.

The Catholic reaction to the threat of liberalism and monarchy to the Church was more clear-cut. Catholic life in the old pre-revolutionary Rhineland states had been smug, comfortable, and without inspiration, and much of this spirit lasted over to damp down early initiatives. But attacks on the Church, first in the Napoleonic period, then by liberal governments in Bavaria and Baden or by the king and civil service in Prussia, shook them awake. The great name in this awakening, particularly on the journalistic side, was that of Görres. There was much confused discussion. 'Realists' such as Franz Baader tried to make a rather exact assessment of the problems and possibilities of the day. Baader was among

163

other things one of the first and most clear-sighted Catholic students of the social problems of modern industry. The 'romantic' school tried instead, often of necessity very tentatively, to define and work for an ideal Christian society. But by the end of the 'forties a pattern began to emerge from this discussion, and German Catholics were awake and ready to act.

Like their co-religionists in Holland or Belgium, they were quite prepared to place this action within the framework of liberalism and political democracy. The liberals' enemy (especially in Prussia) was their enemy, and the liberal freedoms seemed to offer excellent and reliable ground on which Catholics could organise to defend their own rights. When in 1848 revolution broke out, liberal constitutions were promised, and the movement for the economic and political union of Germany entered upon its final stage. Catholics as a body eagerly welcomed this. The first of the annual Catholic Assemblies was held that year. Electoral associations were founded, and a substantial and organised Catholic party appeared at the all-German and Prussian levels. And this party, at least in what is today Germany, was essentially 'realist'. In Austria and Bavaria the romantics played a bigger part. But in Germany, as a whole, under the leadership especially of Fr. Ketteler, later Bishop of Mainz, they were quickly pushed aside.

Bishop Ketteler is the outstanding figure of the whole German Catholic social movement. He began his career as an army officer and civil servant, but resigned from the civil service as a protest against the incidents of 1837 and entered the Church. After serving as curate and parish priest he was elected to the German National Assembly at Frankfurt in 1848, and made his mark there. At the end of the same year he preached in the cathedral at Mainz a series of sermons which have been described as 'a preliminary sketch of the whole doctrine of the Catholic social movement'. Then and thereafter, he marked off Christian social doctrine from liberalism by insisting on the social responsibilities of property, on the dangers of an 'atomised' society, and on the evil effects of unlimited competition, particularly in reducing labour to the status of a commodity. Against the rising Socialist movement he insisted on the need for a wide distribution of property and the dangers of exaggerated State control. Against both he claimed that the social question is primarily moral and religious, and that movements based on the light of nature alone are unlikely to have the wide and clear vision of their task needed to carry it through successfully. He attacked absolutism both in its traditional form and in that of the claim, by followers of the liberals, that the people is the ultimate court of appeal, so that the verdict of the majority can over-ride the Christian's conscience of the divine and natural law. He was impressed, like the British Christian Socialists of about the same period, and like the Socialist

Lassalle and the Protestant Professor Huber in Germany, with the idea of producers' co-operatives as a way of raising the status of the working class. In general, he supported strongly the idea of workers forming their own associations for self-help, and demanded a wide range of social reforms to be realised either in this way or through the State; higher wages, profit-sharing, reasonable working hours, weekly rest days, factory inspection, and special regulation of women's and children's work. He also pressed on his episcopal colleagues, and to some extent achieved, a system by which priests and laymen were set aside to specialise in the study of economic and social questions from the Christian angle, with periodic conferences to bring their work into focus.

Commentators regularly claim that Ketteler was not an original thinker. One can only say, considering the circumstances of his time, that they are judging by a high standard. It is however true that the outstanding feature of Ketteler's life was his ability not merely to formulate objectives but to set on foot action to bring them about. What the leaders of German Catholicism did under his guidance was to accept society, not merely as it traditionally was but as it was coming to be, and then to work to modify it from the inside out. Their 'realism' was shown notably in their social policies. Like the Protestants of the Inland Mission, they had a sense of responsibility for current social problems, and a feeling for the importance of these to new classes not yet won for Christianity. And at least some of them were beginning to look beyond mere charity. It is from this time that Ketteler's first appeals to solve the problems of the working class date; and about this time also, in 1851, Kolping was founding his Journeymen's Associations.

But in noting how German Catholics thus fitted themselves into the typical framework of modern society, with its special problems and techniques, it is essential to underline also how, as with Catholics elsewhere in Europe, this 'yes' was accompanied by an even stronger 'no'. The driving force behind the Catholic effort of these years, as is apparent in the way in which even a man such as Ketteler marked off his position against that of other schools of thought, was not so much a positive vision of the possibilities of a new, fast-moving, and changing social and economic order. It was much more the need to define and defend the rights of the Church against actual or threatening attacks from the upholders of State supremacy; that is the right of Christians to maintain and appeal to their own independent and final standard of judgment. It is significant that Catholic life in Germany, as in France, was marked in these years by ultramontanism. There was a great growth of loyalty to the Pope as Head of the Church, and as symbol of an authority and standards above and beyond the jurisdiction of the State.

Switzerland, finally, is the outstanding example in these years of the

165

paradox that it was very often in withstanding the advance of liberalism that Christians—in this case Catholics—rendered the liberal cause good service. The strength of liberalism had risen in Switzerland by the eighteen-forties to the point where major social and political reforms were clearly on the way. Many of these, such as the strengthening of the Federal government, the unification of the monetary and postal systems, and the abolition of internal customs barriers, were thoroughly justified. But the Catholic cantons feared that reform would give too much to the State, particularly in two directions. First, by unnecessarily interfering with the ancient rights of the cantons themselves. And, secondly, the Liberals, seeing their prevailing temper, and judging by incidents which had already occurred, seemed likely to interfere in the internal jurisdiction of the Church, especially the right to found and extend houses of the religious orders. In 1847 civil war broke out. The Catholic cantons half-seceded into a separate Regional Federation, and a liberal and Protestant army was promptly mobilised against them. They were quickly defeated. But their resistance had shown the victors the red light. Though the Liberals were now masters—they controlled the Swiss Parliament from that date till 1918—they made a moderate settlement which Catholics as well as Protestants have in fact found tolerable. A belated trophy of the liberal victory survives today in a clause of the Swiss constitution which bans the Jesuits, as an order, from Swiss soil. It does not, apparently, ban them as individuals, for many are today openly at work in Swiss parishes and schools.

Swiss Protestants for their part had no difficulty in accepting the liberal ideas of democracy and economic freedom. In the Civil War they and the liberals formed one force. But among Protestants also there began at this time a 'search for the Church' similar to that in Germany: and this, though without much immediate effect on political and social life, had significant long-term consequences. Youth organisations were built up, and the Inland Mission spread into Switzerland. In the 'fifties there were signs of a real break-through on German lines: the youth movements were consolidated nationally, Church charitable unions were founded, and the first meetings of a Churches' Conference were held.

CHAPTER XII

THE RISE OF CHRISTIAN DEMOCRACY, 1820–1880

CHURCH AND STATE (II)

IN TERMS of the characteristic pattern of growth of major social movement, 1820–50 was a typical 'first generation', concerned with the initial discovery of a problem, its discussion and definition, and the fixing of initial positions. By 1850 the problem of Church and State had been well ventilated and was posed in its modern form. 1850–80 was an equally typical 'second generation', when little new appeared on the stage, but the issues outlined by 1850 were fought through to a finish. The characteristic feature of the age, all over Western Europe, was a 'Kulturkampf', or Battle of Ideologies, in which Protestants of strict observance and ultra-montane Catholics, determined to defend the freedom of the Church and their right to obey God rather than men, fought it out with liberals, nationalists, and monarchists equally determined to assert the right of the State (that is of themselves) to override the Church. This battle ended everywhere in a settlement, or the germs of one, along the lines already indicated. On the one hand, Christians accepted modern social techniques and forms of organisation, though often only after a considerable battle among themselves: Belgian and German Catholics, for example, having at times a hard struggle to get their views accepted in more traditionally-minded circles in the Vatican. But on the other hand Christians also succeeded in enforcing their right to maintain, free from State control, the institutions buttressing their independent Christian standard of judgment of the purposes for which the new social techniques were to be used.

In *Italy* the liberal and nationalist movement rose in these years to its climax. Step by step the country was brought under one rule, Rome itself being occupied in 1870. This advance took place, understandably enough, under the sign of anti-clericalism. From the end of the 'forties onwards, beginning in the Kingdom of Piedmont, a series of laws asserted the supremacy of the State over the Church in such matters as education, marriage, and the authorisation or suppression of religious orders. In the eighteen-seventies the often moderate anti-clericals of the earlier days—men who were anti-clerical, but respectful towards Christianity—

began to be replaced by others whose views were more positively anti-Christian.

The Pope on his side, followed by the great majority of Catholic believers, held fast to the course marked out before 1850. He refused to place himself under Italian sovereignty, and when Rome was occupied retired as a voluntary prisoner to the Vatican. Following a formula launched in 1857 by Don Margotti ('neither electors nor elected'), he forbade Italian Catholics to take part in the political life of the new Kingdom. He encouraged them to form, not Christian Democratic movements in the modern sense, but what would today be called movements of Catholic Action, under the direct authority of the Hierarchy. Their attention was thus kept focused on that central core of the Church's teaching and action which is the special responsibility of the clergy, and whose supreme value and independence both Pius IX and his successor Leo XIII deemed it essential to emphasise. The Italian Catholic Youth Movement was founded in 1868, and the first national Catholic Congress was held in 1874. By 1881 there had grown out of this a permanent 'Opera dei Congressi', or Congress Movement, under the direct authority of the Pope. Through the Vatican Council of 1871, which defined the dogma of papal infallibility, Pius IX affirmed the Pope's own personal, final, and supreme authority as Head of the Church. And in 1864, in the Encyclical *Quanta Cura* and the attached 'Syllabus of Errors', he insisted once again that Christian revelation and the natural law provide absolute, ideal standards by which Christians must judge the performance of any social system, and on which no transaction or compromise is possible. It is significant of the intransigence and divisions of the times that these documents were so to speak thrown at the world with little attempt at clarity or at effective communication with either liberals or liberal-minded Catholics. The Syllabus took largely the form of a series of chapter headings or texts drawn from previous documents. It was left to other Catholics, more immediately affected by the misunderstanding and irritation to which its crabbed, obscure and negative presentation gave rise, to try to make its actual meaning clear.

Yet even in Italy this growing intransigence on all sides was merely the crisis before the fever subsided. By 1880 the foundation of reconciliation had been laid. The Pope, so long as the Papal States existed, continued on a course of social and economic reform at least as advanced as anything attempted by the Liberals. In the eighteen-eighties, under a new Pope, the liberal political and social techniques were accepted by the Church, though not yet as applied in the particular case of Italy. The Liberal rulers of the Kingdom of Italy, meantime, offered in a Law of Guarantees to ensure to the Pope what might be called diplomatic though not actually sovereign status; that is independence within the Kingdom in his activities as Head of the Church. The Pope did not feel able to settle for anything less than full sovereignty such as was eventually guaranteed to him in 1929 when the Vatican State was set up. But the essential idea from which this settlement would grow had been born.

In *France* the deep cleavage between Catholics on the one hand and liberals and socialists on the other, created by the events of 1848–50, continued right through the next generation. Catholic leaders continued to insist on the ultimate rights and independence of the Church, and their devotion to Rome and hatred of what they thought of as the Revolution steadily increased. Catholic politicians were overwhelmingly royalist, in an anti-democratic and anti-liberal sense. A little after this time, in 1889, when the country was celebrating the centenary of the Revolution, the leading Catholic social organisations replied by organising on a mass scale the 'Counter-Centenary of the Revolution'. The suppression of the Temporal Power of the Pope by the Italian-national movement was for most of the outstanding French Catholics a major issue. Under their pressure, French troops were sent to the Papal States and staved off their final incorporation with the rest of Italy for several years. As nationalists, Catholics tended to be markedly anti-semitic, a trait which was to come to the surface in an ugly way at the time of the Dreyfus affair in the eighteen-nineties. Catholic liberals remained rare and suspect. And though Catholics' understanding of the special problems of modern social life increased, it continued to issue chiefly in charity, administered by the upper classes within the existing social framework, rather than in forms of Christian Democracy which might call for the use of liberal techniques of political democracy or the socialist techniques of class organisation. Albert de Mun and the Marquis of La Tour du Pin founded in the 'seventies a Workmen's Club Movement which rapidly became important. At its peak at the end of the 'seventies it had probably about 30,000–35,000 members. A variety of friendly societies brought together 30,000–40,000 other workers, and about as many more were reached by a variety of apprentice hostels, evening classes, and so on. A large number of employers came to be associated with the Study Centre which sprang out of the Workmen's Club movement. A number of them experimented with welfare schemes, often extensive and advanced. But all these movements were highly paternalistic. It was French Catholic leaders who in this generation held more than any others to the conception of 'directing classes', with the mission and unchallengeable right to manage the country, and who turned firmly aside from the newer techniques of political and social democracy.

Liberals on their side replied with interest. To some extent, the anti-clericalism of this generation was directed against Catholicism, not against Christianity. The small minority of French Protestants succeeded much better than their Catholic brethren in adapting themselves to the techniques of modern society, and quite a number of them appeared at this point among the liberal leadership. But the essential change in liberalism in this generation was what one writer calls 'a complete renewal of the sources of irreligion'. Previous generations had asserted the rights of society and the State over the Church in the name of, often, a more or less spiritualist philosophy. Now however there appeared a generation trained notably in the school of Auguste Comte, and organised above all in the Masonic lodges. For these men only psychological, social, and technical—in short scientific—facts counted, and they were supremely contemptuous of their own elders as well as of the Church. Papal Infallibility or the Syllabus of Errors appeared to them not merely as misguided but as an insult to scientific intelligence. Christian belief was not merely wrong, though respectable; it was a pernicious and active obstacle to progress, to be swept as quickly and conveniently as might be into the dustbin.

In these views the working-class socialist movement, such as it then was, heartily joined. The Catholic workers' organisations, paternalistic as they were, naturally attracted the pious and weak rather than the militants. And genuine working-class militants' feelings were enflamed by the bloody repression of the Communist rising in Paris in 1871, with a slaughter, under the authority of a Parliament at that moment predominantly Catholic, far exceeding anything committed by the Communists themselves.

But even in France the factual conditions on which a settlement could be based had by 1880 appeared. The General Election of 1876 represented the final and, as quickly appeared, irrevocable victory of liberal democracy. The dream of a restored monarchy could still flutter aristocratic Catholic hearts. But henceforward it was in a democracy that they must live, and a few years later Leo XIII told them squarely to face this fact and adapt themselves to the new republican ways; which from the Church's point of view were as legitimate as any others. Meantime, limited though the impact of the Catholic social movement had been, it had at least cleared the ground of illusions. Paternalism, it had shown, was a dead end; it was not the way to mobilise intelligent and effective social forces. And the social movement had aroused enough interest and trained enough leaders to provide a base from which in the next generation a genuinely Christian Democratic movement could spring. Thus the ground was prepared for French Catholics to accept modern social techniques. And the very clarity and sharpness of the contrast now drawn between the new 'scientistic' liberalism and the independent, uncompromising Catholic upholders of the authority, infallibility, and independence of the Pope, prepared the way for the separation of Church and State in the next generation. In the eighteen-seventies the State in France still paid the Catholic clergy, allowed them official precedence, and had substantial control over their activities. There were liberals who were reluctant to see so powerful a force as the Church slip out of the State's control. There were also Catholics—indeed a large majority of them, until they had actually experienced the benefits of separation—who found it hard to tear their Church away from the fleshpots of civil service status. But by 1880 conditions had been created in which a clear-cut separation, giving the Church its full though unsalaried freedom, would come to seem the solution fairest to both sides.

In *Holland and Belgium* liberals continued through this generation to approve of freedom for the Church from the control of the State. Christians on their side became more confirmed than ever in their view of the value of political democracy and, generally, of the liberal freedoms as means of expressing and enforcing the Christian point of view in the modern world. Christians began, as in France, to move closer to the study of modern social problems, though as yet chiefly by way of charitable organisations. A Federation of Christian Charitable Organisations and Societies was established in Belgium in 1867. A few years later Klaas Kater, a bricklayer, founded the friendly and educational society '*Patrimonium*', the first of the great modern Protestant workers' organisations in Holland: though it is significant of its times that it also took care to have a substantial number of middle-class members.

But a clean-cut break developed between Christian and non-Christian over one major issue where the absolute claims of the liberal State clashed with the demands of Christians' conscience, namely the control of the schools. As in France, Italy, and also Germany, a new generation of 'scientistic' liberals arose, much less inclined than their predecessors to compromise on doubtful points. They did not propose to control the Churches, even when the Churches built schools. But neither did they see why the State should pay for Church teaching, whether in Church or in publicly provided schools. They stood for the 'neutral' school. Christians replied that there is no such thing as a neutral school. One of the chief religious freedoms is the right to transmit the Christian message from each generation to the next, and this requires ideally that every branch of education, in school and family alike, should be centred around Revelation and the Christian tradition and view of life. A 'neutral' school, at best, must fall far short of this ideal. And experience showed in practice, in areas with liberal school administrations, that so-called neutral schools were often in fact used to transmit views contrary to Christianity. It was, Christians argued, an abuse of liberal and democratic principles to use public funds solely for the support of schools which were in fact acceptable, whatever their 'neutral' title, only to the non-Christian section of the population.

Education accordingly became in this generation the dominant issue in

171

both Belgian and Dutch politics. Around this issue in Holland the Anti-Revolutionary Party, sketched out by Groen van Prinsterer, was consolidated in the 'seventies by the greatest leader whom Dutch Protestantism in modern times has produced, Dr. Abraham Kuyper. Kuyper is an outstanding example of the tendency, found throughout the history of the Protestant contribution to Christian Democracy, to combine the battle for the acceptance and good use by Protestants of modern social techniques with that for a better order within the Church, more firmly based on the ultimate foundation of Revelation. Himself a minister and a great theologian, Kuyper led for twenty years a struggle to re-shape the Hervormde Kerk on stricter Calvinist lines. This struggle led in 1886 to the separation from the Hervormde Kerk of the 'Complainants', led by Kuyper, and to the formation of the 'Gereformeerde' churches, which to this day supply the hard core of the Protestant political and social movement. Meantime however Kuyper went into politics, founded in 1872 *De Standaard*, still the chief Anti-Revolutionary paper, and six years later reorganised and consolidated the Anti-Revolutionary group in parliament. Dutch Catholics on their side went through a similar evolution. By the end of the eighteen-fifties they too had come into conflict with the liberals over the schools question. Through the 'sixties and 'seventies this conflict was aggravated by the usual causes, including liberal irritation at the Church's uncompromising statements in the Syllabus and *Quanta Cura*, and over the affirmation of the Pope's infallibility. From the beginning of the 'seventies regional electoral unions were being founded, and in the 'eighties these were consolidated into a party under the leadership of a priest, Dr. Schaepman. Schaepman and Kuyper moved steadily towards an alliance. In 1887–9 Catholics and Protestants together captured a Parliamentary majority, and used it to establish the principle of State support—though not yet of equal support—for the Christian as well as the Government schools.

In *Belgium* friction between Catholics and liberals over the schools question and related issues, including the teaching at State universities and the position of religious orders, grew steadily through the 'fifties and 'sixties. 'A corpse lies across the world barring the road to progress', announced one leader of the new, scientistic, liberals. 'Let us call it squarely by its name—Catholicism.' In 1875 the local liberal associations were linked up into a unitary party. These moves did not prevent Catholics from continuing their support for the liberal constitution. They enthusiastically applauded a statement by Montalembert, at a congress at Liége in 1863, in favour of placing or rather maintaining themselves on the ground of democracy. Cardinal Sterckx, Primate of Belgium, expressly defended this view even at the cost of alarm and despondency in the Vatican, where—it was the year before the publication of the *Syllabus*—

the spirit at that time was intransigent. But against the claims of the liberal party in religious and educational matters the Belgian Catholics proceeded to rally their forces. In 1869 was established a national Federation of Catholic Circles and Conservative Associations, led by Charles Woeste. In 1879 a liberal government tried to create a 'neutral' school system throughout the country, to which alone State support would be given. Catholics boycotted the new schools, and, where formerly Catholic municipal schools were taken over by the State, rapidly created a network of their own. Four years later the reorganised Catholic Party was returned to power with a large majority, and proceeded, as in Holland, to establish the right of the Christian schools to public support.

Switzerland in this generation was settling down after the civil war of 1847. But here also the new, more militant, liberalism made itself felt, and a new though short-lived 'battle of ideologies' broke out in the 'seventies.

It was however in *Germany* that the battle of ideologies took place which has gone down to history above all others, *the* Kulturkampf. This was the generation when Germany was finally united. It was also at this time that Prussia, under Bismarck's leadership, decisively defeated Austria in the battle—the war of 1866—for the leadership of Germany, and that Denmark and France were invaded and Schleswig-Holstein and Alsace-Lorraine annexed. Under the impact of these events national pride and enthusiasm increased and liberals and monarchists drew closer together. A large National Liberal Party came into existence, and by 1874 had acquired 155 out of the 397 seats in the Reichstag. It was on this party above all that Bismarck chose to base his authority in parliament. There also emerged in 1867 a Free Conservative Party, which has been called by one author 'the party of Bismarck *sans phrase*'. So far as the religious situation was concerned, the ideas of the Liberals and of Bismarck and his immediate followers ran together. Neither group was prepared to tolerate a Church which claimed an authority above and beyond that of the State.

The Protestant churches, in spite of their recent and continuing progress towards a new, independent, church order, did not at this stage take up this challenge on any great scale. They were less directly attacked than the Catholic Church, and among Protestants in politics only a few of the old school, such as Gerlach, felt any major principle to be at stake. The firmness even of these Old Conservatives was liable to crumble when challenged in the name of the national interests, real or supposed. Their attitude was often that so unforgettably pictured, among Prussian officers of the old school around the time of the first World War, in Arnold Zweig's *Battle for Sergeant Grischa*. In the social field also Protestant thought had not yet penetrated deep enough to make possible an effective criticism of, for instance, Bismarck's schemes of State-sponsored social reform. Some Protestant social workers and investigators were becoming more sophisticated. Wichern, for instance, sponsored in 1871 what came to be known as the 'October Assembly' at Berlin. Before an audience of some 1,300 church leaders, politicians, civil servants, and professors—labour leaders were characteristically not invited—he insisted on the need to meet the challenge of socialism. For more detailed practical recommendations he passed the word to the economist Adolf Wagner, who put forward a far-reaching programme on wages, hours, social insurance, education, housing, and progressive taxation. It was to be carried out not only by the State, employers, and landowners, but also through trade unions and co-operatives. But Wagner was in advance of his time, and it seems that for the most part his speech went over its hearers' heads. The typical Protestant approach to social reform continued to be by way of moralising, of charity, and of paternal concern by the great landowners, or by employers such as Baron Stumm in the Saar, for their dependents; though more and more reliance was also coming to be placed, always on the general principle of reform from above without democratic participation, on regulation by the State.

But it was against the Catholic Church that Bismarck and his allies directed their heaviest fire. The name 'Kulturkampf' seems to have figured first in a Liberal manifesto in 1873. But by that time the battle was already well under way, chiefly in Prussia, Baden, and Hesse. Diplomatic relations with the Vatican were broken off, and from 1871 through to 1874 a succession of laws and decrees tried to limit Church freedom. State censorship was imposed on sermons and the publication from the pulpit of church documents. State supervision of the schools was stiffened: it was notably on this issue that the Protestant Old Conservatives went into opposition against Bismarck. The Jesuits were expelled from Germany. An attempt was made to establish State control over seminaries, the appointment of clergy, and the internal legislation and discipline of the Church. To a number of these laws the Catholic clergy simply refused obedience, and many of them, including bishops, were declared by the State removed from office. Many were either imprisoned or forced to leave the country. The aim was frankly and openly to nationalise the Church and establish the supremacy over it of the State. A small group of Old Catholics was in fact induced to break off into schism. But they had little following. In the face of Bismarck's challenge not only the Catholic clergy but also the laity stood firmly together. A Centre Party was founded, intended originally to be inter-confessional, but in fact almost wholly Catholic. From 1874 onwards it held in the Reichstag a solid block of 90–100 seats, of which no swing of the electoral pendulum could deprive it.

Here then was the classic case of a Kulturkampf. But Germany also provided the classic example of how such a battle could end, if not in reconciliation, at any rate in an acceptable settlement. The Centre Party was in a strong strategic position. The National Liberal Party crumbled away from the end of the eighties. The Centre Party maintained its strength, and, when it took its stand on civil rights, could expect at least incidental support not only from a number of genuine Liberals and Old Conservatives but also from the small but rapidly growing number of Socialists, against whom Bismarck's legislation had been directed even more strongly than against the Catholics. By the middle of the 'eighties the political situation was such that Bismarck could no longer afford to defy the Centre. The Centre Party itself, meantime, was in no way opposed to a reconciliation. It was neither anti-liberal nor anti-national. A great Catholic leader such as Bishop Ketteler might, and did, condemn the way in which German unity had been brought about and Prussian dominance established. But he was nationalist enough to appreciate both the greatness of the achievement and the possibilities which it opened up. As for liberalism, the Kulturkampf finally and decisively convinced Catholic politicians in Germany—not, it is worth noting, in Austria, which was outside this particular battle—that the liberal freedoms are essential for the defence of Christian interests. It also helped them in their turn to convince Church officials that a liberal and democratic Christian party can be effective only if—working as it is in a field which is the proper responsibility of the laity—it is independent of the clergy. The clergy may indeed join such a party. But they do so as ordinary citizens, within the general framework of the Church's teaching, and not as representatives of the authority by which that teaching is delivered. The principle was not then everywhere understood in clerical circles, and notably not in the Vatican. The Centre Party was at that time essential to the Church in Germany: the Church authorities could not afford to disown or break with it: and Windthorst, its leader, used this strong tactical position to force them to recognise the Party's independence.[1]

Catholics' position in Germany was all the stronger because by this time, following Bishop Ketteler's lead, their movement was developing on the social as well as the political side. It is from this time that the modern Christian workers' movement in Germany dates. The idea of producers' co-operatives was, as has been said, very much in the air, in socialist as well as Christian circles, but remained at the theoretical level. More important was the foundation of a number of actual Christian workers' unions and associations, though these had for the time being a somewhat chequered history. Some small and rather ineffective Catholic workers' societies, largely social and religious, were founded in south Germany from the end of the 'forties. These largely went under, and many workers were caught up in the 'Piusvereine', inter-class associations which

[1] For a further account of this very important and significant episode see below, Chapter XVII, pp. 312–13.

played an important part in getting going the Catholic political movement. The ineffectiveness of these first workers' committees did not, it is ture, stop action on behalf of the working class. The Centre Party showed itself receptive from the start to ideas of social legislation. The clergy were often also sympathetic. But the need was felt more and more for specialised class organisations to define and defend workers' interests, and gradually the movement for these was resumed. From the early 'sixties Catholic miners' associations were being founded in the Ruhr. A little later, towards 1870, there arose 'Christian Social Unions', this time inter-confessional. They met with a good deal of suspicion from both Catholics and Protestants, and had much difficulty in securing good leadership. They found it largely among the clergy, since the Christian workers' movement at that time, as elsewhere in Europe, was not ripe enough to throw up many good leaders of its own. Nevertheless, the Unions attracted some 30,000 members in the Ruhr, and some thousands more elsewhere. They led one or two strikes, and above all succeeded in drafting, and (through the Centre Party) getting discussed in Parliament, a useful programme of social reform on the lines proposed by Ketteler: wages to equal the true value of labour: shorter hours: the exclusion of children and married women from certain types of work: separate workplaces for men and women: Sunday rest: housing programmes: and social insurance and the development of friendly societies. During the Kulturkampf these Unions lost their Protestant members and, like the *Piusvereine* before them, concentrated on the political struggle. Little of their original social and inter-confessional character remained. They had however sowed a seed from which, as will appear, a vast movement was to grow from the 'eighties on. And meantime the organisation of other classes was also beginning. Catholic farmers' unions began to be founded from the early 'seventies, and from this time also dates the Catholic Commercial Union, for principals and employees in the distributive trades.

Thanks to all these developments, the stage was set by the 'eighties for a settlement, or at least for non-belligerent co-existence, between German Catholics on the one hand and the liberal, monarchist, and in many cases nationalist forces on the other, with the Catholics collaborating in the liberal and national culture and the liberals and nationalists admitting the freedom of the Church. Between 1882 and 1887 a series of laws and administrative measures, including the restoration of diplomatic relations with the Vatican, did in fact liquidate the more serious of the attacks of the eighteen-seventies on church freedom. Peace was restored, though even now little love was lost between the opposing parties.

CHAPTER XIII

THE RISE OF CHRISTIAN DEMOCRACY, 1880–1950

INTRODUCTION

THE two generations from 1820 to 1880 were, then, a pilot stage, in which the essential principles of the 'yes' and the 'no' to the ideas characteristic of modern society were established, but the full consequences of this for the construction of Christian Action and Christian Democratic movements had not yet been seen. By 1880 or 1890 there were working patterns of political Christian Democracy in Belgium or Holland or Germany or Switzerland, and in some countries at least the beginnings of a Christian social movement. Christians of all denominations, all over Europe, had found little difficulty in adapting themselves to liberalism in the economic field. But the social movement was as yet feeble; there were countries, notably Italy and France, where Christianity and political liberalism were still at a deadlock, whatever solutions might be dawning on the horizon; and large bodies of Christians, and especially of Protestants, had as yet scarcely been touched by any consciously Christian political, economic, or social movement at all. It was the task of the next two generations to draw together and complete these untidy beginnings, and to build on them by the end of the second World War a movement both comprehensive and reasonably well integrated. Three main developments took place. Protestants in Germany, Switzerland, and France entered the stream, in which their co-religionists in Holland already had an important place. The Christian Democratic social movements, and above all the workers' movements, grew to their full stature and made their weight felt in the political movements. The political movements were completed both by acquiring a broader and firmer base in the social movements and through an increase in their own strength and numbers. In France and Italy, in particular, full-scale Christian Democratic parties now emerged.

These developments took place according to the usual rhythm. There was first an uncertain, experimental generation from the eighteen-eighties to the First World War, during which the new lines of advance were laid out. It was, like that from 1820 to 1850, a time of storm and stress within the Christian movements themselves, a time when interests clashed, misunderstandings were the order of the day, and anathemas rained down. The boundary between dynamic and successful initiative and condemnation and failure often proved, as then, to be narrow. Lamennais in the eighteen-thirties provoked his own condemnation by Rome, and left the Church, while his colleagues Lacordaire and Montalembert continued as leaders of French Catholicism, and the liberal Catholics of Belgium stood out among the Church's most authorised defenders. Seventy years later Fr. Romolo Murri brought about his own excommunication, while his colleague Luigi Sturzo went on to become the elder statesman of the whole Italian Christian Democratic movement, and social doctrines as dynamic as his were the basis, uncondemned, of the Christian workers' movements of Belgium or Germany. The debates over the value and excesses of Catholic liberalism in the earlier period were matched by those over modernism or the 'trade union question' in the later; and equally violent disputes, as will be seen, though in a different context of Church discipline, occurred over the aims and methods of the Protestant social movement. These disputes and experiments gradually settled down, and there emerged broadly agreed lines of action. The story of Christian Democracy in the generation from the First to the Second World War is not so much of the discovery of new policies as of how the policies now generally agreed were given practical effect.

Developments in the generations from 1820 to 1880 pointed forward to something beyond themselves; the organisation of a comprehensive Christian Democratic movement on lines which by 1880 could be guessed. There is reason to think that developments from the eighteen-eighties to the nineteen-forties point forward in their turn to a major reorganisation of at least part of the Christian Democratic movement on lines which developments since the Second World War have begun to make clear, and which may incidentally bring the problems and practice of Continental Christian Democracy much closer to those of the Anglo-Saxon countries than in the past.

CHAPTER XIV

THE RISE OF CHRISTIAN DEMOCRACY, 1880–1950

THE PROTESTANTS ENTER THE STREAM

EXCEPT in Holland, the beginnings of Christian Democracy in 1820–1880 were essentially Catholic. Protestants no doubt adjusted themselves to the democratic tendencies of the times. But not many of them had yet seriously considered how far a Christian needs not merely to accept the techniques current in modern life but to mark off the limits of his acceptance, having regard not only to these techniques but to the beliefs underlying them. Now, however, from 1880 to the nineteen-forties, they too begin in one country after another to follow in the track of the Catholics and of their own co-religionists in Holland. This is true above all of Germany, the nation with the largest Protestant population of those here examined.

GERMANY

The conversion of German Protestants to independent political and social action occurred in three main ways. There arose about 1880, though at first on only a very small scale, a demand for a Protestant political movement, both as an affirmation of the Christian position over against laicist nationalists, liberals, and socialists or communists and as a means of keeping the balance between Protestants and Catholics within the Christian political movement itself. There also arose from about the same date an Evangelical workers' movement, partly independent and partly bound up with the inter-denominational Christian trade unions. Thirdly, and also over the same period, the Protestant churches' search for unity and independence achieved a large measure of success. The Churches were freed from State control, and for their own part came to realise that this freedom must be positively affirmed and used.

The first great name in the Protestant political movement in Germany is that of Adolf Stöcker. After service as an army chaplain, Stöcker was appointed in 1874 as Chaplain to the Emperor at Berlin. This brought him into contact with high politics, and made him acutely aware of the dangers of a situation in which political leaders, whether agnostic or atheist like

179

many liberals or Protestant like many nationalists, recognised no standards of conduct beyond their own judgment, The chief driving force of his activity became the idea that the Church should be free to proclaim the basic principles of political and social life. This was also a point of alliance between him and the small group of Conservatives of the school of Gerlach and Stahl who had survived the nationalist intoxication of 1871. But Stöcker by no means shared the Conservatives' social views. He was a great worker for the Inland Mission. This brought him into close contact with the working class in Berlin, which at that time was rapidly being lost to the Church. A bare quarter of Protestant marriages in Berlin took place in church, and between a quarter and half the children born were not baptised. One factor in this was the Kulturkampf, with the general denigration of the churches which it involved. But another, which Stöcker soon realised to be much more important, was that the Evangelical churches were offering no guidance on the social and political problems which concerned the workers. The workers' guidance on these matters came increasingly from the Social Democrats, who were outspokenly and often offensively anti-religious. If they were to be retained or won for the Church, the Church must learn to speak to them on the things immediately concerning them and in language they could understand.

In 1878 Stöcker took the first steps to found a Christian Social political movement, with a programme of social reform through State intervention. The movement won little support, and that largely middle-class. Stöcker therefore turned to a new line of attack by penetrating the Christian wing of the existing Conservative party. He was elected to the Prussian House of Representatives as a Conservative for a West German constituency in 1879 and to the Reichstag in 1881. There was a time in the early eighteen-nineties, just after the fall of Bismarck, when the leadership of the Conservatives seemed about to drop into his hands. But a reaction set in over the next few years. Big business and, above all, big farming interests captured the party, and in 1896 Stöcker was forced to leave it. He had already lost his Reichstag seat in 1893, and the Emperor (William II) had in 1890 dismissed him from his post as Chaplain. On his parting with the Conservatives, the Emperor telegraphed jubilantly to Baron von Stumm, the then leading industrialist of the Ruhr:

> Stöcker has ended as I said years ago that he would. Political clergy are a monstrosity; whoever is Christian is Social as well. 'Christian-Social' is foolishness. It leads to exaggeration of one's own importance and to intolerance, both directly opposed to Christianity. The reverend clergy should look after the souls of their parishioners and practise charity, but keep clear of politics, which is none of their business. William, R.I.

But Stöcker had not ended. His story joins hands here with that of the Evangelical workers' movement, whose beginnings date from about the same time as those of Stöcker's political movement. From the beginning of the 'eighties workers' unions were springing up under the leadership of Pastor Weber of München-Gladbach, who in many ways saw eye to eye with Stöcker. He too, in his own field, saw very clearly the case for affirming an independent and specifically Christian and Protestant point of view. The rise of this movement took much the same course as that of the Catholic workers' movement, and will be dealt with along with it below. Note here simply that it was coming up fast in the eighteen-nineties and especially after 1900, and was particularly strong in the Protestant districts in the Rhineland and Westphalia. A contributing factor was that a number of these districts had substantial Reformed as well as Lutheran communities, and some ties with the Reformed churches of Holland. Reinhard Mumm, for example, the Elias on whom Stöcker's mantle eventually fell, was a Reformed minister who had himself studied for some time in Holland. It was in this West German area that Stöcker had in any case won his Reichstag and Landtag seats as a Conservative. Now in 1898, in a dramatic battle—his majority was 27 in a poll of 24,000—he won back his Reichstag seat at Siegen on a purely Christian Social platform. He was able to hold and improve his position down to his death in 1909, and Mumm held the seat again from 1912. In 1903 and 1907 two other seats were won for the party in the West, that in 1907 going to Franz Behrens, the first Protestant trade union leader to enter the Reichstag. From then onward till 1933, the Christian Social tendency was always represented there.

By the time of the First World War an independent social-Protestant political movement was thus established, if only on a very small scale, and was flanked by a powerful Protestant workers' movement with some hundreds of thousands of members. But the workers' movement by definition could not, and the Christian Social political movement did not, catch the imagination of the Protestant community as a whole. The political movement's trumpet, in particular, gave forth a very uncertain sound. Its members found it hard to shake themselves free of the State-worship, nationalism, and even racialism then common in German Protestant circles. Stöcker himself, in the eighteen-seventies and eighteen-eighties, had seen much more clearly the need for State intervention than for workers' self-help. He hoped to see the Church attain its freedom not through an affirmation of independence by clergy and laity, but rather through inducing the Emperor, as Head of the Church, to in some way detach himself from the State headed by statesmen of the mind of Bismarck. He and many of his followers were strong, even exaggerated, nationalists and monarchists. He was an anti-semite, not indeed on religious or racial grounds, but because he saw the assimilated Jews of Berlin as conspicuous representatives of the society without roots or absolute standards, concerned only with power and wealth, which seemed to him the menace to Germany and the world: a view very like that taken at the same time by many Catholic nationalists in France. The distinction was too subtle for some of his followers, who took up anti-semitism in its cruder sense. This infected some sections even of the trade union movement, notably among the Protestant clerical workers, who founded their first union at Hamburg in 1893. And not all Stöcker's followers had his clear vision of the essential, independent, role of the Christian in politics or of the consequence to be drawn from it. A large part of the Christian Social movement at the end of the 'nineties followed his disciple Friedrich Naumann along a path which led most of them to the liberal or socialist parties, and some eventually to national socialism. A small but not altogether insignificant 'religious socialist' movement drained off into the socialist party or unions at any rate some potential Christian Social recruits. In 1918–20 much still remained to be done to clear up both the ideas of the Christian Social political movement itself and the attitude towards it of Protestants as a whole.

Very much the same might be said of the position of the evangelical churches themselves in political and social life. The efforts of Stöcker and his then Conservative allies to win more freedom for the Churches in the eighteen-eighties failed in the face of strong opposition from Bismarck, who was prepared to increase State support for them but under no conditions to relax the State's grip. As a Conservative member of the Reichstag said of the increased State grants, 'It looks rather like when the man of the house raises the maid's wages.' The most that was achieved was to establish in 1890 an Evangelical Social Congress, a useful sounding board for independent Church opinion on social matters. A generation later freedom did finally come to the Churches through the collapse of the monarchy in 1918 and the separation under the Weimar Republic of Church and State. But it caught the Churches unprepared, and for some years no very clear lines of policy emerged.

In the thirty years from 1918 till just after the Second World War development proceeded along divergent lines. The workers' movement, hitherto the solidest prop of the movement for independent Protestant action, was suppressed in the Nazi period and was not revived in the same form when it ended. Its trade union section was absorbed into the united German trade union movement, and the remainder of it went through a process of re-thinking and reorganisation, to be considered again below, which for the time being reduced it to insignificance. But with the Churches and the political movement—and it is they that reflect the views of German Protestants as a whole—the story was very different.

First, in these years the Evangelical churches at last acquired a clear sense of their independent mission, and their duty to guide and criticise the State. They were moving that way already by 1918, when the theology of Karl Barth began to be heard of. But the change was completed only during the Nazi period, particularly after the Synod of Barmen from which the Confessing Church was born. After Hitler there could be no further further question that the Protestant Churches and individual Christians must, as such, be prepared to define their own political line and, where necessary, to oppose an emphatic 'no' to the assumptions and practice of governments or parties. Were individual Protestants to do this, however, as Naumann had insisted, as members of any party they might choose to join; or was it advisable, as Stöcker had felt, for Christians to join together to affirm their position in independence? Many still took the first view, and do to this day. But the general trend was towards the second view, even before 1933. In order to take advantage of certain provisions of the new electoral law of the Weimar Republic, the Christian Social parliamentarians joined forces after 1918 with the German National Party, the successor of the Conservatives. Though linked to this party by their nationalism, they presently found their position intolerable, for the same reasons as Stöcker had done in his time. The party was captured by big business and agrarian interests. The Christian Social wing left it, and, after various negotiations, a new independent party known as the Christian Social People's Service emerged in 1929. At the Reichstag elections of 1930 it won 14 seats, and its influence was growing rapidly, especially in West and South Germany. Many contacts were made with Catholic politicians of the Centre Party. The Hitler dictatorship cut this development short. But the current of ideas which it represented spread underground. When in 1945 party formation once more became possible, most of the Protestants of West and South Germany proved to be convinced that the time had come for political action under the Christian label. The Evangelical Churches on the whole encouraged this trend, and also declared in favour of united action between Protestants and Catholics. There was hesitation in the North and East, the areas where the Christian Social message had always had most difficulty in penetrating and where Christian belief and practice were weakest. But substantial support was secured even from there. Today, as will be shown, the degree of support for the C.D.U. is not much less among church-going Protestants in West Germany as a whole than it is among Catholics.

SWITZERLAND

The swing towards independent political action by Protestants has been more complete in Germany than in either Switzerland or France, but the direction of movement in these two countries has been the same. In Switzerland the start before the First World War was slow. Both Stöcker and Naumann came there in the 'eighties and 'nineties and attracted a good deal of attention. But the immediate practical results were small. A few rather weak study circles were founded largely for the clergy, together with some workers' associations. They got little support from the Protestant churches as such. The churches had at that time no central organisation beyond a consultative conference, and had for generations been inactive in the political and social (apart from the charitable) field. There was no question of an independent Protestant political movement, and only the barest beginnings of a trade union. The new workers' associations recommended their members to join the socialist unions, in order not to split the working class, and opposed their joining the Catholic unions, which at this time hoped to become inter-confessional. This line was for the time being all the more convincing because the 'religious socialists' led by the Protestant theologian Ragaz were proportionally more important in Switzerland than in Germany, and for a time won a substantial influence in the socialist movement. Middle-class Protestants continued to vote happily for the Liberals.

However, substantial changes were on the way. In 1907 a tiny handful of anti-socialist Protestant workers around Zurich—two or three hundred —founded an independent mutual aid fund (SESUK), notably to save them from depending in strikes on the funds of the Socialist unions which they were unwilling to join. At the end of the First World War a more substantial number of Evangelical workers began to find the class war, anti-national, and anti-religious attitude of the Social Democrats more than they could stand. The 'religious Socialists' lost a good deal of their credit with the socialist movement through failing to fall in with revolutionary plans, and the lesson was not lost on other Protestants. In 1919 the SESUK was expanded into a new independent trade union, the S.V.E.A., which has become over the years a substantial and still growing force. The Methodist Church backed it from the start, as it had the SESUK. Other Protestant churches were at first sceptical, but were won round, especially through the series of Evangelical Social Congresses which the S.V.E.A. organised from 1922 on. After the first such conference a group of pastors, whose number steadily grew, established an Inter-Church committee in support of the union. A small Evangelical People's Party was also founded about this time, and looked at first as if it might grow into a really substantial body; for the S.V.E.A. saw in it the political counterpart of their own movement, and moved towards an alliance. The E.P.P., unfortunately for itself, did not feel able to meet the S.V.E.A. fully: it remained somewhat Right-wing, and the worker wing which might have given it nation-wide influence never materialised. But the existence of even a small Evangelical party was a portent. The Protestant churches also were on the move. In 1930 they decided to convert their annual conference into a Federation with governing powers. In 1932 the

Federation established a Social Commission, on which duly appeared among others the General Secretary of the S.V.E.A. Through the 'twenties and 'thirties, and especially after the Stockholm Conference of the Life and Work Movement in 1925, the Federation steadily increased its interest in political and social affairs, though it has never gone so far as to impose, or suggest, a general political or social orientation for Church members.

FRANCE

French Protestants are in a basically different position from either German or Swiss, since they are a tiny minority—perhaps half a million practising Protestants in a population of over forty million—who can scarcely achieve much through political or social action on their own. During the nineteenth century they found it on the whole expedient to go along with successive French regimes, taking such advantages as came their way, reacting instinctively when attacked, but having no clear, concerted, or conscious general line. Shortly before the First World War, however, they too—or at any rate their younger generation—began to feel that passivity was no longer enough, and threw up a Christian-social and a nationalist movement. Both were cut short by the war, but the debate was resumed afterwards. There were Christian socialists (like André Philip), Christian monarchists, Christian authoritarians. A large body of opinion, expressed for instance through Denis de Rougemont, insisted that it is the duty of Christians to engage in the search for political solutions, though also that specifically 'Christian' solutions do not exist. The Second World War and the Nazi occupation brought a new clarification, for it forced French—like German—Protestants to see that, whether or not any regimes are specifically Christian, some are specifically un-Christian, and must be condemned and if necessary actively resisted.

> The Church must condemn publicly any State which claims to be the sole warrant for its own actions, and in particular the Nazi regime. (Quoted in Leonard, *Le Protestant Français*, 1953, p. 234.)

On forms of action French Protestants remain today as divided as before the war. Some are in the M.R.P. and C.F.T.C., others are socialist or liberal or conservative or nationalist. But they agree with their Dutch, German, and Swiss brethren that, first, the fact of being a Christian implies a duty to accept a political and social engagement, to search for solutions to political and social problems. And, secondly, while it is permissible in the course of this search to say 'yes' to a wide variety of the techniques and approaches put forward by different parties and groups, the fact of being a Christian also implies in specified circumstances the duty to say 'no', and if necessary to back this 'no' with organised, concerted action. In that sense and to that extent they too have entered the main stream of the Continental Christian social movement.

185

CHAPTER XV

THE RISE OF CHRISTIAN DEMOCRACY,
1880–1950

THE RISE OF THE WORKERS' MOVEMENTS (I)

THE most conspicuous change in the Christian Democratic movement as a whole since 1880 has been the rise of the Christian Democratic political parties to a new power and authority. The most fundamental may well turn out to have been the incorporation into the movement of large new Protestant forces. But neither of these developments would have had anything approaching its actual importance if the political parties had not been reinforced by the rise alongside them of a range of social movements. This is above all true of the workers' movements, which grew first and fastest, and in these two generations changed the whole atmosphere of Christian Democratic thought and action. The rise of the workers' youth movement, and especially of the Y.C.W., has been at least as important as that of the adult movements, and very possibly more so. This chapter will however deal only with the adult movements, leaving the youth movements, whether of the working or of other classes, to be dealt with in the chapter which follows.

THE BEGINNINGS

The years around 1880 are the watershed from which the modern Christian workers' movement begins. There were organisations for Christian workers before that date. But they tended, as has been seen, either to be or to become patronages, under middle and upper class control, directed to keeping the workers out of socialist mischief or to mobilising them for general political ends. The workmen's club movement of de Mun and La Tour du Pin never claimed to be anything more than a protective measure provided by the paternal solicitude of, to quote an early statement of the then very upper-class French Association of Catholic Youth, 'what is known as the ruling class'. The Catholic or mixed workers' associations in Germany tended to become political centres for the general purposes of the Kulturkampf.

But by 1880 this was ending. There was still much middle and upper class initiative in the workers' movement, and often the desire to protect

186

the workers or use them against Socialism. But more and more the movement came to be led by workers themselves in what they saw as the interests of their own class, though within the general framework of the Christian-social movement as a whole. And middle- and upper-class intervention came more and more to be a case of priming the pump for workers' own activity. These were the years when the working class as a whole, not merely its Christian section, was awakening all over Europe and becoming conscious of its strength. And this reflected itself among the Christian workers as elsewhere.

Among German Catholics, the beginning of the new trend dates from 1879, when a Workers' Welfare Association ('Arbeiterwohl') was founded through the initiative of Fr. Hitze. This was a middle and upper class group, whose committee in 1881 included six business men (one of them Chairman), a civil servant, a professor, and a priest (Hitze, as secretary). It went busily about founding workers' associations, intended in the first place as social clubs, friendly societies, and educational centres. The difficulty in equipping these with an authentic working-class leadership was recorded above.[1] But by the eighteen-nineties the ice was breaking. In 1893 Hitze could proclaim that the day of paternalism was over, and set about the foundation alongside the associations of trade union branches. August Brust, a miner, brought into existence an inter-denominational mineworkers' union. In 1895 a Trade Union Federation was established. Brust and the Federation obtained the support (subject to various quarrels to be detailed later) of Pastor Weber and the Protestant workers' associations, which had been developing along much the same lines since around 1880, likewise under largely middle-class or clergy leadership. In 1893 a group of Protestant clerks in Hamburg founded the German Clerical Workers' Union, which in due course became the main centre of Protestant influence in the Christian trade union confederation.

The Swiss, both Catholic and Protestant, followed the German development a little in arrear. Catholic and Protestant workers' associations were coming up through the 'eighties and 'nineties, both with considerable help from the clergy and middle class; the Protestant associations, as recorded above, were weak. Catholic unions began to be formed from 1899, and the first hint of Protestant trade unionism, the SESUK, dates from 1907.

In Belgium the new departures in this period came from two sources. At Ghent in 1878 a group of young workers, alarmed at the progress of socialism, formed a Free Electors' Union, which later developed into the Ghent Anti-Socialist League. They met for this purpose at the Black Cat public house, and were promptly baptised by the Socialists the Kittens. With sage advice from middle-class supporters (often ignored in moments of crisis) the Kittens fought the good fight in municipal and national

[1] Chapter III, pp. 29–30.

politics and helped the birth of Christian trade unionism. The decisive step on that side was in 1882, when Leon Bruggeman, a weaver whose own originally neutral union had been captured by the socialists, set about founding a new union on a Christian basis. The Anti-Socialist League, setting going what was to be a permanent tradition of the Christian Workers' movements in Belgium, in due course also developed a formidable array of services. By 1911 it had 135 employees, its own daily paper and printing works, a co-operative society, friendly society, pension fund, and bank; also a dock workers' employment bureau, set up to break the Socialist monopoly of employment at the Ghent docks. Meantime, on the other side of Belgium, one of the greatest figures of the Belgian Christian social movement, Professor Helleputte, was working outwards from Louvain, founding workers' guilds from which in many places there sprang trade union sections. In 1891 he drew the guilds together into a Belgian Democratic League, the immediate ancestor of the Christian Workers' Movement of today, which quickly attained a membership of over 80,000.

In Holland the Protestant workers' movement goes back to the brick-layer Klaas Kater, who in the eighteen-seventies found the growing Socialist movement not to his taste. In 1876, with middle-class help, he founded the friendly society and educational organisation 'Patrimonium'. This was (and is) a mixed though primarily working-class organisation, with at the outset a middle-class 'advisory committee'. For its first few years it pursued a rather indefinite course. At the beginning of the 'nineties, however, a strong demand for action made itself felt in Patrimonium, and trade union sections began to be founded; the first was in 1890. A social programme was drafted in 1894. Shortly afterwards a new Workmen's Union was founded to cater for Hervormde workers who found Patrimonium too Gereformeerd for their taste. And about this time the Catholic workers' movement also began to get under way. A Catholic People's Union was started at Amsterdam in 1888 as a result of a minor class war in the Catholic ranks themselves. Amsterdam Catholics that year arranged for the tenth year of Leo XIII's pontificate a massive celebration, at which however the entrance prices were too high for the workers and lower middle class. W. J. Pastoors, later a Catholic member of parliament, took advantage of the irritation this caused to form the Union out of members of these two classes. The Union was essentially a 'stand' organisation, not a trade union. In the same year Fr. Ariens founded a workers' league in the textile town of Enschede. It too was essentially a 'stand' organisation, a social club and friendly society with some educational functions, designed to attract workers away from the Marxist and anarchist ideas of the Socialist movement. Two years later, at the end of a hard-fought strike at Enschede, Ariens went on to set up a Catholic textile workers' trade union. He seems to have contemplated from the start unity between Catholic and Protestant workers, and in 1895 his union did in fact federate with a similar Protestant group under the name 'Unitas' and with a common executive and strike fund. The two denominational sections kept their identity within the federation. 'Unitas' became and for several years remained the most effective of the Dutch Christian trade unions, though also, because of its inter-denominational character, the most controversial. From 1891 onwards there sprang up alongside it a number of purely Catholic local unions. By 1895 a first congress of the Catholic workers' movement in Western Holland was able to bring together 49 of these.

In France, as in Germany, the eighteen-eighties were the watershed between the old-style paternalistic movements run for the workers by the upper and middle class and the modern movement run by the workers themselves. The new trend showed itself simultaneously at several points. The most conspicuous at the time was a workers' study circle movement and series of congresses promoted in the 'eighties and 'nineties notably by Leon Harmel, the textile manufacturer of Val-Des-Bois who takes his place alongside Cadbury or Seebohm Rowntree as one of the great pioneers of personnel management. The high point of this movement was reached at a congress at Rheims in 1896, when a Christian Democratic political programme was drafted and an attempt to establish a Christian Democratic political party made. The foundations of a trade union movement were meantime being laid in two main areas. Some small textile unions were struggling into existence in the North of France in the eighteen-nineties. And in 1887 was founded, very modestly, through the initiative of the Christian Brothers at Paris, the Clerical Workers' Union, which was to be the kingpin of French Christian trade unionism for the next sixty years. Christian trade unionism was also growing at this time in Alsace-Lorraine, then however still annexed to Germany.

In Italy, finally, a semi-independent Christian trade union movement began in 1894. At that time the whole political and social effort of Catholic Italy was still centred in the Congress Movement. In the 'seventies and 'eighties this movement promoted co-operative societies, savings banks, friendly societies, and similar institutions for the benefit of workers in the countryside and, to a smaller extent, the towns. In the eighteen-nineties a few union branches began rather timidly to emerge. Many more sprang up at the end of the decade, when the Congress Movement as a whole was stirred up by a ginger group of young Christian Democrats, for the first time officially so-called, led notably by Fr. Romolo Murri.

By the eighteen-nineties, then, the seeds of an independent Christian working-class movement, with on the one hand trade unions and on the other educational, friendly, and service institutions, had everywhere been sown. Between then and the First World War these at first often minute movements grew, consolidated, and took permanent shape, experiencing a series of teething troubles on the way.

(1) *Anti-socialism or a positive Christian policy?*

The first problem was simply to say what the new movements were for: to define their policy. Unlike their paternalistic predecessors, they attracted genuine working-class militants, leaders such as any labour movement might have been proud to own. They came from many different backgrounds. Leon Bruggeman, with his sunken face, his flaming eloquence, and what the chronicler calls his 'earthy language, sometimes picturesquely crude', would have fitted well into the London dock strike of 1889. He was associated in the Ghent movement largely with printers. In France the main support, till the Alsatians came in, came from spinners and weavers in the North and white-collar workers in Paris and the other big towns. It was an interesting combination at a time when life in the textile towns was nasty, brutish, and very often short, whereas white collars were still very white and very high. It was paralleled in Germany, where the main support came from Protestant clerks, usually strong or even extreme nationalists, and from largely Catholic Ruhr miners and steel-workers, deeply suspicious of 'Hurra-Patriotismus' and all it implied. But these, though the main, were far from being the only sources of recruitment in Germany. Stegerwald, the General Secretary of the Christian trade unions for many years, was a carpenter from South Germany. The Protestant Franz Behrens was a gardener. Giesberts, the unions' best journalist in their early days, discovered his talent while stoking the boilers of a printing firm at Cologne. Most of these men came to the Christian workers' movement with disappointed hopes of a comprehensive, united, working-class movement, and a history, often extending over many years, of socialist contempt and persecution which had made their position in united unions intolerable. Bruggeman, Kater, Behrens, Stegerwald, were men with records of this kind. The strong-arm methods with which, after the Christian unions were formed, the Socialists tried for years to break them, also did little to encourage co-operation or respect. There were dramatic moments such as that in 1892 when the banner of the Ghent Anti-Socialist League received its baptism of fire. The League had arranged a big meeting and demonstration at a local hall. The Socialists, with police connivance, garrisoned the entrance to the hall and tried to prevent League supporters from entering. In the pitched battle which followed the League banner was captured and recaptured several times, till at the last the standard-bearer, Victor Van Brakelaere, an ex-Army sergeant, wielding its staff like a medieval mace, broke it over the heads of the opposition and bore what was left of it triumphantly into the hall. Thereafter the Socialists left League meetings alone. But usually there was no such easy end. It was a case of a sneer here, a union card torn up there, and one dark night perhaps a reminder of working-class solidarity weighted with a sock full of nails.[1]

Yet with all this the Christian workers' leaders resolutely refused to pursue a policy of mere anti-socialism. The workers' leagues (understood, their middle-class inspirers)—so August Brust wrote to a colleague in the early days of the Christian miners' movement in the Ruhr—would like to use us against the Socialists, but draw back when it is a question of fighting for the miners' rights. 'On that basis we do not play!' Nor did they. Little by little the Christian unions clarified their own positive doctrine. They agreed with the Socialists that fundamental changes in the existing capitalist order were desirable, but not on what these changes were to be, nor on how they were to be brought about. By the First World War the opposing positions could be summed up in three pairs of contrasting, but on the Christian as on the Socialist side positive, theses.

(1) The Socialists, and particularly the Marxists, saw the right line of development as leading towards *public ownership and national planning*. The Christian movements accepted some degree of this but aimed primarily at a *decentralised order based on industrial self-government*. Firms should be autonomous (and therefore independently owned), with workers' participation in management, ownership, and profits. Industries or professions should be self-governing, on the basis of collaboration between freely organised trade unions and employers' associations. Special attention should be given to the basic unit of social and economic life, the family. There was a particularly marked difference on this last point, as the Socialists' idea of the emancipation of women entailed sharp attacks, on the lines of the Communist Manifesto, on the 'bourgeois family' and the Christian ideal of sex morality.

(2) The Socialist road led through *class war and revolution*. At this time the Socialist movements included not only Social Democrats in the modern sense but also what would now be called Communists, and in some countries, such as France and Spain, substantial bodies of Anarchists. The Christians' aim on the other hand might be described as *collaboration through conflict*. Employer-worker collaboration was possible and indeed necessary, though it could become effective only if each party was ready and able to stand up for its own views and interests.

(3) For the Socialists the forces which counted in society were basically *material* (the economic infrastructure) and in no way supernatural, and reflected themselves in *massive class movements*. The objective was to win the *class* war. The Christians, as trade unionists, were not likely to under-estimate the importance of economic factors or of social classes. But the decisive factor, whether as means or aim, was for them the *quality of individual personalities*. As Cardinal Faulhaber was later to say, 'the soul of culture is the culture of the soul'. And the *Christian revelation* was their guide, with its message on the supernatural as well as the earthly destiny of man.

[1] A favourite weapon in France in those days. Around the turn of the century an important part of the French trade union movement (the 'syndicalist' section) made a positive cult of violence and sabotage.

(2) *For or by the workers?*

If a social class movement, and particularly a trade union, is to have the confidence and support of its constituents, it must have not merely a policy but an independent policy, one made in and by as well as for the class in question. But a whole series of conflicts had to be worked through before the Christian workers' movements won this degree of independence.

First, was an independent, militant, working-class organisation possible, or acceptable, at all? The idea that workers and clerks were incapable of minding their own business died hard. A leader of the Catholic social movements as enlightened and aware as Albert de Mun was won over only around 1912, after seeing how solid and effective the organisation of the French Clerical Workers' Union had proved to be. In Germany the Speyer Congress of the Evangelical Workers' Unions in 1901 had seventy participants, of whom only 17 were workers, and there was no worker on the committee. It was not till several years later that the Evangelical workers became the decisive force in their own organisation. The difficulty of the upper and middle class, including many of the clergy, in seeing the importance to a workers' organisation of being 'of' and 'by' as well as 'for' the workers was shown particularly by the episode of the 'yellow' unions in France. A number of French employers about 1906 promoted what official statistics on the other side of the Rhine euphemistically know as 'economically peaceful' unions.[1] They did not deceive the Christian trade unionists. But they did deceive a large part of the Catholic people generally. Widespread support was given to the yellow unions, notably by the clergy, and the stink which this caused in the nostrils of the French working class poisoned the atmosphere for many years for the Christian trade unions as well.

But assuming that the workers' organisations were to be run by workers, were they to be run on militant lines, complete with strikes and a stout defence of class interests? An ideal widespread among both Catholics and Protestants in the eighteen-eighties and eighteen-nineties was that of the 'mixed corporation' in which, as in the best days of the medieval guilds, employers and workers would collaborate in the service of the public. In quite a few places this formula was actually applied, notably to certain crafts like the goldsmiths' and in agriculture. Klaas Kater tried to form such a corporation in the building trades, and a big debate over this ideal was started in the Dutch Protestant workers' movement by Pastor

[1] Jules Zirnheld has a pleasant little story of how the 'yellow' unions got their name. The second such union to be started in France was at Montceau-les-Mines. One day, the local Socialists heaved bricks through its windows. There were some leaflets lying around printed on yellow paper, and the anti-socialists gummed these over the gaps. The Socialists, noticing this new decor, baptised them the 'yellow' unionists. The new union cheerfully accepted the challenge and took the yellow flower of the broom as its emblem.

Sikkel as late as 1903. In French Switzerland a number of mixed corporations were founded from 1917 onwards by combined Protestant and Catholic groups, beginning in the watch and clock industry. In due course, in the 'thirties and 'forties, there evolved out of them separate employers' associations and trade unions, the employers' associations being initially promoted and (the case must be almost unique) financed by the unions.[1] But the separate associations remained linked by joint machinery as well as by collective contracts, and seem to have retained something of the 'corporative' atmosphere. In Germany the Catholic Commercial Union continues to this day to group shop assistants as well as principals, though, as has been shown, it has now for a generation encouraged its shop assistant members to affiliate also to the appropriate trade union.

The 'mixed corporation' was however yet another case of ignoring the psychological value to workers of having an organisation of their own, and so was also not particularly successful as a means of promoting employer-worker collaboration. By 1900 most of those actively concerned with the Christian workers' movements were convinced that effective and honourable collaboration between classes could be attained only if each class stood firmly on its own feet. It took rather longer, down to about 1910 or 1912, to secure equally general support for the corollary that standing on one's own feet might on occasion entail fighting for one's rights, if necessary with the aid of a strike. The group of Catholic workers' associations centred at Berlin (commonly known as 'Sitz Berlin') managed under upper and middle-class leadership to convince both itself and others that it was in some way wrong for a Catholic organisation to go on strike. This became, for more militant German Catholics, an argument in favour of inter-denominational unions; rather to the surprise and amusement of Catholic trade unionists from Holland, Belgium, and France when Giesberts produced this argument at an international conference in 1908. Neither they nor their theologians saw any objection of principle to strikes, provided that the usual conditions for a 'just war' were fulfilled. And this view soon prevailed generally.

(3) *Relations with the Churches*

In spite of the difficulties it caused, the question whether working-class organisations were to be independent of the upper and middle class was relatively straightforward. Once the issue had been fairly presented, and experience had accumulated, there could not be much doubt of the line to take. A much more awkward and prolonged dispute, one indeed which has been prolonged to the present day, arose over the relation of trade

[1] The story is told in the pamphlet *La Fédération Ouvrière Vaudoise*, published by the Federation in 1949. The Federation is affiliated to the S.V.E.A. (Swiss Protestant unions).

unions and workers' leagues to the Churches and—largely as an incident to this—to each other. There was great initial confusion about this. Some of the trade union movements, for instance, sprang from and remained closely connected with workers' leagues, others arose independently. Some were denominational, even startlingly so. Members of the Clerical Workers' Union in France, for instance, were required in the early days to be members of a religious guild, and when this requirement was abolished it was still insisted that they should be 'notoriously Catholic'. The German unions on the other hand insisted with equal force on the principle of inter-denominationalism. The German chairman of an international trade union congress in 1908, referring to a direction of the Dutch Catholic Bishops that Catholics must join only Catholic unions, exclaimed with what a Dutch author calls 'typically German brutality over against episcopal wishes and decisions':

> There are many Catholics in this room, and I am one myself. But with all honour and respect for our spiritual governors the Bishops, we must say— so far, but no further! (Quoted in Amelink, *Onder Eiger Banier*, 1940, p. 94. The 'Dutch author' quoted is Versluis, *Beknopte Geschiedenis der Katholieke Arbeidersbeweging*, 1949, p. 35.)

Denominational unions might be more, or less, formally under the authority of the clergy. They were under it very formally indeed in the case of the Italian unions, at least after 1902 when the Christian Democratic movement of which many of them formed part was incorporated in the Congress Movement. And in quite a number of cases movements set out on a different path from that which they followed later. The Dutch Catholic unions are today the most denominational in Europe. But in the early days the most impressive bodies of Catholic trade unionists in Holland were to be found in the inter-denominational *Unitas* and the equally inter-denominational miners' union in Limburg. The Protestant unions in Holland and the Catholic unions in Switzerland set out to be inter-denominational but ended by being confined to one denomination (or group of denominations) alone.

The confusion was not only in the minds of trade unionists. Neither Catholic nor Protestant social theorists, not excluding the highest ecclesiastical authorities, were at this stage at all clear about this aspect of the class organisations' relationships. On the one hand, some Christians—the specific reference here is to Catholics—

> Were as much alarmed as [the Christian trade unions'] opponents at their so-called denominationalism . . . many directors of associations and good works, though firmly convinced of the need for a Christian renewal of society and the economy, thought that this could be achieved more easily by the united effort of all 'decent people' than by that of a solidly organised minority, conscious of its doctrine and its own strength. (Zirnheld, *Cinquante Années de Syndicalisme Chrétien*, 1937, p. 140.)

194

This view was taken also by many left-wing Catholics, such as Marc Sangnier of the *Sillon*, the most influential youth movement in France in the early years of the twentieth century. But these were also the years of Pius X's pontificate, when the reaction in the Catholic Church against 'Modernism' was in full swing. Like most reactions, it over-ran itself. 'Integrists' were in high favour, champions of an orthodoxy interpreted with zeal and indiscretion. Spies and informers abounded and anathemas were the order of the day. Even the 'notoriously Catholic' Clerical Workers' Union in France came under suspicion; still more so, then, those who talked of inter-denominationalism or even a-confessionality, that is of movements inspired by Christian principles, but without specific reference to Christianity in their constitution. Similar divisions existed among Protestants, though on that side there was no similar factor operating to aggravate them at that particular time. In Holland, for instance, the rather non-committal constitution of the C.N.V. unions came under heavy fire from the orthodox of the 'Groningen tendency' in the North, and in Germany the debate about the form of the Evangelical Workers' Movement stretched out over more than a decade. Among Protestants even more than among Catholics this strictly religious debate was complicated by the reluctance in any case of middle- and upper-class supporters to see the workers taking their own line.

The debate ran on for ten or fifteen years, down to the First World War, its storm centres being Germany, where the *Gewerkschaftsstreit* (trade union controversy) of these years became one of the landmarks of the whole history of the Christian social movement, and Holland. The debate as a whole did more than any other to clarify the distinction between Christian Democracy and Christian Action. Agreement crystallised in the end, about 1914, round three principles:

(1) There should be what will be called here 'Workers' leagues'; in Germany or Holland they would be called 'class' or 'Stand' organisations. Their business is primarily education and personal formation, for which orthodox doctrine is particularly important, and which is therefore of special interest to the Churches as such. Such leagues accordingly belong properly to Christian Action. They should be organisations of laymen, but under the authority or at least—as it is more correct to say in the case of Protestant bodies—under the very marked influence of the clergy and the Churches as such.

(2) Trade unions on the other hand are concerned chiefly with matters of economic and political technique, which are only indirectly and as regards principles the responsibility of the official Church. Their effectiveness also depends—much more than that of the leagues, which may do their work well even if they recruit only an élite—on the support of a mass of workers, many of them by no means strong believers, whose confidence rests on their conviction that the union is not only a strong but an independent advocate of their interests. Unions therefore belong to the field of Christian Democracy, and can and should have a much slighter official connection

195

with the Churches than workers' leagues. Unions of Catholics or of Protestants are acceptable, but so are inter-denominational or even, as in Britain or America, formally 'neutral' unions: and even unions of members of one denomination are not to be controlled by the clergy or Church as such. Christians should however join only unions which *in fact* base their policy on the Christian revelation and tradition of the natural law, and in which the Christian point of view can be effectively expressed.

(3) The work of friendly societies, co-operative societies, and similar services might at first sight be classified with that of the unions. In practice however it is often convenient to draw a line between services connected with work, such as vocational training, which are best administered by the unions, and other services of use to workers and their families irrespective of their trade, which are best administered by workers' leagues.

By the early 'twenties these principles were being applied according to two different patterns. First, Catholic workers in Holland, Belgium, and Switzerland established about that time—or rather gave definite form to—federated Christian Workers' Movements embracing leagues, unions, and services alike. For Holland the key dates are 1916, when the Bishops gave a ruling on the respective spheres of the workers' leagues (with which went most of the services) and of the trade unions, and 1925, when the two wings were combined under a single Catholic Workers' Federation. A similar Christian Social Workers' Federation was achieved in Switzerland in 1919. The federation of the Christian Workers' Movement in Belgium dates from 1921. In these federations each constituent movement retained, and retains, a high degree of autonomy. All had and have some direct link with the official Church, inasmuch as chaplains are appointed to the different movements. But in the case notably of the trade unions the chaplain's role has come to be a very limited one.

A better understanding was achieved [from 1909 onwards] for the demands of those who wished to see the trade unions independent, and therefore would have preferred to have no chaplains assigned to them. The authoritative leader Poels said: 'Trade unions must not be looked on as a sort of side-chapel to the parish church or even to the cathedral. To be genuinely Catholic they do not need to be church organisations.' And so the unions have had their freedom. The chaplain has remained . . . but on the general understanding that in the case of the unions the chaplain has only an occasional task to fulfil: namely to step in when there is a danger of a positive breach of the moral law. (Versluis, *Beknopte Geschiedenis van de Katholieke Arbeidersbeweging in Nederland*, 1949, p. 38.)

The outstanding fact about these federations is however that though the individual movements are autonomous, they are woven together so as, along with neighbouring movements outside the federations, to create for their members a complete frame of life, specifically and outspokenly Christian. A Belgian worker (Table 1) joins the Christian union, and arranges for his compulsory social insurance to be handled by one of the Christian Workers' Movement's approved societies. His doctor, hospital, or sanatorium, if he falls ill, will probably be those that the Movement suggests to him. He does not, like his Dutch colleague, have the advantage of a specifically Catholic or Protestant broadcasting corporation. But if he happens to be Flemish-speaking there is nothing to stop him tuning in across the border and listening to, among others, programmes sponsored by the Catholic Workers' Movement there. He takes, in any case, his own Movement's own daily paper. If his tastes run to adult education, or to leadership in his union or another working-class organisation, the educational facilities of the Workers' Leagues and the various specialised organisations are at his disposal. If he prefers politics, the Workers' Movement has political committees to pave his way into the Christian Social Party. His savings are in the Movement's savings banks, and his wife joins the Women's League and buys in the Christian co-operatives. Their children go to the Church school, and may in due course find their way to the Catholic University at Louvain. If not, they will presently be active in the Young Christian Workers. When they marry and start a family, the 'Radiant Hearths' movements will help them to find their feet in the early days, and the neutral but Christian-inspired Large Families' League will put the fear of the Lord into such politicians or business men as might be tempted to deny them adequate housing on family allowances. The corresponding network of influences in the Dutch Catholic Workers' Movement (Table 2) is woven even closer, and that in the Swiss Christian Social (primarily Catholic—Table 3) workers' movement only a little less so.

In a complex of associations such as these the role of each organisation depends not only on the cheapness and efficiency with which it performs its own function but also on the contribution which it can make to building up and strengthening the life of the complex as a whole. So for example a study by a leader of the Belgian Christian Workers' Movement discusses on the following lines the case for altering the system of social insurance in force in Belgium.[1] A worker receives with his payslip an insurance check, which he passes on to the friendly society of his choice. The author readily admits that a unified State system of insurance such as exists in Britain, or a 'neutral' system based on the organised industry or profession, might be cheaper and more efficient if the problem was merely to collect contributions and pay them out again. But, he says, insurance has in the experience of the Belgian Christian workers' movement been the starting point of a vast mass of human contacts of great importance to the movement as a whole. The Christian friendly societies are a school for leaders. They have personal contact with their members, and are a main channel for distributing information on social and medical matters. They are an impressive monument of Christian achievement and service, and very

[1] V. L. Heylen, *La Base Idéologique des Services Mutualistes.* Canon Heylen is Chaplain-General of the (Belgian) National Alliance of Christian Friendly Societies.

TABLE 1
The Belgian Christian Workers' Movement

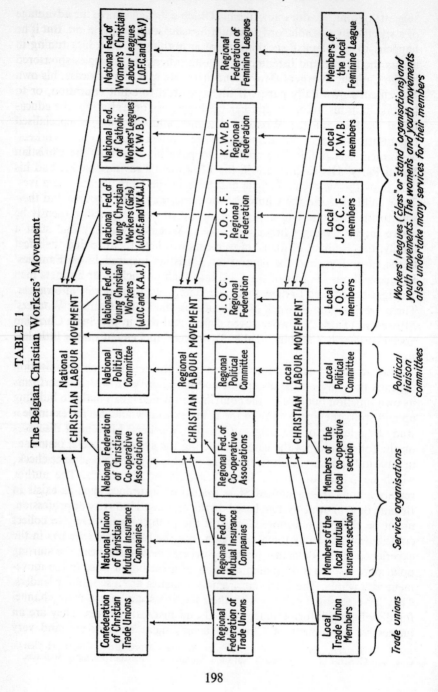

TABLE 2
Catholic Workers' Movement of Holland
(a) National Structure

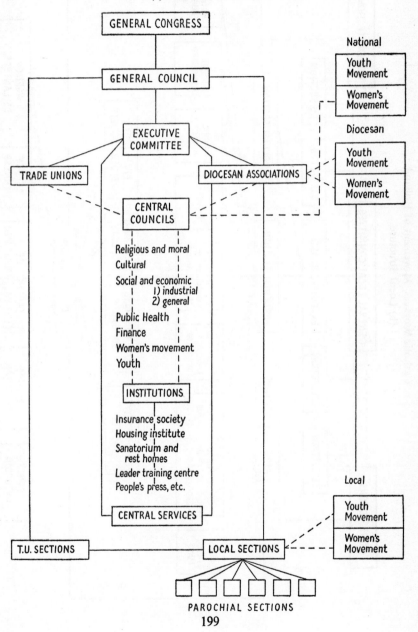

GENERAL CONGRESS

National

Youth Movement

Women's Movement

GENERAL COUNCIL

Diocesan

EXECUTIVE COMMITTEE

Youth Movement

Women's Movement

TRADE UNIONS

DIOCESAN ASSOCIATIONS

CENTRAL COUNCILS

Religious and moral
Cultural
Social and economic
　　1) industrial
　　2) general
Public Health
Finance
Women's movement
Youth

INSTITUTIONS

Insurance society
Housing institute
Sanatorium and
　rest homes
Leader training centre
People's press, etc.

Local

Youth Movement

Women's Movement

CENTRAL SERVICES

T.U. SECTIONS

LOCAL SECTIONS

PAROCHIAL SECTIONS

TABLE 2

Catholic Workers' Movement of Holland

(b) Local Structure

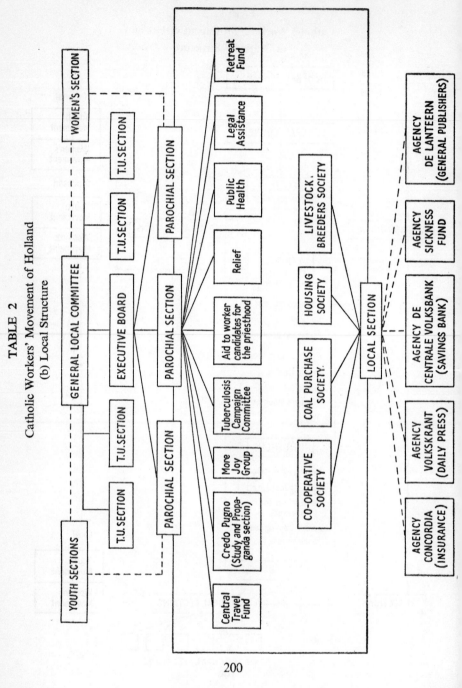

TABLE 3

Structure of the Swiss Christian Social Workers'
Movement (C.A.B.), 1943

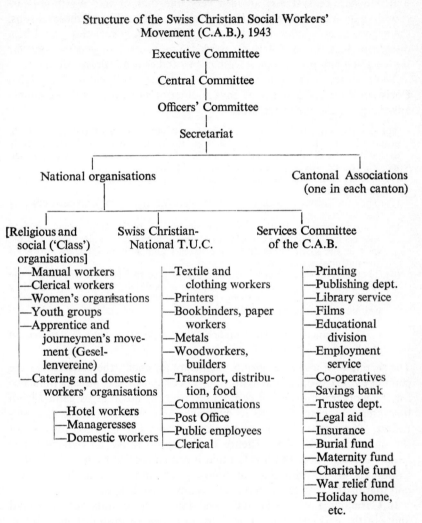

Executive Committee
|
Central Committee
|
Officers' Committee
|
Secretariat
|

National organisations   Cantonal Associations
             (one in each canton)

[Religious and social ('Class') organisations]	Swiss Christian-National T.U.C.	Services Committee of the C.A.B.
—Manual workers	—Textile and clothing workers	—Printing
—Clerical workers	—Printers	—Publishing dept.
—Women's organisations	—Bookbinders, paper workers	—Library service
—Youth groups	—Metals	—Films
—Apprentice and journeymen's movement (Gesellenvereine)	—Woodworkers, builders	—Educational division
—Catering and domestic workers' organisations	—Transport, distribution, food	—Employment service
—Hotel workers	—Communications	—Co-operatives
—Manageresses	—Post Office	—Savings bank
—Domestic workers	—Public employees	—Trustee dept.
	—Clerical	—Legal aid
		—Insurance
		—Burial fund
		—Maternity fund
		—Charitable fund
		—War relief fund
		—Holiday home, etc.

Adapted from Scherrer, *Die Christliche Sozialreform*, 1945, p. 59.

good advertisement especially to those 'ordinary people who get their
ideas on life from life itself'. Around them, thanks to their power and
wealth, has grown up a mass of 'initiatives which, in isolation, would not
be viable'. The choice of a society and the gesture of passing the insurance
cheque over to it is in any case an act of personal and family responsibility

which has some value, and is not called forth in more automatic and united insurance systems: an idea very like that of the 'mystique' surrounding the Young Christian Worker's subscription. For all these reasons, the argument concludes, the abolition of the friendly societies would be a disastrous loss to the Christian workers' movement in general, one far outweighing any possible gain from cheap and easy administration.

The first objective of the co-operative societies affiliated to the Belgian Christian Workers' Movement, says another of its reports, is the economic advantage of the members. But:

> The second objective . . . is the complete emancipation of the workers, in collaboration with the other social organisations. The possibilities are fully as great in this field as in that of material advantages. This task is performed by our co-operatives in various ways, including:
> (1) The co-operatives can give financial help to the social organisations and the workers.
> (2) They multiply the points of contact between the social organisations and the workers.
> (3) They undertake, in the common interest, activities which can serve as models in the economic world, and whose managers can take a responsible part in the institutions and committees which influence the evolution of the national economy.
> (4) They defend in economic life interests whose satisfaction can contribute to a better equilibrium in society. [This is explained as meaning that they develop habits of consumption and saving which are as relevant to workers' welfare as, for example, the recognition of workers' status inside the factory.]
>
> (Mouvement Ouvrier Chrétien, *La Coopération dans le Mouvement Ouvrier Chrétien*, 1952, p. 57.)

The secretary of a savings group, the insurance agent, the assistant on the counter in the Co-op, are so many points of contact and centres of influence for the workers' movement as a whole. And the advantages gained from this interlocking are deemed to outweigh the occasional dangers of confusion. 'The financial support granted to the social organisations is not the only reason for the existence of the co-operative movement.'[1] The danger is recognised. But it is felt that it can be parried by skilful administration and by granting due autonomy to each movement in the complex, and that in any case the gain outweighs any possible loss.

In Germany, France, and Italy, and among Protestants in Switzerland and—in the end—Holland, this tight, in appearance almost monolithic, type of organisation has not met with such favour. Here the unions were by the nineteen-twenties, or became, not merely autonomous within a wider Christian Workers' Movement but entirely independent, and their link with the Churches became much more tenuous. In Germany the unions came to be inter-denominational, and in France and Italy they became what might best be called 'a-confessional'; Christian in only a

[1] Ibid., p. 58.

broad sense, indicated for instance in the 1920 statutes of the French Christian Unions (C.F.T.C.) by a reference to the social Encyclicals of the Popes. It is particularly striking that this should happen in Italy, since there the link with the Church had been specially close. A Social and Economic Union was established there in 1906 to replace the division of the Congress Movement previously responsible for trade union, friendly society, and co-operative work. The Social and Economic Union was a branch of Catholic Action, ultimately controlled by the clergy. A study of the statutes of Christian trade unions just before the First World War showed that over 80% of them could then be classified as denominational. In 1919, however, the Church authorities decided to dissolve the Social and Economic Union and:

> Leave the economic and social organisations organically and technically distinct from Catholic Action, though united to it by the fraternal and moral bond of the common Catholic social programme. . . . (Catholic Action circular quoted in Sanseverino, *Il Movimento Sindacale Cristiano*, 1950, p. 348.)

Notice, in passing, that in this case the services also were cut loose from Catholic Action. The unions forthwith used their new-found freedom:

> While strongly reaffirming their intention to inspire their trade union action with the principles and doctrines of Christianity . . . [to] confirm the a-confessional character of the Confederation . . . and its organs. (Loc. cit. p. 358.)

The Dutch Protestant movements followed a rather different pattern, which in some ways brought them close to the Belgian-Dutch-Swiss Catholic group. Their trade unions became in practice, though not in intention, denominational, and they did for many years, beginning in 1931, maintain a liaison committee between the unions and the workers' leagues (Table 4). To this extent, they followed the Belgian-Dutch-Swiss Catholic pattern. But the liaison between unions and workers' leagues eventually broke down. And one very important characteristic common to them and to the German-Italian-French-Swiss Protestant group was that the trade unions came to overshadow the workers' leagues and equivalent organisations. The cultural and religious side of the Christian workers' movement at the end of the First World War in France, and among Swiss Protestants, was very tenuous. In Italy Catholic Action's religious and cultural work in this field was weakened seriously enough to cause alarm to the Church authorities, expressed notably in a letter by Cardinal Gasparri in May 1921. In Germany the Protestant workers' leagues never regained their pre-war strength, whereas the Protestant component in the trade unions showed at that time no falling off. And in Holland the C.N.V. unions around the end of the First World War won from the Protestant workers' leagues control of the joint local trades councils. The

TABLE 4

The Dutch Protestant Workers' Movement, 1933.

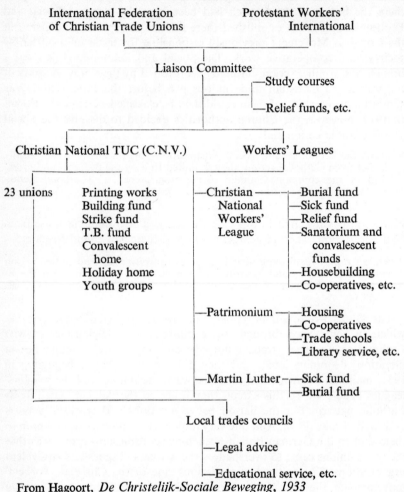

From Hagoort, *De Christelijk-Sociale Beweging, 1933*

unions' membership was by then beginning to swell to a point where it swamped that of the leagues altogether.

In part, this tendency for the unions to overshadow the leagues was due to a wider conception of union work. The unions undertook cultural activities which in Belgium or among Dutch Catholics would be left to the leagues. But it seems also to have been due to the 'materialist temptation', which made trade and legislative action seem more pressing. It was precisely the fear of succumbing to this temptation which led the Dutch, Belgian, and Swiss Catholic workers' movements to take whatever risks there might be in bringing unions and leagues into a single overall organisation. They felt that personal formation, the foundation of a Christian class movement, was likely to be more and more subordinated to current trade activities unless there were some common authority to keep the balance straight.

(4) *Relations with political parties*

One other problem of external relations had to be solved in this period, namely that of the relation of the workers' movements to the Christian political parties. As a general rule they insisted from the start on party-political neutrality. Many of their members were suspicious of the upper- and middle-class leadership of the Christian parties, and supported them only conditionally. In a number of cases—notably in France, Germany, and among Dutch Protestants—their votes were spread over a range of parties, and the workers' movements as such could not afford to commit themselves to any one among these. A special factor in the case of the workers' leagues was that they were Church or quasi-Church organisations, and the Churches were becoming less and less willing to see themselves drawn into party politics. And in the trade unions the conviction grew that union work is one thing and party work another. The union is the defensive organisation of a class, whereas the party is concerned with government, which is responsible for the common good and so is the arbiter between class interests. Both functions are legitimate and necessary. But they are different, and those who have leading responsibilities for one should not try to take on the other as well.

Yet at the same time there were political as well as economic and social purposes for which the workers' movements needed political support, and it was natural to look to the Christian parties for this. For one thing, the workers' movements wanted the vote for the workers on equal terms with the middle and upper class, and worker representatives in Parliament. Belgium and Prussia had down to the First World War plural voting systems, weighted in favour of the middle and upper class. The Catholic Workers' Movement in Germany and the Belgian Democratic League and the Ghent movement were in the forefront of the fight against this. There were also some sharp battles before worker candidates obtained what the workers' movements regarded as an adequate place on the Christian parties' lists of candidates. The Centre and Christian Social parties in Germany seem to have accepted worker candidates without too much difficulty, once the new worker movements were strong enough to make their influence noticeable. But in Belgium, Holland (Protestant as well as Catholic) and Switzerland the incorporation of a 'Christian-social' wing in the existing parties was achieved only after some vigorous exchanges: in the case of the small Swiss Protestant Party, as has been said, it was never achieved at all. The Popular Party in Italy was founded in 1919 complete with a trade union wing. But the evolution leading up to this had been anything but smooth. In the first years of the twentieth century, in particular, the old guard among the clergy and conservative laity neatly out-manoeuvred the promising young Christian Democratic movement, trade union wing and all, and for the time being rendered it, from their point of view, innocuous.

By the end of the First World War the workers' movements had won this particular battle. Henceforward they were sure of understanding and support in parties and parliaments for their views on trade union freedom, labour legislation, social security, and other matters of special concern to them. But this only underlined the difficulty of finding the right relation between the workers' movements as such (as apart from individual parliamentarians drawn from their ranks) and the party machines. It was only after some years that agreement began to focus around the view already outlined in Chapter VII. There should be no organic link. But there should be a relation of friendship and mutual confidence, expressed through more or less formal liaison committees and through such symbolic acts as the exchange of fraternal delegates at conferences.

(5) Organisational problems

It is important to remember that, while the Christian workers' movements were struggling through these various problems of defining their position and establishing their independence, they were also faced with all the organisational problems of building up a new movement with completely inexperienced personnel. Occasionally church backing might help with premises or staff. The Catholic movements in Belgium and Switzerland, for example, had for many years the service as full-time organisers of priests, Fr. Rutten and Fr. Scheiwiler, men of the highest quality, both of whom were later raised to be Bishops. Dr. Poels, in Holland, Fr. Hitze and Mgr. Müller in Germany, are others whose full-time services earned them the movements' deep gratitude. Apart from any question of full-time services, a word in the right place from a parish priest or a Protestant minister could often be decisive for recruitment. Or sometimes an arrangement might be made with some Christian service organisation to make staff available. The first part-time officer of the C.N.V. was a baker in the co-operative society of which the Chairman was manager; the society arranged to give him time off.

In that case, however, the arrangement soon broke down. The service organisations could be milked only within limits. The clergy for their part were not always available or willing to help. And in any case, at a moment when the workers' movements were struggling to establish their independence, heavy reliance on the clergy might well have done more harm than good. This was especially true of the trade unions. Their pioneers were thrown on their own resources, and their biographies have the features familiar in early trade union histories the whole world over. August Brust and his wife used to sell vegetables off the allotment on Saturday to pay for organising trips on Sunday. When payment of expenses and for lost time was introduced, it was not always certain that the cash could be found. Amelink, the historian of the C.N.V., records an early occasion when to get the deputy chairman from Amsterdam to Rotterdam and back nearly proved too much. It was not till around 1905–10, or even later, that most of the Christian trade unions established effective and stable national organisations, though of course some individual unions had established themselves soundly well before that. The Swiss Christian (Catholic) Trade Union Federation dates from 1907, the Catholic federation in Holland from 1908, the C.N.V., the Belgian federation, and the first national federation in Italy from 1909. The French Christian Confederation (C.F.T.C.) and the SVEA (Swiss Protestants) were formed only in 1919. The Germans, having formed their federation in 1895, had a long start of the rest, and tended to dominate such international contacts as there were down to 1914. The small Austrian federation was also founded relatively early, in 1902, but achieved its first national congress only in 1909.

However, by 1914, and still more by 1920, something like the present-day structure of the Christian workers' movements as a whole had emerged. It had three main characteristics:

(1) The structure of the workers' leagues, as Church or quasi-Church organisations, tended to follow the lines of ecclesiastical government, with local or parish groups and, in the Catholic movements, diocesan or regional as well as national groupings.
(2) The trade unions tended to follow industrial lines for manual workers, but to have separate occupational unions for clerical and supervisory grades. They tended to be rather highly centralised in administration and finance, and more and more so as time went on; though the distinction in this respect between the French unions and the rest has been commented on above.
(3) The whole movement laid a great deal of stress on friendly benefits and services.

At the national level, the three groups of activity came to be linked up in certain countries in the way already described. In 1908 was founded an International Secretariat for the trade unions, administered by Germany, and in 1920 an International Federation of Christian Trade Unions. In the course of the 'twenties there were also founded Internationals of respectively the Catholic and the Protestant workers' leagues. The trade union international was flanked and supported, like its socialist opposite number, with a range of international trade federations.

The foundation of these bodies concluded the experimental period of the Christian workers' movements. They had fought their battles, established their autonomy over against other classes, settled their relations among themselves and with the Church and the Christian parties, and built their organisation up to the national and international level.

THE POINT REACHED AT THE END OF THE FIRST GENERATION

The Christian movements had, all in all, in these various ways, made a promising start. But they were still at this point a long way behind the Socialists, particularly if the Socialists' strength was combined with that of the Communists, from whom they were only now beginning to be differentiated. The comparison can be made most simply on the figures for trade union membership.

In *Germany* the Christian unions in the 'twenties had $1\frac{1}{4}$ million members. They had the biggest block of clerical workers: 452,000 in 1928 against 409,000 for the Socialists, 330,000 in the liberal unions, and 189,000 in independent unions. It was on this group, as has been said, that Protestant influence in the Christian unions chiefly depended. Among manual workers the Christians had a strong position in Rhineland-Westphalia, including the Ruhr, with 40–45% of all organised workers; these were mostly Catholics. But in central and Eastern Germany the Christian manual workers' unions were outnumbered by the Socialists by up to twenty or thirty to one. In Germany as a whole the Socialist manual unions outnumbered the Christian by six to one. Civil servants were practically all in independent unions, neither Christian nor Socialist.

In *Austria* the 30,000 survivors of the Austro-Hungarian Christian unions at the end of the war swelled in due course to around 100,000, but were outnumbered by the Socialists by five to one. In *Switzerland* also the Socialists had a crushing majority, the Protestant unions having only just been founded and the Catholics only just become fully independent.

In *Holland* the comparative figures were:

	Thousands		
	1914	1920	1925
NVV (Socialist)	84 ⎫	248 ⎫	184 ⎫
NAS and N.S.V. (Communist-syndicalist)	10 ⎬ 98	52 ⎬ 340	21 ⎬ 245
'Neutral'	4 ⎭	40 ⎭	40 ⎭
C.N.V. (Protestant)	11 ⎫ 40	67 ⎫ 208	50 ⎫ 142
R.K.W. (Catholic)	29 ⎭	141 ⎭	92 ⎭

The Christian unions had crept up by 1925 from two-fifths to three-fifths of the strength of the non-Christian unions, and from under half to four-fifths of that of the Socialists alone. They held a stronger position than the Christian unions of any other country in Europe, but were still some distance from a majority.

In *Belgium* there was a disastrous fall-back during the war years. Just before the war the Christian and Socialist unions were of not very different strength; the former had 102,000 members in 1913, the latter 126,000. But the Christians dropped back by 1920 to 65,000, whereas the Socialists increased to 718,000, a superiority of eleven to one.

In *France*, at the time of the foundation of the C.F.T.C., there were some 156,000 members. Much the biggest block (43,000) were clerical workers; as in Germany, probably the biggest clerical workers' union in the country. The next biggest block was from various trades (notably the railways) in Alsace-Lorraine; and there was a substantial number of textile workers and miners from the North. But overall the Christian unions were crushingly outnumbered by the (till 1921) combined Socialist-Communist unions, which may have had as many as two million members at the peak of the boom, dropping to 600,000 in the slump which followed.

In *Italy* the Christian unions had at the peak about $1\frac{1}{4}$ million members. They were particularly strong among farm workers. But, as in Germany, they were still outnumbered by the Socialist-Communist unions. And above all they had only just attained full freedom of action, and their membership and officials were largely new and inexperienced. Fascism broke over and destroyed them before they had time to settle down.

The *International Federation of Christian Trade Unions* affiliated in 1920 some $3\frac{1}{2}$ million members, including some from countries other than those mentioned. It too was heavily outnumbered, even taking Western Europe alone, by the Communist and Socialist internationals.

Socialist superiority in the trade unions was thus still overwhelming, though the Christian movements were strong in certain categories and areas: among clerical workers generally, and among manual workers in Holland and Flanders, the Ruhr, Alsace, and the North of Italy. All these areas, it is worth noting, lie within the central belt of strong Christian belief and practice described in Chapter I.

The Christian movements' educational and service activities, concentrated in the workers' leagues or in special service organisations, often compared better with those of the Socialists than their trade union strength. This was particularly true of Germany, Holland, and Belgium, the countries which took up earliest and most whole-heartedly the idea, described above in Chapter VI, of a social class, and the working class in particular, as a cultural unit, with a way of life which it is entitled to develop and defend. In Belgium (Table 7, Chapter XVI) the Christian friendly societies had in

1924 a membership equal to rather more than half that of the Socialists, and, after a slump during the First World War, were steadily gaining ground. In the women's movement the Christians were and remained ahead. The membership of the Dutch Protestant workers' leagues varied in the 'twenties and 'thirties round 25,000–30,000. In Germany the combined membership of the Evangelical and Catholic Workers' Movements was over 600,000 in 1913, though it was then severely reduced by the war and only slowly recovered. In Italy also, working on rather different principles, the Christian service organisations built themselves up on a substantial scale. The Christian-inspired 'Italian Cooperative Federation' had in 1920, along with a large number of farmers' and rural credit societies, some 3,200 consumers' societies and 694 producers' co-operatives. The co-operative movement did not cover friendly societies, of which there were by 1911 some 800. There were also at that date 102 savings banks.

But even in the educational and service field, as witness Table 7, the Christian movements' influence often lagged. Overall, taking these activities along with the trade unions, there is no question that the Socialists were well ahead. Could this Socialist superiority have been predicted in the eighteen-eighties? Yes and no. No, inasmuch as the Socialist movement had if anything even greater organisational problems to face than the Christian and started work only a little sooner; and it had far fiercer internal disputes. Yes, in that the Socialists had then one overwhelming advantage; they were an independent working-class movement, and no one could mistake them for anything else. It was the memories, and not only the memories, of patronage and clerical control which applied the brake to the development of the Christian movements. It was only now, at the end of the First World War, that they appeared not only formed and organised, but also as standing on their own feet over against parties, clerics, and the middle and upper classes.

CHAPTER XVI

THE RISE OF THE WORKERS' MOVEMENTS, 1880–1950 (II)

STRENGTH OF THE TRADE UNIONS

THE strength and power of the Christian workers' movements was far greater after the Second World War than after the First. It was in the trade unions that the deficiency was previously greatest, and now it is in their field that there has been the greatest advance. In *Holland and Flanders* the Christian unions are today the largest, and probably come close to an absolute majority (Table 5); for it is known that the Dutch Communist unions have nowhere near the membership they claim. In these countries the Social Democratic unions come second, and the Communists a bad third. In *France and Italy* the Communist-controlled unions come first, but unions under Christian Democratic leadership now have a majority among those workers who join democratic unions of any kind. They make a respectable showing even against the Communists. Here it is the Social Democrats who come at the bottom of the list. In the German-speaking countries—*Germany, Austria, Switzerland*—they come at the top, and the Communists have influence only in a few localities. Christian trade unionists are also a minority, but strongly enough organised, and well enough represented in certain trades and districts, to count for a good deal more than the Communists. In Switzerland there are independent Catholic and Protestant unions, and in Austria a Christian fraction separately organised within the Austrian Trade Union Federation, and strong chiefly in the west of the country. In Germany there have for some years been separate Christian clerical workers' unions. Separate unions for manual workers were started in 1955. In the united unions for manual workers, as they were down to 1955, Christian groups were not formally combined into a fraction of their own, but were noticeable and influential, especially in the Ruhr. About 15% of the officials of the 'neutral' unions were reckoned to be practising Christians. The overwhelming majority were Catholics, who had the support from outside the trade unions of the Catholic Workers' Movement; only about 1% or 2% were Protestants, since the Protestant workers' movement has been passing through a phase of reorientation and reorganisation, to be described below,

TABLE 5

Trade union membership and influence in certain European Countries

Country	Category of Workers	Data based on	Year	Communist	Social Democratic	Christian Democratic	Liberal and independent	Total
Germany	Manual	Till 1955 one federation for all tendencies. Reasonably reliable figures for the C.G.D., the new Christian trade union confederation founded in the autumn of 1955, will be available only when it has existed for a year or two. 1929 figures from *Jahrbuch der Berufsverbände.*	[1929]	[1]	[82]	[14]	[4]	100
	Clerical (not civil service)	Social security elections. % of votes obtained by organisations of each tendency	1953	—	18	28	54	100
Austria	All	One federation. Christian Democratic workers may however *in addition* join the official Christian Democratic 'fraction', the Austrian Manual and Clerical Workers' Union. In 1953 140,000 had done so, or about 11% of the total of all members of the Federation.	1953					
Switzerland	Commercial, clerical, technical	Proportion of *candidates* of each tendency elected to Works Councils	1953–4	5	41	9½	44½*	100
	Manual		1953–4	5	70	4	21*	100
	All	Proportion of *votes* for candidates of each tendency. Chambers of Labour. *Handbuch der Schweizerischen Arbeitnehmerverbände,* and Heil, *Die Christlichen Gewerkschaften.*	1954	10	69	16	5	100
Holland	All	Centraal Bureau voor de Statistiek Percentages	1949	—	381,000 / 68	82,000 / 15	97,000 / 17	560,000 / 100
	All	Percentages	1951	(163,800) / (13½)	405,600 / 33½	533,000 / 44	111,700 / 9	(1,214,100) / 100
	Manual (private firms)	"				43		
	Clerical and administrative (private firms)	"				48		

212

Percentages

		Basis	Year					Public services (manual and clerical) — All
Belgium	All	Estimate by Mouvement Ouvrier Chrétien—two main federations. Percentages	1951	—	575,000 / 51	550,000 / 49	—	1,125,000 / 100
France	All	Social security elections—votes obtained by three main federations as % of votes obtained by these federations	1950	55	17	28	—	44
	Bank and insurance staffs — All	Social security elections: % of total votes	1949–50	23	21	44	11	
Italy	All	Corrected estimate of membership of main confederations. Percentages	1953	(3,000,000) / (60)	(150–400,000) / (5)	(1,900,000) / (35)	—	c. 5,000,000 / 100
	All	Works council elections (3,800 firms) January–October (*Times*, 8.11.55). % of votes obtained.	1955	60	5	30	5	100

Figures bracketed ( ) are doubtful. In the case of Italy the 'Social Democratic' unions (U.I.C.) and Christian Democratic unions (C.I.S.L.) are, formally, mixed or neutral unions. It is however estimated that around 70% of those members of the C.I.S.L. whose beliefs are known are Christian, with 20–25% socialist and 5–10% Republican. The U.I.C. is primarily socialist and Republican. In all other cases except Austria the support recorded for Christian Democratic or Social Democratic unions refers to separate and distinct unions under clearly Social-democratic or Christian-democratic leadership. Socialist unions may have Christian members, and either Christian or socialist unions (may) contain communist or liberal members; just as communist or liberal unions may contain socialist or Christian members. The test is the general colour of the leadership, policy, and statutes.

* It seemed best to refer to these 1929 figures for manual workers in Germany because there is reason to think that the volume of support for Christian leadership in this category may not be very different now from then. At that time 40–45% of the organised manual workers in the Ruhr and Rhineland were in Christian unions. Christian support may well have fallen in the period of enthusiasm for unity after the war, but has been coming up again since. Works Council elections in 1953 and 1955 in the same region show the following percentages of votes received:

		Communist	Social Democratic	Christian	Neutral and independent	Total
Mining—183 pits	1953	20	43	27½*	9½	100
	1955	18½	41	28½*	11½	100
Metal—42 plants	1953	10½	49½	28½	11	100
	1955	12	45	34½	9	100
Other—42 plants	1953	8½	49	31½	11	100
	1955	8½	42	38½	11	100

Quoted in K.N.A./Katholikenausschüsse, Monatsdienst, June–July 1955.

* The figure for the Ruhr mining districts as a whole in 1921 was 17% and in 1925 23¼%. Guillebaud, *The Works Council*, p. 47.

which has for the moment weakened its influence. On the whole, it is in Germany and perhaps Austria that Christian influence in the trade unions has made least progress since the First World War. It may not have much diminished, but can scarcely be said to have increased. Elsewhere, including Switzerland, the increase has been clear and great.

In another sense also Christian trade unionism has widened its influence; it has begun to grow outwards beyond the borders of Europe. A Catholic trade union movement was started in Canada about the time of the First World War. By the end of the nineteen-forties it had overcome its rather numerous teething troubles, built up a membership of 80,000, and become the dominant organisation in French Canada. Shortly after the Second World War the Dutch Protestant unions despatched an organiser to Canada, and as a result of his work a small but increasing number of Protestant locals has been founded. The French and Belgian Christian trade unions (C.F.T.C. and C.S.C.), beginning before the war, have built up substantial memberships in North and Central Africa and Madagascar. A Christian trade union movement appeared in Viet-Nam just after the war, grew rapidly, and by 1953–4 was the biggest and best organised in the country. It suffered a severe blow when a number of strongly Catholic areas were surrendered to the Communists in 1954. A number of these new movements are reaching out beyond Christians and, on the basis that they reflect a 'spiritual' as apart from a 'materialist' view of life, are recruiting from among Moslems and Buddhists as well.

The Christian trade union international (I.F.C.T.U.) has helped this overseas expansion by opening two regional offices for Africa and one for Latin America. The I.F.C.T.U. has also established its position in the various world and regional organisations which touch trade union affairs, though with some difficulty, and in the face of Communist and Socialist hostility. To quote a Socialist historian of the Dutch trade union movement:

> The truth requires us to admit that the International Federation of Trade Unions [the predecessor of the International Confederation of Free Trade Unions] more than once opposed the International Federation of Christian Trade Unions unfairly, above all in the International Labour Organisation. . . . (S. Mok, *De Vakbeweging*, 1953 ed., p. 109.)

The International Confederation of Free Trade Unions has carried on this hostile tradition. The member federations of the Christian international obtain representation at the I.L.O. through their national delegations, though they too have had to struggle for it. A leading case was decided before the Court of International Justice in 1922. The Socialist unions had at that time a majority all over Europe, and claimed that the constitution of the I.L.O. therefore entitled them to a monopoly of trade union representation even from countries, of which Holland was then the leading example, where Christian unions approaching their own strength were to be found. The Dutch Government insisted that in a case such as this the opportunities of representation should be shared proportionally, and the Court agreed that this was in fact consistent with the I.L.O. constitution. One trade union federation under Christian leadership, the Italian C.I.S.L., today escapes difficulties of this kind by being affiliated not to the Christian international but to the larger International Confederation of Free Trade Unions.

STRENGTH OF THE WORKERS' LEAGUES

In the case of the workers' leagues and service organisations, as apart from the trade unions, there is a rather marked difference from the First World War onwards between the experience of Protestants and Catholics. On the Protestant side these organisations made markedly less progress than some of the trade unions. Whereas the Dutch Protestant unions (C.N.V.) went from strength to strength, and the S.V.E.A. unions in Switzerland grew to maturity, the Protestant workers' leagues failed to develop in Switzerland and stagnated in Holland. In Germany the Evangelical Workers' Movement failed to regain its strength as quickly after the First World War as its Catholic opposite number. After the Second World War it revived only slowly and in a vestigial form. There were signs that it would be replaced by a movement of a new type, or rather by a series of movements focussed around the Social Academy set up by the Evangelical Church at Friedewald. But this was something for the future. The movement in its old form was greatly weakened, and till at least the middle of the 'fifties it could not be said that its new forms had had mass impact.

On the Catholic side the workers' leagues and service organisations in this period showed much more dynamism. Their strength and influence, like that of the Christian unions, was in general greater after the Second World War than after the First. In Germany the Catholic Workers' Movement held its ground until 1933, suffered severely during the National Socialist dictatorship, but revived from 1945 in something like its previous strength. Its biggest section, in west and north Germany, had by 1950 some 90% of its 1930 membership: about 180,000, including wives, in nine dioceses. The tightly organised Belgian and Dutch Catholic Workers' Movements have continued to advance both in absolute strength and (Table 7) relatively to the Socialist movements. The Belgian Christian Co-operative movement, for example, which by 1950 was beginning to be of comparable magnitude with the Socialist, is almost entirely a creation of this century, and chiefly of the period since 1921, when the Christian Workers' Movement took its present form. In Italy, the Christian workers' movement, on its educational and service as well as its trade union side,

215

was driven under during the years of Fascism. But Christian Workers' Associations (A.C.L.I.) reappeared forthwith after the collapse of Fascism, and by 1955 had over a million members in 7,000 branches, served by 489 full-time officials. They operated among other things 8,000 advice bureaux, 464 consumers' and 300 producers' co-operatives, 254 building societies, and educational courses with an annual attendance of about 200,000. French Catholics never had, nor have they today, an adult Workers' Movement, outside the trade unions, on the same mass scale as in Italy or Belgium. But there was a marked development of Workers' Catholic Action after the Second World War. It is also in this generation that France acquired, following the example of Belgium, a vast movement of Young Christian Workers (J.O.C.), whose fundamental importance for the Christian workers' movements as a whole will be outlined below in Chapter XIX. The main Christian workers' movements in all these countries are listed in Table 6.

CHANGES IN THE AIMS OF THE WORKERS' MOVEMENTS

The increased absolute and relative strength of the Christian workers' movements, trade union or otherwise, has been the result not of any sharp break in policy, but of building up patiently and steadily on the lines laid down by the early 'twenties. It has indeed been least marked in the country, Germany, where the departure from the practice of that time has been greatest. The various movements' doctrine, in the first place, was developed and matured through this generation without any fundamental change, though with some interesting clarifications and shifts of emphasis. The Dutch and German movements hoped for a time after the First World War to see the immediate practical application of their characteristic ideals of industrial self-government and joint control in the firm. Only partial and temporary success was in fact achieved, but after a pause in the early and middle twenties the advance was pressed on. In 1933 the German Christian trade unions published their 'Essen Principles', a revised and expanded version of their views on joint responsibility in industry. In Holland the new advance which led up eventually to P.B.O. began in the 'thirties with a series of measures on such matters as the legal enforcement of collective bargains or the enforcement of qualifications for new entrants into small business. The Protestant and Catholic workers' movements took an active part in this. In 1938 the Dutch Catholic workers' movement launched, in collaboration with the other main Catholic organisations, a campaign for the 'New Community', directed not only to industrial reform but also to religious and cultural renewal. In France the C.F.T.C. in 1936 published its own 'Plan' for the future of the French economy, and in Switzerland both the Catholic and the Protestant unions

TABLE 6

List of the main Christian or Christian-influenced trade
union federations and other workers' organisations in the
countries studied

	Trade Unions	Cultural and general organisations
Germany		
I.	C.G.D. (German Christian Trade Union Movement)	K.A.B. (Catholic Workers' Movement)
I.	D.H.V. (German Clerical Workers' Union).	Kolping Associations (craft apprentices and journeymen) (C).
I.	V.W.A. (Women Clerical Workers' Union)	C.A.J. (Young Christian Workers) (C). Evangelical Labour Action Committee, grouping the Evangelical Workers' Movement and a number of other movements among Evangelical workers.
Austria		
C.	Austrian Workers' and Clerks' Union—Fraction of the Austrian T.U.C.	
Switzerland		
C.	C.N.G. Swiss Christian National T.U.C.	C.A.B. Swiss Christian Workers' Union (of which C.N.G. is a component) (C)
P.	S.V.E.A. Swiss Federation of Evangelical Workers and Clerks.	
Holland		
C.	K.A.B. (Catholic Labour Movement) (trade union section)	K.A.B. (remaining sections)
P.	C.N.V. (Christian-National, i.e. Protestant, T.U.C.)	Protestant workers' leagues (Patrimonium, Christian Workers' Union, Martin Luther)
Belgium		
C.	C.S.C. (Confederation of Christian Trade Unions)	M.O.C.–K.A.B. (Christian Workers' Movement, of which C.S.C. is a component) (C)
France		
C.	C.F.T.C. (Confederation of French Christian Trade Unions)	A number of guilds and other Catholic Action movements in particular sectors or professions. Workers Catholic Action, Young Christian Workers and Young Christian Farmers. (C)
Italy		
C.	C.I.S.L. (Italian Confederation of Free Trade Unions).	A.C.L.I. (Italian Christian Workers' Associations) (C) Young Christian Workers and Young Christian Farmers (C)

C.=primarily Catholic leadership: P.=Protestant: I.=inter-confessional.

Note. Similar names may cover very different realities. Thus the German Catholic
and Evangelical Workers' Movements are merely one section of the workers' movement
among Catholics or Evangelicals, whereas the C.A.B. in Switzerland or K.A.B. in
Holland or Belgium include all sections of the workers' movement there. For this
reason the Young Christian Workers are mentioned separately for Germany, but not
for these latter countries.

took a leading part at this time in a variety of movements for 'economic renewal'.

These 'Plans' and similar movements reflect the most significant shift of emphasis in the doctrines of the Christian workers' movements at this time, their tendency to converge with those of the Social Democracy. Documents from either source kept, it is true, their characteristic flavour. Some Socialist movements, like the Swiss, still cast their propositions into classic Marxist language about the ever-widening gulf between rich and poor and the 'suppression of the domination of capital by the transfer of the means of production to the property of the people'.[1] In Holland the 1937 revision of the Socialist Party's programme still rested essentially on an analysis of capitalism in the light of the materialist conception of history, whereas the Catholic Workers' Movement's 'New Community' campaign insisted on society's moral and religious foundations. Though the C.F.T.C.'s 'Plan' of 1936 came in many ways very close to that published a year earlier by the General Confederation of Labour (C.G.T.), which was then controlled by the Social Democrats, it placed significantly less stress on the State and more on industrial self-government. It agreed that credit, insurance, fuel and power, transport and tourism, and the health services ought to be operated as public services, or rather as a sort of co-operative wholesale societies under committees representing final consumers, consuming firms, and also workers and the State. But it went out of its way to say that it did not think the 'nationalisation' of these services desirable. By 1945 the C.F.T.C. was no longer afraid of phrases such as 'nationalisation' or 'planned economy'. But it still claimed that its originality as a Christian movement lay not only in its special interest in the family[2] but also in the fact that:

> It defends human personality against the encroachment of the State as well as against the abuses of capital. Its basic orientation is not towards socialism and the reign of collective ownership, but towards professional organisation and the spread of private property. If, finally, it recognises what was too long forgotten, till Karl Marx brought it to the fore, namely the importance of the economic infra-structure for the general evolution of humanity, it nevertheless believes as strongly as ever in the preponderant importance of the moral and spiritual element, and in the need to begin there to build a new world. (*Programme d'Action Ouvrière et d'Organisation Professionelle*, 1945, p. 58.)

'Religious socialist' movements in various countries tried in these years to bridge finally the gap between Christianity and Social Democracy, but found that the time was not yet ripe. We shall come back to these, for they had considerable long-term significance. But they had little importance or success at the time.

[1] *Programme du Parti Socialiste Suisse*, 1935 ed.
[2] Above, Chapter V, p. 49.

218

Yet beneath all these differences of accent and substance, and in spite of apparently unbridgeable gaps, the lines continued to converge. Christians were coming to see the importance of State planning and public ownership—as witness the C.F.T.C., in spite of its verbal reticences—and Socialists that of decentralisation. Socialists saw violence in action under Fascism and in the U.S.S.R., and lost much of their enthusiasm for revolution, class war, and dictatorship. Christians freed themselves finally from illusions about achieving class collaboration without class organisation and conflict. These illusions had in any case never had the same hold in the workers' movement as among middle- and upper-class admirers of the 'mixed corporation'. The Christian movements now saw more clearly, as witness again the C.F.T.C., the importance for personal and social development of mass forces and the economic environment. For many Socialists it was becoming clear that:

> The struggle for social justice is inseparably bound up with respect for human personality. (Dutch Socialist Party, 1937 Programme, par. 33.)

For many of them this lesson of the supreme importance of human personality was underlined by experience in National Socialist concentration camps and in the anti-fascist resistance. The 'religious socialist' movement was one aspect of a much wider movement of dissatisfaction with traditional Marxist materialism. Many Socialists who were not yet ready to accept Christianity were now ready at least to admit that Christianity could be a genuine source of democratic belief, and of action for the common good. The Socialist International formally approved this position after the Second World War.[1]

THE WORKERS' MOVEMENTS AND THE CHURCHES. CONFESSIONAL OR A-CONFESSIONAL?

The relation between the Christian workers' movements and the Churches remained after the Second World War on the whole very much as had been agreed after the First, though not without exceptions and struggles. It came to be more clearly understood what Christian Action and Christian Democracy are, and which movements belong to each: this thanks not only to experience in the movements whose history is being sketched here but also of others, such as the specialised Catholic youth movements, which came up through the 'twenties and 'thirties. On the question whether Christian Democratic and Christian Action workers' movements should be linked under a common roof organisation, the various movements still agreed to differ. The Belgian, Dutch, and Swiss Catholic movements, which had chosen to group leagues and unions in a single, denominational, organisation linked in its entirety to the Church,

[1] Below, p. 383.

concluded from their experience (Table 7) that this was indeed the most effective way of guaranteeing solid personal formation as well as effective trade union action, and therefore of competing with the Marxist movements. Elsewhere, and especially in France, the tendency was precisely the other way. The idea of the French Christian workers' movement was more and more that the machinery of Christian Action and Christian Democracy must be kept separate, that the trade unions should be rigidly a-confessional, and that whatever might suggest that the unions were under clerical influence should be avoided like the plague.

TABLE 7

Membership of the Christian and Socialist workers'
movements in Belgium in certain years

Trade Unions:

Year	Socialist	Christian
1898	13,727	—
1901	21,125	11,000
1910	68,984	49,478
1913	126,745	102,177
1920	718,410	65,000
1922	618,871	162,036
1930	537,379	209,311
1933	629,532	300,713
1939	550,000	350,000
1945	511,851	342,500
1947	500,000	420,022
1951	550,000	575,000

Friendly and approved societies:

Year	Socialist	Christian
1913	109,461	188,690
1920	318,947	132,617
1924	419,268	235,264
1930	500,842	376,024
1937	584,827	502,701

from 1946 onwards: *compulsory* insurance:

1947	793,747	773,274
1949–50	803,000	c.900,000
1952		996,000

Co-operatives

Year	Socialist	Christian
1950–2	c.250,000	445,000

Women's organisations:

Year	'Femmes prévoyantes' (socialist)	Feminine Labour Leagues (Christian)
1922	—	76,000
1928	100,000	114,138
1935	160,000	220,325
1938	179,000	254,000
1946	135,000	281,000
1948	216,576	345,050
1950–2	250,000	371,000

Youth Organisations:

Year	Young Socialists ('Jeunes Gardes Socialistes—the political organisation—the 'Federation d'Education Physique'—the cultural organisations.)	'Young Christian Workers' J.O.C. & J.O.C.F.
1920	13,560	—
1923	36,791	—
1924	29,059	—
1927	23,028	23,700
1930	21,624	70,000
1939	?	80,000
1948	20,000	80,000
1950–2	20,000	84,000

Workers' Adult education:

Year	Socialist	Christian
1941	nil	16,299
1943		26,045
1946		34,344
1949		50,522
1952		69,500

From estimates by the Belgian Christian Workers' Movements.

The question whether the trade unions—whether or not linked to other movements—should have any kind of confessional label led to vigorous debates after the Second World War: indeed, they are not yet ended. The clearer understanding of the meaning of Christian Action and Christian Democracy helped to show in what sense a trade union does *not* need to concern itself with religious matters. As the strength of the Christian unions grew, it began to be argued that they should cease to behave as a minority, drawn in on themselves, and on the defensive, and should instead put themselves at the head of the whole democratic section of the labour movement. And not only was disagreement between Christians and Socialists diminishing; in the age of Fascism and Communism, the line of battle was in any case changing. The prime conflict was no longer between Liberals, Socialists, and Christians. It was between democrats and anti-democrats, a battle for survival in which all democratic groups, Christian, Socialist, or whatever they might be, found themselves on the same side. Even by 1920 the tendency was for the Christian trade unions to drop any specifically confessional test for membership. By the 'thirties, in some countries at least, the question was being reopened whether, in view of the considerations mentioned, the Christian and Socialist unions need or should remain separate. In 1933–4 conversations between the Socialist, Liberal, and Christian unions in Germany showed that a basis for agreement might be found, and in the middle and late 'forties incidental circumstances of the time helped in several countries to bring this question to a head. Comradeship in the resistance, the concentration camps, and the liberation created a general atmosphere of good will and desire to be and to stay together. The unified Anglo-Saxon trade union movements became better known than before the war, thanks to the experience of many Continental leaders in exile and to the many American and British delegations which visited the Continent after the liberation. And in Germany in particular the Allies (including the Americans) used their power as occupying authorities in favour of united trade unions under Socialist leadership.

The upshot, for the time being at least, was to reaffirm the position arrived at in the early 'twenties. Christians should join only unions whose policy in fact conforms to the principles of the Christian revelation and tradition of the natural law, and in which they can make the Christian point of view effectively heard: though, provided these conditions are fufilled, the unions in question need not be denominational, and may be not merely inter-denominational but formally 'neutral'. But the route by which this conclusion was reached was different in the victorious countries, along with neutral Switzerland, from that taken in the defeated countries. In the victorious countries the case for unity made a certain appeal. A few Dutch Catholics, for instance, were attracted to the Communist-led 'Unity Trade Union Centre' (E.V.C.) in the first days after south Holland was liberated. In France a minority in the C.F.T.C., led by members of the teachers' and metal-workers' unions, wished to minimise the specifically Christian character of the unions, to draw in democratically-minded non-Christians on a basis inspired by the American unions and the T.U.C., and to join the International Confederation of Free Trade Unions instead of the Christian international. They were also in favour, as supporters of thorough-going industrial unionism, of breaking up the French Clerical Workers' Union and grouping its members with the manual workers trade by trade. This would incidentally have had the result of wiping out the strongest body of supporters of specifically Christian unionism. But neither in France nor in Holland, nor yet in Belgium or Switzerland, did these tendencies prevail, The C.F.T.C. in 1947 dropped from its constitution a specific reference to the Papal Encyclicals, but kept a more general reference to Christianity. The clerical workers successfully resisted their own annihilation. The Dutch Christian unions refused even to drop their denominational labels. In all these countries the unions remained on a Christian basis and affiliated to the Christian international.

In the defeated countries, on the other hand, it is not unfair to say that the leaders or potential leaders of the Christian workers' movement lost their nerve. They plunged hastily into unity, with results which seem to have been generally satisfactory only in Austria, where the plunge was least complete. Austria has united trade unions, as already described, but with a separately organised and officially recognised Christian fraction, which runs its own candidates at union elections and gains in power from its connection with the Austrian People's Party. In Italy also there was a question at first of retaining a separate identity for Christian trade unionists. In the south, in the first days of liberation, a beginning was made with the reconstitution of actual Christian trade unions. A little later a scheme was put forward for maintaining separate Christian, Socialist, and Communist fractions affiliated to one combined centre. Both these plans were however over-ridden in favour of straightforward unification, and a united trade union movement was set up including Communists, Socialists, and Christians. Its life, under mainly Communist leadership, proved to be nasty and short. The Christians found the Communists' leadership intolerable and broke away in 1948, and the Socialists in 1949. The desire for unity remained, and the C.I.S.L. unions which exist today were set up in 1951 on a formally neutral basis, with a substantial Socialist and Republican as well as Christian membership. They are affiliated to the International Confederation of Free Trade Unions instead of to the Christian International. They are however under predominantly Christian leadership and inspiration. Neutrality in this form is naturally satisfactory to the Christians. What many Socialists and Republicans think of it is shown by the continued existence alongside the C.I.S.L. of a Socialist and Republican union (U.I.L.) with a substantial membership.

In Germany, the third case of a defeated country, the experiment in trade union unity led for several years neither to a clean break, as in Italy, nor to as satisfactory a relationship as in Austria. Catholic trade unionists in particular, though many of them were enthusiastic at the outset, became more and more critical as the years have gone by. By 1955 a substantial proportion of them had come to regret the decision in 1945 not to revive the Christian unions.

The situation in neutral workers' organisations is still more pernicious, that is in the so-called unified trade unions. Here too as well as in neutral political parties or employers' organisations we find people of different religious and political views. Here too the statutes guarantee religious tolerance and political neutrality. In these neutral unions the greater part of the members adhere to the socialist ideology. They are interested only in profiting from their numerical superiority and trying to introduce their ideas, that is their socialist ideals and aims, as the common basis for action. This is noticeable in the allocation of executive positions, in the appointment of officials, and in the delegation of representatives to works councils, firms' Boards, and key posts in the economy. One sees it too in their educational work, the contents of their press, and their efforts to win influence and acquire expert status in every area of life. They take no account of the views of Christian colleagues in the same union, and, in spite of the religious tolerance and political neutrality which is supposed to be guaranteed, try by means of both persuasion and compulsion—whichever happens to serve—to win over the Christians to their socialist views. Drops of water can wear away a stone, and this propaganda, working on Christian workers' minds from dawn to dusk, filters into them more and more of socialist doctrine, and gradually effaces the Christian view of life. That does not prevent the Socialists from making open and unashamed propaganda for their ideas, even though the same statutes apply to them as to Christian members. The complaints which anyone dares to raise against this attitude are violently rejected. The aim, they say, is to defend the workers' interests, which they, the Socialists, can do only by their own programme. Those who have thought that Christians could win influence in the unified union provided that they were active enough have proved to be wrong, for socialist pressure is far too strong, and the Socialists, following their own principles, do not bother themselves with minorities or allow them to make their influence felt. (Johannes Even, Secretary of the Catholic Workers' Movement of West Germany (K.A.B.), address to the conference of the Catholic Workers' International (F.I.M.O.C.), May, 1955.)

The dispute extended not only to the internal affairs of the unions but to policy on such matters as workers' control in the firm. The Catholics, as has been seen, preferred to put the emphasis on the election of representatives by the rank and file, whereas the Socialists insisted on putting the main power of control in the hands of full-time union officials.

Many influential Catholic trade unionists in Germany publicly rejected Johannes Even's view that Catholic participation in the unified unions 'has proved to be wrong'. Among them were Matthias Föcher, Christian Vice-President of the unified unions, and the former trade union leaders Jakob Kaiser, C.D.U. Minister in the Federal government, and Karl Arnold, Prime Minister of the province of North-Rhine-Westphalia. The weight of the Protestant workers' movements was also for long against a split. They pointed out at various times cases where the Socialist leadership of the unions had failed to observe religious or political neutrality. They also claimed the right for Protestant workers to meet and discuss union affairs among themselves. But this referred merely to the right to maintain outside the unions a Protestant Workers' Movement on the lines of the Catholic Workers' Movement, that is a Christian Action organisation; or else to found cells and discussion groups in industry, also on Christian

Action rather than trade union lines. On the question of trade union unity itself, the Evangelical Action Committee, representing all sections of the Protestant workers' movement, resolved in 1953 as follows:

> The delegates, representing all existing Evangelical workers' groups and associations, have agreed to support any action aimed at maintaining the unity of the trade union. (Quoted in G. Heilfurth, *Church and Labour in Western Germany*, paper to the Evanston Assembly of the World Council of Churches, 1954: p. 24.)

This position was later approved by the Social Affairs Committee of the Evangelical Church in Germany.

In the end, there were two major breakaways from the unified unions (D.G.B.). The earliest was that of the clerical workers, among whom, as in France, the question of ideology is complicated by disputes about industrial or occupational unionism. Socialist trade unionists in Germany insist that clerical workers should be grouped with manual workers in industrial unions. Clerical workers themselves prefer their own occupational unions. The result is that the great majority of them have left the D.G.B., the biggest section being now in a neutral union and the next biggest in inter-denominational Christian unions.

Among manual workers a break was finally made in October 1955, being approached in three stages. The first occurred when, after a succession of failures to secure a satisfactory degree of neutrality in the D.G.B. and of autonomy for the Christian groups within it, a number of Christian workers' movements agreed to set up a joint action committee. This included the Catholic Workers' Movement, Kolping, the Young Christian Workers, the small Protestant Workers' Movement, and the more important Men's Industrial Movement (Betriebsmännerwerk) of the Evangelical Church. The 'social committees' through which the Christian Democratic Union keeps in touch with industrial life were not represented at first—not surprisingly, seeing the attitude of Christian labour politicians like Kaiser and Arnold—but later sent an observer. The joint committee still failed to get satisfaction from the unified unions, and as a next step set up a research group to sample opinion in plants all over Germany. It claimed as a result that nuclei for a new Christian trade union movement could be found in several hundred plants. Further efforts were made to reach agreement with the executive of the D.G.B. on the basis of a formula on Austrian lines, leaving the Christian fraction free to organise its own educational and press services and to have its own international affiliations. The executive went so far as to suspend some of its officials whose activity had been particularly offensive to the Christian group, notably Viktor Agartz, the head of its Research Department. But it did not accept the main Christian demands. The rank and file of the Christian movement were now becoming impatient. Negotiations broke down, and at delegate meetings at Essen on October 15th and 30th it was decided to set up a new German Christian Trade Union Movement (C.G.D.).

The initial list of C.G.D. members was about three-fifths Catholic and two-fifths Protestant. About half the first recruits held no trade union card at that time, a quarter were former members of the D.G.B. Metal Workers' Union, and a fifth from the Transport and Public Employees' Union. About 8% were from the Distributive, Bank, and Insurance Workers' Union—that is, from that minority of the white-collar professions who had remained with unified unions up till then. It is significant, seeing the attitude of some Christian labour politicians, that the Chairmen of the three governing bodies of the new federation, the General Council, Executive Committee, and Advisory Council, were all Christian Democratic members of parliament.

It remains to be seen what strength the C.G.D. will build up, in the face of some opposition from within the Catholic Church and more from within the Evangelical Church. No doubt it will be several years before its true strength can be judged. One thing is, however, obvious to anyone who has followed its growth at all carefully. The split among German manual workers, like that among clerical workers, and like the split which produced the C.I.S.L. in Italy, rests on the will of the rank and file. It is not a manoeuvre from above; indeed, to a great extent (unlike the Italian case) it represents the repudiation by the Christian rank and file of such presumed leaders of their own as Matthias Föcher. It is possible that the unity of the German unions can be restored. But, if so, it will have to be done by a genuine new deal and not by a tactical arrangement.

RELATIONS WITH THE POLITICAL PARTIES

Relations between the Christian workers' movements and political parties have continued in general on the lines laid down by the early 'twenties, becoming more or less formal and cordial according to the circumstances of the time. In 1945, for example, when the M.R.P. was founded, as the first Christian Democratic party in France to have first-rate political importance, the C.F.T.C. unions lifted their normal ban on combining a full-time union post with membership of Parliament. Several C.F.T.C. leaders were in fact elected. But the decision was strictly qualified. Officials who benefited by it were to appeal for votes purely in their personal and civic capacity, and must not involve the C.F.T.C. itself in party politics. This distinction was obviously hard to preserve, and in 1946, under pressure from its left wing, the C.F.T.C. ruled that national officials and members of the National Executive must not hold office in any public authority or political party, even at the local level. Trade and regional federations and union branches were advised to apply the same rule. A few years later, after the strike wave of 1953, in which the M.R.P.

was widely felt to have betrayed the workers, a position was reached in which:

> A Christian trade unionist, above all if he belongs to the militant wing of the C.F.T.C., would think it an insult to be confused with a member of the M.R.P. (Étienne Borne in *Recherches*, Jan.–Feb. 1955, p. 27.)

ORGANISATION

In the organisation of the workers' movements, the most original departure in this generation was that already mentioned in the case of the German Protestant movement. The failure of the Protestant Workers' Movement in Germany to revive in its traditional strength and form after 1945 seems to have been due largely to scepticism about the value of class-based mass organisations for other than trade union purposes. By 1945–50 it was being argued in many circles of the Evangelical Church in Germany that the future of cultural and educational work lay not with mass workers' leagues on the lines of the Protestant and Catholic Workers' Movements but with much smaller groups of neighbours and friends, or with factory and department 'cells': little groups, linked through the parish, and better able to adapt to the more diversified and geographically, socially, and occupationally mobile populations of today. Experiment was going on actively through the Evangelical Social Academy at Friedewald and the workers' action section of the Church Men's Action of the Evangelical Church. The more traditional Protestant Workers' Movement, though weakened, was not out of the picture, and was grouped with the other two movements in the Evangelical Action Committee for Labour Questions. What final form of organisation will emerge from this ferment remains to be seen.

On the Catholic side also there was a tendency by the nineteen-forties to put a new emphasis on small, informal, groups; particularly in the family movement, which will be referred to again below. But by and large the Catholic Workers' leagues, as well as the Catholic or largely Catholic trade unions, carried on along their previous lines. Small-group work and more differentiation were no doubt necessary, but—except in parts of the family movement—there seemed to be no necessary contradiction between this and the maintenance of larger-scale organisations to link the small groups up. Most of what reorganisation there was took the form of tidying up and consolidation—usually with a marked tendency to centralisation— or of additions along established lines, rather than of radical new departures. In Switzerland the organisation chart of the Catholic Workers' Movement was tidied up in 1937 by eliminating what by then had become a superfluous 'Central Association' linking some of its components. In Holland in 1945 the Catholic Workers' Movement was re-baptised with that name, and reorganised as no longer a federation, in which a worker

227

THE RISE OF THE WORKERS' MOVEMENTS, 1880–1950 (II)

could join the trade unions but not the workers' leagues (or vice versa), but a unified though decentralised organisation in which joining either branch entailed also joining the other. In Germany the Catholic workers' movements—Kolping and the K.A.B.—became after the war, along with Men's Catholic Action (the 'Männerwerk'), the chief pillars of the 'social seminars' developed by Catholic Action in the industrial districts. The 'Männerwerk' itself set up an Industrial Action branch. In Belgium also the Christian Workers' Movement launched in 1941 (Flanders) and 1947 (Wallonia) an important adult education scheme designed to raise the cultural standards and militancy not only of its officials but of the mass of its members. The way in which the Belgian Christian trade unions were gradually centralised over these years was recorded above.[1]

The same process of centralisation developed in other branches of the Belgian Christian Workers' Movement as well. So for instance its consumers' co-operative movements had succeeded by 1939 in concentrating the commercial operation of the vast majority of its stores in the hands of two societies, though in the case of the larger of these societies the actual owners of the stores usually continued to be the regional and local societies.

The C.F.T.C. was increasingly centralised and unified in this period. It was this effort to increase cohesion and discipline which, says Zirnheld, ensured the C.F.T.C.'s safety and survival 'even under the worst strains of June 1936'. These 'strains of June 1936' were due to the forward movement which arose spontaneously in the French working class at the beginning of the Popular Front government of Leon Blum. The membership of all trade unions rocketed, the number of the C.F.T.C.'s own branches rising between its Congress in 1936 and May 1937 from 803 to 2,048. At this date, however, though the Christian clerical workers had long been established as the leading organisation in their field, the Christian manual workers' unions were still not accepted as a permanent feature of the French trade union world. The Socialists now took advantage of the wave of militancy to make one last attempt to squeeze them out. Strong-arm methods were used against C.F.T.C. members. C.F.T.C. leaders were kept off the strike committees, and the Socialists refused to admit them to sign the Matignon Agreements by which the strike wave was ended. But the C.F.T.C. stood its ground and took its share of the general growth in membership. The test was decisive. The C.F.T.C.'s right to be present on the trade union stage and to speak for its members of all grades was not again seriously challenged.

The organisation and scope of the Italian Christian Workers' Associations (A.C.L.I.), on their establishment in 1944 as a new branch of Catholic

[1] Chapter VI, p. 81.

Action, quickly developed on the lines by that time traditional in other Catholic workers' movements. At the start their work was:

> Directed clearly—apart from organising activity—to workers' education, to their preparation for trade unionism—very necessary after the fascist period—and to steering them into the unified trade unions. (A.C.L.I.—*Le A.C.L.I.*, *Principi-Attività-Struttura*, 1950.)

But events quickly forced the A.C.L.I. into a more active role in the unions, for the Communist Party quickly penetrated these and captured them. Faced with 'political strikes, statements of policy on clearly Communist lines, violence, demagoguery, and undemocratic methods of capturing control of the union machinery' (ibid., p. 6), the A.C.L.I. in 1946 redefined their function as 'the expression of the Christian tendency in the trade union field'. In this capacity they first of all led the fight against the Communists within the unions, and then, after a revolutionary strike called by the Communist leadership in 1948, took the initiative in leading the Catholic workers out of the C.G.I.L. and founding new unions. When in due course the C.I.S.L. unions were constituted under mainly Christian leadership, the A.C.L.I. again withdrew from direct participation in trade union affairs. But they did not return to their original limited function. They now defined themselves as 'the Christian workers' social movement'. They were now, besides undertaking educational, social service, and leisure activities, to maintain 'a general activity of orientation' (ibid., p. 37) in the trade union field, though 'without concerning themselves directly with day to day trade union problems'. They have in fact acted as a ginger group, concerned particularly with keeping C.I.S.L. policy not only active but oriented along the lines of Christian social theory. Though they were bound to no political party, and did not intervene in general politics, they were prepared to take political action in matters affecting workers' interests, such as land reform or the reform of social security. They were to be a comprehensive movement, concerned actively with every area of working-class life, very much on the lines of the Catholic Workers' Movements of Germany; or, except that the A.C.L.I. now had no organic link with the trade unions, of Holland or Belgium. In the A.C.L.I.'s own statement of aims and methods the views of Mgr. Brys, the Chaplain-General of the Belgian Christian Workers' Movement, on the need for such a movement to be comprehensive—one activity supporting another—were now quoted with strong approval (ibid., pp. 22–3). For this comprehensive activity the A.C.L.I. equipped themselves with the usual structure of parish, diocesan, regional and national committees, with women's, youth, and trade sections, local social service, bureaux, and factory cells.

THE FASCIST INTERLUDE AND ITS CONSEQUENCES

The period of fascism and war from 1922 until 1945 provided a severe and searching test for the whole organisation and policy of the Christian labour movements whatever their country or denomination. By the middle 'thirties the trade unions in Italy, Germany, and Austria had been driven underground by the Fascists and Nazis. In the next few years those of Belgium, Holland, Luxembourg, and France shared the same fate. In one way, these dissolutions and curtailments hit the Christian movements harder than the Socialist or Communist, since the latter retained their most important bases in the British Isles, Sweden, North America, and the U.S.S.R., whereas the Christian movement was at that time strongly represented outside Europe only in Canada. A proposal to move the office of the Christian trade union international from Holland to North America was turned down by its executive only a few weeks before the Nazi forces moved in.

The Christian workers' movements did not entirely disappear. The activity of the workers' leagues and service organisations continued in some countries to some extent, under the protection of the Church, though it was severely curtailed, and that of the trade unions was kept up underground. Many both of the movements and of their individual militants joined actively in the resistance of Nazism. In one country, Austria, a substantial number of Christian trade unionists collaborated with a Fascist regime. They were promptly disowned by the International, and collaboration even in their case was confined to the native Austrian fascism of Dollfuss and Schuschnigg. After the German invasion of 1938 this group too joined in the resistance. However, in spite of these various efforts to keep the pot boiling, the Fascist period represented a major interruption in the life of the various movements; their reconstitution after the war thus offered an opportunity, if one were needed, for radical reorganisation. It is significant that it was not generally taken, and that what happened on the whole was not so much reorganisation as consolidation. The trend of development in the Christian labour movements was continuous in spite of the Fascist interlude.

Supposing that these movements were developing at the generation-to-generation pace usual in large social movement of any kind, it might have been expected, in the absence of Fascism and war, that their steady, unspectacular gains in power, organisation, and clarity of view through the 'twenties and 'thirties would lead in the 'forties to a stage of consolidation, preparatory to a sharply different phase characterised by radical new departures. And that is precisely what seems to have happened, in spite of all interruptions. The reasons for thinking that a radically new phase may be imminent, and indeed may already have begun, will be set out below.[1] The consolidation in the 'forties is already a matter of history. The most marked new departures from the older patterns at that time, the entry of Christian trade unionists into unified unions in Germany, Austria, and Italy, and the change in the organisation of the Protestant workers' movement in Germany, may themselves have been less significant than they seemed. This is particularly true of the unification of the trade unions. It may be that this represented the premature birth of a form of organisation to which Christian Democrats in general will rally at some time in the future. But for many of those immediately involved it seems, to change the metaphor a little, to have been a case of marrying in haste and repenting at leisure: a temporary distortion due to shock rather than a real change of trend.

[1] Chapter XXIII.

CHAPTER XVII

1880–1950: MANAGEMENT, MIDDLE-CLASS, AND FARMERS' MOVEMENTS (I)

I N THE seventy years from 1880 to 1950 there grew up not only the modern Christian workers' movements but also a series of movements for the middle-class professions and for farmers. On the whole, though some of these movements are powerful and comprehensive, their development has been less thorough and complete than that of the workers' movements. A glance at Table 8 is enough to show that far more of them confine their activities to educational work, with perhaps the provision of some incidental services, and do not undertake the equivalent on the employer's or small business man's side of trade union work. Strong and well-organised Christian trade and farmers' associations exist in Holland and Belgium, but not elsewhere; and even in Holland and Belgium they tend to have a less strong hold in their own field—this applies less to the farmers' than to the employers' or middle-class organisations—than the trade unions do in theirs. The organisations which concentrate on educational work and general services often have less impact on their members' lives than the corresponding workers' leagues and related movements. It is very doubtful, for instance, whether the general run of members of the Catholic employers' associations in Germany or even Belgium are as much under their organisations' influence as are members of the Catholic Workers' Movement in Germany or, still more, the Christian Workers' Movement in Belgium. In general, the organisation of non-working-class groups tends to be patchy and weak by comparison with that of the workers.

The reason for this seems to have been twofold. The first is that a number of movements, particularly those for medium and big employers, seem to have found it even harder than in the case of the workers' movement to decide just what model of Christian conduct they were there to promote. And secondly, there have been more doubts than on the workers' side as to whether organisation was needed at all, at least by employers, and especially about the need for organisation on a Christian basis.

232

TABLE 8

Christian movements for employers and managers, business middle-class, the professions and farmers in certain European countries, about 1950

	Both Trade association and cultural and general functions	Christian organisations have:			No organisations of any importance on Christian basis exist
		With substantial influence in 'neutral' trade associations or political circles	Cultural and general functions only: With some influence of that kind: solid base on which to build	Cultural and general functions only: Beginnings only: some organisation exists	
Large and medium employers and managers	Holland (Protestant and Catholic)	Belgium France	Italy Germany (Catholic)	Switzerland (Catholic) Germany (Protestant)	
Business middle class	Holland (Protestant and Catholic)	Germany (Catholic craftsmen only)	Germany (Catholic shopkeepers and assistants)	Italy (crafts-men only) France Switzerland (Catholic)	Italy (commercial) Germany (Protestant)
Professions	Belgium	Italy (teachers)	Holland (Catholic)	France Italy (other than teachers) Germany (Catholic)	
Farmers	Holland (Protestant and Catholic) Belgium		France Switzerland (Catholic) Germany (Catholic)		Germany (Protestant)

233

THE EMPLOYERS' MOVEMENTS: FROM PATERNALISM TO LEADERSHIP

One cannot help being struck, in reading the early records of the Christian Democratic movements, by the essentially correct instinct of the workers' leaders for the use to be made of class organisations, and the correspondingly incorrect view of the bigger employers. Collaboration was the end in view, but the way to it led through putting each partner in a position to stand on his own feet and defend his own interests and dignity; and workers could expect to achieve this only through collective action and the free choice of their own representatives. Employers, even Christian, showed over and over again that they simply could not see this point. Henri Rollet, himself a leader of the French Catholic employers today, sums up thus the efforts of the Catholic employers of the North of France in the eighteen-eighties and eighteen-nineties.

> The chief limit on their work lay in its spirit. At the congress of Mouvaux in 1895, Camille Feron-Vrau said: 'We must educate the workers further, and accustom them to respect the sphere reserved for the employer'. We touch here on the sore point. This 'sphere' reserved for the employers, of which the workers must become used to having no knowledge, is the expression of a whole way of thinking of which the examples have repeatedly appeared in these pages: the employer's wife who comes into the plant and dismisses the non-Catholic women, the chaplain at Fourmies who preaches the peace of the Gospels in the works council, the Roubaix employers who repress spending at the public house instead of increasing wages—always the idea of the worker as a minor, a child to be looked after. He is to be trained from infancy; so is his wife, as witness the nuns employed to sort out domestic disputes. In the Vrau factory the Sisters take the mother's place in training the children. The employers in the North thought of themselves as the fathers of their workers, accepting all the resulting duties, but also insisting on exercising all the resulting rights. It is for this type of behaviour that the condemnatory term 'paternalism' has been coined. One cannot condemn the paternalism of the employers in the North *a priori*. It inspired important and valuable services and relieved much misery. It originated various institutions accepted today. But in itself it is an obsolete, out of date, conception of employer-worker relations, and progress has turned away from it. . . . It was growing obsolete from 1885 to 1895. It was acceptable at the first date, combated at the second. At that point its rigidity and tenacity helped to prevent the fusion of new ideas with the old. . . . It rendered great services, which it would be unjust to forget. But its condemnation lies in the fact that it made it impossible to unite the organised Catholic forces in industry. (Rollet, *L'Action Sociale des Catholiques en France, 1871–1901*, p. 322, 1947.)

This passage refers to what were then the most advanced employers of Catholic France, men who knew and personally respected their workers and their families. Camille Feron-Vrau, for instance, respected the workers at his own factory enough to leave them free to elect their own representatives to the works council, instead of hand-picking them himself; a policy which seemed revolutionary even to his colleagues in the Social Studies Conference. When he defended his view there, the minutes recorded 'general cries of dissent'. And note that the sting of Rollet's condemnation lies in its tail. The curse of paternalism was that the employers could not reach a sound conception of trade or class organisation even on their own side until they understood the framework of collaboration, on a basis of mutual respect, into which it must fit.

The Christian employers' movement has come far since then. What it understands by the employer's function today is illustrated by an article with that title by A. C. J. Rottier which appeared in the Bulletin of U.N.I.A.P.A.C. for March 1952. Not so long ago, says Rottier, the employer was thought of as an individual, as a dictator, and as concerned essentially with the direction of his firm. He might also have incidental attributes, such for instance as supplying capital or starting a firm. Within the firm, his function was thought of primarily in economic terms and from the angle of profitability. Contrast with this his position today! Inside his firm, the employer is expected to discharge a range of 'social' functions connected not merely with profitability but with the welfare of all engaged in the firm; selection and training, safety and health, a family wage, and a host of other matters. Even more important, he has now to realise that the firm has become the most important unit in the social structure as a whole, whether from the economic or the social point of view: 'more and more, it gains significance from the contribution it makes to the whole'. He has therefore to think in terms of full employment and inflation, of the balance of payments, of national investment policy as well as of the welfare of his own firm. And he has to recognise, fit in with, and play his very important part in shaping the norms of the society surrounding him. This requires that he become no longer a dictator but a constitutional leader, taking account of and in many respects formally bound by the views of others: notably of trade unions or the government. Constitutional leadership is not easy, since there are many interests to reconcile even within the firm—those not only of capital and workers but also of technical, and supervisory, and managerial grades. Often interests have a different degree of pull at different levels. P.B.O., for instance, gives a very heavy weight to labour, whereas capital has a strong position under company law. A further complication is that the 'employer' is often no longer one person. Managerial responsibility in a firm is spread over a group, not concentrated in one man; and so, still more, is the responsibility for making, notably through P.B.O. or employers' associations, management's contribution to the welfare of society as a whole. The employer today, in short, must be a man of wide views, a group leader rather than an individualist, capable of collaborating at many levels in an enterprise where many interests are concerned. And the employer's position has to be justified by his ability to reconcile and lead. He can claim no right to dictate. No doubt he is entitled to claim the degree of authority needed

235

to carry out his particular tasks; the Christian Democratic view on this was described above. But this is always within and subject to the wider whole. And if he fails in his task, says Rottier, society will rightly call him to account.

> Employers claim to play a leading part in economic life, or rather in both economic and social life. They must now either abandon this claim or accept all those obligations which this role of leadership implies.

This is essentially the same ideal as emerges from modern management literature: the ideal of the manager as a professional man, who admits and understands his responsibility to every section of the community, and is skilled in extracting a coherent policy from all the maze of influences—the many 'moral systems', in Chester Barnard's phrase—in which he is involved. It is one very far removed from the inturned, paternalistic, primarily economic outlook characteristic of managers in Feron-Vrau's day. It is difficult to put exact dates to the transition. Rottier does not claim that all Catholic (or Protestant) employers yet live up to the modern ideal. But it is clear that whereas the attitudes Rollet describes were characteristic of organised Christian employers in the eighteen-eighties, by the end of the Second World War the ideal, if not always the reality, was much nearer that described by Rottier. Points of difference remained with the Christian workers' movement, notably over the extent of workers' control in the firm, as apart from the organised profession. But the whole atmosphere in which employers and managers were prepared to discuss these differences had changed. It is not till this transition was well advanced that the Christian employers' movement as it is now known could emerge.

THE AIM OF THE FARMERS' AND MIDDLE-CLASS ORGANISATIONS

The farmers' and middle-class organisations have of course had much less reason to be paternally-minded than the organisations for big employers. Their members have relatively few employees, and their prime task has been seen from the start, as in the workers' movements, as being to defend members' interests and undertake their personal formation: not to run the lives of some other social class. We have noted earlier the conception of the ideal farmer, held in the Belgian and Dutch farmers' union, and the pride with which they look back on their achievements in building up farmers' character and widening their outlook. More striking to an outside observer, particularly from Britain, is the positive and constructive outlook of the business middle-class organisations on the role of the Small Man. Economic textbooks in all countries tend to present the small shopkeeper, for instance, as the ball on the end of the chain which industry and society drag behind them. He is obsolete, reactionary, individualistic, and unproductive, a prime cause of the high cost of living, and a man whose only interest in government is to keep down the rates. And no doubt there is much truth in this, as the Christian middle-class organisations on the Continent are very ready to admit. As regards individualism, for instance, it is pointed out in Holland that the percentage of members of the business middle class who join their trade organisations is only about half as high (around 30–40%) as the figure for farmers or bigger employers. There is in Holland since 1937 a law requiring that anyone proposing to set up in business must be able to show that he has an adequate background knowledge of that field of business, as well as specific knowledge of his trade. The intention was to raise not only the technical but the general educational standards of shopkeepers and similar grades. But the official, including Catholic and Protestant, schools, which try to provide a broad and thorough education of the whole man, have had from the start to meet the competition of correspondence colleges whose only interest is to cram their victims through the necessary examinations: and it is the short and narrow path that the prospective shopkeeper or independent craftsman still tends to prefer. 72% of all candidates passed through the official schools in 1938, before the correspondence colleges were awake to their opportunity, but only 25% in 1953.

But this does not stop the Dutch from looking back over the sixty years of effort to change the temper and outlook of the business middle class and concluding that it can be done; or from holding up, on the ground of this experience, a positive and inspiring ideal of what the small business man can become. There is a tradition in the Christian social movement that the ideal citizen is one who works with his own hands, yet owns his own tools and makes his own decisions. There is an Eric Gill-like quality about some recent Dutch reports on this; though with a wealth of supporting experience, not always found in the poets of distributism, to show how the Small Man's productivity can be raised, and how he can learn to manage his business on modern lines and make a positive contribution to industrial and social relations. Also to show how he can do this primarily through co-operation, with only an initial stimulus from outside.

THE GENERAL DIFFICULTY OF RECRUITMENT IN THE MIDDLE CLASS

The Christian farmers' and business middle-class organisations have thus seen fairly clearly what they had to do. But, like the workers' movements—often indeed rather more than the workers' movements—they have been held back by doubts among potential recruits as to whether organisation on a Christian (or, often, on any) basis is necessary, and what form it should take. This has also been a supplementary cause for delay in the case of larger employers and of higher technical and managerial grades. There are several obvious reasons why employers, farmers, and higher-grade and independent workers should be slower than manual and clerical workers to organise. They are independent, accustomed to solving their own problems, and largely in a position to do so. They are highly differentiated, with widely varying needs not always easy to cater for in a large organisation. They are not usually under such severe economic pressure as rank and file workers, though slumps due to the trade cycle or changes in the long-term pattern of demand may change this. The rise of the farmers' movement, for example, was encouraged by the fact that the end of the nineteenth century was a time of severe economic pressure on farmers; and the two world wars and the slump of the 'thirties contributed a great deal to the rise of the employers' movement in general. These are reasons for delay in *any* organisation for independents. As regards organisation on a specifically religious basis there are two further points. Independent and higher-grade workers live and work largely on their own; they can more easily escape from those pressures of a non-Christian environment which workers' leaders like Bruggeman or Stegerwald found so intolerable. And they have been in less danger of being cut off from the official Church organisation. Table 9 is a striking illustration of this; the management of Evangelical parishes in Westphalia has become in effect a middle-class monopoly. For France an exceptionally well qualified observer, Joseph Folliet, Secretary of the *Semaines Sociales de France*, comments that:

> No Catholic Action movement has as yet succeeded in organising the middle class effectively; craftsmen, shopkeepers . . . free professions. That is paradoxical, for it is just this class of people which swarms into our parishes and practically takes them over. Why the difference? It is easy to talk about the indiscipline and individualism of the middle classes; that is fair enough, but it is not the whole truth. This group does after all give a great deal to Catholic Action in other fields, to youth and social movements; and not long ago it used to be the great source of recruitment for study circles. The truth seems to be that up to now the right formula for specialised Catholic Action in these classes has not been found. . . . (*Présence de l'Église*, 1949, pp. 108–9.)

Attention in Christian circles in France, he suggests, has been turned rather too exclusively to problems of the working class. But also, and more generally, Catholic Action has failed to cater enough for the variety and differentiation which exists within the middle class:

> One reason for the relative failure of Catholic Action in the middle and parts of the upper middle class seems to be an over-simplified conception of the way of life of the middle class, which is confused with a 'class' whose definition really fits only capitalist employers, a minority of the upper middle class. Not enough allowance has been made for the fact that the upper middle and the middle class include an infinite number of sub-classes, almost shut off from one another. . . . Think of such well-marked environments as those of university professors, school teachers, journalism, the Bar, the arts, the theatre. We have not seen clearly enough that the middle class is perpetually in the process of becoming, whereas the working class is relatively fixed. . . . (ibid., p. 116.)

TABLE 9

Social structure of 100 Evangelical churches in Westphalia, 1953

Class	Percentage of each of the following categories who belong to each class:		
	Baptised Evangelicals known as such to the minister	Church-goers	Elders (Church Council members)
Workers:			
Settled	35	5	0
Casual and refugee	10	0	0
Lower middle class (including tradesmen, craftsmen, and more established workers)	25	65	85
Intermediate 'intellectual' grades (e.g. journalists)	5	2	0
Upper middle class	5	15	15
Others	20	13	0
Total	100	100	100

From an estimate by K. von Bismarck. Cyclostyled report of a lecture in Berlin, January 9th, 1954, on *Was hat die Kirche an den Arbeiterschaft versäumt?*

CASE HISTORY: THE C.W.V.

How these difficulties in getting employers and independents organised have looked from the Protestant side can be shown by a pair of case histories, from respectively a farmers' organisation and one for medium and large employers. The first comes from the Christian Employers' Association (C.W.V.) in Holland, which published just before the war a pamphlet by its chairman, A. Borst, under the title *Hold the Fort!*, giving the Association's view of its aims and problems. Christian principles, says Borst, cannot have their full impact unless they are lived out in a visible community; one visible in each area of life. To give them effect requires organised power. It must be power organised specifically on the basis of God's absolute sovereignty over all. Not much good has come of the 'little grains of salt' who have tried to add savour to 'neutral' organisations. There is a whole range of issues on which the Protestant employers' organisations differ from the 'neutral' bodies, which, whether or not they contain Christian members, are in fact 'liberal' in the sense in which that word is understood on the Continent. Examples are schemes for works councils, for making collective agreements legally binding, for insisting on proper qualifications for those who propose to set up small businesses,

239

or for paying family allowances or discouraging the work of married women. On all these matters, and on schemes for industrial self-government, the Protestant employers' organisations are in favour, the 'liberal' organisations against. The Protestant organisations have moreover a special role inside their church. Being specifically Protestant, they are well placed to keep the official Church informed about economic needs, and to collaborate with other Protestant organisations—especially the trade unions and political parties—and so promote good will among Christians and reduce conflict. And the prestige of each Protestant group in its own field is increased through belonging to the Protestant social movement as a whole. In that sense the presence of the C.W.V. in its own field helps the work of other Protestant groups in theirs, just as their presence in their own fields helps that of the C.W.V.

But to define these principles is one thing and to get them recognised is another. The attitude of many Protestant employers is illustrated, Borst writes, by the story of Pastor Reflective ('Ds. Nadenker') and his congregation. The deacons are in session, and Brother Workman's case comes up. He has joined the Socialist union. Deacon Pillar, the pride and joy of the chapel, himself a big local employer, undertakes to see him. But when he and the minister go round, Brother Workman quickly turns the tables. For he is aware that Pillar is in the 'neutral' trade association, and matches argument with argument to show that what is sauce for the boss is sauce for the worker as well. Pastor Reflective goes home, and reflects. Whatever the reason, says Borst—there is Barthian theology in it, as well as sheer reaction—a high though diminishing proportion of all Protestant employers insist that business is business, with its own laws which can be observed as well by a neutral as by a Protestant organisation.

Perhaps, he suggests, they might have been less inclined to take this view if the C.W.V. itself had always been clear just what it was trying to do. The original Dutch Protestant employers' association, 'Boaz', split in 1918 not merely because it was too unspecialised, but also because it was too much of a debating society. Employers' real interest went to the organisations where practical, day to day affairs were debated. But even after the split the C.W.V. was not at first clear whether it was in fact to act as a 'social class' organisation without trade functions, like the workers' leagues, or to undertake trade association work as well. By 1920 it made up its mind that trade association work should be done by *a* Protestant employers' organisation, but not by the C.W.V.; the idea preferred was that of a separate Protestant central trade association affiliating trade groups both from the large and medium employers' side and from that of the business middle class. A central association of that sort was set up, but died in the early 'thirties. Employers were canny with their subscriptions. The tendency, as the later Prime Minister Colijn put it in a speech to the C.W.V. and business middle-class organisations in 1923, was to 'refuse the horse who must do the work his oats'. Meantime the C.W.V. havered, and in 1929 brought out a report, which was however never adopted as official policy, in effect approving the neutralist doctrine that 'business is business'. Borst, who signed it, confesses nine years later that he is thoroughly ashamed of it. It was not till 1936 that the C.W.V. finally and decisively took in hand the building up of trade groups of its own with full trade association functions. The effective organisation of large and medium Protestant employers in Holland, on the lines today accepted as standard, dates only from that year. The previous discussion and experience had however ensured that, when it did begin, it had solid support behind it. Experience after the date of Borst's pamphlet confirmed this. The general enthusiasm for unity at the end of the Second World War made little impact on the C.W.V., which not only held its ground but grew.

CASE HISTORY: THE C.B.T.B.

The second case comes from the Dutch Protestant farmers' organisation, the C.B.T.B. To judge by its official history, the C.B.T.B. does not seem to have suffered from the same confusions as the C.W.V. about the form of organisation to adopt or its relation to other bodies. Early in its career it laid down that it proposed to leave to genuinely neutral organisations such strictly technical functions as operating creameries or beet-sugar factories. For the rest, however, it proposed to offer its members all the services which might normally be expected of a farmers' union. It would see to such things as prices or trade policy, and also matters of social policy such as the administration of the industry's social insurance scheme. It justified its own existence by much the same arguments as the C.W.V. The Protestant farm-workers' unions needed a counterpart on the employers' side. The Protestant political parties would be helped by a Protestant farmers' organisation, and it by them. Noting that certain 'neutral' groups wished to set up a Farmers' party, the C.B.T.B. commented that it felt agriculture would be better served by retaining strong farm contingents in each of the established general parties, and notably of the Protestant parties. Protestants needed to appear among the farmers' associations as an organised force, since many neutral organisations were reluctant to allow their Protestant members to exert effective influence.

> There were associations in which, when officers and committees were appointed, members from the Christian side were systematically excluded. They applied a Liberal Monroe doctrine; the farmers' unions for the free-thinkers. (*Gedenkboek C.B.T.B.*, 1948, p. 29.)

By a curious coincidence, Protestant committee-men began to be elected in a number of these organisations shortly after the C.B.T.B. established itself as a competitor. And, the C.B.T.B. insisted, the Christian conception of industrial self-government, as ultimately realised in P.B.O., had to be defended against the liberal anti-interventionists on one flank as strongly as against socialist enthusiasts for 'nationalised farming' on the other.

But the battle to get potential members to accept these principles and come into the organisation spread out over years. There seem to have been four or five main currents of thought which ran counter to the C.B.T.B.'s propaganda in its first years. The theology of Karl Barth proved as embarrassing to the Dutch farmers as to most other Protestant social organisations. Suppose that Karl Barth is right—so the C.B.T.B.'s official history puts it—and that revelation is delivered directly to each individual, like a flash of lightning, with reference to a concrete situation; and that any attempt on that individual's part to derive general principles from it, or to apply it to other situations, is a mere human construction which can in no sense or degree claim the authority of a divine message? Then, clearly, an organisation based on so-called Christian principles is a monstrosity, indeed little short of a blasphemy. It is claiming to be something which by definition no organisation can be. These Barthian subtleties might not make much immediate impact on the mass of potential members. But the C.B.T.B.'s leadership were afraid of the indirect influence which might emanate from Protestant intellectuals and clergy, and found it necessary therefore to take up a theological position against them. The Barthian argument rested on the conception of an absolute distinction between God and nature,

> There is an immeasurable gulf between God and the world . . . the division commonly called the 'deadline'. On the earthly side of this deadline is sin and injustice. All is accursed and lies under the judgment of death, under the curse. There is nothing on that side which does not lie under this judgment. Therefore, it is said, one cannot speak of anything as 'Christian', not even of a Christian marriage or Christian family. (Loc. cit., p. 65.)

The C.B.T.B. on the contrary took up the position that:

> God sent His Son to redeem the world . . . and it is redeemed by Him. Sin still goes its destructive way, but in principle the world is redeemed, and can again do God's will. It is still full of sin and defect, and we still continually do evil even when we wish to do good. But that does not change the fact that creation is redeemed, and God wills to dwell on earth with His grace and spirit. Therefore the deadline . . . no longer exists. . . . It follows . . . that this is a world once again turned to God, or must become it. Our vocation is to work at this. (Pp. 66–7.)

And whereas the Barthian theology denies that anything about God's will can be learnt from nature, the C.B.T.B. points in reply to the Confession of Faith of the Dutch churches, which specifically rejects this view on the authority of St. Paul.

A related religious difficulty proved to be, throughout the C.B.T.B.'s history, what the official history calls the 'Baptist deposit' among many members of the churches; not particularly, it notes, of the Baptist denomination. That is the tendency on religious grounds to treat the world as of little importance compared to the life of the spirit, and therefore to stand aside not merely from specifically Christian but from any organised social activity. This view leads on easily to one of two others. One is that of plain indifference. 'The lukewarm, the indifferent, the Bileamites, have always been the most serious threat to our organisation.' (p. 71.)

> The church that was in Laodicea has disappeared, but any number of Protestant communities could still be classed from their behaviour as colonies of Laodicea. (P. 70.)

Or alternatively, there is the attitude of Moral Rearmament, which the C.B.T.B. found a considerable nuisance just before the Second World War. Here too it became necessary to define the organisation's position formally. The C.B.T.B.'s executive had no objection to criticism and recalls to duty. But, they asked, to what duty? Rightly understood, to that of understanding and obeying Scripture in all its implications, and wielding the sword of the Spirit accordingly. A vague religiosity, embracing all men but with no clear direction or doctrinal backbone, was not enough either for individuals or for organisations.

Yet another tendency to break away from the Protestant conception of a farmers' union, this time one peculiar to the farming world, came from what was known to the C.B.T.B. as the 'physiocratic' trend. This was the tendency to regard the farmer as the one true foundation of society, and to play down farmers' obligation towards the rest of the community. This view flourished among many Dutch farmers under the strains and genuine injustices of the slump of the 'thirties. It was complicated at the end of the 'thirties by the growth of National-Socialist doctrines of 'blood and soil', which made a considerable impact in North and East Holland. The Friesland branch of the 'neutral' union distinguished itself by electing a Nazi chairman, to the considerable disgust of its Protestant members. The Nazi occupation of course killed this tendency outright.

In general, the C.B.T.B.'s experience was that in the first period after the split in 'Boaz', that is from 1918 to the early 'thirties, its potential recruits found it hard to see that the work of a farmers' union involved Christian principles at all. In the 'thirties the line shifted. It came to be agreed that principles were involved, only now it was argued that they were adequately safeguarded in the 'neutral' organisations, which by this time were trying to meet C.B.T.B. competition by such measures as electing Protestants to prominent positions and refraining from Sunday activities. At this point the C.B.T.B. had to meet, in addition to the arguments already mentioned, complaints that it was weakening Christian influence in the farming world by withdrawing its members into a comfortable isolation in which they could no longer act as the 'leaven in the lump'. The C.B.T.B.'s reply was that independent Christian organisation was anything but an easy or comfortable road, and that the lump had never shown so many signs of being leavened as since it found its Protestant members being drawn off from it.

Little by little, the C.B.T.B.'s counter-attack against these various types of propaganda took effect. This was helped by certain organisational changes in the late 'twenties and 'thirties, including the installation of a permanent secretary, and the strengthening of the union's branch organisation, particularly important for recruitment. Thanks to the combination of organisation and propaganda the curve of membership turned upwards, and the advance has since continued unchecked. In 1945, when the liberation honeymoon was on among employers as among workers, there was a moment of anxiety. Would particularly the young farmers, who had come up during the years of Nazi occupation, come to the Protestant or the 'neutral' organisations? The event showed that the pre-war effort of organisation and propaganda had been successful. The old members came back, new members were added, and by the end of 1946 membership was already a third higher than in 1939.

CHAPTER XVIII

1880–1950: MANAGEMENT, MIDDLE-CLASS, AND FARMERS' MOVEMENTS (II)

T HE time-table of the rise of the movements covered in this chapter, against the general background outlined in the last, is not very different from that of the workers' movements. The foundations were laid in the last quarter of the nineteenth century. There was a general consolidation around the time of the First World War, and then a progressive build-up to a new consolidation, which took place from the end of the 'thirties till just after the Second World War. The results in most cases were less impressive than those of the workers' movements, but the shape of development was the same.

THE FARMERS' MOVEMENTS

The farmers' movements go back to the eighteen-sixties, when rural credit co-operatives began to be founded in *Germany* by the Protestant William Raiffeisen. He quickly received strong support from the Catholic clergy of Rhineland-Westphalia, and by 1895 there were some 3,100 societies with 270,000 members, making loans at the rate of around £3,000,000 a year; say £10–12,000,000 at present prices. Farmers' unions also began to be founded in West Germany, about the same time as the credit co-operatives, notably by the Catholic Baron Schorlemer-Alst. These also grew rapidly and by 1903 had 250,000 members. The German example was widely followed. In *Italy* Fr. Cerrutti founded the first rural credit co-operative in 1880 near Venice. Friendly societies had already been spreading through the countryside, and now farmers' unions and a variety of other types of co-operative society—insurance, purchasing, smallholders'—also began to be founded. All this activity was co-ordinated, and largely inspired, by the Italian Catholics' general Congress Movement. By 1920 there were 2,116 rural credit societies and some 800 farmers' unions affiliated to the Italian Catholic Co-operative Union. In *France* a farmers' union movement grew up from the eighteen-eighties. Lay Catholics were largely responsible for it The clergy for their part took up on a big scale, beginning in 1890, Raiffeisen's idea of credit co-operatives; by 1898 it is estimated that there were some 425 of these in active existence.

245

In *Belgium* the present Farmers' Union was founded in 1889 by a priest, Fr. Mellaerts, and two laymen, Helleputte and Schollaert, as an all-purpose organisation with educational as well as economic ends. When Fr. Mellaerts retired in 1902 there were already some 359 local branches or 'guilds'. In *Holland* the Catholic Farmers' Union began in 1896 and, like its Belgian opposite number, quickly obtained a substantial membership. Efforts to organise Dutch Protestant farmers were rather less successful, thanks to what in due course proved to be an error of tactics by the Protestant social movement as a whole. In 1892 was founded a society known as 'Boaz', arising out of meetings between Dutch Protestant employers of all sizes and trades at the first general Christian Social Congress in 1891, one of the landmarks in the Protestant social movement's history.[1] This society was intended as a centre for the discussion of Protestant social principles as applied to the problems facing employers in general. It proved in fact too heterogeneous to be effective. Its maximum membership, including shopkeepers and farmers, was a little over 2,800 in 1895; 343 of these were farmers and market gardeners. It has to be mentioned for the historical record rather than for anything very important it achieved.

With this exception, all the farmers' movements mentioned were well established by the First World War. A number of them were by that time ready to draw breath and consolidate. The Belgian Farmers' Union was consolidated and centralised, largely during the war, with particular attention to developing its educational and social as well as its economic activities. In Italy in 1919 what was left of the Congress Movement was dissolved and the co-operatives and friendly societies, like the trade unions, were given their independence. The Co-operative Union referred to above as existing in 1920 was an independent organisation, founded in 1919, no longer formally subordinate to the official Church. The Dutch Protestants also took occasion from the war to put their organisation on a sounder basis. In 1918, under the leadership of Dr. Colijn, Boaz was split into three independent movements for large employers, the business middle class, and farmers. Boaz itself retained a shadowy existence for some years longer as, in principle, a co-ordinating body. The farmers', or to be strictly accurate, the farmers' and market gardeners', section, the C.B.T.B., quickly built up a membership of between two and three thousand; far less than the Catholic or neutral organisations, but enough to enable it to work effectively and obtain official recognition.

---

[1] Professor Diepenhorst recalls a pleasant little incident at the foundation of Boaz; also rather instructive as the atmosphere in which the pioneers of the Protestant social movement worked, and from which they were trying to get away. The meeting was held at the Bible Hotel at Amsterdam. At a certain point a Bible was required. The management was acutely embarrassed to produce one until a waiter saved the situation by bringing out his own.

From 1920 to 1950 there were a variety of reorganisations and additions. The C.B.T.B., for instance, at the end of the 'twenties broke up its previously rather centralised organisation, which it found to be hampering recruitment and educational work. A few years later it was appointing a full-time secretary and staff; the Executive Committee is said to have made sure that the candidate appointed not only had a law degree but also knew how to milk a cow. There was a general tendency as the farmers' unions grew more mature, and especially after the Second World War, to pay more attention to altering the structure within which farmers operate: as apart from simply helping farmers to become individually efficient, or from action, as in the slump of the 'thirties, to ward off an immediate emergency. Matters which have come in for attention in recent years include P.B.O.—on which the Secretary of the C.B.T.B., the same who knows how to milk a cow, wrote his doctoral thesis—a Green Pool for Europe, and the unification of the market for Benelux. On the social side several movements, and notably the French Rural Family Movement to be mentioned below, have been working on the structure of rural communities and how best it can be adapted to modern needs: matters such as physical planning, leisure activities, local government, and the activities of and relations between social groups.

In Switzerland a Catholic Farmers' Union was founded in 1942 to work within the neutral Swiss Farmers' Union; it is also closely linked to the Conservative [Catholic] People's Party. In Austria a Farmers' Union, whose origin goes back to before the First World War, is today a component part—on the same basis as the Christian workers' fraction of the Austrian trade unions—of the Austrian People's Party.

> The function of the Austrian Farmers' Union is to bring together farmers, their workers, and their families, to promote their strength through mutual aid, to reinforce pride of class and function, to defend the farmer's well-earned possessions, and to guarantee them against debt, exploitation, and waste. The Farmers' Union is intended also to ensure its members a reliable, decent, living, to stop the flight from the land, to meet the shortage of labour, to maintain sound Christian customs and ways of life among country people, to reinforce love for the land, the farmer's calling, and the community to which each belongs . . . and to promote the rural co-operative movement. (Kasamas, *Programm Oesterreich* (Austrian People's Party), 1949, p. 18.)

But the main feature of the years from 1920 to 1950 was the working out of a divergence between two main groups of the Christian farmers' organisations over the proper limit of their functions and their relation to the Church; a divergence already implicit by 1920, and very like that which arose in the workers' movement between the Belgian, Dutch, and Swiss Catholic movements and the rest. It can be seen that the Christian contribution to the organisation of farmers had everywhere and from the start a very practical slant. It was a movement to put more fertilisers on the land and to bring down interest rates from thirty per cent to three. Fr. Mellaerts made his first conquests among the Belgian farmers because he knew his chemistry as well as his religion. This practical and economic interest did not prevent most of the movements mentioned from having at the start a strong denominational slant, or from taking an active interest in personal formation and general not merely technical education. The Belgian, Dutch, and (till 1919) the Italian farmers' organisations sailed under a specifically denominational flag, and so, *de facto* if not always *de jure*, did a great many of the rural credit societies. The farmers' unions in France and Germany were often the creation of 'notorious Catholics' and were so regarded by the general public. A typical incident illustrating this occurred when some of the promoters of the movements in Brittany launched a very well-conceived and unsectarian scheme of agricultural education for primary schools. The 'free' (Catholic) schools took it up. The lay, municipal schools, seeing who its authors were, stood suspiciously aside.

But from the time of the First World War a division became apparent between the Dutch (Protestant and Catholic) and Belgian movements on the one hand and those in France, Germany, and Italy on the other. The former maintained and even accentuated their educational work and their religious character. In the two Catholic movements the clergy passed, it is true, rather more into the background once the movements were launched. The Belgian Farmers' Union was reorganised at the end of the 'thirties following the failure of the union's central bank. There ceased to be a majority of clergy on the central committee, and the Union's technical services were given more autonomy. But suggestions which arose from time to time that the Union should become a-confessional were firmly beaten off, and there was no question of succumbing to the 'materialist temptation'. The French, German, and Italian movements, by contrast, became overwhelmingly concerned with economics and lost most of their confessional and general-educational character. What remained was a matter of personal influence within organisations now formally neutral, and this influence, even when exerted by men who personally were excellent Christians, often lacked a clear direction. So for instance a great deal of the leadership in the French farmers' unions has always been Christian, but often rather traditionalist in outlook; not well equipped, in any case, to give the sort of lead called for by the modern Christian social movements. A determined effort was made by non-Christian left-wing groups in 1944–5, at the time of the Liberation, to squeeze these conservative and Christian leaders out, but without success.

This change of direction by the French, German, and Italian farmers' unions had more far-reaching effects, and led to a more marked abandonment of educational work, than the decision of Christian trade unionists in Germany or Italy or Austria to join a-confessional or neutral unions after the Second World War. The Catholic who joined a 'neutral', actually Socialist, trade union in Germany in 1945 still had at his service the Catholic Workers' Movement, with its educational functions and, incidentally, its ability to act on occasion as a pressure group. The Italian who joins the a-confessional C.I.S.L. today is still backed by the A.C.L.I. workers' leagues, as his French colleague in the C.F.T.C. is backed by Workers' Catholic Action. But at the time when the farmers' unions in France and Germany and Italy dropped the torch of Christian formation and education, there was at first no rural equivalent of the workers' leagues to pick it up. Canon Boulard's *Missionary Problems of Rural France* presents the picture of a countryside where credit may indeed be available and farmers are a powerfully organised economic and political force, but where the task of giving them and other country dwellers a Christian formation has been long and disastrously neglected. There could scarcely be a sharper contrast with Belgium, where the Farmers' Union, with its educational as well as its trade functions, has as its ideal the countryman who is not only skilled in farming (though that is part of the ideal), but has also the social skills, the knowledge of his religion, and the wide horizons and general flexibility needed to live a Christian life in the modern world. In Germany the Catholic *Volksverein*, of which more below,[1] began in the first years of the twentieth century to work at adult education in the rural areas. But its approach, in the words of a leader of the modern German Catholic rural movement whose own experience reaches back to the First World War, was 'somewhat static', concerned too much with maintaining or bringing back to life the village customs of the past.

It was in Germany that these deficiencies first began to be made good. The *Volksverein* revised its methods after 1918, a flourishing Young Farmers' Movement grew up, with an interest both in modern technology and in its relation to spiritual values, and a series of Rural High Schools were set up for adult education. A similar Evangelical movement developed, and by 1933 more than thirty Rural High Schools of the two denominations were in operation. During the Nazi period the *Volksverein* and most of the activities it sponsored were suppressed. However, by shifting to a strictly religious basis some of the leaders of the rural movement were able to keep the flag flying. The circulation of one Catholic Action pamphlet series under the title 'Landmann Gottes' (God's Countryman) ran to 600,000; it was eventually banned by the Nazis. After 1945 the movement revived, and by 1951 was strong enough to consolidate itself, in a Congress happily placed at the Gates of Heaven (Himmelspforten) near Würzburg, into a new German Catholic Rural Movement (K.L.D.). The K.L.D. is a

---

[1] Part IV, pp. 427-8.

movement of Catholic Action, under lay leadership, but ultimately under the authority of the clergy, which addresses itself to all who live in the country, but especially to the farming population. Its statutes debar it from economic activities, but for the rest it concerns itself, primarily from the educational angle, with all aspects of the social and religious life of each village. It has women's and Young Farmers' movements, and some 16 adult education centres. By 1954 it could be claimed in the Archdiocese of Cologne that two-thirds of all rural parishes had Farmers' Committees within the framework of the K.L.D.

Italy also has today the beginnings of a Young Christian Farmers' Movement, as well as a powerful general development of Catholic Action in rural parishes. In France the educational task was taken up first of all, in the 'thirties, by the Young Christian Farmers, and then, chiefly since the Second World War, by the Rural Family Movement to which they gave rise. Both of these will be dealt with at more length below.[1]

Fifteen or twenty years ago, if one asked which were the most successful and promising of the European Christian farmers' movements, there could be little doubt of the answer. The prize went to the Belgian and Dutch farmers' unions, Protestant as well as Catholic, on the ground of their double success in assisting their members economically and also raising their religious and cultural level. If there is more doubt about who should take the prize today, it is not because these movements have lost ground. On the contrary. The Belgian *Boerenbond*, and its associated *Alliance Agricole* for the French-speaking districts, are overwhelmingly the most important farmers' organisations in the country. In Holland also the Catholic Farmers' and Market Gardeners' Union (K.N.B.T.B.) is the largest, with about 48% of all organised farmers in 1953. The Protestant C.B.T.B.'s membership began to rise fast about 1930: it reached 18,764 in 1939 and 25,571 in 1947, and by 1953 had 16% of the total of organised farmers. Combining this with the membership of the K.N.B.T.B., it appears that nearly twice as many farmers join the Christian organisations as the neutral Royal Dutch Agricultural Committee.

But today it is at least arguable, in the light of experience, that as good results, or better, can be obtained on both counts—economic and cultural or religious—by training a Christian élite in a separate Christian Action organisation to act as a leaven in a neutral farmers' union, as by the Dutch and Belgian technique of the specifically Christian union combining educational with trade functions. The French Young Christian Farmers have, as they justifiably claim, shaped a whole new generation of leaders who will be rising to influence over the next few decades, with further help and training from the adult Rural Family Movement. The question whether and when the Belgian-Dutch or the French and German approach

---

[1] Chapter XIX.

pays best must for the moment be left open. It will take at least another generation to answer it.

THE EMPLOYERS', MANAGERS', AND BUSINESS MIDDLE-CLASS MOVEMENTS. THE FIRST GENERATION: TO 1920

This group of movements was very much a thing of bits and pieces until the First World War. The most substantial of its sections, at least among the bigger firms, was that in *France*. The Catholic employers in the North of France, especially in the textile industry, were beginning in the eighteen-seventies to feel the need for concerted action to express their obligation as employers and Christians. The greatest of them, Leon Harmel of Val-des-Bois, was at this time building up an impressive system of welfare services and joint consultation, and others were beginning to look to his example. In 1884 was founded a Catholic Employers' Association for the North of France which acquired a wide influence. It was dissolved in 1892 by order of the courts, as its religious objects at that time put it outside the law permitting trade unions. But it was revived in another form, as a 'Social Studies Conference'. A number of its members did in fact follow Harmel's example in developing welfare services, personnel management, and joint consultation. They also promoted a number of 'mixed unions' of the kind already described. These assembled some thousands of workers as well as employers, and did valuable work in the field of mutual insurance, consumers' co-operation, housing, and to some extent also joint consultation and conciliation and arbitration.

In the course of 1889–91 Harmel collaborated with a priest at Paris, Fr. Alet, to found a 'Fraternal Union of Trade and Industry', which published a Catholic trade directory, provided information for its members on various trade matters—advertising, insurance, transport, taxation—and also undertook their personal and religious formation. By 1895 the Union had some 1,200 members in Paris alone; its peak membership in France as a whole was 7,000. It recruited in practice mainly shopkeepers, with a certain number of small manufacturers and a few large; very like Boaz, and not much more effective. In 1896 an important section, the builders, broke off because they wished to take a more specific and positive line in trade matters. Other similarly minded groups linked up with these, notably through the work of Fr. Puppey-Girard, and in 1901 was founded a 'Central Association of Federated Unions', based on some 26 trade groups combined into federations of associated trades. This established itself firmly, especially at Paris, and in the next few years took an active line on such issues as legal provision for arbitration, workers' pensions, and Sunday observance. Its building federation in 1902 organised a joint conference with the Clerical Workers' and associated unions; this was among the first, if not actually the first, case of joint action between

251

employers' and independent clerical and manual workers' unions in the French Christian social movement. Fr. Puppey-Girard was also responsible for the foundation in 1892 of what presently became the 'Catholic Engineers' Social Union' (U.S.I.C.). Formed originally as a religious association for graduates of one of the main engineering schools (Central) it constituted itself legally as a trade union in 1902, and in 1905 extended its recruitment to all Catholic engineers. By 1911 it had about a thousand members. Some other professional groups, such as that of the journalists, were also beginning to come up from the eighteen-eighties.

By the end of the First World War these various groups in France were beginning, like the farmers' movements, to settle down and consolidate. The 'Fraternal Union' and 'Central Association of Federated Unions' combined in 1926 into what is today the leading organisation for French Catholic employers, the French Christian Employers' Centre (C.F.P.C.); the title was less openly confessional in 1926. The Engineers' Social Union, which includes also managers if they happen to be technicians, gave birth to a separate Salaried Engineers' Social Union, and the organisation of intellectual workers also made rapid strides. A Catholic Intellectuals' Professional Association (C.P.I.C.) was founded in 1921, and received the support of a number of teachers', writers', doctors', and other 'intellectual' groups. The number of such groups was now becoming substantial.

In *Germany* no Christian movement for the larger employers had yet developed. An emissary was despatched there from the Dutch employers just after the First World War, and interviewed the leading Catholic economist, Fr. Heinrich Pesch.

> A Catholic employers' association? Don't start that in Germany! Till 1912 we had here the unfortunate battle between the Cologne and Berlin tendencies [the *Gewerkschaftsstreit* referred to above]. Start a Catholic employers' association and the old battle will blaze up again.(Quoted in Allgemeine Katholieke Werkgeversvereniging, *Waarvoor Wij Staan*, 1950, p. 80.)

But Germany did have, and even from before this generation, important organisations for the business middle class. The oldest, the *Kolpingsfamilie* or Journeymen's Association, dates from as far back as 1844–5. It is primarily a youth organisation, catering for young craftsmen just out of their time; chiefly for those likely to set up for themselves, though also today for those who will remain wage-earners. Its proper place is therefore in the next chapter. But it is one of those youth organisations, like the Young Christian Farmers in France, of which it can be said that they have made their spirit penetrate into the whole of that part of the adult world in which their past members move. The 'old boys' of Kolping are grouped in *Meistervereine* or Masters' Associations. But it has never seemed worth while for these to go beyond educational and social functions

252

and set up as guilds or trade associations on their own. There are in Germany statutory guilds, which are neutral. There has been plenty of non-Christian influence in them, and Kolping and ex-Kolping members have been very critical of it; of a tendency, that is, as they see it, to subordinate wider consideration to the search for profit at any price. But they have been strong and confident enough to feel justified in leaving trade functions to the neutral guilds, in which their point of view is in fact very effectively represented. The influence of Kolping extends also to Switzerland and Austria, and at various times has been significant in Holland and Hungary. It has been felt at one time or another in all the countries of continental Europe which have a Catholic social movement at all.

In 1877 was founded in Germany a Catholic Commercial Union (K.K.V.), for principals and assistants in the distributive trades. It arose out of a series of purely religious groupings, the Marian Congregations for young men in the distributive trades, of which the first was founded at Aachen in 1854. The K.K.V. was and is, like Kolping, a social and educational body, not a trade association or trade union. It grew steadily though modestly, and by the turn of the century had some 14,000 members. It is interesting as one of the few successful and lasting applications of the 'mixed guild' ideas common in those days, for it has never ceased to include both owners and managers on the one hand and clerks and assistants on the other. Difficulties arose over this when the white-collar workers began to organise their own unions, and in 1920 it was agreed that the K.K.V.'s employee members were to be encouraged to belong to one of the Christian white-collar unions as well.

In *Holland* 'Boaz' included Protestant employers and members of business middle class of all kinds from 1892, but, as was said in connection with the farmers, to no very practical effect. It was not till 'Boaz' was split in 1918, and a Christian Employers' Association and Christian Middle Class Union were formed out of it as well as the C.B.T.B., that the way to successful and permanent organisation was opened. The new employers' and middle-class organisations became solidly established in due course with trade as well as educational and social functions; but their course at first, as has been seen from the case-history of the C.W.V., was not at all clear.

The Dutch Catholic employers' and business middle-class movement developed with fewer setbacks, though at first in a very fragmentary way. A Catholic employers' association—of cigar-makers—was founded in North Brabant some time before 1907. This was an association with trade functions. An association with social and educational functions, the forerunner of an employers' 'social class' or 'Stand' organisation, was set up by pottery and engineering firms at Venlo in 1910. By that time there were also a number of local associations of Catholic craftsmen and shop-keepers, which by 1912 had developed far enough to justify establishing diocesan federations. In 1915 these diocesan federations were combined into the present Dutch Catholic Middle Class Union, which has both trade and educational or social functions, though these are operated through distinct organisational channels. It has one pyramid of trade associations and another of local clubs and diocesan unions, culminating in a common national committee. The bigger employers followed suit a little later. In 1915 it was possible to form a 'social class' organisation of employers, with educational and social functions; the present A.K.W.V. or 'General Association for Catholic Employers'. (Plate opposite.) By 1919 there were also enough Catholic trade groups, in the cigar, leather, biscuit, pottery, printing, engineering, and textile trades, to justify setting up a Federation of Catholic Trade Associations with trade functions. In 1921 this and the A.K.W.V. were brought together in a personal union, with a common address and the same officials, though retaining separate constitutions and letter-heads.

The spark also leapt over at this time into *Belgium*, where there seems previously to have been nothing, at least for the larger employers, beyond an ephemeral Catholic Employers' Association of which all that is known is that it existed in the early 'nineties. But in 1920 there was a new start. The chaplain of the Dutch Catholic employers in Limburg visited Liége and Louvain to investigate the possibilities of a Belgian Catholic employers' organisation. He visited among others a professor of the Catholic University of Louvain, a man also largely responsible for developing the then new coalfields of the Campine.

Nothing doing! The interview lasted two minutes, on the doorstep. The Professor simply could not see what it was about. A Catholic organisation for leaders in business life? But that sort of leadership had nothing to do with Catholic principles! (*Waarvoor wij Staan*, Allgemeine Katholieke Werkgevers-vereniging 1950, p. 79.)

It seems that the failure was due not only to lack of enthusiasm for the idea of a Christian employers' organisation but also to political disputes between Belgium and Holland. Certain Belgian claims on Holland, going back to the war of liberation in 1830, had at that time flared up again. In East Belgium, on the scene of this dispute, the chaplain from Limburg seems not to have been the man to calm the storm. But at the other end of the country there was more success. Dutch contacts, notably through cigar firms with factories in both countries, touched off a Catholic employers' association at Antwerp in 1923. Another came up at Courtrai about the same time, and what later became the Catholic Employers' and Engineers' Association (A.P.I.C.) was founded at Brussels in 1920–3. The latter was purely an educational and service—'social class'—organisation,

DUTCH CATHOLIC EMPLOYERS' MOVEMENT

NATIONAL COMMITTEE

FEDERATION OF CATHOLIC TRADE ASSOCIATIONS

EXECUTIVE COMMITTEE

OFFICERS

GENERAL SECRETARIAT

DE KATHOLIEKE WERKGEVER

The Federation of Catholic Trade Associations is a national grouping of Trade associations, whose members are firms as such

FEDERATION COMMITTEE

NATIONAL ASSOCIATION OF CATHOLIC EMPLOYERS (A.K.W.V.)

Friesland Circle · Groningen Circle · Gelder/Ov. Circle · Utrecht Circle · Twente Section

Alkmaar Circle · Amsterdam Circle · Haarlem Circle · Leiden Circle · The Hague Circle · Rotterdam Schiedam Circle · Study Circle · Study Circle

Venlo Circle · Weert Circle · Roermond Circle · Maastricht Circle · Study Circle · Study Circle

Bostel Circle · Eindhoven Circle · Helmond Circle · 's Hertogenbosch Circle · Nijmegen Circle · Tilburg Circle · Study Circle · Study Circle II

A.K.W.V. Archdiocese of Utrecht.

A.K.W.V. Diocese of Haarlem

A.K.W.V. Diocese of Limburg

A.K.W.V. Diocese of Breda

A.K.W.V. Diocese of 's Hertogenbosch

The National Association of Catholic Employers is a national organisation grouping five diocesan associations, which employers join as individuals whereas the Antwerp group intended at first to develop also trade association functions on the Dutch model. And about this time were also laid the foundations of what are now the leading Christian business middle-class associations in Belgium.

With this wave of new foundations, the employers' and middle-class movements began to take shape. By the early 'twenties movements of all the classes covered in this section—employers, business middle class, the professions—were established in one country or another. The distinction familiar in the trade unions and farmers' movements between Belgium and Holland and the rest was now emerging in the employers' and middle-class movements as well. The Belgian and Dutch organisations so far mentioned, except A.P.I.C., aimed at least at the start at providing their members both with trade services and with general services and personal formation. The French and German organisations on the other hand, except for the Salaried Engineers' Union, which was a trade union rather than an employers' association, were educational and general service bodies. U.S.I.C. and C.F.P. have both done a vast amount to educate their members and the general public, including non-Christian employers. They express their views on matters of industrial policy, and they run their conferences, schools, and so on. But they are not trade associations, any more than the K.K.V. or Kolping. That is left to neutral groups in which the Catholic bodies try (today with substantial success) to ensure that their views are represented.

THE EMPLOYERS' MOVEMENT: 1920–50

Even after the new foundations and consolidations of 1915–25, the Christian employers' and middle-class movements were in much less finished form than, at the same date, the farmers' or workers' movement. It is not surprising that the next generation saw much more marked extensions and modifications.

First, the *Catholic employers*' movement now extended itself all over Europe, and indeed outside it, notably to Canada and South America. Swiss (V.C.U.), German (B.K.U.), Italian (U.C.I.D.), and also British Catholic employers' associations emerged about or just after the Second World War; the British indeed enjoying the luxury of two, a Catholic Industrialists' Conference, which is officially recognized by the Catholic employers' international, and an Association of Catholic Managers and Employers. All these are primarily educational organisations, concerned with such things as management training or the promotion of human relations in industry. Various developments also took place in the existing French and Belgian movements. In France was founded in 1936 the neutral but Christian-inspired 'Young Employers' Movement', and in 1948 the C.F.P. adopted the frank title of 'Christian', so coming into line with its sister organisations in other countries. In Belgium the Flemish groups federated in 1935 into a 'General National Catholic Employers' Association'. They experimented for a time with trade association work in the cigar, brick, brewing, and food wholesaling trades, but eventually were won over to the A.P.I.C.'s view and decided to concentrate entirely on education and general services, including family allowances, mutual insurance, and advice to members on taxation and labour problems. In 1937 they combined with the A.P.I.C. to establish a Federation of Belgian Catholic Employers (F.E.P.A.C.), which received permanent form in 1945. The F.E.P.A.C. and its constituent Walloon (A.P.I.C.) and Flemish groups now form the only exception to the rule that the Christian Social organisations in Holland and Belgium, whether on the management or on the workers' side, have trade as well as educational functions. The Dutch Catholic employers' association has continued to have functions of both kinds. So has its Protestant opposite number, the C.W.V., where recent history was sketched in the last Chapter.

The Catholic employers' organisations and the Protestant C.W.V., as they stand today, do effective work, though usually within fairly narrow limits. In Holland, where the functions of the Christian employers' movements are widest, the neutral organisations are still the most important, and the Protestant and Catholic associations together have been able to claim only two out of the nine employers' seats on the National Economic Council. But both have been coming up fast in recent years, more particularly among medium employers. (Plate overleaf.) Though the very largest employers still tend to hold off from them, the wind is blowing their way. Elsewhere in Europe the Catholic employers' organisations, though they confine themselves to educational and other non-trade functions and are nowhere dominant, are present, dynamic, and influential everywhere. The C.F.P.C. in France had by 1949 a membership of 10,000 and the Young Employers' Centre 4,000. Both bodies are represented in the national executive of the neutral National Federation of French Employers (C.N.P.F.), and their members have leading positions in a number of other neutral bodies. The C.F.P.C.'s management training programmes are particularly highly developed. In Belgium the F.E.P.A.C. is a constituent member of the Federation of Belgian Industry, and a very active and influential one. Its chairman is at the time of writing also chairman of the F.B.I. The B.K.U. in Germany has a relatively small membership. But it is active on the educational side, often in co-operation with the Catholic Workers' Movement. Its political influence, which is considerable, illustrates the principle which occurs again and again in the history of Christian Democracy, that the strength of the Christian movements depends not only on their own membership and resources but also on the existence of other like-minded movements to which they can turn.

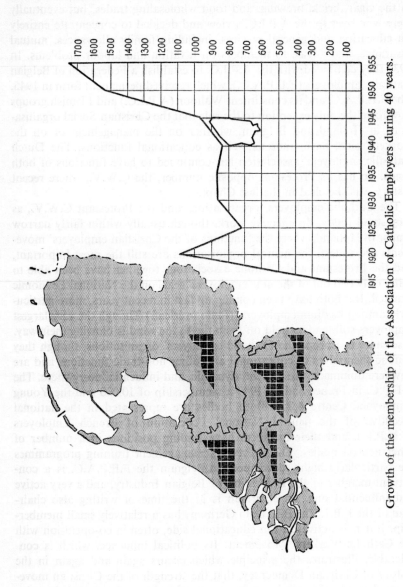

Growth of the membership of the Association of Catholic Employers during 40 years.

258

Several B.K.U. members are in parliament, and with other sympathisers constitute a parliamentary group within the Christian Democratic Union, which has been the leading Government party ever since democratic government in Germany was restored. In Italy, finally, the U.C.I.D., in spite of its youth, is already well established and is growing fast in all the main industrial districts. It has considerable and growing influence, through personal connections, in the main neutral organisations in industry and in large-scale commerce and agriculture.

The Catholic employers have an International (U.N.I.A.P.A.C.), moves for whose establishment go back to 1920–4. The International itself regards as its origin a meeting in January 1924 at Antwerp between the Dutch and the Belgians.

> Our efforts were then turned to Flanders, where it finally proved possible to lay the foundations of our international. . . . On a cold and foggy day in January 1924 we travelled to Antwerp with the Chairman of the A.K.W.V., J. Asselbergs, and Dr. Kortenhorst, to the 'Kalkoensche Haan' restaurant, where a meeting of Catholic employers at Antwerp was being held. It was a modest start in an appalling room, chilly, and discouraging. But it was still Christmas-time, and we drew the parallel of the Stable at Bethlehem . . . whereupon they replied that in that case we must be the Three Wise Men from the North. (Cassianus Hentzen, O.F.M., in A.K.W.V., op. cit., p. 81.)

Actually, this started merely a link, not a formal association. That did not come till 1930–1, when formal discussions took place between representatives from Belgium, Holland, and France. A German delegate represented, not indeed a German Catholic Employers' Association, since there was none, but the Catholic employers' group associated with the Centre Party. It was not at that time possible to set the International on a permanent footing, as the Vatican preferred to wait for a time to see how a series of 'International Conferences' of the associations worked out. It was not till 1949 that the International Association of Catholic Employers' Organisations (U.N.I.A.P.A.C.) was finally founded.

THE BUSINESS MIDDLE-CLASS MOVEMENTS, 1920–50

The *business middle-class movements* have also not been idle. They did not extend into new countries after 1920. But the middle-class (shopkeepers' and craftsmen's) organisation in Holland and Belgium, which as has been said have full trade association as well as educational and political functions, have increased and multiplied until they are the most powerful in their respective countries. The business middle class are a hard group to organise in any country, and Holland and Belgium are no exceptions. It is reckoned in Holland that 70% of farmers and 85–90% of all medium to large employers join trade organisations, but only about 30–40% of all employers in the business middle class. In Belgium the proportion joining is still lower. But among those who do join, in both countries, the Christian

Democratic organisations have the leading place. The Dutch Catholic Middle Class Union claims to have the biggest membership in Holland, and the Protestant 'Christian Middle Class Union' has substantial and increasing support. The two together lead the field. The two largest Belgian organisations for the business middle class, the National Federation of the Middle Classes (French-speaking) and the Christian National Middle Class Union (Flemish), with a combined total of 70,000 members, are both of Christian inspiration. The French-speaking organisation finds that it has to play down any formally Christian element in deference to the large mass of floating voters, always ready to join the unorganised majority, whose politics are liberal and whose motto is 'business is business'. Many outside observers therefore regard the National Federation as a liberal rather than a Christian organisation. This seems however to be a confusion between the tactics adopted by the leadership and the strategy behind them. Strategically, the aims of the leadership seem clearly to be such as to bring them into the Christian Democratic fold. Like the farmers' organisations, the middle-class organisations have full trade association functions. By 1950 the Dutch and Belgian middle-class movements had not merely established their own organisation firmly but also won their preliminary battle in public affairs. They had obtained for the affairs of the middle class the same sort of considerations from State departments as is normally given to those of industry, farmers, and labour.

In Germany Kolping and the K.K.V. have continued on their way, though both suffered severely during the Nazi period. Kolping recovered rapidly after 1945, thanks to the continuing loyalty of its 'old boys'. The K.K.V.'s recovery was slower; it had 45,000 members in 1934, at the beginning of the Nazi regime, and had regained only 12,000 by 1949. In 1955 an International Catholic Movement for the Middle Class (I.K.M.B.) was formed, bringing together the Catholic organisations in Holland, Belgium, and Germany. The Dutch Catholic Middle Class Union supplies the secretariat.

Business middle-class groups on a Christian basis are now to be found in other countries besides these, and some at least are influential. The Swiss Conservative People's Party, for instance, includes a 'Business Middle Class Group' which works in and with the neutral Swiss Crafts' and Commercial Union (Schweizerische Gewerbeverband). One of the components of the Austrian People's Party is the 'Economic Union', which represents craftsmen and shopkeepers, and also the free professions, as well as the bigger employers. Italy has a Catholic-inspired National Craftsmen's Centre. France has a number of fairly effective Catholic groups, with educational not trade functions, in trades such as printing, or butchery, or among department store staffs. There is a general Catholic

Action movement for the Independent Classes (ACI), which by 1949 had a membership of 20,000. Of these French movements, however, the most that can be said is that they provide a sound foundation on which to build. They have not yet grown far enough to have any very great influence themselves, and many of them show little promise of ever doing so. Powerful and effective business middle-class organisations do exist in France. The General Confederation of Small and Medium Businesses had in 1949 some 120,000 members on the manufacturing and craft side and 600,000 on the commercial side. More recently, in 1954–5, the shopkeepers' revolt led by M. Poujade—it is probably nearer the mark to speak of it as a revolt than as an organised and considered movement—has proved to be a force in French politics. But Christian influence in these movements has been at best sporadic.

1920–1950: PROFESSIONAL AND MANAGERIAL WORKERS

It is on coming to the 'intellectual' professions that one realises most fully the truth of Joseph Folliet's comment on the difficulty of organising this variegated and immensely differentiated category; though also, on the other hand, the great strides made in the last generation towards doing so. In Holland the Catholic 'St. Adalbert Association' groups for cultural and social purposes some 3,000 members of the intellectual professions, and there is a variety of specialised groups for all and sundry, from town clerks to that 'lively and original body' (as the chronicler puts it), the Catholic Cultural Association of Teachers of Dancing. The Evangelical Church in Germany has made since the Second World War a remarkable effort to stimulate self-education among members of all social groups, and of the intellectual professions in particular, through its 'Academies' or discussion centres; the Academy movement has since been taken up by the Catholic Church in Germany as well. In France specialised groups cater for a number of the free professions, such as doctors (3,200 members in 1949), pharmacists (1,700 out of a possible 13,000), journalists, artists, lawyers, and so on. Catholic Action for the Independent Classes covers the free professions as well as the business middle class. The Catholic Engineers' Social Union (U.S.I.C.) and the Salaried Engineers' Union have continued to build up their influence. At the end of the Second World War the Salaried Engineers' Union took a leading part in founding the Staffs' Federation (C.G.C.), which has its place alongside the C.F.T.C., C.G.T., and Force Ouvrière as one of the main French trade union centres. It is a neutral organisation, but one in which technicians and managers from the Christian organisations hold many leading positions. On the educational side, U.S.I.C. came at the same time to be flanked by the 'Catholic Action Movement for Engineers and Employers' (M.I.C.I.A.C.). MICIAC specialises in training managers and supervisors—or, to be more exact, in helping managers and supervisors to train themselves—to solve their own immediate problems. USIC is more concerned with big public issues, statements of policy, and training for leadership in the neutral employers' and managers' organisations. A 'Young USIC' group has been formed to supply recruits to both USIC and MICIAC. USIC set out after the Second World War to form an international association of Catholic engineers and managers. It has held two international conferences, which attracted support from groups in these grades all over Western Europe, particularly in Germany, Holland, and Italy.

In quite a different sphere, one of the most numerous and impressive professional groups recorded in the Annual of French Catholic Action is that of the (employed) social workers, with 12,000 members in 1949. This is a group which tends to be well organised everywhere, helped of course by the place which the Churches themselves hold in the social services. In the official Church Year Book of the Catholic Church in Germany the list headed 'The Church and Social Service' includes some 72 separate national and regional organisations, most of them grouped round the 'Caritasverband'. In Holland and to a less extent in Belgium many even of the statutory social services—the hospital service, for example—are organised on denominational lines. The Dutch Catholic Bishops sponsored just after the Second World War a major research project on the availability and distribution of Catholic doctors, which led among other things to the creation of a medical faculty at the Catholic University of Nijmegen. It has been noted earlier how under the Belgian system of national insurance workers organised in the Christian trade unions normally register with an approved society on a specifically Christian basis, and, having done so, naturally find themselves guided to Christian practitioners in medicine, the social services, and the rest. The Catholic International Union of Social Service, at any rate, however, to whatever its influence may be due, affiliated in 1954 some 93 schools for social workers, nine other training centres, and 27 social workers' associations. The majority— 56 schools, 4 other centres, and 16 associations—were in Europe.

Teachers are another group often well organised. In Italy Giorgio Candeloro, author of the Communist Party's handbook on Catholic Action, has to admit with regret that Catholic Action's movements for teachers, the *Movimento Maestri* and the two separate associations for secondary and university teachers, are strong enough to permeate the whole policy of the neutral teachers' trade unions. The *Movimento Laureati* or 'Graduates' Movement', to which the associations of secondary and University teachers are affiliated, groups also separate organisations for Catholic 'technicians'—understood rather widely to cover all the technical professions, including doctors—and for lawyers, artists, publicists, and pharmacists. Internationally, Catholic graduates of

262

all faculties are linked up through *Pax Romana* which also includes students. This movement is strongly represented all over Europe, and has its centre at Fribourg in Switzerland.

This list is selective, a matter of examples. It shows something of the variety and strength of the development in these various fields in the last generation; it cannot show anything like the whole of it.

CONCLUSION

What is difficult to bring out fully in a short summary such as this is the difference, in spite of the multiplication of organisations, between the stage of development reached by the middle-class movements, other perhaps than that of the farmers, and that reached by the workers' movements. The workers' movements' age of experiment lies forty or fifty years in the past. They have chosen their road, built their machinery, and settled down in their ways. A new stage of development may be dawning for them; but meantime they have in recent years shown themselves relatively stable and mature. The farmers' unions or Kolping give this impression as well. But when one comes to the employers' movements or, still more, to those for intellectual and professional workers, the impression is still very much one of a formative stage. No doubt certain tendencies are visible already. It is clear that, for the reasons set out in the last chapter, specifically Christian movements tend in these fields, much more than in that of the workers' or farmers' movements, to confine themselves to educational and general service activities; it is a question of Christian penetration of more or less neutral environments or organisations, rather than of Christians setting up their own professional or trade associations. Perhaps one should say that this is a matter of degree rather than of kind, for there are workers' and farmers' movements even in Continental Europe which prefer to rely on the method of penetration, just as there are employers' and business middle-class groups in Holland or Belgium which prefer to stand completely on their own. The all-pervading difference between Dutch and Belgian practice and that of the rest of Christian Europe cuts across the distinction between workers and farmers and the rest of the middle class. It may also be that the tendency to limit the role of specifically Christian organisations is due to the relatively late growth and weakness of the Christian movements for the middle class, as well as to a different view of what in any case is the right approach. But the dominant impression in this field is not in any case one of fixed aims and agreed methods. It is one of expansion and multiplication—very rapid since the Second World War—and of experiment. And for that reason the middle-class movements constitute today an exciting field, in a way which they certainly did not a generation ago.

CHAPTER XIX

THE RISE OF CHRISTIAN DEMOCRACY, 1880–1950

THE YOUTH AND FAMILY MOVEMENTS

THE YOUTH MOVEMENTS

(a) The beginnings: to the First World War

WE ARE concerned here, as before, with Christian youth movements only in so far as they have a substantial impact on social action. One or two movements with a substantial social content have a history running back to the eighteen-forties or 'fifties. On the Protestant side, the Y.M.C.A., Y.W.C.A., and similar groupings under other names originated at that time. They tended to appeal mainly to white-collar people and craftsmen, and were primarily and essentially a religious, apostolic, movement. But they had a certain social content even—sometimes, in fact, particularly—in the early days. In Switzerland, for instance, the historian of the Evangelical Workers' Movement sees them as the forerunners of the Evangelical Workers' Leagues founded at the end of the nineteenth century. He shows how in the 'eighties and 'nineties a movement developed to re-group the members of the Swiss Y.M.C.A. on occupational lines. There was at that time a good deal of exchange of views within the association on trade matters and the development of the working-class movement. In 1906 and 1907 it was on the initiative of Methodist members of the Y.M.C.A. that the 'SESUK' friendly society, the predecessor of the S.V.E.A. trade unions, was brought into existence. Once, however, the Evangelical workers' movement was launched, the Y.M.C.A. tended to concentrate again on 'their original main purpose, the spreading of the Gospel among young people'.

On the Catholic side the great name from the early years is that of Adolf Kolping. As curate at Elberfeld in the Ruhr he started in 1844–5 a group of young craftsmen; not factory workers, but men in the traditional craft trades. From 1849, when Fr. Kolping was transferred to the cathedral at Cologne, the movement rapidly took hold. It was from the start a Catholic Action movement, concerned essentially with education rather than with social policy.

264

[Kolping] used every available means of education. Far from regarding religious and moral teaching as sufficient, he brought to bear the whole arsenal of educational techniques to turn his young journeymen into all-round, fully developed personalities; good Christians, good fathers of their families, good craftsmen, good members of the nation and the state. He put chaplains at their disposal to carry on the direct work of education, demanding that the chaplains should keep the closest possible contact with these young person-alities and, so to speak, give them their hearts in pledge. He created for them a new, family-like, community . . . he built them centres and hostels for when they were away from their family home. He knew how to use courses and conferences to take hold of all their interests in life on earth—their family, craft, class, national, and political interests—and to help them to success. He worked to take hold of their emotions through song and enjoyment, through celebrations and national customs, so as to root the whole man fast in nation and land, in class and craft, in Church and society. (*Handbuch des Katholischen Gesellenvereins*, Swiss ed., 1945, pp. 83–4.)

As with all Catholic Action movements, the control of the Kolping Associations is essentially in the hands of the chaplains, though over the years their day to day running has come to be largely in the hands of their members. Their growth was checked for a time by the Kulturkampf, during which police action was taken against them on a number of occasions. But by 1885, when the Kulturkampf was easing off, there were nearly 30,000 members in Germany and about 8,500 elsewhere; mainly in Austria-Hungary, though with smaller contingents in Switzerland and Holland. These figures now included a number of factory workers; for in 1870, though still considering that men in the independent crafts were its main target, the associations' Congress agreed that craftsmen in factories might be brought in as well.

But Kolping's work, though outstandingly successful, also remained for a generation unique. The beginning of the greater part of the modern Catholic political and social youth movements goes back to the familiar period in the eighteen-seventies and 'eighties when so many of the other Catholic social movements also had their rise, and their growth shows the usual two-phase pattern. The outstanding feature of the first generation, to just before the First World War, was the success in several countries of all-purpose, largely middle- and upper-class movements. In the second generation growth was spread more evenly between classes, and specialisa-tion by class and to some extent by purpose—political or social—increased.

The first major movement to be founded was the Italian Catholic Action Youth, the G.I.A.C. It was started in 1868 as a means of rallying Catholic forces in defence of the temporal power of the Pope. The G.I.A.C. was at first small—it had only 72 local groups by 1874—but became and has remained influential. In 1874 it was responsible for bringing together the first national congress of Italian Catholics, the beginning of the Congress Movement which was to dominate Italian Catholic social and political action for the next thirty years. Between then and 1890 a number of similar movements were founded by young Catholics in other countries. What is now 'Catholic Action for French Youth' (A.C.J.F.) was started in 1886, being touched off by the example of the Swiss Catholic youth movement by then already flourishing, and the corresponding Belgian organisation (A.C.J.B.) also dates from this period.

These movements were primarily upper and upper middle-class, recruiting largely from students. Their history is even more liberally adorned than that of most Catholic organisations of the time with the names of Princes and Counts. The A.C.J.F. said quite frankly in 1890 that:

> For the moment, the Association is chiefly concerned with recruiting in the so-called ruling classes, that is among young people who have had a secondary education or its equivalent. (*L'A.C.J.F.*, fiftieth centenary publication of the Association, 1936, p. 8.)

But this was a temporary phase. The A.C.J.F., though concerned on the one hand with problems special to upper- and middle-class life ('to tear the bourgeois from their pleasures, their fashions, their fripperies . . . and remind them that they will have to give a final account of all that'), was also much interested in the growing problems of the working class.

> The common people, gentlemen, the workers in the towns, the factories, and the fields—there is the great problem which should fill your thoughts. (From an address to the A.C.J.F. by Albert de Mun, loc. cit., p. 10.)

In 1896 there arose alongside the A.C.J.F. another Catholic youth movement, the *Sillon* or 'Furrow', which is the direct ancestor of modern French Christian Democracy. The *Sillon*'s defects were numerous and glaring. It did not suffer over-much from democracy itself. It was founded by and remained centred around one man, Marc Sangnier, who had an immense capacity for attracting personal attachment, but almost none for building a permanent and stable organisation. Its doctrine was often gaseous and sentimental, with an absence of hard edges. We have quoted above Jules Zirnheld's comment on how Marc Sangnier's vacillation and initial woolly idealism damaged the Christian trade unions at a critical period of their growth. Emmanuel Mounier, for several years editor of *Esprit* and one of the most dynamic figures in French Catholic life, used to describe the French Christian Democrats' political attitude as characteristically 'soft': and this 'softness' was inherited from the Sangnier age. And Sangnier failed to keep a clear distinction between the role of an educational organisation, belonging like the A.C.J.F. to Catholic Action and responsible to the official Church, and that of an independent, lay, political party, which the *Sillon* tended to become. Some of its members, though not Sangnier himself, followed 'modernists' such as Loisy into definite theological error. In the end, in 1910, the Church authorities took

266

matters into their own hands and required the *Sillon* in its existing form to be broken up. Its members could pursue political action if they so wished. But the danger of theological error and confusion with Catholic Action must end. *Sillon* groups, as such, must become formally part of Catholic Action, under the authority of and responsible to the Bishops.

Yet in spite of all this woolliness, Sangnier's remarkable personality won his movement an immense influence. With its left wing idealism it focused attention on social problems and on the case for political action to solve them. It also showed the need to extend the youth movement to cover (as the *Sillon* itself soon came to do) all social classes. The *Sillon*, says Joseph Folliet, is sometimes compared to *L'Avenir*, and Sangnier to Lamennais: but it is a superficial comparison, for the influence of the *Sillon* was in fact far wider and deeper. It set going a genuine mass movement, whose influence is not yet exhausted. When it broke up, its members scattered into an enormous variety of other movements:

> One finds them at the origin of one movement after another. The Scouts, with Lucien Goualle . . . at the origins of the Y.C.W. and specialised Catholic Action, with Fr. Guerin . . . of Christian trade unionism, with Marcel Poimboeuf, Georges Torcq, and many others . . . of the pacifist movement . . . at the beginnings of the Youth Hostel movement . . . of the renewal of parish life with Fr. Remillieux. One finds them in publishing . . . in journalism, with Francisque Gay, founder of *La Vie Catholique and L'Aube*, and with the *Ouest-Éclair* group: in literature, with Francois Mauriac . . . in philosophy . . . in economic and social thought . . . in social action. (Joseph Folliet in *Chronique Sociale de France*, March–April, 1950, pp. 127–8.)

Under this impulse the A.C.J.F. also fell into line. Between 1899 and 1904 its basis of recruitment was completely transformed. Workers, clerks, and young farmers poured in, and the number of affiliated branches leapt from one hundred to eleven hundred. It is significant that the theme of its annual congress was 'Trade Unionism' in 1903 and 'Labour Conditions of Young Workers' in 1905. By 1911 it was estimated that some 512 branches had founded between them:

> 26 trade union branches
> 150 branches of farmers' unions
> 20 co-operative societies
> 118 friendly societies
> 8 social service bureaux
> An unspecified number of allotment societies, housing societies, and credit and insurance societies.
>
> <div align="right">(<i>L'A.C.J.F.</i>, 1936, p. 467.)</div>

And 53 Mayors then in office had been trained in the A.C.J.F.'s ranks.

It was not only in France that new currents were flowing. In Italy also it was in the youth movements that modern conceptions of Christian Democratic politics were born. A main carrier of these ideas was the

Italian University Catholic Federation (F.U.C.I.), founded in 1896. But the G.I.A.C. also played an important part in the ferment of new political ideas which arose in the Congress movement around the turn of the century. In Italy as in France, and indeed all over Catholic Europe, this free flow of new ideas among the youth movements was rather sharply checked in the period of 'integrist', orthodox, reaction under Pius X. The A.C.J.F., for example, though proud of having always maintained rigorous orthodoxy, was forced to curtail its activities in order to escape denunciations and condemnations. It was skilfully led through the most difficult period by Pierre Gerlier, whose orthodoxy proved strong enough in due course to cause him not only to enter the Church but to rise to be Bishop and Cardinal. But even he could not prevent drastic purges; in the strongly Catholic Vendée, for example, 92 out of 180 local branches were dissolved.

(b) The rise of specialisation: from the First World War to 1950

However, this was only a temporary check. A new trend was on the way. Most of the organisations mentioned so far in this chapter, whether Catholic or Protestant, were general-purpose bodies, though this did not of course prevent them from recruiting at this or that moment from a given class, or from concentrating for a time on some particular group of problems. By now, however, by the time of the First World War, the general organisations themselves, like the A.C.J.F. and the *Sillon*, were beginning to glimpse the case for the 'apostolate of like to like'. And now that the Christian trade unions, workers' leagues, and farmers' organisations were also well under way, was it not time—their example suggested —to start a similar specialisation in the youth movement as well?

(c) Specialisation: (1) the Protestant movements

The Protestant response to this challenge was very small in Germany and Switzerland, and was only partly successful in Holland. It also came rather late, the first effective action being taken only at the end of the eighteenth century. The *C.N.V. trade unions* in Holland discussed the question of youth organisation on and off from 1910 onwards. It was not till 1931, however, that it was finally decided to set up youth clubs, union by union—some individual unions had already experimented with these— wherever there were enough young members to support them. Much effort went into these clubs, but by 1939 the movement was practically dead. The clubs were usually too small to be lively, and their range of activities was restricted. They were intended to discuss trade questions and carry on social and economic education, but were expected to keep out of the field of the general Protestant youth organisations, concerned with religious and leisure interests. And they were kept firmly under adult

268

leadership. In 1940 it was decided to make a new start with joint clubs covering, if necessary, the young members of all the unions in each town or area. But the invasion cut this experiment short.

The *Dutch Protestant farmers'* youth movement did better. It was launched in 1929 to meet the competition of other young farmers' leagues. The C.B.T.B. hoped that, while the older farmers were proving reluctant to leave the 'neutral' organisations, the younger men could be won more easily. It also realised that in a world of change young people needed more deliberate training in the application of Christian principles to economic and social problems than they had been getting hitherto. Like the C.N.V.'s youth groups, the Young Protestant Farmers were expected to play second fiddle to the general Protestant youth organisations, and to keep to technical, economic, and social matters. But these matters seem to have provided more attractive food for thought for the young farmers than for young trade unionists. The Young Farmers seem also to have been given more freedom, and there was no question of splitting them up in any locality between several different clubs. The organisation took root, and in 1938 a separate girls' league was founded; with very good results, the official account says, on the morale of the young men. Neither body achieved as high a membership as its Catholic opposite number. But they have remained active and reasonably well-supported.

(d) Specialisation: (2) the German Catholic movements

On the Catholic side the move towards specialisation was much more marked, and also began much earlier. The Germans were the pioneers, particularly as regards young workers. The Kolping Associations constituted a specialised Catholic Action youth movement a lifetime before that label was thought of. Their first, formative, generation was completed by the time of the Kulturkampf. Through their second generation, down to about 1900–5, they consolidated their organisation without dramatic new departures. Regulations were made stricter now that the associations were well enough established to be able to afford to discipline their more lukewarm members. Religious instruction, for instance, was made not merely regular but compulsory, and the official history contains a number of entries such as 'restriction of festivities, namely dances' (1891). Following on the decision to admit factory workers (1870), the Associations in due course took a line in support of the rising forces of Christian trade unionism (1900), as well as of guild organisation for the independent crafts (1895). Their membership in Germany rose to what proved for the moment to be a peak of between 55,000 and 60,000 and their international membership reached between 70,000 and 80,000; about double the figure for 1885. From around 1900–5 they entered into a new phase characterised by international expansion, but also by certain important developments in

Germany. There was some democratisation. Members, as well as the clergy directing the Association, were to have a voice at the general congress. A new statute was passed in 1925. And before the First World War a move was set on foot to make Kolping a general organisation for all working youth of pre-trade union or workers' league age.

The two World Wars checked the international expansion of the Kolpingsfamilie. The building in Brussels where it had made a modest start was confiscated as enemy property after the First World War; it became for a time the headquarters of, among others, the Young Christian Workers. After the Second World War Kolping also withdrew from Holland, where it had been more solidly based, leaving only one section in Nijmegen. Hungary, Rumania, and Poland, where the movement had developed well, passed under Communist control. Outside links remained however, notably with Austria and Switzerland, and within Germany membership rose further. In 1954 there were 150,000 members of the ordinary—young craftsmen's—section, and 80,000 in the senior section for married craftsmen and those established on their own. But this membership still consisted wholly of craftsmen, and the plan to make Kolping a general movement came to nothing; for already by the First World War the Catholic Workers' Movement had set up its own organisations for working youth in general. The history of these has been briefly sketched already. The first attempt was in the eighteen-eighties; about 6,000 members were collected in 37 branches. This attempt failed through too much patronage, and too little freedom for the members themselves. The same mistake wrecked another attempt after 1907; the peak membership this time, in 1911, was 11,000. But in 1925 it proved possible to make a new start. The *Werkjugend* grew up out of informal readers' groups attached to the paper of that name. It was (and under the new name of Werkmannschaft is) a largely self-governing, primarily educational movement, in many ways very like the Young Christian Workers who began in Belgium and France about the same time. And it quickly built up not merely a substantial membership—50,000 by 1932, Kolping's membership in 1929 being 90,000 for Germany and 117,000 overall—but one active and interested, and promising to bring forward a fine new generation of leaders, genuine militants, for the workers' movement as a whole. The inter-denominational Christian trade unions also began to run youth congresses of their own.

All this flourishing movement was suppressed in the Nazi period. It was revived at the end of the war, and reinforced by the importation of the Young Christian Workers' Movement from Belgium and France. The *Werkjugend*, reborn as the *Werkmannschaft*, recruits young men from 25 to 35, and the Y.C.W. (in Germany C.A.J.) those under 25. But the reborn movement took some time to get into its stride again. By 1950 the

West German *Werkmannschaft* had recovered only to 3,300 members. In any case, the lost years after 1933 were vital ones: just those in which the Y.C.W. was expanding fastest elsewhere. Though the Germans were the pioneers in the organisation of young workers, the lead—and this refers even more to dynamism than to numbers—has now passed to other countries.

The Germans were also the pioneers in organising 'independent' youth, that is young people from the business middle class. The Catholic Commercial Union laid heavy stress, from the eighties onwards, on the technical and social education of its younger supporters. At first this was conceived essentially as an activity *for* younger members of the profession. From about 1893, however, 'apprentice sections' began to be founded in the Union's branches. By about 1906 the idea of a separate Youth Federation was beginning to make its way, and in 1913 it was finally decided to form one and to appoint a full-time organiser—a priest—to take charge of it. The Federation appeared in public for the first time at the Union's congress in 1914. It had little time to develop before the war, but was revived immediately after it at a congress at Hildesheim.

> From the Union's congress at Hildesheim date the first independent life and struggles of the Youth Federation. Our young people turned more and more strongly against the idea that they were a mere source of recruits for the main body of the Union, and sought instead for new forms of independent youth activity within the Union. This new assertion of youth within the K.K.V. was very closely connected with the general trend in the German youth movement, which took on a new impetus shortly after the First World War, presented itself as a living protest against the superficial culture of that time, and stood for a more youthful, freer, pattern of life. Under this influence youth found its appropriate expression in the 'Wander' movement; this made itself felt also among the K.K.V. youth, who established a 'Wander' movement of their own. (*Geschichte des Verbandes K.K.V.*, 1952, p. 95.)

The independence and self-confidence of the K.K.V. Youth Federation seems to have been fully achieved—as in the case of the *Werkjugend*—by about 1930–2. The Youth Federation congresses of these years were, the official history says, a clear recognition by the K.K.V. youth that 'the age of welfare work for youth is over'. In full independence the Federation adopted statutes defining its aim as:

> To work with all its power to shape the personality of young Catholics in German commerce; to make them Catholic, manly, and true, sound in body and mind, fit to make their way in life and to serve God, the people, and all humanity in their vocation of commerce.
>
> To fight with the force of unity and the full support of each member for the freedom of Christ's Church and the application of Her doctrine in social, political, and economic life.
>
> To support the reconstruction of society and the economy on vocational lines, and to establish good order in the vocation of commerce.
>
> To fight without reservation for clean, honest, honourable dealing in

commerce, and against professional incompetence and the unrestricted pursuit of profit.

To defend the Christian family, as the basis of a healthy society.

To help to maintain the determination and tenseness of German youth, and to win wider space for its development.

(Loc. cit., p. 100.)

Its members had religious obligations, and were also required to follow a course of professional training, stimulated and often provided by the K.K.V. itself, leading to a National Certificate. At this time also full co-ordination was finally established between the 'Wander' movement, with its emphasis on the open-air life, and the more commercially-minded section of the membership. The Wanderers had at one time threatened to split off. After going under in the Nazi period, the Youth Federation was revived in 1948.

(e) Specialisation: (3) *Holland, Belgium, France. The Y.C.W.*

In Holland, Belgium, and France specialisation came rather later. The Catholic farmers' organisations in Holland and Belgium set up after the First World War what in due course became flourishing Young Farmers' Leagues. In France in 1924 the A.C.J.F. equipped itself with a rural secretariat, though as yet this was merely an office, not a young farmers' movement. Among the Catholic or Catholic-inspired workers' movements of these countries specialisation began to come in around the First World War. The C.F.T.C., in France, tried from 1924 to establish 'Young Trade Unionists' groups. These succeeded quite noticeably in the women's unions, and made at least a beginning among young men. But they had little time to develop in most parts of the country before being overtaken by the rise of the Young Christian Workers, which has proved the most revolutionary influence not only in the organisation of young workers but also in the whole Catholic conception of work among young farmers and the middle class.

The beginnings of the Young Christian Workers go back to 1912, when the then Fr. Cardijn was appointed curate of Laeken at Brussels, and was put in charge of the various women's Associations. He presently built up a group of girls from the local workshops and factories. Like Kolping, he did not concentrate unduly on the catechism, but took his start from questions of daily life. 'Where do you work?' 'What do you do?' 'When do you get up?' 'Where do you wash?' He himself was a great enquirer into facts, going continually to look at social conditions and organisations; the British trade unions among others. The facts led on to a judgment, and the judgment to the suggestion of what the young people themselves might do to remedy what was wrong. The Enquiry Method and its famous 'See-Judge-Act' formula was born. Cardijn had faith in young people's ability to help themselves ('among them, by them, for them'—the movement's second great slogan), and he soon attracted lay assistants who shared his views. The first was Fernand Tonnet, a bank clerk and Christian trade unionist, who however found the unions at that time not radical enough. During the war he was mobilised, and Cardijn himself was interned after 1916. But from 1918 the work was resumed, and Cardijn and Tonnet were joined by another bank clerk, Paul Garcet, and a locksmith, Jacques Meert. From September 1920 the three laymen began to publish *La Jeunesse Syndicaliste* (Trade Union Youth) as the organ of the movement. Their grammar and spelling were home-made, but they wrote and talked a language young workers could understand. They and Cardijn asked a great deal; not only action but a full range of leisure interests, along with intensive study, a high degree of religious life, and often great personal sacrifice. And the Trade Union Youth, unlike the similarly named affiliates of the C.N.V. or C.F.T.C., intended to cater for all these lines of interest themselves. There was no question of leaving the religious and leisure interests of the young worker to one organisation, as in the C.N.V. experiment, and passing over his formation as a trade unionist and citizen to another. The young worker's life was one and indivisible and— a third main formula of the movement—could be catered for effectively only as a whole.

Experience gradually proved that their approach paid. By May 1921 membership had crept up to 300; curious characters, some of them, looking more like the fishermen of Galilee than the members of conventional Christian youth movements. The movement began to come out of its shell and become known in public. There began what Tonnet's biographer calls an 'interminable series of discussions' with the A.C.J.B., to make it possible for the Trade Union Youth to affiliate without giving up the freedom in their own affairs which their founders deemed essential. Other arguments took place with the trade unions. The T.U.Y. leaders, as their name showed, were strong supporters of trade unionism, more particularly of Christian trade unionism. But they insisted to the unions that young workers up to, say, the age of 25 needed a place apart of their own, something more than ordinary trade union membership. They had interests of their own which often either were not or could not be catered for by unions concerned—quite properly—mainly with their adult members. The trade unions did not necessarily object to youth having their place apart. But their conception of what this should be corresponded at first to that of the C.N.V. or the C.F.T.C. rather than that of the T.U.Y. Here also a hard struggle was needed to convince the unions that the fuller independence and the more comprehensive, less union-centred, type of organisation called for by the T.U.Y. were right.

By 1924 things were moving. The T.U.Y. decided to take its present more general title of the 'Young Christian Workers'. New members were won outside Brussels, and the Y.C.W. felt its way towards the awkward problem of fitting itself into the normal run of parish activities; awkward because of the comprehensive, one might almost say totalitarian claims of the Y.C.W., which made an arrangement with religious sodalities or with movements like the Boy Scouts hard to come to. A meeting of priests from all over French-speaking Belgium was held at Brussels; it was at this point that the Y.C.W. was accorded the definite right of entry into the parishes. A high pressure campaign followed, the officers organising some 300 meetings up and down the country in six months. In September 1924 was held a mass demonstration at Charleroi, when for the first time the Y.C.W. appeared publicly under its new name. Early in 1925 the Y.C.W. finally affiliated to the A.C.J.B., and a girls' section was started. In April 1925 the first National Congress was held, with 500 present; the total membership may then have been 15,000–20,000. Statutes and a programme were adopted, on lines in all essentials similar to those in force today; as regards, that is, not only the objects—set out in earlier chapters of this book—but also the form of government and relation to the Church.

From here on all was, if not exactly plain sailing, at any rate a matter of straightforward development. Membership of the Y.C.W. itself continued to rise in Belgium, and in due course the whole organisation of the Belgian Christian youth movement fell into line with Y.C.W. conceptions. The A.C.J.B. remains the co-ordinating body, under which, with a great deal of autonomy, appear separate organisations for young workers, independents, students, and also farmers. The Young Farmers' Leagues started by the Belgian Farmers' Union affiliated to the A.C.J.B. in 1928. In 1941 they were detached from the Farmers' Union and established as an autonomous organisation, like the Y.C.W., within the A.C.J.B.'s framework. There is some reason to think that the Belgian Christian youth movements as a whole, and the Y.C.W. in particular, reached in the early 'fifties a plateau or ceiling of development: a time when the movements' initial possibilities had been used up and their dynamism seemed to diminish. It is not yet clear where the resulting reassessment of aims and methods will lead.

The Y.C.W. entered *France* in 1926 through the initiative of four young workers at Clichy, in the industrial belt of Paris, who heard of what was going on in Belgium and set out eagerly to apply the same idea themselves. Within a year there were 120 local sections, and inside four years the whole A.C.J.F. was reorganised on Y.C.W. lines. The Young Christian Farmers, Young Christian Sailors, and Christian Student Movement were founded in 1929–30, and the Young Independents' Movement—for the middle class—a year or two later. The A.C.J.F. became and has remained a federation of these four movements, along with the Young Christian

Workers, each movement being autonomous in its own sphere. For a number of years the leadership of the federation remained student and middle class. But after the Second World War the new balance of forces within it was recognised by an understanding that henceforward the Chairman would normally be, in turn, from the Young Workers' and the Young Farmers' movements.

Holland also acquired in the 'thirties and after the Second World War strong and active Young Christian Workers', Young Independents', and also Young Employers' Movements—in France, as was mentioned earlier, the Young Employers' Movement is Christian-inspired but not formally Christian—in addition to the (Catholic) Young Farmers' movement already mentioned.

(f) Against Specialisation: Italy

Among the countries covered in this book, the one where the Catholic youth organisations remained most markedly impervious to the trend towards specialisation was Italy. The G.I.A.C. did indeed on various occasions show a tendency to specialise. In 1931, for instance, its Rome regional federation incurred violent attacks from the Fascist press by suggesting to its branches that they set up 'workers' secretariats', to be co-ordinated by a Workers' National Secretariat at G.I.A.C. headquarters. But there precisely was the rub. In the face of fascist attacks, it proved necessary to drop any question of specialisation and of intervention in social policy. Ecclesiastical control of the G.I.A.C. was tightened, its branches remained on an inter-class basis, and its work was kept strictly to the religious sphere. As the years went by this policy left a stamp on the mentality of those concerned with the Italian Catholic youth movement which can be appreciated best by comparing the autobiography of Luigi Gedda, for many years President of the G.I.A.C., with the classic of the French Y.C.W., Van der Meersch's *Fishers of Men*. Practically every episode in Van der Meersch's story of the battle for the rights of the working class in the streets and factories of Lille, and between the different tendencies within the working-class movement itself, would in Italy have attracted the attention of the O.V.R.A., the fascist political police whose caricature so engagingly decorates Gedda's dust-cover. It is understandable in the circumstances that Gedda's book shows much less concern for concrete, detailed, social problems or for the type of youth organisation needed to deal with them. It is shot through with a general, rather vague, spirit of inter-class good will, reminiscent in a rather different style of Marc Sangnier's, and very different from the style of the Young Christian Workers or Young Christian Farmers. Both these latter movements were in due course founded in Italy after the Second World War, but were very slow to take hold.

(g) The political youth movements, 1920–50

But if Italy has been backward in following the trend towards specialisation, it has been well in the forefront in another more recent development in the Christian youth movements, namely the rise of mass political youth movements from 1945 onwards. These are Christian Democratic movements entirely independent of the Churches, not movements of Christian Action. The Youth Groups of the *Democrazia Cristiana* claimed by 1952 some 300,000 members, which made them so far as is known the largest youth movement attached to any democratic political party in the world. According to the Youth Groups' own account of themselves, they represent the 'third generation' of anti-fascism; that which

> Met democracy not at school or at home, but in the mountains at the time of the underground battle against Nazis and Fascists. Young people in Italy have looked to democracy as an entirely new ideal, decisively revolutionary over against the past. (Article by P. E. Taviani in *L'Europe, Patrie de l'Avenir*, publication of the International Union of Young Christian Democrats, 1952, p. 39.)

Their chief initial aim was to develop a sense of social responsibility and solidarity among all classes of Italian youth. 'The solidarity of youth' was the great slogan, the idea being to draw together, for example, students and young workers in a common consciousness of the possibility and need, by a united effort, to 'overcome the capitalist structures of society and construct a new order'. This educational stage was to be followed by a drive for achievement; but education must come first.

That, essentially, has also been the position of the only other Christian Democratic political youth movement on a scale comparable to that in Italy, the 'Junge Union' attached to the C.D.U./C.S.U. in Germany. Like the C.D.U., this is a mixed Protestant and Catholic body founded after the collapse of Nazism. It claimed in 1952 some 120,000 members, a total built up with considerable difficulty in the face of the widespread political indifference among German youth after the collapse of Nazism. It is linked with the slightly smaller Social Democratic youth movement and the much smaller Liberal movement in the 'Ring Politischer Jugend', a united front of the democratic youth movements against left and right wing extremism.

The other Christian Democratic political youth movements are much smaller, though in one form or another they have often a long history. In France, for example, this history can be traced back under one name or another to the time of the *Sillon*, and indeed to the early days of the A.C.J.F. Before the Second World War there was no formal link between the movements in the various countries. After it there occurred a number of informal meetings, either of young people alone or on the occasion of various gatherings of the political parties and the European Movement.

The first formal international congress was held at Fiuggi near Rome in 1948, and later that year the present International Union of Young Christian Democrats was founded. At later conferences it drafted itself a programme and social charter. It has also played an active part in the movement for European unity; notably in the European Youth Campaign, started by the European Movement in 1951.

(h) The youth movements: summary and conclusion

The Christian Action and Christian Democratic youth movements have grown piecemeal, and there are still wide differences between the practice of different denominations and countries. There is much more specialisation among the Catholic movements than among the Protestant. Germany and Italy have strong political movements, but are definitely backward (Italy) or have tended to lose their original impetus (Germany) on the social side; whereas in France or Belgium the political movements are weak but the social movements are extremely strong. Germany has no Young Christian Farmers' Movement, and Italy none of much importance; the Young Christian Workers have flourished much more in Belgium and France than in Germany or even in Holland.

But in spite of this piecemeal character, the Christian youth movements make up an impressive picture when all their statistics are drawn together. The political movements (Table 10) have a total membership of half a million, and their influence stretches (Table 11) into a number of fields not obviously or at first sight political.[1] The strength of the social movements is sometimes less easy to assess, since the larger part of the Christian youth movements in Western Europe is concerned with general and religious education or with leisure and sport. Its purpose is not specific enough to bring it under the umbrella of Christian Democracy. In Germany the Catholic youth movements had in 1954 some 1,012,000 members; but only 175,000 of these were in movements with other than sport, leisure, and religious interests. In Holland there are 400,000 members of Catholic youth organisations, but only 120,000 in movements relevant here. There is also sometimes a certain haziness about youth movements' statistics. The Young Christian Workers (Girls' Section) in France had for instance in 1950 some 225 Federations with 'approximately' 2,000 sections and 'about 100 girls', on the average, being 'influenced by' each section. However, the data in Table 12 are accurate enough to give a fair

---

[1] The Christian Democrats appear actually to be slightly under-represented in the Italian Universities, with 33–34% of the votes as compared with 36–40% at the local government and parliamentary elections of 1951–3. Seeing the social composition of Italian students, it is not surprising that the Communist Party and its allies win much less support than in the country at large, whereas Fascists and near-Fascists win much more. There is a strong Liberal and middle-class element also in the laicist-democratic groups ('Goliardi'), which are also over-represented compared to the country at large.

TABLE 10

Data on certain political youth movements in Europe

Germany	The Junge Union (youth section of the C.D.U./C.S.U.) claimed in 1952 120,000 members.
Austria	Membership of the Youth Section of the Austrian People's Party, 1952, 25,000.
Switzerland	Membership of the Christian Conservative and Social Youth Movement (autonomous, but linked to the Swiss Conservative Party), 1952: 20,000.
Holland	The Youth Section of the Catholic People's Party had in 1952 3,000 members. The Christian Democratic Youth Movement in Holland also includes the Youth Sections of the Anti-Revolutionary and Christian-Historical (i.e. Protestant) parties.
Belgium	The youth groups associated with the Christian Social Party have around 2,000 members, compared with about 13,000 for the Young Liberals and 30,000 for the Socialist youth movement. But the majority of young Christian political leaders emerge from the much larger social and economic movements such as the Young Christian Workers.
France	The order of importance of the political youth movements in 1954 was:
	Communists (UJRF). Dropping, but probably still the most numerous; well organised and influential.
	M.R.P. Not very numerous, but have influence among students and in the Christian workers' movement.
	Socialist youth. Few, but active and influential in the North, and in some areas (notably Paris and Toulouse) among students.
	Radical Party (liberal) youth. 'Neither very many nor very young', but active notably in propagating the idea of united Europe.
	Right-wing groups (R.P.F.—i.e. Gaullist—and remnants of Action Française and similar groups). Few but noisy.
Italy	The Youth Section of the Christian Democratic Party claimed 350,000 members in 1954; probably more numerous than the only other mass political youth movement, that of the Communists, but less effectively organised.

Based on the Union of Christian-Democratic Youth's pamphlet *L'Europe—Patrie de l'Avenir*, 1952, and on private information.

TABLE 11

Results of elections to student representative Councils in Italy,
1952–3 and 1953–4

	1952–3	1953–4
Number of universities for which results received	24	21
Percentage of seats won by:		
Communists	10	9
'Goliardi' (democratic, laicist: include liberals, republicans, socialists)	28	35
Catholics	34	33
Monarchists	4	4
Fascists	20	13
Independents	4	7
	100	100

As given by *Civitas*, June 1954, pp. 28–9.

general impression. Young workers' movements (including those Kolping craftsmen who will eventually set up on their own) reach something of the order of three-quarters of a million boys, young men, and girls. Young Christian Farmers' movements reach somewhere around half a million. Christian organisation among young 'independents' and employers or managers is much weaker, in line with what has already been said about organisation among adults of this group. But here also there are some substantial Christian groupings, as well as a number of fascinating side-lines which lead too far out of the way of Christian Democracy to be followed up; the Catholic Society Girls in France, for example, whose task is the conversion of the upper middle class and aristocracy, or the 'Catholic Young Ladies of Italy', who follow the same attractive though not easy apostolate there.

The importance which these movements have had for Christian Democracy as a whole can scarcely be over-estimated. Several of them are in their second or later generations. They have solved or helped to solve a number of problems directly on their own; the contribution of the Young Farmers' Movements, for instance, to raising standards of productivity, or of the young workers' movements, including Kolping, to improving young workers' conditions. But over and above this they have peopled the 'adult' movements with a new generation of well-educated, trained, apostolically-minded leaders, well aware of the work to be done and with the will to do it. The list of A.C.J.F. leaders between the First World War and 1936, for example, includes the names of men such as Charles Flory, later for

279

TABLE 12

Data on certain young workers', farmers', and business
middle-class youth movements in Europe

Young workers and craftsmen

Kolping Germany	1954	150,000

Werkmannschaft
(Catholic Workers'
Movement youth
groups, Germany)   1950   3,300

Young Christian Workers (*Catholic*)

Germany	1954	10,000
Holland	1954	51,000 boys and young men
Belgium	1952	84,000
France	1950	200,000 girls
		? ? boys and young men

Young Farmers

Holland	1948	5,400 Protestant
	1954	25,000 Catholic—boys and young men
Belgium	1952	47,000 both sexes
France	1950	410,000 (250,000 boys and young men)

Managers and business middle class

Germany	1954	13,000 Catholic Commercial Union
Holland	1954	2,200 Catholic business middle class
	1954	275 Association of Young Catholic Employers
France	1950	18,000 Independent classes (Catholic)
	1949	4,000 Young Employers (officially non-confessional).

In most cases the absence of figure for a given class of movement in a given
country (e.g. for Young Farmers in Germany) means that no substantial movement on a Christian basis exists. Exceptions to this include Kolping in Switzerland
and the Catholic girls' and most of the Protestant youth movements in Holland;
in the two latter cases the organisations are unspecialised, and it is not possible
to separate out a Christian Democratic wing.

N.B. that what is meant by 'membership', or by the figures given, varies a
good deal from case to case. E.g. the Y.C.W. figures for France are for young
people *influenced*, whereas those for the independent classes are for *effective*
members.

many years Chairman of the Semaines Sociales de France, or of M.R.P. leaders like André Colin (General Secretary of the M.R.P. from its foundation), Georges Bidault, and François de Menthon. And so also the Christian trade unions and farmers' organisations are today increasingly led by those who made their name and got their training in the youth movements. It is when one studies the early history of the Christian social movements, their difficulty in finding competent organisers or in arousing understanding of the purpose these movements were to serve, that one best realises how important this contribution of the youth movements to the leadership and membership of the present generation has been.

THE FAMILY MOVEMENTS

(a) *The contribution of the women's movements*

There have been movements *for* the family—for charitable aid, for moral welfare, later against depopulation—at all times in the history of the Christian churches. There have also been in a sense movements of the family, for the many and flourishing Christian women's movement might well be classified as such. In modern times women's movements for Christian Action and Christian Democracy have come up rapidly, especially since the turn of the century. Sometimes it has been a case of what might be called the Christian Action or Christian Democratic aspect of general women's organisations such as the Italian Catholic Women's League, founded in 1908 as a breakaway from the National Italian Council of Women,[1] or the French Women's Catholic Action League. These general organisations for women are often of great strength. The Italian leagues have half a million members, the French two and a half million. The Catholic Women's League in Germany was dissolved by the Nazi police in 1939, and took some time to recover after the war: but it too had built up by 1954 to a total of 1,200 local sections and 250,000 members. Their objects are also very wide; so wide that they often, as with many of the general Christian youth movements, take them outside the scope of a work on Christian Democracy altogether. The French Women's League for Catholic Action, for instance, states as its objects:

(1) To collaborate in the Church's apostolic mission, in its present efforts to renew the parish community:
by inspiring a more conscious and intense Christian life in the parish
by building teams of active workers in the parish, on a street and neighbourhood basis
by specially training these active workers to develop, in and through their daily lives, missionary action among all the people of the street or neighbourhood for which they are responsible

[1] The breakaway occurred because the Council came out for the abolition of religious instruction in schools.

by providing active workers with the necessary tools, through various special services (library, family movements, mutual aid, documentation)

by collaborating with all the various Catholic movements engaged in the re-conversion of France.

(2) To bring the weight of its 2,200,000 members to bear on public opinion and institutions. As an organisation of general Catholic Action, the League is required to:

defend the rights of religion in the social order

undertake positive and constructive action as a Catholic group with responsibilities in the social order.

(Statement in the *Annuaire* of Catholic Action in France, 1950 ed., p. 83.)

To 'inspire a more conscious and intense Christian life in the parish' is not part of the work of Christian Democracy. But to 'build teams of active workers', who will among other things 'undertake positive and constructive action' on behalf notably of mothers and children, might be very much part of it.

In other cases the women's organisations have followed the general trend towards specialisation. So for example the Belgian Farmers' Union established a Countrywomen's League in 1912, and the C.B.T.B. in the 'thirties. The Catholic workers' leagues in Germany began recruiting a few women after 1900, and by 1931 had built up a membership of some 18,000, overwhelmingly in South Germany. The West German leagues, though by far the largest in the country—their total membership was nearly 200,000—had recruited only 1,100 women. After the collapse of Nazism, when the leagues were revived, women workers were still very reluctant to come in, but workers' wives came in in masses. In 1950 the West German leagues, exclusive of the diocese of Trier, had recruited 120,000 men. Alongside these were fewer than a thousand working women, but nearly 60,000 wives of Catholic workers. In Belgium the Christian Women's Leagues of the Christian Workers' Movement were founded before the First World War, federated in 1921 when the Workers' Movement itself was unified, and by 1951 had reached the respectable membership of 371,000. They claimed by then to have organised over a third of all the working-class married women in the country. In France women played a prominent part in the early days of the trade union movement, the first independent women's unions having been founded at Lyons, Paris, and Voiron (Isère) at various dates between 1899 and 1906. It was from these women s unions that the immediate initiative for the foundation of the C.F.T.C. went out. A new and dramatic increase in women's and girls' participation in, in this case, Catholic Action, occurred later when specialisation developed in the French Catholic youth movements.

Alongside the boys' and men's movements arose organisations for girls; the Girls' Sections of the Y.C.W., Young Christian Farmers, Christian Students' Movement, and Young Christian Independents—and the expansion of these Catholic Action movements represented a victory for feminism. The original

Catholic social movement was supported by only a small number of women; trade unionists, pioneers of social service, supporters of the Women's Civic and Social Union. Now however the Church found itself invaded by a mass of girls of very different type from those of the last generation—from those good, passive, souls, members of pious sodalities, or alternatively from the Lady Bountifuls, the 'mothers of the Church'. Here too the laity came of age in the field of the apostolate. (Folliet, *Présence de l'Église*, 1949, p. 60.)

France has also produced a particularly effective Christian feminist organisation in the Women's Civic and Social Union which Folliet mentions; by its French initials, the U.F.C.S. The impulse for this was given by an international feminist congress in 1900. A few French Catholic women were present, but found themselves outnumbered and isolated among a remarkable salad of laicists, anarchists, and freemasons. After the congress they got together to exchange their views and plan for action on their own. From this there arose by 1914 a variety of women's social action groups, consumers' leagues, and a series of 'St. Joan Congresses'. In 1925 the U.F.C.S. was founded to tie all this movement together. It developed steadily through the years, and in 1948 was recognised by the Assembly of the Cardinals and Archbishops of France as the Catholic women's movement with special responsibility for:

> Activities in pursuit of technical solutions in the temporal sphere.
> Approaches for this purpose to public authorities and other institutions.
> Training and support for women engaged in public work (local authorities, food committees, and so on).
> Propagation among the general public of the principles of the natural law as defined, completed, and adapted by the Church, without however engaging the responsibility of the Hierarchy. (*Chronique Sociale de France*, March–April, 1950, p. 133.)

Austria also has an effective Women's Movement associated with the Austrian People's Party. Before 1914:

> The pioneers of the Austrian women's movement, tame imitators of the English suffragettes, never came near the dynamism of the Anglo-Saxon or Scandinavian feminists. There was at that time no powerful enough pressure, no chronic surplus of women, in our latitudes. Christian women, looking to the Right, played no small part in the battle for political rights. But it was precisely the Christian women, as apart from the Socialists, who lacked a political concept of their own. They were perfect subjects of the Crown, but not yet, most of them, awakened to the need for political action. (Gilda Götzen, cyclostyled note on *Entwicklungsgeschichte der Christlich Demokratischen Frauenbewegung in Österreich*, Central Office of the Austrian Women's Movement, Wien, 1955.)

The Church women's movements, Protestant as well as Catholic, were concerned with spiritual formation rather than with 'activating women to the secular duties bound up with it'. After the First World War and the fall of the Habsburg Monarchy the Christian as well as the Socialist parties recognised women's right to the vote and to political responsibility. But:

> The transformation from subject to citizen, amid the chaos following the collapse of a centuries-old tradition, was understandably harder for Christian women, the roots of whose loyalty ran deep, than for other groups less attached to these values or positively opposed to them. (Ibid.)

It was not till the Nazi occupation after 1938, which 'degraded women to a lower class of humanity', that a new generation of Christian Women 'ripened in the resistance'. The Austrian Women's Movement was founded in 1945 as one of the main constituents of the Austrian People's Party. It acts as a recruiting and propaganda agency for the party, and also as a pressure group within it, concerned with winning for women not only formal political rights but also actual representation in parliament and local authorities. The latter task, the Movement's own note underlines, is not always easy. In 1955 the Austrian Women's movement took the initiative in bringing together similarly minded women's groups from Germany, Italy, and other European countries in a European Women's Union.

It is not surprising that a feature common to all these women's movements, in whatever country, has been a deep concern for the family. Here for example is Germaine Peyroles presenting the M.R.P.'s case for votes for women at the French Constituent Assembly in 1946.

> The right to vote for which we French women have waited so patiently . . . is not something which we wish to exercise casually or on the side, something which has little to do with reality. It is for us a means of achieving, concretely, what we feel and think and demand. . . . Above and beyond all ideologies and parties, women's votes have a meaning of their own. They may help to accent such vital themes as international peace and social justice. . . . And, gentlemen —for it is to the men particularly that I am speaking—if there is in the heart of the women of our country one single object of our inborn and unshakeable devotion, it is, for each one of us, our family. For her family a woman of France will sacrifice her leisure, her health, and if necessary her life. Do not then be surprised if the vote is in her hands a weapon, defensive and offensive, in the service of that to which she holds above anything else in the world. . . . (Quoted in *Chronique Sociale*, loc. cit., p. 137.)

And so also one finds, for example, the Women's Leagues of the Belgian Christian Workers' Movement providing 'special educational action for young married women' and a variety of health, mutual aid, holiday, and other services for families, in addition to representing members', and particularly family, interests in a variety of public bodies and in the Christian Workers' Movement itself.

(b) *The family movement properly so-called: The first generation in France*, 1887–1920

But though the Christian women's organisations, Protestant as well as Catholic, are deeply concerned with the family and tend to think of all problems from the family angle, they are still not strictly family organisations; that is organisations of as well as for families as such. The family movement in that sense has a different and separate history.

Its pioneers seem to have been the French, with the Belgians second. The lead in France came from the Protestants, who were founding family associations from as early as 1887. But the biggest development occurred necessarily on a Catholic or inter-confessional basis. One line of growth began in 1902 at Plaisance, in Paris, at that time a district of bad slums, largely of common lodging houses. A Catholic curate, Fr. Viollet, in collaboration with the local Protestant pastor and with a group of workers, brought into existence what came to be known as the 'Moulin-Vert Family Association', from the name of the street where the headquarters were established. The problems of housing, furnishing, education, holidays, and health with which the association proposed to deal were what might be expected. Its method was more novel. It was interested not so much in helping a family as in equipping the family to help itself. And it saw the essential aid for this purpose as coming, not from some social service agency, but from other similar families in the neighbourhood. The problem was one not of assistance but of mutual aid. Fr. Viollet also seems to have had from the start a clearer understanding of what is meant by 'Christian' in, respectively, Christian Action and Christian Democratic organisations than was usual at that date. When later on he founded another type of family group, the Christian Marriage Association, concerned with the spirituality of the family—that is a Christian Action organisation—he was careful to keep it on a denominational basis; 'Under the patronage of the Cardinals of France', as the Association's publicity material says today. But he saw the original Moulin-Vert type of association as essentially a families' trade union and friendly society, which could and should be kept on an a-confessional basis, open to people of all religions or none; though no doubt led and inspired by those of Christian faith. This distinction has been very widely accepted in the Christian family movements in Europe, even in a country such as Belgium where the tendency to give organisations at least in practice a denominational tinge has been strong. It was also distinctive of Fr. Viollet's movement that it was not only concerned with 'normal' or large families. It aimed at recruiting families of all shapes and sizes, and indeed particularly at bringing in the young married couples on whom the educational work of the Associations was likely to have most effect. Associations of the Moulin-

285

Vert type spread steadily, and in 1919 there were enough of them to form a General Confederation of Families (C.G.F.).

Meantime another type of family trade union had grown up, inspired partly by fears of a fall in the birth-rate, and partly by a desire to improve the standard of living of families with a 'normal' or large number of children: what was in due course expressed as the principle of equal standard of living for equal work. The movements of this type also were a-confessional, though under Christian inspiration and leadership. In 1908 Captain Maire started the 'Large Families League', open to the fathers of at least three children. In 1916, going one better, was started a body with the happy name of 'The Still Larger Family' ('La plus grande famille'), for families with not less than five children. In 1921 a number of 'large family' movements on Captain Maire's model, though excluding at that time the 'Still Larger Family', were drawn together into the so-called Large Families' Federation. By 1939 this grew into a powerful and influential body with several hundred thousand subscribing members. Certain denominational movements were also started around the time of the First World War, notably the Catholic Association of Heads of Families (1911) and Fr. Viollet's Christian Marriage Association just mentioned. In 1920 all the existing family movements of whatever type, whether C.G.F., 'Large Family', or denominational, together with a number of other movements 'for' the family as apart from 'of' families, combined to support a Declaration of the Rights of the Family agreed at a congress at Lille. This laid down the family's right to protection against public immorality and social disorganisation, as for instance through unemployment: also the right of parents to determine the general character of their children's schooling: the right to earn, save, and inherit, and to fair treatment for the family in the matter of taxes and allowances: and the right to political representation for the family, notably through extra votes for fathers of families.

It is important to bear in mind the different strands—spirituality of the family, marriage guidance, co-operation among young families, fiscal and social justice for the family with several children, fear of a falling birth-rate—which have woven together into the French family movement. There is a common but wrong impression that the main impulse behind that movement has been the desire to keep the population up. That has certainly been one motive, and a very useful one to emphasise when trying to obtain political support. But it is very far from having been the main motive among the founders of family associations themselves, and its importance even as a means of persuading politicians has tended to diminish with time. The widespread concern with the family in France today is due primarily, as in other countries, to a new appreciation of the importance of the family as such. The French family movement has in any case discovered the danger of using arguments and a vocabulary most likely to appeal to the political Right.

> The French family movement was in the first place a reaction against the individualism of the nineteenth century. It defended the family *en bloc*, as something existing in the nature of things and as the basic unit of the community. It had no time to analyse or explain the deep springs of its own action. Many people, especially in intellectual or political circles, thus got the impression that it was more concerned with defending what existed than with adjusting to new conditions. On this rests the charge of conservatism often, wrongly, brought against the family movement in the past. It did, it is true, often use a vocabulary more usual on the political Right. But it was led and inspired from the start by outstanding personalities with a lively social sense, and its recruits came from every class in society . . . (Article by Eugène Dary in *Dokumente*, 1952, p. 519.)

Reading today the 1920 Declaration of the Rights of the Family, one can easily see what M. Dary has in mind when he talks of a vocabulary more usual on the Right. There are references to 'the family, hierarchically constituted under the father's authority', or to the right to transmit family property and estates, which anyone on the political left would certainly wish to qualify, and which today seem curiously out of place in the light of changing views on the family in the Christian Democratic world itself.[1]

(c) The second generation in France, 1920–50: consolidation and specialisation

By the middle 'twenties the French family movement had become a powerful force, able to get results. One of the most striking was the generalisation of family allowances. These originated in France in the First World War. Real wages had fallen, a general wage increase was ruled out by war conditions, and certain Catholic employers paid allowances to relieve the strain on families with several children. The system caught on, and, under pressure from the family movement and the Christian trade unions and employers, was made compulsory throughout French industry in 1932. In 1938 was enacted a 'Family Code' which, among other things, greatly improved the family's position in the matter of taxes and allowances.

The most remarkable achievement of the French family movement occurred however during the 'forties, when for the first time in the history of any country it won for associations representing the family an official status in French public life not unlike that given to employers' associations and trade unions in Holland under P.B.O. It is of the essence of P.B.O. that the different interest groups in industry should be represented by their own voluntary and independent associations. But official recognition

[1] See Chapter V.

and legal powers of self-government are granted, not directly to these associations, but to joint public bodies to which each interest group nominates members. That is exactly the position of the family movement in France today. The voluntary associations continue to exist, and indeed, under the stimulus of an opportunity for public representation, have increased and flourished. It is estimated that from 1945 to 1947, when the new official structure was being set up, the number of local associations or branches of associations qualified for representation in it rose from 800 to 6,000; though this may have been in part merely a recovery from the war or a question of change of names. It is reckoned that in the early 'fifties there were 12,000. In each Department (county) the voluntary associations come together to constitute a Departmental Union, each association having votes in proportion to its membership. The Departmental Unions in turn elect a National Union of Family Associations. And it is these joint Unions which are recognised by Government departments and other public bodies as the qualified representatives of family interests. Through these arrangements France has officially recognised that the family, like the working class, is today no longer a ward of society. It has come of age, and is entitled to participate in its own right and through its own representatives in all public business which touches its interests.

The most important development among the voluntary associations towards the end of this first generation was a move, as in other branches of Christian social action, towards specialisation by social class or environment. There came up first of all a number of family associations for members of particular professions, most of them middle class, such as medicine, the law, banking, and the civil service; though also including railwaymen and staff of other semi-public services. These associations distinguished themselves notably as a ground for experiment. One or other of them was the first to try out a great many services which later became standard in France, such as maternity loans, marriage allowances, and certain types of housing scheme.

Of more general importance was a series of movements formed by young married couples trained in the specialised youth organisations set up at the end of the 'twenties. These organisations were from the start closely concerned with the family, and their militants turned naturally to the family movement as they married and left the youth organisations behind. From the Young Christian Workers emerged a Christian Workers' league (L.O.C.), which later became the People's Family Movement (M.P.F.), and later again, in 1950, the People's Liberation Movement (M.L.P.). From the Young Christian Farmers came a Christian Farmers' League (L.A.C.), which likewise renamed itself, just before the Second World War, the Rural Family Movement (M.F.R.). The M.F.R., like the Young

Christian Farmers, is a Catholic Action movement concerned with education and personal formation rather than with political or trade union action. Alongside it has come into existence a 'National Confederation of Rural Families', which, like the 'Large Family' movements or Fr. Viollet's original movement, is a-confessional, and concerned with trade union action and mutual aid.

The M.P.F./M.L.P. began, like the M.F.R., as a Catholic Action movement. But, like the *Sillon* in its time, it drifted towards politics and direct action (it took in particular a leading part in the French squatters' movement) under the pressure of its markedly left-wing militants. After the war, by agreement with the Catholic Hierarchy, it divested itself of its Catholic Action character and became a fully independent movement with the same status or lack of status in relation to the official church as, for instance, the M.R.P. or C.F.T.C. In 1949 it also broke away from the National Union of Family Associations, feeling, as it put it, that the U.N.A.F. was 'merely another trade union' engaged in reformist action within the capitalist system. It felt unable to pursue its work for the family in isolation from the general problem of the liberation of the proletariat. The M.L.P. is not itself a grouping of family associations, but has given rise to a National Confederation of Workers' Family Associations operating from the same address. And meantime a new movement of 'Workers' Catholic Action' has been started to do the work given up by the M.P.F./M.L.P. in the field of Christian personal formation and training. In 1953 this movement had about a thousand local groups and 14,000 active members.

With the establishment in the countryside of the National Confederation and the Rural Family Movement, and among the more class-conscious workers of the M.L.P. and Workers' Catholic Action, the voluntary organisations in the French family movement have begun to show the same pattern as is usual in the trade union field; a-confessional 'trade unions', specialised by class, and dealing with families' secular interests, alongside specialised Catholic Action movements catering for the Christian formation and training of the same groups. The movement as a whole, however, has not accepted specialisation by class or environment, though it does accept the distinction between trade union and Christian Action activities. The chief unspecialised family movements with trade union or friendly society aims—Fr. Viollet's original C.G.F., the 'Large Families' Federation', and the 'Still Larger Family'—were fused in 1947 into a 'French Families' Federation', which remains concerned with the interests of families of every social class. Like its component movements, it is of the a-confessional trade union type. The Catholic Association of Heads of Families and the Protestant family associations continue to exist alongside it. Christian Action activities parallel to it, that is, not in principle specialised by class, are carried on by, among other agencies, a large and growing number of associations and groups of families, which operate on a small scale and are concerned with the spirituality of the family and with personal formation. These groups and the spirit behind them will be considered further in a moment.

(d) Belgium: 1920 and after

The French family movement has been described at length, because it has the longest history and, in terms of results achieved, whether materially or spiritually, has been in many ways the most effective. Its nearest rival has been the movement in Belgium. This began in 1921 with the foundation of a Large Families' League. Membership in this was not absolutely confined to 'heads' of large families. As its Director, Fr. Fallon, observed to a congress in 1947, the fact that he was a member of the League did not necessarily imply that he had four or more children. Like the main French trade union and mutual aid movements, the League is a-confessional, though under strong Catholic influence. By 1946 the League could claim 183,000 subscribing members, representing with their families about a million and a quarter people. By the 'fifties it reached 250,000. In a country the size of Belgium this has been enough to make it very much a power in the land, and in such matters as taxation, family allowances, or reduced railway rates it has served its members very well. After the Second World War it secured the establishment by the Government of a National Family Council and of a special section for family affairs in the Ministry of Health. Indeed, until the end of the 'forties, it was commonly and perhaps not unjustly accused of concentrating too exclusively on these material and administrative aspects of family life.

In the course of the 'thirties and 'forties there grew up in Belgium a number of other family movements, likewise parallel to those in France. In 1943 was started what came presently to be known as the Catholic Families' Association, parallel in many ways to Fr. Viollet's C.G.F. It concerned itself with families of all sizes, and with young married couples in particular. Around the same time there also emerged a Belgian version of the M.P.F., which however failed to establish itself permanently. And there came to be the same flurry as in France of small, informal, family groups, concerned mainly with personal formation and spirituality. Often in fact their groups were a legacy from the short-lived Belgian M.P.F. But the middle-class 'Golden Ring' and 'Equipes Notre Dame' were the Belgian end of French movements, and the 'Companions of St. Francis' (all class) were the prolongation of what was originally launched as a youth movement in France in the 'twenties by Joseph Folliet.

An article by P. Ranwez in *Lumen Vitae* (1949, No. 2), though written primarily in the light of Belgian practice, brings out the spirit behind these groups in France as well. They too, like the M.F.R. or M.P.F., followed on from young people's experience in the new youth movements of the 'twenties and 'thirties. Young married couples, ex-members of these movements, tended—unless they dropped out of the Christian social movement altogether—to re-think their participation in Christian social activity along two divergent lines. Some preferred 'activist' movements, including under this title not only the Christian Democratic but also the adult specialised Catholic Action movements. Others, looking at these movements, noted the danger of a too 'organisational' and 'conquering' approach: too great a tendency to 'capture' souls for Christ instead of winning them by force of example. There was also another danger registered by an attitude survey in 1946:

> Many young people trained by Catholic Action were unconsciously seeing in their Christianity the completion and crown of their life on earth. Their ideal seemed in a way to be that of an earthly paradise. (Ranwez, loc. cit., p. 241.)

Conscious of these dangers, many felt the need to turn inwards and deepen their understanding of Christianity; though in the expectation of again turning outwards to a new, less formal, apostolate. And they found the ideal means of doing so in small groups of half a dozen to a dozen married couples, usually young; some of the groups being linked to wider movements, some on their own; immensely varied and experimental, and having their value just in that fact.

> The specialised Catholic Action movements are intended to put back the Christian stamp on the various social classes and professional groups. . . . This task is indispensable and as yet far from being completed. But it must not make us forget that the different groups in society cannot live in isolation. At the Congress of the *Union des Œuvres* at Lille in 1948 a leader of M.P.F. spoke proudly of her 'caste spirit'. We understand the greatness of heart behind this affirmation, but insist that it is in itself incomplete. Christian charity which—so Christ desired—unites all humanity, must be realised in practice. It develops in the intimacy of the family, radiates and is diffused through hospitality, friendship, aid, and devoted love. It leaps over the barriers of formality, hostility, and competition. It unites what was separated. May not the true vocation of groups of families be to link together the various sections of humanity which live in mutual ignorance or mistrust—social classes, nations, races? A vocation complementary to that of the specialised movements of Catholic Action. (Loc. cit., p. 244.)

Statistics are not easy to come by. But it is known that in Brussels in 1953, for instance, about 1,500 families were involved in groups of this kind.

(e) Other Countries

Luxemburg has a flourishing Workers' Family Movement (M.O.F.) which emerged from the Young Christian Workers. In *Switzerland* also a family movement was touched off in the 'twenties by the example of France. The first association in French Switzerland was started in the canton of Vaud in 1923. In due course a Large Families' League was also started in German Switzerland, and later also an M.P.F. These bodies have never become as powerful as in Belgium or France, partly at least because of a rather hostile public opinion. Swiss opinion is favourable to family welfare measures, but not, in a country very heavily populated in relation to its resources, to measures specially favourable to large families.

In Germany, Italy, and Holland the family movement properly so-called, as apart from incidental activities of the women's or workers' leagues, took hold only after the Second World War. In *Holland* it could be said as late as 1952 that families were only just:

> Beginning to stir and to feel the need to fight for their own interests. Families are now everywhere beginning to link up in groups, spontaneously, to discuss the spiritual problems of marriage. (*Dokumente*, 1952, VI, p. 530.)

In *Italy* an imposing 'Family Front' under Catholic inspiration mushroomed into a membership of millions when the new Italian Constitution was being hammered out after the war, and issues such as that of permitting or forbidding divorce were being faced. It was and is a-confessional and non-political, and has a programme broadly on the lines of the Lille Charter. Constitutionally, it is a typical family trade union of the kind developed in Belgium and France. It has proved, like most mushrooms, to contain a great deal of water; more Front than Families. But it retains enough support to have a substantial influence in legislation and public affairs.

The 1952 report quoted above for Holland complained that 'the *German family* is silent' (p. 564). Perhaps the German family's voice was not very loud. But to say that it was 'silent' was surely by that date a little pessimistic. A 'German Family Union' was founded in 1949, and by 1952 had built up a substantial membership. It was and is another typical family trade union, a-confessional and a-political, concerned with the family's economic and social interests. Alongside it grew up the usual swarm of small, informal, groups, strongly influenced by the (Catholic) youth movements, and concerned particularly with developing the spiritual side of family life. Watching this initial experience, the Catholic Bishops in Germany seem to have taken a less favourable view than their French or Belgian colleagues of a-confessional family trade unions, and of the ability of the smaller, informal, spiritually minded groups to make good their deficiencies. They therefore encouraged the formation in 1953 of a German Catholic Families' League, which quickly, by 1955, built up a membership of 870,000. In defending the family's economic and social interests the League works closely with the German Family Union and with the Evangelical Action Committee for Family Questions, which is a movement *for* and not *of* the family. The rise of these movements is one main symptom of the transformation, recorded earlier, of the atmosphere in which family policy is discussed in Germany in the last few years.

(f) Conclusion: the source of the family movement

It should finally be recorded that the main drive in the family movement has throughout, and in all countries, come from Catholics. The relative backwardness of countries such as Holland, Germany, and Switzerland in the family movement is largely due to the slowness of Protestants to take up this form of Christian social action. The early start made by them in France seems to have been altogether exceptional. Humanists and agnostics have also made relatively little contribution. They have on the whole been more concerned with problems such as those of birth control, divorce, and women's civic and industrial rights than with fair shares for the family or improvement in human relations within it. The conception of the family as dynamic and autonomous, not so much protected by society as shaping society to the pattern families themselves deem best, is almost exclusively a Christian and particularly a Catholic discovery.

CHAPTER XX

1880–1950: THE CHRISTIAN DEMOCRATIC POLITICAL PARTIES (I)

THE Christian Democratic political parties are today the most prominent and in many countries the most powerful and characteristic manifestation of the whole Christian Democratic movement. Foreigners may indeed easily over-estimate their importance compared to that of the social movements, less well known outside their own environment. The main pillar of Christian Democracy in France is not the M.R.P., important though that party is. It is probable that far more real weight attaches to the Christian trade unions (C.F.T.C.) or to the youth movements, such as the Young Christian Farmers or Workers, grouped in the A.C.J.F. But the parties are in any case important enough for their role to need no exaggeration. The Christian Democratic Union in Germany, the *Democrazia Cristiana* in Italy, and the Christian Social Party in Belgium have been consistently the largest parties in their respective Parliaments, and have at one time or another held absolute majorities. The three leading Christian Democratic parties of Holland (the Catholic People's Party and the Anti-Revolutionary Party and Christian Historical Union, which are Protestant) hold a permanent majority in their parliament, though they have not always acted together as a block to exploit it. The Austrian People's Party and the Christian Social Party in Luxemburg have never quite attained an absolute majority, but have been the largest parties in their respective parliaments. The M.R.P. (Popular Republican Movement) in France holds a mere $13\frac{1}{2}\%$ of the seats in the French Chamber of Deputies. But they happen to be key seats, in that central area of which André Siegfried said, in the days when it was monopolised by the Radicals, that its yield of ministerial portfolios to the square yard was the highest in the Chamber. The M.R.P. has been represented in nearly every French government since the war, the only important exception being the Mendes-France government of 1954–5. It has had a particularly great influence on foreign affairs. The Conservative People's Party of Switzerland, which is based mainly on Catholic support, has likewise only 25% of the deputies in the Swiss lower house. But, as a centre party, it has, like the M.R.P., a key position, and is permanently represented in the government.

Taking all these eight countries together (Table 13), and adding in various small splinter parties mentioned at the foot of the table, the Christian Democrats held early in 1954 some 37% of all the seats in the lower houses of parliament; half as many again as the next largest fraction, the Socialists. Among the parties whose belief in democracy is clear and beyond question—excluding, that is, the Communists and extremer conservatives and nationalists—the Christian Democrats held an absolute majority. In 1954 the members nominated by the national parliaments of

TABLE 13

Seats in the Lower Houses of the Parliaments of
certain European countries

Country	Date of elections	Communists	Social Democrats	Christian Democrats	Liberals	Conservative or Nationalist	Other	Total
Germany	1953	–	150	247	48	15	27	487
Austria	1953	4	73	74	–	–	14	165
Switzerland	1951	5	49	49	93	–	–	196
Holland	1952	6	30	55	9	–	–	100
Belgium	1954	4	86	97	25	–	–	212
Luxemburg	1951	4	19	21	8	–	–	52
France	1951	103	104	85	94	216	24	626
Italy	1953	218*	19	262	19	69	3	590
Total		344	530	890	296	300	68	2428
Percentages:		14	23	37	12	12	3	100

* Including the Italian Socialist Party, allied with the Communists in the 'social communist' block.

There is an element of estimation in the distribution of, e.g., the various French parties between such categories as 'liberal' or 'conservative'. Dissident Christian groups (Centre in Germany, KNP in Holland, dissidents from the PSC in Belgium) have been grouped with the Christian Democrats. The number of seats involved is:

Centre 3

KNP 2

Belgian dissidents 2

The Dutch K.N.P. was formally dissolved in October 1955, and its members reunited with the Catholic People's Party.

295

France, Italy, Germany, Belgium, Holland and Luxemburg to the Common Assembly of the European Coal and Steel Community formed themselves into international groups. The extreme parties being absent, the result was:

Christian Democrats	38
Socialists	23
Liberals	11
	72

But this power and influence is largely new, a creation of the last two generations. Compared to what it later became, the Christian political movement in the eighteen-eighties was crude and negative in outlook and limited in extent. Political parties of Catholic inspiration existed in Belgium, Holland, and Germany. One was founded during the eighteen-eighties in Austria. An important Protestant party existed in Holland. But no move to found one had yet been made in Switzerland, and Adolf Stöcker was only just beginning his work in Germany. In France, Italy, and Switzerland Catholics were a force to be reckoned with in politics, but parties such as exist in those countries today had not yet been set up.

There was also a lack of what Christian Democrats today would regard as a clear or satisfactory policy. The parties which then existed had grown, as has been said, on the basis of an acceptance and a rejection. They rejected the totalitarian claims of the Liberals, particularly as these affected the right of the Churches to go about their work of education and the propagation of the faith, but accepted many of the liberal social techniques, based on the principle of freedom and competition. But this positive attitude to liberalism was itself, as regards the work of governments and political parties, essentially negative, for liberalism laid down with much more assurance what governments should not do than what they should. And liberalism was in its origins essentially a middle-class creed, propped up by middle-class support and, usually, by a restricted franchise. Liberals, and the Christian parties who followed their line, had it is true come round by the eighteen-eighties to accepting a fair amount of social legislation. The marked social element in the German Centre Party was commented on above, and in Belgium the first great wave of social legislation in the 'eighties was carried through by the Catholic Prime Minister Beernaert. But in general the Christian parties at that time were middle and upper class in their outlook, negative in their social policies, and confessional in the sense, not indeed that they took orders from Bishops, but that the centre of their thinking was the defence of ecclesiastical interests.

Over the next sixty or seventy years, down to the end of the Second World War, these deficiencies were made good. The existing parties became more socially-minded, had less reason to preoccupy themselves with ecclesiastical interests, and lost much of their confessional character. They absorbed the lessons of the socialist age, together with the federalist ideas worked out in the Christian social movements and in regional and national movements such as those of Flanders or of south Germany and Austria. They opened their ranks and their minds to all classes, particularly to the working class, and some of them were reorganised so as to cater more precisely for regional or denominational differences among their own supporters. And the number of parties increased to include all the countries covered in this study, and Protestants (outside Holland) as well as Catholics.

The battle over the principle of these developments was fought out, as elsewhere in the Christian social movement, mainly in the generation to the First World War. The history from then on is of the growth of the seeds sown by the early 'twenties and the projection of the trends then apparent; until in 1945, for the first time for three centuries, movements based explicitly and effectively on Christian principles, and socially and not merely liberally minded, emerged as the major political force in Western Europe. The process of growth was the usual one in two stages: one generation to formulate new problems and agree on a new approach, another to carry the new development to its conclusion.

THE SOCIAL ELEMENT IN THE OLDER PARTIES

(a) Belgium

There was no need, in the eighteen-eighties, to convince Belgian Catholics of the virtues of democratic government. They remained convinced, as they had long been, that in the modern world democracy, in the sense of the liberal freedoms, was the regime under which Christians were most likely to live their life and practise their religion in the way they desired and to influence their environment. But democracy as preached by the Socialists, a democracy which might call, in the interests of the people, for far-reaching intervention by trade unions or the State in the free play of social and economic life, was another matter altogether. Down to the eighteen-nineties the dominant view in the Catholic party was that of Charles Woeste, a stout opponent of all kinds of State intervention and therefore of most kinds of social reform. There was it is true a second current, more realist, led by M. Beernaert, which in favourable conditions succeeded in drawing the party after it in matters of social policy. But it was not till the 'nineties that there arose forces powerful enough to change the party's character permanently.

The first of these was *Belgian Democratic League* (L.D.B.), the ancestor of the present Christian Workers' Movement, founded by J. Helleputte in 1891. Helleputte and his followers were no revolutionaries. Within their own ranks they were inclined to play down awkward issues; and, when they won a place in Parliament, they refused to constitute a group apart from, or even within, the Catholic Party. But they were resolute for social reform, for the right to proclaim their own economic and social programme, and for Christian Democratic and particularly working-class representation in parliament. In 1907, to the intense fury of the Catholic press, they brought down a Catholic government on the issue of the eight-hour day for miners. A more strictly political movement of the 'Young Right' also arose in 1891, led notably by a group of young Catholic deputies from Brussels and by Fr. Rutten, who later became the first General Secretary of the Belgian Christian trade unions. This group was if anything more radical than the L.D.B., and stood for such things as universal suffrage, military service to be performed in person and without replacement (a sore point with workers, who were forced to serve while the middle class bought their way out), progressive taxation, death duties, the closed shop, and the family living wage. There was also a small, short-lived, Flemish Christian People's Party led by Fr. Daens, which affiliated for a time to the L.D.B. but was presently expelled. It was accused of promoting the class war, of being too exclusively political, and of following a line dangerous to Catholics' political unity.

Already in the eighteen-nineties these new trends had their effect on party policy. A new programme issued in 1896 expressed the Catholic Party's belief in social insurance and factory legislation (these were Beernaert's special contribution, and Woeste's special *bête noire*), and its support for an 'Immediate Social Programme' just issued by the Belgian Bishops, which among other things called for the development of trade unions and farmers' co-operatives. In 1893 the Cardinal-Archbishop of Malines issued a statement on the importance of:

(1) Recognising the independence in the economic field of the various groups which agree on the main questions of religious and governmental policy.
(2) Ensuring, when lists of candidates are being drafted, representation for the major social interest groups, and notably for labour.
(3) Securing agreement, for electoral purposes, between all those associations and groups whose purpose is to defend religion, property, and the family, whether this agreement is reached through joint committees or otherwise.
(Quoted in Verhaegen, *25 Années d'Action Sociale*, c. 1912, p. 259.)

The problem was to find an organisational formula in which this policy could be expressed. Woeste, expressing in this what came later to be the general view in the Christian Democratic political world, opposed the formation within the party of anything in the nature of organised interest groups. A preliminary attempt at a joint committee, including not only the party (the 'Federation of Catholic Clubs and of Constitutional and Conservative Associations'—the name speaks volumes) but also the

L.D.B. and the Belgian Farmers' Union, broke down over this in 1899. But in 1907 a Catholic prime minister for the first time included in his Cabinet representatives of the L.D.B. and the 'Young Right', and it was agreed that the L.D.B. should henceforward nominate its own candidates on the common party list. In 1921 was formed a 'Catholic Union', including the Federation, the Farmers' Union, the Federation of the Middle Classes, and the Christian Workers' Movement which in that year succeeded the L.D.B. The Union was at first loose, but from 1932 its Committee obtained the right to give binding decisions in disputes between its member movements. Meantime, during the First World War, Socialists had for the first time entered the government, and collaboration between Catholics and Socialists became a practical possibility. After the war there came a variety of governments, Catholic-Liberal-Socialist, Catholic-Liberal, Catholic-Socialist. But through them all the Catholic Party remained the pivot, and a steady stream of political and social reforms came forward; universal suffrage (though not yet for women), progressive taxation, housing policy, old age pensions, the eight-hour day, and protection for unions' right to organise.

But the Catholic Party was not yet out of the wood. Co-ordination through the Catholic Union was unsatisfactory, often leading to a compromise rather than a true synthesis between the views of member groups. And there arose a new cause of division in the Flemish question. The effort of certain groups in Flanders to establish equality between their culture and that of French-speaking Belgium went back to the eighteen-seventies, and over the course of the years achieved important successes; the use of Flemish in the schools and for administrative purposes, and, after the war, the conversion into a Flemish-language university of the University of Ghent. Now, however, there began to be talk of political independence as well, or at least of converting Belgium into a Flemish-Walloon federation. The Flemish cultural movement had strong support throughout from the Catholic Party, and the new political movement attracted a good deal of Catholic support, above all from the Belgian Farmers' Union. The Catholic Party as a whole did not accept the idea of the division of Belgium, but was itself almost torn apart by it. In 1936 it split, in effect, into separate Flemish and Walloon parties, each with its separate organisation, though linked by joint committees and a Congress.

These divisions and defects of co-ordination were unsatisfactory. At the end of the Second World War the Catholic Party was accordingly reconstituted in not merely an a-confessional—we return to this below—but a more unified form. Its programme was still of the Centre, with a strong social element; indeed a rather stronger social element than before the war. It also continued its support for the cultural autonomy of

Flanders. But its own organisation was now concentrated on the lines already described. Its national Congress divided for certain purposes into Flemish and Walloon 'wings' (Table 14). But there was now only one Congress and set of executive officers and committees. And the former organic link with the social movements was replaced by arrangements for liaison, of which the Christian Workers' Movement says:

> The Movement has set up an organisation for liaison with . . . the Christian Social Party. This is not a mass organisation; simply a committee. It is *not* the wing or section of any party. It is composed of members of our Movement and of the Party. . . . They examine and study current social problems and achievements, explain the Movement's attitude on these matters, consider what political action might be taken on them, and present to the . . . Party the views and requests approved. . . . The . . . Party gives them a hearing, and then decides and acts under its own authority and responsibility. (Brys, *The Christian Labour Movement of Belgium*, 1952, p. 31, Cyclostyled.)

(b) Holland

Dutch Catholics, like Belgian, tended till the eighteen-nineties or even later to follow a liberal-conservative line in social matters. Mgr. Schaepman, the founder of their party, was a man of a very different stamp. But many stories are told of how in social matters he failed to carry his followers with him. In the eighteen-nineties, during a discussion on extending the franchise, the question was raised of how to keep slum-dwellers from voting. Schaepman suggested that the best way might be to abolish the slums. The remark was not well received in his own ranks. A few years later a Liberal government brought forward proposals for

TABLE 14

Christian Social Party (Belgium). Constitution
of the National Committee

	Nationality of members	
Members elected by	Flemish	Walloon
National Congress	Chairman (from either wing)	
National Congress (Flemish Wing)	7	–
National Congress (Walloon Wing)	–	7
Parliamentary group (Senate)	3	3
Parliamentary group (Chamber)	3	3
National Committee—coopted members		
Flemish Wing	2	–
Walloon Wing	–	2
	15 1	15

From the Party Statutes, 1951 ed.

compulsory schooling. Schaepman and one other member were alone in the Catholic parliamentary group in supporting them, and the mass of Catholic opinion outside parliament and of the Catholic press was against them. As in Belgium, the system whereby the rich could buy their way out of conscription was yet another stumbling block.

However, as in other countries, the rise of the social and particularly the workers' movements changed this state of affairs. There was the usual difficulty in finding the right formula in which to express these movements' new political importance. It was not till 1918–23 that, in a series of steps, a solution was reached not unlike that arrived at in Belgium a generation later. In 1918 the Bishops confirmed what was in any case already the normal practice of the social movements. They were not to take part directly in politics, nor to discuss candidatures, nor to use their weight and influence in support of any candidate. Four years later the Catholic Party invited the social movements to join a committee, to be responsible for drafting the preliminary lists of candidates. In the light of the decision of 1918 they refused. But this did not prevent them from approaching the party as occasion might offer to put their point of view on particular issues, nor the party from approaching them. Nor did it prevent them from encouraging their members to join the Catholic electors' associations, inside which there developed in practice a vigorous struggle between different interest groups. Farmers and workers in this way acquired and have maintained a powerful influence in the party and substantial representation in Parliament. The first fruits of this development appeared just after 1918, when one of the leaders of the social wing of Dutch Catholicism, Professor Aalberse, was responsible for the introduction of the statutory eight-hour day and a range of other social reforms.

The *Dutch Protestant* political movement had from the start at least a few leaders with a strong social sense. This was particularly true of Abraham Kuyper himself. He was responsible, along with *Patrimonium*, for bringing together the Christian Social Congress of 1891, the most remarkable event of its kind in Dutch history. The speech with which he opened it is read and re-read to this day. As a statement of Christian social principles and policy it is worthy of the year which also saw the appearance of *Rerum Novarum*. *Patrimonium* itself, as the first major element in the Protestant workers' movement, helped to reinforce this trend. It adopted its first social programme in 1894, and in 1901 two of its leaders entered Parliament. One of them, the Rev. A. S. Talma, who besides his personal experience as a pastor had been influenced by the efforts of Stöcker in Germany and of Maurice and Kingsley in England, in due course entered the Cabinet and made an important contribution to social legislation.

But, when seen through the eyes of the C.N.V. trade unions, by far the most active and dynamic section of the Protestant workers' movement, these influences in the Protestant parties did not amount to much. Kuyper, like his Catholic opposite number Schaepman, found it easier to make speeches about social policy than to induce his more liberal or conservative colleagues to take action on them. And though Talma's work continued to give satisfaction to the workers' movement, that of his colleague Van Vliet at times did not. In 1911, for example, when the C.N.V. petitioned parliament for certain, by modern standards, very modest improvements in the Dutch labour code—a ten-hour day for example, a free Saturday afternoon, and two days' paid holiday a year—Van Vliet 'could only express his regret that certain leaders of Christian organisations were thus competing' with the Socialists. In the next few years sharp criticism was several times expressed of the attitude of both the Protestant and the Catholic parties, and various formulas for better contact and stronger influence were discussed. The Seamen's Union at one point suggested a standing joint committee with the Christian parliamentary parties, including the Catholic Party. This suggestion was not taken up. Opinion was more in favour of the idea that the parties themselves should include adequate working-class representation, and that the views of the unions should be expressed through these representatives. This was to be representation within the existing parties; the possibility of a re-grouping of parties was not ruled out, but that of a class-based Labour Party, and still more of a party run by the unions themselves, was excluded as contrary to the Christian Democratic conception of political action. It 'could be logically defended only on social democratic principles'.

In 1918 the C.N.V. drafted its own political programme, covering such matters as education, housing, social insurance, progressive taxation, price control, nationalisation, factory legislation, arbitration, and legal backing for collective contracts. The programme seems to have aroused a certain amount of alarm among Protestants outside the trade union movement. However, the C.N.V. proceeded to back it with action to get its own candidates adopted for the 1918 elections. Pressure was put particularly on the Anti-Revolutionary Party, to which at that time most of the leaders of the Protestant trade unions belonged. In acting in this way the C.N.V. leaders were careful to make it clear that they did so in their personal capacity, as A.R.P. members, not as leaders of the formally non-political trade unions: the distinction, evidently, was somewhat academic. The A.R.P. offered one seat, and the C.N.V. leaders thereupon protested publicly, to the considerable annoyance of, notably, Abraham Kuyper. Indeed, the C.N.V. went further; it directed its members how to vote, irrespective of the wishes of the party leadership, so as to give a chance to other C.N.V. candidates who would otherwise have been too far down the party lists to be in the running. Enough followed this advice to make two other trade unionists runners-up on their respective lists, and of these one quickly entered parliament to fill a vacancy. The total number of A.R.P. seats in the Lower House at that time was 13. The battle for fuller representation went on, and a settlement seems to have been reached only in the 'thirties.

One difficulty on the Protestant side which did not exist on the Catholic was that what might be called the Liberal and Conservative wings of the political movement were from 1894 in separate parties. In economic and social matters the A.R.P. was the Liberal wing, with both the advantages and the disadvantages which that implies. Colijn, its leader in the 'twenties and 'thirties, was very well aware of the significance of the rise of the various workers' movements. The turning point, as he told the Protestant employers' organisations in 1923, was not 1918 but the eighteen-nineties. Its significance was that the Fourth Estate proposed now to follow the rise in income and social position accomplished by the Third Estate earlier in the nineteenth century; and this ambition, Colijn added, had behind it not merely force but justice. But Colijn, as has been shown, remained wedded to an extreme Gladstonian conception of economics, and it was not until his reign ended, about the time of the Second World War, that the 'social' tendency in the party became dominant. The Christian Historical Union on the other hand drained off from the A.R.P. elements who in Britain would have found their place in the Conservative Party; less intellectually sharp, one might say, than their liberal colleagues but more adaptable (as the party's name implies) to the march of events. The C.H.U. thus had room for many 'socially progressive' elements, as that term was understood down to the Second World War, including quite a number of those who after the Second World War went to make up the Protestant group in the neutral Dutch Labour Party.

(c) *Germany*

It would be going too far to say that the *Protestant political movement in Germany* started on the Left. Stöcker's Socialism was distinctly National. He and his party were markedly anti-semitic and it was not till the beginning of the 'twenties that his successors definitely broke with the 'German Nationalist' party which later helped Hitler so conspicuously towards his majority in 1933. However, there was nothing false or assumed about Stöcker's own concern for social legislation, and, as has been shown, he quickly won support from the rising Protestant workers' movement. When in the 'twenties the stage of experiment ended and the Christian Social People's Service was founded, it could quite fairly be described as a Centre or even Centre-Left party of the same character as the P.D.P. in France or the P.P.I. in Italy. The problem of the Protestant political movement in Germany has not therefore been to insert a social and democratic element into a pre-existing Christian party. As in France and

303

Italy, it has been to win politically moderate or right-wing churchmen's support for a movement which was markedly Christian Democratic from the start, and decidedly so after its first generation.

Of all the Christian parties existing before the First World War, that of the *German Catholics*, the Centre Party, came closest to what today is the standard pattern of Christian Democracy. Though forced by events into the position of a Catholic party, it was in principle a-confessional. It stood, like the Christian Democratic parties today, midway between the conservative and liberal Right and the Marxist Left, and was a main pillar of democracy in Germany. The high points of its history were reached when it served, as the *Democrazia Cristiana* in Italy or the M.R.P. in France—it is significant how often the thought of Alcide De Gasperi throughout the generation for which he led the *Democrazia Cristiana* came back to the example of the Centre—as a rallying point for the forces of democracy against attacks from one flank or the other. During the *Kulturkampf* it stood with the Left against the assaults of right-wing nationalists; notably, it refused to accept Bismarck's laws against the Socialists. When the German Empire was succeeded in 1918 by the Weimar Republic, the Centre became the king pin of an alliance between liberals, Social Democrats, and Christian Democrats, against the assaults first of Communists and later again of nationalists. And its greatest failure occurred when, after 1929, it abandoned its focal role and, particularly, its alliance with the Social Democrats. The Centre did not ally itself with the National Socialists. But, by abandoning its own traditional policy, it allowed the democratic forces in Germany to meet the challenge of National Socialism dispersed and divided, and to be defeated accordingly.

The Centre also resembled the modern Christian Democratic parties in that it had from the start a strong interest in social and economic policy and, particularly, in the social problems created by modern industry. In its initial draft programme of 1870 it made in particular three points, centred round the idea of an equilibrium between the interests of land, labour, and capital.

(1) The predominance of landed and farming interests had in the past led to social stagnation. More recently however 'the theories of the economists, industrialism, unlimited occupational mobility, and the concentration of capitalist power' had swung the pendulum to the other extreme. It was particularly important to ensure that this new 'fever' of development should not lead to the destruction of the family farm and the business middle class.
(2) Special attention should also be given to problems of wages and social security in industry, and the impact of industrial conditions on family life.
(3) The action required should not come solely or even mainly from the State. Voluntary organisations should be encouraged to play their part. (Summary of s. 7 of the programme, as reprinted in Salomon, *Die Deutschen Parteiprogramme*, 1932 ed., p. 161.)

In 1877 the Centre group in the Reichstag moved a comprehensive resolution in favour of arbitration boards 'including freely elected workers' representatives', of a ban on Sunday work and on industrial work by children under 14, of a variety of other measures of factory legislation, and of co-operative (it might be better to say 'corporative') organisation for the craft industries. A year later it was opposing unlimited free trade. Its first worker member was elected—against, it should be added, the wishes of the party machine—in 1877; a turner, Gerhard Stötzel, from Krupp's, put up for an Essen seat by one of the earliest successful Catholic workers' leagues.

However, even the Centre needed time to work its ideas out. Its early social programmes were sketchy. It was not till 1894 that there appeared a comprehensive 'Catholic Social Programme', of more or less the standard Christian Democratic type. This was not, strictly, a programme of the Centre Party, but the influential group of Catholic social thinkers and practitioners from whom it emanated was representative of Centre Party views. It followed the characteristic line of the 'realist' school of men such as Franz Hitze, who by that time dominated the Catholic social movement. The ultimate aim, it suggested, was a co-operative social and industrial order, based on self-government in industry and the professions. But the road to this lay, not through comprehensive and revolutionary change, but through a series of immediate and detailed practical reforms.

Even this, however, was still not a workers' programme, in the sense of one made or substantially contributed to by workers. It was not till at or after the end of the century that the Christian trade unions and the Catholic workers' leagues were powerful enough to make their own weight fully felt in the party. By that time the members of the leagues were sufficiently awakened to be demanding political education and action. Personal contacts were built up with the Centre Party, and from 1914 these were formalised through the creation of 'political committees' in the leagues. There was an obvious contradiction here with the principle that the leagues, as what would later have been called Catholic Action organisations, responsible to the Bishops and committing them by their acts, should refrain from party politics. This contradiction became flagrant when, in the course of the war, there arose a battle for equal voting rights, with no weighting in favour of wealth or education. The political committees joined in with full force, and the Church authorities stepped in and insisted that they cease to be agencies of the leagues. But this merely meant that they became independent. They did not disappear, and it is from about this time, as in so many other Christian Democratic parties, that worker influence in the party can be regarded as established. Trade union and workers' league officials such as Adam Stegerwald, Joseph

Joos, and Heinrich Brüning played henceforward a very prominent part in the Centre.

For eight years continuously, from 1920 to 1928, a Centre Party deputy, Fr. Heinrich Brauns, was Reich Minister of Labour. Under his rule German legislation in such matters as social insurance, factory regulation, works councils, and protection against arbitrary dismissal can fairly be said to have led the world. Brauns' policy was in the direct line of that outlined by Hitze and his colleagues a generation earlier; fundamental change in the structure of the capitalist economy as the end, but gradual, step by step alteration as the means. His changes still left the overall management of the economy and of individual firms and industries to the choice, though no doubt the increasingly restricted choice, of managers and owners. But quantitative change eventually becomes qualitative, and by the time he left office an important younger group of German Catholics was beginning to speak disparagingly of his policy as mere 'repair work' on the capitalist system, and to suggest that the time had now come for a decisive move towards what had all along been the final objective; sharing the control of overall policy with workers, above all at the level of the industry, but also at that of the firm. Catholics were also beginning to take socialist claims more seriously, and to understand better the Socialist case for overall State control of the economy. Debate on these matters was just getting going in the Centre Party, as in the rest of the Catholic social movement in Germany, when it was cut short by the National Socialist dictatorship. But the movement of ideas continued underground, and emerged again after 1945 in the C.D.U. Certain aspects of it, such as the case for State planning against unemployment or for industry-wide organisation on P.B.O. lines, did not seem relevant in the years of reconstruction, though P.B.O. or its German equivalent was formally endorsed by the Catholic Workers' Movement, by the general *Katholikentag* at Bochum in 1949, and by the C.D.U. in its earlier programmes before reconstruction got going in 1949. But it has been seen what a substantial increase, as compared with the years before 1933, has taken place under the C.D.U.'s rule in workers' control and influence over firms' policy; as well as—in practice, not so much in theory—in Government responsibility for the good management of the economy as a whole.

The Centre Party and C.D.U., like their colleagues in Belgium or Switzerland, have had throughout their history to accommodate themselves not only to varying class interests but also to the clash of regional interests, leading in some cases to federalist or even separatist demands. Bavarian Catholics in particular have consistently affirmed their identity and autonomy. In the early days they had their own Bavarian Patriotic Party, and for a time also a Catholic People's Party which branched off from it. It was not till 1887 that the Patriotic Party became the Bavarian

Centre Party. At the end of the First World War was founded a Bavarian People's Party, which became the most important in the country. At one moment there was a question of a federation between Bavaria and Austria. When that hope faded, there remained a sharp conflict between the federalist wishes of most Catholic and many Protestant electors in Bavaria and the tendency of the Reich government, strongly supported at that moment by the Centre Party, to centralise one service after another. The Socialists, who entered the Reich government at the end of the war, were always a centralising party. But other parties also were impressed with the need for strong central control to consolidate the new Weimar Republic, and also—Heinrich Brauns' view, for instance—to enforce adequate standards of social legislation and policy throughout the land. The Bavarians, at any rate, did not share these views. Their People's Party worked with the Centre for a year or two, but then, as the tendency to concentrate more and more power in Berlin became apparent, became estranged from it till the end of the 'twenties. In due course the breach was made up, and when after the Hitler period a new Christian Social Union was founded in Bavaria it entered a standing alliance with the C.D.U. But the difference of name remains significant of a feeling of separate identity and resentment of national interference, of which the C.D.U. has to take account.

(d) Austria

There is a real difference of political views behind the desire of the South Germans for autonomy: one which comes out even more sharply when the history of the Centre and C.D.U. is compared with that of their opposite numbers in *Austria*. The Catholic political movement, as it existed in Austria in 1880, was conservative and monarchist, with a strong respect for tradition, authority, and vested interests. In that year there began what came to be known as the 'Vienna Movement', an Austrian and Catholic version of Stöcker's Christian-Social movement, by which it was in fact partly inspired. Like Stöcker's movement in its initial stages, it was strongly anti-semitic: though, as in Stöcker's case, on the ground not of race or religion but of the role played by Jews in Austrian culture at that date. In 1887 this movement gave rise to the 'Christian Social Union', led by Karl Lueger. Elected Mayor of Vienna in 1897, Lueger proved to be one of the outstanding municipal administrators of his day. He let the anti-semitic side of his movement gradually drop, and when in 1906 universal suffrage was introduced in Austria was able to spread his movement throughout the country. The whole Catholic political movement, in effect, was absorbed into the Christian-Social Party.

But here appears the difference in climate between the Catholics of South Germany and of the North. By the standards of the Centre Party the intellectual leaders of the Christian Social movement in Austria were intransigent, men of the thesis rather than the hypothesis; inclined to leap straight over to the co-operative, decentralised economic and social order which the Catholic social movement as a whole took as its aim, and much less inclined than the Centre to feel their way along the earthier paths of experience. They were, many of them, less fully convinced than the Centre politicians of the virtues of democracy, more inclined to idealise the social order of the past. On both counts, many of them inclined to a political system built up on the representation of interests, and particularly of industrial or guild interests, rather than on the individual citizen's vote. These views might have been corrected if the party had had a strong working-class component. But industrial workers never, in fact, till the Second World War, won as effective a voice in the policy of the Catholic political movement in Austria as they did in that of the Centre. Landowners, farmers, and the business middle class were dominant. Nor was there a non-Christian democratic labour movement capable of influencing the Christian Social party from outside, for the Austrian Socialist Party bore much the same relation to German Socialism as the Christian Social Party did to the Centre. It too was marked off from its German opposite number by its intransigence, its conservatism—in the sense of its slowness to move on from the traditions of the Early Marxist age—and its belief in strong-arm methods in the factories and private armies in the streets. When the Austrian Empire collapsed in 1918, Social Democrats and Christian Socialists were left in control of the country, the two parties being about equally balanced, each strong enough to checkmate the other. Neither, as can be seen, was well equipped for a common effort in defence of democracy and social progress. In due course, in 1934, civil war broke out between them. The Christian Socialists emerged as victors and imposed the corporative constitution already described; only to be swept away in their turn a few years later, with little sympathy from the outside world, by the National Socialists. It is not certain whether a united front of Socialists and Christian Socialists could have saved Austrian democracy or independence, in the face of armed invasion from Germany. But it is clear that the conservatism and lack of realism of the two great Austrian parties made any attempt to do so hopeless.

In the light of this history it can be understood why the Austrian People's Party today insists that:

> The Austrian People's Party is a new party. It has no connection with any political formation in the past, nor could it. . . . (Kasamas, *Programm Österreich*, 1949, p. 17.)

The O.V.P. is genuinely attached to democracy, and has a realistic policy, effective representation of all classes, including the workers, and a strong social sense. There is also, thanks particularly to the experience of the resistance and Russian occupation, and to the 'deconfessionalisation' of the O.V.P. described below, much greater tolerance and collaboration between the O.V.P. and the Socialist Party. But it remains true that it has taken much longer to reach this point in Austria than in any of the other countries studied here. Elsewhere the transition from conservative to social and democratic policies was mainly completed between 1880 and 1920, the generation from 1920 to 1950 providing only some finishing touches. In Austria on the other hand the capture of the Catholic political movement by the 'Vienna Movement' took the transition only half way and the decisive step was left until after the Second World War.

(e) Switzerland

The case of Swiss Catholics, unlike that of Austrian, runs very much to rule. The Catholics of Switzerland had their parliamentary fraction right from the start of the present Swiss constitution in 1848, though at first it was very small; eight out of 111 members of the first National Council elected under the new constitution. Gradually this fraction strengthened its position, until in 1891 it was able to capture for the first time one of the seven seats in the Cabinet, the Federal Council.[1] As yet there was no organised national party behind this fraction. The Social Democrats were the first to found such a party in Switzerland, in 1888. In 1894 the Liberal parties of the various cantons federated into a national party, and in 1912 the Catholics finally did the same. Seven years later, in 1919, the balance of power in Swiss politics, and the position of the Conservative People's Party in particular, was revolutionised by the first general election under proportional representation. The Liberal majority which had prevailed since 1848 ended, the Liberal Party itself split, the Socialists more than doubled their representation, and the Catholics emerged in a key position in the centre of the political scene. In due course the Federal Council also was adapted to the new situation. There too the Liberals finally lost their majority in 1943, the membership then being three liberals, two Catholics, and one each from the Socialists and the (dissident liberal) Farmers' Party. But this was an after-effect, delayed by the conventions of the Swiss Constitution. The essential changes—the rise of national parties and the change in the balance of political forces—took place in the generation from 1880 to the First World War. Since then the balance of Swiss politics has scarcely altered.

1919 is the date not only of the revolution in the balance of power

[1] The seven members of the Federal Council are in principle re-elected every four years. In practice a member once elected remains as long as age permits. The government is thus permanent, irrespective of what happens in Parliament. From 1848 to 1952 only 67 persons were members of the Swiss Federal Council, including the seven incumbents in 1952.

in Swiss politics but also of the decisive establishment of a 'social' wing within the Conservative People's Party. A few individuals actively interested in social reform had begun to appear in the Catholic party, or fraction as it then was, in the last quarter of the nineteenth century.

> Before the creation of an actual Christian-social parliamentary group [i.e. a group within the Conservative People's Party] there was in the Catholic Conservative fraction a group of socially-minded individuals, who kept in touch with the Christian social movements and defended their views on social policy in parliament; a task which Catholic parliamentarians at that time were not always too thankful to take up . . . (Scherrer, *Die Christliche Sozialreform*, Swiss Christian Social Workers' League, 1944, p. 25.)

These contacts involved some half-dozen members of the Catholic fraction, and were concerned notably with social insurance and factory legislation. The most distinguished lay leader of the 'social' tendency among Swiss Catholics at that time, in the political as well as the economic and social field, was Kaspar Decurtins, who belonged to the group (Fribourg Union) which prepared the way for the Encyclical *Rerum Novarum*. He also took a prominent part in the early efforts at international labour legislation from which eventually emerged the International Labour Organisation.

The big change came, however, when the Christian workers' movement developed in the first two decades of the twentieth century. There was now a source from which a permanent Christian-social wing of the party could grow, and a force to support it. From the end of the First World War a permanent parliamentary group accordingly came into existence. One Christian-social deputy was elected in 1917, and four in 1919. By 1943 the group had risen to 14, out of 43 Conservative People's Party members at that date.

(f) Conclusion

The increasingly 'social' character of the older Christian Democratic parties does not mean that they have become Socialist, nor even that they can be treated as the political arm of the Christian labour movement. The battle between left and right goes on within them. An outstanding example of the differences between them and the Christian labour movement is the question of co-responsibility and workers' control, which was discussed in detail above. But their 'social' element is today strong enough to make them genuinely what they claim to be, parties of the centre, in which all classes and groups have an assured place and an effective voice. They have, as the statistics quoted below (Chapter XXII) will show, the support of those workers who are practising Christians as well as of the middle class. It may have been possible in the nineteenth century for a Christian party to attract working-class support without a marked and genuine social policy. It is certainly not possible today, as the Evangelical People's Party in Switzerland has found to its cost.

From the point of view of relations with other parties, the parties in this group have found a position in the centre of the political stage, flanked normally by Liberals and Conservatives on one side and Social Democrats on the other, as satisfactory as any: short, that is, of the ideal situation in which a Christian Democratic party could by itself dominate the political stage.[1] If opinion in and out of a Christian Democratic party is swinging to the left, it can incline to the left itself, work with the Social Democrats, or at least compete with them effectively. If the swing is to the right, there is the possibility of a similar relation with Liberals and Conservatives. In either case the swing of public opinion is duly reflected in parliament, the government of the country is carried on by a democratic party or coalition, and Christian Democracy remains powerful and influential. The condition of this happy state of affairs is of course that the Christian Democrats' alternative partners to the left and the right should be strong enough both to influence them effectively and to govern in combination with them. In the past this condition has not always been fulfilled. A case in point was the situation in Germany in 1932, when the National-Socialist party alone held as many seats as the Christian Democrats and Social Democrats together, the Communist party also being strongly represented on the other wing. The case of two countries, France and Italy, where Christian Democracy has suffered through its not being fulfilled in recent years, will be examined in the next chapter. An attempt will then be made, in Chapter XXIII, to draw some general conclusions from the experience of Christian Democracy as a whole.

A-CONFESSIONALITY—THE OLDER PARTIES

(a) Germany

It is significant that of the ten major Christian Democratic parties in the countries studied here only one, the Catholic People's Party in Holland, carries today an obvious denominational label. There were some even of the nineteenth century parties which, though called into existence to meet a challenge to ecclesiastical and denominational interests, were anxious to enlarge their policy and affirm their independence of the ecclesiastical authorities. This was particularly true of the German *Centre Party*. Operating as they did in a State of mixed religions, with a Protestant majority, the Centre leaders recognised from the start that their appeal to be fully effective must be directed to churchmen of all denominations, and based on something more than the defence of the Catholic schools or the

---

[1] An ideal which in Christian Democratic theory itself should be unattainable, since the time would then have come for the unique Christian Democratic party to divide into two or more competing with one another. See below, Chapter XXIII, p. 391.

right of Catholic bishops to discipline their clergy. In its early programmes the Centre gave a prominent place to the defence of specifically Church interests, but in language which contrasted sharply with that of the more denominationally minded Catholics of South Germany and Austria. Its election programme of 1870, for instance, called for:

> Maintenance of the constitutionally guaranteed independence and rights of the Church, and the defeat of all attacks on the independence of church institutions, the development of religious life, and the activities of Christian charity. (Quoted in Salomon, op. cit., p. 163.)

Contrast this with the corresponding paragraph of the draft programme for a Christian Social Party in Bavaria prepared about 1875 by Prince Karl zu Löwenstein, for many years organiser of the annual 'Catholic Assemblies' in Germany:

> We reject and oppose the modern, undenominational State, which in its enlightened agnosticism denies that the Church is founded by God and enjoys the rights following from that fact. The Christian State, on the other hand, our ideal, will:
>
> (1) Recognise the divine mission of the Church, its inner autonomy and external independence, and its claim to the protection and aid of the secular arm in the fulfilment of its task.
> (2) Recognise the right of the Church to define for itself the boundary of the sphere of activity assigned to it by Christ.
> (3) Guarantee the Catholic Church full freedom within this sphere.
> (4) Recognise the Church's right of supervision and control over the excesses of science and art. . . .
> (5) Hand over to the Church the direction of denominational educational establishments and the administration of Catholic school funds.
> (6) Hand over to the Church all welfare funds and institutions supported by the State, if their founders intended them to have a Catholic character, or if, having regard to the proportion of Catholics in the population, they should properly serve Catholics.
> (7) The Christian State will tolerate people of other beliefs in so far as they do not deny God or the principles of the natural law, and will recognise their historically acquired rights. (Salomon, op. cit., II, 32–2.)

In 1887 there arose the important opportunity referred to earlier for the Centre to define its position in relation to the Church authorities. The *Kulturkampf* was running to an end, and as part of the settlement the Church authorities agreed with Bismarck, over the heads of the Centre leaders, that if certain anti-religious laws were withdrawn the Centre would vote for Bismarck's military budget, to which on general political grounds they were opposed. The Centre leaders immediately made their position clear in letters to the ecclesiastics concerned. In matters of internal church government, or of the relation of the Church as such to the government of the State, they agreed that final responsibility must lie with the Bishops and Pope. The Centre might protest against a decision in these matters if it seemed politically inopportune, but would accept it, and defend it in Parliament, if the Church authorities insisted. But 'it is absolutely impossible for the Centre to accept directives in matters of non-ecclesiastical legislation', and if the Pope or Bishops insisted on issuing such directives the party would break up. The right of Bishops to define the principles by which Christian politicians must be guided was one thing. The right to say which Act should be passed through Parliament at a particular time, except in that small though vital range of 'ecclesiastical' matters where the Church has in any case direct authority, was quite another. The Pope and Bishops did not insist further.

The Centre did in fact at all times attract some Protestant support. But a series of accidents prevented this from growing into a true Evangelical wing of the party. When the party was starting, Pius IX's *Syllabus of Errors* and his definition of Papal infallibility rankled in many Protestant minds. Then came the *Kulturkampf*, and again many Protestants were frightened off. Towards the end of the century a new drive was made to emphasise the inter-denominational character of the Centre. This was expressed notably in a famous article by Julius Bachem in 1906, with the title 'We Must Fight in the Open Field' (*Wir Müssen aus dem Turm heraus*). The defensive battle, focused on Catholic church interests, was won. Now, Bachem argued, was the time for the Centre to come out of its entrenchments and make its general political programme the rallying point for all men of good will, and in the first place for Protestants as well as Catholics. In 1909 the party leadership again solemnly reaffirmed that:

> The Centre Party is basically a political and not a confessional party. It takes its stand on the German Constitution, which requires deputies to regard themselves as representatives of the people as a whole. (Salomon, op. cit., II, p. 65.)

But this new forward move coincided with the pontificate of Pius X, the counter-attack of the Catholic Church against 'Modernism', and the 'Trade Union Conflict' in Germany. In the Centre Party also voices were raised calling for a more definite Catholic character for the party. Once again, Protestants were frightened off.

In the end, it was not until Protestants themselves had awakened to the case for party formation on a specifically Christian basis, and had formed their own party and built up their own self-confidence, that the ideal of an inter-denominational party in Germany came near to realisation. The deputies of the Evangelical People's Service regularly voted with the Centre in the early 'thirties, and built up good personal connections with Centre leaders. As already explained, it was the experience of the Nazi period which finally convinced the mass of church-going Protestants in Germany of the case for Christian political action; and the contacts established before 1933, along with the inter-confessional tradition of the

313

Centre Party, helped to ensure that this should take the form of a Protestant wing in the united C.D.U. The Centre Party was re-founded separately from the C.D.U., but never acquired either much influence or a very clear policy. There were those who wanted Catholic-Protestant collaboration, but between independent Catholic and Protestant parties. There were others who wished to go back on the trend to inter-confessionality and use the revived Centre Party to press Catholic claims, now that the amputation of East Germany had created an approximately equal balance of the denominations. Others were afraid of the Right-wing tradition of most Protestants in politics, and saw in a revived Centre the possibility of a German Labour Party, a-confessional, drawing support from socialists as well as from Catholics and left-wing Protestants. But all these confused and contradictory tendencies were swept away in the general movement of opinion in favour of a united Christian party, with a general and not merely an ecclesiastical programme, independent of the official Churches, and drawing its support from all classes and denominations.

(b) Switzerland

The course of events among *Catholics in Switzerland* recalls in many ways that in Germany. The Conservative People's Party is primarily a party of Catholics, but has always aimed at being inter-confessional. Its statutes lay down its objective as being to organise 'the Catholics of Switzerland and those who stand with them in politics'. The party arose out of the defence of cantonal rights against Liberal tendencies to central-isation, as well as of Catholic rights in the face of Liberal measures against religion: when in 1912 it was formally constituted, the title 'Catholic' was deliberately rejected, and that of 'Conservative', underlining the party's defence of the historic Swiss way of life, was chosen instead. There have in fact always been active Protestant members of the party. But Switzer-land, unlike Germany, has never had more than the embryo of a Protestant political movement, whether in association with the Conservative People's Party or otherwise. Swiss Protestants have on the whole remained un-awakened to the case for independent Christian political action, and so the possibility of an effectively inter-confessional party has never arisen.

(c) Austria, Belgium, Holland

In *Austria, Belgium,* and *Holland,* by contrast with Germany and Switzerland, the Christian parties both before and after the First World War were frankly denominational. The Catholic Party in *Belgium* reached the height of its power in the eighteen-nineties. It has been said of its most powerful leader at that time, Charles Woeste, that 'he was interested in nothing but increasing the budget for the Churches and the State grants to the Catholic schools'. Ministers, a little later:

314

Were no longer even the instruments of the majority in the Chamber. They were those of the Federation of Catholic Clubs. Carefully, methodically, the Cabinet used its formidable and mysterious 'fourth power', that of the administration, to people the public service with its creatures. In the phrase of Paul Hymans, it divided Belgium into two camps, that of the orthodox and that of the heretics. (Van Kalken, *La Belgique Contemporaine*, 1950, p. 154.)

The rise of the Christian social movements changed this a good deal. With the Christian trade unions and workers' leagues and the Belgian Farmers' Union hammering at the door, the party leaders could no longer 'be interested in nothing but increasing the budget for the Churches'. The influence of the social organisations was taking effect by the time of the First World War. The movement of ideas went on, and around the time of the Second World War there came a further change, similar to that expressed in the Centre Party by the slogan 'We must fight in the open field'. To quote the present-day Christian Social Party's own statement on this:

From the middle of the nineteenth century till the war of 1940, our Catholics traditionally grouped themselves in a denominational party known as the 'Catholic Party'.... In spite of this strong tradition, the post-war years did not see the rebirth of the old Catholic Party. From 1945, the great majority of Christian believers and a minority of non-Christians grouped themselves in an undenominational party which bases its policy on the personalist principles inherited from Christianity. The old Catholic Party was a federation, on a denominational basis, of political associations of the middle class, workers, and farmers, each giving expression to its own social and economic aspirations. At the end of the war the denominational link, which arose out of the battles of the past over the schools question, seemed to Christians obsolete in the light of changing ideas, and also inadequate as a response to the general desire for the reconstruction of western civilisation. Abandoning denominationalism, the Christian Social Party has adopted a common foundation on which it hopes to group, round a programme aiming at the common good, citizens without distinction of religion, class, or economic interest. Its programme is centred on the development of human personality, on the family, and on pluralism, and is in general inspired by the social doctrine of the Encyclicals. It is this that ensures the Party a vigorous doctrine, in which must be seen the essential reason for its unity. (Reply by the P.S.C. to questionnaire by the N.E.I. for the Annual Congress of the N.E.I. at Fribourg, 1952.)

For the *Austrian* Christian Democratic movement also the Second World War was in this respect the turning point. 'Clericalism', as the Austrian People's Party defines it, exists:

When the Church exerts political power through the channel of a government or party, or inserts its influence in fields where it is not entitled to any.... Our party takes the view that religious societies, in their own interest, should not attempt to influence the current course of politics, and that it is not desirable that positions of political power should be held by ecclesiastics. (Kasamas, *Programm Österreich*, 1949, p. 125.)

The Catholic and the (in Austria) much smaller Evangelical Church both

315

issued official statements, just after the war, that they proposed to keep out of politics and to forbid their clergy to hold political office. By the agreement even of the Austrian People's Party's anti-clerical opponents, this undertaking has been honourably kept.[1] It has not of course prevented the Churches from continuing to make statements of principle which incidentally affect political practice. As in Italy, there has been a certain tendency for Catholic Action to put forward political demands and serve as a channel for 'clerical' views.

The same tendency to de-confessionalisation has made itself felt also in *Holland*, though less forcibly. On the Catholic side a change of climate began at the end of the First World War, when the main ecclesiastical issue on which the party had been built up, the schools question, was in great part settled. An Act of 1920 established absolute financial equality between Government and Church primary schools. Secondary, higher, and technical education remained a matter for dispute: but the main principle was decided. The main change in the party constitution following from this alteration of climate came at the end of the Second World War. The question was then raised whether the pre-war Catholic Party should be revived, or Catholics should instead join new groupings of the sort which will be discussed below. It was finally agreed to revive it, but in a new and less confessional form.

> Our Party is not a Church party; its members are expected to join it because they accept its programme, and in this way non-Catholics as well as Catholics should be able to join. (Resolution reprinted on p. 1 of *Reglementen van de Katholieke Volkspartij*, Pt. I.)

What was needed was a party based on the natural law and Revelation (note the non-denominational phrasing), equipped with a progressive social policy attractive also to non-Catholics. The party's title does, however, remain 'Catholic', though this is something of an accident,[2] and its rules refer to 'the teaching authority of the Church'. It is not subject to ecclesiastical authority even to the limited extent described already in the case of the Dutch Catholic Trade unions. But it gets open and explicit support from the Catholic Bishops, on which more below: sometimes, indeed, to an extent the party finds embarrassing. It has, therefore, still a substantially denominational character, and it is not surprising that its efforts to attract non-Catholic support have had rather little effect. Nevertheless, the changes made in 1945 have been a substantial step towards the inter-confessional or a-confessional pattern now normal elsewhere.

[1] See notably the statement by the Austrian Socialist Party to the Socialist International's conference on Socialism and Religion, Bentveld, 1953.

[2] The obvious a-confessional alternative was 'Christian', which had to be turned down because of a trick of the Dutch language. 'Christelijk', in Dutch public life, usually means 'Protestant'.

The Dutch Protestant parties are the clearest exception to the general trend, for they have become in some ways more denominational through the years. In the 'eighties there was only one such party, the Anti-Revolutionary. In the course of the 'nineties there split off from the Anti-Revolutionaries the groups which later made up the Christian Historical Union. This was partly, as has been said, a question of liberal or conservative politics. But there was also theology in it. Kuyper, the leader of the Anti-Revolutionaries, was also in his theological capacity the leader of the 'Complainants' of 1886 and of the new, strict Calvinist, Gereformeerde churches which grew out of it. The Christian Historicals tended to be Hervormd, resentful of the 'Complaint', and to draw their doctrine from the natural law to an extent hard to reconcile with strict Calvinist orthodoxy. Theology again played a part later in the formation of the small, rigidly Calvinist, and rather markedly anti-Catholic 'Political *Gereformeerde* Party'. It may be that these theological distinctions were significant less in themselves than as pegs on which to hang personal and political differences. It is known for instance that Baron de Savornin Lohman, the founder of the Christian Historical Union, felt towards the end of his life that they could and should be bridged again. But there remains a distinct difference of theological as well as political climate between the Protestant parties, and all of them keep in their rules or statutes their characteristically Protestant formulas. There has been less change on their side than among the Catholics: less, in fact, than in any of the other major Christian Democratic political movements mentioned here.

CHAPTER XXI

1880–1950: THE POLITICAL PARTIES (II)

T HE political movements just described started this period as, except in Austria, convinced adherents of liberal democracy, but had still much to learn about democracy in the social and economic field, as well—several of them—as about the danger of being too closely identified with church affairs and an ecclesiastical hierarchy. The new Christian Democratic parties which arose in these generations in Italy and France might be said in these respects to be born with a silver spoon in their mouths, since they came late enough to be from the start not merely liberal and democratic but also a-confessional and socially aware. The difficulty in their case was rather that an immense effort was needed to bring them to birth at all.

ITALY

The problem in Italy was not so much to bring Catholics as an organised and united force onto the political stage as to decide what form this force was to take. For a generation after the unification of Italy and the end of the Papal States, the main Catholic forces in Italy remained united under the direct authority of the Church, until 1904 through the Congress Movement, and then, after a short interregnum, through the machinery of what now came to be called Catholic Action. In principle, their central concern was with the question of the Temporal Power, and a formal ban (the 'non-expedit') was imposed by successive Popes on participation by Catholics in Italian national politics. But as the years went by the question of the Temporal Power came in practice to be seen more and more as one to be settled between the ecclesiastical authorities and the government, certainly not as one which called for the exclusive concentration of lay Catholics' political effort. The more conservative Catholics, intransigent on the Temporal Power, kept control of the Congress Movement till 1904, and unquestionably rendered great services to what was later to become the cause of Christian Democracy. They established and maintained the idea of a distinctive Christian position in public life. They built up around this idea a following in certain areas—the Veneto, for instance—where Christian Democracy still has its most secure bases. And the Congress

Movement, under their control, did valuable pioneering work in Catholic social theory and, to a smaller extent, practice.

But the fact remained that the intransigents' position rested on a refusal to accept the ordinary responsibilities of public life, and from the eighteen-nineties two strong currents developed in favour of more normal participation in public affairs. One, the older—traces of it go back to the 'seventies, and beyond—was essentially liberal. It appreciated the liberal social order, was anxious to defend it against the rising forces of socialism, and wished for that reason to collaborate with the laicist liberal governing class of the time. It met with increasing understanding from the Liberals, who were tending to become a conservative force, reluctant to lose good allies over what by now were beginning to seem somewhat old-fashioned ecclesiastical quarrels. The most characteristic leader of this group was Filippo Meda.

The second current, whose most prominent leader in the early days was Fr. Romolo Murri, was known at the time as 'Christian Democratic'. Its spirit can be seen best from the 'Programme of the Young Christian Democrats' published at Turin in 1899.

(1) We demand the organisation of society, step by step, into corporative associations for each profession: autonomous, comprehensive, and statutory. . . . Therefore we call on the State and all other subordinate public authorities to favour in every way this tendency to corporative organisation, especially by allowing full freedom and legal recognition to the trade unions and trade associations which are being formed through private initiative.

(2) We demand the proportional representation of parties in parliament and local authorities as a closer approach to fair representation, and as a step towards the proportional representation of social interests, which will be the effect of corporative social organisation.

(3) We demand extensive decentralisation of the administration, as a step towards real autonomy for local and regional authorities, though tempered by regard for the genuinely national requirements of the State.

(4) We demand effective legal protection for labour: restrictions on night work and on the work of women and children: compulsory Sunday rest: accident, sickness, and old age insurance: a fixed maximum of hours per day and a fixed minimum wage. We insist that the practical application of these general rules, to be laid down by law . . . be entrusted to the corporative organisations of the professions.

(5) We demand serious protection and effective promotion of the country people and their interests: of small property . . . of collective and especially local authorities' property: more rational legislation on tenancy agreements: the extension of agricultural education: the establishment of Chambers of Agriculture and of arbitration machinery.

(6) We demand serious protection and efficient promotion of the interests of industry and commerce: vocational education for the masses: producers', consumers', and credit co-operatives: friendly societies and workers' housing societies. We call for the establishment of a Ministry of Labour, of Chambers of Industry, and of industrial arbitration machinery. We wish to see the promotion and development of the merchant navy and the development of trade outlets.

319

(7) We call for a sharp and progressive reduction in military charges and taxation; for economy in all the unproductive services of the administrative bureaucracy.

(8) We wish for a reform of taxation in line with the requirements of justice . . . the abolition of consumption taxes, the limitation of tariffs to what is strictly necessary to the national economy, and the abolition or at least reduction of the taxes on real property; the institution of a moderate and progressive income tax, with exemption for the minimum necessary for existence.

(9) We wish for the suppression of usury, of stock exchange gambling, and of capitalist speculation . . . and the lowering of the legal rate of interest.

(10) We wish to see civil and political liberties protected: freedom of teaching, of the press, of association, of meeting, of organisation: liberty and extension of the franchise: the development of the nation's culture and of education on religious, civic, and popular lines.

(11) We wish for general and progressive disarmament, the brotherhood of peoples, and arbitration between nations.

We demand all this as Christian Democrats, because the reforms for which we call correspond at once to the aspirations of a true democracy and to the social principles of Christianity. Christian Democracy means the wholehearted application of Christianity, that is of Catholicism, to the whole of modern public and private life, and to all its forms of progress.

As Italian Christian Democrats we wish to see an end to the antagonism between the political and civic institutions of our country and the Catholic Church and Roman Pontiff, which are the historic, moral, and political centre of the Italian nation. We wish for the unity, freedom and independence of the Church.

We therefore call for a transformation in the conscience of the nation, such as will lead it to see its special mission, and the best guarantee of its greatness and prosperity, there where it is really to be found: in making itself the centre and auxiliary, along with the Pontiff, of a universal renewal of Christian and popular humanism: in promoting, that is, that international Christian Democracy which, thanks to the pressure of social advance, and in accordance with the desire of such men of genius as Gladstone, Leo XIII, and Guiseppe Toniolo, will be the glory of the twentieth century. (Text as reprinted in Tupini, *I Democratici Cristiani*, 1954, pp. 326–8.)

What the devil is Gladstone doing in this galley? There is more than a little in this manifesto to make one smile. But there is no question of its impact, or rather of the impact of the movement from which it came, on Catholic Italy around the turn of the century. The Christian Democrats were radicals. It was not enough to reform the liberal and economic social order, as the liberal Catholics were also willing to do. To encourage friendly societies and co-operatives, to let trade unions grow, was all very well. But it was necessary to cut deeper, to substitute for the free play of interests the statutory organisation of corporations, and the idea of Christian charity and co-operation for the common good. The State must where necessary be brought in to enforce a new order. Property rights must be seen as subject to a 'social mortgage', and there must be a guaranteed family living wage; demands which in that time and place seemed not merely radical but revolutionary. Italian society as a whole must be reshaped into a truly Christian order, reconciled to and centred around the Pope. These ideas, like those of Sangnier in France, proved immensely stimulating and won a wide audience. For several years the debates of the Congress Movement turned around them.

Murri, like Sangnier, was a man whose generous disposition sometimes outran his practical and intellectual capacity. A careful examination of the Young Christian Democrats' manifesto brings out certain points personal to him, and much less characteristic of his colleagues or of the Christian Democrats who came after him. It has been said of Murri that he was even more of a theocrat than a democrat, and his conception of theocracy was one which confused the spheres of Church and State and entailed serious dangers for both. He agreed with the intransigents that it was right for Catholics to withdraw from public life while the question of the Temporal Power remained unsettled. But he did not agree that the settlement of this question was merely a matter of a transaction such as led eventually to the creation of the State of Vatican City. The value of the 'non expedit' lay not merely in preparing the way for a territorial settlement, but also and even more in allowing Catholics to rally their forces for the annihilation of a bourgeois State in which they had neither lot nor part. Proposals, such as appealed to the school of Meda, to rally to the defence of the liberal State for the sake of the positive good it contained, made little impression on Murri. The enemy, indeed, tended to become the State as such, not merely its liberal form. If Murri emphasised decentralisation and local autonomy, it was not merely because of the usual pluralist assumptions of Christian Democracy. It was because he doubted whether there was in any case room in Italy for a strong State—even one inspired by Christianity—as well as a strong Church. He cast the Papacy for a role like that envisaged by the neo-Guelfs before 1848, as the focus of the country's temporal as well as spiritual life.

> He was not a politician but a sort of missionary. . . . The vision he saw was of one, unique, *societas perfecta*, that of the Church. He conceived the existence of only one party, that which he was building within the Church. And since . . . he realised that the achievement of such a programme depended on the support of the mass of the people and on accepting the standards and methods of political and cultural action characteristic of modern thought, he introduced in practice, modernist heresy into the Italian laity. For the Church, to govern in the political sphere, would have had to earn by politics the support of the mass of the people, and therefore to accept . . . something of the ideas, the intentions, and the tendencies of secularism and bourgeois democracy, at the cost of endlessly compromising religion, which would be forced, so to speak, to do work not its own. (G. de Rosa, *L'Azione Cattolica*, Vol. I, 1953, pp. 217–18.)

Murri's 'modernist' views led early in the new century to his excommunication. He returned to the Church before his death. But as a force in Catholic politics he had ended his career.

His work was carried forward, however, by a colleague, Fr. Luigi Sturzo, who largely shared his views on social policy—on the need to break up the excessive centralisation of the Italian State, for example, and win 'the support of the mass of the people'—but without their modernist overtones or confusion of State and Church. A Sicilian, and a leading figure in local government, Fr. Sturzo was working from at least 1905 for an a-confessional, socially progressive party of Christian inspiration. It was round this conception, with Sturzo as leader, that the liberal Catholics and the Christian Democrats were eventually able to unite.

Step by step, the Vatican relaxed its ban on Catholic participation in politics; a little in 1904, rather more in 1909, a very long way in 1913. These moves were not due to recognition of the value of Christian Democracy as Sturzo, still less Murri, understood it. They came on the one hand from purely diplomatic motives, the recognition by the Pope that the fall of the Temporal Power in its old form was now an accomplished fact, to which it was necessary to adjust; and on the other from fear of the rising tide of socialism, and the desire therefore to work more closely with the Liberals. The symbol of the new policy was the 'Gentiloni Pact' of 1913 which brought Catholics and Liberals into an electoral alliance. The immediate victory therefore went to the Catholic liberal school of Meda; but the incidental result was to open the road to Sturzo, who reaped the ultimate benefit.

The final steps were taken in 1918, when Benedict XV agreed to release the whole complex of what would nowadays be called Christian Democratic activities in Italy—trade unions, co-operatives, friendly societies, as well as political action—from ecclesiastical control. Catholic Action in Italy ceased to enter into politics—at least directly—and the road was finally open for an autonomous Christian Democratic party such as Sturzo proposed. Catholic support for such a party was much more readily forthcoming than before the war, since the alliance of Catholics with Liberals, from whom all of them differed on Church policy and very many on social policy, had aroused widespread dissatisfaction. Revolution was in the air, and the political problems of the post-war world were pressing from all sides. Full-scale Catholic participation in Italian politics was clearly urgent. At a private meeting in November 1918 the leaders of the Catholic social organisations thrashed out the various possibilities. Were Catholics to spread their forces over the various existing parties, to concentrate on some one of them, or to form a new party of their own? Under Sturzo's leadership the idea of a new party was accepted, and the Catholic liberals, including Meda himself, for the most part rallied to it. The newly autonomous Christian trade unions and co-operative movements gave the new party their general support, though without becoming formally affiliated with it. In 1921 the unions and co-operatives agreed with the P.P.I. that their objectives were the same, that the party would support no unions or co-operatives other than the Christian ones, and that these in their turn, without assuming political responsibilities, would look to the P.P.I. in the political field. Union leaders such as Achille Grandi and Giovanni Gronchi figured prominently in the P.P.I's leadership, equipping it from the start with an influential 'social' wing. At the beginning of 1919 the Italian Popular Party (P.P.I.) was formally launched, and met an immediate response. At the elections of 1919 it won 100 seats. The Socialists also made a big advance, the conservative-liberal groups which before the war had dominated parliament were reduced to a minority, and the Popular Party was left holding the balance of power.

On the face of it, the new party was well equipped to fit into a democratic political system. Though not Liberal, it was essentially liberal in the sense of being deeply attached to political democracy and all that it implies. The youthful enthusiasm of 1899 for a corporative parliament based on the 'proportional representation of social interests' had died away. The party could make its own now what were later to be the formative ideas of the *Democrazia Cristiana*, and were already those of the Christian Democratic parties of Germany, Switzerland, Belgium, and Holland:

> The indispensable condition and necessary safeguard of the inviolable rights of the human person, and of all civil liberty, is political freedom. . . .
> Representative democracy, expressed through universal suffrage, based on the equality of rights and duties, and animated by the spirit of brotherhood, which is the vital ferment of Christian civilisation: this must be the regime of tomorrow. . . .
> In the face of every intolerance of race or religion, the democratic regime will maintain the most rigorous respect for freedom of conscience. . . . (Manifesto on *Idee Ricostruttive della Democrazia Cristiana*, circulated in the resistance years, 1943–5.)

The Popular Party was also federalist, and keenly interested (which the Liberals officially so-called were not) in local government and regional decentralisation. Like the Socialists, it stood for social security, a national investment policy, and the rehabilitation of Italy's depressed areas.

The *Popolari* also had their hands free in the matter of ecclesiastical affairs and clerical control. There were indeed those who would have liked to see them take a more strongly denominational line. Fr. Gemelli, for example, the later founder of the Catholic University at Milan, along with another ebullient friar (the phrase is Jacini's), launched a strong attack on the original programme of the P.P.I. on the ground that it should have made the Catholic faith its ground of differentiation from other parties, and should have declared war on the liberal-democratic state and put the question of the temporal power of the Pope at the head of its programme. But this attack had lost much of its fire by the time it was carried into the

323

first Party Congress, and the Congress preferred to follow the view set out then and earlier by Fr. Sturzo. The Church unites, politics divide: a political party is something essentially different from an organisation for Catholic Action. It was dangerous, Sturzo argued, to involve the Church authorities in the mistakes and prejudices of politics. It was also dangerous to make Catholicism or the defence of ecclesiastical interests the party's ground of differentiation; for that would bring into the party Catholics unlikely to accept the social-economic or democratic programme which was in fact the P.P.I.'s distinctive mark. The Temporal Power was no doubt an important problem, but it was one for the ecclesiastical authorities to settle directly with the government of the day.

The situation of the P.P.I. was nevertheless uncomfortable, since on neither side could it find stable or reliable allies. The Socialists were in a revolutionary mood, the Liberals were led by old men of no great political stature, more familiar with the personal intrigues of the pre-war regime than with deliberate, co-ordinated programmes of social reform and development of the type for which the P.P.I. stood. In 1924, when fascism was near its final victory, the chance of an understanding between the P.P.I. and the Socialists came up. But here the Vatican stepped in. The ecclesiastical authorities no longer had direct power to intervene in the P.P.I. But they had a good deal of influence, for, while Sturzo and his followers intended to re-establish the traditional distinction between the spheres of clergy and laity and of the spiritual and temporal powers, they had no intention of setting up a rigid separation between them. The Church authorities were less interested in Christian Democracy or aware of the dangers of right-wing totalitarianism than they later became. In this respect Stefano Jacini, himself a P.P.I. leader and the semi-official historian of the party, passes a particularly severe judgment on Pius XI, who succeeded Benedict XV in 1922.

> The new Pontiff was, let us not forget, by origin a typical Lombard and conservative. As a Lombard he had observed in his youth the regrettable conflict between intransigent and liberal Catholics at Milan, and so came to desire above all things a reconciliation, political and legal, with the Italian State; a direct renewal of contact, in which the existence of an independent party of Catholics might in some circumstances help, but might also stand in the way. As a conservative he could never hide a certain distrust of Christian democracy, of which the P.P.I. was in its way the concrete political expression. To this prejudice was added an almost physical horror of Bolshevism . . . and therefore an instinctive sympathy towards those forces, whatever they might be, which seemed to oppose Bolshevism most energetically and effectively. All this . . . goes to explain how in the first part of Pius XI's pontificate he lent an ear to the views of those who saw in the rising star of fascism above all the defeat of traditional Liberalism; and how he supported those elements in the Church which were not hostile to the developing dictatorship, and that small group in the P.P.I. which was least violently opposed to it. Jacini, *Storia del Partito Popolare Italiano*, 1951, pp. 115–16.)

It was more than once made clear, in the face of the Fascist threat, that from the Church's point of view the P.P.I. was expendable. And at the moment when an understanding with the Socialists seemed possible, the Pope intervened formally against it.

In these circumstances it proved impossible to build stable or effective governments. Italian democracy survived after a fashion the first, Socialist and Communist, wave of violence after the war, but succumbed to the Fascist wave which followed it. The P.P.I.'s history in effect ended on January 16th, 1926, when its parliamentary group were beaten up by the Fascists in the Chamber of Deputies and, in the most literal sense, thrown out.

But the party had laid firm foundations. Its leadership was not destroyed. Fr. Sturzo by 1926 was already in exile. His successor in the leadership, Alcide de Gasperi, after a spell in a Fascist jail, found refuge as a cataloguer in the Vatican library. Both went on with their political work, and so did many minor figures up and down the country. The dictatorship itself cleared away one major obstacle to Catholic political action when, in the Lateran Pacts of 1929, it finally guaranteed to the Pope his own independent State in a form consistent with Italian national unity. The Catholic Action organisations, though remaining strictly neutral in politics, provided at least a frame for personal contact among former members of the P.P.I. The Church's attitude to Fascism—and not least that of Pius XI —hardened as its character became clearer. When in 1943 the Fascist regime crumbled and armed resistance began, the Christian Democrats played a leading part in it. Their forces mobilised in the North are reckoned to have amounted to about 65,000 men, rising to 80,000 at peak periods, and there were some 4,800 casualties. By the time the war ended a new Christian Democratic Party had arisen and been consolidated on the ruins of the P.P.I., and De Gasperi was again its leader. It had, this time, the backing of the Church and Catholic Action, though not in the sense that the ecclesiastical authorities directed it or were committed by its acts. It was rather that the Church was now prepared to treat resistance to positively anti-democratic forces—though not, of course, the choice between democratic parties themselves—as a matter of clear moral obligation. In this sense and to this extent, the organisations of Catholic Action now became important and reliable, if sometimes rather embarrassing, auxiliaries of the party.

The policy of the new party was broadly in line both with that of the P.P.I. and with the general, international, policy of Christian Democracy as described in earlier chapters. The *Democrazia Cristiana* was liberal and democratic—some key passages were quoted above (p. 323)—and it had, like the P.P.I., a strong and vocal 'social' wing. The old trade unionist Giovanni Gronchi, after serving for several years as Speaker of the lower house of parliament, was elected in 1955 as the first Christian Democratic President of the Italian Republic. Among the several trade unionists whose names figure on the Executive of the *Democrazia Cristiana* is Giulio Pastore, General Secretary and in effect founder of the C.I.S.L. trade unions. But both the party's policy and its tactics have carried a special stamp, for two reasons. It, and especially its first leader, De Gasperi, remained deeply marked by the memory of the resistance years, and also of those earlier decades when democracy was undermined; originally by the lack of common ground between Liberals and Catholics, and then, after 1918, by the violent opposition of revolutionaries and reactionaries, which the P.P.I. tried in vain to bridge. And secondly, the natural laicist allies of the Christian Democrats in the defence of democracy, the Liberals and Social-Democrats, have collapsed and shrunk to a shadow of their former selves.[1]

The threat to democracy was not dead with the defeat of Fascism, nor is it now. A third of the Italian electors have continued to vote 'Social-communist' or Communist, and a smaller but significant number for Right-wing parties whose allegiance to democracy is at any rate doubtful. During and immediately after the Resistance period, the Christian Democrats neutralised the main danger, from the Communists, from within Liberation Committees and then Governments based on the three mass parties—Communists, Socialists, and themselves. But Communist influence in this tripartite system was great, and in 1947 the Christian Democrats felt strong and established enough to break with it. The condition of doing this, however, seeing how small the democratic forces other than the Christian Democrats themselves today are, was to maintain a united front among all the democratic parties, from the Liberals on the right to the Social Democrats on the left, and above all to prevent the re-opening of a line of division, splitting the democratic front, between clericals and anti-clericals. Henceforward it became a fixed principle of Christian Democratic strategy to do this. This policy was maintained even in 1948–53, when the Christian Democratic party on its own held an absolute majority in parliament; still more, of course, after that majority was lost. It proved very effective for establishing and maintaining a democratic state in Italy. It also permitted a strong and agreed foreign

[1] Voting in the 1953 elections:

	%
Christian-Democrats	40.1
Social-Democrats	4.5
Liberals and Republicans	4.6
Communist and Social-Communist	35.4
Monarchist and neo-Fascist	12.7
Miscellaneous	2.7
	100.0

policy. But it proved, not surprisingly, much less satisfactory in the field of social policy.

Manifestoes circulated by the Christian Democrats during the resistance went some way beyond the programme of the P.P.I. in such directions as workers' control in industry, P.B.O., or State economic planning. Workers' control, for instance, was called for by the Christian trade unions in 1919, but was absent from the P.P.I.'s initial manifesto and was taken up only, so to speak, as an afterthought. Now the P.P.I.'s successors took it up vigorously and from the start. But when it came to the point of legislation, policies such as these ran into a double difficulty. They met, naturally, with opposition from right-wing elements in the Christian Democratic party itself. This might have been overcome. But they met with even stronger opposition from the Christian Democrats' right-wing democratic allies, and threatened to divert an uncomfortably large number of votes to the right-wing non-democrats. And at the same time the existence of a very powerful anti-democratic opposition on the left made it necessary to move cautiously with reforms, such as joint control in industry, which—however sound in themselves—could be used by this opposition to create disorder and obstruction with a view to undermining the democratic state itself. Up to about 1950 these difficulties were secondary, since problems of constitution-making, of restoring Italy's position among the nations, and of sheer physical reconstruction in a country reckoned to have had a third of its capital assets destroyed in the war took precedence of everything else. Since then, however, they have given rise to a continuous debate, not yet ended, between the centre or 'united front' section of Christian Democracy and the party's left and right wings. They have not prevented certain major social reforms, notably the introduction on a massive scale of land reform and regional development schemes, which were also a key point in the P.P.I.'s programme. Sturzo, after all, was from the South. But in many other directions they have undoubtedly led to a certain 'immobilism', sharply criticised, above all, by the Christian labour movements, C.I.S.L. trade unionists and members of the A.C.L.I. workers' leagues.

This 'immobilism' has been aggravated by difficulties which have arisen over keeping the party fully a-confessional. The *Democrazia Cristiana* has maintained Sturzo's conception of a party of Christians, inspired no doubt by the teaching of the Church, but acting on their own in that wide sphere which the Church itself recognises as the independent responsibility of the State, that of the 'things that are Caesar's'. In the light of Italian history of the last three-quarters of a century, this view needs little justification. There may indeed have been some advantage to secular politics and social action, quite apart from the question of the Temporal Power itself, in the concentration of Catholics' political interest from 1870 to 1904 on an ecclesiastical issue and under ecclesiastical direction. It diverted to problems of local government and of trade union and co-operative organisation the attention of many Catholics who might otherwise have neglected them, and it allowed the new Liberal state to run itself in without the distraction of a powerful and, at that time, irreconcilable opposition. But in general it is impossible to regard as healthy a state of affairs in which half the citizens of Italy denied the authority of their government and its contribution to the common good,[1] and considered public problems —officially at least—not on their own merits but as counters in successive manoeuvres over the Temporal Power. When Sturzo insisted that the P.P.I. should operate within the established Italian State and leave the question of the Temporal Power to be negotiated by the Church, he restored, though too late, the basis for a healthy development of Italian politics. And there is no reason to think that his action in any way delayed the solution of the question of the Temporal Power itself.

But this lesson, though it has not been forgotten by the *Democrazia Cristiana*, has sometimes been overlooked, or at least under-emphasised, by others. The most important case is that of the Civic Committees established by Italian Catholic Action—though they are not formally part of it—in 1948. Catholic Action, as an agency of the official Church under the direct authority of the Bishops, is politically neutral. But Catholic Action and the Church itself claim, like any other non-political interest group, the right to intervene in politics when and in so far as their own particular interests are directly involved. In the particular case of Italy since the Second World War, the effective choice before the citizens has lain between the group of democratic parties headed by the Christian Democrats —liberals, social-democrats, and Christians—and the 'social-communist' block. Looking at the experience of other countries, Italian Catholics can reasonably assume that a Communist victory would be followed by the closing or confiscation of their schools and Universities, the suppression of their organisations for youth and the Christian apostolate, and of their press, and the progressive strangulation of even the purely religious activities of their clergy. The Church's interests are manifestly involved in the most direct way possible. Accordingly in 1948 Catholic Action came together with the Catholic workers' leagues (A.C.L.I.—themselves a branch, though a largely autonomous one, of Catholic Action) and the Christian Democratic Party to found 'Civic Committees', of which there were presently some 24,000 at the parish level and 304 at the diocesan level. These committees carry on anti-communist propaganda at election times and get out the anti-communist vote.

So far, so good. But the road proved to be short from intervention

---

[1] The great distinction at the time was between the 'country as it really is' and 'the country as by law established'.

against Communism to intervention *for* some other specified party, meaning in practice the Christian Democrats, and the intervention could be very direct and conspicuous. In an Italian town at election time, pick the building with the greatest number of *Democrazia Cristiana* posters: it is probably the convent. From this point a still shorter road leads on to attempts to influence the policy of the party supported. There have been signs that the national leaders of the Civic Committees would like to see the Christian Democrats take a more denominational line, laying more weight on ecclesiastical interests, making Catholicism the dividing line between themselves and other parties, and also laying more stress on anti-Communism. This policy, conceived from a narrowly ecclesiastical point of view, evidently cuts across Sturzo's and De Gasperi's grand design for a party which would bridge the gap between lay and Christian democrats and between left and right. In the conception of these political leaders Christian Democracy was to be differentiated from other parties by its political and social rather than its Church policy. Given the existing balance of political forces in Italy, successive Christian Democratic governments have in any case found it difficult to move ahead fast enough in social policy to make this differentiation clear. And this difficulty has been increased by the pressure put on them, through the Civic Committees, to concentrate in any case on a policy of quite another kind.

FRANCE

Modern French Christian Democracy comes from a variety of sources, not all of them either Christian or Democratic. By the eighteen-eighties most French Catholics had come very comfortably to terms with economic and social liberalism, though it was beginning to be seen, in the studies of La Tour du Pin or the first green shoots of the Christian employers' and trade union movements, that it might also be necessary for Christians to mark out their own special and separate position in these matters. In politics they had not yet come to terms with liberalism; for the question of the monarchy and the Counter-Revolution (understood, the Revolution of 1789) played much the same part for many of them as that of the Temporal Power did for many Catholics in Italy. They could still, as has been said, celebrate in 1889, with pomp and circumstance, the Counter-Centenary of the Revolution. They recognised, as did their more liberal colleagues in Belgium or Switzerland or Holland or Germany, that in modern politics as well as in social and economic affairs it was necessary for Christians to mark out their special position and not merely let themselves be absorbed and carried along by such political movements as the circumstances of the time might throw up. But, unlike these other Catholics, they had not yet seen how this could be done without throwing overboard the whole inheritance of the Revolution; not merely its materialist principles, but also its democracy and all that is implied in a Liberal economic and social order.

However, from the end of the eighteen-seventies the democratic Republic in France was, as it proved, finally established, and, since there was in fact nothing offensive to Christianity about democracy or republics as such, the question of coming to terms with it could not be delayed much longer. When in 1892 the Pope himself advised French Catholics to do this, there appeared among them three currents of thought, very much resembling those present from about the same time in Italy. First, there were the intransigents; a French parallel to the conservative anti-participationists who led the Congress Movement in Italy down to 1904, and from whom in due course came the Catholic supporters or at least tolerators of Fascism. The intransigents in France rendered Christian Democracy the same three major services as in Italy, though some at least among French Christian Democrats would like to forget it. They established a distinctive Christian position in public life, built round this idea an electoral following from which Christian Democracy still benefits, and promoted much valuable pioneering in Catholic social theory: particularly the work of La Tour du Pin. But these services dated essentially from before 1892. It is difficult to distinguish any constructive role among the representatives of this current after that date. They remained strong enough for another generation to prevent any mass rally of Catholics to the democratic Republic, and they contributed great numbers of recruits to authoritarian movements; particularly, from 1898 onwards, to Charles Maurras' monarchist *Action Française*. Though the philosophy of the *Action Française* leaders was basically materialist, they made great play with the claim that their movement was Catholic. In 1926 it was condemned by the Church, and Catholics forbidden to belong to it; though later, when the movement had ceased to be of major importance, the ban was relaxed. With the condemnation went a series of measures to remove sympathisers of the *Action Française* and, generally, of the intransigent trend from key posts in the Church; bishoprics, teaching posts, directors of Catholic Action. The intransigent current survived, and has in particular contributed a good deal to the various forms of the Gaullist movement since the war. But from that time, or thereabouts, it ceased to dominate French Catholic affairs.

Secondly, there appeared a current in French Catholicism very like that which led to the 'Gentiloni Pact' in Italy. It included Catholics ready to collaborate with Liberals on conditions, though often, it must be admitted, unrealistic ones: friendly to liberalism, but to liberalism interpreted usually in a socially conservative sense. There was very limited support for this view in the eighteen-nineties, as election results showed, and what little there was collapsed as a result of the Dreyfus case, in which

Catholic opinion as a whole swung sharply against Dreyfus. From the end of the century, however, this current revived. A small group of Catholic parliamentarians formed in 1899 a Liberal Action group, from which emerged in 1901 a nation-wide organisation, led chiefly by Jacques Piou and Albert de Mun, known as Popular Liberal Action (A.L.P.). This developed substantially for several years, and lasted till after the First World War. In parliament it was partly an independent and partly an inter-party group; the maximum number of deputies directly influenced by it seems to have been around a hundred. All were from the Right or Right-Centre, a fact, however, which in a country where the main dividing line was the issue of Church and State, did not have the significance normal in Anglo-Saxon countries. The group was drawn together originally, like the Catholic liberals in Italy, by a not very well-defined desire to defend the interests of the Church against the violent attacks then proceeding—it was in these years that the separation of Church and State was carried through—and to defeat revolutionary Socialism. But it took care to place itself on an a-confessional basis, and over the years developed an extensive programme of political and social reform. Among the items of this were:

Support for trade unionism: P.B.O.: factory legislation (notably on hours, Sunday rest, and safety and health): minimum wages: old age, sickness, accident, and unemployment insurance.

restriction of speculation, notably on the Stock Exchange: promotion of co-operatives and friendly societies: encouragement of family property, notably in land.

proportional representation: compulsory voting: action against fraud and undue pressure at elections: creation of a proper status for the Civil Service: abolition of the spoils system: election of the President on American lines (an electoral college, itself directly elected): a Charter of Human Rights with legal force, and a Supreme Court on American lines to enforce it: introduction of the referendum.

local autonomy: regionalism.

freedom of conscience: freedom of association for all, including the Church: freedom to teach, and distribution of State grants to schools in proportion to their number of scholars. (Based on the collection of data in Moon, *The Labour Problem and the Social Catholic Movement in France*, 1921, Ch. IX.)

The A.L.P.'s a-confessional character and its social and political programme, implying at least acceptance of political as well as social democracy, would seem to put the party well in the stream of the Christian Democratic movement. In fact however it cannot be called strictly 'Democratic', for membership of it did not imply any belief in the principle of democracy. It was a case rather of taking as a fact the existence of a democratic Republic in France, and making the best of it. There was also in the early years still a marked tendency towards paternalism in social policy; to talk of the role of the 'governing classes', or to prefer 'mixed' trade unions to the distinct and militant workers' and employers' associations for which the Christian Democrats then so-called were fighting. It also proved extremely hard for the A.L.P. to make an effective impact in parliament. On the major issue of French politics at that time, the right of the Church to organise its own services, schools, and religious orders, the A.L.P. deputies were permanently in the minority, and the general prejudice aroused by the religious issue made even their proposals for social legislation suspect. In the history of French politics the A.L.P. thus figures rather little, and in that of Christian Democracy it often gets no more than a mention in passing. It is said unkindly by one author that Popular Liberal Action was so called because it was inactive, illiberal, and not particularly popular.

Such a judgment however goes much too far. The achievement of the A.L.P. was certainly limited at the time, but was significant for the long run. As the party's life continued the monarchist element died out of it and the social and democratic element grew, notably by absorption from the officially Christian Democratic movement to be described in a moment. Valuable work was done in educating middle-of-the-road Catholic politicians in the policies and attitudes appropriate to modern conditions. This education owed a good deal to the efficiency and good documentation of the party's central office, which in many ways seems to have been well ahead of other French parties at the time. This educational work was extended into the country through provincial and regional federations and local branches, whose membership in 1911 reached 265,000. There was likewise a youth organisation and a series of links with women's and working class associations. Even those who judge most severely the A.L.P.'s parliamentary achievements agree that in political education and the defence of religious interests its organisation in the country did yeoman work.[1] By the end of the nineteen-twenties, and particularly after the condemnation of the *Action Française* in 1926, 'moderate' Catholics had grown from a fraction to a majority of the whole French Catholic body.

The quarter from which there finally appeared a force capable of giving a permanent lead to the 'moderates' as well as to those on their left was that of Christian Democracy properly so-called. The first stirrings appeared, as in Italy, in the eighteen-nineties, coming out of the workers' study circle movement started by Harmel—a genuine working-class movement, always to be carefully distinguished from the paternalistic 'workers' club' movement of de Mun and La Tour du Pin—and from the energetic propaganda of a group of young clergy, the 'abbés démocrates'. A Christian Democratic Party was actually founded at Rheims in 1896. It

[1] See for instance Dansette, *Histoire Religieuse de la France Contemporaine*, II, 298.

was radical in social policy, opposed to paternalism in industry, and made up (unlike the A.L.P.) of convinced believers in the value of government by as well as of and for the people. It was also, less happily, markedly anti-semitic. But as a party it failed to establish itself, though one or two representative figures of this first phase did at one time or another find their way into parliament; notably Fr. Lemire, for many years deputy for Hazebrouck in Flanders, and a prominent figure in the Chamber. Another powerful thrust forward came after 1900 from Marc Sangnier and the *Sillon*. The *Sillon's* influence in turning the younger Catholics towards democratic politics and social affairs was immense, and when it was dissolved Sangnier founded a 'Young Republic League' to carry this side of the good work on. The war interrupted progress. But in 1919 some thirty or forty followers of the ideas of the *Sillon* and Christian Democracy, Marc Sangnier himself among them, were returned to the Chamber of Deputies on various lists. A local 'Federation of Democratic Republicans' had been founded by ex-Sillonists in Brittany in 1911; now two more were added in the Paris region and in Normandy. These Federations and the Young Republic League joined up temporarily in 1921–2 in a National Democratic League, which however the Young Republic League presently left to promote the cause of pacifism. In 1922, at the annual Social Week at Strasbourg, the General Secretary of the 'Social Weeks', Adeodat Boissard, the then Chairman of the A.C.J.F., Charles Flory, the General Secretary of the C.F.T.C., Gaston Tessier, and a former leader of Popular Liberal Action, Jean Lerolle, agreed together to form a Civic Action Bureau. At the elections of 1924 several of the existing sympathisers with Christian Democracy in the Chamber were defeated, including Sangnier. But about a dozen of the remainder, from traditionally Christian constituencies in Brittany, Alsace-Lorraine and the Ardennes, and the Basque country, now decided to form a Parliamentary group of their own. And this group in November 1924 linked up with the National Democratic League and the Civic Action Bureau to form a Popular Democratic Party (P.D.P.), the first effective Christian Democratic party in France.

The P.D.P. belonged, like all the Christian Democratic parties, essentially to the Centre. Its leaders and origins were on the centre-left, its programme was broadly that of Christian Democracy everywhere, and its electorate, drawn from all classes, tended if anything to the centre-right; notably among that by this time large though shapeless mass of Catholics, just described, who were ready to accept the democratic Republic but had no strong social line of their own. The party itself, like previous Christian Democrats, accepted the Republic not merely in practice but in principle. It was a-confessional, partly on grounds of principle—the need to keep the distinction clear between Catholic Action

333

and Christian Democracy—and partly from fear of too close a link with
the official Church, by this time thoroughly and, so far as France was
concerned, correctly identified in the minds of the French public with
political reaction. It did not, however, throw up any outstanding leader.
It had no Sturzo or De Gasperi, and those who later became the leaders
of the M.R.P. were at this time still busy in the youth movements. And it
was a phenomenon hard to fit into the established pattern of French
politics. The intransigents were still strong enough to make an honestly
democratic and republican, socially progressive, centre party look curiously out of place in appealing for the Catholic vote. Laicist Liberals and
Socialists found it hard to accept a party of Christian inspiration as
belonging to their own world. The resulting confusion and embarrassment
comes out very well in André Siegfried's classic *Tableau des Partis en
France*, written in 1930. Siegfried sees and admits that the P.D.P. is all
that it claims to be, but still classes it as a party of the Right. For, he says,
though the ancient tradition which makes religion and not social policy
the line of division between left and right in France *can* be broken through,
he will believe it when he sees it and not before. Down to 1939 the P.D.P.
never much exceeded its original parliamentary strength.

In France as in Italy, the resistance contributed greatly to the rebirth
of Christian Democracy after 1944. The P.D.P. parliamentary group voted
in majority against Pétain's demand for full powers after the collapse of
1940, and P.D.P. supporters played an active part in the Resistance
throughout. One, Georges Bidault, became President of the National
Council of the Resistance. Contacts were kept up and memoranda
exchanged, and in 1944 the new Popular Republican Movement (M.R.P.)
was founded: a-confessional, like the P.D.P., and with a similar though
fuller and in some ways more advanced programme. It looked at first a
bigger affair than it was, since the right-wing parties—more or less
democratic, as the case might be—took some time to re-emerge. Meantime,
right-wing electors tended to vote M.R.P., as the lesser evil. With this
reinforcement, the M.R.P. vote for the first two or three years after the
Liberation ran around 25–30% of the total. By the elections of 1951,
however, this fortuitous support had gone to its proper home, and the
party was left with 12–13% of the national vote and some 85 seats in
Parliament.

Like the P.D.P., the M.R.P. found itself in a key position at the centre
of the Chamber. Unlike the P.D.P., it was strong enough to use this
position so as to make a major impact on policy. Its social policy was and
is as 'advanced' as that of the Socialists, though with the usual differences
of emphasis. It played a large part in the reform of social security and
family allowances and in the nationalisation and national investment
policies introduced just after the war, and a no less important, though

334

less spectacular, part in safeguarding these gains in later years when liberalism and conservatism revived and French politics swung back to the Right. It has pressed for co-responsibility in the firm and Industry Councils on P.B.O. lines,[1] and has become more and more convinced over the years of the need for far-reaching policies of State planning and investment. The Ministry of Foreign Affairs was for many years almost an M.R.P. monopoly, and it used this position to take the lead in, particularly, moves for the unification of Europe. It was Robert Schuman's position as an M.R.P. leader which opened the way for him to launch the European Coal-Steel Community.

The M.R.P. can also claim to have contributed as much as any party, in very difficult conditions, towards establishing and maintaining democratic government in France, and to have proved its members' republican and democratic convictions beyond all reasonable doubt. It was, it is true, rather uncertain at the start which way to turn in the constitutional field.

> It has become—alas—a commonplace to say that the M.R.P., though innovating boldly in the matter of social policy, seems strangely moderate in the political and institutional field: moderate because timid, and timid because it is not at its ease in a field which it has not sufficiently explored. (Biton, *La Démocratie Chrétienne*, 1954, p. 84.)

The M.R.P. had come to power too quickly to be sure of itself. But its views soon settled down. In the debates over the new French Constitution, it supported democracy in a sense which represented a marked break with French tradition. Traditionally, sovereign power in France belongs to the nation, incarnate today in parliament. This 'decapitated monarchy', as Sangnier had called it, had made little appeal to Christian Democrats. The truly 'democratic' republic, for him, was that in which:

> Each citizen will feel that he has a share in power; and the power which is granted to us every four years (at election times) is no more than a ridiculous caricature of this. (Quoted in Biton, op. cit., p. 87.)

The M.R.P., following in this tradition, showed itself keenly interested in developing popular control of parliament through such devices as the referendum, proportional representation, and the design of party machinery so as to ensure effective contact between the leadership and the rank and file, and with different interest groups: though it did not go so far towards rank and file control as the Socialists. It was careful to weight the higher organs in its own constitution so as to leave what by British as well as French standards would be regarded as adequate freedom of action, within the broad orientations established by the party congress, for the party leadership and parliamentary group.

[1] See above, Chapter VI, pp. 63 and 75–6.

The new democratic constitution was far from secure. The M.R.P., like the *Democrazia Cristiana*, found itself with a large share of responsibility not only for creating but for maintaining and operating it. On the left were the Communists, strongly entrenched in Parliament[1] and the trade unions. During the time when Communist ministers were in the government their men also penetrated deeply into the administration. In due course, and especially after the General Election of 1951, there appeared on the Right another large party, General de Gaulle's French Union (R.P.F.),[2] containing elements whose allegiance to democracy was dubious. The General Election of 1956 left the Gaullists weakened: but the gap was filled by another party of small traders and related groups, more definitely opposed to parliamentary government, and led by M. Poujade. Like the *Democrazia Cristiana*, the M.R.P. tried at first to neutralise Communist influence from within a tripartite government. In 1946 it broke with the Communists, and in 1947 with what was then emerging as the Gaullist movement. Henceforward it aimed, again like De Gasperi in Italy, to become the king pin of a 'third force' including Liberals, who were now coming back to the surface after being submerged just after the war, Christian Democrats, and Social Democrats.

But it turned out to be even more difficult to operate such a policy in France than in Italy. Was the 'third force' to follow a progressive social policy? Such a policy must rest chiefly on two parties, the M.R.P. itself and the Socialists. But French Socialism, though not so miserably shrunken as Italian, is a poor and weedy growth compared to the Socialism of Belgium, Holland, the German-speaking countries, or Scandinavia or Britain. 'Laicist' French workers vote in large majority for the Communist Party, and join Communist unions. Communist collaboration could be had at a price, but one which neither the M.R.P. nor the Socialists were willing to pay: abandoning plans to unite Europe, refusing economic and military collaboration with America, and admitting Communists to the levers of power, with dangers to democracy made clear by experience not only in France but in Czecho-Slovakia and elsewhere in Eastern Europe. The M.R.P. itself was in a weaker position than the *Democrazia Cristiana*, since it had far less hold on its voters. Practising Christians in France are less attached to their Christian Democratic party than those of any of the other countries studied here. The effective competitors, moreover, are on the Right. The M.R.P. leadership, in social matters, has usually been well ahead of that large block of 'moderate' electors which it inherited from the A.L.P. Many voters from this block were lost in 1951: a strong left-wing policy might well lose more.

The number of votes available in parliament to any possible 'progressive

[1] Figures in Chapter XX, Table 13.
[2] Literally 'French People's Assembly'. Renamed 'Social Republicans' in 1955.

democratic' coalition was thus limited: and it was also even harder than in Italy to hold such a coalition together. French Liberals and Socialists, as well as Communists, retain their conviction that public funds should be reserved for those parents who do not want their children taught religion in school. In Italy the Concordat attached to the Lateran Treaty of 1929 guarantees that religious teaching shall be available in State schools; the Treaty and Concordat were incorporated after the war in the new Republican Constitution by Communist as well as Catholic votes. But in France the secularist tradition stands firm. When religion comes in at the door of the school, public funds fly out at the window. The Catholic schools have as a result been in serious financial difficulties in recent years. In 1951 the conservative and nationalist Right raised, not perhaps without a certain malice aforethought, the question of grants to them. Communist propagandists took care that the issue was duly underlined. One of the main reasons for the M.R.P.'s existence has been to bridge the traditional gap between clericals and anti-clericals, and therefore to avoid raising issues of this kind. But, once the question was brought forward, the M.R.P. could not fail to support a cause on which most of its voters felt keenly. Its solidarity with Liberals and Socialists was severely shaken.

There have also been difficulties over colonial policy. The M.R.P.'s policy for the colonies has been parallel to its policy for Europe and France. To federate Algeria with France has seemed as natural and useful as to federate France with the rest of Europe, and to stop Communism on the frontier of Viet-Nam as right and obvious as to stop it on the Elbe. But a policy of this kind has won, naturally, more support on the Right than among traditionally anti-colonialist Socialists, especially as its execution has been in many ways incompetent and oppressive.

All these obstacles have stood in the way of an effective Centre-Left policy. But an alliance between the M.R.P. and the Right has been equally unattractive. It meant social immobility, a possible danger to democracy, and a danger to the M.R.P.'s policy for united Europe, which has been no more attractive to right wing nationalists than to the Communist Party. To steer a clear course and take effective action amid these conflicting pressures has called for more skill than the M.R.P.'s leaders, most of them relatively inexperienced in politics, possessed. For one moment, in 1954 and 1955, the way ahead seemed to open. The main Liberal party, the Radicals, split into a conservative and a progressive wing. There was a chance of an effective and dynamic, as well as democratic, centre coalition of progressive liberals, Christian Democrats, and Social Democrats, capable perhaps of capturing enough votes from the Communists to give itself a firm base. But the price for the M.R.P. was to compromise on Europe, accepting what exists today as Western European Union instead of a full federal Europe, and to liquidate many of the party's colonial policies. The clerical-anti-clerical issue also played its part. The chief immediate issue was Europe, and on this the M.R.P. leaders preferred to go down with their ship. At the Bruges Congress of Christian Democratic parties of Europe in 1954, the M.R.P. delegates represented the extreme limit of intransigence on this issue. The opportunity of a re-grouping in French politics was missed.

The M.R.P.'s difficulty in recent years in taking the lead in a positive and effective social policy has caused a good deal of alarm and despondency among its more militant and left-wing members, notably those in the Christian labour movement; rather more, it may well be, than has been caused in the *Democrazia Cristiana* by the corresponding difficulty in Italy. The *Democrazia Cristiana* can point to substantial achievements, in the rehabilitation of depressed areas, the redistribution of land, or the recovery of the country from the war, which have unquestionably occurred under its leadership. And its leaders, De Gasperi above all, in any case started with the clear determination to make the defence of democracy, and therefore the maintenance of an alliance with liberals as well as Socialists, the consideration which must take precedence of all others. The early documents of the M.R.P. emphasised much more policies of social reform. There was to be a break with the capitalist past and the evil ways of the Third Republic. The M.R.P. was to be a great revolutionary party competing with the Communists on Christian principles, but on their own ground. These views were often rather vague, sometimes sentimental, after the manner of Sangnier and the A.C.J.F., but they were very sincerely held. The lack of dramatic achievements under this head, at least after the first year or two, has seemed to many a betrayal of the M.R.P.'s first purpose. The question has more than once been raised of building a new Labour Party containing elements of the M.R.P., of the Socialists, and perhaps of the various liberal parties—more particularly, in that case, farming elements. But there has not yet seemed to be enough prospect of a departure of this kind leading to a genuinely new situation in French politics to bring it to life.

To an outside observer, it is in any case not at all certain that those who regard the M.R.P.'s deficiencies as a failure of principle are correct, or that a new and even less experienced party would do better. The road to hell is paved with good intentions. What seems to have happened to the M.R.P. is not that it has abandoned its principles, but that it has lacked the political skill to apply them in an extremely difficult situation. It has practised too little of 'la politique politicienne', not too much. Its history is in fact the clearest and most extreme example of the tendency, noted by Houben[1] in all countries, for Christian Democratic politicians to treat

[1] Above, Chapter II, p. 24.

politics as an exercise in pure principle on the one hand and day to day tactics on the other. The tendency is to forget, or not to think through sufficiently, the intermediate level of strategy, the 'hypothesis', or middle 'principles'. Old and experienced Christian Democratic parties like those of Holland do not suffer much from this deficiency. The M.R.P., true to its rather woolly antecedents, has suffered from it a great deal.

339

CHAPTER XXII

IS A NEW ORIENTATION IN SIGHT?

THE fourfold process described in the last chapters—the incorporation of Protestants (especially in Germany), the founding of new parties, the 'new look' in social policy, and the reduction in parties' denominational ties—has led the Christian Democratic political movements over the last two generations to remarkable heights of power (Table 15). They have also become conscious of themselves as never before as an international movement, with a point of keen common concern in the movement for European unity. Members of Christian Democratic parties can still be found holding quite startling misconceptions about the policy and practice of similar parties in other countries. But the air has begun to be cleared, particularly since the foundation in 1947 of the Christian Democratic political international, the Union of Christian Democrats or Nouvelles Equipes Internationales (N.E.I.), followed by the foundation of the corresponding youth international in 1948. The N.E.I. is not, in form, an alliance of parties. It is an association of national groups made up of individuals interested in Christian Democratic politics and international co-operation. In practice, of course, this means groups associated with and financed and serviced by the parties where these exist; though the formula also makes it possible to bring in groups of East European or Spanish exiles, or delegations from countries such as Great Britain which have never had a Christian Democratic party, at any rate in the Continental sense. For some years the N.E.I. found it hard to fix its proper sphere of work. At times it touched directly on current politics; providing, for instance, an opportunity for German politicians to meet their opposite numbers from other countries on an equal footing, in the years just after the war when such opportunities were not easily to be had. But its most effective work has been as a forum for the exchange of ideas among people in the various parties and groups who are concerned with programme-building and education; the back-room boys, so to speak, as apart from those making current political decisions.

To this growth in the strength and unity of the political movements, add the advances made by the social movements and recorded in previous chapters. These movements too have been growing together internationally,

TABLE 15

The changing strength of Christian Democracy in Politics

*Position of Christian Democratic Parties or their
predecessors in:*

Country	1880s	1950s
Germany	Centre Party (Catholic) an important factor in politics, but not yet involved in government formation.	C.D.U. (inter-denominational) has absolute parliamentary majority. Major governmental party throughout postwar period.
Austria	Genuinely Christian Democratic forces very small. Main Christian force monarchist, feudal, counter-revolutionary, essentially outside the life of the modern world.	Austrian People's Party genuinely Christian Democratic, and just short of an absolute parliamentary majority. Permanently in government.
Switzerland	Catholic fraction, informally organised, not yet represented in government.	Fully organised Catholic party with 2 out of 7 seats on the Federal Council. Small Evangelical party.
Holland	Catholic-Protestant coalition able from time to time to form a government.	Catholic and Protestant parties dominate Parliament when they choose to work together. Regularly represented in government.
Belgium	Catholic Party organised and powerful, capable of forming a government on its own.	P.S.C. remains largest party in the country, with absolute majority 1949–53.
France	See Austria.	M.R.P. a key factor in most governmental combinations, though having smaller electoral support than the Christian Democrats in any of the other countries mentioned.
Italy	Still in the 'intransigent' period. Catholics refuse, at least officially, to participate in the life of the Liberal state.	*Democrazia Cristiana* the largest party in the country: absolute majority 1948–53: leading government party throughout postwar period.

not only movement by movement but also overall. The Congress of Catholic International Organisations, founded after the Second World War, brings together some 31 internationals, from the Young Christian Workers and the International Union of Catholic Employers' Associations (UNIAPAC) to the World Union of Catholic Philosophical Societies (Table 16). The Congress analyses one main subject each year; that for 1954, for example, being 'Technique and Productivity', with special reference to their impact on human relations.

Add, also, the support which political and social movements alike receive from an important section of the Press (Table 17), from the part of the educational system influenced by the Church (Table 18), from the wide range of organisations[1] connected with the churches for analysing, defining, codifying, and propagating the principles of social action; and, of course, from the churches themselves. The churches do not run the Christian Democratic movements, though they do those of Christian Action. But even in the case of the Christian Democratic movement they help in a vital way to clarify and unify doctrine. This contribution is particularly obvious on the Catholic side, and particularly liable to be misunderstood. Georges Bernanos, in his *Diary of a Country Priest*, makes one of his characters speak of the impact of Leo XIII's Encyclical *Rerum Novarum*:

> You read it quietly today, skimming through it, like any Lenten pastoral. But when it came out, my friend, we seemed to feel the earth rock under our feet. Talk about enthusiasm! I was parish priest of Norenfontes then, right in the coalfield. That simple idea that labour is not a commodity subject to the law of supply and demand, that it is wrong to speculate in wages or men's lives as if they were wheat or sugar or coffee—believe me, it shook people's consciences! (*Journal d'un Curé de Campagne*, 1936, pp. 72–3.)

Reading the history of the various Catholic social movements, one often gets this impression of a flash of revealing light; a feeling that the social movement might well be dated before and after *Rerum Novarum*. But the impression is misleading. *Rerum Novarum* marked a turning point, it did not create one. Like all the Papal social encyclicals, it represented the summing up of a certain stage of thought and discussion about social problems among Catholics, both clerical and lay. A picture of new problems and solutions was emerging from this discussion. A transition was under way from one major stage in the growth of Christian Democracy to another. *Rerum Novarum* represented the turn of the screw which brought one part of the new picture finally into focus. And it is just in this ability to focus discussion that the great service of the Encyclicals and the other official interventions of the Church has lain. As a comprehensive and authoritative summary of the present state of each problem in

[1] See Part IV, p. 427 ff.

TABLE 16

List of organisations associated with the Conference
of Catholic International Organisations, 1954

	Headquarters
Study and Education	
International Centre for Religious Studies (including religious sociology) and Education	Brussels
International Catholic Federation for Physical Education	Paris
International Federation of Catholic Universities	Rome
International Catholic Education Office	The Hague
International Union of Social Studies	Brussels
World Union of Catholic Teachers	Rome
World Union of Catholic Philosophic Societies	Fribourg
Youth	
International Federation of Catholic Youth	Rome
International Federation of Catholic Girls' Movements	Ghent
Young Christian Workers' International	Brussels
Pax Romana (Catholic Students)	Fribourg
General adult organisations	
International Federation of Catholic Men	Rome
Pax Romana (Catholic graduates)	Fribourg
World Union of Catholic Women's Organisations	Paris
Social Service	
Apostolate of the Sea	Rome
Catholic International Association of Girls' Protection Societies	Fribourg
Ladies of Charity of St. Vincent de Paul	Paris
Society of St. Vincent de Paul	Paris
Society of St. Vincent de Paul (women's section)	Bologna
Catholic International Child Care Bureau	Paris
International Catholic Committee on Migration	Geneva
Catholic International Committee for Nurses and Therapists	Paris
International Conference of Catholic Charitable Organisations	Rome
International Catholic Temperance League	Fribourg
Catholic International Union of Social Service	Brussels
Economic and Social action	
International Christian Social Union (including the Catholic workers', farmers', and business middle class organisations)	Brussels
Catholic International Union of Employers' Associations	Scheveningen
Communications media	
International Committee of Catholic Editors	Paris
International Federation of Catholic Journalists	Paris
International Catholic Film Bureau	Brussels
UNDA (International Catholic Association for Radio and Television)	Fribourg

TABLE 17

Christian Democracy and the press

			Communist	Socialist	Christian and Christian Democratic	Liberal	Independent	
Germany (Federal Republic only)	1954	The percentage of daily papers with various political or ideological lines was:	1½	4½	15	3	76	Excluding papers which made no return

The Christian group represent 12.6% of the total number of daily papers, and have 13.3% of the total circulation. Another study (N.E.I.) claims that 55–60% of the general newspaper circulation in Germany is of papers with a tendency favourable to Christianity. The Christian papers are 6.5% (of total of all papers) general Christian', 1.2% Catholic, 4.9% specifically C.D.U.: total 12.6%. The 4.9% C.D.U. compares with 1.4% Communist, 3.5% Socialist Party, 0.1% Liberal Party.

1954	Periodicals

General and illustrated papers have a circulation of 17,900,000, and specifically religious papers (not clear if this includes religious-inclined general illustrateds) something over 12,800,000. The latter figure relates to some 80% of the religious papers. The religious press includes 524 papers. 263 are Evangelical, 198 Catholic, 63 other. Circulation (80% only of papers of each denomination) —Evangelical 4,300,000, Catholic 7,400,000, others 1,100,000. Technical, trade, trade union, etc. papers are excluded from all this calculation.

Switzerland	1951

Claims to have more newspapers per 10,000 inhabitants than any other country in the world. Of the dailies and periodicals dealing with politics, 76 (33%) are Catholic: 24 dailies, with a circulation of 180,000, and 52 local papers with a circulation of 150,000. There is a close link between Catholic press readership and Catholic-Conservative voting.

Luxemburg	1951

The Catholic 'Luxemburger Wort' claims double the combined circulation of all other political dailies.

Holland	1951

3 main Catholic dailies, and 20 regional dailies, altogether 35% of the total circulation of all Dutch dailies. One main Protestant daily and 8 regional, altogether 12% of the total circulation. About 300 other Catholic periodicals.

Belgium	1951

9 Christian-tendency dailies in French, 10 in Flemish, representing altogether a large fraction of the whole circulation of dailies. One in each language is associated with the Christian trade unions. Also a number of influential high-level reviews.

France	1951

Specifically Catholic press has a monthly circulation of about 10,000,000 including the Church press. Biggest circulation, over 2,000,000, is *Echo des Françaises*, of the Catholic Women's League. The Catholic press reaches all regions and social groups, and includes several widely read weeklies and digests. But it is weak in dailies, especially at Paris. There are several good Protestant reviews, notably *Réforme* (circulation 20,000) and *Christianisme Social*.

Italy	1951

Catholic Action operates 8 small-circulation dailies, 6 being in the north. The Christian Democratic Party has one main and a number of regional papers. There is also the usual network of specialised and Church papers.

Based mainly on an enquiry in 1951 by the Nouvelles Equipes Internationales. Also on *Die Deutsche Presse* 1954, Berlin 1954.

the light of the general beliefs and teaching of the Church, they have given the Catholic social movement a clarity and sense of purpose which could have been attained in no other way. On the Protestant side it is above all in the great series of conferences which led up to the meetings of the World Council of Churches in 1948 and 1954—the world missionary conferences from 1910 onwards, the Life and Work movement, the Faith and Order movement—that a common doctrine and purpose have been hammered out. These meetings belong, like the Papal Encyclicals, to the ecclesiastical history of the Protestant Churches as much as to their social history.

Take all these things together, and the picture of the strength and cohesion of the Christian Democratic movements and the related movements of Christian Action, and of their growth in the last sixty or seventy years, is undeniably impressive. And yet in spite, or perhaps because, of this growth and success the question of a new orientation for Continental Christian Democracy is now beginning to be raised. Should there not be a further stage of development, occupying the next generations just as the last occupied the generations from the eighteen-eighties to the nineteen-forties? This new stage might not perhaps require new policies. The main lines of Christian Democratic policy, as described in Part II, seem likely to stand. But might it not call for a 'break-through'—the name used for the new orientation by those who have been discussing it in Holland—to new forms of organisation? Several factors have helped to bring this question of a 'break-through' to the front. The first is the success of at any rate some of the Christian Democratic movements in recruiting up to the limits of what must be their natural constituency so long as they are constituted as they now are; the body of Christian believers, who make up what might be called these movements' 'Christian base'.

THE LIMITS OF RECRUITMENT—THE SIZE OF THE 'CHRISTIAN BASE'

Statistics on the number of practising believers in different countries are extremely tricky. In the case of the Protestant churches it is difficult to attach any absolute meaning even to such figures as exist, since these churches have no clear-cut standard of what constitutes a 'practising' member. The Catholic Church does have an apparently clear-cut standard; a practising Catholic is one who, as a minimum, has been baptised, is married in church, goes to Mass on Sunday, and goes to confession and Communion at least once a year, about Easter. But even this test has more pitfalls than might be supposed. A literal reading, for instance, of the very precise statistics in the *Kirchliches Jahrbuch* for Germany, grossed up by the factor proposed in its text, would suggest that no less than 115% of the Catholics of the city of Passau fulfilled their Easter duties in 1948; an exemplary performance indeed. However, there is no need here to have

345

TABLE 18
The Churches' stake in education

Country	Date						
Germany	1948	Statistics for primary schools for all West German Länder except Bavaria (which has a Catholic majority, and schools satisfactory from a Christian point of view) show: 16,781 schools of which 7,565 non-confessional, 9,216 confessional (5,264 Evangelical, 3,952 Catholic). For 1949–50 in North Rhine/Westphalia, which has 5,824 of these 16,781 primary schools, 95% of all Catholic children attended Catholic primary schools and 64% of all Evangelical children Evangelical schools.					
Switzerland	1951	Public primary schools are officially neutral, in practice tend to be satisfactory to Catholics in the Catholic Cantons, but elsewhere to be secularist. A substantial proportion of Catholic secondary students are in Catholic schools. There is a Catholic university at Fribourg.					

			Public (neutral) schools	Private schools	Of which:		
					Catholic	Protestant	Other
Holland	1951	Students in:					
		Kindergartens	56,379	285,105	156,855	82,362	45,888
		Primary schools	392,832	1,014,678	602,050	381,206	31,422
		Technical, etc.	23,030	235,831	63,839	21,498	150,494 (no complete figures for agricultural, etc., education, which is excluded)
		Secondary	42,853	56,746	27,894	16,137	12,715
		University and other Higher Education	23,779	4,471	1,968	1,435	1,068
		Seminaries	—	9,947	9,563	371+	13 + (figures for 1949)
		Teacher training	4,742	13,745	7,255	5,167	1,323

346

Belgium 1948–9 'Free' schools, with a few exceptions (the most important is the University of Brussels), are Catholic. 'Communal' or 'State' schools are neutral, but in small towns and villages are often in practice Catholic. Subject to this, the statistics are:

Students in:	Communal or State Schools	Free Schools
Kindergarten	72,888	191,376
Primary	337,653	437,725
Secondary	55,694	65,044
University	5,505	8,416 (Catholic University of Louvain and related establishments).
	+4,273 for the Free University of Brussels	

France 1951 Little separate Protestant education. Public schools are in principle neutral, in practice largely secularist, though decreasingly so. An increasing number of Christian teachers are making their influence felt in them at all levels, from the primary schools to the University. A separate, privately supported Catholic school system exists, with the following number of students:

Primary	approx. 1,000,000 (60% of all school attenders in Brittany and Vendée: high proportion in other Western dioceses and Alsace-Lorraine, the only area where confessional schools—Protestant also—are publicly financed on any large scale)
Secondary	312,000
Technical	115,000 (out of national total of 500,000)
University, seminary, and other higher	24,500
Agricultural	20 secondary and 8 higher schools.

To all the above must be added adult education centres, such as the Thomas More Academy (Catholic) or the Evangelical Academies in Germany: these have developed rapidly in recent years. Also the great variety of schools and training centres operated by the specialised Christian movements.

347

figures reliable to the last place of decimals. It is important in discussing Christian Democracy in, say, France, to know whether the proportion of Christian believers is 10%, 50%, or 90%, and how they are distributed about the country. It is not important, in a study on as broad a scale as this, to know whether the proportion is, say, 42% or 43½%. And broadly accurate figures do in fact exist for the whole Catholic population of France, Belgium, Holland, Germany, and many parts of Italy. There is also a good deal of information about Protestant belief and practice in Germany and Holland.

RELIGIOUS PRACTICE AMONG CATHOLICS

The number of regular Sunday churchgoers is probably the best single index to use, as it permits comparison between churches whose views on the nature and significance of the communion service differ violently, but which agree on the duty to keep holy the Sabbath. Among Catholics in France and French-speaking Belgium something like 35% or 40%—Table 19—would seem to be regular churchgoers. These include more women than men—Table 20—and more than their share of older people, people from the smaller towns and countryside, and non-manual workers. But this must not be over-stressed; for the table also shows that regular church-goers include substantial numbers from all areas and classes. For Italy there are no complete figures, and those that are available come largely from problem areas such as Rome or Milan. The most illuminating figures are those from Fr. Leoni's study of the diocese of Mantua, which lies sandwiched between areas of high observance to the North and others of notoriously low observance southwards towards Bologna. Fr. Leoni studied only the country districts; taking good and bad together, his figure for regular churchgoers comes out very close to that found by Canon Boulard in the French country districts. There was a particularly marked surplus of men over women in the parishes of lowest observance, and a general tendency for white-collar workers and proprietors to show higher percentages of attendance than manual workers (Table 21). It would probably not be far wrong to assume that regular Mass attendance in Italy is of the same order as in France. In Germany, on the other hand, it is markedly higher, quite possibly of the order of 55–60%. There are no separate figures for church attendance by Catholic and Protestant men and women in Germany. But taking the two denominations together (Table 22) there are rather more women than men regularly attending. The proportions from high and low income groups are about equal. In Flanders the proportion of regular attenders to the whole population under obligation rises to about 60%. Though there are no complete Mass attendance figures for Holland, the high proportion of Catholics who complete their Easter duties suggests that—except in the coastal belt which includes Amsterdam and Rotterdam—regular Mass attendance may be a good deal higher there than even in Flanders.

So far as possible these are percentages of those who are actually obliged by Church law to attend Mass—that is, are not exempt by reason of age, health, or work or domestic responsibilities. But it should be stressed that all the figures given are built up to some extent by estimation and approximation. And these broad, nation-wide averages, like the three great international zones marked out in Chapter I—the central belt, the northern Protestant and southern and western Catholic deserts—naturally conceal great local variations. A zone of relatively high practice stands out in the north-west of France (Brittany, Vendée, parts of Normandy), right outside the central belt. Belgium, on the other hand, is right in the belt, but Liége and much of the mining area on both sides of the frontier near Mons and Charleroi are in matters of religion depressed areas. It is possible to quote country districts, some of them large—as in the centre of France—which have in effect reverted to paganism, and also town working-class parishes where practising Catholics can be counted almost on one hand. In three Rouen parishes, with a total working-class population aged 14 and over of around 9,500, Michel Quoist found 3% of the workers at Mass on Sunday, including one docker out of 661 in the district. $2\frac{1}{2}\%$ of miners working underground at Lens practise their religion, and $2\frac{1}{4}\%$ also ($1\frac{1}{4}\%$ of men alone) of workers in a working-class suburb at Puteaux, Paris. In general, observance is weak in the big residential and industrial towns which have grown up through the last century, and to whose conditions the Church has been slow to adapt itself. It tends to be weaker among manual than among white-collar workers, and among men than among women. 'Weak' means here a comparison by the standards of the surrounding culture. Catholic observance in Amsterdam is very poor indeed by Dutch standards, but would stand out as a triumph of Christian evangelism in Paris.

RELIGIOUS PRACTICE AMONG PROTESTANTS

The data for the Protestant churches are much less revealing, and it is important to remember the difference of church practice and discipline. For a Catholic, to fail to attend church on Sunday is a mortal sin. For a Protestant it is certainly an offence, but one more easily excused. When using church attendance data as an index of religious belief and practice, it is probably fair to equate regular attendance by Catholics with regular *or periodic* attendance by Protestants. The figures suggest (rather than prove) that the proportion of active members in this sense of the Protestant churches tends to equal or exceed that of the Catholic Church where Protestantism is a minority, but to fall short where it is dominant. There are probably not more than a million Frenchmen in any way attached to

349

TABLE 19

Proportion of baptised Catholics who practise their religion

All figures relate, unless otherwise stated, to those members of the Catholic population who are obliged by Church law to attend Mass on Sunday and confession and Communion at Easter

Country	Date	Source and notes	Occasional Conformists		Regular Sunday Mass %	Easter Duties %	Notes
			Great occasions of life (marriage, birth, death) %	Great feasts			
Germany	1949	*Kirchliches Jahrbuch.* The overall figures are dragged down by those for three dioceses (Berlin, Breslau [German section], and Meissen [Saxony]) in East Germany. The best and worst dioceses in West Germany are: Trier (incl. Saar and Koblenz) Passau (Bavaria) Hildesheim (Brunswick-Hannover)			59 76 69 45	65 80 95 52	Sunday Mass attendances are *actual* attendances on two Sundays in each year, and thus probably overestimate the number of *regular* attenders. All figures are grossed up by *national* factors which may not be fully applicable to *individual* dioceses.
	1952	Poll by Institut für Demoskopie, Allensbach, March 1952. West Germany only. Adults (voting age) [Corresponding Protestant figures]	19 [38]	23 [27]	48 [14]		The Institute's categories are 'Seldom', 'Irregular or occasional', and 'Regular' churchgoers. The poll was of adults of voting age.
Holland	1946	Katholiek Sociaal-Kerkelijk Instituut. Dioceses of: S'Hertogenbosch (S.E.) Breda (S.W.) Utrecht (Centre & North) Haarlem (West coast) Towns of:— Amsterdam Rotterdam				97 97 92 76 62 59	}All in the diocese of Haarlem.

350

	Date	Source	%	%	Notes
Belgium	1946–51	*Lumen Vitae*, Oct/Dec. 1952			Figures of varying reliability, relating to Sunday attendance, not necessarily to regular attendance.
Regions:					
Flanders			50		
Brussels			60		
Wallonia			41		
of which:—					
Liége			45		
Hainaut (Mons-Tournai-Charleroi)			26		
Province of Namur			63		
Province of Luxemburg			76		
France— rural	1939	Boulard, *Problèmes Missionaires de la France Rurale*, Vol.I, p.136 (1946)	←— 59 —→	←— 39 —→	Categories are 'practising' and 'occasionally conforming'.
all	1952	Poll by Institut Français de l'Opinion Publique			Those who attend regularly at Sunday Mass are also assumed to perform their Easter duties. So 51% who perform E. duties (including the 40% of Mass-goers) and 34% conformists plus 15% living outside religion = 100% of all baptised Catholics.
Regions:					
Brittany, Vendée, parts of Normandy			51	60	
East (Alsace, Lorraine, etc.) and North (Depts. of Nord and Pas-de-Calais)			40	c.50	
Paris			9	25	
Rest			25	c.35	
Italy—					
Mantua (diocese)	1948	Leoni, *Sociologia e Geografia Religiosa di una Diocesi*, 1952	37	60	very rough figures.
Rome	c.1950–1	Droulers and Rimoldi, *La Sociologia Religiosa in Italia*, in *La Scuola Cattolica*, 1952	25–30	35–40	
Milan	1949		20–30		
Emilia, Tuscany, Liguria	1941–7		10–30		
Veneto and adjacent districts	1941–7		80–100		

TABLE 20

Characteristics of regular adult Mass attenders, France, 1952

	Percentage of:	
	All regular Mass attenders	*Whole adult population*
Men	34	48
Women	66	52
Aged:		
20–34	28	33
35–49	30	30
50+	42	37
Class:		
Workers	17	
Clerks, civil servants	16	
Independents (traders, etc.), professional, managerial	17	
Farmers	27	
Retired, not gainfully occupied	23	
From places with:		
under 5,000 inhabitants	60	53
5,000–100,000	26	31
over 100,000	14	16

Source as for Table 19

Of baptised adult Catholics, the poll showed the following proportions to regard themselves as "lukewarm" or "non-practising":

	Percentages	
	Lukewarm	*Non-practising*
All	17	26
Workers	20	35
Clerks	18	31
Independents, professional, managerial, etc.	n.a.	24
Farmers	18	n.a.
No profession	n.a.	18

TABLE 21

Sunday Mass attendance by Catholics in the diocese of Mantua.
1948. Rural districts only

	Percentage of each category in each part of the diocese who attend Sunday Mass			
	Upper Mantua	Middle	Lower Mantua	Whole diocese
Sex				
Men and boys	37	25	16	27
Women and girls	58	47	36	46
Total	47	36	26	37
Age				
7–14	57	50	38	49
15–21	50	45	31	42
22 and over	45	29	21	31
Occupation (adults over 21 only)				
Owner—farmers, landlords	57	63	54	57
Civil servants, clerical workers	69	52	48	56
Tenant farmers	63	57	43	54
Business owners and managers: traders: independent craftsmen	43	40	31	37
Skilled workers: shop assistants	41	32	24	34
Semi- and unskilled workers	36	28	23	28

From Leoni, *Sociologia e Geografia Religiosa di una Diocesi*, 1952 (Rome, Gregorian University), pp. 58 ff.

the Protestant churches, a very small minority. The French Protestant churches themselves claim only about 800,000 members. But of these as many as two-thirds may be in some sense practising; as compared with the 40% or so of Catholics who are fully practising, and the 50% or 60% who attend at least an occasional—usually Christmas or Easter—Mass. In Holland the 'Gereformeerd' churches, with 10% of the total population nominally attached to them, have a high standard of practice. On the other hand the Dutch national church, the Hervormde Kerk, has shown till recently a marked lack of solidity in its own ranks, and has been the

TABLE 22

Proportion of men and women of high and low incomes in
Western Germany who are churchgoers (Catholic and Protestant
together). Sept.–Nov. 1952

	Number in Sample	Churchgoing (%):				
		Regular	Irregular	Seldom	Never	Total
Higher incomes (at least 250 DM a month)						
Men	1,427	24	23	28	26	100
Women	1,455	34	25	29	12	100
Lower incomes (below 250 DM a month)						
Men	971	26	24	29	21	100
Women	1,339	38	25	27	10	100
Total	5,192	31	24	28	17	100

From polls by the Institut für Demoskopie, Allensbach. Figures refer to men and women of voting age.

main source (Table 23) of recruits for the growing army of the 'churchless'; that is of those who in filling in their Census forms no longer claim to belong to any church community. A study by Professor Kruyt about 1930 showed church attendance among the Hervormde to be typically from 5% to 20% of church members in the mainly Protestant regions, dropping to as little as 4% in Amsterdam. It was much higher, up to 60% and more, in predominantly Catholic areas.

So also in Germany. The poll (Table 19) which showed in March 1952 that 48% of all Catholic voters claimed to be regular churchgoers put only 14% of Protestants in the same category. If 'regular' and 'occasional' are taken together the figure is still 71% for Catholics against 41% for Protestants. Data on the main acts of 'occasional conformity' point the same way. It seems (Table 24) that not more than 5–10% of Catholic couples fail to marry in church; this even after the events of the war and postwar years, which led among other things to a fair number of Catholics obtaining civil divorces and then 're-marrying' (being ineligible for a church marriage) before the civil authorities. In the Evangelical churches, on the other hand, 15–20% of the couples in which both partners were Evangelical married outside the church in the early 'thirties. After recovering to 5–10% in 1933–6 this proportion shot up to 32% in 1939. Though it later recovered,

TABLE 23

Source of growth in the number of 'churchless'
Dutchmen, 1930–1947

(a) *Increase in the number of 'churchless'*		496,000
of whom:		
Natural growth of the 'churchless' population (14·4% of the total population in 1930)	160,000	
Net transfer from Catholic Church (36·4% of the population in 1930)	80,000	
Net transfer from the Hervormde Kerk (34·5% of the population in 1930)	250,000	

(b) *Net gains and losses to the Hervormde Kerk, 1930–47*

Losses		*Gains*	
By transfer to other Reformed Churches	10,000	By natural increase	520,000
Transfer to Remonstrants	7,500	Reaffiliation of the 'Hersteld Verband'	8,000
Transfer to other religious groups	2,500		
Loss to 'churchless'	258,000		
Balance: net increase	250,000		
	528,000		528,000

Losses and gains are given *net*. E.g. loss to 'churchless' = transfers to 'churchless' minus transfers from them.

All figures are approximate estimates by J. P. Kruijt, in *Sociologisch Bulletin*, published by Kerk en Wereld, 1949, No. 3.

it has never again equalled the Catholic figure. In addition to being generally lower, Protestant Church attendance seems (Table 9, Ch. 17) to be very sharply biased towards the middle class.

OTHERS: THE CHURCHLESS

The total of Protestants and Catholics does not of course add up to the whole number of people in western Europe. But it does take in the great majority; for the number of Orthodox, Jews, and Moslems, is negligible, and only a small (though probably still a growing) minority denies a connection with any religious group at all (Table 25). In the West German Census of 1950 certain places turned out to have a substantial proportion of 'free religionists and free-thinkers'. Hamburg, for instance, had $13\frac{1}{2}\%$.

TABLE 24

Proportion of marriages between two Catholics or
two Evangelicals (i.e. mixed marriages excluded)
not celebrated in church. Germany

		%
Catholic couples	1948	5–10
Evangelical couples	1930	18
	1934	7
	1937	15
	1939	32

From *Kirchliches Jahrbuch* (Evangelical), 1950, p. 466, and *Kirchliches Handbuch* (Catholic), 1944–51, p. 277.

The *Kirchliches Jahrbuch*, 1951, pp. 349 ff., shows that from 1940 onwards the proportion of Evangelical marriages celebrated in church rose again, and may by 1945 have been not far above the figure for 1930.

But the proportion for the Federal Republic as a whole was only 3·2%; though even this proportion added up to the substantial absolute total of 1,525,000. Holland has some 17% (from the Census of 1947) of 'churchless', mainly along the north and west coast. In France it seems that around 20%—very approximately—of the people are either instructed in no religion, or else baptised Christians who would now declare themselves frankly atheists. A further 5% or so, more or less, are baptised Christians who, without being declared atheists, might well come within the Dutch definition of 'churchless'.

SUMMARY

It is clear from these various figures that though Christian Democracy's 'natural constituency' is limited it is still substantial. Upwards of 40%—in many regions far more—of the adult baptised Catholics of the countries for which statistics exist, and a substantial number of Protestants, are actively enough in touch with the Churches to rank as regular churchgoers, and there is a further fringe of occasional conformists. And though churchgoing is more marked in some regions and classes than in others, and has died altogether in particular small districts and sections of the people, there is still a good deal of it to be found in every *large* region and social group. A churchgoer is not necessarily a democrat, or even in more than a formal sense a Christian. But there is at any rate a greater *prima facie* chance of his being open to the appeal of Christian Democratic principles—presented specifically as such—than there is in the case of those who refuse the name of Christian and the right and duty of participation in Christian worship.

TABLE 25

People with no religious affiliation.
France, Holland, Germany

	Number	% of total or local population
W. Germany, Census of 1950		
Total	1,525,200	3·2
Highest 'Land' (Hamburg)		13·6
Lowest 'Lands' (Bavaria and Württemberg)		1·1
West Berlin, Census of 1950	324,950	15·1
Holland, total, Census of 1879		0·3
1889		1·5
1899		2·3
1909		5·0
1920		7·8
1930	1,144,600	14·4
1947	1,641,300	17·0
Highest province, 1947 (North Holland)		34·1
Lowest province, 1947 (Limburg)		1·3
France, Institute of Public Opinion poll, 1952. Very approximate.		15–25

The German and Dutch figures refer to those who returned themselves as 'free-thinkers', 'no fixed religion', or 'churchless' at the Census. The French figures are made up of two components, 'instructed in no religion' and 'baptised Catholics living outside any religion—atheists'. Both components are estimated.

THE ACTUAL MEMBERSHIP OF THE CHRISTIAN DEMOCRATIC ORGANISATIONS

But what proportion of Christian believers do actually support the Christian Democratic organisations, and does this support come, as does that for Christianity itself—with however many deficiencies in this territory or that—from all classes? This question can most easily be answered in the case of the Christian Democratic political parties. Politics is an activity which in a modern democratic state interests the whole adult population, and in which the majority, usually the very large majority, take at least a minimum part. It is also an extremely important activity, and for that reason well documented. Full statistics are not available for all countries of Western Europe. But there are enough available to show rather clearly what the position is.

The political parties: Catholic support

Among adult Catholics who are regular churchgoers, in all countries for which figures are available, over half—and usually much higher proportions than this—support Christian Democratic parties. The highest figures come from *Holland*, where (Table 26) the Catholic parties have the vote of over 90% of the *whole* Catholic adult population, not simply of the churchgoing population; though in Holland there is less difference between the two figures than anywhere else in Europe. Those who vote for other parties are found chiefly in the big towns where Catholic observance is (by Dutch standards) low, and most of them can be assumed to be lukewarm or non-practising. The 'break-through' movement has thrown up in recent years, among both Catholics and Protestants, groups of sincere and orthodox believers who are convinced that the day of denominational parties is done. But these groups' Catholic wing, though it has been a major cause of argument in Dutch politics, has not to the time of writing made a serious dent in the solid support of Left- as well as Right-Wing Dutch Catholics for the Catholic People's Party.

Though there are no exact figures for *Italy*, it is safe to assume that the support given to Christian Democracy by regular Catholic churchgoers there is not far off that found in Holland, though some are certainly drawn off by the Monarchist and other right-wing parties. Italy is of all countries in Europe the one where the closest connection has existed since the war between politics and the ecclesiastical authorities. The Christian Democratic Party in Italy is not itself a 'Church' party. But the clergy, and the 'civic committees' set up under their direction by Catholic Action, have been main agents in recruiting voters for it. Comparing the Christian Democratic vote (40% in 1953) with the figures of Table 19 for regular churchgoing in Italy, it is reasonable to assume that 'regular churchgoer' and 'Christian democratic voter' are normally interchangeable terms.

In *Germany* the proportion of Catholic churchgoers who vote Christian Democratic drops to about two-thirds (Table 27). It was rather higher, probably, at the General Election of 1953, in which the Christian Democrats did decidedly better than appears from the public opinion poll figures for 1952; but the 1952 figures are probably again representative for more recent years. And in France rather more than half of all regular Catholic churchgoers claimed in 1952 to vote for the M.R.P. (Table 28). Baptised Catholics constitute 80–85% of the adult population of France, and about 35–40% of the baptised (Table 19) are regular churchgoers. This would make the M.R.P. vote a minimum of 15% of the vote for all parties, which is a good deal more than the 12% which the M.R.P. received out of the votes actually cast at the elections of 1951. The two figures may both be correct; for there were several areas where in 1951 the M.R.P.

358

TABLE 26

Dutch voters in 1948

	Catholics	Gerefor-meerde (strict observ-ance)	Calvinists Hervormde (National Church)	No Religion	Total
Out of every 1,000 voters there were	335	95	370	180	1,000
And these voted for:					
Catholic Parties					
KVP (Catholic People's Party)	310	—	—	—	310
KNP (Right-Wing Catholics)	15	—	—	—	15
Protestant Parties					
AR (Anti-Revolu-tionary)	—	80	50	—	130
CHU (Christian Historical Union)	—	—	90	—	90
SGP (Strict Calvinist	—	10	15	—	25
Other Democratic Parties					
VVD (Liberals)	5	—	45	30	80
Miscellaneous	—	—	5	10	15
P. v.d. A (Labour)	20	5	150	80	255
Communist Party (CPN)	5	—	15	60	80
Totals	355	95	370	180	1000

From a Report by the research centre of the Dutch Labour Party.

put up no candidates, and between 1951 and 1952 there may well have been a swing towards the M.R.P. from, for example, the Right-Wing nationalists (R.P.F.). Table 29 shows that in 1952 a very much higher proportion of M.R.P. voters than of any other party claimed to be 'much' or 'substantially' influenced by the advice of the Church in making their decision to vote. It is therefore not surprising to find in Maps I and II that the distribution of M.R.P. voting corresponds substantially with that

TABLE 27

Churchgoers' political views, Germany, 1952

Party	Percentage supporting each party out of voters whose church attendance is:			
	Regular	Irregular	Seldom	Never
(a) *Christian-Democrats*				
Catholics	67	28	25	14
Protestants	40	27	18	7
Both together	57	28	17	10
(b) *Social-Democrats*				
Catholics	16	39	54	45
Protestants	21	34	43	44
Both together	18	36	46	45
(c) *Liberal*				
Catholics	3	7	13	16
Protestants	26	21	17	15
Both together	9	16	19	18
(d) *Other Parties*				
Catholics	14	26	8	25
Protestants	13	18	22	34
Both together				
Bavarian regionalist	4	6	2	1
German Party	2	3	5	5
Communist Party	1	1	1	6
Other	9	10	10	15
Totals for Catholics, for Protestants, and for both together add to:	100	100	100	100

From a poll by the Institut für Demoskopie, Allensbach. 'Christian-Democratic' includes here only the C.D.U./C.S.U. The small Centre Party is counted under 'other'.

of high Catholic observance. There are however also important discrepancies, showing that 'practising Catholic' and 'M.R.P. voter' are by no means labels which cover one another. In the west the zone of relatively high M.R.P. voting stretches a good deal further into the centre of France than does that of high religious observance. In the north-east there are two departments with high M.R.P. votes and moderate or low observance. In the south and in Brittany can be found large areas of high observance

TABLE 28

Political views of Catholics in France, 1952

*Percentage of all regular Catholic churchgoers
who would vote:*

Communist	1
Socialist	5
Liberal (radical)	2
Christian-Democrat (M.R.P.)	54
Conservative (Moderates, Independent)	20
Nationalist (R.P.F.)	18

*Of all Catholics voting for each group (not
only regular churchgoers) there claim to be:*

	Fervent Catholics	'Normal' Catholics	Lukewarm	Non-practising
Communist	1	5	8	79
Socialist	1	15	23	49
Liberal (radical)	'about half'		'about half'	
Christian-Democratic	'over half'			
Conservative				
Nationalist				

Poll by French Institute of Public Opinion. Quoted in *Réalités*, Nov. 1952.

TABLE 29

Percentage of baptised Catholic supporters of different French
parties who claimed in 1952 to be influenced to some extent
by the advice of the Church in their decision to vote

Party supported	*% of voters influenced by Church's advice*		
	Much	A little	Total
Communist	6	1	7
Socialist	2	9	11
Liberal (radical)	0	13	13
Christian-Democratic (M.R.P.)	43	39	82
Conservative (Moderate, Independent)	26	36	62
Nationalist (R.P.F.)	18	38	56

From a poll by the French Institute of Public Opinion.

but negligible support for the M.R.P. And along the Swiss frontier it is possible to find the rather startling juxtaposition of a low-observance department with high M.R.P. voting and a high-observance department where M.R.P. voting is below the national average.

The political parties: Protestant support

Churchgoing Protestants, at least in Holland and Germany, are more likely to support the Christian Democratic parties than any others. But they are not as likely to support them as Catholics. The highest percentages are found in Holland (Table 26), where the stricter Calvinists, the Geer-formeerde, support Protestant parties with the same enthusiasm which Catholics show for the Catholic parties. Among Protestants in the national church, on the other hand—the Hervormde Kerk—only a little over 40% vote for Christian parties. This 40% is actually a more impressive figure than it looks, since it is a percentage of all who regard themselves as even nominally attached to the Hervormde Kerk, not merely of the active churchgoing population. Taking both Protestant groups together, it seems that 50–55% of all nominal Dutch Protestants vote for Christian parties; an impressive figure but still far short of the corresponding figure for Catholics. The balance who vote for other parties includes two main groups: nominal and indifferent Christians, and a number of believing but modernist (the Dutch word is 'free-thinking') Churchmen who have among other things played a remarkable part in the evangelisation of the Dutch Labour Party. As among Catholics, a small number of orthodox believers have in recent years become strong Labour supporters.

In *Germany* more churchgoing Protestants support the Christian Democrats than any other party, indeed almost twice as many. But in 1952 the proportion of Christian Democratic voters among Protestant churchgoers was even so only 40%; a smaller figure than for Catholics (67%), and much smaller than the corresponding proportion of Protestant *churchgoers* in Holland. Table 30 shows how in North-Rhine/Westphalia the degree of support for the Christian Democratic parties (the Christian Democratic Union and the Centre Party) falls off as the proportion of Catholics in the population dies away. Looking at the right-hand columns of the table, it is obvious that in areas where a very high proportion of the population is Catholic there is a substantial number of Catholics who do not vote Christian Democratic; for the total of Christian Democratic votes in many of these districts, including any which may come from Protestants, is equivalent to only two-thirds or even a half of the number of Catholic electors. Looking at the left-hand side of the table, it can be seen that in areas where the Catholic population falls to as little as 5%, 10%, or 15% of the total there is still a substantial Christian Democratic vote, which must come from Protestants. But with all these reservations,

MAP I

Departments in which the French Christian Democrats (M.R.P.) polled above the national average for their party, General Election of 1951

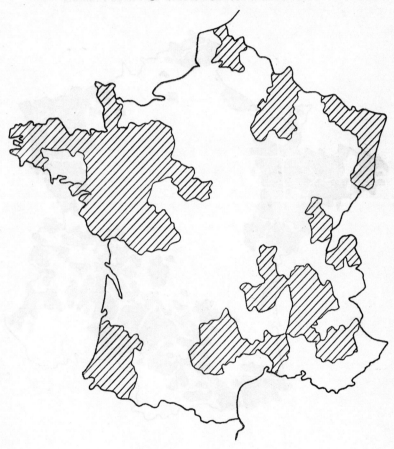

MAP II

Religious practice in the French countryside, about 1945.
From Boulard, Essor ou Déclin du Clergé Français

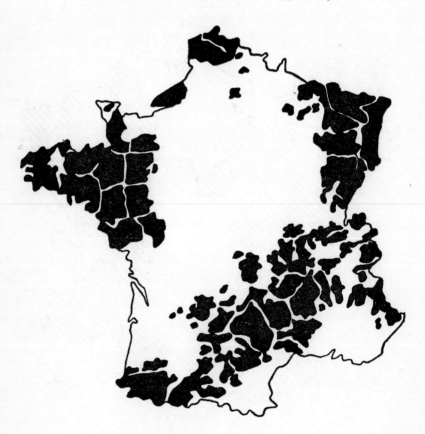

TABLE 30

North-Rhine/Westphalia. Christian Democratic votes and Catholic population. Provincial elections, 1954

	Number of constituencies in which:					
Percentage of voters voting C.D.U. or Centre Party was:	Percentage of population who are Catholic (1950 Census) is:					
	0–19	20–39	40–59	60–79	80+	Total
20–29	13	3	—	—	—	16
30–39	1	26	15	—	—	42
40–49	1	—	26	13	3	43
50–59	—	—	1	13	12	26
60–69	—	—	—	3	9	12
70–79	—	—	—	—	10	10
Total	15	29	42	29	34	149

From a press release by the Katholische Nachrichten-Agentur, Bonn and Munich.

there is no mistaking the significance of the march of Christian Democratic voting percentages diagonally across the page, rising step by step with the percentage of Catholic electors. In that area at least, the first condition for a really high Christian Democratic poll is a high proportion of Catholics in the population. Table 31 shows how the early membership of the C.D.U. came predominantly from Catholics, even in much of Protestant North Germany.

In *Switzerland*, finally, which has the third largest Protestant population among the countries studied here, there is only one small Protestant party in Federal politics, far too small to have a substantial influence. The main Swiss Christian Democratic party is Catholic, and Protestants spread their votes over a variety of non-confessional parties.

The political parties: the 'dissidents'

When Christians in these various countries do not vote Christian Democratic, which parties do they support? Protestant regular churchgoers in *Germany* are most likely to vote Liberal, and next most likely to vote Socialist. Less regular churchgoers are much more likely to be Socialist voters; the percentage of Liberals among them is much smaller. This may also be the pattern among Protestants in *Holland*, where the statistics lump regular and irregular churchgoers together. Of all the (from the Christian Democrats' point of view) dissident Dutch Protestants, about 20% vote Liberal and 70% Socialist. The balance vote for the Communist

365

TABLE 31

Membership of the Christian Democratic Union (Germany) 1947–8

	North Rhine Province	Hanover	Bremen	Sachsen Anhalt (Soviet zone)	Berlin (All zones)
(a) Catholics and Protestants[6]					
Catholics as % of:					
Population (1946)	64	19[1]	9		
Party members (1947–8)	86	59	46		
Protestants as % of:					
Population (1946)	30	76[1]	86		
Party members (1947–8)	14	41	53		
(b) Social class. Percentage of party members					
Manual workers	22	17		13	10
Clerical and managerial:					
Clerks[4]	16 ⎫	11 ⎫		18 ⎫	10 ⎫
Civil servants	7 ⎬ 24	6 ⎬ 17		8 ⎬ 26	30 ⎬ 40
Managers, employers	1 ⎭	—[2] ⎭		—[2] ⎭	— ⎭
Independents:					
Tradesmen and craftsmen	18 ⎫	15 ⎫		10[3] ⎫	13 ⎫
Professional (incl. students)	5 ⎬ 35	8 ⎬ 43		9 ⎬ 33	9 ⎬ 22
Farmers	12 ⎭	20 ⎭		14 ⎭	— ⎭
Pensioners, rentiers	11	3		4	8
Housewives, women not otherwise employed	—[2] [5]	21		25	19
Misc., unknown	8	—		—	—
Total	100	100		100	100

From Wieck, *Die Entstehung der C.D.U.* 1953, pp. 220–222.

Notes: [1] *Whole* of Niedersachsen.

[2] No separate figure given.

[3] Craftsmen only. Not clear where tradesmen are entered.

[4] 'Clerks' in private industry only: 'civil servants' including clerks in public enterprises.

[5] Housewives seem here to be included in previous figures, treated as representing social category, not occupation.

[6] There were also a few party members, and a fair number of people in the whole population, of other or no known religious belief.

and various miscellaneous parties. German Protestants provide a fair amount of support for Right-wing conservative and nationalist parties as well as for the Liberals and Socialists; but this, as Table 27 shows, comes chiefly from among nominal Protestants, whose churchgoing is 'seldom' or 'never'. Among Catholics, dissidents in both Germany and Holland usually vote Socialist. In striking contrast to what happens among Protestants, rather few support the Liberals. The number of dissident regular Protestant churchgoers in Germany who support respectively the Socialists and the Liberals is not far from equal; but among Catholic churchgoers there are only 3% of Liberal voters, as compared with 16% who vote Socialist. German Catholics also provide a fair amount of support for Conservatives of regionalist groups such as the Bavarian Party. But there are not as many Catholic voters for these parties as for the Socialists.

In *France*, unlike Germany and Holland, it is the Right-wing parties which attract most of the dissident Catholic vote. Only 8% of Catholic churchgoing electors in France in 1952 (Table 28) claimed to support the Liberals, Socialists, or Communists. Conversely the vast majority of the supporters of these parties, if they were baptised Catholics at all, put themselves down as 'lukewarm' or 'non-practising'. No less than 38% of regular Catholic churchgoers, on the other hand, claimed to be right-wing (Conservative or nationalist) voters, and over half the support for these parties came from Catholics who claimed to be 'normal' or 'fervent'. The fact that dissident Catholics in France tend to vote to the Right, whereas those in Germany or Holland tend to vote to the Left, does not of course necessarily mean that French Catholics are more conservative than German or Dutch. It may, and to a large extent, does, mean that Christian Democracy in France is further to the Left than the corresponding parties in Holland or Germany, so that it is particularly the right-wingers who are likely to be tempted to stay out of it or break away.

Looking at the countries studied here as a whole, the one clear distinction which emerges among those churchgoing Christians who dissent from Christian Democracy is that Protestants are more likely to vote Liberal than Catholics. Otherwise, dissidents of both denominations fan out from Christian Democracy in all directions, towards socialism on one side and liberalism, conservatism, and nationalism on the other, emphasising the Christian Democratic parties' central position in the political world.

The political parties: non-Christian support

The converse of the fact that the Christian Democratic parties group a large fraction—a majority, in the case of Catholics—of all practising Christians in their countries is that they attract only a comparatively small degree of support from non-Christians or inactive Christians, in spite of their efforts in recent years to divest themselves of any denominational or even, in some cases, any specifically Christian character. When after the Second World War the Dutch Labour Party opened a campaign for a 'break-through' of the existing political structure, Professor Romme, the Parliamentary leader of the Catholic People's Party, replied that, if Socialists were so anxious for unity with Catholics, there was nothing in the Catholic People's Party's constitution to stop them from joining it. He was formally correct, but the Socialists were not convinced. In actual practice, rather few of the definitely irreligious join the Christian parties. In Germany (Table 27) only 7% of non-practising Protestants claimed in 1952 to support the C.D.U., and 14% of non-practising Catholics; though in a country as large as Germany these figures of course represent considerable numbers. Occasional ('seldom') churchgoers are more likely to give support; but still only a small minority of them. In Holland there is for practical purposes no such thing as a voter of 'no religion' who supports a Christian party; though these parties certainly have the support of some pretty lukewarm Christians. For France Table 27 is eloquent. If 82% of M.R.P. voters claim to be under Church influence, that leaves only 18% for possible independents, and it is reasonably certain that these too will include some Christian believers.

The political parties: class representation

The Christian Democratic parties do not merely group a large number of Christians; they draw them from all classes. In *Germany* the Christian Democratic Union (Table 32) has about an equal share of high and low income voters, whereas the Liberals are overbalanced on the side of the high incomes and the Socialists on that of the lower-income groups. (See also Table 31.) The C.D.U. has a relatively high proportion of women voters, and in this respect is unbalanced compared to the Liberals; though not as compared with the Social Democrats, who have a similar but opposite excess of men. In *Holland* votes for the Christian parties mirror almost exactly the occupational structure of the population as a whole (Table 33); they have rather more than their share of farmers, and fractionally more than their share of independent traders and professional men, but on the other hand have as near as makes no difference exactly their share of manual and white-collar workers and managers. The Liberal, Communist, and to a less extent the Labour Parties are by contrast class parties. The Labour Party is weak among farmers. The Communist Party gets its support from manual workers and pensioners. The Liberals have about their share of white-collar workers, but far more than their share of the independent middle class and farmers, along with a great under-representation of manual workers.

TABLE 32

Voters by age, sex, and income. Germany, 1952

	Percentage of all electors who would vote for:				
	Social Democrats	Christian Democrats (C.D.U. only)	Liberals	Other parties	Total
All	36	33	13	18	100
Men	43	24	13	20	100
Women	30	42	12	16	100
Monthly income:					
Under 250 DM.	41	32	7	20	100
250 DM or more	33	34	17	16	100

From a poll by the Institute für Demoskopie, Allensbach.

TABLE 33

How various classes in Holland distributed their
political support, 1948

	Communist	Labour	Liberals	KVP	CHU	AR	Total
Manual Workers	45	135	5	135	35	55	410
Clerical workers and managerial workers	5	75	15	70	20	20	205
Independents: Shop-keepers, professions, etc.	5	30	40	50	20	30	175
Farmers	—	5	15	40	10	15	85
Pensioners	15	15	5	25	15	10	85
Belonging to other parties (not analysed)							40
	70	260	80	320	100	130	1000

Source: As for Table 26.

TABLE 34

How different classes distributed their political support in France, 1952

	Percentage of voters in each party who come from each class:					
	Com- munist	Socialist	Liberal (radical)	Christian Dem- ocratic	Conserv- ative	Nation- alist (R.P.F.)
Manual workers:						
general	38 ⎱46	21 ⎱27	9 ⎱13	19 ⎱21	9 ⎱11	15 ⎱18
farm	8 ⎰	6 ⎰	4 ⎰	2 ⎰	2 ⎰	3 ⎰
Clerical and managerial:						
clerks	8	6	1	15	4	10
civil servants	5 ⎬14	13 ⎬23	8 ⎬13	4 ⎬22	7 ⎬20	3 ⎬19
managers, employers	1	4	4	3	9	6
Independents:						
tradesmen	5	5	10	8	11	10
professions, incl. students	3 ⎬13	1 ⎬14	1 ⎬39	3 ⎬29	3 ⎬45	1 ⎬27
farmers	5	8	28	18	31	16
Pensioners, rentiers	5	10	19	8	10	6
Women not otherwise employed	22	26	16	20	14	30
	100	100	100	100	100	100
Votes for each party as % of those actually cast for all parties General Election, 1951	25	14	10	12½	11½	22

From a poll by the French Institute of Public Opinion, published in *Réalités*, May, 1952. Voting statistics as re-worked by Goguel, *Géographie des Elections Françaises*, 1951, p. 141.

In *France*, the M.R.P. has (Tables 34, 35, 36):

A relatively high proportion of:

    women voters
    young and middle-aged voters
    people from small towns and the countryside
    clerical workers
    independent middle class (tradesmen, professions)
    farmers
    manual workers (general)

TABLE 35

Proportion of supporters of each French political
party who have certain attributes: 1952

	Com-munist	Socialist	Liberal (radical)	Christian Demo-cratic (M.R.P.)	Conserv-ative	Nation-alist. (R.P.F.)
Women voters	30	32	27	44	41	46
Voters under 35	42	30	11	31	30	28
35–49	35	33	24	35	25	35
over 50	23	37	65	34	45	37
Proportion who:						
own property	18	32	57	44	58	47
have a car	11	21	30	21	43	33
have a servant	3	5	20	15	31	17
Living in districts:						
under 5,000 people	48	50	60	53	55	45
5,000–100,000	32	34	17	28	16	33
over 100,000	20	16	23	19	29	22

Source: As for Table 34.

*A proportion corresponding to its overall ranking (4th) among the six parties
tabulated of:*

> property and car owners: people with servants
> people from middle-sized towns
> pensioners, people living on their own means
> women "not otherwise employed"

A relatively low proportion of:

> elderly voters
> people from big towns
> civil servants
> managers
> manual workers (farm)

What stands out, however, is not so much that the M.R.P. has more of
this or less of that, but rather (Table 36) that there are very few groups in
which it is either clearly at the top or clearly at the bottom of the list.
It has very little support from farm workers. Conversely, it has very strong
support from clerical workers, thanks no doubt largely to the very strong
position of the Christian trade unions in this group. But these are rare
extremes. Of all major French parties, the M.R.P. is the one which has the
most balanced representation of all classes or groups. Though exact

TABLE 36

Ranking of the M.R.P. among the six political
groups referred to in Tables 34 and 35 in
respect of certain criteria. 1952

	Rank
Proportion of women voters	2
Voters under 35	2
35–49	1–3
over 50	5
Proportion who:	
own property	4
have a car	4–5
have a servant	4
Living in places	
under 5,000 inhabitants	3
5,000–100,000	4
over 100,000	5
Proportion of:	
Manual workers—general	3
farm	5–6
Clerical and { clerks	1
managerial { civil servants	5
{ managers, etc.	5
Independents—tradesmen	2–3
professions, students	1–3
farmers	3
Pensioners, rentiers	4
Women not otherwise employed	4
Total vote	4

figures are not available, it is known that the same holds of the Christian
Democratic parties in *Belgium, Switzerland,* and *Italy.* Variations appear
in these countries as in France: a rather high proportion of women's,
white-collar, and independent middle-class or farming votes, a rather low
proportion of at least some categories of manual workers'. But the over-
shadowing fact everywhere is that of balance between the classes, not of
excess or deficiency in one or another.

THE SOCIAL ORGANISATIONS

How far have the Christian Democratic social and economic organisations occupied their 'Christian base'? It is much harder to answer such

372

questions in their case than in that of the political parties. In the first place there are fewer sources of information. Poll experts swarm around politics like flies, but show much less interest in (for example) the doings of Protestant employers in Holland. Secondly, a study on the same basis as for the political parties, and permitting a fair comparison with them, is possible only in the case of those social organisations which, like the parties, have executive functions and do not stop at education and miscellaneous services. A Christian trade union, or a body such as the Belgian Farmers' Union, is *the* organisation to defend its members' daily needs in its own sphere, just as a Christian Democratic party does in the world of politics. But a body such as the Catholic Workers' Movement of Germany stands alongside and to a great extent outside its members' day to day interests, which in that case are represented (at least for manual workers) by the neutral German T.U.C. All experience suggests that it is unlikely that more than a minority of those who join an organisation attending to their daily needs will also join an organisation on the side lines even if, like the Catholic Workers' Associations in Italy, it sets out to attract a mass membership through friendly society or leisure activities. And thirdly, it is in any case harder to say in the case of most social organisations than it is in a count of political voters what constitutes a full or satisfactory measure of participation. Nearly everyone has political opinions, and the great majority express them at least at general elections. But trade union membership, for example, varies greatly from trade to trade and from country to country. In a trade where membership of all unions is low, a Christian union may have occupied its base to an extent which compares well with other unions even though only a fraction of the believing Christians in the trade have joined it.

Though all these difficulties are present, the *workers' movements* are on the whole the easiest to analyse. In France, if the Christian trade unions secured the support of all regular Catholic churchgoers among the working class, but of no others, they would recruit (Table 37) about 25–30% of all manual workers and 35–40% of all clerical workers. Actual membership is vague and shifting. But it has been shown here (Table 5, Chapter XVI) that at the social security elections of 1950 the Christian unions secured 28% of all votes cast for the main trade union federations, and no less than 44% of those cast in the case of bank and insurance staffs. The Christian unions do not of course secure the support *only* of regular churchgoers, or of Catholics. Like the M.R.P., the C.F.T.C. sets out today to attract all those, Christians or not, who support its programme, or who take a 'spiritual' as apart from a 'materialist' view of trade union problems. Its ranks have been open, as has been said, to Moslems in North Africa and to Buddhists in Indo-China. It is not certain how much of the membership is accounted for by this non-Christian support. But, considering only

373

TABLE 37

Calculation of the proportion of regular churchgoers among French workers, 1952

(1) Proportion of workers in French Institute of Public Opinion's sample:

$$\text{manual (not farming) } 20\cdot4\%$$
$$\text{clerical } \qquad\qquad 13\cdot8\%$$

(2) Given that:

45% of all adult Catholic-baptised manual workers fulfil their Easter duties

51% of all adult Catholic-baptised clerical workers fulfil their Easter duties

80% of all Catholics who fulfil their Easter duties are regular Mass attenders—this figure is assumed to apply to both manual and clerical workers

baptised Catholics represent 83% of the whole adult population—this figure is assumed to apply to both manual and clerical workers

16% of all regular Catholic churchgoers are clerical workers
17% of all regular Catholic churchgoers are manual workers
40% of all baptised adult Catholics are regular churchgoers

(3) then the proportion of all manual workers who are regular churchgoers is either:

$$0\cdot45\times0\cdot8\times0\cdot83 \text{ of the total adult manual worker population:} = 29\cdot8\%$$

or:

$$\frac{100(0\cdot17\times0\cdot4\times0\cdot83)}{20\cdot4} \text{ of the total adult manual worker}$$
$$\text{population:} = 28\%$$

(4) And the proportion of all clerical workers who are regular churchgoers is either:

$$0\cdot51\times0\cdot8\times0\cdot83 \text{ of the total adult clerical worker population:} = 34\cdot0\%$$

or:

$$100(0\cdot16\times0\cdot4\times0\cdot83) \text{ of the total adult clerical worker}$$
$$\text{population:} = 38\cdot4\%$$

(5) Therefore the proportion of all manual and clerical workers who are regular churchgoers is either:

$$\frac{(13\cdot8\times34\cdot0)+(20\cdot4\times29\cdot8)}{13\cdot8+20\cdot4} = 31\tfrac{1}{2}\%$$

or:

$$\frac{(13\cdot8\times38\cdot4)+(20\cdot4\times28\cdot0)}{13\cdot8+20\cdot4} = 32\%$$

Christian members, it may well be that in the case of bank, insurance, and certain other categories of clerical workers—though not of civil servants, who are more likely to support the Socialists—the C.F.T.C. has been winning recruits and votes up to near the limits of its 'natural' constituency. In the case of manual workers it has probably not reached the limits of its constituency but is getting within striking distance of it. In Belgium and Italy also, though only fragmentary statistics are available, it is safe to assume that the very great majority of organised workers who are also churchgoers support Christian or Christian-led unions.

In Holland and Germany it is possible to compare the experience of Protestant and Catholic workers' movements. As in the case of political parties, the solidest support for the Christian organisations comes from the Catholics. About 33% of all Dutch workers (manual or clerical) vote for the Catholic People's Party, and about this proportion of all organised workers are in the Catholic trade unions. To be exact, Catholic trade unionists in 1953 were 31% of the nominal total of all organised workers, and 35% of the number of non-Communist workers. The correct overall figure lies somewhere between these two, since there is reason to think that the numbers officially declared by the Communist unions are inflated. Since it is known that only a small fraction of even nominal Catholics in Holland vote for non-Catholic parties, the Catholic unions must be recruiting up to near the limits of their natural constituency. The Protestant unions in Holland also have a substantial membership, between $16\frac{1}{2}$% and 19% of the total of all organised workers. But 21% of all workers vote for Protestant parties, and these parties themselves have the support of little more than half the number of the country's nominal Protestants. It is quite possible that, if tested by the proportion of regular churchgoers recruited, the Dutch Protestant unions would compare well with, say, the French Christian unions. But by the more stringent test of recruitment among all workers who are nominal members of their church they fall seriously short of the Dutch Catholic unions. They themselves reckoned in 1953 that at least half of all nominal Protestant workers were unorganised or (from the Protestant unions' point of view) wrongly organised.

Christian trade unions existed in Germany till 1955 only for clerical workers, of whom 28% voted for Christian lists at the social security elections of 1953. This figure obviously includes a certain number of lukewarm Christians and even more probably of non-Christians. Allowing for this, it looks as if the Christian unions may be still some way from recruiting the whole number of regular churchgoers in their field; for at the end of 1952 regular churchgoers amounted to about 25% of all adult men in Germany, and 35–40% of women. The shortfall may well be of the same order as in the case of the Christian manual workers' unions in France.

In the wider, neutral German trade union movement, covering all classes of workers, it is possible to compare Catholic and Protestant influence on the basis of the figures already quoted for the number of practising Catholics and Protestants among full-time union officials. 15% were practising Catholics in 1954, and only about 1% to 2% Protestants. This seems to have been due to two inter-dependent factors: the practical collapse since 1933 of the Evangelical Workers' Movement, and the small participation (Table 9, Chapter XVII) of semi- and unskilled workers in Evangelical parish life.

In the case of Christian Democratic *social organisations other than trade unions* it would not be useful, with the figures at present available, to go beyond the scraps of information already collected in previous chapters. The most that can be said is that some few of these organisations have expanded to their 'natural' limit, or near it, but that most have not done so. Taking first support from Catholics, it is known that the Catholic farmers' movements in Holland and Belgium, and the Dutch Catholic employers' movement, recruit or at least have the support of a large majority of the practising Catholics in their respective fields. So, probably, does the officially neutral but in fact Christian Large Families' League in Belgium: it in fact recruits the majority of all eligible families, Christian or not. It is not known exactly what proportion of the Kolpingsfamilie represent of the younger Catholic craftsmen in Germany, but it too must be substantial. The Catholic business middle-class organisations in both Holland and Belgium have, as has been shown, a higher degree of support among all people in this class, and therefore presumably among Catholics, than organisations of any other kind. But, since organisation of any kind is weak in this group, their members quite possibly are only a minority even of believing Catholics in their class.

Protestants, as in the case of the trade unions and political parties, give less support to organisations of these various kinds than do Catholics. In Holland, the Protestant farmers', business middle-class, and employers' organisations have had a harder fight than their Catholic opposite numbers to convince even practising members of the Protestant churches that organisation 'under their own flag' is best. The middle-class organisation reckons that it could multiply its membership by four or five—in spite of a very rapid growth already recorded in recent years—if all eligible recruits came in. The employers' organisation has reached perhaps half of its potential constituents, and that at the price of allowing many of them to maintain a second membership in 'neutral' organisations. In Germany it is significant that efforts to found an Evangelical organisation of the type of the Kolpingsfamilie have had little success: any more than the somewhat sporadic efforts to organise Protestant employers.

CHAPTER XXIII

IS THERE A NEW ORIENTATION?

THE fact that some at least of the Christian Democratic movements, in such important fields as politics or the labour movement, have expanded to, or within striking distance of, the natural limits of their recruitment, obviously poses a question. Where next? If their influence is to go on growing, are new sources of membership to be tapped, or is it enough to strengthen the various movements within their existing limits and add to their alliances outside? Should the existing structure of Christian parties and social movements, recruiting in fact if not in theory overwhelmingly from Christian believers, be 'broken through'?

The same question is posed by a number of other developments touched on in earlier chapters. One or two of the political parties, especially the M.R.P. in France and the *Democrazia Cristiana* in Italy, have run themselves into a position where, so long as the political structure remains as at present, they can do little to advance social reform. In many fields of both politics and economic and social action the lines dividing Christians from Social Democrats and Liberals have faded, while the consciousness of all three of the need to stand together against totalitarianism from the left and the right has grown. Christian and particularly Catholic Action has grown to a new stature; there are far more facilities available today than fifty years ago for equipping Christians to hold their own in 'neutral' parties or social organisations, and the pressure to maintain Christian Democratic movements on a confessional, specifically Christian, basis has been correspondingly reduced. The Christian social movements have widened out in the last generation to provide on a large scale for the middle class, for youth, and for families, and these groups often take a different view of organisation on a confessional basis from that of the older political and labour movements. The middle-class movements, outside Holland and Belgium, show little wish to go beyond the educational work of Christian Action and to found Christian Democratic trade or professional associations. This attitude has even, as in the case of the Belgian Catholic employers, made some inroads into the Dutch-speaking countries themselves. Many of the family movements take the same view, as well as many of the dynamic, apostolic, and excellently trained militants of the youth

377

movements. 'Christian trade unions and trade associations?' said a chaplain of the French Catholic youth movement (A.C.J.F.) when asked about his militants' views: 'Ils s'en moquent'.[1]

Above all, there is the major change which, as was pointed out in Chapter II, has come over the Christian Democratic movements as a result of their rise to new strength and power in the last two generations. Their interest today goes beyond the defence of ecclesiastical interests, the affirmation of Christian principles, or even the creation of strong and stable organisations. All these, necessary in their time, were essentially defensive operations; aspects of a struggle to survive within an order established apart from Christianity and often against it. Today the accent has passed from defence to attack. The problem is to find the strategy by which the militant Christian laity, now powerful and aware of their objectives, can transform the society around them. This shift from defence to attack is the hallmark of the rising generation of Christian militants in the countries studied here, and of what may well be called the Third Age of Christian Democracy. And inevitably it raises the question whether the traditional forms of organisation, springing as they often did from considerations of defence and survival, are adequate for the tasks of today.

It has been shown how at the end of the Second World War these and other, more temporary, factors led to a movement for unity among the trade unions of a number of countries, and how, in spite of the strong and effective resistance put up against this trend in the victorious and neutral countries, and the later reaction against it in those which had been defeated, something of the spirit which inspired it remains. There is the growing minority in the French Christian unions which wishes to widen these unions' appeal by finally dropping the 'Christian' label. There is the strong group of Catholic trade unionists in Germany who, with the full support of their Protestant colleagues, delayed for years the break-up of the united German Trade Union Federation (D.G.B.), and the similar group in Austria. There is also the Catholic group in Italy, led by Giulio Pastore, which will not indeed unite with the Communists, but is very satisfied with the C.I.S.L. unions, which draw in Social Democrats and Liberals—though under mainly Catholic leadership—and refuse to affiliate to the Christian trade union international.

Similar pressures have made themselves felt in politics. Julius Bachem's slogan about fighting in the open field is being pressed as never before. Considering the growth of Communism, the gap between the Churches and at least some sections of the workers, and the difficulty of social reform, many not only in the political world but in the trade unions have been specially attracted by the idea of an equivalent of the British Labour Party. This would group together social democrats, Christian democrats

---

[1] 'They laugh at them.'

(or at least their left wing), and perhaps also some liberals and farmers. The idea of a party of this kind was raised in Germany by Jakob Kaiser and other Christian and Liberal trade unionists just after the war, as part of the same movement which led to the creation of the united German trade unions. The Social Democrats however refused to support it, and Kaiser, with his colleague Ernst Lemmer of the former Liberal (Hirsch-Duncker) trade unions, thereupon joined in setting up the C.D.U. In Holland at the same time the Socialist Party reconstituted itself as a Labour Party on a basis such that Christians could join it, and a number did. And more recently the question of a Labour Party such as Kaiser had in mind has received strong support from working-class and a number of middle-class Christian Democrats in France. There have been hints of a move in that direction in Italy.

THE CASE FOR A 'BREAK-THROUGH': (1) HOLLAND. THE 'RELIGIOUS
SOCIALIST' MOVEMENT

The question of a 'break-through' deserves to be studied in detail, for on it the whole future organisation of Christian Democracy may depend. This can best be done by taking one or two case-histories, and in the first place that of the narrowing of the gap, in politics at least, between Christianity and Socialism in Holland. Traditionally, believing Christians in Holland vote for Christian parties. There have always been some who voted for other parties, but they have tended to be people whose orthodoxy was doubtful and their religious practice weak; liberal or modernist Protestant theologians, members of the national church whose religion amounted to little more than writing 'Hervormd' on a Census form, nominal Catholics from the three big cities of Holland where leakage is large and religious practice often poorly kept up. The new feature since the war has been the appearance of an important though not yet massive body of both Catholics and Protestants, people whose loyalty to their church is beyond question, who nevertheless demand that the traditional framework of Dutch politics be broken through; and it is particularly in the movement for a reformed Labour Party that this group has made its weight felt.

The supporters of a 'break-through' have been influenced by considerations of very much the kind already outlined in the case of the trade unions. The whole atmosphere of discussion has been changed by the events of recent years, and particularly of the resistance. It is doubtful whether the resistance and the concentration camps widened the common ground already existing in Holland between Christians of different denominations, or between them and 'humanists'. But it did make them aware as never before of human personality, the importance of basic human rights, and the need for social reform. And this change of atmosphere has helped to make operative a change in several more fundamental factors. Some are religious. Catholics have become more sharply aware of the distinction between the religious and denominational task of Catholic Action and the a-confessional aims of the Christian in politics; especially since Christians in Holland have won their battle over the schools and the relation of Church and State, and need no longer give much attention to these issues of a directly ecclesiastical kind. Protestants have been influenced by the Barthian denial, already outlined in the case of the C.B.T.B., of the right of any party to arrogate the name of Christian. And Catholics and Protestants alike have been influenced by the spirit of 'We Must Fight in the Open Field', or, in more traditional Christian terms, by the desire to go out into the highways and byways and bring the separated, in this case Socialist, brethren in. There is in the 'break-through' movement a great sense of the Christian's mission in public life, both as one who promotes certain policies and as the bearer of a religious message: a sense of the universality of the Church and of the need for Christians to keep contact even with those outside the fold.

There is a certain inconsistency in these religious positions. One cannot be entirely happy with a movement in which one set of voices proclaims the mission—and the mission in a religious, not only a political, sense—of the Christian politician, while another denies that there can be such a thing as 'Christian' politics at all. But though the premises differ the conclusion is agreed; the Christian parties must go and neutral parties take their place. And this conclusion is supported, as in the working-class movements, by the more material argument that all left-wing democratic forces must be grouped to ensure a dynamic social policy. This line of argument was heard especially just after the war, when the memory of Colijn's liberalism was still strong in the land. But it still remains important today.

The move towards unity has also been helped by the tendency, more marked in Holland than in any other part of Europe, for the differences between Christians and Socialists in both politics and industrial matters to grow much smaller over the last sixty years. A glance at the Dutch Socialist cartoons of the eighteen-eighties and eighteen-nineties is enough to show why Christians, however socially minded, could not come together with Socialists in those days. Militarism, Monarchy, Modern Prostitution, and a variety of intriguing characters in Roman tiaras and Geneva gowns, stunned by the blows of whiskery proletarians with nothing to lose but their chains, drown in the wake of the good ship Organisation with Nemesis rather indecently exposed at her prow. In politics as in industry the Socialism of those days stood for revolution rather than for democratic change, for State collectivism rather than for 'sovereignty in one's own sphere', and for resolute opposition to the Christian revelation at best as irrelevant, and more usually as a pernicious error to be rooted out.

An important part in the transformation which has taken place in Dutch Socialism since that time has been due to the 'religious socialist' movement, the Dutch end of a much wider movement covering all Europe. Religious socialist movements have a long history; it will be remembered, for example, how the group of religious socialists around the 'Atelier' played a significant part in the revolution of 1848 in France. But the religious socialist movement in its modern form dates from the eighteen-eighties and eighteen-nineties. A small number of individuals and little groups, made up notably from the Protestant clergy, began at that time to see the future of Christian political and social action as lying in the Social Democratic movement, and sought to build a bridge between that movement and the Christian world. Groups of this kind appeared in Germany, Switzerland, France, French-speaking Belgium, and Holland. Nearly always, even in Belgium and France, the initiative came from Protestants, though there were one or two isolated Catholic contributors, notably Fr. Hohoff in Germany. Some of the initiators joined the Socialist Party; but not all went even as far as this. By far the most effective movements were in Holland and Switzerland. The various Dutch groups, in particular, laid solid though as yet narrow foundations with a Fabian tenacity of purpose. They had three main points of departure. In 1902 a group of young 'free-thinking'—in England one would say rather 'liberal' or 'modernist'—Protestant pastors in Friesland began to publish *The Joyful World*, a title directly copied from *Merrie England*, famous in the early days of British socialism. This paper still appears as *Time and Task*. In recent years this group has returned towards orthodox Protestantism and played a notable part in the renewal of the Hervormde Kerk. In 1908 another, at that time more orthodox, group founded a Christian Socialist Union. And there also began before the First World War the 'Woodbrook Workers' Community', an adult education movement inspired by the English Quakers and now centred at Bentveld, near Haarlem. Its leader between the two wars was J. W. Banning, later a Professor of Theology at Leiden, who also from 1932 to 1950 edited *Time and Task*.

In the course of religious socialism's second generation, from the First World War through to around 1950, its weight in different countries changed a good deal. Little more was heard from Belgium, and in Switzerland the movement lost much of its influence in the Socialist Party when it refused to join in plans for a revolution at the end of the 1914–18 war. The French religious socialists acquired some influence among Protestants, and threw up one or two notable leaders; particularly André Philip, who has played a prominent though, in his own party, rather isolated part in postwar French politics and in the European Movement.

In Germany religious socialism grew by the end of the Second World War into an accepted feature of the Socialist party scene. In Austria there arose an interesting though short-lived movement, distinguished by being both working-class—unlike the mainly intellectual movements elsewhere—and Catholic. It was founded by an engineering worker, Otto Bauer (not to be confused with Dr. Otto Bauer, at that time leader of the Austrian Socialist Party), and won a good deal of working-class support, as well as sympathy from both Catholic and Social Democratic leaders who saw in it a real possibility of bridging the gap between the two great trends in Austrian political and social life. It stood for a co-operative, decentralised industrial order, with nationalisation only of key industries, and made clear that the owner-farmer or small independent business man had nothing to fear from it. It accepted the idea of a class struggle, but interpreted in the sense of a battle for the common good by way of the defence of class interests. It was in some ways rather confused over the historic necessity of Socialism and over the role of the Church. It did however draft its programme on cultural matters, notably on the schools questions and on sex, so as to meet Christian views. It also insisted on maintaining its independent existence as a fraction within the Socialist party. But in 1931 it was crippled by Pius XI's declaration, in *Quadragesimo Anno*, that it is impossible for a Catholic to be both a sincere socialist and a true member of the Church. It is possible that if Bauer's movement had stood on its own it would have been covered by the series of rulings by Church authorities on the British Labour Party, to the effect that a politician who calls himself a socialist is not necessarily a socialist within the meaning of *Quadragesimo Anno*. But Bauer and his followers, however well-intentioned in themselves, were members of the fanatically anti-religious Austrian Social Democratic Party, with its tradition not merely of the defence of class interests but of organised violence and if necessary civil war. Therefore they fell under the ban. Though Bauer himself went on with his work, his prospects of any wide success were gone.

However, Bauer's movement pointed the way down a road which the mainly Protestant religious socialists of Holland were presently to follow more successfully. By the nineteen-thirties they had made themselves an established place in the Dutch socialist movement, and in 1937 J. W. Banning was elected to the Socialist party executive. At this point the work of the religious socialists was reinforced by two other influences. First, after some decades' experience, the socialist movements, including the trade unions, were becoming convinced that Christians could never be recruited *en masse* unless they were allowed to come in 'under their own flag'; which meant not merely that they must not be offended by party or union policy, but also that they must be allowed to preserve their independent, organised existence as a Christian group or groups within the

382

Socialist organisations. And secondly, Social Democrats' own views were changing. Many socialist intellectuals were beginning to look for a philosophy which would underline the cultural task of socialism, one less purely rationalist and materialist than Marxism. This led some at least of them, by way of a vague 'world religion', towards Christianity. Among working class socialists there arose:

> An intense need for the ultimate and deepest certainty . . . the urge towards God came up, even though workers themselves seldom or never spoke that prejudice-laden name. (Wilzen and Van Biemen, *Samen op Weg*, 1953, p. 155.)

Party members had for many years been becoming aware of the dryness and lack of depth in Marxism. Now came the collapse of the Italian and later of the powerful and famous Austrian and German socialist movements, and the outstanding embodiments of the democratic Marxist ideal crumbled into dust overnight. Then, further, came the invasion and resistance in Holland itself. Socialists who had once looked on Christians as 'worthy but spineless' now noted with astonishment their firm principles and the sources of inner strength on which they drew. Whence, they began to ask, did these come?

Influences like these were at work all over the Socialist movement in Europe. In conferences at Frankfurt in 1951 and Bentveld in 1953 the Socialist International formally agreed that socialism must not be regarded as in itself an ethic or philosophy of life. It was the practical expression in current conditions of an ethic whose roots might run back to various sources. The source for a particular individual might be Marxist or Kantian 'humanism', or it might be Christianity. Either, for socialists, was equally respectable; for the unifying factor in socialism was its programme, not an identity of ethical or theological beliefs. It was, however, apparent at these conferences that this view was held with very different intensity in different countries. For French or Belgian or Spanish socialists it was little more than a formality. Their anti-religious and above all anti-clerical views remained as before, and their delegates showed little awareness of the conditions on which it was in fact likely that Christians and social democrats could be brought within one organisation. The Belgian delegation at Bentveld, for example, left an impression that the way to attract Catholics was to appeal to them over the heads of their Bishops, on a programme in which items such as attacks on the Catholic schools were apparently to remain unchanged. It is difficult to imagine this line making much impression on the militants of the Belgian Christian Workers' Movement. But it was apparent that in Germany, and to a less extent in Austria, the Socialist party leaders—the same could not always be said of their subordinates or of the rank and file—were making a genuine attempt to understand and meet the Christian point of view. In Holland the shift of socialist opinion had by that time reached the point of a revolution in the Socialist Party's constitution and programme.

This revolution was carried out when the party was being rebuilt after the Second World War. Three main points in particular were clarified.

(1) The Party is now decisively on the side of democracy and law and order. It has become strongly anti-Communist, gives full support to national defence, and has abandoned all thought of revolutionary action. The last occasion when there was any serious suggestion of a Socialist attempt at revolution in Holland was in 1918.

(2) The Party is no longer State socialist in the full sense, nor exclusively concerned with working-class interests. The family, the problems of self-government in the firm and industry, and the interests of farmers and the middle classes now have a large part in its programme.

(3) It is no longer a party of Marxist or indeed any other philosophy, and this is symbolised in the change of its name from 'Social-Democratic Labour Party' to 'Labour Party' without qualification. In line with the Frankfurt and Bentveld resolutions, the party sees itself as simply the meeting place of those who agree on a progressive political programme. The collaboration of these people is valuable only if they have strong principles, rooted in a philosophy of life which they must seek outside the Labour movement. It is expected therefore that each member of the party will be a Catholic, a Protestant, or a 'humanist', and will behave and wish to be treated accordingly.

This implies:

(a) that party members will wish to follow the directions of their Church or equivalent group in political, economic, and social matters. It is explicitly recognised that it is not, for example, 'political Catholicism' for the Pope to issue an Encyclical or the Bishops a Pastoral, and for Catholic members of the party to conform to it.

(b) that Catholic, Protestant, or humanist members of the party will wish to form an organised fraction within the party, since only in this way can their voice be effectively heard. 'Working groups' for each of these denominations are provided for in the party constitution.

(c) that citizens who hold each of these philosophies of life will wish to perpetuate them into the next generation, and have a right to do so. The Party therefore agrees that the adherents of each body of belief are entitled to send their children to schools of their own choice. It is the government's duty to support these schools equally with its own.

On this basis the Labour Party has been able to win the support of a body of both Catholics and Protestants impressive by their quality, though not as yet by their quantity. The Protestant Working Group within the party had by 1954 some 4,500 members, and the Catholic around 800.

THE CASE FOR A BREAK-THROUGH: (2) FRANCE

The initiative for a combined Christian and Socialist Labour Party has come in Holland from the Socialists. In France there has been a corresponding initiative, but coming from the Christian side; that is from Christian trade unionists dissatisfied with the lack of dynamism not only in trade union affairs but also in the social and economic policies of the existing French political parties. The M.R.P. has been informally linked with the C.F.T.C. unions ever since the party began. But dissatisfaction with the M.R.P. as well as with other parties came to a head during the strike wave of August 1953, when M.R.P. leaders failed to give the strikers the support which they and their unions thought right. It achieved concrete formulation through the work of various groups, whose contributions are summed up in the C.F.T.C.'s official discussion organ *Recherches* for January 1955. One group, in Alsace, brought together not only C.F.T.C. militants but also a number of members of the staff of the University of Strasbourg. Another has been based largely on the engineers' and teachers' unions and centred round the review 'Reconstruction', inspired particularly by Paul Vignaux. The C.F.T.C. is strongly represented in the north of France, and several contributions have come from there. Others again have been made from the side of the M.R.P.

Common to all these contributions has been the idea that the tide of social progress can best be set going again in France by strengthening the influence in politics of the democratic trade unions, and in the first place of the largest of them, the C.F.T.C. As to how this is to be done, opinions differ. One school still emphasises, as do the supporters of the Christian parties in Holland, the policies which Christian trade unionists and Christian Democratic politicians have in common; and which they continue to have in common even when, to quote again Etienne Borne's contribution to this discussion, 'a Christian trade unionist regards it as an insult to be identified with the M.R.P.' The problem for this school is not to found a new party but to strengthen the C.F.T.C.'s influence within the M.R.P., on the assumption that in any case a specially close link between the two Christian movements is desirable. As Borne points out, it is largely through the incompetence in political matters of the C.F.T.C.'s own leaders that their influence in the party has been limited since the war. And a policy of regaining influence in the M.R.P. would have at least one obvious advantage over one of establishing a new and more strictly working-class formation. The M.R.P. has a substantial block of middle-class supporters. Many or most of these would be permanently lost to the Right if the working-class wing of the party were to split away on its own; whereas, if that wing can strengthen its influence in the party, the party as a whole, and its middle-class voters and deputies with it, can be swung in favour of the policies which Christian trade unionists have in mind.

Others, however, attach much less importance to the specifically Christian elements in policy which can be taken to be common to the M.R.P. and C.F.T.C. The trouble about the M.R.P. seems to them (it is Sturzo's criticism over again, and that brought against Catholic Action in

2c—C.D. 385

Italy today) to be that it wins support too much on a basis of vague religiosity, and not enough on the soundness and current relevance of its policy. In any case, given the tradition of French politics, the most characteristically Christian elements in policy, such as the schools question, are probably best treated, on this group's view, as Sturzo treated that of the Temporal Power. Let them be left to the ecclesiastical authorities to negotiate as best they may, but be put, so far as Christian politicians are concerned, into cold storage. For their urgency is not absolute and compelling, and to bring them forward in present conditions in France arouses violent prejudice among just those laicist elements of the democratic centre and left whose support is vital for a sound social policy.

If the views summarised in the last paragraph are right, the argument could lead on in either of two directions. On one view, represented notably by the 'Reconstruction' group, the best line is for the trade unions, not indeed to enter politics directly, but to try to win more influence in all the centre or left-wing democratic parties, including the Liberals; in any case, not only in the M.R.P. The first step would be an educational campaign in the unions themselves, to bring home to leaders and members the political meaning of trade union objectives. On this would then be built an attempt to influence political parties in an organised way, after the fashion of the American trade unions. There would be election manifestoes, approaches to candidates and deputies, press campaigns, and all the customary activities of pressure groups; techniques already of course in use, only now their use would be more organised and more skilfully directed. This policy, like that of association with the M.R.P., would have the advantage of allowing the unions to influence middle-class as well as working-class votes by way of the existing parties.

But on another view, represented particularly by the Alsace group, the right policy would be to go over directly to form a Labour Party on British lines, promoted by though not identical with the trade unions. This group is sceptical about the possibilities of influencing political parties from the outside. The unions can effectively control their own party, but not someone else's. And they see in the idea of a Labour Party one special and very great advantage which would probably not follow from either of the other formulas just described. A chief reason why social and economic policy has tended to be less dynamic in France than in, say, Holland, has been that in France the vast majority of the non-Christian Left are Communists, with whom the democratic parties find it difficult to work, whereas in Holland they are Social Democrats with whom Christian Democrats or Liberals can and do work perfectly well. The problem in France is to find a way of attracting out of the Communist Party a large body of workers who are unlikely to support a party which is either Christian or largely middle-class. The Socialist Party has lost a great deal of its working-class support,[1] and would probably no longer constitute a suitable nucleus; especially as it would be important to attract also the support of Christian workers, to whom the Socialist Party appears as one of the main pillars, past and present, of anti-clerical 'humanism'. The answer would appear to be a new Labour Party. The Alsace group feel that such a party, rather on Dutch Labour Party lines, could in fact win enough support among the democratic Left and Centre, and recapture enough Communist voters for democracy, to transform the face of French politics. The choice between these various views remains to be made. There has not yet been, as in Holland, an actual 'break-through' on the Left, though there is a long-standing one on the Right: for right-wing French Catholics group themselves freely with non-Christians in conservative and nationalist parties, though they do not, traditionally, join the liberals in the Radical Party.

THE CASE AGAINST THE BREAK-THROUGH: HOLLAND

The case against the break-through has been most fully set out in Holland, where the great majority of both Protestant and Catholic leaders have refused to accept the Labour Party's argument. They claim, first, that on a wide range of issues Christians as such—irrespective of any differences which may exist between various Christian groups—are likely to disagree with the policy pursued by even the reformed Labour Party. There are questions concerning the family, such as family allowances, or divorce, or the suppression of indecent publications, or parents' right to a choice of schools; on this latter point Christian politicians prefer to rely more on their own strong right arms than on the assurances of other parties. There is the question of 'subsidiarity' or 'sovereignty in one's own sphere', and of going far enough but not too far in the field of nationalisation. There are problems of property formation and of making adequate the payment for skilled work, on which the Labour Party has been by the Christian parties' standards lukewarm. And there are various questions of foreign policy on which Christians have felt they had a distinctive contribution to make; as for instance United Nations or UNESCO policies on education and birth control.

It could evidently be argued that on issues like these Christians can make their weight felt through participation in neutral parties as well as through possessing parties of their own. But it is argued that in the particular circumstances of Holland, and of the Labour Party in particular, this is unlikely to be the case. Christian influence in politics is likely to be strong to the extent that Christians are a strong and organised force, made up of men and women soaked in Christian principles, and in a position to demonstrate their principles in action; for example counts

[1] See the analysis of class support for various parties in Chapter XXII, Table 34.

more than moralising. In none of these respects, it is said, is a Christian in the Labour Party as well placed as a Christian in the Catholic or one of the Protestant parties.

First, though Christians in the 'working groups' of the Labour Party are an organised force, they are a small minority (there is an obvious parallel here with Bauer's movement) in a party whose majority is still overwhelmingly 'humanist'. Moreover, working groups exist in the Labour Party only at national headquarters and in a few local centres, so that Christian organisation in the party is very incomplete. The working groups are also an extra complication in an already very complicated party machine, so that in practice their contact with and influence on the party executive can be only occasional. In the Christian parties, on the other hand, Protestants and Catholics have organisations which are Christian to the core and solidly organised, and, when they act together, can dominate Dutch politics. Even separately, the Catholic and Protestant parties are powerful political forces, well able to demonstrate their principles in action. Christians in the Labour Party themselves agree that in many respects they have failed to pass their views into the party's programme or into the actions of the Ministers it has contributed to various governments. By contrast, the Anti-Revolutionaries or the Catholic People's Party have printed their mark deeply on four generations of Dutch political history, and not least on that of the Labour Party itself. The strong and independent stand taken by Christians in politics has contributed as much as any other factor, as has been seen, to the Labour Party's own internal revolution.

As for individuals being 'soaked in Christian principles', it is of course true that Christians in the Dutch Labour Party can and do meet other Christians for discussion at the level of principles. They can also read the Christian press, listen to Christian broadcasts, support Christian schools, and meet among themselves to hammer out their Christian principles in relation to Labour Party policy. But, being involved to the extent that they are with non-Christians, they do not live in so Christian an atmosphere, and are not so soaked in Christian principles, as people who belong to a Christian party. And those who give up their adherence to a Christian party will not necessarily continue their support for other Christian institutions. As Dutch Christians of all denominations traditionally insist, the various institutions of Christian life depend on and support one another. The press supports the unions and the unions support the party, and so on; all combining to ensure that members' political, economic, and social decisions are taken against a thoroughly Christian background. Each influence gains in strength from its combination with others. And this argument also works in reverse. Breaking away from the Christian parties may be the thin end of the wedge. Those who take the first step may take others, to the non-Christian trade unions or press or schools; and the whole Christian environment of their life and decisions then breaks up.

But, the supporters of the break-through argue, even supposing that a Christian party is the best means of promoting the policies characteristic of Christians as such, what of that much wider and very important range of issues on which opinions are divided among Christians as among others? The Christian parties take up a dead-centre position, drawing members from both Left and Right. Does experience not prove that this attempt to keep a balance leads to immobility in social policy? Is it not possible that a clear Left-Right division would secure a more dynamic social policy, though no doubt with its intervals of conservatism and consolidation?

Supporters of the Christian parties reply that it is precisely since they became powerful in the land, in the eighteen-seventies and eighteen-eighties, that Holland has ceased to be an economic and social backwater and become in many ways a model of social progress to the rest of the world. The danger of social immobility is parried in two ways. First, the Christian social organisations are themselves well able to press their interests within the Christian parties. The incorporation of a 'social' wing in the older Christian parties was described in Chapter XIX. In the particular case of Holland, the transformation within the last ten or fifteen years in the social and economic policies of the Anti-Revolutionaries has already been recorded. On the Catholic side the general election of 1952 led to a good illustration of how the pressure of interest groups works. Before the elections there was dissatisfaction on both the left and the right wing of the party. Some right-wing elements broke away and founded what was in effect a Catholic liberal party, the K.N.P., which had some success at the elections.[1] On the left there was talk of a Catholic labour party based on the trade unions, and a number of Catholic workers seem in fact to have broken away and voted for the Dutch Labour Party. Weakened in these ways, the Catholic People's Party suffered what in a country with proportional representation must be regarded as relatively severe losses. Waking up on the morning after this performance, all concerned experienced a severe shock. New efforts were made to meet the claims of both wings. A network of local study groups was set up to keep the party leadership in closer touch with the rank and file. Through this and other measures a generally acceptable balance in the party's policy was restored.

But also, and secondly, the fact that the vast majority of non-Christian left-wingers in Holland vote for a democratic party means that the dilemma

[1] Its two members of parliament have since joined up again with the Catholic People's Party.

389

faced by Christian Democrats in France or Italy, of alliance with democratic but immobile centre or centre-right parties or with socially dynamic but anti-democratic parties of the left, does not arise. When the balance of political forces tilts that way, there is nothing to prevent an alliance between the Labour Party and one or all of the Christian Democratic parties, usually in practice first and foremost the Catholic Party; and governments based on such an alliance and having a correspondingly 'progressive' policy have in fact been a regular feature of the Dutch political scene since the Second World War.

The stand taken by the majority of Dutch Catholic and Protestant politicians received the backing in the spring of 1954 of a strongly worded pastoral letter from the Dutch Catholic Bishops, which, without actually forbidding Catholics to join the Labour Party, severely censured those who had done so. The principles of the Pastoral received strong support from Protestant as well as Catholic commentators, though the fact that a political decision appeared in this case to be imposed by the Bishops proved embarrassing to the Catholic People's Party itself; and its leader made clear that he did not propose to use the Pastoral as an electoral argument. The Catholic working group of the Labour Party, seeing the question as one of political tactics rather than of religious principle, reconsidered it on that basis and decided to abide by their own judgment and remain in the Labour Party. There at the time of writing the matter rests.

OPTIONS FOR THE FUTURE

Where does all this leave us? The debate over 'We Must Fight in the Open Field' is still very much alive, not only in politics but among the social organisations. It does not apply to Christian Action, which by general agreement is and must remain a denominational activity. But it does arise over the whole front of Christian Democracy. There are strong partisans on both sides, prepared to defend their views as a matter of principle. It is unlikely that there will be any sudden, mass, conversion of Christian Democrats from one view to the other. The case of the Dutch Labour Party is instructive on this. The religious socialist movement and the shift in views among Socialists and Christian Democrats of which it took advantage to begin the 'break-through' evolved over some sixty years, at the usual generation-to-generation pace; one generation to establish the religious socialist groups, another for them to build outwards from this foundation and win a wide influence. That is still the pace of evolution to be expected. But it is clear that the argument will go on and that there will be evolution in one direction or another. Therefore it is worth while, at the risk of some repetition, to set out more formally the options implicit both in the French and Dutch cases just discussed and in the debate in the Christian social movement as a whole. There would seem to be four:

(1) Christian parties or social organisations, as at present established; disregarding for the moment the exact degree of a-confessionality which each has attained.
(2) Christian 'working groups', as in the Dutch Labour Party or the Austrian trade unions, within neutral parties or organisations.
(3) Christians in neutral parties or organisations, without any groups of fractions of their own, but continuing as at present to receive personal training for public life through some form of Christian Action.
(4) Christians in neutral parties or organisations, without either working groups or special training from Christian Action.

According to the Christian Democrats' own theorists, the choice between these is a matter of circumstances and tactics; for each of the two poles and of the intermediate solutions may be appropriate in particular circumstances. In a society in which all were convinced and practising Christians, so Fr. Oswald von Nell-Breuning has argued, the normal formula would be (4). Political and social problems would then in any case be discussed in the light of Christian standards, and no special, separate, organisation of Christians would be required. The choice of formulas in the actual and existing world would seem, in the light not only of theory but of the arguments actually used in the debates in Holland, France, or Germany, to turn on a mixture of considerations of ends and means.

THE CHOICE AS DETERMINED BY AIMS

First, how many and how important are the political or social issues—that is the issues within the ordinary field of Christian Democracy—on which Christians as such, or substantial bodies of them drawn from different classes or political directions, agree among themselves, but disagree with non-Christians of the same country or party? How important are such issues, compared with others on which Christians differ among themselves but agree with this or that party or fraction among non-Christians? It is easy to imagine circumstances in which differences between Christians and non-Christians would have very little importance. The 'Christian' character of Christian Democratic programmes lies after all essentially in their catholicity—their completeness and balance—rather than in the inclusion in them of items which non-Christians could not accept. Others besides Christian Democrats may stand and have stood for political and industrial democracy, a decentralised economy, a strong family policy, and respect for the rights of different 'spiritual families', including the right of parents to choose their children's schools. Christian Democracy has certainly in the past made a characteristic contribution to European political thought, in the shape of its pluralist or federal conception of economic, social, and political policy: the belief that stress should be laid on the whole range of social units from the individual to international society, instead of being concentrated with Liberals on the individual or with Socialists on the State. But this conception, like the liberal, socialist, and conservative ideals before it, is today becoming part of the common fund on which Western democrats of all ideologies draw. As the Dutch case or the analysis of labour movements shows, democratic non-Christians have in many ways modified their views in recent years to meet Christian objections. With the clearer distinction today between Christian Action and Christian Democracy, there is less danger than there was for example in the times of the Italian Congress Movement or of the beginnings of the Clerical Workers' Union in France of burdening Christian Democracy with what is properly a part of Christian Action's specifically religious mission. And some of the ecclesiastical problems hitherto most characteristic of the Christian political parties, such as that of Christian teaching in the schools, are beginning to appear in a new and less prominent perspective. Where, as in France, the schools problem is not solved, it goes without saying that Christian believers still regard the Christian school as worth fighting for. But the Christian family and youth movements now offer many alternative channels for winning young people for Christianity. Is the Christian school still important enough, it begins to be asked, to justify sacrificing the chances of social progress, or risking the revival of anti-clerical prejudice against the other work of the Church, in what may be a vain effort to attain it?

The question is thus one of fact. How big is the difference in aims between Christians and 'humanists' of one shade or another? Most people connected with the Christian Democratic political and labour movements in Western Europe, and a great many of those connected with the other Christian social movements, would still say that the differences remain wide enough, here and now, to justify keeping their movements on at least an a-confessional Christian basis. A Christian Democratic politician is likely to support this view over against other democratic parties with arguments like those quoted above for Holland. In countries like Italy and perhaps France—Germany in the period of reconstruction has been another such case—where democracy itself is insecure, he may push the argument deeper. Here, he will say, the special service of independent Christian parties is to act as a bridge between Left and Right and as the cement in a democratic alliance: a task for which the 'centre' character of these parties specially qualifies them. And, he may add, the question is not merely whether differences between Christians and non-Christians *do* exist. It is also whether they *might* exist. Christians are very conscious of being in some countries a minority, and in all faced with a 'humanism' which:

Takes in principle no account of the existence of a personal God . . . which in practice amounts to denying God. Insofar as it is based on sound natural reasoning, and, unconsciously, on Christian traditions, it may perhaps for a time offer some hand-hold to people who have no other. But in the end, and sooner rather than later, the attempt will prove to have been idle. Humanism treats good and evil as relative, takes no or insufficient account of original sin and human weakness, and above all conduces to a morality without God: an attempt as futile as to try to create or maintain the world without its first and deepest cause, God. Of this humanism may be said with Jeremias: 'Me they forsook, the fountain of living water, and thereupon they dug cisterns of their own, leaking cisterns, that had no water to give them.' (Jer. 2.13.) Though the purpose may be other and perhaps better, this is basically a new attempt to build a Tower of Babel. . . . History repeats itself: to build a society without God has always led to tragic failure. (*De Katholiek in het Openbare Leven van deze Tijd*, 1954, p. 39.)

Where 'humanism' will lead is not clear. But a good many Christians are taking no risks. They prefer to remain a power in their own right, not beholden to others.

THE CHOICE AS DETERMINED BY MEANS

But supposing that Christians as such have in fact a distinctive view to put, how can it be put most effectively? There seem to be four main considerations.

The first is the percentage of Christians in the population, and the way in which the electoral system and other features of the social structure allow them to bring their influence to bear. The Christian Democratic parties and social organisations in Western Europe arose in their present form because Christians' numbers and the conditions of political and social action were such as to allow them to be a powerful force if, but only if, they acted together as a body. Dutch Catholics, to quote their argument again, have been numerous enough to constitute under proportional representation the most powerful political force in the country; but they are still a minority, and one which, in the conditions of the past, would have met with little consideration in combined movements in which the majority was 'humanist' or even Protestant. Reference has also been made to the C.B.T.B.'s argument that it was only after a Protestant farmers' organisation was founded that Protestant farmers began to be elected to positions in the 'neutral' organisation. One of the chief points in dispute between supporters and opponents of the 'break-through' is whether Christians are or are not today strong enough to be powerful even when distributed among a number of neutral parties or organisations.

The answer to this question depends, secondly, not only on numbers and voting or organising arrangements but on Christians' personal and social formation. Though supporters of the break-through deny the value

393

of Christian parties and trade unions, and many of them doubt the need even for Christians in neutral organisations such as the Dutch Labour Party to form working parties or groups, not many go so far as to deny the value of any organisation at all for Christians in public life. It is generally agreed that, if the Christians' voice is to be effectively heard in the complicated and organised life of today, they must receive personal, individual, initial training through Catholic Action and the (approximately) corresponding Protestant movements, and have further opportunities for discussion and reflection in the light of Christian principles as their experience grows. But this training may issue in social action at two very different levels. At the lower level it may make people aware enough of the implications of their faith to stand together with other Christians in matters of clear common concern, and to follow a Christian line so long as they have support and encouragement from their environment. At the higher level it may make them fit to carry on an apostolate or develop a Christian line in a neutral or hostile environment even without the immediate support of an organised body of fellow-Christians. The practical question is whether the Christians in a given environment are numerous and highly enough trained, and have enough backing from the educational Christian Action organisations to be able to take and hold to a Christian line without further organised support.

Opponents of the break-through do not necessarily deny that there is scope for small numbers of highly-trained apostles and specialists to move ahead of the general mass of Christians and penetrate neutral or 'humanist' organisations. But they are very much aware of the danger that even specialists may fail to maintain a genuinely Christian line in a colourless or anti-Christian environment. The most striking example of this in recent years was the collapse in 1953 of the first phase of the worker-priests' movement in France. Worker-priests were launched into a largely pagan environment subject to highly-organised Marxist influence. Many of them had inadequate initial training and little opportunity of maintaining, so to speak, contact with their base. A number as a result were penetrated by their environment instead of penetrating it, and the scheme in its original form had to be wound up and replaced by another. In the opinion of, for example, the Belgian Christian Workers' Movement or the main Dutch Protestant and Catholic movements, the place even of the Christian élite in the modern, largely de-Christianised world is in Christian organisations where they can have the support of their environment in working out and applying Christian principles; and this applies still more to the weaker vessels, the general mass of Christians. And—the argument has already been set out in the Dutch case above—Christians are more likely to be a shining light and to influence non-Christians effectively, if they band together to demonstrate their principles in action than if they lose themselves promiscuously in the non-Christian mass. The unit of the apostolate is not the individual Christian but the Christian community: the Church that is in parliament, or in the labour force of a particular factory, or among the young people of a town or parish. By all means let there be co-operation between Christians and non-Christians; but let it be between organised groups in which each can sail 'under his own flag'. It is significant that in Holland, where the problems of the break-through have been most fully worked through, even its supporters do not deny that in modern conditions Christians must appear in a neutral organisation as an organised body if they want their voice to be effectively heard. The only presumable exception would be in cases like those of the family movements or the C.I.S.L. unions where Christians have so large a share in the leadership that a 'neutral' organisation is in effect Christian.

If organisation and the environment matter so much, it follows, thirdly, that in discussing the case for a break-through neither politics nor any other sort of social activity can be treated in isolation. They are part of a complex which includes not only the whole range of Christian Democratic activities but also those of Christian Action, the Christian press and schools, and the Churches themselves. It may be, as the Belgians and the Dutch so often point out, a case of hanging together or hanging separately; knock one key item out of the complex of influences which help Christians of a given country or class to live their lives and make their decisions in the light of their principles, and the complex as a whole will fall to pieces. The argument can also cut the other way. If the interests of Christian families, for example, are being looked after by a powerful family movement able to make its influence felt among politicians of all shades, there is less need for a Christian political party with a special family programme. But either way, it is by reference to the whole complex of Christian interventions in social life that the rightness or wrongness of a change in any one form of intervention must be judged.

Fourthly, the way in which Christians should organise depends on the balance of power and form of organisation among non-Christians. As the case of Holland or Belgium shows, the Christian Democratic parties' desire to represent all classes and to take up a centre position in politics is perfectly compatible with a dynamic social policy provided that an external as well as an internal condition is fulfilled. The internal condition is that just considered. A party must not be isolated: all the relevant interests among Christians themselves must be organised enough to make their influence felt within it. There must be a strong 'social' as well as a conservative wing. The external condition is that democrats and progressives—those who belong to the democratic wing of what is sometimes called the 'Party of Movement'—outside the Christian ranks should also be effectively organised, and able either to stimulate the Christian Demo-crats through competition or to form a powerful alliance with them. It is quite possible for the conception of a Christian centre party to be workable in a country where this condition is fulfilled, but not in a country like Italy, where there are eight or nine Communist or Social-Communist votes for every one for a democratic Socialist: or like France. In these latter cases a conception like that of the Alsace group of the C.F.T.C. may turn out to be the best; one, that is, which involves splitting Christian Democrats between a neutral Labour Party, better able than a specifically Christian or a weak Social Democratic party to win over potential Communist voters, and another neutral party to its right.

CONCLUSION

It would take a bold man to guess where the present debate over confessional organisation and the 'break-through' will end. Either approach can be justified in particular cases, and indeed there is no particular reason why, as is in practice happening in Holland, the two should not be com-bined. It is commonplace to think of the propagation of the Christian religion as a process in which the existing Christian community is organised in parishes, while missionaries feel their way among the rest of society and try to establish Christian groups of some sort there. Only later will these in their turn be consolidated into parishes, which may or may not be made up of the same sort of people or undertake activities of the same kind as the previously existing parishes, or be formally linked to them; as apart, that is, from their common membership in the Church as a whole. So also in the political and social world it may be perfectly in order for the mass of those who already think as Christians in their social or political relations to stand together in a body, while a select band of missionaries feels its way ahead into groups of other traditions and tries to plant the ideas of Christian Democracy there. The result may be to bring more recruits to the existing Christian parties or social organisations. It may instead be to build Christian or Christian-inspired groups or fractions of a new type.

What seems on the whole most probable is that there will be no clear victory for any one formula, but that there will come in due course to be more flexibility; a clearer understanding of the usefulness of different formulas in different times and places, and more readiness to switch from one to another as occasion demands. It is perfectly possible for the same structure of Christian Democracy which serves Holland well to serve France badly. Dutch politics, with a Christian Democratic core and Liberal and Social Democratic wings, are among the most stable, yet also progressive, in the world. The French political system too has a Christian Democratic party near its centre, but the results have hardly been so happy. And it is perfectly possible also that the organisation which suited the last generation of French or Dutch Christians will not fit the problems of the next. It may well be the task of the present and coming generation of Christians in Europe to reduce such empirical findings as these to order, and to build on them a general theory of the organisation and methods of Christian Democracy; a strategy of organisation, to set alongside the 'middle principles', or strategy of ideas, with which Part II of this book was concerned. For though the raw materials for such a theory of organisation are available, they have not yet been put together. The 'break-through' controversy may be the occasion for doing so.

PART IV

PART IV

CHAPTER XXIV

CHRISTIAN DEMOCRACY IN THE PER-
SPECTIVE OF CHURCH HISTORY

THE Christian Democratic movements, as has been seen, refer on the one hand—directly or indirectly—to the Christian revelation and the tradition of the Church, and on the other to the practical experience of lay Christians during the last four or five generations. From this combination of revelation and historical experience they have built up a set of principles for handling modern political, economic, and social problems; a comprehensive, genuinely catholic synthesis, drawing on all the main currents of modern social thought. A movement with characteristics of these kinds has a clearly identifiable place in the general history of the Christian Churches. We have considered it so far in a relatively short perspective, covering only those few generations in which Christian Democracy has actually been coming to birth. It remains now to situate it in the longer perspective of Christianity as a whole.

EARLY CHRISTIANITY: ACCENT ON REVELATION

The growth and spread of Christianity is sometimes compared to an incoming tide, in which waves may run forward or back, but each wave, up to the present day, has left its mark higher than the last. Or it might be better to think of it as a series of tides, starting from the neap and moving upwards to the spring. For besides the short-term, often localised gains and losses which can properly be represented by waves, there have been ebbs and flows. But always each flow runs higher up the beach, or floods out over more new lands, than the last.

The first of these tides ran in during the five centuries from the birth of Christ to the end of the Western Roman Empire. The achievement of the Church in this time was the work mainly of what today are the Orthodox churches. They stood under the immediate impact of revelation and were busy working out its implications for doctrine and worship. The fundamental importance of revelation, as apart from natural reasoning, is brought out by St. Paul in his first Epistle to the Corinthians.

So we read in Scripture, I will confound the wisdom of the wise men, disappoint the calculations of the prudent. What has become of the wise men, the scribes, and the philosophers of this age we live in? Must we not say that God has turned our worldly wisdom to folly? When God showed us his wisdom the world, with all its wisdom, could not find its way to God; and now God would use a foolish thing, our preaching, to save those who will believe in it. Here are the Jews asking for signs and wonders, here are the Greeks intent on their philosophy. But what we preach is Christ crucified, to the Jews a discouragement, to the Gentiles mere folly; but to us who have been called, Jews and Gentiles alike, Christ the power of God, Christ the wisdom of God. So much wiser than men is God's foolishness, so much stronger than men is God's weakness.

In the main stream of Christian thought it has always been clear that revelation completes natural knowledge but does not replace it. To have a full picture of the world, one which will allow Christians to take hold of their surroundings and shape them according to their principles, the broad and long views of revelation must be filled in with the detail of purely human science, experience, and intuition. But revelation, as St. Paul says, is primary and basic, and the early Church had plenty on its hands without proceeding far beyond it towards a synthesis of revealed and natural knowledge. It had to make the message of revelation known for the first time. It had to establish and confirm the authority—bishops, councils, the ultimate appeal to Rome—by which the once-for-all deposit of revelation was to be safeguarded and defined. It had to work out, with immense controversy, what the basic doctrines to be derived from revelation actually were. It had to build from nothing the necessary structures of church organisation, and worship. Persecuted at one time, stifled by the protection of the Emperors at another, it faced immense difficulties both internal and external, of doctrine, management, and bare survival. It is not surprising that the early Christians tended to let the world around them look after itself, with only the minimum of protest against its grosser abuses. They preferred to concentrate on Revelation and life after death, rather than attempt to grasp the world and thoroughly transform it with the aid of natural reasoning.

Bit by bit, however, under the pressures of day to day life, and of the need to define and defend the Church's position in reasonable terms, the idea of a synthesis of natural reasoning and revelation made its way. This was true of the high levels of philosophy and history. It was also true of social affairs. Is wealth—or power—worth having? What constitutes true wealth? May the Church own property? How is it to be administered? What value is to be attached to work, to particular worldly callings, to particular types of income—notably from interest on money? Granted that it is right to work and earn an income, how much may one keep for oneself? How much should be redistributed for the benefit of those less well off, or of the clergy? What about the State and taxes? Is communism the ideal? Such problems as these were by no means at the centre of the

Church's thought even, say, in the third or fourth century after Christ. But they were coming to be treated more and more thoroughly with a combination of Scriptural reference and sturdy common sense, backed by subtler natural law arguments taken over from the Greek and Roman philosophers.

These excursions into natural reasoning were not always happy. Tertullian, who produced a devastating broadside under the title of *The Way Women Get Themselves Up*, observed that if God had meant people to wear gorgeous blue and purple, he would have made sheep grow purple and blue wool. A number of other Fathers propounded in effect the following theory. Suppose that a man and wife have £X a year, and the surplus above their reasonable needs, which they ought for the good of their souls to devote to the relief of the poor, is £Y. Then, if four children are born to them, the poor ought to get £$3Y$ per annum; for now there are six souls to be saved instead of two, that is three times as many. One does not need to be a welfare economist to see where the logic has slipped. Gradually, however, a solid body of doctrine emerged, at the practical as well as the speculative level. When in the fifth century St. Augustine summed up and clarified what had gone before, the starting-point of the medieval Catholic synthesis was well established. The greatest good of mankind is peace in a harmonious order; one in which every man, and every thing, has found the right place, and fills it fully and competently. What is this order? It is defined first of all by the divine law, the relation of men and things to God. Secondly, the ideal as defined by the divine law can in many cases be read out of the world of nature, by purely natural reasoning. Thirdly, however, sin—sin on the spot, so to speak, or the results of past sin, whether by those currently involved in a problem or by others—often makes it impossible to achieve the ideal of the divine and natural law on earth. In any given set of earthly conditions, there is a best possible solution to current problems, one which comes nearest to the ideal: but this will not necessarily correspond with the ideal itself. Such a solution may emerge even from the hands of men who are not aiming at the ideal, but have some lower and perhaps opposite aim in mind; men who, personally, will have no place in the eternal City of God. It is not for that reason alone to be despised by Christians, living as they do in an imperfect world. Here is the famous distinction, which runs through all later Christian discussion, between the ideal *thesis* and the concession to the hardness of human hearts, the *hypothesis*.

THE MIDDLE AGES: THE CATHOLIC SYNTHESIS

In due course the first high tide of Christianity ebbed. The life of the Church sank in many places, particularly in the West, to a low level. Much of what had been Christian territory in the Middle East, North

Africa, or Spain was lost to the Moslems. The Christian faith, established and defined within the political and social framework of the Roman Empire, had not penetrated this framework deeply enough to inspire an order capable of standing its ground in the face of barbarian or Moslem attacks. But presently the ebb also ended in its turn, and from the tenth to the thirteenth century the tide again flowed in. The lead now passed from the Eastern Churches to those of the West, and what are now the Orthodox Churches broke away from the Catholic Church; temporarily in the ninth century, permanently in the eleventh. Geographically, this age saw Christianity spread wider than ever before, from Greenland across to China, and much ground lost to the Moslems was won back. On the side of doctrine, the Catholic Church now moved on from the point reached by St. Augustine to establish a comprehensive synthesis of revealed and natural knowledge; one capable of carrying Christian thought into each corner of everyday life.

The medieval synthesis was a colossal achievement, attained by facing squarely the conditions which making and defending such a synthesis implies. It must, first of all, be immensely detailed. Consider for example the medieval doctrine of the Just Price. Such a price will involve payment in accordance with the true long-term value to consumers of the goods or services supplied, disregarding elements of monopoly, temporary gluts and famines, and the ignorance and eagerness of particular buyers. It will enable the producer, provided he is of standard efficiency, to earn whatever society regards as a reasonable return for a man of his skill and social standing, allowing for his family as well as his personal needs, and for all necessary costs. It will take account of the wider repercussions of each transaction on society as a whole; we would think, in modern times, of such problems as town planning, unemployment, or inflation. It will look to the future as well as the present; the needs of investment, for example. What, in any specific case, each of these rules implies, may be decided in the market, or by public authority, or by common opinion and discussion. Each phrase here opens out whole text-books of economic and social analysis. And the complexity is due to the nature of the problem, not to the enthusiasm of scholastics for debates on how many angels can dance on the point of a pin. Nineteenth-century economic analysis showed a smooth but quite deceptive simplicity. For many years now the rocks of reality have been emerging piecemeal from its receding tide. And the picture which now emerges begins to look like that of Thomas Aquinas, not of Ricardo or Carl Menger or of Stanley Jevons.

A complete synthesis of revelation and natural reasoning must also be prepared to move in the world of the hypothesis as well as of the thesis; to say what is the best of a bad job. It is no doubt regrettable, for instance, that business men, if they are to stay in business in certain times and places, should have to falsify their tax returns, defraud the Customs, or deliver nine cubic yards where they have invoiced ten. But there may quite genuinely be justification for it.[1] Yet at the same time ideal standards must be upheld; first of all because they are the ideal, and efforts must be made at least to move in their direction; and secondly because they are in fact often attainable, and, if so, should be attained.

A synthesis which is so complicated, and needs such varied interpretation according to time and place, must also have an authority to define and interpret it. This authority must be prepared to go further into the world of natural reasoning, and of the hypothesis as well as the thesis, than would be needed to safeguard and interpret the deposit of revealed truth alone. It may be of more than one kind, and indeed two or more types of authority may be used at once. It may be, as in the Middle Ages, a Pope and Curia. It may be, as in the modern world of science, the common opinion of experts, focussed through machinery for organised discussion. The latter, as the example of science shows, can be effective as well as the former. An authority, however, there must in either case be, to prevent confusion and safeguard established truth.

The medieval synthesis met these three conditions, and illustrated both the advantages and the dangers which they imply. It avoided the danger of a position like that taken up by the early Church, with its heavy reliance on revelation; that is, of leaving the ordinary affairs of life to settle themselves, or else to be judged by the absolute standard of the divine law without regard for the actual conditions of the world. These are the characteristic faults of the 'sect' type of Christianity, which in all ages has been deeply suspicious of Church authority, of elaborate chains of natural reasoning, and of the apparent betrayal of ideals by those who argue realistically in the 'hypothesis'. Of such Christians it can quite fairly be said that they can save themselves, but others they cannot save. They can build an admirable small world of their own, and live in it in a way which may be, and has again and again been, an inspiration to others. But history shows that a Christianity which is to take hold of the general mass of a people, not merely of the perfect few, must be of the 'Church' type, ready to mobilise detailed reasoning from experience or first principles, to move in the world of reality as well as of the ideal, and equipped with strong organisation and authority. These conditions the medieval synthesis admirably fulfilled.

On the other hand, the fears of the 'sectarian' Christians of all ages, and of those of like mind, such as the early Franciscans, who have kept their place in the Church, have not been idle. The Church of the Middle Ages,

[1] These cases are taken from the textbook by Fr. Albert Müller, S.J., on *La Morale et la Vie des Affaires*, Casterman, 1951: published by the Belgian Catholic employers' association (French-speaking section: A.P.I.C.).

precisely because of its success in linking natural reasoning to revelation, risked going too far down that road. It was in danger of not seeing the wood for the trees; of forgetting the guiding lines of revelation and the prime importance of moral and religious factors. A great Pope like Hildebrand (St. Gregory VII), in the eleventh century, might fight his battles in a high spiritual cause and with mainly spiritual weapons. His successors were not always easy to distinguish from the other intriguing lay princes of the time. 'Realism' gained ground at the expense of ideals. And, with its towering hierarchy, its canon law, and its swelling Civil Service, the Church at certain moments looked more like a lawyer's office, or a branch of big business, than the community of the believers in Christ. The sins of pride and materialism flourished nowhere more strongly than at Rome.

This was a short-fall by comparison with the standards of the Early Church. The medieval Church, however, also fell short in one respect where the early Church too had provided no solution. In principle, the medieval synthesis was capable of adjustment to any new or changing social circumstances. The divine and natural law, its authors recognised, remains the same in all times and cultures. But its application varies according to physical, biological, and social circumstances. This is true of points of detailed application, which raise no issue of principle; whether, as it might be, the rule of the road is to drive on the left or the right. It is also true of the 'middle principles' which represent the general lines of action suitable to a particular culture. 'Middle principles' are the characteristic expression of the 'hypothesis', the nearest approximation to ideal standards possible in a particular age and place, in the actual conditions of an imperfect world. Though, therefore, they may remain constant for years on end, and perhaps for the whole life of a culture, they have no *absolute* value. In the end they change. All this was, in principle, fully agreed by the authors of the medieval synthesis. Individuals who followed on in their tradition—St. Antonino in Florence, for instance, or Lessius in Belgium—did in fact in later centuries do a great deal to adapt the thought of the Middle Ages to changing social conditions. But the adaptation of so vast a body of ideas needs not merely agreement in principle, plus the effort of a few pioneers, but also, so to speak, built-in mechanisms of change, to ensure that the current synthesis is up to date. It is here that medieval thought fell short, and that, on the contrary, Reformed Christianity made its greatest contribution.

THE REFORMATION: DYNAMIC ADAPTATION AND THE ROLE OF THE LAITY

This contribution emerged from what in itself was a disaster to Christianity. From the end of the thirteenth to the sixteenth century the Christian tide again ran out. The defects of the medieval approach made themselves felt. Christianity in the previous centuries had taken a firmer grip on nature and society; but society and nature in their turn seemed in these two centuries to have Christianity by the throat. Church leadership was worldly, when not positively corrupt, and one materialist Beelzebub resolutely refused to be cast out by another. Externally, Christianity was weakened and lost much ground. All over Asia it was either weakened or wiped out. The Western Church tried to raise a force to save the Byzantine Empire, but failed. The Empire finally went under in 1453. Though the Orthodox Church survived, its leadership fell more and more to its Russian branch, and turned still further away from the West: for the Greek Churches were now under the Turks, whereas the Russian Church was associated with a State not only Christian but independent and powerful.

The Western Church itself ended this period of decline with a threefold failure. In the first place, it split into two main branches, Protestant and Catholic, with various further sub-divisions on the Protestant side. The Catholic Church kept the fullness of the faith. But it was Reformed Christianity, as will be shown, which pioneered the strategy and tactics by which Christian influence could best be brought to bear on the problems of what was coming to be a rapidly changing world. Neither Protestant nor Catholic, in these circumstances, could give the world all that Christianity should have been able to offer.

Secondly, in the face of new developments in natural reasoning—in philosophy, theology, politics, or science—the Church failed to show clearly and forcibly how these developments were relevant to revelation, and revelation to them. It was not quick enough to take up the new threads and weave them into its own pattern of thought. As a result, these developments tended to proceed independently of, and to some extent in opposition to, Christianity.

Thirdly, the Church's worldliness and political intrigues undermined its spiritual authority to the point where, in public affairs at least, it in effect collapsed. The religious and moral authority of the Popes stood high enough in the twelfth century to be imposed even on kings. The churches of the sixteenth century or later, Catholic and Protestant alike, were more likely to find themselves 'protected' by some monarch in a sense equivalent to 'annexed'. The Thirty Years' War was wound up on the formula that the people's religion should follow the king's. This principle was in honour outside as well as in Germany, and was pursued as eagerly by the Protestant Elizabeth I of England as by the Catholic Philip II of Spain.

Nevertheless, from this disastrous period there emerged at least one important new acquisition, namely the techniques, pioneered by the new Protestant Churches, for coping with a world of change. It was in these centuries that the pace of economic and social innovation was beginning to accelerate sharply, marking the transition from the relative stability of society in the Middle Ages to the continuous process of change in which we live today. And there is no question that Protestantism, with its fresh approach, was for centuries more successful than Catholicism in maintaining Christian belief and influence on social policies in the face of this growing flood of innovation. Catholic countries tended either to be influenced little and late by the new developments, especially those of the Industrial Revolution, or to be unsuccessful in understanding and controlling them.

The reason why Protestantism was so much more successful in maintaining Christian penetration into the life of a changing world has often been obscured by concentrating on the association between Protestantism and capitalism. It is perfectly true that Protestantism did contribute to the rise of capitalism, and may even have been the decisive factor in it. Max Weber's demonstration of this has often been attacked, but never overthrown. It ranks indeed as probably the most important illustration in social science of the primacy of moral and religious over social and material factors in social change. But nothing that Max Weber or anyone else has said indicates that, if Christian influence for between three and four hundred years kept pace with social change in Reformed more than in Catholic countries, this was merely because it was a capitalist age and capitalism and Protestantism went well together. The greater Christian penetration in the Reformed countries showed itself as much in the growth and success of labour and anti-capitalist movements as in anything else. It is more significant to show, as notably Robert Merton has done, that Protestantism in its early days proved better able than Catholicism to make its influence felt in the world of science. Protestants preponderated among the early scientists, and, population for population, made more use than Catholics of technical and 'real' education. The essential point is that Protestants long showed more ability than Catholics to discover the growing points of society, absorb new ideas and experiences into their own thought, and so fit themselves to impose on new developments the shape they themselves desired. And they did this by the process of experiment and practical verification which is characteristic of science. Naturally, it is not every group of Protestants of whom this could be said. It could be said, for instance, rather less of the Lutheran churches than of the Calvinist, or, often, of the smaller sects. There were Protestants who were slow to meet new developments, as indeed there were Catholics who welcomed them with open arms. But of the general contrast between Catholics and Protestants there is no doubt.

The superiority of Protestantism in this respect rested firstly on the role assigned by it to the laity. One aspect of this was the idea of the layman's 'calling' in his ordinary duties in life. God, it has been said, is manifested in the Protestant and particularly the Calvinist tradition as the Lawgiver, directing action, rather than through love, demanding surrender and contemplation. The life of contemplation, to which Catholic thought gives the highest place, is seen as not necessarily or even commonly superior to the life of action. In whatever sphere of useful work a man finds to his hand, he is to work tirelessly for the glory of God. He is also to work disinterestedly. The Protestant tradition has as little to say as the Catholic or the Orthodox in favour of the mere accumulation of personal wealth. It stresses the community, towards which all have duties, including the duty to share out any surplus of wealth for the community's purposes, and on which all in return have claims. Primarily, this applies to the community of the faithful. But since in practice it is not possible to distinguish who are and are not the true faithful chosen by God, the idea of the community spreads out eventually to cover all those who are in fact present in a particular group.

The success of Protestantism in adapting to new conditions was due, secondly, to the way it related lay to clerical action, as can be seen notably in the Anglo-Saxon countries. The religious situation in these countries in, say, the nineteenth century corresponded very much to the Christian Democrats' conception of 'vertical pluralism'. It was not one of toleration, since there was little or no toleration of those who attacked, at any rate publicly and noticeably, the strong core of beliefs and moral attitudes common to the main denominations. It took six years, in the eighteen-eighties, for the British Parliament to decide to admit the duly elected but atheist member for Northampton, Charles Bradlaugh, to take his seat. A few years later, Parnell's divorce broke up the Irish Party and set back the cause of Home Rule for Ireland by a generation. Church, State, and public opinion combined in the Anglo-Saxon as in other parts of the Protestant world to impose a central core of Christian profession and attitudes on all. This general Christian discipline was supplemented with the more particular demands made by individual churches on their own members. But to decide what precisely membership of a Church implied for the day-to-day conduct of an individual layman, or for collectivities of laymen such as firms or Governments, was much more a matter for the laity in the Protestant churches than in the Catholic. The Lutheran churches from the start threw on governments the responsibility for discovering for themselves the principles of divine and natural law by which they were to operate. The Calvinist churches began, certainly, with the idea of close unity between Church and State, with the Church holding the whip hand. Geneva in the early days was as near to a theocracy as any society in history. But gradually, under the pressure of experience, Calvinism absorbed many of the characteristics of 'sectarian' Christianity, including the idea of the free Church, separated and standing somewhat back from the State, and of democracy and freedom of judgment and expression in Church and State alike.

The result, whether in the Lutheran, the Calvinist, or the 'sectarian' tradition, was that laymen were expected, to a much greater extent than in the Catholic Church, not merely to apply Christian principles in their daily lives but to discover what these principles were, and which principles were applicable in each field. They did so, it is true, within the general framework of Christian belief and ethics. In the last resort, they were expected to apply basic, agreed Christian standards of reference, and would be sharply called to order if they did not. Limits were set to error. But, within this very general framework, they were expected to do much more than merely take over and apply a body of established rules from the church or the clergy, along with the necessary interpretations. To a great extent, they were required to make and interpret their rules for themselves. To define 'middle principles' was their business, not that of the clergy.

In those countries where it was fully applied this method of working proved extremely fruitful, for it offered just the combination of authority and freedom which an age of change required. As was said earlier, major social movements tend to move in steps of a generation at a time, each concerned with a limited range of problems. It takes a generation or so simply to define each complex of problems, and arrive at the first reasonably reliable pointers to solutions. It may then take another generation to verify the proposed solutions and apply them on a mass scale. During the first generation it is practically impossible, and during the second not at all easy, for anyone not actually engaged as a practitioner in the work of a movement to grasp what is going on. Methods are disputed or undefined; assumptions are only partly explicit. Only at the end, when the movement's formative period is over and the textbooks record it in perspective, can an outsider, however firm his grasp of principle, pass anything like an informed and sound judgment on it. This is true not only of the outsider but of the insider, who can see his own part of the field, but cannot be expected to grasp the whole until the formative period is complete. Till that time comes, the nearest it is possible to come to a reliable judgment is to pool the ideas and experience of all who are contributing to a particular field of development and arrive in this way at a common opinion. This is in fact the method of science: successive approximation to a solution, through decentralised experiment, and the widest possible pooling of ideas, relying on the common opinion of experts to keep the line of progress straight.

The Christian expert has a special part to play in this process. For though the study of society is in part a science of facts, the order and combination in which facts are studied, and the conclusions drawn from them about what ought to be done, will depend on a man's view of life. It is in that sense that one can speak of a Christian or a Marxist or a 'humanist' sociology. But the Christian plays his part here as an expert with a Christian background: it is his expert status, which normally means his status as a layman in the Church, which qualifies him to intervene.

And this defines the position of the Christian clergy in relation to social change in a dynamic society. The clergy as a body have their own special and full-time task in connection with worship and with studying, defending, and teaching the message of Revelation, along with those general principles of conduct which follow directly from it or can be deduced from first principles by natural reasoning. They may reasonably protest when a social movement, on the face of it, violates one or other of these central principles. But they are by definition outsiders in relation to any particular movement, and during a movement's formative period can speak only with much caution where 'middle principles', which require experience for their definition, are concerned. Individual clergy may actually be experts in particular social fields. But even then they are in the position of insiders who can see only one part of the field, and must in many respects bow to the common opinion of the group. They may make an invaluable contribution by bringing out the way in which particular proposals or policies relate to that central Christian message which is the clergy's special concern. But when it comes to 'middle principles', they must wait like everyone else for history to clarify the data on which a final judgment can be based. In a relatively slow-changing age, like the Middle Ages, the clergy may be able, even without help from lay practitioners, to speak with authority on almost the whole field of current affairs. For the problems to be solved and the solutions to be applied are of long standing, and have been thoroughly thrashed out. In a fast-moving age, when the problems of each generation are largely new, this is not possible. It is necessary to rely in such an age for the nearest practicable approach to an authoritative definition of 'middle principles', on the common opinion of practitioners, including those clergy specially competent in each field. The role of the clergy in general, or of the appropriate authority among them, must be chiefly to help in summing up or drawing out this emerging common opinion—the essential role in modern times of the Papal Encyclicals—and to suggest points where it may be inconsistent with the central truths of Christianity. The question of their stepping in with the weight of authority to correct the common opinion can usually arise, in the first generation or two of a problem's active consideration, only when the inconsistency with revelation and the Christian tradition is gross. It was the great achievement of Reformed Christianity to pioneer a relationship of this sort between clergy and laity in the age when the tide of social change was rising to a flood.

This achievement, like that of the medieval Church and of early (and Orthodox) Christianity, has proved in due course to have the defects of

411

its qualities. In its pre-occupation with current, practical affairs, Protestantism in various times and places has lost its grip on the spirit and even the doctrine of the Gospel:

> From the purely religious standpoint its tendency to legalism and pharisaism, to feverish activity and a mechanical outlook, is very far from being in complete agreement with the deepest Christian ideas. (Troeltsch, *Social Teaching of the Christian Churches*, p. 1012.)

Protestantism has been governed not only by Luther and Calvin but by Babbitt and Bishop Barnes; it is not surprising if the relevance of Revelation has at times been forgotten or even denied. The Catholic Church, as Fr. Congar has pointed out, may indeed have in this case or that fallen short in practice: as, notably, by failing to encourage the laity to take the full part in the life of the Church to which they are called. But it has never denied the Faith or any part of it, or fallen into formal error on the Church, its nature, and the layman's place in it. Protestantism, on the other hand, achieved greater practical efficiency—for a time at least—at the cost not only of neglect but of denial of much that belongs to the Christian tradition.

Even on the side of practical activity, one misses in Protestant history the superb architecture of the medieval synthesis. It is striking how in the nineteenth and early twentieth centuries the formulation of Protestant social doctrine lagged behind that of Catholicism even in countries, such as the United States or Britain, where the social effectiveness of Protestantism was far ahead of that achieved by Catholics anywhere. This lack of formal doctrine may have done little harm in countries where Protestant belief was dominant or rising fast, and where social development was continuous enough for tradition, established or gradually emerging, to take the place of textbooks. Its dangers have shown much more clearly where the course of development is less stable, or where Christianity has to meet the challenge of fully thought out principles of other schools: as for instance in Germany between the two World Wars.

THE SIXTEENTH TO THE EIGHTEENTH CENTURY: CONSOLIDATION AND DEFENCE

But let us turn back to the more general history of the Christian churches. The four centuries since the age of the Reformation have been, on the whole, a time of recovery from that age's disasters, a new flowing of the Christian tide. Christianity has expanded in these centuries from an overwhelmingly European religion to one genuinely world-wide. Absolutely, and in proportion to population, it has reached more people than ever before. There is some reason to believe that the percentage of convinced as apart from 'customary' Christians has risen. It is certain, at any rate, that in all communions membership of a church, and conversion to it, has tended to become much more a matter of individual conviction than in previous ages. It is also certain that the Christian churches, clergy and laymen together, have advanced greatly in their ability to grasp, analyse, and solve the types of problem facing them in the modern world. But this recovery has not gone smoothly or evenly. It falls into two waves of very different kinds, separated by a pause or recession.

First, under the immediate shock of the Reformation, from the sixteenth on throughout the seventeenth century, both Protestants and Catholics worked hard to define and consolidate their respective positions. The classics of Protestant theology, of Luther and Calvin and the rest, belong to this period. The Council of Trent re-stated the essential Catholic positions in Christian doctrine, and Catholic church practice and discipline were drastically reformed. Later Popes might be charged with narrowness, and lack of vision for the needs of their time, or with too heavy an emphasis on personal religion as apart from social action; but never again, by any serious investigator, with the worldliness of their Renaissance predecessors. The Orthodox Church in its turn was stimulated to draft important re-statements of its belief, not least under the influence of personal contact with the Reformed churches. A Patriarch of Constantinople was deeply influenced by his travels to Geneva and Germany; and among the posts honourably filled by Balliol men is that of Patriarch of Alexandria under the Grand Turk in the seventeenth century. From all three main stems of Christianity there also went out in these two centuries a massive missionary effort, more particularly in North and South America, India, China, and Russia. The losses of the previous centuries in number and geographical extension were far outweighed by the new missionary gains.

But this activity tended by the eighteenth century to die down. Missionary effort, especially Catholic, wilted. Spain and Portugal, sources of much of the drive of the previous years, were now in decay, and it became obvious that the missions in most of the world were still unhealthily dependent on overseas support. Only in North America, the area where settlers and missionaries had been thrown most firmly on their own, with the least effective supervision from their home countries, was Christianity in the new countries fully able to stand on its own feet and indeed to initiate new departures. On the Catholic side the Society of Jesus, the most effective single order in both the missionary field and the defence of the Catholic Church in its homelands, was dissolved by the Pope under political pressure in 1773. In many countries theology and social conscious-ness were at a low ebb in both the Protestant and the Catholic Churches, and remained so into the nineteenth century. It is useless, writes Hagoort, the historian of the Dutch Protestant social movement, to look for fore-runners of this movement among the official leaders and synods of the Dutch Reformed Church. Members of that Church were indeed preparing the way for a revival on both the religious and the social front; but they did so as individuals, in the face of an organised church which to all

413

intents and purposes was dead. Catholics in Holland were still fighting for emancipation: they had as yet no independent role to play. In German Protestantism:

> The traditional creeds had been undermined and their defenders had propped them up with very shaky supports. Deism was itself dying of inanity. In the light of Kant's *Critique* the great speculative systems now appeared as castles in the air. Kant's own attempt to save belief in the three essentials of rational theology by making them postulates of the practical reason had subordinated religion to morality. . . . Theology was discredited both as to content and as to method. (Quoted in Drummond, *German Protestantism since Luther*, p. 104.)

Socially, the German Protestant clergy figured as the 'black police'. In Austria their Catholic brethren had the same unpleasant reputation. The Emperor Joseph II combined the social and philosophic outlook of Voltaire with the standing and powers of a Catholic King, and treated the Church as 'primarily a department of State whose office was the promotion of moral order'.[1] Austria became the classic example of the 'religion-gendarme'. In the ecclesiastical principalities on the Rhine the Catholic clergy did not dishonour the Church in this way. But in the drowsy peace of the Rhineland they contributed little or nothing positively to the Church's advancement.

In France the Catholic clergy before the Revolution were most of them honourable and devoted, and their files show that the practice of religion among the general body of their followers, so far as it can be measured by statistics of attendance at Mass and reception of the Sacraments, reached probably a higher level in the early eighteenth century than ever before or since. But, particularly in the higher ranks, they were more well-fed than apostolic. Many of them were interested in current problems of philosophy and social life, but this usually reflected non-Christian or anti-Christian reasoning, rather than a serious effort to think out a Christian position. The life of prayer, contemplation, and asceticism was discredited by heresy and scandals. And presently the French Revolution deprived the Church of its schools, hospitals, and properties, shattered its organisation, almost wiped out for a time its religious orders, and halved the number of its parish clergy. The influence of the Revolution spread beyond the borders of France, sometimes indeed with advantage to one or other of the Churches—Dutch Catholics owed the beginning of their emancipation to it—but more often to the contrary. Swiss Catholics had their civil war to fight against the liberals as late as 1848. And when presently the Church in France, after being crushed in the Revolution, was restored by Napoleon, it found itself a tool in a policy after Joseph II's own heart. 'There is a connection, gentlemen,' wrote Napoleon's Minister of Police to the French Bishops, 'between my functions and yours: our

---

[1] Philip Hughes, S.J. *Popular History of the Church*, p. 224.

414

common purpose is to promote the security of the Empire in the midst of order and virtue'.[1] 'With good police and a good clergy', exclaimed the Cardinal Archbishop of Paris on another occasion, 'the Emperor can always be sure of public order; for an archbishop is likewise a commissioner of police'.[2] Nor did this state of mind end with Napoleon. Even at the end of the nineteenth century, the reluctance of the French Bishops to strike out a line of their own provoked Cardinal Lavigerie's famous description of his colleagues as 'hares in mitres'.[3]

In short, from the sixteenth to the eighteenth centuries Catholics and Protestants alike, and to a less extent also the Orthodox, dug in on the positions they occupied about the time of the Reformation. They stopped the previous rot, showed new vitality, even made new gains in the mission field. But they none of them solved fundamentally the problems whose neglect led to the sixteenth-century disasters. They did not establish the independent spiritual, non-political, authority of the Church against the State. They did not show themselves able to extend the Christian synthesis to include the ideas and cover the needs of a new and rapidly changing age, or at least of doing so without incurring those characteristic defects of Protestantism described above. Protestantism might indeed in the short run be more successful than Catholicism in adapting to a world of change. But by the end of the eighteenth century it was obvious that this suppleness had been bought at the cost of the sense of direction, the full and firm grasp of revelation and the Christian tradition, which remained with the Catholic Church alone. And the Protestant, Catholic, and Orthodox traditions still went their separated and only too often hostile ways.

Summing up his vast study of *The Social Teaching of the Christian Churches*, Troeltsch observed that 'the Church-type'—Catholic or Protestant—'has been going through a process of decay and even of destruction'.[4] The social philosophy of the Christian Church 'has suffered an undeniable disintegration'.[5] Both its Catholic and its Protestant types 'have now spent their force'.[6] Social theory 'has far out-distanced the social philosophy of the Church'.[7] Troeltsch's study ends early in the nineteenth century, and it is first and foremost to that period that these judgments relate. If Christianity is the salt of society, it had at that time certainly lost its savour. And this could be said of the purely religious as well as of the social field.

THE NINETEENTH AND TWENTIETH CENTURIES. THE NEW ADVANCE: (1) THE TAIL OF THE EBB AND THE TURN OF THE TIDE

However, in the course of the nineteenth century the tide again turned, though for many contemporaries in Western Europe—the qualification

---

[1] [2] [3] All these quotations are from Dansette, *Histoire Religieuse de la France Contemporaine*.
[4] P. 1008.   [5] P. 991.   [6] P. 1012.   [7] P. 991.

should be underlined—the turn was for the moment masked. Even to Troeltsch, who wrote at the beginning of the twentieth century, such a statement as that Christianity 'was more potent in the affairs of man'[1] in 1944 than in 1914 would have seemed wildly paradoxical. For in this century and a half the results of earlier failures were working themselves out, even while new foundations were being laid for the future. In the parts of Europe with which this study is concerned, the number of Christian believers and the extent of Christian practice were diminishing, if not absolutely, then at any rate in proportion to the population as a whole.

Among Catholics most of the harm seems to have been done by the end of the eighteenth century. From then on the story was not so much of losses in new quarters as of lost opportunities of penetrating into new fields, of losses due to the impact of current politics on occasional conformity, or of the working out of other, more genuine, losses for which the stage by then had already been set.

The development in France was characteristic. In the countryside and small towns the map of religious practice among Catholics looked much the same in the middle of the twentieth century as early in the nineteenth, only the influences at work in 1800 had by 1950 come more clearly to the surface. In some rural areas belief had been weakened to the point of mere 'conformity'; birth, marriage, and death, the great feasts, and a vaguely religious ethic. It now became apparent that in many such areas it had dropped below the point at which it could maintain itself without new and well-planned reinforcements from outside. Regions which were 'conformist' in the eighteen-fifties were liable to be 'mission country' by the early twentieth century; and 'mission' meant here what it means in Central Africa, not what it means in the ordinary life of a settled Church. Revivalists, with a notable stress on death and hell fire—one cleric preached in the cemetery by night, with a death's head on each grave, made of a hollow pumpkin with a candle inside—scored mighty successes in many parts of the French countryside after Napoleon's collapse. But even by the eighteen-eighties and eighteen-nineties they were finding in certain regions, as for instance near Limoges, that they could no longer draw an audience, and had given up the struggle. In other sections of French society a change in the social and political atmosphere allowed many who in the early nineteenth century would have been occasional conformists to drift out of the Church altogether: a loss to Christianity more apparent than real, but still not to be ignored. In the eighteen-twenties, in the pious atmosphere of the Bourbon restoration, many a sound atheist felt that his job was worth a procession and a candle. Under the violently anti-clerical governments around 1900 the pendulum swung the other way. 'It happened

[1] Latourette, *History of the Expansion of Christianity*, Vol. VII, p. 410.

often enough', wrote the head of the Masonic spy service in the Army, 'that one saw an officer who in 1901 had his sons at a Jesuit school and openly displayed sentiments hostile to the Government, in 1902 sending his sons to the *lycée*, and in 1903 expressing his respect for our institutions'.[1] A much more serious failure was that the Church did not keep pace with the growth of new concentrations of population in the big towns of France, and especially around Paris. *Christ in the Suburbs*, to borrow the title of a work in 1927 which focused attention on this problem, was often more of a wish than a reality. But this was a new problem, relating to areas never penetrated by Christianity. Like Alice at the Mad Hatter's tea party, one cannot have less of anything (only Alice was interested in 'more') until one has had some of it. There were some important gains to the Catholic Church in France to offset these various failures. In particular, the middle and upper middle class and the world of intellect, apparently hopelessly lost to Christianity in 1800 or 1820, had by 1950 been largely won back. But the general picture is of the slow erosion of ground already undermined by 1800, plus the missing of important new opportunities arising since that date.

Such data as there are on the Catholic populations of other West European countries point the same way. As in France, the level of belief recorded in 1950 does not seem to have represented a spectacular loss of ground as compared with the positions actually held by Christianity a hundred and fifty years before. But at various points structures already weakened collapsed, and new opportunities of which advantage might have been taken were missed.

In Germany it seems that the percentage of Catholics who fulfilled their Easter duties dropped through the First World War, rose again by the 'thirties, both before and during the Nazi period, to a level higher than that in the first recorded statistics, dropped through the Second World War, and by 1949 was again rising steadily towards its pre-war level. As in France, the statistics show a conspicuous failure to catch up with the concentration of population in the big towns. A secondary problem, before and still more since the Second World War, has been the difficulty of providing for Catholics scattered in mainly Protestant areas. This may well account for the rather slower recovery after 1945 than after 1918, because of the much greater problem of Catholic refugees scattered through Protestant territory. The rather encouraging fact that, with temporary fluctuation, the level of practice among Catholics in Germany has been maintained, would of course mean little if large numbers of the weaker vessels had been leaving the Church and dropping out of the statistics altogether. But in fact this is not so. A few Catholics have in recent decades turned completely away from Christianity, and there has been a slight balance of conversions in

---

[1] Quoted in Brogan, *Development of Modern France*, p. 383.

favour of Protestantism. But neither source of loss has been on a big scale.

In Holland, as in Germany and France, the Catholic Church seems to have been relatively unsuccessful—though probably more successful in Holland than in either of the other two countries—in solving the new problems created by the growth of big towns. Over the last thirty years the proportion of Catholics in the big Dutch towns who practise their religion has fallen somewhat, and the figure even in the nineteen-twenties was well below that for the smaller towns and the country. Even in the big towns, however, at least 60–70% of Catholics today fulfil their Easter duties. Elsewhere, as has been shown, the figures are much higher. And the leakage of Catholics who either leave the Church altogether or join a Protestant communion is very small. Dutch Catholicism, one might say, has slipped a little, but not very far. For Eastern Belgium, around Liége, a recent study brings out very well both the usual pattern of erosion and of failure to keep up with the growth of the big towns and also the way in which the rot was eventually stopped. For many years, as industrialisation developed, anti-religious influences worked gradually out from town to town and village to village from Liége, largely through the agency of the Socialist unions. But in the course of the 'twenties and 'thirties the Christian social movements in their turn came into action, and the tide was stopped and even turned: though Liége itself, and its suburbs, still stand out as an area of poor religious practice.

In several of the countries covered here Protestant belief and practice may have diminished between 1800 and 1950 more than Catholic; even omitting the cases where Protestantism, like Catholicism, did not so much lose ground as fail to occupy new ground open to it. An analysis of this kind for Protestantism is as has been said a back-breaking task, since there is no accepted minimum standard of practice. The fact that 40% of Lutherans in Hanover took communion in 1932, but only 11% of Calvinists, tells one more about their respective theologies than about the fervour of their faith. But some indications are too clear to be overlooked. In Germany it seems that the proportion of communicants in the Evangelical churches —a test described in their own *Kirchliches Jahrbuch* as the 'best thermometer of Church life'—fell from 45% in 1889 to 17% in 1940. It dropped still further during the war years, though it then, like the corresponding Catholic figure, began to rise again. These absolute percentages should be quoted only with care, for they relate to the *whole* membership of each Evangelical 'community', only part of whom are eligible for communion. But this does not alter the *relative* movement. The percentage of communicants in recent years has been two-fifths, or less, of what it was sixty or seventy years ago.

It does not seem that there has been a very great loss to German

Protestantism, any more than to German Catholicism, through people giving up Church membership altogether. In the West German census of 1950 only 3·2% of the population claimed to be attached to no church. In Holland on the other hand a substantial number of Protestants have abandoned Church membership; notably in the Hervormde Kerk, which can still, in spite of competition from stricter Protestant groups, claim to be the 'national' Protestant church. The proportion of Dutchmen who return themselves as belonging to no church was negligible at the Census of 1880, reached 2·3% in 1900, and has since risen steadily to 17·0% in 1947. The overwhelming bulk of this loss seems to have been at the expense of the Hervormde Kerk; though, once again, one must beware of describing as a loss the failure of this church, as of all the other main churches of Europe, to keep pace with the growth of new concentrations of population. It seems that there has also been some fall in the intensity of practice in the Hervormde Kerk, though on this the statistics are not clear. And the social atmosphere has changed in Holland, as elsewhere, and made it easier for occasional conformists to become non-practitioners or open atheists. A study of Dutch elections shows a marked correlation between radical (notably Communist) voting today and the proportion of the people in each district shown by the Census of twenty years ago to have abandoned church membership. But there is no correlation at all between radical voting today, or the increase in it over these twenty years, and the *increase* in the percentage of non-church members within this period. It looks as if in the past those who rejected membership of, notably, the Hervormde Kerk were likely to do so only on thought-out grounds which also affected their political behaviour; the social resistance to quitting the church was too strong to allow a merely casual departure. Today it is easier simply to drift out without any strong conviction either way.

This picture of the change in religious practice in countries covered by the present study is on the whole dull and depressing. It is easy to see why Troeltsch, and others living in these countries a generation or two ago, took so poor a view of the prospects of Christianity. But their pessimistic view needs to be corrected in two ways. If, first, still counting heads, one looks outside the group of West European countries with which this study is concerned, one finds a somewhat uncertain balance of gains and losses in which however the gains may well predominate. Areas where there have been recent losses include the Iron Curtain countries, and also (among Protestants) Great Britain and Scandinavia. It is not always certain that there has been a net loss in these countries since 1800, as apart from a decline from some peak of religious observance reached more recently. Observance among British Protestants may well have reached a peak in the nineteenth century, and then dropped back; though whether it has dropped to a lower point than that at which Wesley found it is rather doubtful. In

China there were great gains down to the arrival of Communism, and Communism has not entirely cancelled them. In any case, there are vast and clear gains to record in India and Africa. From the seventeenth to the nineteenth centuries the Churches there were purely and strictly missionary. Today they are coming to have their own full range of clergy and to stand on their own feet. There have been remarkable advances also in some European countries, notably by the Catholic Church in Britain, which has succeeded in keeping pace with a mass movement of population from Ireland, incidentally for the most part into big towns, and in holding a large part of the immigrants and their descendants to their faith. In the United States the proportion of Church members to the whole population rose from 5% in 1790 to 43½% in 1910 and 1920 and over 50% in 1941–2. Readers of *Middletown*, or of a Catholic study such as *Southern Parish*, will not over-value the quality of much of this membership. But the achievement simply of gathering them all into the fold is impressive, especially when it is borne in mind that the rules of various churches exclude many people—children, for instance—from the full church membership which alone is counted in the statistics.

But the lesson which stands out above all from church history since 1800 is that church life, and above all Church leadership, clerical and lay alike, have gone through a qualitative revolution, of a kind which cannot in the first instance be measured by the counting of heads. It should of course, and indeed if this movement is genuine it must, be possible to measure it in that way once it has had time to make itself fully felt. But 'time' in this case, as with all profound mass movements of opinion, means at least several generations. The Orthodox Churches, and especially the greatest of them, the Russian Church, have suffered too much from political control and direct attack to be able to take their full part in this revolution, though there are signs that they would have done far more had they had the chance. But if one looks at Protestantism or Catholicism, the change for the better in the last century leaps immediately to view.

First, these churches show a new independence and self-confidence in their dealings with the State. There is, it is true, a sense in which the Christian churches have not so much recovered their independence of mind as been compelled to recover it. The Catholic Church in France fought to the last ditch against disestablishment in the early twentieth century, a move which, seen in the perspective of later years, has proved one of the greatest blessings in that Church's history. The German Evangelical Church found its soul again, a little perhaps at the time of the separation of Church and State in 1918, but most of all when the *Confessing Church* emerged in resistance to Nazi attacks. But whether the independence of the Churches has emerged, as in these countries, through violent dispute, or has come by peaceable development as in the Church of England or (so far as it has come there at all) in Scandinavia, the churches today in the free countries speak with a clarity and confidence very different from their uncertain sound a hundred or a hundred and fifty years earlier. It is here above all that there is a painful contrast between Protestants and Catholics on the one hand and the main body of the Orthodox Churches on the other.

Secondly, the churches have taken a firm grip on the characteristic problems of modern times. One may agree or disagree with Christian positions in history, or science, or social affairs. What is no longer possible is to treat the Catholic or Protestant churches as historical survivals whose views in these fields intelligent men can neglect. In one field, that of social affairs, the facts gathered in this study are a demonstration of this.

Thirdly, the Reformation and pre-Reformation division between the three great traditions of Christianity, the failure of each to profit by the experience of the others, has begun to break down. And here lies the key to the two previous changes. For if the churches feel new confidence, or grasp modern problems more firmly, this turns out on examination to be essentially because the representatives of each of these traditions have covered the weak points in their own position with reinforcements borrowed from, suggested by, or at any rate previously characteristic of the others: the practical efficiency of Protestantism, the spirituality of the Orthodox, and the full Catholic grasp of the Faith in general and of the nature and purpose of the Church in particular.

Some Churches have set out deliberately to learn from others. This is true especially of the Protestant Churches, which are in increasingly close contact with one another and with Orthodoxy, especially through the Ecumenical Movement. Some of these churches, as notably the Church of England, have also paid close attention over the last century to the Catholic Church. It has been all the easier for them to do so because the Catholic Church has reappeared in force in this time, notably in Holland, Britain, and the United States, in several countries in which it had been banished or repressed, or was present on only a negligible scale. In other cases, and notably in the Catholic Church, the process has been different. There has been little, if any, attempt deliberately to learn from other churches. There has probably been a fair amount of unconscious absorption of lessons from others. It is difficult to believe, for instance, that in half a century's close collaboration between the Catholic and Protestant trade union movements in Holland the influence has all been one way. And an English Catholic who visits Continental Catholic congresses very quickly becomes conscious of how much he himself has absorbed—and often gained—from the Protestant culture surrounding him at home. First and foremost, however, the change in Catholicism has been a matter of internal experience and growth; of meeting new problems, working out appropriate solutions, and then finding after the event that these look strikingly like those traditional in the other Christian churches.

THE NINETEENTH AND TWENTIETH CENTURIES: (2) THE NEW SYNTHESIS

(a) Unity, authority, and synthesis: chiefly Protestant

This recovery by the various churches of neglected features in each other's tradition has occurred at three chief points. First, they have learnt more and more the value of unity in doctrine and action, of an authority to promote and define this, and in general of the Church as such. This movement came first among Catholics. A return to the Church was, as has been shown, an essential part of Catholics' effort to affirm their independent position in the new Liberal world of the first part of the nineteenth century. Negatively, this took shape in the collapse of the various movements—Gallicanism, Josephism, Febronianism—which had tried in the eighteenth century and earlier to 'nationalise' the Catholic Church in France or Austria or the Rhineland and to drive a wedge between the national churches and Rome. Positively, Catholics came to appreciate the value of the international Church and the Pope as the foundation and guide to their effort at independent political and social expression. Their devotion to the Pope increased, and a large part of their political activity in the middle of the century, and onwards into 'eighties and 'nineties, was concerned with guaranteeing him the political freedom needed for his work as international Head of the Church. This 'ultramontane' movement was striking enough at the time. But it was, basically, merely the re-affirmation of a principle which Catholics might neglect but which they had never abandoned. The corresponding Protestant movement came later, and in terms of Protestant theology and church practice was much more revolutionary.

It has been shown how in Germany the growth of an independent Protestant political and social movement has gone hand in hand with growing unity in the Protestant churches and independence of the churches from the State. The creation of the Inland Mission, which was the effective beginning of the social movement, was also part of one and the same operation with the founding of the Evangelical Church Assemblies and the Eisenach Assemblies. When the 'Caesaro-Papism' of the Kulturkampf began to arouse uneasiness in a section of Church opinion, Adolf Stöcker was setting out on his initially even more modest attempt to create an independent Protestant political movement. When this movement at last, after the First World War, swelled to a size at which it began to count in national politics, this was just when the Churches were for the first time freed from State control and becoming conscious of the problems of independence. A German Church Federation was founded, and there was a tendency to discredit modernist theology and to return, not only to the

Bible direct, but also to the historic Confessions which summarise the orthodoxy of the Lutheran and Reformed churches. In the course of the next generation German Protestants were converted *en masse* to the Christian political movement: and this was also the time of the Confessing Church, that is of the decisive affirmation of the Church's independent and organised authority over against the State. It was at the end of this period that the federated churches were further linked up into the Evangelical Church in Germany. And it can be shown that these coincidences were no accident. Protestants' intervention in the political and social field would not have taken place had it not been for their awakening to a new sense of community and independent identity in the Church. And this awakening was stimulated at point after point by events in the political and social field: the Kulturkampf, the rise of the workers' movement, and so on. The changes in Protestantism in church life and social action were two sides of the same medal.

So also in Switzerland the establishment of the S.V.E.A. unions and the Evangelical People's Party at the end of the First World War coincided, and not by chance, with the creation of an Evangelical Churches' Federation and of a new, comprehensive, organisation for church social work. In Holland it can scarcely be said that the Protestant churches have found unity over the years. But it is certainly true that their growing dynamism and independence, even when expressed in divisions and secessions, has contributed immensely to the Protestant political and social movement. The contributions in this respect of the 'Separation' of the 'thirties and 'forties of the nineteenth century and the 'Complaint' of the 'eighties have been mentioned in their place. And there have been significant moves even in Holland towards the new unity being achieved in Germany and Switzerland. Mention has for instance been made of how one group of clergy, prominently associated with the 'break-through' movement, has over the years turned back from modernism to orthodoxy, and has played an important part in the revival in recent years of the national Hervormde Church. And the Dutch churches have taken a prominent part in the world-wide Ecumenical Movement.

Isolated moves towards a world-wide association of the Protestant churches began late in the eighteenth and early in the nineteenth century. As the nineteenth century went on, related churches and movements in different countries organised on an international scale. Examples are the Lambeth Conferences of the churches of the Anglican Communion, of which the first was in 1867, or the creation of the Baptist World Alliance in 1905: or, on a different plane, the world-wide federation of the Y.M.C.A. in 1855 or the Y.W.C.A. in 1894. There also gradually came up moves towards inter-denominational co-operation. Missionaries, for whom the division of the churches was a particularly serious obstacle in their daily work, played a great part in these. Important inter-denominational missionary conferences were held at New York in 1854 and Liverpool in 1860, and were followed by others, including several in the mission fields themselves. These culminated in the World Missionary Conference at Edinburgh in 1910. There were also a number of moves, like those already mentioned in Germany and Switzerland, towards inter-denominational co-operation within the European and North American countries.

From the Edinburgh conference onwards the pace quickened. Within a number of countries the movement to fuse or federate Protestant churches developed fast. But the most striking developments were international. The Edinburgh conference itself led to the formation of the International Missionary Council (1921), after a delay due to the First World War. The Council was the first inter-church international body with a full-time secretariat, and has since gone from strength to strength. It also represented the transition to a more fundamental level of discussion.

> It became clear that at the latter (Edinburgh) gathering the basic questions of faith and order which had historically separated the churches were not being faced. With the purpose of obtaining the fullest possible co-operation those concerned with the expansion of Christianity were consciously avoiding the issues which had been traditional sources of division and were seeking to rise above them in meeting together the tasks which all had in common. Yet these issues remained and prevented the full achievement of a united front. Questions of fundamental belief concerning the Christian faith, the Holy Communion of Lord's Supper, the nature of the ministry, the ordination of the ministry, and the organisation of the Church would not down. It was felt that representatives of the Church should frankly face them together ... (Latourette, *History of the Expansion of Christianity*, Vol. VII, p. 30.)

If these differences could not be reconciled, they could at least be understood; and who could tell where understanding might lead? It was from this feeling, expressed notably but not exclusively as a result of the Edinburgh meeting, that world conferences on Faith and Order were held at Lausanne in 1927 (after which a 'continuing organisation' and secretariat were set up) and at Edinburgh in 1937. The delegates at these meetings officially represented their churches. They came from a wide range of Protestant churches, and there were some from the Orthodox churches.

Another, converging, line of development began when from the eighteennineties onwards there grew up in the United States a Protestant peace movement. From this emerged in 1914 a Church Peace Union. The Union planned an international conference in Switzerland for August 1914: not, as it turned out, an auspicious moment. But the Union was not discouraged. It converted itself into a World Alliance for International Friendship Through the Churches and went on with its work. It linked up with similarly minded forces in other countries. Archbishop Soederblom, Primate of Sweden, gave strong support. In Britain the wish of the Protestant churches to work together and exchange ideas on social affairs was shown notably in the Conference on Christian Politics, Economics, and Citizenship, usually known as COPEC, at Birmingham in 1924. From all this there emerged a Universal Conference of the Church of Christ on Life and Work, at Stockholm in 1925. This conference set up a Continuation Committee, and in 1937, the same year as the Faith and Order Conference at Edinburgh, a further world conference on Life and Work was held at Oxford. The coincidence of the two Conferences was no accident. They were arranged in close collaboration, their membership largely overlapped, and the opportunity was taken to improve contact between the two movements. In each, the conviction had grown that the two constituted essentially one movement. *Life and Work* could operate effectively only with the guidance of *Faith and Order*, while *Faith and Order* needed to find part at least of its fulfilment in *Life and Work*. It was accordingly agreed to set up a permanent World Council of Churches, with a permanent secretariat. Once again war delayed progress. But in 1948 the first assembly of the World Council duly met at Amsterdam, and in 1954 the second at Evanston in the United States.

The World Council has no power of compulsion. It is an association of churches, not a super-church, and there is no question of drafting a creed and imposing it on any Church. To one who is used to the full and rounded statement of the Faith in the Catholic Church, the formulae on which the World Council and its predecessors have been able to agree must seem limited and the gaps wide. But it would be quite misleading to think of the Ecumenical Movement as being, as it were, a movement of laymen anxious to gloss over the occasions for theological hair-splitting, to secure unity of action by emptying out the content of belief. The movement originated mainly with the clergy. It represents a serious attempt, massive and well-planned, to confront and, if possible, reconcile divergent views without confounding them. It has already contributed a good deal to the unity of doctrine and worship, and of understanding and good will: though, as even some Protestants would say, unity has at times been bought at the price of doctrine.[1] Above all, it has underlined for many in certain churches, particularly the missionary churches, a truth which we are inclined to neglect, namely, that there is

> No mere consequential relation between Gospel and Church but a relation which is both integral and constitutive.[2]

The Church, that is, is not a convenience for preaching the Gospel, to be shaped and reshaped like any other administrative structure. To belong to a Church with a definite unity, authority, and tradition is an essential part of being a Christian. And though the World Council's authority is

[1] The reference is particularly to the Church of South India.
[2] P. O. Devanandan, in *The Universal Church in God's Design*, World Council of Churches, 1948, p. 149.

purely moral, it is substantial and increasing. Through it the Protestant and part of the Orthodox world are acquiring a central authority, though not indeed of the kind held by the Pope in the Catholic Church; it is one based on consent, of the sort which rules the world of science.

(b) Learning from experience: the role of the laity: chiefly Catholic

While Protestants have been moving towards unity and authority, the Catholic Church has turned towards Protestant techniques for establishing and applying 'middle principles', the realistic 'hypothesis' in any given situation, as apart from the ideal 'thesis'. There is nothing new to Catholicism in these efforts to define middle principles, nor is it new to work them out by experience and natural reasoning, as well as from the light of revelation, before finally and formally incorporating them as part of the Church's current synthesis. That is how the medieval synthesis was built up. What is new among Catholics, though not among Protestants, is what were called earlier the built-in mechanisms for coping with a *continuous* stream of change.

First, the machinery for formally incorporating new findings into the Church's current synthesis, and for giving such guidance as the Pope and clergy appropriately can during the time when ideas are being shaped, has itself been overhauled, speeded up, and adapted to the wide audience and enormous variety of movements in the Church today. This is true especially of the final authority, that of the Pope. From the time of Leo XIII, in the last quarter of the nineteenth century, the output of formal Encyclicals has been greatly increased, and more and more use has been made by the Popes of formal or informal addresses, interviews, press releases, and radio messages. Leo XIII in 1893 launched his encyclical *Au Milieu des Sollicitudes,* on the duty of French Catholics to accept loyally the Republic, in an interview with a mass-circulation paper. The event was a sensation. In 1952 his fourth successor, Pius XII, delivered some 13 radio speeches, 57 addresses to groups of all kinds, from cardinals to the Rome telegraph boys, and published 37 documents and directives; and this apart from personal and private interviews and correspondence.

Behind these official statements of Church policy there is today a far more impressive machine than in the past for studying current experience in social affairs, deriving principles of action in the light of Catholic theology and philosophy, and relaying these principles back to the action level. A great deal of work of this kind is of course done directly by the social movements themselves, and particularly by the large and growing body of clergy attached to them as chaplains or, in the case of the Christian Democratic movements, as what the Dutch call 'spiritual advisers'. But there have also grown up in the last two generations three main types of organisation with a more general responsibility.

First, there are the various Catholic centres of research, beginning with those in which theologians and philosophers make a special study of social affairs from the angle of their own science. Probably the most influential single school of this kind, one whose views have shaped both Papal statements and practical programmes, has been that of the German and Austrian Jesuits. The six founders of this school, whose chief work fell into the period from 1868 to the First World War—Frs. Meyer, Costa-Rossetti, Lehmkuhl, Biederlack, Cathrein, and Pesch—re-worked the traditional Catholic doctrine of the natural law, and its application to modern life, on lines which the rest of the Church has followed ever since. Fr. Pesch in particular worked out on a massive scale the philosophy of 'Solidarism', which is none other than the political and social theory underlying the Christian Democratic programme today. Other countries have had their distinguished contributors to the formation and statement of Catholic social theory. France most of all: one thinks of such obvious names in recent years as Etienne Gilson, Jacques Maritain, or Yves Congar, or of the vast analysis of Papal social teaching recently published by the Jesuit Fr. Villain. And other religious orders besides the Jesuits have had their schools of social thought, notably the Dominicans. But there is no school anywhere that has flourished so continuously through wars and upheavals as that of the German-language Jesuits, or has produced so many standard works, reprinted again and again and used throughout the world as university and seminary textbooks. Its outstanding representatives today are probably Frs. Gundlach, von Nell-Breuning, and Messner.

Research by Catholics is of course not confined to philosophy and theology. The Catholic Universities of Louvain, or Fribourg, or Milan, or Nijmegen, or the Catholic Institutes in France—to mention only universities in the countries studied here—have flourishing schools of social science, and many Catholic scholars in other universities are carrying on research in similar fields. And within the last generation has arisen the 'religious sociology' movement, concerned with studying social situations specifically from the point of view of their impact on religious belief and practice. This grew up first in France, but is today probably most solidly rooted in Holland. It is, in any case, represented in all the countries covered here.

Nearer to the level of action are to be found a number of what might be called 'institutes of social action', concerned with inspiring and stimulating, advising, but also learning from the social organisations themselves. The most successful institute of this kind was the German *Volksverein*, or People's Union, founded by Franz Hitze in 1890. For many years, indeed right down to its dissolution by the Nazis in 1933, its headquarters at München-Gladbach was in effect the brains trust of the entire German Catholic social movement. In a typical early year, 1903, it had 300,000 members, including some 10,000 militants holding local office. It circulated the respectable total of 13½ million copies of its publications, provided regular series of articles to the Catholic press, sponsored 1,400 public meetings, and supplied three series of speakers' notes. It acted as an enquiry bureau on social matters and apologetics, and had started and in many cases gave financial support to thirty social secretariats[1] and seven other bureaux specialising in labour matters. It held each year a two-and-a-half-month course for labour leaders, through which most of the leading Catholic figures in the German labour movement passed.

The *Volksverein* found several imitators elsewhere. In Italy, after the Congress Movement was dissolved in 1904, one of the agencies by which it was presently replaced was a 'Unione Popolare' modelled on the *Volksverein*. 1906 was an unfortunate date for a would-be dynamic agency of social inspiration and instruction to be born, in the middle of the 'modernist' controversy and under the immediate and suspicious eye of Rome. The *Unione* never obtained as wide an influence as the *Volksverein*. It was dissolved in 1923, its work being transferred after an interval to what is now Catholic Action's 'Catholic Institute of Social Action'. Swiss Catholics acquired a *Volksverein* in 1904. For the French-speaking countries similar work is done by *Action Populaire*, started in 1903 in Belgium, transferred in 1907 to Rheims, and then, after its office there was destroyed in the First World War, to Paris. Like the *Unione Popolare*, *Action Populaire* suffered a good deal from the modernist controversy. But it survived, went from strength to strength, and has taken a leading part in all the major social movements of French Catholicism to this day: not least, perhaps, through the some two hundred priests who have trained in its office and passed on to other work. It is also the French who in recent years have developed furthest the idea of Catholic 'social secretariats', which they themselves got notably from Belgium. The nearest equivalent in British terms would be a Council of Social Service. In France these Secretariats began in a number of big towns—the first was at Lyons—between 1901 and 1914. They were intended, to quote one of their leaders, to:

> Support institutions, organisations, and activities in the social field, and help them in their work and propaganda.
> Initiate action where required.
> Wherever possible, establish useful contacts between the social organisations.
> (Quoted in *Chronique Sociale de France*, 1952, 2, 220.)

As time went on and the Christian Democratic and Catholic Action organisations grew, it became less and less necessary for the Secretariats themselves to undertake activities or to act as enquiry bureaux. After the Second World War, about 1945-7, they were accordingly turned more specifically into a sort of local general staff for the various Catholic social

---

[1] See below on the Social Secretariats in France.

movements: though 'general staff' is a misleading expression, since they have no actual authority over the movements. They are, so they say themselves, organs of the official Church, and as such are bound to refrain from direct participation in political, trade union, and similar activities, and also to respect the autonomy of in particular the Christian Democratic movements. Their organisation typically includes:

A central group of laymen and clergy which reviews current economic and social developments, accepts responsibility for all aspects of it, provides adequate documentation, forms committees, links up experiments, decides on lines of social action, of propaganda, and of revision of social theory. . . .

Committees devoted to particular problems, or as occasion may demand, usually cutting across social groups . . . searching for . . . clarification through objective information, with technical knowledge cooling off emotions. . . .

Activities initiated by the Secretariat. . . . Once they have grown and developed their technique they usually become independent, or link up with other organisations already existing. . . . (Loc. cit., pp. 221–2.)

In between the theoreticians of philosophy and social science on the one hand and the institutes of social action on the other appears a third group of agencies concerned with reflecting on and codifying current experience at a level more academic than that of the institutes, yet nearer to current affairs than the work of the theologians or the university scientists. Most of the countries studied here have today 'Social Weeks', an annual course of lectures and seminars at which Catholics interested in social action meet for a refreshing experience of reflection and instruction. The most famous of these is probably the *Semaine Sociale de France*. In a sense, the history of the *Semaine* runs back to de Mun's and La Tour du Pin's 'Workers' Club Movement' of the eighteen-seventies. That movement established a Research Committee, which in turn was replaced by a 'Study Union', whose chairman just after the beginning of the century was Henri Lorin. With the rise of Christian Democracy it became apparent that debates behind closed doors were not enough; it was necessary to carry out the conclusions to the much wider circle of people from all classes who were now taking an active hand in the Catholic social movement, and to draw in turn on their ideas and experience. At this point Lorin linked up with Marius Gonin, editor of the *Chronique du Sud-Est*, which as the *Chronique Sociale de France* is still the official paper of the *Semaine*, and founder of the Social Secretariat at Lyons. From these two men's collaboration arose the first *Semaine* in 1904. The series has been annual ever since, broken only by the two World Wars. In Italy the *Unione Popolare* started a similar Social Week, on the French model, in 1907, and these too have run through to the present day. In Belgium the corresponding initiative was taken by the Christian Workers' Movement. In Germany social topics have frequently been taken up at the annual Catholic Assemblies; the Bochum resolution on workers' control, for example, quoted above, came out of a seminar at the 1949 *Katholikentag*, which was entirely devoted to problems of social justice. A separate German Social Week has also been started since the Second World War. Swiss Catholics also have a Social Week of their own.

And meantime other groups have carried forward the less conspicuous work of clarification and codification illustrated by the work of the 'Study Union' in France. The ground for the Encyclical *Rerum Novarum* was prepared in the eighteen-eighties by a small group of laymen and clergy meeting informally at Fribourg in Switzerland with the later Cardinal Mermillod as Chairman. The example has not been forgotten. Between the two wars another similar group was started, not very success-fully, at Fribourg, and at the end of the Second World War the University of Fribourg established an Institute to serve as a centre for international collaboration in the social science field. Meantime, in Belgium, Cardinal Mercier was inspired in 1920 by Professor Helleputte, who had been a member of the original Fribourg group—it is difficult to get away from Helleputte in anything to do with the foundations of Christian social action in Belgium—and by Eugène Duthoit, at that time Chairman of the *Semaines Sociales* in France, to call together a similar group at Malines. This 'Union of Malines', or more officially 'International Union of Social Studies', has produced a series of Codes on social principles, international ethics, and the family, as well as a number of shorter declarations on current topics such as workers' control or world popula-tion and food resources. After Cardinal Mercier's death it was carried on by his successor, Cardinal Van Roey.

All these measures for increasing the sensitivity of the official Church to current social trends and problems, and its capacity to give relevant guidance to those engaged in solving them, are important. But they are not by any means the most important of the moves made to equip Catholicism as a whole, not only the official Church, with built-in mechanisms for coping with social change. The vital change has been to put the accent more and more on the action and 'calling' of the Catholic laity, and less exclusively on that of the clergy. The calling of the laity may be to Catholic Action in the strict sense, under the direct control of the clergy. Table 38 presents the chart of Catholic Action in one particu-larly well-organised diocese. In other cases, in the field of Christian Democracy, it is to independent lay responsibility, subject only to the ordinary teaching authority of the Church. In either case, lay people are called to play a larger part in the Church than was customary in the nineteenth century, or at any time since the Reformation. A great deal of effort has gone into defining the right relation between clergy and laity in this new situation, and, in particular, a new 'theology of the layman's role' has grown up.

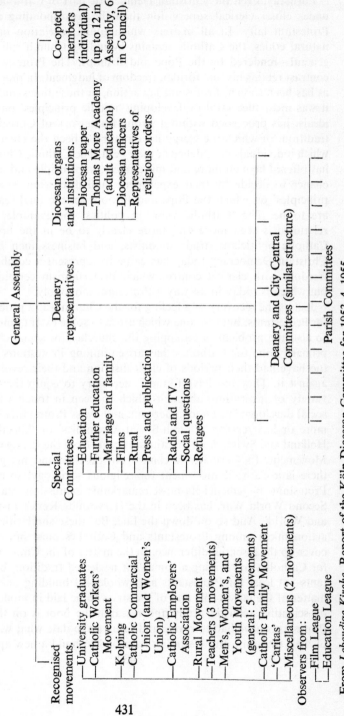

TABLE 38

Organisation of Catholic Action in the Archdiocese of Cologne

Archbishop

Executive Committee

Council ('Leaders' Circle')

General Assembly

Special Committees.
- Education
- Further education
- Marriage and family
- Films
- Rural
- Press and publication
- Radio and TV.
- Social questions
- Refugees

Deanery representatives.

Diocesan organs and institutions.
- Diocesan paper
- Thomas More Academy (adult education)
- Diocesan officers
- Representatives of religious orders

Co-opted members (individual) (up to 12 in Assembly, 6 in Council).

Recognised movements.
- University graduates
- Catholic Workers' Movement
- Kolping
- Catholic Commercial Union (and Women's Union)
- Catholic Employers' Association
- Rural Movement
- Teachers (3 movements)
- Men's, Women's, and Youth Movements (general: 5 movements)
- Catholic Family Movement
- 'Caritas'
- Miscellaneous (2 movements)

Observers from:
- Film League
- Education League

Deanery and City Central Committees (similar structure)

Parish Committees

From *Lebendige Kirche*, Report of the Köln Diocesan Committee for 1953-4, 1955.

CHRISTIAN DEMOCRACY IN THE PERSPECTIVE OF CHURCH HISTORY

Formally, even the Christian Democratic part of Catholic lay action is under closer clerical supervision than the corresponding action by the Protestant laity. In all matters which touch revelation or ethics, even natural ethics, the Catholic remains bound by Church rulings—however general—rendered by the Pope and Bishops. The Protestant layman by contrast retains his full, formal, freedom of judgment. In practice, however, as has been shown, Protestant lay action, in those times and places where it was most successful in developing 'middle principles' out of Christian ideals, has proceeded within a strong framework of Christian belief and tradition, of which the clergy have naturally been the chief support, and which individuals have defied at their peril. The Catholic Church on its side has offered laymen more and more freely, in principle and in practice, the chance to decide by their experiments and discussion what the 'middle principles' on which the Pope and Bishops set the final seal of approval are to be. The 'Catholic view' in politics, for example, or industrial relations, is seen more and more clearly to be in the first place what Catholic politicians, trade unionists, and business men have made it. Christian Democracy today has come to represent a combination of lay freedom with clerical control which Protestantism certainly pioneered, but which is today in no way a Protestant monopoly.

Just as the recovery of a feeling for the Church was a problem primarily for Protestants, but also one which arose to some extent among Catholics, so also the problem of equipping the churches for social change, though primarily one for Catholics, has arisen among Protestants as well. They too have had their periods of clericalisation and their revolts by the laity against it. They too have found it necessary to equip themselves with a variety of institutions through which to keep in touch with and assess social development. Dutch, German, and Swiss Protestants have had their more or less regular 'Church Social Assemblies' or 'Social Courses'. In Holland and Switzerland the stimulus came from the Evangelical Workers' Movement. In Germany it came from Stöcker and his group. Just as there is a Catholic movement for religious sociology, so also there is a Protestant movement: its most remarkable expression, started since the Second World War, has been in the Hervormde Kerk's institute 'Church and World'. And so on down the line. But these similarities between the action taken among Protestants and Catholics must not be allowed to cover up the essential difference. In the matter of the Church, it was a case for Catholics of reviving a somewhat neglected tradition, but for Protestants—at least for Protestants as a whole—of building one anew. In the matter of the laity's role and of the stress to be laid in modern conditions on scientific, realistic, study and research the boot is on the other foot. Protestants have had to revive and bring up to date what was always part of their tradition. But Catholics have had to build a new approach, or at

432

least to unearth a tradition which has been underground at least since the highly clerical Counter-Reformation.

(c) The relevance of revelation

There is finally a sense in which both Protestants and Catholics have turned back to the tradition of the Early Church, with its stress on the key importance of revelation for both the Church and the individual believer. Both the Protestant and the Catholic worlds, in the first place, have seen important fresh departures in theology in the last three or four generations. A key date on the Catholic side is 1879, when Leo XIII published his Encyclical *Aeterni Patris*, to restore St. Thomas Aquinas to his central place in Catholic philosophy. In the Protestant world there have been several major theological movements, including notably in the last generation that led by Karl Barth. Barth's theology insists that it is the Word of God, not the word of man, that is essential for understanding the Christian's place in the world. His destiny depends, not on any truth which can be read by natural reasoning out of history, but on the will and grace of God, knowledge of which is conveyed by Revelation. Barth's views, taken in detail, are not every Protestant's. But they are one sign among many of Protestant interest not merely in church or social organisation, or in building outwards from Revelation by natural reasoning, but in defining and proclaiming the central message of Revelation itself. The whole Faith and Order movement points the same way: above all the passage to the more fundamental discussion of doctrines after the Edinburgh Missionary Conference of 1910.

In both the Protestant and the Catholic world there has also been an immense growth of Bible studies in the last hundred and fifty years, as well as in efforts to spread popular knowledge and use of the Bible. In the Catholic Church this movement came rather later than among Protestants, but no less strongly. It was vigorously promoted by Encyclicals of Leo XIII, in 1893, and Pius XII in 1943. Like its Protestant counterpart, it has had its lighter moments. Protestant Higher Criticism has offered a happy hunting-ground for Miss Dorothy Sayers (in her satirical spare time) and Mgr. Ronald Knox. On the Catholic side, it was none other than the great Mgr. Duchesne who took time off from debunking pious legends to do the same for the policies of the then current Pope. There was the encyclical *Digitus in Oculo*. And there was the barque of Peter 'menée à coups de gaffe'.[1] But among Catholics as among Protestants, these have been merely the by-products of an immense and constructive effort to increase understanding of the basic message of Revelation.

And both Catholicism and Protestantism have seen a vast amount of renewal and experiment in the field of prayer and worship. Pius X initiated

[1] Both quotations from Dansette, op. cit.

a far-reaching overhaul of the Catholic liturgy. Since his time a great effort has been made to adapt the forms of Catholic prayer and worship to the special needs of particular groups, including notably workers' groups. More use has been made of local languages and of new forms of prayer. Congregations have been helped to co-operate more actively in services. Particular stress has been laid on prayer and worship in small groups, where face to face relations are easy and the message of Revelation can be lived out simply and directly. Catholics, notably in France, have spent vast efforts in re-working the idea of the parish and the various specialised groups and movements attached to it. On the Protestant side Barth's theology emphasises particularly the role of the 'community', meaning the parish or other local Church community. And a striking feature among Protestants has been—over and above the development of new forms— the stream of revivals and awakenings, often leading to new sects or to splits in churches, which has run strongly to the present day.

CONCLUSION. THE PLACE OF CHRISTIAN DEMOCRACY IN THE HISTORY OF CHRISTIANITY

It is now possible to draw this chapter together and show the place of Christian Democracy in the general development of Christianity. When Troeltsch, writing fifty years ago, passed his gloomy verdict on the present and future of the Christian churches, he saw no clear way out. 'Thoughts will be necessary which have not yet been thought.'[1] In the rather longer perspective in which we today can see events since the early nineteenth century, it is possible to correct his judgment in two ways.

First, there has in fact been a Christian revival: indeed, it was going on even in Troeltsch's own time. Christianity today has become a force to be reckoned with, intellectually and in social and political affairs. A century and a half ago it had much support from tradition and inertia, but little apparent future. Today it is a fighting force well planted in the modern world, capable of grasping and solving the world's problems and of taking an independent stand on them. There is no longer any doubt that it has a future, though, as yet, its strength is too new for all the losses and missed opportunities of the past to have been made good.

Secondly, this has happened, not through 'thinking new thoughts', but through joining that which was separated in the centuries down to the Reformation: through drawing together the three great streams of the Christian tradition and making them reinforce one another. The new wave of recovery and advance in Christianity in the last hundred years can be literally and precisely described as ecumenical or catholic, taking both words in their dictionary sense. For it is due to a return towards the full unity of the Christian tradition.

[1] *Social Teaching of the Christian Churches*, p. 1012.

Christian Democracy fits into this pattern exactly. Its characteristics are that it insists on the relevance both of revelation and of practical, historical, experience, particularly that of the laity; and that, from this, it derives a broad catholic synthesis in the political, economic, and social field. But to stress revelation, or realistic adaptation and the role of the laity, or the catholic synthesis, are precisely the characteristics of the three great Christian traditions, Orthodox, Protestant, and Catholic. Christian Democracy can, therefore, be said to represent the current drawing together of these traditions so far as this is relevant to political, economic, and social affairs. And it will be apparent from what has been said in this and earlier chapters that this is not a mere analogy or coincidence. The Protestant contribution to the Christian Democratic movements would not have been possible without Protestants' new awareness of the Church as an organised body and of their own responsibilities as members of it. Their awakening as Churchmen and their awakening to Christian responsibility in the political and social field are, as has been said, two sides of the same medal. Catholics for their part could have contributed little to Christian Democracy if they had not taken over from Protestantism its tradition of flexible adaptation to current trends and, in particular, its traditional emphasis on the role of the laity. And it is enough to know the Catholic and Protestant political and social movements even superficially to realise that their dynamism is drawn above all from the substitution of living, thought-out, and deeply felt personal religion for the traditional conformity of the not so very distant past. This last argument can also be turned the other way round. There has been a religious revival in the Christian churches. It is difficult to see how this revival could have proceeded as far as it has done if it had not found an outlet and stimulus in concern for the problems of life on earth; where, as in Heaven, Christians pray that the Kingdom may come.

In short: Christian Democracy can be re-defined as *that aspect of the ecumenical or catholic movement in modern Christianity* which is concerned with the application of Christian principles in the areas of political, economic, and social life for which the Christian laity has independent responsibility.

BIBLIOGRAPHY

THIS bibliography is neither select nor complete. It represents the material of which it was possible to make use for this book, with a few additional references to books not obtainable in this country, or which were published or noted after the main draft was finished. It is not generally cross-referenced, so that for any particular subject or country it is advisable to refer to the 'general' sections as well as to the particular sections concerned.

INTERNATIONAL AND GENERAL

GENERAL

J. Moody (ed.), *Church and Society*, Arts inc., 1953 (collection of articles on the Catholic Social movement in different countries. See especially the book-length section on Germany).

S. Z. Ehler and J. B. Morrall, *Church and State through the Centuries* (documents), Burns, Oates, 1954.

L. Sturzo, *Church and State*, Geoffrey Bles, 1939.

E. Troeltsch. *The Social Teaching of the Christian Churches*, 2 vols., George Allen and Unwin, 1931.

Y. Congar, Vraie et Fausse Réforme dans l'Église, *Unam Sanctam*, 1951. Jalons Pour Une Théologie du Läicat, *Unam Sanctam*, 1954.

K. S. Latourette, *History of the Expansion of Christianity*, Vols. 3–7, Eyre and Spottiswoode, 1939–45.

P. Hughes, *Popular History of the Catholic Church*, Burns, Oates, 1947 ed.

H. Somerville, *Studies in the Catholic Social Movement*, Burns, Oates, 1933.

Catholic Truth Society, collections of Papal Encyclicals:
    (1) *The Pope and the People* (1878–1922).
    (2) *Selected Encyclicals* (1928–32).
    (3) *Mit Brennender Sorge*, 1937 (National Socialism).
    (4) *Firmissimam Constantiam*, 1937 (Mexico—the right to resist).
    (5) *Divini Redemptoris*, 1937 (Communism).
    (6) *Selected Letters and Addresses of Pius XII*.

Pontifical Court Club, *Catholic Documents* (periodical).

Collections and commentaries on Catholic social doctrine such as:
    J. Messner, *Social Ethics*, St. Louis, 1949.
    International Union of Social Studies:
        (1) *Code of Social Principles*, 3rd ed., English translation published by Catholic Social Guild, 1952.
        (2) *Code of International Ethics*, American translation, cf. 1951 ed.
        (3) *Code Familial*, French ed. Spes (Paris) and Erasme (Brussels), 1951.

J. Villain, *L'Enseignement Social de l'Église*, 3 vols., Spes, to 1954.

J. F. Cronin, *Catholic Social Principles*, Bruce (Milwaukee), 1950.

Moody, *op. cit.*, has good bibliographies, especially of the German Jesuit School led notably by Heinrich Pesch.

There is no equally authoritative summary of Protestant social doctrine and its development. A brief summary, specially relevant to the European movements discussed here, is:

J. C. C. Rupp, *De Sociaal-Economische Boodschap der Protestantse Kerken*, Albani, Den Haag, no date.

See also the reports and papers of the meetings of the World Council of Churches at Amsterdam, 1948, and Evanston, 1954, and of the conferences which led up to it:

Life and Work (Stockholm 1925 and Oxford 1937).

Faith and Order (Lausanne 1927, and Edinburgh 1937).

Missionary (Edinburgh 1910, Madras 1938).

RELIGIOUS SOCIOLOGY

Lumen Vitae, Special number *on Modern Environment and Religion* (review of progress of religious sociology), VI (1951), 1–2.

Sociologie Religieuse et Sciences Sociales. (Report of IV International Congress of Religious Sociology.) Paris: Éditions Ouvrières, 1955.

POLITICS

Nouvelles Équipes Internationales (Union of Christian Democrats):

(1) Statutes.

(2) Papers of Congresses (cyclostyled), especially:

(a) Fribourg, 1952, 'Strength and Weakness of Christians in European Democracy' (including reports on current representation in schools, press, etc., as well as the political field).

(b) Bruges, 1954, 'Economic and Social Policy of Christian Democracy' (including questionnaire replies from individual countries).

(3) Summer school papers, especially 'La Place du Travail dans la Société', 1955.

R. Houben:

(1) 'Réflexions sur la Doctrine Politique Chrétienne', *Revue Politique*, October 1951.

(2) 'Force et Faiblesse des Chrétiens sur le Plan de la Doctrine', *Revue Politique*, December, 1952 (the gist of the main report at the N.E.I.'s Fribourg conference).

(3) 'Les Chrétiens devant la Politique', *Revue Politique*, October 1953.

P. C. van Gestel, *Het Religieus-Socialisme*, Louvain, 1932.

Socialist International:

(1) *Declaration on the Aims and Tasks of Socialism*, Frankfurt, 1951.

(2) Papers and conclusions (cyclostyled) of the conference on Socialism and Religion, Bentveld (Holland), 1953.

BIBLIOGRAPHY

WORKERS' MOVEMENT

International Federation of Christian Trade Unions:
  (1) Programmes.
  (2) Congress reports.
  (3) Periodicals *Labor* and *Christlabor*.

International Federation of Evangelical Workers' Associations:
  (1) Congress reports (notably IV Congress, Copenhagen, 1950).
  (2) Pamphlets and periodical *Evangelisch-Soziale Welt*.

Katholische Arbeiterinternationale (between the two wars):
  (1) Report of 1st Congress, Köln, 1928.
  (2) Report of 2nd Congress, Utrecht, 1931.
  (3) Statutes.

International Christian Social Union (St. Gall International) (immediately post-Second World War: main support from workers' organisations). Congress papers (Cyclostyled) and *Bulletin*.

Féderation Internationale des Mouvements Ouvriers Catholiques (developed out of workers' section of St. Gall International).
  (1) Periodical *Tour d'Horizon*.
  (2) Special series *Études et Expériences*.

MIDDLE CLASS, ETC.

Union Internationale des Associations Patronales Catholiques:
  (1) Report of Rome Congress, 1949.
  (2) Study session reports:
      (a) *L'Entreprise Privée*, 1948.
      (b) *L'Organisation Professionnelle*, 1950.
      (c) *Les Données Actuelles de l'Économie*, 1951
      (d) *Progrès Économique et Progrès Social*, 1952.
  (3) Papers of sessions on Unemployment, The Hague, 1954, and Paris, 1955.
  (4) *Bulletin*.

Union Catholique Internationale de Service Social. Progress report, 1950–3.

YOUTH AND FAMILY

Jeunesse Ouvrière Chrétienne:
  (1) *L'Église Face au Problème de la Jeunesse Travailleuse*, Brussels, 1949.
  (2) *Semaine d'Études Internationale*, 1935.
  (3) *Une Étape de l'Internationale Jociste*, 1950.

Union des Jeunes Democrates-Chrétiens: *L'Europe, Patrie de l'Avenir*, Bonn, 1952 (includes statistics of membership).

International Union of Family Organisations:
  (1) *Organisations Familiales dans le Monde*. Report of 1947 Congress.
  (2) Policy statements on the Bill of Rights of the Family; Family Allowances: The Financing of Family Housing.
  (3) Quarterly *Familles dans le Monde* and pamphlets and conference reports.

438

Die Lage der Familie in Europa: Dokumente, 1952:6
Lumen Vitae, VII (1952), 2, special number on 'La Formation Religieuse au Foyer'.

FRANCE

GENERAL

J. B. Duroselle, *Les Débuts du Catholicisme Social en France*, Presses Universitaires de France, 1950.

H. Rollet, *L'Action Sociale des Catholiques en France*, Éditions Contemporaines, 1947.

G. Hoog, *Histoire du Catholicisme Social en France*, Domat-Montchrestien, 1946.

P. T. Moon, *The Labor Problem and the Social Catholic Movement in France*, New York, Macmillan, 1926.

E. Leonard, *Le Protestant Français*, Presses Universitaires de France, 1953.

A. Dansette, *Histoire Religieuse de la France Contemporaine*, Flammarion, 2 vols., 1948 and 1951.

Chronique Sociale de France, 1952, II, Étapes Sociales Catholiques.

La Nef, *Problèmes du Catholicisme Français*, Julliard, 1953.

J. Folliet, 'Présence de l'Église', *Chronique Sociale de France*, 1949.

PERIODICALS

Chronique Sociale de France (regular articles on all aspects of French Catholic social action. Drawn on repeatedly in this book, in addition to the special references below).

Revue de l'Action Populaire.

Semaines Sociales de France, reports of annual meetings.

See also *Semaines Sociales de France—Origines, Méthodes, Développements*, published by *Chronique Sociale de France*, 1936.

Annuaire des Services Generaux de l'Épiscopat: Mouvements d'Action Catholique —Œuvres Diverses.

Periodicals specialising in the trade-union and working-class movement include:

Syndicalisme ⎫
Recherches ⎬ C.F.T.C.
Reconstruction (C.F.T.C. minority).
Masses Ouvrières.

RELIGIOUS SOCIOLOGY

Le Bras, *Introduction à l'Histoire de la Pratique Religieuse en France*, Paris, 1942 and 1945.

F. Boulard, *Problèmes Missionaires de la France Rurale*, Éditions du Cerf, 2 vols., 1945.

F. Boulard, *Essor ou Déclin du Clergé Français*, Éditions du Cerf, 1950.

Y. Daniel, *Aspects de la Pratique Religieuse à Paris*, Éditions Ouvrières, 1952.

S. Ligier. *Recherches Sociologiques sur la Pratique Religieuse au Jura*, cyclostyled, 1952.

M. Quoist, *La Ville et l'Homme* (Rouen), Éditions Ouvrières, 1952.

M. Ward, *France Pagan*, Sheed and Ward, 1949: English translation of and commentary on Godin and Daniel, *'France, Pays de Mission?'*

BIBLIOGRAPHY

M. R. Loew,
   (1) 'Les Dockers de Marseille'⎫ *Économie et*
   (2) 'En Mission Prolétarienne' ⎭ *Humanisme.*
M. Aumont, *Femmes en Usine*, Spes, 1953.
Virton, *Études de Sociologie Paroissiale*, Spes, 1954.
See also the poll report in *Réalités*, November, 1952, 'La Vérité sur les Sentiments Religieux des Français'.
On techniques see, for example:
   Économie et Humanisme: (1) 'Au Contact des Forces Vivantes', 1951.
                              (2) 'Collection de Sociologie Religieuse' (instructions for survey), 1952.
   F. Boulard, 'Premiers Itinéraires en Sociologie Religieuse', *Économie et Humanisme*, and Éditions Ouvrières, 1954.

POLITICAL

H. Rollet, *Albert de Mun et le Parti Catholique*, Éditions Contemporaines, 1949.
H. de Gailhard-Bancel, *Quatorze Années de Défense Religieuse à la Chambre des Députés*, 1901–1914, Spes, 1928.
A. Siegfried, *Tableau des Partis en France*, Grasset, 1930.
M. Darbon, *Le Conflit Entre la Droite et la Gauche dans le Catholicisme Français, 1830–1953*, Privat, 1953.
Mouvement Républicain Populaire, *Statuts* (1950 ed.).
F. Goguel, 'Christian Democracy in France', in Einaudi and Goguel, *Christian Democracy in Italy and France*, University of Notre Dame, 1952.
F. Goguel, *Géographie des Elections Françaises, 1870–1951*, Armand Colin, 1951.
L. Biton, *La Démocratie Chrétienne dans la Politique Française*, Siraudeau (Augers), 1954.
Sondages, 1952: 3, special number on the electorate of French parties. See also the reports of polls in *Réalités*, May and November, 1952.
Forces Nouvelles (party paper of the M.R.P.). See especially the numbers published before the general election of 1951, and the special series of reports to the Party's X Congress in 1954.

TRADE UNIONS

J. Montreuil, *Histoire du Mouvement Ouvrier en France*, Aubier, 1947.
G. Lefranc, *Les Expériences Syndicales en France de 1939 à 1950*, Aubier, 1950.
M. Turmann, *Le Syndicalisme Chrétien en France*, Valois, 1929.
O. Jean, *Le Syndicalisme*, Action Populaire, 5th ed., 1922.
J. Zirnheld, *Cinquante Années de Syndicalisme Chrétien*, Spes, 1937.
G. Levard, *Chances et Périls du Syndicalisme Chrétien*, Fayard, 1955.
Trade Unions and Employers' Associations, text of a letter from the Sacred Congregation of the Council to the Bishop of Lille, English ed. by Catholic Social Guild, 1929.
G. Lecordier, *Syndicaliste Chrétien—Pourquoi? La Réponse d'un Catholique*, Laboureur, 1945.
C. Deguy, *Syndicaliste Chrétien—Pourquoi? La Réponse d'une Protestante*, Laboureur, 1945.
Confédération Française des Travailleurs Chrétiens, *Statuts*.

BIBLIOGRAPHY

Congress reports and programmes of the C.F.T.C., particularly:

Plan de la C.F.T.C. 1936.
Programme d'Action Ouvrière et d'Organisation Professionnelle, 1945.
Unité Syndicale ou Unité d'Action, 1945.
Problèmes du Syndicalisme Ouvrier International, 1945.
Pour un Nouveau Plan de la C.F.T.C.—La C.F.T.C. Face aux Responsabilités du Syndicalisme Moderne, 1953.
Pour un Syndicalisme Moderne, 1955.
Rapport Moral at successive Congresses.

MIDDLE CLASS, FARMERS, ETC.

Henry, *Mouvement Patronal Chrétien Français*, I.L.O.
J. Zamanski, *L'Avenir de l'Entreprise—un Patronat qui s'Engage*, E.P.E.E., 1948.
G. Lecordier:

(1) *Les Classes Moyennes en Marche*, Bloud et Gay, 1950.
(2) *Le Monde Rural en Marche*, Éditions I.G.C., 1954.
(3) *Le Mouvement Patronal*, Chronique Sociale de France, 1949, I.

YOUTH AND FAMILY MOVEMENTS

Action Catholique des Jeunes Français:

(1) *L'A.C.J.F.—Cinquante Années d'Action*, Spes, 1936.
(2) *Sept Ans d'Histoire*, Éditions de l'Epi, 1946.
(3) Reports to the Federal Council, especially:
   1948. *L'A.C.J.F. et l'Évolution des Structures Sociales*.
   1949. *Perspectives, 1950*.
   1950. *Devenir Membre Actif de la Société des Hommes*.
   1951. *Nos Raisons d'Agir*.

Jeunesse Ouvrière Chrétienne, Jocisme Français, 1927–1939, cyclostyled, available at JOC headquarters, Brussels.
M. Van der Meersch, *Pêcheurs d'Hommes*, Albin Michel, 1940.
Masses Ouvrières, issues of August–September, 1947, and May, 1952, on the J.O.C.
Chronique Sociale de France:

1950, II, special number on the 'Cinquantenaire du Sillon'.
1950, series by G. Lecordier on the 'Mouvement Féministe', and special number on 'La Femme Française'.

S. de Lestapis, *Amour et Institution Familiale*, Spes, 1948.
P. Ranwez, *Promotion de la Famille*, Lumen Vitae, IV (1949), 2.
Reports and circulars of the Mouvement Populaire des Familles/Mouvement de la Libération du Peuple.
Association du Mariage Chrétien and Association Catholique des Chefs de Famille: periodicals and leaflets.
Les Droits de la Famille: charter agreed by the main French family organisations in 1920.
Comment Fondre et faire Vivre une Association Familiale, Éditions Sociales du Nord, 1947.
Union Nationale d'Associations Familiales: periodicals and reports.

BIBLIOGRAPHY

BELGIUM

GENERAL

Van Kalken, *La Belgique Contemporaine*, Colin.
A. Verhaegen, *25 Années d'Action Sociale*, De Wit, 1911.
R. C. K. Ensor, *Belgium*, Home University Library, 1915.
See also the section on Belgium in Moody (ed.), *Church and Society*, Arts Inc., 1953.

PERIODICALS

La Revue Politique (from 1951).
Bulletin d'Information of the *Parti Social Chrétien*.
Bulletin Social des Industriels (Catholic employers' organisation).

RELIGIOUS SOCIOLOGY

E. Collard, map of religious practice in Belgium, *Lumen Vitae*, Oct.–Dec., 1952.
J. Kerkhofs, *Godsdienstpraktijk en Sociaal Milieu*, Louvain, 1953.
G. Hoyois, *L'Ardenne*, Éditions Universitaires, Brussels, esp. Vol. II.
N. Devolder, *De Godsdienstigheid der Intellectuellen*, Beyaert, Bruges, 1947.

POLITICAL

Parti Social Chrétien:

    (1) *Statuts Nationaux*, 1951 ed.
    (2) *Les Chantiers sont Ouverts*, 1945 (party programme).
    (3) *Parti Social Chrétien–1949* (election handbook).
    (4) *Bulletin d'Information*, Annual and Extraordinary Congress reports.

Melot, *Le Parti Catholique en Belgique*, Rex (Louvain), 1934.
Mishaegen, *Le Parti Catholique Belge de 1830 à 1884*, Larcier, 1946.

WORKERS' MOVEMENT

A. Brys, *The Principles and Organisation of the Christian Labour Movement of Belgium*, Mouvement Ouvrier Chrétien, cyclostyled (the gist of this is also published in Moody (ed.), *Church and Society*, Arts Inc., 1953).
Mouvement Ouvrier Chrétien. Documents and Congress reports, particularly:
    XV Congress, 1947.
        (1) General report.
        (2) Hulpiau, report on 'Le M.O.C. Devant les Problèmes de l'Heure'.
        (3) *Notre Politique Familiale*.
    XVI Congress, 1952.
        (1) *Rapport Moral*.
        (2) *Orientation*.
        (3) *La Co-opération dans le Mouvement Ouvrier Chrétien*.
        (4) *Les Vacances des Travailleurs dans le Cadre des Loisirs*.
V. L. Heylen, *La Base Idéologique des Services Mutualistes* (post-war, no date).
I.S.C. (periodical issued by the International Federation of Christian Trade Unions) May, 1949:
    La Montée de la C.S.C. Belge.
Centre Libre de l'Orientation Professionnelle, *Les Principes de l'Orientation Professionnelle Libre*. No date.

442

Confédération des Syndicats Chrétiens de Belgique:

    XV Congress, 1947: report on 'Le Syndicalisme'.

    XVI Congress, 1949.

        (1) *L'Activité de la C.S.C. de 1947 à 1949.*

        (2) *La Politique Syndicale en Matière de Salaires.*

    XVII Congress 1951.

        (1) *L'Activité de la C.S.C. de 1949 à 1951.*

        (2) *Le Syndicalisme Chrétien: sa Nature et sa Mission.*

    Prospérité et Plein Emploi, 1953 (Immediate Programme for 1954).

    Déclaration Commune sur la Productivité (jointly with the Socialist unions and the employers) 1954.

Semaine Sociale Wallonne, 1950. Cyclostyled reports by:

    Canon Leclercq, *L'Évolution de la Question Sociale.*

    E. Baussart, *Les Mouvements Ouvriers.*

    (No author's name) *Problèmes du Mouvement Ouvrier.*

MIDDLE CLASS, FARMERS, ETC.

Boerenbond Belge:

    (1) *Soixante Ans d'Activité*, Louvain, 1950.

    (2) Annual reports.

A. Varzim, *Le Boerenbond Belge*, Desclée Brouwer (Paris), 1934.

Association des Patrons et Ingénieurs Catholiques de Belgique:

    (1) *L'Entreprise et son Destin*, 1949.

    (2) A. Müller, *La Morale et la Vie des Affaires*, Casterman, 1951.

Fédération Nationale des Classes Moyennes:

    (1) *Les Travailleurs Indépendants dans l'Économie Nationale*, 1953 (special number of Bulletin d'Information).

    (2) J. P. de Crayencour, *L'Organisation Professionnelle* (report to Brussels Congress, 1953).

F. Collin, *Rapport sur les Classes Moyennes Artisanales et Commerçantes*, Larcier, 1937.

H. Lambrechts, *Trente Années au Service des Classes Moyennes*, Winandy, Digon, n.d.

Report of the 'Congrès International des Classes Moyennes et du Travail Indépendant', Louvain, 1946.

YOUTH AND FAMILY

M. Fiévez, *La Vie de Fernand Tonnet*, Éditions Jocistes, 1947.

Jeunesse Ouvrière Chrétienne:

    (1) *Manuel*, 1925 and 1930 eds.

    (2) Reports of the annual national 'Semaine d'Études de Godinne': e.g. Cardijn, *The Hour of the Working Class* (1948, Australian ed.).

    (3) *Statut de la Jeunesse Travailleuse*, 1944.

The account of the early history of the J.O.C. in the text is built up largely from the periodicals *Jeunesse Syndicaliste* (1920–4), *Jeunesse Ouvrière* (1924 ff.), *Bulletin des Dirigeants*, and *Notes de Pastorale Jociste.* See also the International section.

BIBLIOGRAPHY

J. Meert:

(1) Jocisme, *Mouvement de Conversion*, Éditions Jocistes, no date.
(2) *Vraie et Fausse Réforme du Jocisme*, cyclostyled, 1952.

J. Mazioux, *Entre vos Mains*, Éditions Ouvrières and Éditions Jocistes, 1941.

HOLLAND

GENERAL

R. Hagoort, *De Christelijk-Sociale Beweging*, Edecea, 1933 (new ed. 1955).
Reports of the Christian-Social (Protestant) Congresses, especially 1891.
Rogier, *Beknopte Nederlandse Kerkgeschiedenis*, *Urbi et Orbi*, Amsterdam, 1945.
R. Kothen, *La Vie Catholique en Hollande*, Éditions des Fiches Documentaires, Louvain, 1951.
Catholic Bishops of Holland, *De Katholiek in het Openbare Leven van deze Tijd*, 1954 (French translation as *Le Catholique dans la Vie Publique Actuelle*).
Dutch Catholic Action, *De Katholieke Actie in Nederland*: seven-language short guide to Dutch Catholic Action (no date).
J. Veraart, *Beginselen der Publiekrechtelijke Bedrijfsorganisatie*, Bussum, 1947.
See also the text of the Industrial Organisation Act, 1950.

RELIGIOUS SOCIOLOGY

Het Katholiek Sociaal—Kerkelijk Instituut, no date, published by the Institute.
Early publications of the Institute include:

(1) *L'Église Catholique aux Pays-Bas* (cyclostyled).
(2) G. H. L. Zeegers, 'Sociological Analyses of the Religious and Social Position in the Netherlands', *Lumen Vitae* VI (1951), 1–2.
(3) Linus Grond, 'Nature and Function of a District in a City', ibid.

The Sociological Institute of the Dutch Reformed Church, 1951 ed. (see also its *Sociologisch Bulletin*).
Reports of the Institute (cyclostyled) such as:

(1) *Sociografische Schets van de gemeente Kempen*.
(2) *Rapport betreffende de herorientatie van het diaconele Werk en het jeugdwerk den Ned. Hervormde Gemeente te Gorcum*.

J. P. Kruijt, Thesis (1933) on the growth of indifference in the Protestant churches.

POLITICAL

Brom, *Schaepman*, Haarlem, 1936.
L. C. Suttorp, *De Savornin Lohman*, Hague, 1948.
P. Kasteel, *Abraham Kuyper*, Kok, Kempen, 1938.
J. A. de Wilde and C. Smeenk, *Het Volk ten Baat* (Anti-Revolutionary party history), Groningen, 1949.
Laman, *Groen van Prinsterer als Volksvertegenwoordiger, 1862–5*, no date (postwar).
Brief summaries of party histories in:

(1) *Nederlandse Politiek-Religieuze Ontwikkeling in de 19ᵉ Eeuw Anti-Revolutionaire Staatkunde*, July, 1948.

444

(2) Catholic People's Party,

    (a) *Van het Verleden naar het Heden* (no date: postwar).

    (b) *De Schoolstrijd*, 1948.

    (c) A. Veldtman, *Enige Hoofdstukken uit de Politieke Geschiedenis*, 1948.

(3) *Christelijk-Historische Unie, C.H.V., 1908–1948*.

H. J. Wilzen and A. Van Biemen, *Samen op Weg* (the 'religious socialist' movement), N. V. de Arbeiderspers, Amsterdam, 1953.

W. Banning (ed.) *Socialistische Documenten*, N.V. de Arbeiderspers, 1952 (contains a number of documents on the Christian movements). See also the revised (1947) Programme of Principles of the Partij van de Arbeid.

Wiardi-Beckman Stichting, *Verkiezingen in Nederland*, 1951 (cyclostyled).

Catholic People's Party:

    (1) *Reglementen*.

    (2) *Algemeen Staatkundig Program*.

    (3) *Urgentie-Program*, 1946—*Verkiezings Manifest*, 1948.

    (4) *Verkiezings program*, 1952.

    (5) C. P. M. Romme, 'Eenheid in de Politiek', *Katholiek Staatkundig Maandschrift*, May, 1952.

Centrum voor Staatkundige Vorming (Catholic), *Staatkundige Eenheid der Katholieke Nederlanders*, 1954.

C. P. M. Romme, *Katholieke Politiek*, Spectrum, Utrecht, 1953.

Anti-Revolutionaire Partij:

    (1) *Beginselprogram*, 1934 ed.

    (2) *Program van Actie* (no date: postwar).

    (3) *Handboekje voor de Huisbezoekers*, 1952.

Christelijk-Historische Unie:

    (1) *Program van Beginselen*, 1951 ed.

    (2) *Sociaal-Economisch Program*, 1950.

    (3) *Jaarboekje 1952* (includes reprints of Principles and Programme).

W. Banning:

    (1) *Taak en Arbeid van het Religeus-Socialisme, Arbeidersgemeenschap der Woodbrookers*, about 1925.

    (2) *Ons Werk*, same publisher.

See also the pamphlet series of the various parties and movements, and periodicals such as *Katholieke Staatkundig Maandschrift, Anti-Revolutionaire Staatkunde*, and *Tijd en Taak*.

WORKERS' MOVEMENT

L. G. S. Verberne, *De Nederlandse Arbeidersbeweging in de 19ᵉ Eeuw*, Van Kampen, Amsterdam, 1950.

S. Mok, *De Vakbeweging*, Albani, 1953 ed.

C. Lammers, *De Vakbeweging en haar Problemen*, N.V. de Arbeiderspers, 1951 ed.

M. Ruppert, *De Nederlandse Vakbeweging*, 2 vols. Haarlem, Volksuniversiteit, 1953.

Centraal Bureau voor de Statistiek. Annual report on 'Omvang der Vakbeweging'.

BIBLIOGRAPHY

C. J. Kuiper, *Uit het Rijk van de Arbeid*, 2 vols, 1925–7.

W. G. Versluis, *Beknopte Geschiedenis van de Katholieke Arbeidersbeweging in Nederland*, Dekker and Van de Vegt, 1949.

C. du Bois de Vroylande, *L'Organisation du Milieu Ouvrier en Hollande-Standsorganisatie*, Spes, Paris, 1925 (shorter French version of the original Dutch publication by the same author).

Stokman, *De Katholieke Arbeidersbeweging in Oorlogstijd*, Utrecht, 1947.

E. van Iersel, *Signaal op Rood*, Spectrum, Utrecht, 1950.

See also, among other reports and pamphlets of the Catholic Workers' Movement, 'A View of the KAB', short English-language introduction to the movement.

R. Hagoort, *Patrimonium*, published by Patrimonium, 1927.

H. Amelink:

   (1) *Onder Eigen Banier*   ⎱ Edecea,
   (2) *Met Ontplooide Banieren* ⎰ 1950.

Christelijk Nationaal Vakverbond in Nederland, *Le CNV aux Pays-Bas*, Vooruitgang, Courtrai, no date (postwar).

The C.N.V. also prints a useful list of dates in its official Diary. See also its monthly *Evangelie en Maatschappij*.

Foundation of Labour, published by the Foundation, no date.

MIDDLE CLASS, ETC.

Middenstandsnota, 1954. Staatsdrukkerij, The Hague.

Reports of the Christelijke Middenstandsbond and Nederlandse Katholieke Middenstandsbond.

N.R.K.M. and Katholieke Volkspartij, *Middenstandsbeleid op Hoger Plan*, 1953.

Katholieke Volkspartij. Reports of the Commissie voor de Middengroepen.

Christelijk-Historische Unie, *Middenstandsrapport*, no date.

Algemeene Katholieke Werkgeversvereniging, *Waarvoor Wij Staan*, A.K.W.V., 1950.

   See also the A.K.W.V.'s annual reports and periodical *De Katholieke Werkgever*.

J. H. Derksen, 'Die Schaffung von Eigentum in Arbeiterhand'. In circular of Bund Katholischer Unternehmer, Köln, April, 1952.

Christelijke Werkgevers-Verbond:

   (1) *What We Believe and What We Do* (c. 1938).
   (2) *Statutes* (postwar ed.).
   (3) *Action programmes*, 1937 and 1946.
   (4) H. Colijn, address at annual meeting, 1923.
   (5) Series of reports of jubilee celebrations in *Standaard*, 23–5 February and 7–8 March, 1938.
   (6) Addresses at further jubilee meeting, March 1948:
      J. Meynen, 'The Calvinist Ideology'.
      G. Vixseboxse, 'Wages as a Social, Economic, and Cultural Factor'.
   (7) A. Borst, 'Bewaart de Vesting!' (prewar pamphlet).
   (8) 'Doel' (pamphlet, 1946).
   (9) Annual reports.

Christelijke Boeren—en Tuindersbond, *Gedenkboek 1918–1948*, The Hague, 1948. See also the C.B.T.B. weekly, *Ons Platteland*.

W. Rip, *Landbouw en Publiekrechtelijke Bedrijfsorganisatie*, Veenman, Wageningen, 1952.

Katholieke Nederlandse Boeren—en Tuindersbond, Sociaal-Economische Beleidsprogramma, 1955.

FAMILY AND YOUTH

Ministry of Education, *Youth Problems in the Netherlands*, 1954.

GERMANY AND AUSTRIA

GENERAL

Articles in *Staatslexikon (Görresgesellschaft)*, and in *Die Religion in Geschichte und Gegenwart-Handwörterbuch für Theologie und Religionswissenschaft*, Mohr, Tübingen, 1927.

F. Schnabel, *Deutsche Geschichte*, Vol. IV, Herder, 1951 ed.

G. Goyau:
    (1) *Bismarck et l'Église*, Paris, 1911–13.
    (2) *L'Allemagne Religieuse*, 1898.

Ritter, *Die Katholisch-Soziale Bewegung in Deutschland im 19 Jahrhundert und der Volksverein*, Köln, 1954.

A. Pieper, *Le Mouvement Catholique Social en Allemagne*, 1903.

J. Schlüter, *Die Katholisch-Soziale Bewegung in Deutschland seit der Jahrhundertwende*, 1928.

Paul Jostock, *Der Deutsche Katholizismus und die Überwindung des Kapitalismus*, Regensburg, 1932.

W. Schwer and F. Müller, *Der Deutsche Katholizismus im Zeitalter des Kapitalismus*, Augsburg, 1932.

J. Dobretsberger, *Katholische Sozialpolitik am Scheidewege*, Graz, 1947.

A. Geck, 'Revival of Social Catholicism in Germany', *Lumen Vitae*, VI (1951), 1–2.

Report of the 73rd Deutsche Katholikentag, Bochum, 1949.

Katholisches Jahrbuch, 1948–9:
    (1) Article by P. Jostock on 'Die Soziale Frage in Deutschland und der Katholizismus'.
    (2) Chart, aims and statistics of Catholic organisations in Germany.

A. L. Drummond, *German Protestantism since Luther*, Epworth Press, 1951.

M. Gerhardt, *Innere Mission*, 2 Vols., Bertelsmann, Gütersloh, 1948.

F. Karrenberg, *Christentum, Kapitalismus, und Sozialismus*, Berlin, 1932.

E. zur Nieden, *Versäumte Chance? Bilanz der Kirche nach 5 Jahren*, Stuttgart, 1950.

Kirchliches Jahrbuch fur die Evangelische Kirche in Deutschland, articles on development during and since the war.

A. Piettre, *L'Économie Allemande Contemporaine, 1945–52*, Paris, 1952.

R. Kothen, *Aperçu sur la Situation de l'Allemagne en 1950*, Fiches Documentaires, Louvain, 1950.

Diözesankomitee der Katholikenausschüsse, Köln, and *Katholische Nachrichten-Agentur*: monthly press releases.

RELIGIOUS SOCIOLOGY

Evangelische Kirche in Deutschland, Kirchenstatistisches Amt.:

(1) *Kirchliches Jahrbuch*

(2) Series of offprints of statistical articles from various journals published in the 'Schnelldienst' service.

K. von Bismarck:

(1) *Kirche und Gemeinde in Soziologischer Sicht.*

(2) *Was hat die Kirche an der Arbeiterschaft Versäumt*?

Zentralstelle für Kirchliche Statistik des Katholischen Deutschlands:

(1) *Kirchliches Handbuch.*

(2) *Informations-dienst.* See especially No. 2, October 1952, 'Das Religionsbekenntnis und die Politische Einstellung der Bevölkerung im Bundesgebiet'. Further data on this are available from the Institut für Demoskopie, Allensbach.

Lebendige Seelsorge, Sept. 1952: Special number on 'Pfarrseelsorge nach Mass'.

POLITICS

L. Bergsträsser:

(1) *Geschichte der Politischen Parteien in Deutschland*, Isar, Munich, 1952 ed.

(2) *Aus Geschichte und Politik.*

Salomon, *Die Deutschen Parteiprogramme*, Teubner, 1932 ed.

Mommsen, *Deutsche Parteiprogramme*, 2 vols.

Heydte und Sacherl, *Soziologie der Deutschen Parteien*, Munich, 1955.

K. Buchheim, *Geschichte des Christlichen Parteien in Deutschland*, Kösel, Munich, 1953.

K. Bechem, *Vorgeschichte, Geschichte, und Politik der deutschen Zentrumspartei*, 8 vols., 1927–31.

H. G. Wieck, *Die Entstehung der C.D.U.*, 1945. Droste-Verlag, 1953.

Christlich-Demokratische Union:

(1) *Geschichte und Wesen des C.D.U.* (includes text of Kölner Leitsätze and Ahlener Programme), 1949.

(2) *Was will die C.D.U.?* (Programme, 1949).

(3) *Düsseldorfer Leitsätze*, 1949.

(4) *Hamburger Programm*, 1953.

(5) Congress reports, particularly first (Goslar) and fourth (Hamburg).

(6) *Zentrum gegen Zentrum*, 1948.

O. Von Nell-Breuning, *Zur Programmatik Politischer Parteien*, Köln, 1946.

Osterreichische Volkspartei: A. Kasamas, *Programm Österreich*, 1949. See also the party periodical, *Österreichische Monatshefte*.

WORKERS' MOVEMENT

H. F. Zeck, *Vom Werden und Wachsen der Katholischen Arbeiterbewegung*, Köln, 1932.

O. Müller, *Die Christliche Gewerkschaftsbewegung Deutschlands*, 1905.

W. Wiedfeld, *Der Deutsche Gewerkschaftsbund*, Leipzig, 1933.

BIBLIOGRAPHY

Deutsche Gewerkschaftsbund der Christlich-Nationalen Gewerkschaften:
Jubiläumschrift, Berlin, 1924 (short biographies of the leaders and founders: also published as separate pamphlets).

J. Deutz, *Adam Stegerwald*, Köln, 1952.

Articles in *Jahrbuch der Christlichen Gewerkschaften*, 1909 and 1911: *Arbeiter-Taschenbuch* of Kartellverband Katholischer Arbeitervereine, 1913: pamphlets of the Volksverein für das Katholische Deutschland on the Socialist women's and youth movements, 1913. See especially *Jahrbuch der Christlichen Gewerkschaften*, 1909, article on the trade-union question in the Evangelical workers' movement.

Handbuch der Christlichen Gewerkschaften Deutschlands, 1905. Statutes, and 'Programm der Christlichen Gewerkschaften'.

Der Kölner Gewerkschaftsprozess, 1913.

J. Windolph, *Der Deutsche Protestantismus und die Christlichen Gewerkschaften*, 1909.

Report of the IV Deutsche Arbeiterkongress, 1917.

Jahrbuch der Berufsverbände im Deutschen Reiche, 1930 ed.

G. W. Guillebaud, *The Works Council*, Cambridge, 1928.

Frey, *Die Stellung der Christlichen Gewerkschaften Deutschlands zu der Politischen Parteien, Christliche Gewerkschaft-Verlag*, Berlin, 1931.

DGB (Christian trade unions), *Die Essener Richtlinien*, 1933.

J. Joos, *Am Räderwerk der Zeit*, Augsburg, 1949.

G. Briefs, *Zwischen Kapitalismus und Syndikalismus—die Gewerkschaften am Scheideweg*, Munich, 1952.

Frings, Cardinal, *Verantwortung und Mitverantwortung in der Wirtschaft*, Bachem, Köln, 1949.

Katholische Arbeiterbewegung (K.A.B.):

(1) Report of the Würzburg Congress, 1921 (includes Würzburg Programme).

(2) Reports of Präsidestage, 1918 ff.

(3) *Der Verbandstag zu Gelsenkirchen*, 1950.

(4) *Programm der K.A.B.*, 1950 (Gelsenkirchen Programme).

(5) *Gewerkschaften im Zwielicht*, c. 1952.

(6) H. Reichel, *Die Deutsche Einheitsgewerkschaft und ihr Geistigen Standort*, 1952.

(7) *Der Betriebsverfassungsgesetz*, 1952.

(8) *Unser Weg zur Sozialen Neuordnung*, 1953.

See also periodical *Priester und Arbeiter*.

Deutsche Gewerkschaftsbund: H. Böchler, 'Aufgaben der Deutschen Gewerkschaften' (Chairman's address at foundation congress, 1949).

Evangelische Soziale Akademie: G. Heilfurth, 'Church and Labour in Western Germany' (message to the World Council of Churches, Evanston, 1954).
See also periodicals *Die Mitarbeit* (*Evangelische Aktionsgemeinschaft für Arbeiterfragen*) and *Arbeiterbrief* of the Männerarbeit of the Evangelical Church in Germany.

E. Müller, *Recht und Gerechtigkeit in der Mitbestimmung*, Stuttgart, 1950.

Österreichische Arbeiter-und Angestelltenbund, *Wiener Programm der Österreichischen Arbeiterschaft*, Wien, 1946.

L. Weinberger, *Tatsachen, Begegungen, und Gespräche*, Wien, 1948.

BIBLIOGRAPHY

MIDDLE CLASS, ETC.

Verband Katholischer Kaufmännischer Vereine Deutschlands:
   (1) *Geschichte des Verbandes, K.K.V. 1877–1952*, 1952.
   (2) Congress reports.
   (3) Jubilee pamphlets of local branches.
   (4) B. Pfister, *Wirtschaftsfreiheit—Wirtschaftsbindung*.
Bund Katholischer Unternehme, circulars and pamphlets.
Männerarbeit der Evangelischen Kirche in Deutschland, Bauernbrief.
Das Dorf, periodical of the Katholische Landvolkbewegung Deutschlands.

YOUTH AND FAMILY

Schäffer, *Adolf Kolping*, Kolping-Verlag, Köln, 7th ed., 1952.
Nattermann, *Adolf Kolping als Sozialpädagoge*, Leipzig, 1925.
Vitus, *Die Anfänge der Katholischen Gesellenvereinen*, Bergland, Wuppertal, 1934.
Wernet, *Handwerkspolitik*, 1951.
Deutsche Kolpingsfamilie:
   (1) A. Kolping, *Der Gesellenverein*, 1952 ed.
   (2) A. Kolping, *Der Gesellenverein und seine Aufgabe*, 1952 ed.
   (3) F. J. Wothe, *Vater Kolping*, 1948.
   (4) *Werkende Hand, Wirkender Geist*, 1951.
Katholische Kaufmännische Verein, youth organisation pamphlet. 'Besinnung und Aufbruch'. No date.
See also G. Heilfurth (ed.), *Jugend ohne Geborgenheit*, Wichern-Verlag, Berlin, 1952.
Familienbund der Deutschen Katholiken, *Zur Katholischen Familienarbeit in Deutschland* (for the Stuttgart Congress of the International Union of Family Organisations, 1954).
Pro Familia, special publication for the Stuttgart Congress of the I.U.F.O., 1954.

SWITZERLAND

GENERAL

E. Bonjour, H. S. Offler, and G. R. Potter, *History of Switzerland*, Oxford University Press, 1952.
A. R. Ziegler, *Die Evangelisch-Soziale Bewegung der Schweiz*, S.V.E.A.—Verlag, 1939.

POLITICAL

M. Rosenberg:
   (1) 'Die Politische Lage in Zahlen', in *Civitas*, December, 1951.
   (2) 'Les Partis Politiques en Suisse', in *Revue Politique*, II (1952), 2.
Schweizerische Konservative Volkspartei, *Standort und Programm*, 1951.
Evangelische Volkspartei, *Partei-Programm und Statuten*, 1951 ed.

WORKERS' MOVEMENT

Handbuch der Schweizerischen Arbeitnehmerverbände, 1949.
J. Scherrer, *Die Christliche Sozialreform*, Christlichsozialer Arbeiterbund der Schweiz, 1945.
A. Heil, *Die Christlichen Gewerkschaften, in Völker an der Arbeit*, Zürich, 1951.

Schweizerische Verband Evangelischer Arbeiter und Angestellter:
  (1) *Richtlinien,* no date.
  (2) *Gesamtarbeitsvertrag und Betriebliche Arbeitsgemeinschaft.*
  (3) Pamphlet series, 'Evangelisch-Soziale Schriften'.
  (4) Annual reports.
Fédération Ouvrière Vaudoise (S.V.E.A.): *La Fédération Ouvrière Vaudoise,* 1935–49.

YOUTH AND FAMILY

Schweizerischer Katholischer Gesellenverein (Kolping):
  Lebensmeisterschaft-Handbuch des Katholischen Gesellenvereins, 1945 ed.

ITALY

GENERAL

G. de Rosa, *L'Azione Cattolica, 1874–1904,* Laterza, 1953.
G. Candeloro, *L'Azione Cattolica in Italia,* Edizioni di Cultura Sociale, 2nd ed., approx. 1950.
Magri, *L'Azione Cattolica in Italia,* Milan, 1953, 2 vols.
L. Civardi, *Manuale di Azione Cattolica,* 12th edn., Rome, 1952.
R. Kothen, 'Notes sur la Situation Sociale et Religieuse de l'Italie', 1948–9. *Fiches Documentaires,* VII, 1.5.
A. Canaletti Gaudenti (ed.), *Verso il Corporativismo Democratico,* Cacucci, Bari, 1951.
See also the reports of the annual Settimane Sociale dei Cattolici d'Italia, Edizioni dell' ICAS, Rome.

RELIGIOUS SOCIOLOGY

A. Leoni, *Sociologia e Geografia Religiosa di una Diocesi,* Rome, Gregorian University, 1952.
P. Droulers and A. Rimoldi, *La Sociologia Religiosa in Italia.* Reprint from *La Scuola Cattolica,* 1952.

POLITICAL

A. C. Jemolo, *Chiesa e Stato in Italia negli ultimi Cento Anni,* Einaudi, 1952.
S. Jacini, *Storia del Partito Popolare Italiano,* Garzanti, 1951.
D. A. Binchy, *Church and State in Fascist Italy,* Oxford, 1941.
M. Einaudi, in Einaudi and Goguel, *Christian Democracy in Italy and France,* Notre Dame, 1952 (with very full bibliography).
A. de Gasperi, *Studi ed Appelli della Lunga Vigilia,* Cappelli, 1953.
G. Tupini, *I Democratici Cristiani,* Ganzanti, 1954.
L. Somma, *De Gasperi o Gronchi,* Corso, 1953.
Democrazia Cristiana:
  (1) *Statuto del Partito,* 1950.
  (2) G. Gonella, *Il Programma della D.C. per la Nuova Costituzione,* 1946.
  (3) P. E. Taviani, *Problemi del Lavoro,* 1947.
  (4) Congress reports.
  (5) Monthly *Libertas.*
Magri, *La Democrazia Cristiana in Italia, 1897–1954,* Milan, 1954.
See also the complete edition of works by Luigi Sturzo, published by Zanichelli for the Istituto Luigi Sturzo.

BIBLIOGRAPHY

WORKERS' MOVEMENT

Rigola, *Storia del Movimento Operaio Italiana* (to 1926), Milan, 1947.

G. Candeloro, *Il Movimento Sindacale in Italia*, ed. di Cultura Sociale, 1950.

Associazioni Cristiane Lavoratori Italiani:

    (1) *Le A.C.L.I.—Principi, Attività, Struttura*, 1950.

    (2) *Le A.C.L.I. e i Problemi del Lavoro*, 1950.

    (3) 'Le A.C.L.I.—Movimento Sociale dei Lavoratori Cristiani', 1950 (propaganda pamphlet).

    (4) *Appunti sull' Evoluzione del Sindacato*, Milan, 1951—prepared by Istituto Sociale Ambrosiano.

    (5) *Dieci Anni di Vita e di Opere*, 1955.

Confederazione Italiana Sindacati Lavoratori, Congress reports and leaflets.

Comitato Civico Nazionale, 'Prospettive Sindacale', pamphlet, no date, approx. 1948.

MIDDLE CLASS, ETC.

Unione Cristiana Imprenditori Dirigenti:

    (1) 'La U.C.I.D.' (introductory pamphlet), 1953

    (2) Congress reports, particularly:

        IV (1951)—*La Disoccupazione nella Vita Economica e Sociale Italiana.*

        V (1952)—*La Formazione Sociale dei Soggetti dell' Impresa.*

        VI (1954)—*La Collaborazione Aziendale nell' Impresa Industriale ed Agricola.*

    (3) E. Soave, *La Riforma Agraria in Italia*, 1953.

    (4) Review *Operare.*

YOUTH

L. Gedda, *Addio Gioventù*, Rome, 1947.

GENERAL INDEX

Aalberse, Prof., 301
Academy Movement, 261
Action Française, 330, 332
Action Populaire, 25, 428
Agartz, V., 225
Ahlen Programme, 72
Alet, Fr., 251
Amelink, H., 31, 207
Amsterdam, 188, 425
Antwerp, 259
Aquinas, Thomas, 404, 433
Ariens, Fr., 188
Asselbergs, J., 259
Atomisation, 42
Aumont, M., 123
Austria, 47, 132, 208, 211, 307, 314
Automisation, 41

Baader, F., 163
Bachem, J., 313
Barmen, Synod of, 183
Barnard, Chester, 36
Barth, Karl, 18, 183, 242, 433
Bauer, O., 382
Beerenbrouck, Ruys van, 91
Behrens, F., 181, 190
Belgium, 27, 101, 157–8, 171, 209–11, 246, 259, 290, 297, 314
Benedict XV, 322
Bernanos, G., 342
Bethmann-Hollweg, M. von, 162
Bidault, G., 281, 334
Biederlack, 427
Bismarck, Prince, 104, 173–5, 181, 312
—, K. von, 239
Biton, L., 22
Blum, Leon, 228
'Boaz', 246, 253
Bochum, 65, 306
Boissard, A., 333
Borne, E., 227
Borst, A., 239
Boulard, Canon, 83, 84, 101, 249
Brauns, Fr. H., 306
'Break-through', 377 *et seq.*
Brentano, H. von, 96

Britain, Great, 81, 222, 256, 425
Bruges, 25, 67, 94, 99, 106–11, 139, 338
Bruggeman, L., 188, 190, 238
Brüning, H., 306
Brust, A., 187, 191, 207
Brys, Mgr., 38, 300
Buber, M., 124
Bureaucracy, 135
Bye, M., 144

Cadbury, 189
Canada, 214, 230, 256
Candeloro, G., 262
Cardijn, Fr., 272
Cathrein, Fr., 427
Cerrutti, Fr., 245
Charleroi, 274
Charter of Human Rights, U.N., 49
Christian Student Movement, 274
Church History, 401 *et seq.*
Civardi, L., 145
Clark, Colin, 111, 114 *et seq.*
Coal and Steel Community, 139, 296, 335
Colijn, Dr., 140, 246, 303
Colin, André, 281
Communist Party, 119, 134, 139, 209, 222, 262, 270, 277*n*., 311, 326, 336, 386, 420
Competition, 59, 130 *et seq.*
Confessional Movements, 163, 219, 296, 311, 316, 317, 331, 393
Congar, Fr., Y., 412, 427
Congo, 97
Consultation, 133, 137
Consumption and Work, 114 *et seq.*
Controls, Social, 112 *et seq.*, 131
Co-operative movement, 202, 215, 245
Corten, Fr., 92
Costa-Rossetti, Fr., 427
Council of Europe, 49
Coux, C. de, 155

Daens, Fr., 298
Dary, E., 287
Decurtins, K., 310
De Standaard, 172
Devanandan, P. O., 425*n*.

453

456

INDEX TO NATIONAL ORGANISATIONS

See also 'International' and 'Trade Unions' in the General Index

458